"If you are looking for a job ... before you go to the newspapers and the help-wanted ads, listen to Bob Adams, publisher of *The Metropolitan New York JobBank.*"
        -Tom Brokaw, *NBC*

"One of the better publishers of employment almanacs is Adams Media Corporation ... publisher of *The Metropolitan New York JobBank* and similarly named directories of employers in Texas, Boston, Chicago, Northern and Southern California, and Washington DC. A good buy ..."
        -Wall Street Journal's
        National Business Employment Weekly

"A timely book for Chicago job hunters follows books from the same publisher that were well received in New York and Boston ... [*The Chicago JobBank* is] a fine tool for job hunters ..."
        -Clarence Peterson, *Chicago Tribune*

"Because our listing is seen by people across the nation, it generates lots of resumes for us. We encourage unsolicited resumes. We'll always be listed [in *The Chicago JobBank*] as long as I'm in this career."
        -Tom Fitzpatrick, Director of Human Resources
        Merchandise Mart Properties, Inc.

"Job hunting is never fun, but this book can ease the ordeal ... [*The Los Angeles JobBank*] will help allay fears, build confidence, and avoid wheel-spinning."
        -Robert W. Ross, *Los Angeles Times*

"Job hunters can't afford to waste time. *The Minneapolis-St. Paul JobBank* contains information that used to require hours of research in the library."
        -Carmella Zagone
        Minneapolis-based Human Resources Administrator

"*The Florida JobBank* is an invaluable job-search reference tool. It provides the most up-to-date information and contact names available for companies in Florida. I should know--it worked for me!"
        -Rhonda Cody, Human Resources Consultant
        Aetna Life and Casualty

"*The Boston JobBank* provides a handy map of employment possibilities in Greater Boston. This book can help in the initial steps of a job search by locating major employers, describing their business activities, and for most firms, by naming the contact person and listing typical professional positions. For recent college graduates, as well as experienced professionals, *The Boston JobBank* is an excellent place to begin a job search."

-Juliet F. Brudney, Career Columnist
Boston Globe

"No longer can jobseekers feel secure about finding employment just through want ads. With the tough competition in the job market, particularly in the Boston area, they need much more help. For this reason, *The Boston JobBank* will have a wide and appreciative audience of new graduates, job changers, and people relocating to Boston. It provides a good place to start a search for entry-level professional positions."

-*Journal of College Placement*

"*The Phoenix JobBank* is a first-class publication. The information provided is useful and current."

-Lyndon Denton
Director of Human Resources and Materials Management
Apache Nitrogen Products, Inc.

"[*The Ohio JobBank* is] a good resource for the job hunter."

-Virginia Tyler, Human Resources Manager
Battelle Columbus Operations/Ohio

"*The Ohio JobBank* is a very helpful tool for locating and researching potential employers. It's easy to use and even gives advice on winning the job."

-Judith G. Bishop, Manager of Employment
Barberton Citizens Hospital

"*The Seattle JobBank* is an essential resource for job hunters."

-Gil Lopez, Staffing Team Manager
Battelle Pacific Northwest Laboratories

"I read through the "Basics of Job Winning" and "Resumes" sections [in *The Dallas-Ft. Worth JobBank*] and found them to be very informative, with some positive tips for the job searcher. I believe the strategies outlined will bring success to any determined candidate."

-Camilla Norder, Professional Recruiter
Presbyterian Hospital of Dallas

"Through *The Dallas-Ft. Worth JobBank,* we've been able to attract high-quality candidates for several positions."

-Rob Bertino, Southern States Sales Manager
CompuServe

What makes the JobBank series the nation's premier line of employment guides?

With vital employment information on thousands of employers across the nation, the JobBank series is the most comprehensive and authoritative set of career directories available today.

Each book in the series provides information on **dozens of different industries** in a given city or area, with the primary employer listings providing contact information, telephone numbers, addresses, a summary of the firm's business, and in many cases descriptions of the firm's typical professional job categories, the principal educational backgrounds sought, and the fringe benefits offered.

In addition to the **detailed primary employer listings,** the 1996 JobBank books give telephone numbers and addresses for **thousands of additional employers.**

All of the reference information in the JobBank series is as up-to-date and accurate as possible. Every year, the entire database is thoroughly researched and verified by mail and by telephone. Adams Media Corporation publishes **more local employment guides more often** than any other publisher of career directories.

In addition, the JobBank series features important information about the local job scene -- **forecasts on which industries are the hottest, overviews of local economic trends,** and **lists of regional professional associations,** so you can get your job hunt started off right.

Hundreds of discussions with job hunters show that they prefer information organized geographically, because most people look for jobs in specific areas. The JobBank series offers **20 regional titles,** from Minneapolis to Houston, and from Boston to San Francisco. Jobseekers moving to a particular area can review the local employment data not only for information on the type of industry most common to that region, but also for names of specific companies.

A condensed, but thorough, review of the entire job search process is presented in the chapter **The Basics of Job Winning**, a feature which has received many compliments from career counselors. In addition, each JobBank directory includes a section on **resumes and cover letters** the *New York Times* has acclaimed as "excellent."

The JobBank series gives job hunters the most comprehensive, timely, and accurate career information, organized and indexed to facilitate the job search. An entire career reference library, JobBank books are the consummate employment guides.

Published by Adams Media Corporation
260 Center Street, Holbrook, MA 02343

Manufactured in the United States of America.

Because addresses and telephone numbers of smaller companies change rapidly, we recommend you call each company and verify the information before mailing to the employers listed in this book. Mass mailings are not recommended.

While the publisher has made every reasonable effort to obtain and verify accurate information, occasional errors are inevitable due to the magnitude of the database. Should you discover an error, or if a company is missing, please write the editors at the above address so that we may update future editions.

Cover photo courtesy of North Carolina Travel and Tourism Division.

ISBN: 1-55850-603-9

This book is available at quantity discounts for bulk purchases.
For information, call 800/872-5627.

Visit our home page at http://www.adamsjobbank.com

The
Carolina
JobBank
4th Edition

Reference Editor
Steven Graber

Series Editor
Jennifer J. Pfalzgraf

Associate Editor
Marcie DiPietro

Editorial Assistants
Tami M. Forman
Lissa Harnish
Andy Richardson

ADAMS MEDIA CORPORATION
Holbrook, Massachusetts

Top career publications from Adams Media Corporation

The JobBank Series:
each JobBank book is $15.95

The Atlanta JobBank, 1996
The Boston JobBank, 1996
The Carolina JobBank, 4th Ed.
The Chicago JobBank, 1996
The Dallas-Ft. Worth JobBank, 1996
The Denver JobBank, 8th Ed.
The Detroit JobBank, 6th Ed.
The Florida JobBank, 1996
The Houston JobBank, 1996
The Los Angeles JobBank, 1996
The Minneapolis-St. Paul JobBank, 1996
The Missouri JobBank, 1st Ed.
The Metropolitan New York JobBank, 1996
The Ohio JobBank, 1996
The Greater Philadelphia JobBank, 1996
The Phoenix JobBank, 6th Ed.
The San Francisco Bay Area JobBank, 1996
The Seattle JobBank, 1996
The Tennessee JobBank, 3rd Ed.
The Metropolitan Washington JobBank, 1996

The National JobBank, 1996
(Covers the entire U.S.: $270.00 hc)

The JobBank Guide to Employment Services, 1996-1997
(Covers the entire U.S.: $160.00 hc)

Other Career Titles:

The Adams Cover Letter Almanac ($10.95)
The Adams Jobs Almanac, 1996 ($15.95)
The Adams Resume Almanac ($10.95)

America's Fastest Growing Employers, 2nd Ed. ($16.00 pb, $30.00 hc)
Career Shifting ($9.95)
Careers and the College Grad ($12.95)
Careers and the Engineer ($12.95)
Careers and the MBA ($12.95)
Cold Calling Techniques (That Really Work!), 3rd Ed. ($7.95)
The Complete Resume & Job Search Book for College Students ($9.95)
Cover Letters That Knock 'em Dead, 2nd Ed. ($10.95)
Every Woman's Essential Job Hunting & Resume Book ($10.95)
The Harvard Guide to Careers in the Mass Media ($7.95)
High Impact Telephone Networking for Job Hunters ($6.95)
How to Become Successfully Self-Employed, 2nd Ed. ($9.95)
The Job Hunter's Checklist ($5.95)
The Job Search Handbook ($6.95)
Knock 'em Dead, The Ultimate Jobseeker's Handbook, 1996 ($12.95)
The Lifetime Career Manager ($20.00 hc)
The MBA Advantage ($12.95)
The Minority Career Book ($9.95)
The National Jobline Directory ($7.95)
The New Rules of the Job Search Game ($10.95)
Outplace Yourself ($15.95 pb)
Over 40 and Looking for Work? ($7.95)
Reengineering Yourself ($12.95)
The Resume Handbook, 2nd Ed. ($7.95)
Resumes That Knock 'em Dead, 2nd Ed. ($10.95)
300 New Ways to Get a Better Job ($7.95)

TABLE OF CONTENTS

SECTION FOUR: EMPLOYMENT SERVICES

SECTION FIVE: INDEX

HOW TO USE THIS BOOK

Right now, you hold in your hands one of the most effective job hunting tools available anywhere. In *The Carolina JobBank*, you will find a wide array of valuable information to help you launch or continue a rewarding career. But before you open to the book's employer listings and start calling about current job openings, take a few minutes to learn how best to put the resources presented in *The Carolina JobBank* to work for you.

The Carolina JobBank will help you to stand out from other jobseekers. While many people looking for a new job rely solely on newspaper help-wanted ads, this book offers you a much more effective job-search method -- direct contact. The direct contact method has been proven twice as effective as scanning the help-wanted ads. Instead of waiting for employers to come looking for you, you'll be far more effective going to them. While many of your competitors will use trial and error methods in trying to set up interviews, you'll learn not only how to get interviews, but what to expect once you've got them.

In the next few pages, we'll take you through each section of the book so you'll be prepared to get a jump-start on your competition:

The Carolina Job Market: An Overview

To get a feel for the state of the local job scene, read the introductory section called *The Carolina Job Market*. In it, we'll recap the economy's recent performance and the steps that local governments and business leaders are taking to bring new jobs to the area.

Even more importantly, you'll learn where the local economy is headed. What are the prospects for the industries that form the core of the region's economy? Which industries are growing fastest and which ones are laying off? Are there any companies or industries that are especially hot?

To answer these questions for you, we've pored over local business journals and newspapers and interviewed local business leaders and labor analysts. Whether you are new to the area and need a source of regional information, or are a life-long resident just looking for a fresh start in a new job, you'll find this section to be a concise thumbnail sketch of where the jobs are.

This type of information is potent ammunition to bring into an interview. Showing that you're well versed in current industry trends helps give you an edge over job applicants who haven't done their homework.

Basics of Job Winning

Preparation. Strategy. Time-Management. These are three of the most important elements of a successful job search. *Basics of Job Winning* helps you address these and all the other elements needed to find the right job.

One of your first priorities should be to define your personal career objectives. What qualities make a job desirable to you? Creativity? High pay?

Prestige? Use *Basics of Job Winning* to weigh these questions. Then use the rest of the chapter to design a strategy to find a job that matches your criteria.

In *Basics of Job Winning*, you'll learn which job-hunting techniques work, and which don't. We've reviewed the pros and cons of mass mailings, help-wanted ads and direct contact. We'll show you how to develop and approach contacts in your field; how to research a prospective employer; and how to use that information to get an interview and the job.

Also included in *Basics of Job Winning*: interview dress code and etiquette, the "do's and don'ts" of interviewing, sample interview questions, and the often forgotten art of what to do <u>after</u> the interview. We also deal with some of the unique problems faced by those jobseekers who are currently employed, those who have lost a job, and college students conducting their first job search.

Resumes and Cover Letters

The approach you take to writing your resume and cover letter can often mean the difference between getting an interview and never being noticed. In this section, we discuss different formats, as well as what to put on (and what to leave off) your resume. We review the benefits and drawbacks of professional resume writers, and the importance of a follow-up letter. Also included in this section are sample resumes and cover letters which you can use as models.

The Employer Listings

Employers are listed alphabetically by industry, and within each industry, by company names. When a company does business under a person's name, like "John Smith & Co.", the company is usually listed by the surname's spelling (in this case "S"). Exceptions occur when a company's name is widely recognized, like "JCPenney" or "Howard Johnson Motor Lodge." In those cases, the company's first name is the key ("J" and "H" respectively).

The Carolina JobBank covers a very wide range of industries. Each company profile is assigned to one of the industry chapters listed below.

Accounting and Management Consulting
Advertising/Marketing and Public Relations
Aerospace
Apparel and Textiles
Architecture, Construction, and Engineering
Arts and Entertainment/Recreation
Automotive
Banking/Savings and Loans
Biotechnology, Pharmaceuticals and Scientific R&D
Business Services and Non-Scientific Research
Charities and Social Services

Chemicals/Rubber and Plastics
Communications: Telecommunications and Broadcasting
Computer Hardware, Software and Services
Educational Services
Electronic/Industrial Electrical Equipment
Environmental and Waste Management Services
Fabricated/Primary Metals and Products
Financial Services
Food and Beverage/Agriculture
Government

*Health Care: Services, Equipment and
    Products
Hotels and Restaurants
Insurance
Legal Services
Manufacturing and Wholesaling: Misc.
    Consumer
Manufacturing and Wholesaling: Misc.
    Industrial*

*Mining/Gas/Petroleum/Energy Related
Paper and Wood Products
Printing and Publishing
Real Estate
Retail
Stone, Clay, Glass and Concrete Products
Transportation
Utilities: Electric/Gas/Water*

Many of the company listings offer detailed company profiles. In addition to company names, addresses, and phone numbers, these listings also include contact names or hiring departments, and descriptions of each company's products and/or services. Many of these listings also include a variety of additional information including:

Common positions - A list of job titles that the company commonly fills when it is hiring, organized in alphabetical order from Accountant to X-ray Technician. Note: Keep in mind that *The Carolina JobBank* is a directory of major employers in the area, not a directory of openings currently available. Many of the companies listed will be hiring, others will not. However, since most professional job openings are filled without the placement of help-wanted ads, contacting the employers in this book directly is still a more effective method than browsing the Sunday papers.

Educational backgrounds sought - A list of educational backgrounds that companies seek when hiring.

Benefits - What kind of benefits packages are available from these employers? Here you'll find a broad range of benefits, from the relatively common (medical insurance) to those that are much more rare (health club membership; child daycare assistance).

Special programs - Does the company offer training programs, internships or apprenticeships? These programs can be important to first time jobseekers and college students looking for practical work experience. Many employer profiles will include information on these programs.

Parent company - If an employer is a subsidiary of a larger company, the name of that parent company will often be listed here. Use this information to supplement your company research before contacting the employer.

Number of employees - The number of workers a company employs.

Companies may also include information on other U.S. locations and any stock exchange the firm may be listed on.

Because so many job openings are with small and mid-sized employers, we've also included the addresses and phone numbers of such employers. While none of these listings include any additional hiring information, many of them do offer rewarding career opportunities. These companies are found under each industry heading. Within each industry, they are organized by the type of product or service offered.

A note on all employer listings that appear in *The Carolina JobBank*. This book is intended as a starting point. It is not intended to replace any effort that you, the jobseeker, should devote to your job hunt. Keep in mind that while a great deal of effort has been put into collecting and verifying the company profiles provided in this book, addresses and contact names change regularly. Inevitably, some contact names listed herein have changed even before you read this. We recommend you contact a company before mailing your resume to ensure nothing has changed.

At the end of each industry section, we have included a directory of other industry-specific resources to help you in your job search. These include: professional and industrial associations, many of which can provide employment advice and job search help; magazines that cover the industry; and additional directories that may supplement the employer listings in this book.

Employment Services

Immediately following the employer listings section of this book are listings of local employment services firms. Many jobseekers supplement their own efforts by contracting "temp" services, head hunters, and other employment search firms to generate potential job opportunities.

This section is a comprehensive listing of such firms, arranged alphabetically under the headings Employment Agencies, Temporary Agencies, and Executive Search Firms. Each listing includes the firm's name, address, telephone number and contact person. Most listings also include the industries the firm specializes in, the type of positions commonly filled, and the number of jobs filled annually.

Index

The Carolina JobBank index is a straight alphabetical listing.

THE CAROLINA JOB MARKET: AN OVERVIEW

North and South Carolina cover a vast expanse of the eastern U.S. coastline, incorporating a melange of businesses and lifestyles. A typical Carolinian may live in a buzzing metropolis, a sophisticated smaller city, a neighborly village, or in the rural countryside. Career choices stretch from farmer to businessperson to high-tech researcher and developer.

Among the strengths of the North Carolina economy are the rich high-tech business opportunities in the Raleigh-Durham-Chapel Hill area. South Carolina's fertility is more literal -- agriculture is the cornerstone of the state's economy, with manufacturing playing a strong supporting role. Both states enjoy a low cost of living, balmy temperatures for much of the year, and affordable housing. To examine the Carolina job market, let's take a closer look at each state.

NORTH CAROLINA

Raleigh-Durham and the Research Triangle

The backbone of North Carolina's economy is found at its capital and the surrounding Wake County. Raleigh appeals to businesses and individuals alike, earning recognition for its top-notch workforce pool, pro-business atmosphere, medical care, and quality of life. Business publications have showered praise on the city for years: *Fortune* has called Raleigh the best city in America for "knowledge workers," and it has been hailed by *Entrepreneur* for its nurturing atmosphere for start-up companies. *World Trade* has called it a hot spot for international companies. *Money* has rated it as the best place to live and the *Wall Street Journal's National Business Employment Weekly* has rated greater Raleigh the fourth-best market in the country for new graduates.

The prosperity of Raleigh and Wake County is spurred by talent at three distinguished universities -- **Duke University** in Durham, the **University of North Carolina** at Chapel Hill, and **North Carolina State University** in Raleigh. The three schools mark the points forming the technology-laden Research Triangle Park, home to over 70 U.S. and foreign companies. The presence of these and other local colleges and universities helps the Triangle maintain one of the highest concentrations of highly-qualified college graduates in the country. After graduating from local universities, students find a plethora of opportunities in highly technical, information-related fields. As Research Triangle businesses eagerly hire fresh recruits and experienced transplants, the economy is also given a boost. Most workers employed by high-tech businesses earn above-average salaries, which translates into more discretionary income that can be funneled back into area businesses.

Although the Raleigh-Durham area avoided the national recession of the early '90s, its economy is now thriving in a recovery-like manner. *The Triangle Business Journal* reported that as of January 1995, North Carolina's 3.3 percent unemployment rate was the lowest of the nation's largest 11 states, and the only one below 4 percent.

Health care, telecommunications, biotech, and software companies dominate the Research Triangle. Most of **IBM**'s personal computer operations are here, along with over 10,000 employees. Other big names include **Glaxo**, the developers of AZT. Durham, formerly known as "Tobacco City," now claims to be the "City of Medicine," supported by the **Duke University Medical Center**. According to *Carolina Business*, one in three people in Durham works in a health-related field, and the physician-to-population ratio is five times the national average.

Accolades for the Research Triangle continue to draw high-tech companies from other parts of the country. In 1993, 38 new companies relocated or started up in the area, creating 1,150 new jobs. The big news in 1994 was **Motorola**'s purchase of a semiconductor manufacturing site originally owned by General Electric, and most recently owned by Harris Semiconductor. Motorola retained all Harris employees and hired 75 more, bringing total employment to 250. Jobseekers should keep an eye on this company.

On the Wake County side of Research Triangle Park, **NetEdge Systems, Inc.**, a computer network developer, began building a new research facility in late 1994. Several other high-tech companies followed suit in the spring of 1995. Among them: **Cisco Systems**, **Corning BioPro**, and **Biogen**. Over 1,000 jobs should result from these openings in 1996 and 1997. Other good bets for jobseekers in the Research Triangle: Michigan-based **Syntel Inc.** has chosen Cary's Crossroads Corporate Park for the site of its new development center, and hopes to employ 325 workers there. **Strategic Technologies** in Cary, a company that sells and integrates corporate information systems, was recently listed as one of the fastest-growing companies in the U.S. by *Inc.* magazine.

Charlotte

The prosperity of Raleigh-Durham spills into the rest of the state's economy as well. In 1994, the Tar Heel State was among the top five for population emigration from other states. That trend still continues today, as the state's growth rate races on far beyond the national average. As North Carolina's largest city with just under 400,000 residents, Charlotte is seeing particularly marked growth, as over 400 companies started up, expanded, or relocated to the city in the early '90s. John Rees, head of geography at **UNC Greensboro**, sees Charlotte not only growing but acting as a magnetic pole drawing on Raleigh. He sees the two cities growing toward one another, eventually becoming a single, "linear city."

Supported by the cotton and textile industries, Charlotte also has become the third-largest financial center in the United States, after New York and San Francisco. Two *Fortune* 500 banks are headquartered in town -- **First Union** and **NationsBank**. Electronics, printing and publishing, and medical services also abound as this city draws relocating companies from around the globe.

However, it is still the textile industry that dominates. **Speizman Industries**, a distributor of textile machinery for the hosiery industry, was recently named by *Business Week* one of the hottest companies in America. And

Collins and Aikman, the *Fortune* 500 company that manufactures wall-coverings, home fabrics, and auto fabrics, is also based in Charlotte. Other large Charlotte employers include **National Gypsum**, a producer of structural metal work, and **Nucor**, a manufacturer of steel and steel products. A potentially good bet for jobseekers: **Cogentrix**, a power plant operator. This fast-growing company topped the *Inc.* 500 list two years in a row -- in the midst of the early '90s recession.

Other opportunities

With giants such as **Standard Commercial**, a tobacco leaf merchant in Wilson, and apparel manufacturers **Burlington Industries** and **Unifi**, both of Greensboro, textile manufacturing and tobacco still rank among the largest employers in other regions of the state. However, there are additional opportunities emerging if one knows where to look. Some of the more interesting high-growth companies include Asheville's **HydroLogic**, a company that provides water-quality environmental services; **Sports Endeavors** of Hillsborough, a mail-order catalog company specializing in sports apparel; Pineville's **Sound Choice Accompaniment Tracks**, a manufacturer and distributor of software for the karaoke industry; and **Protech Communications** of Burlington, involved in the sales and service of communications systems.

SOUTH CAROLINA

While South Carolina's job market has not boomed the way North Carolina's has in recent years, the Palmetto State still boasts one of the stronger local economies in the nation. South Carolina's service sector added 10,900 new jobs between September 1994 and September 1995, and the wholesale and retail trade added another 10,000. Population is expected to increase steadily through the turn of the century, reaching 4 million shortly after the year 2000. The state's three major business centers -- Greenville, Columbia, and Charleston -- have all shown substantial growth. Furthermore, South Carolina is an agreeable place to live, with a low cost of living and a beautiful coastline.

Despite its important role in the state's economy, the manufacturing sector is not doing exceptionally well here. In total, between September 1994 and September 1995, South Carolina manufacturers laid off 7,200 workers. The bulk of the losses occurred in apparel and textile manufacturing, where 3,100 jobs were cut. However, the industrial machinery and equipment sector performed much better, gaining 1,600 jobs.

Charleston and the coast

Traditionally, the military has also played an important economic role in the coastal region of South Carolina. The area is home to the **Charleston Naval Base** and **Charleston Air Force Base**. The **Marine Corps Recruit Depot** at Parris Island and the **Marine Corps Air Command** site at Beaufort are also nearby. Unfortunately, the military cannot always be counted on as a stable employer here. In April 1996, the Charleston Naval Base is scheduled to close. The closing is projected to cost the state as many as 22,000 jobs.

There has been some good news for jobseekers in this region, however. Berkeley County won out over West Point, Virginia, as home to **Nucor Corporation**'s third steel mini-mill. The mini-mill is expected to generate about 500 high-paying jobs, in addition to creating satellite industries.

As much of an economic lift as the new Nucor mill will be, an even bigger boost to Charleston and the surrounding coastal region comes from tourism. More than 5 million tourists visit the state every year, drawn to the coast's many golf courses and beautiful, warm-water beaches. Charleston is particularly well-known for its preserved and restored historic buildings. Myrtle Beach has benefited from the boom in country music as tourists have flocked to the area's country music theaters.

Columbia

Capital city Columbia, the largest city in the state and home of the **University of South Carolina**, serves as the state's government, services, and transportation center, with these sources providing the bulk of the city's employment.

Although South Carolina is not as well-known for its high-tech companies as its neighbor to the north is, there are a number of businesses in the greater Columbia area that jobseekers should investigate. **Policy Management Systems**, a *Business Week* 1000 company, is a Blythewood computer software firm specializing in developing systems for insurance companies. Also, **Computer Professionals**, a provider of information, as well as consulting and integration services, has shown substantial job growth in recent years.

Looking to the future, the employment outlook for South Carolina remains promising, with the state expecting to gain 28,000 non-farm jobs through the year 2005. Population growth and rising disposable income will make services -- social, management consulting, business, legal, and health -- the fastest-growing sector in the state. As is true nationwide, an aging population and advances in medical technology will increase the demand for health-related workers, such as physical therapists and home health aides. Other fast-growing occupations in South Carolina include human service workers, machine tool setters and operators, and data processing equipment repairers.

For further information, jobseekers can contact:

Employment Security Commission of North Carolina
P.O. Box 25903
Raleigh NC 27611
919/733-3098

Greater Raleigh Chamber of Commerce
P.O. Box 2978
Raleigh NC 27602
919/664-7040

South Carolina Employment Security Commission
Labor Market Information Division
P.O. Box 995
Columbia SC 29202
803/737-2660

THE JOB SEARCH

THE BASICS OF JOB WINNING: A CONDENSED REVIEW

This chapter is divided into four sections. The first section explains the fundamentals that every jobseeker should know, especially first-time jobseekers. The following three sections deal with special situations faced by specific types of jobseekers: those who are currently employed, those who have lost a job, and college students.

THE BASICS:
Things Everyone Needs To Know

Career Planning   The first step to finding your ideal job is to clearly define your objectives. This is better known as career planning (or life planning if you wish to emphasize the importance of combining the two). Career planning has become a field of study in and of itself.

If you are thinking of choosing or switching careers, we particularly emphasize two things. First, choose a career where you will enjoy most of the day-to-day tasks. This sounds obvious, but most of us have at one point or another been attracted by a glamour industry or a prestigious job title without thinking of the most important consideration: Would we enjoy performing the everyday tasks the position entails?

The second key consideration is that you are not merely choosing a career, but also a lifestyle. Career counselors indicate that one of the most common problems people encounter in job-seeking is that they fail to consider how well-suited they are for a particular position or career. For example, some people, attracted to management consulting by good salaries, early responsibility, and high-level corporate exposure, do not adapt well to the long hours, heavy travel demands, and constant pressure to produce. Be sure to ask yourself how you might adapt to not only the day-to-day duties and working environment that a specific position entails, but also how you might adapt to the demands of that career or industry choice as a whole.

Choosing Your Strategy   Assuming that you've established your career objectives, the next step of the job search is to develop a strategy. If you don't take the time to develop a strategy and lay out a plan, you may find yourself going in circles after several weeks of randomly searching for opportunities that always seem just beyond your reach.

The most common job-seeking techniques are:

- following up on help-wanted advertisements
- using employment services
- relying on personal contacts
- contacting employers directly (the Direct Contact method)

Many professionals have been successful in finding better jobs using each one of these approaches. However, the Direct Contact method boasts twice the success rate of the others. So unless you have specific reasons to believe that other strategies would work best for you, Direct Contact should form the foundation of your job search.

If you prefer to use other methods as well, try to expend at least half your effort on Direct Contact, spending the rest on all of the other methods combined. Millions of other jobseekers have already proven that Direct Contact has been twice as effective in obtaining employment, so why not benefit from their experience?

With your strategy in mind, the next step is to work out the details of **Setting** your search. The most important detail is setting up a schedule. Of course, **Your** since job searches aren't something most people do regularly, it may be **Schedule** hard to estimate how long each step will take. Nonetheless, it is important to have a plan so that you can monitor your progress.

When outlining your job search schedule, have a realistic time frame in mind. If you will be job-searching full-time, your search could take at least two months or more. If you can only devote part-time effort, it will probably take at least four months.

You probably know a few currently employed people who seem to spend their whole lives searching for a better job in their spare time. Don't be one of them. If you are presently working and don't feel like devoting a lot of energy to job-seeking right now, then wait. Focus on enjoying your present position,

> **The first step in beginning your job search is to clearly define your objectives.**

performing your best on the job, and storing up energy for when you are really ready to begin your job search.

Those of you who are currently unemployed should remember that job-hunting is tough work physically and emotionally. It is also intellectually demanding work that requires you to be at your best. So don't tire yourself out by working on your job campaign around the clock. At the same time, be sure to discipline yourself. The most logical way to manage your time while looking for a job is to keep your regular working hours.

If you are searching full-time and have decided to choose several different contact methods, we recommend that you divide up each week, designating some time for each method. By trying several approaches at once, you can evaluate how promising each seems and alter your schedule accordingly. But be careful -- don't judge the success of a particular technique just by the sheer number of interviews you obtain. Positions advertised in the newspaper, for instance, are likely to generate many more interviews per opening than positions that are filled without being advertised.

If you are searching part-time and decide to try several different contact methods, we recommend that you try them sequentially. You simply won't have enough time to put a meaningful amount of effort into more than one method at once. Estimate the length of your job search, and then allocate so many weeks or months for each contact method, beginning with Direct Contact.

And remember that all schedules are meant to be broken. The purpose of setting a schedule is not to rush you to your goal but to help you periodically evaluate how you're progressing.

The Direct Contact Method

Once you have scheduled your time, you are ready to begin your search in earnest. If you decide to begin with the Direct Contact method, the first step is to develop a checklist for categorizing the types of firms for which you'd like to work. You might categorize firms by product line, size, customer-type (such as industrial or consumer), growth prospects, or geographical location. Your list of important criteria might be very short. If it is, good! The shorter it is, the easier it will be to locate a company that is right for you.

Now you will want to use this *JobBank* book to assemble your list of potential employers. Choose firms where *you* are most likely to be able to find a job. Try matching your skills with those that a specific job demands. Consider where your skills might be in demand, the degree of competition for employment, and the employment outlook at each company.

Separate your prospect list into three groups. The first 25 percent will be your primary target group, the next 25 percent will be your secondary group, and the remaining names you can keep in reserve.

After you form your prospect list, begin work on your resume. Refer to the Resumes and Cover Letters section following this chapter to get ideas.

Once your resume is complete, begin researching your first batch of prospective employers. You will want to determine whether you would be happy working at the firms you are researching and to get a better idea of what their employment needs might be. You also need to obtain enough information to sound highly informed about the company during phone conversations and in mail correspondence. But don't go all out on your research yet! You probably won't be able to arrange interviews with some of these firms, so save your big research effort until you start to arrange interviews. Nevertheless, you should plan to spend several hours researching each firm. Do your research in batches to save time and energy. Start with this book, and find out what you can about each of the firms in your primary target group. Contact any pertinent professional associations that may be able to help you learn more about an employer. Read industry

> **The more you know about a company, the more likely you are to catch an interviewer's eye. (You'll also face fewer surprises once you get the job!)**

publications looking for articles on the firm. (Addresses of associations and names of important publications are listed after each industrial section of employer listings in this book.) Then try additional resources at your local library. Keep organized, and maintain a folder on each firm.

If you discover something that really disturbs you about the firm (they are about to close their only local office), or if you discover that your chances of getting a job there are practically nil (they have just instituted a hiring freeze), then cross them off your prospect list. If possible,

---

DEVELOPING YOUR CONTACTS: NETWORKING

Some career counselors feel that the best route to a better job is through somebody you already know or through somebody to whom you can be introduced. These counselors recommend that you build your contact base beyond your current acquaintances by asking each one to introduce you, or refer you, to additional people in your field of interest.

The theory goes like this: You might start with 15 personal contacts, each of whom introduces you to three additional people, for a total of 45 additional contacts. Then each of these people introduces you to three additional people, which adds 135 additional contacts. Theoretically, you will soon know every person in the industry.

Of course, developing your personal contacts does not work quite as smoothly as the theory suggests because some people will not be able to introduce you to anyone. The further you stray from your initial contact base, the weaker your references may be. So, if you do try developing your own contacts, try to begin with as many people that you know personally as you can. Dig into your personal phone book and your holiday greeting card list and locate old classmates from school. Be particularly sure to approach people who perform your personal business such as your lawyer, accountant, banker, doctor, stockbroker, and insurance agent. These people develop a very broad contact base due to the nature of their professions.

---

supplement your research efforts by contacting individuals who know the firm well. Ideally you should make an informal contact with someone at that particular firm, but often a direct competitor, or a major supplier or customer, will be able to supply you with just as much information. At the very least, try to obtain whatever printed information the company has available -- not just annual reports, but product brochures and any other printed materials that the firm may have to offer, either about its operations or about career opportunities.

Getting The Interview   Now it is time to arrange an interview, time to make the Direct Contact. If you have read many books on job-searching, you may have noticed that most of these books tell you to avoid the personnel office like the plague. It is said that the personnel office never hires people; they screen candidates. Unfortunately, this is often the case. If you can identify the appropriate manager with the authority to hire you, you should try to contact that person directly. However, this will take a lot of time in each case, and often you'll be bounced back to personnel despite your efforts. So we suggest that initially you begin your Direct Contact campaign through personnel offices. If it seems that the firms on your prospect list do little hiring through personnel, you might consider some alternative courses of action.

The three obvious means of initiating Direct Contact are:

- Showing up unannounced
- Mail
- Phone calls

Cross out the first one right away. You should never show up to seek a professional position without an appointment. Even if you are somehow lucky enough to obtain an interview, you will appear so unprofessional that you will not be seriously considered.

Mail contact seems to be a good choice if you have not been in the job market for a while. You can take your time to prepare a letter, say exactly what you want, and of course include your resume. Remember that employers receive many resumes every day. Don't be surprised if you do not get a response to your inquiry, and don't spend weeks waiting for responses that may never come. If you do send a letter, follow it up (or precede it) with a phone call. This will increase your impact, and because of the initial research you did, will underscore both your familiarity with and your interest in the firm.

Another alternative is to make a "Cover Call." Your Cover Call should be just like your cover letter: concise. Your first statement should interest the employer in you. Then try to subtly mention your familiarity with the firm. Don't be overbearing; keep your introduction to three sentences or less. Be pleasant, self-confident, and relaxed. This will greatly increase the chances of the person at the other end of the line developing the conversation. But don't press. If you are asked to follow up with "something in the mail," this signals the conversation's natural end. Don't try to prolong the conversation once it has ended, and don't ask what they want to receive in the mail. Always send your resume and a highly personalized follow-up letter, reminding the addressee of the phone conversation. *Always* include a cover letter if you are asked to send a resume.

> **Always include a cover letter if you are asked to send a resume.**

Unless you are in telephone sales, making smooth and relaxed cover calls will probably not come easily. Practice them on your own, and then with your friends or relatives.

If you obtain an interview as a result of a telephone conversation, be sure to send a thank-you note reiterating the points you made during the

DON'T BOTHER WITH MASS MAILINGS OR BARRAGES OF PHONE CALLS

Direct Contact does not mean burying every firm within a hundred miles with mail and phone calls. Mass mailings rarely work in the job hunt. This also applies to those letters that are personalized -- but dehumanized -- on an automatic typewriter or computer. Don't waste your time or money on such a project; you will fool no one but yourself.

The worst part of sending out mass mailings, or making unplanned phone calls to companies you have not researched, is that you are likely to be remembered as someone with little genuine interest in the firm, who lacks sincerity -- somebody that nobody wants to hire.

HELP WANTED ADVERTISEMENTS

Only a small fraction of professional job openings are advertised. Yet the majority of jobseekers -- and quite a few people not in the job market -- spend a lot of time studying the help wanted ads. As a result, the competition for advertised openings is often very severe.

A moderate-sized employer told us about their experience advertising in the help wanted section of a major Sunday newspaper:

It was a disaster. We had over 500 responses from this relatively small ad in just one week. We have only two phone lines in this office and one was totally knocked out. We'll never advertise for professional help again.

If you insist on following up on help wanted ads, then research a firm before you reply to an ad. Preliminary research might help to separate you from all of the other professionals responding to that ad, many of whom will have only a passing interest in the opportunity. It will also give you insight about a particular firm, to help you determine if it is potentially a good match. That said, your chances of obtaining a job through the want ads are still much smaller than they are with the Direct Contact method.

conversation. You will appear more professional and increase your impact. However, unless specifically requested, don't mail your resume once an interview has been arranged. Take it with you to the interview instead.

Preparing For The Interview
Once the interview has been arranged, begin your in-depth research. You should arrive at an interview knowing the company upside-down and inside-out. You need to know the company's products, types of customers, subsidiaries, parent company, principal locations, rank in the industry, sales and profit trends, type of ownership, size, current plans, and much more. By this time you have probably narrowed your job search to one industry. Even if you haven't, you should still be familiar with the trends in the firm's industry, the firm's principal competitors and their relative performance, and the direction in which the industry leaders are headed.

Dig into every resource you can! Read the company literature, the trade press, the business press, and if the company is public, call your stockbroker (if you have one) and ask for additional information. If possible, speak to someone at the firm before the interview, or if not, speak to someone at a competing firm. The more time you spend, the better. Even if you feel extremely pressed for time, you should set aside several hours for pre-interview research.

> You should arrive at an interview knowing the company upside-down and inside-out.

If you have been out of the job market for some time, don't be surprised if you find yourself tense during your first few interviews. It will probably happen every time you re-enter the market, not just when you seek your first job after getting out of school.

Tension is natural during an interview, but knowing you have done a thorough research job should put you more at ease. Make a list of questions that you think might be asked in each interview. Think out your answers carefully and practice them with a friend. Tape record your responses to the problem questions. If you feel particularly unsure of your interviewing skills, arrange your first interviews at firms you are not as interested in. (But remember it is common courtesy to seem enthusiastic about the possibility of working for any firm at which you interview.) Practice again on your own after these first few interviews. Go over the difficult questions that you were asked.

Interview Attire
How important is the proper dress for a job interview? Buying a complete wardrobe of Brooks Brothers pinstripes or Donna Karan suits, donning new wing tips or pumps, and having your hair styled every morning are not enough to guarantee you a career position as an investment banker. But on the other hand, if you can't find a clean, conservative suit or won't take the time to wash your hair, then you are just wasting your time by interviewing at all.

Top personal grooming is as important as finding appropriate clothes for a job interview. Careful grooming indicates both a sense of thoroughness and self-confidence. This is not the time to make a statement -- take out the extra earrings and avoid any garish hair colors not found in nature. Women should not wear excessive makeup, and both men and women should refrain from wearing any perfume or cologne (it only takes a small spritz to leave an allergic interviewer with a fit of sneezing and a bad impression of your meeting). Men should be freshly shaven, even if the interview is late in the day, and men with long hair should have it pulled back and neat.

Men applying for any professional position should wear a suit, preferably in a conservative color such as navy or charcoal gray. It is easy to get away with wearing the same dark suit to consecutive interviews at the same company; just be sure to wear a different shirt and tie for each interview.

Women should also wear a businesslike suit. Professionalism still dictates a suit with a skirt, rather than slacks, as proper interview garb for women. This is usually true even at companies where pants are acceptable attire for female employees. As much as you may disagree with this guideline, the more prudent time to fight this standard is after you land the job.

SKIRT VS. PANTS:
An Interview Dilemma

For those women who are still convinced that pants are acceptable interview attire, listen to the words of one career counselor from a prestigious New England college:

I had a student who told me that since she knew women in her industry often wore pants to work, she was going to wear pants to her interviews. Almost every recruiter commented that her pants were "too casual," and even referred to her as "the one with the pants." The funny thing was that one of the recruiters who commented on her pants had been wearing jeans!

The final selection of candidates for a job opening won't be determined by dress, of course. However, inappropriate dress can quickly eliminate a first-round candidate. So while you shouldn't spend a fortune on a new wardrobe, you should be sure that your clothes are adequate. The key is to dress at least as formally or slightly more formally and more conservatively than the position would suggest.

What To Bring   Be complete. Everyone needs a watch, a pen, and a notepad. Finally, a briefcase or a leather-bound folder (containing extra, *unfolded*, copies of your resume) will help complete the look of professionalism.

Sometimes the interviewer will be running behind schedule. Don't be upset, be sympathetic. There is often pressure to interview a lot of candidates and to quickly fill a demanding position. So be sure to come to your interview with good reading material to keep yourself occupied and relaxed.

The Interview   The very beginning of the interview is the most important part because it determines the tone for the rest of it. Those first few moments are especially crucial. Do you smile when you meet? Do you establish enough eye contact, but not too much? Do you walk into the office with a self-assured and confident stride? Do you shake hands firmly? Do you

---

BE PREPARED:
Some Common Interview Questions

Tell me about yourself...

Why did you leave your last job?

What excites you in your current job?

Where would you like to be in five years?

How much overtime are you willing to work?

What would your previous/present employer tell me about you?

Tell me about a difficult situation that you
faced at your previous/present job.

What are your greatest strengths?

What are your greatest weaknesses?

Describe a work situation where you took initiative
and went beyond your normal responsibilities.

Why do you wish to work for this firm?

Why should we hire you?

make small talk easily without being garrulous? It is human nature to judge people by that first impression, so make sure it is a good one. But most of all, try to be yourself.

Often the interviewer will begin, after the small talk, by telling you about the company, the division, the department, or perhaps, the position. Because of your detailed research, the information about the company should be repetitive for you, and the interviewer would probably like nothing better than to avoid this regurgitation of the company biography. So if you can do so tactfully, indicate to the interviewer that you are very familiar with the firm. If he or she seems intent on providing you with background information, despite your hints, then acquiesce.

But be sure to remain attentive. If you can manage to generate a brief discussion of the company or the industry at this point, without being forceful, great. It will help to further build rapport, underscore your interest, and increase your impact.

Soon (if it didn't begin that way) the interviewer will begin the questions, many of which you will have already practiced. This period of the interview usually falls into one of two categories (or somewhere in between): either a structured interview, where the interviewer has a prescribed set of questions to ask; or an unstructured interview, where the interviewer will ask only leading questions to get you to talk about

> **The interviewer's job is to find a reason to turn you down; your job is to not provide that reason.**
>
> -John L. LaFevre, author,
> *How You Really Get Hired*
>
> Reprinted from the 1989/90 *CPC Annual,* with permission of the National Association of Colleges and Employers (formerly College Placement Council, Inc.), copyright holder.

yourself, your experiences, and your goals. Try to sense as quickly as possible in which direction the interviewer wishes to proceed. This will make the interviewer feel more relaxed and in control of the situation.

Remember to keep attuned to the interviewer and make the length of your answers appropriate to the situation. If you are really unsure as to how detailed a response the interviewer is seeking, then ask.

As the interview progresses, the interviewer will probably mention some of the most important responsibilities of the position. If applicable, draw parallels between your experience and the demands of the position as detailed by the interviewer. Describe your past experience in the same manner that you do on your resume: emphasizing results and achievements and not merely describing activities. But don't exaggerate. Be on the level about your abilities.

The first interview is often the toughest, where many candidates are screened out. If you are interviewing for a very competitive position, you will have to make an impression that will last. Focus on a few of your greatest strengths that are relevant to the position. Develop these points carefully, state them again in different words, and then try to summarize them briefly at the end of the interview.

Often the interviewer will pause toward the end and ask if you have any questions. Particularly in a structured interview, this might be the one chance to really show your knowledge of and interest in the firm. Have a list prepared of specific questions that are of real interest to you. Let your questions subtly show your research and your knowledge of the firm's activities. It is wise to have an extensive list of questions, as several of them may be answered during the interview.

> **Getting a job offer is a lot like getting a marriage proposal. Someone is not going to offer it unless they're pretty sure you're going to accept it.**
>
> -Marilyn Hill,
> Associate Director,
> Career Center,
> Carleton College

Do not turn your opportunity to ask questions into an interrogation. Avoid reading directly from your list of questions, and ask questions that you are fairly certain the interviewer can answer (remember how you feel when you cannot answer a question during an interview).

Even if you are unable to determine the salary range beforehand, do not ask about it during the first interview. You can always ask about it later. Above all, don't ask about fringe benefits until you have been offered a position. (Then be sure to get all the details.)

Try not to be negative about anything during the interview (particularly any past employer or any previous job). Be cheerful. Everyone likes to work with someone who seems to be happy.

Don't let a tough question throw you off base. If you don't know the answer to a question, simply say so -- do not apologize. Just smile. Nobody can answer every question -- particularly some of the questions that are asked in job interviews.

Before your first interview, you may be able to determine how many rounds of interviews there usually are for positions at your level. (Of course it may differ quite a bit even within the different levels of one firm.) Usually you can count on attending at least two or three interviews, although some firms are known to give a minimum of six interviews for all professional positions. While you should be more relaxed as you return for subsequent interviews, the pressure will be on. The more prepared you are, the better.

Depending on what information you are able to obtain, you might want to vary your strategy quite a bit from interview to interview. For instance, if the first interview is a screening interview, then be sure a few of your strengths really stand out. On the other hand, if later interviews are primarily with people who are in a position to veto your hiring, but not to push it forward, then you should primarily focus on building rapport as opposed to reiterating and developing your key strengths.

If it looks as though your skills and background do not match the position the interviewer was hoping to fill, ask him or her if there is another division or subsidiary that perhaps could profit from your talents.

Write a follow-up letter immediately after the interview, while it is still fresh in the interviewer's mind (see the sample follow-up letter format found in the Resumes and Cover Letters chapter). Then, if you haven't heard from the interviewer within a week, call to stress your continued interest in the firm, and the position, and request a second interview.

After The Interview

THE BALANCING ACT:
Looking For A New Job While Currently Employed

For those of you who are still employed, job-searching will be particularly tiring because it must be done in addition to your normal work responsibilities. So don't overwork yourself to the point where you show up to interviews looking exhausted and start to slip behind at your current job. On the other hand, don't be tempted to quit your present job! The long hours are worth it. Searching for a job while you have one puts you in a position of strength.

If you're expected to be in your office during the business day, then you have additional problems to deal with. How can you work interviews into the business day? And if you work in an open office, how can you even call to set up interviews? As much as possible you should keep up the effort and the appearances on your present job. So maximize your use of the lunch hour, early mornings, and late afternoons for calling. If you keep trying, you'll be surprised how often you will be able to reach the executive you are trying to contact during your out-of-office hours. You can catch people as early as 8 a.m. and as late as 6 p.m. on frequent occasions.

Making Contact

Your inability to interview at any time other than lunch just might work to your advantage. If you can, try to set up as many interviews as possible for your lunch hour. This will go a long way to creating a relaxed atmosphere. (Who isn't happy when eating?) But be sure the interviews don't stray too far from the agenda on hand.

Scheduling Interviews

Lunchtime interviews are much easier to obtain if you have substantial career experience. People with less experience will often find no alternative to taking time off for interviews. If you have to take time off, you have to take time off. But try to do this as little as possible. Try to take the whole day off in order to avoid being blatantly obvious about your job search, and try to schedule two to three interviews for the same day. (It is

> **Try calling as early as 8 a.m. and as late as 6 p.m. You'll be surprised how often you will be able to reach the executive you want during these times of the day**

very difficult to maintain an optimum level of energy at more than three interviews in one day.) Explain to the interviewer why you might have to juggle your interview schedule -- he/she should honor the respect you're showing your current employer by minimizing your days off and will probably appreciate the fact that another prospective employer is interested in you.

References   What do you tell an interviewer who asks for references? Just say that while you are happy to have your former employers contacted, you are trying to keep your job search confidential and would rather that your current employer not be contacted until you have been given a firm offer.

IF YOU'RE FIRED OR LAID OFF:
Picking Yourself Up and Dusting Yourself Off

If you've been fired or laid off, you are not the first and will not be the last to go through this traumatic experience. In today's changing economy, thousands of professionals lose their jobs every year. Even if you were terminated with just cause, do not lose heart. Remember, being fired is not a reflection on you as a person. It is usually a reflection of your company's staffing needs and its perception of your recent job performance and attitude. And if you were not performing up to par or enjoying your work, then you will probably be better off at another company anyway.

> **Be prepared for the question "Why were you fired?" during job interviews.**

A thorough job search could take months, so be sure to negotiate a reasonable severance package, if possible, and determine what benefits, such as health insurance, you are still legally entitled to. Also, register for unemployment compensation immediately. Don't be surprised to find other professionals collecting unemployment compensation -- it is for everyone who has lost their job.

Don't start your job search with a flurry of unplanned activity. Start by choosing a strategy and working out a plan. Now is not the time for major changes in your life. If possible, remain in the same career and in the same geographical location, at least until you have been working again for a while. On the other hand, if the only industry for which you are trained is leaving, or is severely depressed in your area, then you should give prompt consideration to moving or switching careers.

Avoid mentioning you were fired when arranging interviews, but be prepared for the question "Why were you fired?" during an interview. If you were laid off as a result of downsizing, briefly explain, being sure to reinforce that your job loss was not due to performance. If you were in fact fired, be honest, but try to detail the reason as favorably as possible and portray what you have learned from your mistakes. If you are confident one of your past managers will give you a good reference, tell the interviewer to contact that person. Do not to speak negatively of your past employer and try not to sound particularly worried about your status of being temporarily unemployed. .

Finally, don't spend too much time reflecting on why you were let go or how you might have avoided it. Think positively, look to the future, and be sure to follow a careful plan during your job search.

THE COLLEGE STUDENT:
How To Conduct Your First Job Search

While you will be able to apply many of the basics covered earlier in this chapter to your job search, there are some situations unique to the college student's job search.

Gaining Experience Perhaps the biggest problem college students face is lack of experience. Many schools have internship programs designed to give students exposure to the field of their choice, as well as the opportunity to make valuable contacts. Check out your school's career services department to see what internships are available. If your school does not have a formal internship program, or if there are no available internships that appeal to you, try contacting local businesses and offering your services -- often, businesses will be more than willing to have any extra pair of hands (especially if those hands are unpaid!) for a day or two each week. Or try contacting school alumni to see if you can "shadow" them for a few days, and see what their day-to-day duties are like. Either way, try to begin building experience as early as possible in your college career.

THE GPA QUESTION

You are interviewing for the job of your dreams. Everything is going well: you've established a good rapport, the interviewer seems impressed with your qualifications, and you're almost positive the job is yours. Then you're asked about your GPA, which is pitifully low. Do you tell the truth and watch your dream job fly out the window?

Never lie about your GPA (they may request your transcript, and no company will hire a liar). You can, however, explain if there is a reason you don't feel your grades reflect your abilities, and mention any other impressive statistics. For example, if you have a high GPA in your major, or in the last few semesters (as opposed to your cumulative college career), you can use that fact to your advantage.

What do you do if, for whatever reason, you weren't able to get experience directly related to your desired career? First, look at your previous jobs and see if there's anything you can highlight. Did you supervise or train other employees? Did you reorganize the accounting system, or boost productivity in some way? Accomplishments like these demonstrate leadership, responsibility, and innovation -- qualities that most companies look for in employees. And don't forget volunteer activities and school clubs, which can also showcase these traits.

On-Campus Recruiting   Companies will often send recruiters to interview on-site at various colleges. This gives students a chance to get interviews at companies that may not have interviewed them otherwise, particularly if the company schedules "open" interviews, in which the only screening process is who is first in line at the sign-ups. Of course, since many more applicants gain interviews in this format, this also means that many more people are rejected. The on-campus interview is generally a screening interview, to see if it is worth the company's time to invite you in for a second interview. So do everything possible to make yourself stand out from the crowd.

The first step, of course, is to check out any and all information your school's career center has on the company. If the information seems out of date, call the company's headquarters and ask to be sent the latest annual report, or any other printed information.

Many companies will host an informational meeting for interviewees, often the evening before interviews are scheduled to take place. DO NOT MISS THIS MEETING. The recruiter will almost certainly ask if you attended. Make an effort to stay after the meeting and talk with the company's representatives. Not only does this give you an opportunity to find out more information about both the company and the position, it also makes you stand out in the recruiter's mind. If there's a particular company that you had your heart set on, but you weren't able to get an interview with them, attend the information session anyway. You may be able to convince the recruiter to squeeze you into the schedule. (Or you may discover that the company really isn't suited for you after all.)

Try to check out the interview site beforehand. Some colleges may conduct "mock" interviews that take place in one of the standard interview rooms. Or you may be able to convince a career counselor (or even a custodian) to let you sneak a peek during off-hours. Either way, having an idea of the room's setup will help you to mentally prepare.

Be sure to be at least 15 minutes early to the interview. The recruiter may be running ahead of schedule, and might like to take you early. But don't be surprised if previous interviews have run over, resulting in your 30-minute slot being reduced to 20 minutes (or less). Don't complain; just use whatever time you do have as efficiently as possible to showcase the reasons *you* are the ideal candidate.

LAST WORDS

A parting word of advice. Again and again during your job search you will be rejected. You will be rejected when you apply for interviews. You will be rejected after interviews. For every job offer you finally receive, you probably will have been rejected a multitude of times. Don't let rejections slow you down. Keep reminding yourself that the sooner you go out and get started on your job search, and get those rejections flowing in, the closer you will be to obtaining the job you want.

RESUMES AND COVER LETTERS

When filling a position, a recruiter will often have 100-plus applicants, but time to interview only a handful of the most promising ones. As a result, he or she will reject most applicants after only briefly skimming their resumes.

Unless you have phoned and talked to the recruiter -- which you should do whenever you can -- you will be chosen or rejected for an interview entirely on the basis of your resume and cover letter. Your cover letter must catch the recruiter's attention, and your resume must hold it. (But remember -- a resume is no substitute for a job search campaign. *You* must seek a job. Your resume is only one tool.)

RESUME FORMAT:
Mechanics of a First Impression

The Basics

Recruiters dislike long resumes, so unless you have an unusually strong background with many years of experience and a diversity of outstanding achievements, keep your resume length to one page. If you must squeeze in more information than would otherwise fit, try using a smaller typeface or changing the margins.

Keep your resume on standard 8-1/2" x 11" paper. Since recruiters often get resumes in batches of hundreds, a smaller-sized resume may get lost in the pile. Oversized resumes are likely to get crumpled at the edges, and won't fit easily in their files.

First impressions matter, so make sure the recruiter's first impression of your resume is a good one. Print your resume on quality paper that has weight and texture, in a conservative color such as white, ivory, or pale gray. Use matching paper and envelopes for both your resume and cover letter.

Getting It On Paper

Modern photocomposition typesetting gives you the clearest, sharpest image, a wide variety of type styles, and effects such as italics, bold-facing, and book-like justified margins. It is also much too expensive for many jobseekers. And improvements in laser printers mean that a computer-generated resume can look just as impressive as one that has been professionally typeset.

A computer or word processor is the most flexible way to type your resume. This will allow you to make changes almost instantly and to store different drafts on disk. Word processing and desktop publishing systems also offer many different fonts to choose from, each taking up different amounts of space. (It is generally best to stay between 9-point and 12-point font size.) Many other options are also available, such as bold-facing for emphasis, justified margins, and the ability to change and manipulate spacing.

The end result, however, will be largely determined by the quality of the printer you use. You need at least "letter quality" type for your resume. Do not use a "near letter quality" or dot matrix printer. Laser printers will generally provide the best quality.

Household typewriters and office typewriters with nylon or other cloth ribbons are *not* good enough for typing your resume. If you don't have access to a quality word processor, hire a professional who can prepare your resume with a word processor or typesetting machine.

Don't make your copies on an office photocopier. Only the personnel office may see the resume you mail. Everyone else may see only a copy of it, and copies of copies quickly become unreadable. Either print out each copy individually, or take your resume to a professional copy shop, which generally use professionally-maintained, extra-high-quality photocopiers and charge fairly reasonable prices.

Proof With Care Whether you typed it yourself or paid to have it produced professionally, mistakes on resumes are not only embarrassing, but will usually remove you from further consideration (particularly if something obvious such as your name is misspelled). No matter how much you paid someone else to type, write, or typeset your resume, *you* lose if there is a mistake. So proofread it as carefully as possible. Get a friend to help you. Read your draft aloud as your friend checks the proof copy. Then have your friend read aloud while you check. Next, read it letter by letter to check spelling and punctuation.

If you are having it typed or typeset by a resume service or a printer, and you can't bring a friend or take the time during the day to proof it, pay for it and take it home. Proof it there and bring it back later to get it corrected and printed.

> The one piece of advice I give to everyone about their resume is: show it to people, show it to people, show it to people. Before you ever send out a resume, show it to at least a dozen people.
>
> -Cate Talbot Ashton,
> Associate Director,
> Career Services,
> Colby College

If you wrote your resume on a word processing program, also use that program's built-in spell checker to double-check for spelling errors. But keep in mind that a spell checker will not find errors such as "to" for "two" or "wok" for "work." It's important that you still proofread your resume, even after it has been spell-checked.

Types Of Resumes The two most common resume formats are the functional resume and the chronological resume (examples of both types can be found at the end of this chapter). A functional resume focuses on skills and de-emphasizes job titles, employers, etc. A functional resume is best if you have been out of the work force for a long time and/or if you want to highlight specific skills and strengths that your most recent jobs don't necessarily reflect.

Choose a chronological format if you are currently working or were working recently, and if your most recent experiences relate to your desired field. Use reverse chronological order. To a recruiter your last job and your latest schooling are the most important, so put the last first and list the rest going back in time.

Organization

Your name, phone number, and a complete address should be at the top of your resume. Try to make your name stand out by using a slightly larger font size or all capital letters. Be sure to spell out everything -- never abbreviate St. for Street or Rd. for Road. If you are a college student, you should also put your home address and phone number at the top.

Next, list your experience, then your education. If you are a recent graduate, list your education first, unless your experience is more important than your education. (For example, if you have just graduated from a teaching school, have some business experience, and are applying for a job in business, you would list your business experience first.)

Keep everything easy to find. Put the dates of your employment and education on the left of the page. Put the names of the companies you worked for and the schools you attended a few spaces to the right of the dates. Put the city and state, or the city and country, where you studied or worked to the right of the page.

This is just one suggestion that may work for you. The important thing is simply to break up the text in some way that makes your resume visually attractive and easy to scan, so experiment to see which layout works best for your resume. However you set it up, stay consistent. Inconsistencies in fonts, spacing, or tenses will make your resume look sloppy. Also, be sure to use tabs to keep your information vertically lined up, rather than the less precise space bar.

RESUME CONTENT:
Say It With Style

Sell Yourself

You are selling your skills and accomplishments in your resume, so it is important to inventory yourself and know yourself. If you have achieved something, say so. Put it in the best possible light. But avoid subjective statements, such as "I am a hard worker" or "I get along well with my coworkers." Just stick to the facts.

While you shouldn't hold back or be modest, don't exaggerate your achievements to the point of misrepresentation. Be honest. Many companies will immediately drop an applicant from consideration (or fire a current employee) if inaccurate information is discovered on a resume or other application material.

Keep It Brief   Write down the important (and pertinent) things you have done, but do it in as few words as possible. Your resume will be scanned, not read, and short, concise phrases are much more effective than long-winded sentences. Avoid the use of "I" when emphasizing your accomplishments. Instead, use brief phrases beginning with action verbs.

While some technical terms will be unavoidable, you should try to avoid excessive "technicalese." Keep in mind that the first person to see your resume may be a human resources person who won't necessarily know all the jargon -- and how can they be impressed by something they don't understand?

Also, try to keep your paragraphs at six lines or shorter. If you have more than six lines of information about one job or school, put it in two or more paragraphs. The shorter your resume is, the more carefully it will be examined. Remember: your resume usually has between eight and 45 seconds to catch an employer's eye. So make every second count.

Job Objective   A functional resume may require a job objective to give it focus. One or two sentences describing the job you are seeking can clarify in what capacity your skills will be best put to use.

Examples: An entry-level position in the publishing industry.
A challenging position requiring analytical thought and excellent writing skills.

Don't include a job objective in a chronological resume. Even if you are certain of exactly what type of job you desire, the presence of a job objective might eliminate you from consideration for other positions that a recruiter feels are a better match for your qualifications. But even though you may not put an objective on paper, having a career goal in mind as you write can help give your resume a sense of direction.

Work Experience   Some jobseekers may choose to include both "Relevant Experience" and "Additional Experience" sections. This can be useful, as it allows the jobseeker to place more emphasis on certain experiences and to de-emphasize others.

Emphasize continued experience in a particular job area or continued interest in a particular industry. De-emphasize irrelevant positions. Delete positions that you held for less than four months (unless you are a very recent college grad or still in school).Stress your results, elaborating on how you contributed in your previous jobs. Did you increase sales, reduce costs, improve a product, implement a new program? Were you promoted? Use specific numbers (i.e., quantities, percentages, dollar amounts) whenever possible.

Mention all relevant responsibilities. Be specific, and slant your past accomplishments toward the position that you hope to obtain. For example, do you hope to supervise people? If so, then state how many people, performing what function, you have supervised.

Keep it brief if you have more than two years of career experience. **Education** Elaborate more if you have less experience. If you are a recent grad with two or more years of college, you may choose to include any high school activities that are directly relevant to your career. If you've been out of school for awhile, list post-secondary education only.

Mention degrees received and any honors or special awards. Note individual courses or research projects you participated in that might be relevant for employers. For example, if you are an English major applying for a position as a business writer, be sure to mention any business or economics courses.

USE ACTION VERBS

How you write your resume is just as important as *what* you write. The strongest resumes use short phrases beginning with action verbs. Below, we've listed a few of the action verbs you may want to use. (This list is not all-inclusive.)

achieved	developed	integrated	purchased
administered	devised	interpreted	reduced
advised	directed	interviewed	regulated
analyzed	discovered	invented	reorganized
arranged	distributed	launched	represented
assembled	eliminated	maintained	researched
assisted	established	managed	resolved
attained	evaluated	marketed	restored
budgeted	examined	mediated	restructured
built	executed	monitored	revised
calculated	expanded	negotiated	scheduled
collaborated	expedited	obtained	selected
collected	facilitated	operated	served
compiled	formulated	ordered	sold
completed	founded	organized	solved
computed	generated	participated	streamlined
conducted	headed	performed	studied
consolidated	identified	planned	supervised
constructed	implemented	prepared	supplied
consulted	improved	presented	supported
controlled	increased	processed	tested
coordinated	initiated	produced	trained
created	installed	proposed	updated
designed	instituted	provided	upgraded
determined	instructed	published	wrote

Highlight Impressive Skills   Be sure to mention any computer skills you may have. You may wish to include a section entitled "Additional Skills" or "Computer Skills," in which you list any software programs you know. An additional skills section is also an ideal place to mention fluency in a foreign language.

Personal Data   This section is optional, but if you choose to include it, keep it very brief (two lines maximum). A one-word mention of hobbies such as fishing, chess, baseball, cooking, etc., can give the person who will interview you a good way to open up the conversation. It doesn't hurt to include activities that are unusual (fencing, bungee jumping, snake-charming) or that somehow relate to the position or the company you're applying to (for instance, if you are a member of a professional organization in your industry). Never include information about your age, health, physical characteristics, marital status, or religious affiliation.

References   The most that is needed is the sentence, "References available upon request," at the bottom of your resume. If you choose to leave it out, that's fine.

HIRING A RESUME WRITER:
Is It The Right Choice for You?

If you write reasonably well, it is to your advantage to write your own resume. Writing your resume forces you to review your experience and figure out how to explain your accomplishments in clear, brief phrases. This will help you when you explain your work to interviewers.

If you write your resume, everything will be in your own words -- it will sound like you. It will say what you want it to say. If you are a good writer, know yourself well, and have a good idea of which parts of your background employers are looking for, you should be able to write your own resume better than

> **Those things [marital status, church affiliations, etc.] have no place on a resume. Those are illegal questions, so why even put that information on your resume?**
>
> -Becky Hayes, Career Counselor
> Career Services, Rice University

anyone else can. If you decide to write your resume yourself, have as many people review and proofread it as possible. Welcome objective opinions and other perspectives.

When To Get Help   If you have difficulty writing in "resume style" (which is quite unlike normal written language), if you are unsure of which parts of your background you should emphasize, or if you think your resume would make your case better if it did not follow one of the standard forms outlined either here or in a book on resumes, then you should consider having it professionally written.

There are two reasons even some professional resume writers we know have had their resumes written with the help of fellow professionals. First, they may need the help of someone who can be objective about their background, and second, they may want an experienced sounding board to help focus their thoughts.

The best way to choose a writer is by reputation -- the **If You Hire** recommendation of a friend, a personnel director, your school placement **A Pro** officer, or someone else knowledgeable in the field.

Important questions:
- "How long have you been writing resumes?"
- "If I'm not satisfied with what you write, will you go over it with me and change it?"
- "Do you charge by the hour or a flat rate?"

There is no sure relation between price and quality, except that you are unlikely to get a good writer for less than $50 for an uncomplicated resume and you shouldn't have to pay more than $300 unless your experience is very extensive or complicated. There will be additional charges for printing.

Few resume services will give you a firm price over the phone, simply because some resumes are too complicated and take too long to do for a predetermined price. Some services will quote you a price that applies to almost all of their customers. Once you decide to use a specific writer, you should insist on a firm price quote before engaging their services. Also, find out how expensive minor changes will be.

COVER LETTERS:
Quick, Clear, and Concise

Always mail a cover letter with your resume. In a cover letter you can show an interest in the company that you can't show in a resume. You can also point out one or two skills or accomplishments the company can put to good use.

The more personal you can get, the better. If someone known to the **Make It** person you are writing has recommended that you contact the company, **Personal** get permission to include his/her name in the letter. If you have the name of a person to send the letter to, address it directly to that person (after first calling the company to verify the spelling of the person's name, correct title, and mailing address). Be sure to put the person's name and title on both the letter and the envelope. This will ensure that your letter will get through to the proper person, even if a new person now occupies this position. But even if you don't have a contact name and are simply addressing it to the "Personnel Director" or the "Hiring Partner," definitely send a letter.

Type cover letters in full. Don't try the cheap and easy ways, like using a computer mail merge program, or photocopying the body of your letter and typing in the inside address and salutation. You will give the impression that you are mailing to a host of companies and have no particular interest in any one.

Cover letter do's and don'ts

- *Do* keep your cover letter brief and to the point.
- *Do* be sure it is error-free.
- *Don't* just repeat information verbatim from your resume.
- *Don't* overuse the personal pronoun "I."
- *Don't* send a generic cover letter -- show your personal knowledge of and interest in that particular company.
- *Do* accentuate what you can offer the company, not what you hope to gain from them.

FUNCTIONAL RESUME
(Prepared on a word processor
and laser printed.)

PENELOPE FRANCES PANZ
430 Miller's Crossing
Essex Junction VT 05452
802/555-9354

Objective
A position as a graphic designer commensurate with my acquired skills and expertise.

Summary
Extensive experience in plate making, separations, color matching, background definition, printing, mechanicals, color corrections, and personnel supervision. A highly motivated manager and effective communicator. Proven ability to:

- **Create Commercial Graphics**
- **Produce Embossed Drawings**
- **Color Separate**
- **Control Quality**
- **Resolve Printing Problems**
- **Analyze Customer Satisfaction**

Qualifications

Printing:
Knowledgeable in black and white as well as color printing. Excellent judgment in determining acceptability of color reproduction through comparison with original. Proficient at producing four or five color corrections on all media, as well as restyling previously reproduced four-color artwork.

Customer Relations:
Routinely work closely with customers to ensure specifications are met. Capable of striking a balance between technical printing capabilities and need for customer satisfaction through entire production process.

Specialties:
Practiced at creating silk screen overlays for a multitude of processes including velo bind, GBC bind, and perfect bind. Creative design and timely preparation of posters, flyers, and personalized stationery.

Personnel Supervision:
Skillful at fostering atmosphere that encourages highly talented artists to balance high-level creativity with maximum production. Consistently meet or beat production deadlines. Instruct new employees, apprentices, and students in both artistry and technical operations.

Experience
Graphic Arts Professor, University of Vermont, Burlington VT (1987-1993).
Manager, Design Graphics, Barre VT (1993-present).

Education
Massachusetts Conservatory of Art, Ph.D. 1987
University of Massachusetts, B.A. 1984

CHRONOLOGICAL RESUME
(Prepared on a word processor
and laser printed.)

MAURICE DUPETREAUX
412 Maple Court
Seattle, WA 98404
(206) 555-6584

EXPERIENCE

THE CENTER COMPANY   Seattle, WA
Systems Programmer   1993-present
- Develop and maintain over 100 assembler modules.
- Create screen manager programs, using Assembler and Natural languages, to trace input and output to the VTAM buffer.
- Install and customize Omegamon 695 and 700 on IBM mainframes.
- Develop programs to monitor complete security control blocks, using Assembler and Natural.
- Produce stand-alone IPLs and create backrests on IBM 3380 DASD.

INFO TECH, INC.   Seattle, WA
Technical Manager   1991-1993
- Designed and managed the implementation of a network providing the legal community with a direct line to Supreme Court cases, using Clipper on IBM 386s.
- Developed a system which catalogued entire library inventory, using Turbo Pascal on IBM AT.
- Used C to create a registration system for university registrar on IBM AT.

EDUCATION

SALEM STATE UNIVERSITY   Salem, OR
    B.S. in Computer Science.   1989
    M.S. in Computer Science.   1991

COMPUTER SKILLS

- Programming Languages: C, C++, Assembler, COBOL, Natural, Turbo Pascal, dBASE III+, and Clipper.
- Software: VTAM, Complete, TSO, JES 2, ACF 2, Omegamon 695 and 700, and Adabas.
- Operating Systems: MVS/XA, MVS/SP, MS-DOS, and VMS.

FUNCTIONAL RESUME
(Prepared on an office-quality typewriter)

LORRAINE AVAKIAN
70 Monback Avenue
Oshkosh, WI 54901
(608) 586-1243

OBJECTIVE:
To contribute over eight years of experience in promotion, communications, and administration to an entry-level position in advertising.

SUMMARY OF QUALIFICATIONS:
- Performed advertising duties for small business.
- Experience in business writing and communications skills.
- General knowledge of office management.
- Demonstrated ability to work well with others, in both supervisory and support staff roles.
- Type 75 words per minute.

SELECTED ACHIEVEMENTS AND RESULTS:
Promotion:
Composing, editing, and proofreading correspondence and PR materials for own catering service. Large-scale mailings.

Communication:
Instruction; curriculum and lesson planning; student evaluation; parent-teacher conferences; development of educational materials. Training and supervising clerks.

Computer Skills:
Proficient in MS Word, Lotus 1-2-3, Excel, and Filemaker Pro.

Administration:
Record-keeping and file maintenance. Data processing and computer operations, accounts receivable, accounts payable, inventory control, and customer relations. Scheduling, office management, and telephone reception.

WORK HISTORY:
Teacher; Self-Employed (owner of catering service); Floor Manager; Administrative Assistant; Accounting Clerk.

EDUCATION:
Beloit College, Beloit, WI, BA in Education, 1987

CHRONOLOGICAL RESUME
(Prepared on a word processor
and laser printed)

T. WILLIAM MAGUIRE
16 Charles Street
Marlborough CT 06447
203/555-9641

EDUCATION

Keene State College, Keene NH
Bachelor of Arts in Elementary Education, 1995
- Graduated *magna cum laude*
- English minor
- Kappa Delta Pi member, inducted 1993

EXPERIENCE
September 1995-
Present

Elmer T. Thienes Elementary School, Marlborough CT
Part-time Kindergarten Teacher
- Instruct kindergartners in reading, spelling, language arts, and music.
- Participate in the selection of textbooks and learning aids.
- Organize and supervise class field trips and coordinate in-class presentations.

Summers
1993-1995

Keene YMCA, Youth Division, Keene NH
Child-care Counselor
- Oversaw summer program for low-income youth.
- Budgeted and coordinated special events and field trips, working with Program Director to initiate variations in the program.
- Served as Youth Advocate in cooperation with social worker to address the social needs and problems of participants.

Spring 1995

Wheelock Elementary School, Keene NH
Student Teacher
- Taught third-grade class in all elementary subjects.
- Designed and implemented a two-week unit on Native Americans.
- Assisted in revision of third-grade curriculum.

Fall 1994

Child Development Center, Keene NH
Daycare Worker
- Supervised preschool children on the playground and during art activities.
- Created a "Peter Rabbit Corner," where children could quietly look at books or take a voluntary "time-out."

ADDITIONAL INTERESTS

Martial arts, skiing, politics, reading, writing.

GENERAL MODEL
FOR A COVER LETTER

Your mailing address
Date

Contact's name
Contact's title
Company
Company's mailing address

Dear Mr./Ms. _____:

Immediately explain why your background makes you the best candidate for the position that you are applying for. Describe what prompted you to write (want ad, article you read about the company, networking contact, etc.). Keep the first paragraph short and hard-hitting.

Detail what you could contribute to this company. Show how your qualifications will benefit this firm. Describe your interest in the corporation. Subtly emphasizing your knowledge about this firm and your familiarity with the industry will set you apart from other candidates. Remember to keep this letter short; few recruiters will read a cover letter longer than half a page.

If possible, your closing paragraph should request specific action on the part of the reader. Include your phone number and the hours when you can be reached. Mention that if you do not hear from the reader by a specific date, you will follow up with a phone call. Lastly, thank the reader for their time, consideration, etc.

Sincerely,

(signature)

Your full name (typed)

Enclosure (use this if there are other materials, such as your resume, that are included in the same envelope)

SAMPLE COVER LETTER

16 Charles Street
Marlborough CT 06447
March 16, 1996

Ms. Lia Marcusson
Assistant Principal
Jonathon Daniels Elementary School
43 Mayflower Drive
Keene NH 03431

Dear Ms. Marcusson:

Janet Newell recently informed me of a possible opening for a third grade teacher at Jonathon Daniels Elementary School. With my experience instructing third-graders, both in schools and in summer programs, I feel I would be an ideal candidate for the position. Please accept this letter and the enclosed resume as my application.

Jonathon Daniels' educational philosophy that every child can learn and succeed interests me, since it mirrors my own. My current position at Elmer T. Thienes Elementary has reinforced this philosophy, heightening my awareness of the different styles and paces of learning and increasing my sensitivity toward special needs children. Furthermore, as a direct result of my student teaching experience at Wheelock Elementary School, I am comfortable, confident, and knowledgeable working with third-graders.

I look forward to discussing the position and my qualifications for it in more detail. I can be reached at 203/555-9641 evenings or 203/555-0248 weekdays. If I do not hear from you before Tuesday of next week, I will call to see if we can schedule a time to meet. Thank you for your time and consideration.

Sincerely,

Bill Maguire

T. William Maguire

Enclosure

GENERAL MODEL FOR A
FOLLOW-UP LETTER

Your mailing address
Date

Contact's name
Contact's title
Company
Company's mailing address

Dear Mr./Ms._____:

Remind the interviewer of the reason (i.e., a specific opening, an informational interview, etc.) you were interviewed, as well as the date. Thank him/her for the interview, and try to personalize your thanks by mentioning some specific aspect of the interview.

Confirm your interest in the organization (and in the opening, if you were interviewing for a particular position). Use specifics to re-emphasize that you have researched the firm in detail and have considered how you would fit into the company and the position. This is a good time to say anything you wish you had said in the initial meeting. Be sure to keep this letter brief; a half-page is plenty.

If appropriate, close with a suggestion for further action, such as a desire to have an additional interview, if possible. Mention your phone number and the hours that you can be reached. Alternatively, you may prefer to mention that you will follow up with a phone call in several days. Once again, thank the person for meeting with you, and state that you would be happy to provide any additional information about your qualifications.

Sincerely,

(signature)

Your full name (typed)

PRIMARY EMPLOYERS

ACCOUNTING AND MANAGEMENT CONSULTING

 *As the number of accounting graduates drops and the economy strengthens, all types of accounting professionals will benefit. According to the Bureau of Labor Statistics, the number of accounting jobs may grow by as much as 40 percent by the year 2005. A recent survey conducted by Robert Half International found that the best opportunities for accountants were in the financial, insurance, and real estate sector, followed by the retail and wholesale industries.*

Even faster growth is projected for the management consulting industry, where the number of jobs is expected to grow almost three times faster than the rate for all industries. The increasing complexity of business will contribute to industry growth. Among other things, today's managers must worry about rapid technological innovations, changes in government regulations, growing environmental concerns, continuing reduction of trade barriers, and globalization of markets. Because it has become difficult to keep abreast of these changing conditions, corporations, institutions, and governments will increasingly need the aid of well-trained, well-informed management consulting professionals.

North Carolina

COOPERS & LYBRAND
100 North Tryon Street, Suite 3400, Charlotte NC 28202. 704/375-8414. **Contact:** Leigh Anne Beck, Assistant to Human Resources. **Description:** One of the Big Six certified public accounting firms, providing a broad range of services in the areas of accounting and auditing; taxation; management consulting; and actuarial, benefits, and compensation consulting. Coopers & Lybrand operates 100 offices in the U.S. and more than 700 offices in 112 foreign locations. **Number of employees worldwide:** 65,000.

DELOITTE & TOUCHE
P.O. Box 2778, Raleigh NC 27602-2778. 919/546-8000. **Contact:** Duane Barrett, Office Administrator. **Description:** An international firm of certified public accountants, providing professional accounting, auditing, tax, and management consulting services to widely diversified clients. Deloitte & Touche operates more than 500 offices throughout the world, and has a specialized program consisting of some 25 national industry groups and 50 functional (technical) groups that cross industry lines. Groups are involved in various disciplines, including accounting, auditing, taxation, management advisory services, small and growing businesses, mergers and acquisitions, and computer applications. **Benefits:** Dental Insurance; Disability Coverage; Life Insurance; Medical Insurance; Tuition Assistance. **Corporate headquarters location:** Wilton CT.

ERNST & YOUNG
P.O. Box 40789, Raleigh NC 27629-0789. 919/981-2800. **Contact:** Joanne Jamrozy, Human Resources. **Description:** A certified public accounting firm. Ernst & Young also provides its clients with management consulting services. The company operates more than 300 offices with 16,000 personnel in 70 countries worldwide, including more than 8,500 employees in the United States. The consulting staff is comprised of more than 1,000 consultants and support staff worldwide, and is involved in such fields as data processing, financial modeling, financial feasibility studies, production planning and inventory management, management sciences, health care planning, human resources, and cost accounting and budgeting systems. Ernst & Young provides

services to numerous industries, including health care, financial institutions, insurance, manufacturing, retail, government, utilities, and transportation.

HAY GROUP INC.
212 South Tryon Street, Suite 1370, Charlotte NC 28281. 704/333-1591. **Contact:** Office Manager. **Description:** An international human resources and management consulting firm that provides services ranging from total compensation planning to strategic management, business culture, employee surveys, and outplacement. The Hay Group has 18 field offices located throughout the United States. **Benefits:** Dental Insurance; Disability Coverage; Life Insurance; Medical Insurance; Pension Plan; Tuition Assistance. **Corporate headquarters location:** Philadelphia PA.

KPMG PEAT MARWICK
301 North Elm Street, Greensboro NC 27262. 910/884-1220. **Contact:** Robert Pompey, Manager. **Description:** A large certified public accounting firm providing auditing, assurance, management consulting, and tax services, with more than 1,900 partners and principals in the United States. KPMG Peat Marwick operates approximately 135 offices nationwide, and approximately 1,100 offices in 131 countries. **Benefits:** Dental Insurance; Disability Coverage; Life Insurance; Medical Insurance; Pension Plan; Savings Plan. **Corporate headquarters location:** New York NY.

McGLADREY & PULLEN
P.O. Box 2470, Greensboro NC 27401. 910/273-4461. **Contact:** Timothy Hansen, Personnel Partner. **Description:** A certified public accounting firm providing audit, tax, management, data processing, and cost systems services. **Common positions include:** Accountant/Auditor. **Educational backgrounds include:** Accounting. **Benefits:** 401K; Dental Insurance; Life Insurance; Medical Insurance. **Special Programs:** Training Programs.

Note: Because addresses and telephone numbers of smaller companies change rapidly, we recommend you call each company to verify the information below before inquiring about job opportunities. Mass mailings are not recommended.

Additional employers with under 250 employees:

ACCOUNTING, AUDITING, AND BOOKKEEPING SERVICES

Arthur Andersen & Co.
100 N Tryon St, Suite 3800, Charlotte NC 28202-4000. 704/332-0092.

Deloitte & Touche
227 W Trade St, Suite 1100, Charlotte NC 28202-1675. 704/372-3560.

Ernst & Young
101 N Tryon St, Suite 1100, Charlotte NC 28246-1100. 704/372-6300.

Price Waterhouse
100 N Tryon St, Suite 5400, Charlotte NC 28202-4019. 704/372-9020.

Arthur Andersen & Co.
One Hannover Square Suite 1100, Raleigh NC 27610. 919/832-5400.

Arthur Andersen & Co.
301 N Elm St, Suite 300, Greensboro NC 27401-2149. 910/378-1445.

Blackman & Sloop CPAs
NationsBank Plaza, Durham NC 27701. 919/682-4071.

Payroll 1
810 Tyvola Rd, Charlotte NC 28217-3536. 704/523-8434.

Medaphis Physician Service
1110 Navaho Dr, Raleigh NC 27609-7322. 919/878-8582.

MANAGEMENT SERVICES

Food Masters Inc.
5017 Memory Rd, Raleigh NC 27609-5410. 919/876-0957.

Mattlin Corp.
2703 Lake Forest Dr, Greensboro NC 27408-3804. 910/288-8689.

BUSINESS CONSULTING SERVICES

Development Dimension International
1712 Euclid Ave, Suite 202, Charlotte NC 28203-4700. 704/358-8985.

Gibbens Co. Inc.
4909 Waters Edge Dr, Raleigh NC 27606-2462. 919/851-0141.

Hayes Seay Mattern & Mattern
2300 W Meadowview Rd, Suite 110, Greensboro NC 27407-3711. 910/855-8422.

Mantech Services Corp.
210 Stonebridge Sq, Havelock NC 28532-9505. 919/447-0878.

Management Resources Associates
8848 Red Oak Blvd, Charlotte NC 28217-5518. 704/522-8682.

Maritz Performance Improvement Co.
205 Regency Executive Park Dr, Charlotte NC 28217-3989. 704/527-2202.

CMS
400 Silver Cedar Ct, Chapel Hill NC 27514-1512. 919/933-1118.

Alexander Group
1033 Dresser Ct, Raleigh NC 27609-7323. 919/872-2280.

Charmes Inc.
1479 Lake Meadow Ct, Kernersville NC 27284-7557. 910/993-8640.

Shelton Companies Inc.
301 S College St, Suite
3600, Charlotte NC 28202-
6000. 704/348-2200.

Fieldstudio
410 Oberlin Rd, Raleigh NC
27605-1352. 919/839-
5554.

Sigcom Inc.
4413 W Market St,
Greensboro NC 27407-1305.
910/547-9700.

ERM-Southeast Inc.
7300 Carmel Executive Park,
Charlotte NC 28226.
704/541-8345.

S&ME Inc.
3100 Spring Forest Rd,
Raleigh NC 27604-2880.
919/872-2660.

South Carolina

AUTOMATION RESEARCH SYSTEMS
3937 Sunset Boulevard, West Columbia SC 29169. 803/739-7019. **Contact:** Human Resources. **Description:** Provides consulting services for the health care industry.

ELLIOT DAVIS & COMPANY LLP
1901 Main Street, 11th Floor, Columbia SC 29202. 803/256-0002. **Contact:** Nancy Browder, Office Manager. **Description:** A corporate accounting firm.

HOSPITALITY RESOURCES INC. (HRI)
822 South Guingard Drive, Sumter SC 29150. **Contact:** Maxine Harrington, Payroll Manager. **Description:** Performs general accounting functions, as well as payroll and workmen's compensation, for other corporations.

For more information on career opportunities in accounting and management consulting:

Associations

AMERICAN ACCOUNTING ASSOCIATION
5717 Bessie Drive, Sarasota FL 34233.
813/921-7747. An academically-oriented accounting association that offers two quarterly journals, a semi-annual journal, a newsletter, and a wide variety of continuing education programs.

AMERICAN INSTITUTE OF CERTIFIED PUBLIC ACCOUNTANTS
1211 Avenue of the Americas, New York NY 10036. 212/596-6200. A national professional organization for all CPAs. AICPA offers a comprehensive career package to students.

AMERICAN MANAGEMENT ASSOCIATION
Management Information Service, 135 West 50th Street, New York NY 10020.
212/586-8100. Provides a variety of publications, training videos, and courses, as well as an Information Resource Center, which provides management information, and a library service.

ASSOCIATION OF GOVERNMENT ACCOUNTANTS
2200 Mount Vernon Avenue, Alexandria VA 22301. 703/684-6931.

ASSOCIATION OF MANAGEMENT CONSULTING FIRMS
521 Fifth Avenue, 35th Floor, New York NY 10175. 212/697-9693. Offers certification programs.

INSTITUTE OF INTERNAL AUDITORS
49 Maitland Avenue, Altamont Springs FL 32701. 407/830-7600. Publishes magazines and newsletters. Provides information on current issues, a network of more than 50,000 members in 100 countries, and professional development and research services.

INSTITUTE OF MANAGEMENT ACCOUNTANTS
10 Paragon Drive, Box 433, Montvale NJ 07645-1760. 201/573-9000. Offers a Certified Management Accountant Program, periodicals, seminars, educational programs, a research program, a financial management network, and networking services.

INSTITUTE OF MANAGEMENT CONSULTANTS
521 Fifth Avenue, 35th Floor, New York NY 10175. 212/697-8262. Offers certification and professional development and a directory of members.

NATIONAL ASSOCIATION OF TAX PRACTITIONERS
720 Association Drive, Appleton WI 54914. 414/749-1040. Offers seminars, research, newsletters, preparer worksheets, state chapters, insurance, and other tax-related services.

NATIONAL BUSINESSWOMEN'S LEADERSHIP ASSOCIATION
6901 West 63rd Street, P.O. Box 2949, Shawnee Mission KS 66201-1349. World Wide Web address:
http://www.natsem.com. A professional organization dedicated to advancing the careers of women in management.

NATIONAL SOCIETY OF PUBLIC ACCOUNTANTS
1010 North Fairfax Street, Alexandria VA 22314. 703/549-6400. Offers professional development services, government representation, a variety of publications, practice aids, low-cost group insurance, and annual seminars.

Directories

AICPA DIRECTORY OF ACCOUNTING EDUCATION
American Institute of Certified Public

Accountants, 1211 Avenue of the Americas, New York NY 10036. 212/596-6200. $150.00. Only available to AICPA members.

ACCOUNTING FIRMS AND PRACTITIONERS
American Institute of Certified Public Accountants, 1211 Avenue of the Americas, New York NY 10036. 212/596-6200. $150.00. Only available to AICPA members.

Magazines

CPA JOURNAL
530 Fifth Avenue, New York NY 10136. 212/719-8300. Published monthly by The New York State Society.

CPA LETTER
American Institute of Certified Public Accountants, 1211 Avenue of the Americas, New York NY 10036. 212/596-6200.

JOURNAL OF ACCOUNTANCY
American Institute of Certified Public Accountants, 1211 Avenue of the Americas, New York NY 10036. 212/596-6200.

MANAGEMENT ACCOUNTING
Institute of Management Accounting, 10 Paragon Drive, Montvale NJ 07645. 201/573-9000.

WENDELL'S REPORT FOR CONTROLLERS
Warren, Gorham, and Lamont, Inc., 210 South Street, Boston MA 02111. 617/423-2020.

ADVERTISING, MARKETING, AND PUBLIC RELATIONS

Due to several trends shaping the industry, finding a job in advertising is as tough today as it has ever been. To remain competitive, the industry's largest firms have been downsizing to save money for larger campaigns. On the other hand, smaller agencies are increasingly specializing in fields such as direct marketing and public relations in order to gain a stronger presence in the market. Meanwhile, the growing cable industry has opened the door to new business opportunities, as has the Internet. Increasingly, advertisers are using the information highway to conduct business, as well as to target specific "digital" audiences.

In the public relations field, there has been an explosion in the number and range of consultants in the marketplace. Partially as a result of the recession of the early '90s, many senior executives who were released from their contracts at major firms have launched companies of their own.

North Carolina

ADSTREET
1145-D Executive Circle, Cary NC 27511. 919/481-3004. **Contact:** Rich Styles, President. **Description:** AdStreet is a small, full-service advertising and public relations agency. The company does its own creative advertising work and also offers media buying services.

BOZELL WORLDWIDE, INC.
205 Regency Executive Park Drive, Suite 207, Charlotte NC 28217. 704/527-2990. **Contact:** Human Resources. **Description:** One of 63 international full-service advertising offices. Bozell also offers public relations services such as corporate relations, marketing support, employee relations, financial relations, government affairs, and community relations. The staff includes specialists in marketing, media, account service, creative work, research, public relations, finance, agriculture, and broadcast affairs. **Corporate headquarters location:** New York NY.

CADMUS DIRECT MARKETING, INC.
1123 South Church Street, Charlotte NC 28203-2801. 704/334-5371. **Contact:** Human Resources. **Description:** Cadmus Direct Marketing provides strategic consulting, integrated marketing, database analysis and management, data processing, direct mail production, telemarketing, and fulfillment services. The company is a full-service marketer operating on a national basis. **Parent company:** Cadmus Communications Corporation in Richmond VA is a graphic communications company offering specialized products and services in three broad areas: printing, marketing, and publishing. Cadmus is one of the largest graphic communications companies in North America. Product lines include annual reports, catalogs, direct marketing, financial printing, point-of-sale marketing, promotional printing, publishing, research journals, specialty magazines, and specialty packaging. Other subsidiaries of Cadmus Communications Corporation include: American Graphics, Inc. (Atlanta GA); Cadmus Color Center, Inc. (Richmond VA); Cadmus Interactive (Tucker GA); Cadmus Journal Services (Linthicum MD, Easton MD, and Richmond VA); Central Florida Press, L.C. (Orlando FL); Expert Brown (Richmond VA); Garamond, Inc. (Baltimore MD); Graphtech Corporation (Charlotte NC); Marblehead Communications, Inc. (Boston MA); Three Score, Inc. (Tucker GA); Tuff Stuff Publications, Inc. (Richmond VA); Washburn Graphics, Inc. (Charlotte NC); The William Byrd Press (Richmond VA). **Listed on:** NASDAQ. **Number of employees nationwide:** 2,500.

DONNELLEY MARKETING INC.

200 Creekside Drive, Washington NC 27889. 919/946-8200. **Contact:** Donna Allen, Human Resources Manager. **Description:** Donnelley Marketing Inc. operates in three divisions: Carroll Wright, the company's sales division, sends advertising coupons to residences; Donnelley Consumer Promotions sends promotions through the mail such as soap and detergent products; and the Donnelley Direct Database division provides maintenance services of databases. Donnelley Marketing Inc. also offers a complete line of demographic information services for consumer marketers. **Corporate headquarters location:** New York NY. **Other U.S. locations:** Orange CA; Stamford CT. **Parent company:** Dun & Bradstreet. **Operations at this facility include:** Advertising; Direct Mail; Distribution; Manufacturing; Marketing; Purchasing; Sales Management; Strategic Planning; Telemarketing.

NATIONWIDE ADVERTISING SERVICE INC.

3100 Smoketree Court, Suite 809, Raleigh NC 27604-1053. 919/872-6800. **Contact:** Judy Wilson, Regional Manager. **Description:** With offices in 36 major U.S. and Canadian cities, Nationwide Advertising Service is one of the largest and oldest independent, full-service advertising agencies exclusively specializing in human resource communications, promotions, and advertising. The company offers consultation, campaign planning, ad placement, research, and creative production. **Corporate headquarters location:** Cleveland OH.

Note: Because addresses and telephone numbers of smaller companies change rapidly, we recommend you call each company to verify the information below before inquiring about job opportunities. Mass mailings are not recommended.

Additional employers with under 250 employees:

MISC. ADVERTISING SERVICES

Long Haymes Carr Lintas
P.O. Box 5627, Winston-Salem NC 27113-5627. 910/765-3630.

McKinney & Silver
333 Fayetteville Street Mall, Raleigh NC 27601-1738. 919/828-0691.

Speidel Group
2608 Mayview Rd, Raleigh NC 27607-6917. 919/834-8999.

William Cook Agency
S College St, Charlotte NC 28282. 704/377-7083.

Cable-Ad-Net-Durham
4000 Westchase Blvd, Suite 350, Raleigh NC 27607-3943. 919/834-9488.

News & Record
2579 Eric Ln, Suite M, Burlington NC 27215-5416. 910/229-7301.

Hanes Printables
521 Northridge Park Dr, Rural Hall NC 27045-9575. 910/519-4908.

DIRECT MAIL ADVERTISING SERVICES

Action Performance Sales
415G Minuet Ln, Charlotte NC 28217-2718. 704/525-0300.

KPC Delivery Target Market Coverage
600 S Tryon St, Charlotte NC 28202-1842. 704/358-5968.

Professional Mail Services
5608 Spring Ct, Raleigh NC 27604-2966. 919/876-9651.

Symbol Technologies
4101 Lake Boone Trl, Raleigh NC 27607-7506. 919/571-0235.

Dun & Bradstreet Information Service
5835 Executive Center Dr, Suite 1, Charlotte NC 28212-8849. 704/535-2270.

South Carolina

ADVO, INC.

3937D Sunset Boulevard, West Columbia SC 29169. 803/739-0142. **Contact:** Human Resources. **Description:** A direct mail advertising company. **Corporate headquarters location:** Windsor CT. **Listed on:** New York Stock Exchange. **Number of employees nationwide:** 5,500.

McLEOD AND ASSOCIATES

P.O. Box 3518, West Columbia SC 29169. 803/739-6900. **Contact:** Steve Gardner, Office Manager. **Description:** Advertises for realtors, welcoming newcomers to the Columbia area through three publications.

For more information on career opportunities in advertising, marketing, and public relations:

Associations

ADVERTISING RESEARCH FOUNDATION
641 Lexington Avenue, New York NY
10022. 212/751-5656. Fax: 212/319-
5265. World Wide Web address:
http://www.arfsite.org/arf. A nonprofit
organization comprised of advertising,
marketing, and media research companies.
For institutions only.

AMERICAN ASSOCIATION OF ADVERTISING AGENCIES
666 Third Avenue, New York NY 10017.
212/682-2500. Offers educational and
enrichment benefits such as publications,
videos, and conferences.

AMERICAN MARKETING ASSOCIATION
250 South Wacker Drive, Suite 200,
Chicago IL 60606-5819. 312/831-2764.
Fax: 312/648-5625. World Wide Web
address: http://www.ama.org. An
association with nearly 50,000 members
worldwide. Offers 25 annual conferences,
library and research services, and 25 annual
issues of *Marketing News*.

DIRECT MARKETING ASSOCIATION
1120 Avenue of Americas, New York NY
10036-6700. 212/768-7277. Offers
monthly newsletters, seminars, and
conferences.

INTERNATIONAL ADVERTISING ASSOCIATION
521 Fifth Avenue, Suite 1807, New York
NY 10175. 212/557-1133.

LEAGUE OF ADVERTISING AGENCIES
2 South End Avenue #4C, New York NY
10280. 212/945-4991. Seminars available.

MARKETING RESEARCH ASSOCIATION
2189 Silas Deane Highway, Suite #5,
Rocky Hill CT 06067. 860/257-4008.
Publishes several magazines and
newsletters.

PUBLIC RELATIONS SOCIETY OF AMERICA
33 Irving Place, New York NY 10003.
212/995-2230. Publishes three magazines
for public relations professionals.

Directories

AAAA ROSTER AND ORGANIZATION
American Association of Advertising
Agencies, 666 Third Avenue, 13th Floor,
New York NY 10017. 212/682-2500.

DIRECTORY OF MINORITY PUBLIC RELATIONS PROFESSIONALS
Public Relations Society of America, 33

Irving Place, New York NY 10003.
212/995-2230.

O'DWYER'S DIRECTORY OF PUBLIC RELATIONS FIRMS
J. R. O'Dwyer Company, 271 Madison
Avenue, Room 600, New York NY 10016.
212/679-2471.

PUBLIC RELATIONS CONSULTANTS DIRECTORY
American Business Directories, Division of
American Business Lists, 5711 South 86th
Circle, Omaha NE 68127. 402/593-4500.

PUBLIC RELATIONS JOURNAL/REGISTER ISSUE
Public Relations Society of America, 33
Irving Place, New York NY 10003.
212/995-2230.

STANDARD DIRECTORY OF ADVERTISING AGENCIES
Reed Reference Publishing Company, P.O.
Box 31, New Providence NJ 07974.
800/521-8110.

Magazines

ADVERTISING AGE
Crain Communications, 740 North Rush
Street, Chicago IL 60611. 312/649-5316.

ADWEEK
BPI, 1515 Broadway, 12th Floor, New York
NY 10036-8986. 212/536-5336.

BUSINESS MARKETING
Crain Communications, 740 North Rush
Street, Chicago IL 60611. 312/649-5260.

JOURNAL OF MARKETING
American Marketing Association, 250 South
Wacker Drive, Suite 200, Chicago IL
60606. 312/648-0536.

THE MARKETING NEWS
American Marketing Association, 250 South
Wacker Drive, Suite 200, Chicago IL
60606. 312/648-0536.

PR REPORTER
PR Publishing Company, P.O. Box 600,
Exeter NH 03833. 603/778-0514.

PUBLIC RELATIONS JOURNAL
Public Relations Society of America, 33
Irving Place, New York NY 10003.
212/995-2230.

PUBLIC RELATIONS NEWS
Phillips Publishing Inc., 1202 Seven Locks
Road, Suite 300, Potomac MD 20854.
301/340-1520.

AEROSPACE

The aerospace industry, wracked by layoffs throughout the early '90s, has yet to pull out of its tailspin. As ever, the slump is being fueled by declining commercial aircraft orders and further defense cuts. As a result, research and development dollars have been trimmed, and many of the biggest firms in the industry have now merged. As of early 1996, the industry was continuing to shrink -- and is now dominated by fewer, larger companies.

While this consolidation has led to a surge in profits, it also means that rapid downsizing will continue. Some analysts believe that even though the defense industry has cut well over 1 million jobs since the late '80s, the industry still needs to cut its workforce by another 30 percent.

Many companies are trying to shift to commercial production, reducing their dependence on dwindling defense contracts. Even so, defense purchases still support a significant number of aerospace workers. Over the long haul, the industry's focus on advanced technology will mean more professional and technical positions -- with engineers leading the way.

North Carolina

ALLIEDSIGNAL EQUIPMENT SYSTEMS
3475 North Wesleyan Boulevard, Rocky Mount NC 27804. 919/977-2100. **Contact:** Ron Savino, Human Resources. **Description:** Manufactures aircraft parts and equipment. **Parent company:** AlliedSignal Corporation serves a broad spectrum of industries through its more than 40 strategic businesses, which are grouped into three sectors: Aerospace; Automotive; and Engineered Materials. AlliedSignal Corporation is one of the nation's largest industrial organizations.

BURNS AEROSPACE CORPORATION
1455 Fairchild Road, Winston-Salem NC 27105-4588. 910/767-2000. **Fax:** 910/744-1009. **Contact:** Bill Englebert, Human Resources Manager. **Description:** A manufacturer of airline seating. **Common positions include:** Blue-Collar Worker Supervisor; Buyer; Computer Programmer; Customer Service Representative; Human Resources Specialist; Industrial Engineer; Purchasing Agent and Manager; Quality Control Supervisor. **Educational backgrounds include:** Computer Science; Engineering; Liberal Arts. **Benefits:** 401K; Dental Insurance; Disability Coverage; Employee Discounts; Life Insurance; Pension Plan; Profit Sharing; Savings Plan. **Corporate headquarters location:** This Location. **Other U.S. locations:** Inglewood CA. **Parent company:** Eagle Industries. **Operations at this facility include:** Administration; Divisional Headquarters; Manufacturing; Regional Headquarters; Research and Development; Sales; Service. **Listed on:** Privately held. **Number of employees at this location:** 561. **Number of employees nationwide:** 700.

CURTISS WRIGHT FLIGHT SYSTEMS
201 Old Boiling Springs Road, Shelby NC 28152. 704/481-1150. **Contact:** Anita Ross, Director of Human Resources. **Description:** Manufactures actuation flight control systems for aircraft.

WALTER KIDDE AEROSPACE, INC.
4200 Airport Drive NW, Wilson NC 27896. 919/237-7004. **Contact:** Jan Kemp, Director of Human Resources. **Description:** Develops and manufactures fire detection and suppression equipment for use in aerospace and marine applications. Products are sold to aircraft manufacturers and to airlines as replacement/repair parts, and are used in defense applications. **Common positions include:** Accountant/Auditor; Aerospace Engineer; Computer Programmer; Electrical/Electronics Engineer; Industrial Engineer; Mechanical Engineer. **Educational backgrounds include:** Business Administration; Engineering. **Benefits:** Dental Insurance; Disability Coverage; Life Insurance; Medical Insurance; Pension Plan; Savings Plan; Tuition Assistance. **Special Programs:** Training

Programs. **Corporate headquarters location:** Boston MA. **Parent company:** William Holding Company. **Operations at this facility include:** Administration; Manufacturing; Research and Development; Sales; Service. **Number of employees at this location:** 240.

South Carolina

ABEX NWL AEROSPACE
302 Parker Drive, Beaufort SC 29902. 803/846-3208. **Contact:** Mark Sedky, Human Resources. **Description:** Abex NWL Aerospace is a designer and manufacturer of flight, missile, and engine controls for both commercial and military programs. The product lines consist of electronics, hydraulics, and electrohydraulic components. **Benefits:** 401K; Dental Insurance; Life Insurance; Medical Insurance; Pension Plan; Tuition Assistance. **Corporate headquarters location:** Hampton NH. **Parent company:** Abex Inc. **Listed on:** New York Stock Exchange. **Number of employees nationwide:** 1,068.

CHAMPION AVIATION PRODUCTS
P.O. Box 686, Liberty SC 29657-0686. 864/843-1162. **Contact:** Human Resources. **Description:** Champion Aviation Products manufactures aircraft parts and equipment.

LOCKHEED AEROMOD CENTER INC.
244 Terminal Road, Greenville SC 29605. 864/299-3350. **Contact:** Mr. Terry York, Director of Human Resources. **Description:** Manufactures aircraft parts and equipment. **Parent company:** Lockheed Martin Corporation is a diversified defense contractor with businesses in engineering contracting, civil space programs, government services, commercial electronics, aeronautical systems, avionics, aerodynamics, and materials. Subsidiaries include a missiles and space systems group; an aeronautical systems group; a technology services group; an electronic systems group; and Lockheed Financial Corporation.

STARCRAFT AEROSPACE INC.
305 Florida Street, Greenville SC 29605. 864/299-5444. **Contact:** Human Resources. **Description:** Performs aircraft control and repair services.

For more information on career opportunities in aerospace:

Associations

AIR TRANSPORT ASSOCIATION OF AMERICA
1301 Pennsylvania Avenue NW, Suite 1100, Washington DC 20004. 202/626-4000. A trade association for the major U.S. airlines.

AMERICAN INSTITUTE OF AERONAUTICS AND ASTRONAUTICS
85 John Street, 4th Floor, New York NY 10038. 212/349-1120. Membership required. Publishes six journals and books.

FUTURE AVIATION PROFESSIONALS OF AMERICA
4959 Massachusetts Boulevard, Atlanta GA 30337. 770/997-8097. Publishes a monthly newsletter which monitors the job market for flying jobs; a pilot employment guide, outlining what is required to become a pilot; and a directory of aviation employers.

NATIONAL AERONAUTIC ASSOCIATION OF USA
1815 North Fort Meyer Drive, Suite 700, Arlington VA 22209. 703/527-0226. Publishes a magazine. Membership required.

PROFESSIONAL AVIATION MAINTENANCE ASSOCIATION
500 NW Plaza, Suite 1016, St. Ann MO 63074. 314/739-2580. Members' resumes are distributed to companies who advise the organization of employment opportunities. Many local chapters also provide job referrals. Members have access to the Worldwide Membership Directory.

APPAREL AND TEXTILES

The apparel industry is facing an uncertain future. Women's apparel prices dropped 4.4 percent in 1994, and many experts expect continued deflation through 1996. Consumers have remained disinterested in new fashions and refuse to pay higher prices. Textile and apparel mills are under pressure from the other end of the supply chain as well -- the cost of cotton and other raw materials has remained at close to record highs, with raw cotton prices jumping 35 percent in 1994. As a result, many textile producers have recently reported significant drops in earnings. However, improved consumer confidence, more attractive fashions, and lower prices may prod consumers to buy. This will eventually increase business for mills. Especially hot: sales of men's suits. This trend is expected to continue as men look for upscale casual wear to accommodate more relaxed dress codes. The highest consumer demand in apparel will probably be for lower-priced clothing produced for discount stores.

North Carolina

ALBA-WALDENSIAN, INC.
P.O. Box 100, 201 St. Germain SW, Valdese NC 28690. 704/874-2191. **Contact:** Warren Nesbitt, Human Resources Manager. **Description:** Founded in 1901 as Waldensian Hosiery Mills, Alba-Waldensian has grown into a national, multi-facility apparel manufacturing company offering a variety of knit products. The company primarily produces women's knit hosiery and stretch panties. Since 1974, Alba-Waldensian has also produced knit health products, which are used in hospitals and nursing homes and are distributed throughout the United States, Canada, England, Europe, and the Middle East. In 1989, the company formed Alba Direct, a telemarketing division, which sells the company's products to small retail and export accounts. In 1992, the company acquired Byford Apparel, a marketer of English men's socks and sweaters to department stores, specialty stores, and the golf trade. **Corporate headquarters location:** This Location. **Listed on:** American Stock Exchange. **Number of employees nationwide:** 850.

ALLIEDSIGNAL CORPORATION
338 Pea Ridge Road, Moncure NC 27559. 919/542-2200. **Contact:** John Williamson, Manager/Personnel Department. **Description:** This location manufactures polyester filament yarns for seat belts, cordage, and other industrial applications, and also produces polyester resins. Overall, AlliedSignal Corporation serves a broad spectrum of industries through its more than 40 strategic businesses, which are grouped into three sectors: Aerospace; Automotive; and Engineered Materials. AlliedSignal Corporation is one of the nation's largest industrial organizations.

AMERICAN & EFIRD, INC.
P.O. Box 507, Mount Holly NC 28120. 704/597-7717. **Contact:** Ms. Eunice Price, Director/Personnel Department. **Description:** Manufactures and distributes sewing thread for worldwide industrial and consumer markets. American & Efird, Inc. has 12 manufacturing facilities in North Carolina. **NOTE:** All hiring for American & Efird, Inc. is done at this location, not at the offices of the parent company (Ruddick Corporation). **Parent company:** Ruddick Corporation is a diversified holding company operating through wholly-owned subsidiaries American & Efird, Inc.; Harris Teeter, Inc.; and Ruddick Investment Company. Harris Teeter, Inc., located in Charlotte, NC, operates a regional supermarket chain and handles its own hiring as well. Ruddick Investment Company employs less than ten people.

ARDEN BENHAR MILLS
633 Chatham Street, Sanford NC 27330-4838. 919/774-5900. **Contact:** Barbara Clack, Human Resources Manager. **Description:** A broadwoven fabric mill. Arden

Benhar Mills manufactures potholders, mittens, aprons, chef's attire, and a wide variety of other related products for consumers, kitchens, and restaurants.

ARROWOOD MILLS, INC.
P.O. Box 908, Mount Pleasant NC 28124. 704/436-9351. **Contact:** Linda Bridges, Personnel Director. **Description:** Arrowood Mills, Inc. is a manufacturer and wholesaler of women's sheer hosiery. **Benefits:** Dental Insurance; Employee Discounts; Life Insurance; Medical Insurance; Pension Plan; Savings Plan. **Corporate headquarters location:** This Location. **Operations at this facility include:** Manufacturing; Sales. **Number of employees at this location:** 200.

BALI COMPANY
P.O. Box 5100, Winston-Salem NC 27113-5100. 910/519-6053. **Contact:** Ms. Lee Fittro, Employee Relations Assistant. **Description:** Bali Company manufactures women's intimate apparel. **Parent company:** Sara Lee Corporation is a diversified producer of consumer products including food products.

BURKE MILLS, INC.
P.O. Box 190, Valdese NC 28690. 704/874-2261. **Contact:** Maggie Hughes, Human Resources Manager. **Description:** Burke Mills, Inc. is engaged in twisting, texturing, winding, dyeing, processing, and selling filament, novelty, and spun yarns and also in the dyeing and processing of these yarns for others on a commission basis. The principal markets served by the company are the upholstery, apparel, and knitting and weaving industries. The company's products are sold in highly competitive markets throughout the United States. These products are distributed through salesmen, primarily in the eastern United States, and other commissioned workers. **Corporate headquarters location:** This Location. **Listed on:** NASDAQ.

BURLINGTON INDUSTRIES EQUITY
3330 West Friendly Avenue, Greensboro NC 27410. 910/379-2000. **Contact:** Jim Guin, Director of Human Resources. **Description:** Formerly known as Burlington Industries, Inc., Burlington Industries Equity is a major producer of textiles, including apparel and interior furnishings. Apparel products, which are designed, manufactured, and sold by five divisions within the company, include yarns, wools, woven synthetics, denims, industrial uniforms, and sportswear. The interior furnishings division includes Burlington House, which manufactures drapes, upholstery, and bedroom ensembles; the carpet division, which uses the Lees brand name; and the Burlington House Area Rugs unit. **Educational backgrounds include:** Computer Science; Engineering; Finance; Manufacturing Management; Marketing. **Corporate headquarters location:** This Location. **Listed on:** New York Stock Exchange.

CHF INDUSTRIES, INC.
8701 Red Oak Boulevard, Charlotte NC 28217. 704/522-5000. **Contact:** Ms. Pat Phifer, Human Resources Specialist. **Description:** CHF Industries, Inc. operates in three divisions: Aberdeen Manufacturing Corporation, designers and manufacturers of curtains, draperies, bedspreads, comforters, and shower curtains; Cameo, designers and manufacturers of curtains, draperies, bedspreads, and comforters; and Joanna, producers of window shades, blinds, and shutters. **Corporate headquarters location:** This Location. **Other U.S. locations:** New York NY.

CHARLES CRAFT
P.O. Box 370, Wadesboro NC 28170. 704/694-5121. **Contact:** Debby Wright, Payroll Clerk. **Description:** Charles Craft manufactures and wholesales cotton yarn. **Common positions include:** Accountant/Auditor; Administrator; Attorney; Blue-Collar Worker Supervisor; Buyer; Computer Programmer; Customer Service Representative; Department Manager; Financial Analyst; General Manager; Human Resources Specialist; Industrial Engineer; Manufacturer's/Wholesaler's Sales Rep.; Mechanical Engineer; Operations/Production Manager; Purchasing Agent and Manager; Quality Control Supervisor. **Educational backgrounds include:** Accounting; Business Administration; Computer Science; Engineering. **Benefits:** Life Insurance; Medical Insurance; Pension Plan; Savings Plan. **Corporate headquarters location:** This Location. **Operations at this facility include:** Manufacturing; Sales; Service.

COATS NORTH AMERICA
4135 South Stream Boulevard, Charlotte NC 28217. 704/329-5800. **Contact:** Administrator. **Description:** Coats North America is a manufacturer and supplier of sewing thread and associated products for the industrial and consumer products markets. The company is also engaged in manufacturing cotton and synthetic thread and yarn; metal and coil slide fasteners, tapes, trimmings, and small die castings; wood turnings and novelties; and special machinery spools, nylon travelers, and other

plastic injection moldings. **Common positions include:** Accountant/Auditor; Chemical Engineer; Computer Programmer; Computer Systems Analyst; Credit Manager; Customer Service Representative; Economist/Market Research Analyst; Human Resources Specialist; Industrial Production Manager; Manufacturer's/Wholesaler's Sales Rep.; Purchasing Agent and Manager; Quality Control Supervisor. **Educational backgrounds include:** Accounting; Business Administration; Chemistry; Marketing. **Benefits:** 401K; Dental Insurance; Disability Coverage; Life Insurance; Matching Gift; Medical Insurance; Pension Plan; Tuition Assistance. **Corporate headquarters location:** This Location. **Other U.S. locations:** Acworth GA; Albany GA; Cleveland GA; Rossville GA; Thomasville GA; Toccoa GA; Gastonia NC; Marble NC; Marlon NC; Old Fort NC; Rosman NC; Stanley NC; New York NY; Bristol RI; Greer SC; Lake City SC. **Subsidiaries include:** Coats & Clark, Inc. (Greenville, SC). **Operations at this facility include:** Administration; Sales; Service. **Number of employees at this location:** 215. **Number of employees nationwide:** 6,700.

COLLINS & AIKMAN HOLDINGS CORPORATION
P.O. Box 32665, Charlotte NC 28232. 704/548-2350. **Contact:** Ms. Delette Bost, Manager of Personnel. **Description:** Collins & Aikman Holdings Corporation and its subsidiaries manufacture commercial floor coverings, home furnishings, and consumer hosiery products, as well as textile products for major automobile manufacturers. The home furnishings division produces and sells decorative upholstery fabrics through 15 manufacturing facilities and 11 showrooms across the nation. Consumer legwear includes the brand name No-Nonsense. **Corporate headquarters location:** This Location. **Listed on:** American Stock Exchange.

CONE MILLS
1201 Maple Street, Greensboro NC 27405. 910/379-6220. **Contact:** Cathy Allen, Director of Human Resources. **Description:** Cone Mills is a major manufacturer of denim and home furnishing fabrics with a worldwide sales and marketing force. The denim division produces about 400 styles and is the largest supplier to Levi Strauss & Company. The division also manufactures specialty fabrics including plaids, chamois flannel, and uniform and sportswear fabrics. The home furnishings segment markets its products through Carlisle Finishing Company, the largest U.S. commission printer of home furnishing fabrics; John Wolf Decorative Fabrics, a maker of fabrics for upholstery, drapes, and bedrooms products; and Olympic Products Company, a subsidiary which manufactures foams for beds, carpets, and furniture used in the medical and consumer markets. **Corporate headquarters location:** This Location. **Listed on:** New York Stock Exchange.

CONTEMPORA FABRICS INC.
351 Contempora Drive, Lumberton NC 28358. 910/738-7131. **Contact:** Teresa Johnson, Human Resources. **Description:** A commissioned textile manufacturer.

CULP TICKING
P.O. Box 488, Stokesdale NC 27357-0488. 910/643-7751. **Contact:** Mr. Barrett L. Brown, Human Resources Manager. **Description:** Manufacturers of mattress and other upholstery ticking. **Common positions include:** Account Manager; Blue-Collar Worker Supervisor; Buyer; Commercial Artist; Customer Service Representative; Department Manager; Human Resources Specialist; Industrial Engineer; Manufacturer's/Wholesaler's Sales Rep.; Purchasing Agent and Manager; Quality Control Supervisor. **Educational backgrounds include:** Accounting; Art/Design; Business Administration; Computer Science; Industrial Design; Marketing. **Benefits:** Dental Insurance; Disability Coverage; Medical Insurance; Tuition Assistance. **Corporate headquarters location:** High Point NC. **Other U.S. locations:** Graham NC; Anderson SC; Pageland SC. **Operations at this facility include:** Administration; Manufacturing; Sales. **Number of employees at this location:** 150.

FIELDCREST CANNON, INC.
326 East Stadium Drive, Amp Building, Eden NC 27288. 910/627-3000. **Contact:** Dr. Brian Bergman, Manager of Executive Employment. **Description:** Fieldcrest Cannon is an international manufacturer of home textiles which distributes its products through accounts with department stores, catalog merchandisers, specialty stores, and mass retailers, as well as institutional, government, and corporate clients. The bath segment manufactures bath towels, rugs, and kitchen products, and the bed segment produces blankets, throws, bedding, and decorative window treatments. **Common positions include:** Accountant/Auditor; Chemist; Computer Programmer; Electrical/Electronics Engineer; Industrial Agent/Broker; Management Trainee; Manufacturer's/Wholesaler's Sales Rep.; Mechanical Engineer; Operations/Production Manager; Textile Manager. **Educational backgrounds include:** Accounting; Business Administration; Chemistry; Computer Science; Engineering; Liberal Arts; Management/Planning; Marketing;

Textiles. **Benefits:** Dental Insurance; Disability Coverage; Employee Discounts; Life Insurance; Medical Insurance; Pension Plan; Savings Plan; Tuition Assistance. **Special Programs:** Internships. **Corporate headquarters location:** This Location. **Operations at this facility include:** Administration; Divisional Headquarters; Manufacturing; Regional Headquarters; Service. **Listed on:** New York Stock Exchange.

FREUDENBERG SPUNWEB COMPANY
P.O. Box 15910, Durham NC 27704. 919/479-7226. **Fax:** 919/471-2516. **Contact:** Winston Roberts, Director of Personnel. **Description:** Manufactures nonwoven fabrics. **Common positions include:** Accountant/Auditor; Electrical/Electronics Engineer; Mechanical Engineer. **Educational backgrounds include:** Accounting; Engineering; Finance; Marketing. **Benefits:** Dental Insurance; Disability Coverage; Life Insurance; Medical Insurance; Pension Plan; Savings Plan; Tuition Assistance. **Corporate headquarters location:** This Location. **Operations at this facility include:** Administration; Manufacturing; Research and Development; Sales. **Number of employees at this location:** 145.

GALEY & LORD
P.O. Box 250, Marion NC 28752. 704/652-3448. **Contact:** Ron Hickman, Personnel Manager. **Description:** Galey & Lord is a leading manufacturer and marketer of apparel fabric sold to clothing manufacturers. The company is a major producer of Wrinkle-Free, 100 percent cotton fabrics for the uniform trade. The company's products are produced at seven manufacturing facilities located in North Carolina, South Carolina, and Georgia. Other branch offices are located in Los Angeles, San Diego, and Chicago. **Corporate headquarters location:** New York NY.

GENERAL TEXTILE PRINT COMPANY
P.O. Box 1620, Rocky Mount NC 27802. 919/977-0631. **Fax:** 919/977-2389. **Contact:** Martin Imhoff, Human Resources Director. **Description:** Engaged in the bleaching and preparation of woven textiles for printing, primarily for garment manufacturers. **Common positions include:** Textile Manager. **Educational backgrounds include:** Textiles. **Benefits:** Dental Insurance; Life Insurance; Medical Insurance; Profit Sharing; Savings Plan; Tuition Assistance. **Corporate headquarters location:** This Location. **Operations at this facility include:** Administration; Manufacturing. **Listed on:** Privately held. **Number of employees at this location:** 270. **Number of employees nationwide:** 350.

GLEN RAVEN MILLS, INC.
1831 North Park Avenue, Glen Raven NC 27217. 910/227-6211. **Fax:** 910/227-5650. **Contact:** Elizabeth Coble, Personnel and Development Manager. **Description:** Engaged in the textile dyeing and finishing of knit, woven, and nonwoven fabrics. **Common positions include:** Blue-Collar Worker Supervisor; Clerical Supervisor; Computer Programmer; Customer Service Representative; Electrical/Electronics Engineer; General Manager; Human Resources Specialist; Inspector/Tester/Grader; Marketing/Advertising/PR Manager; Quality Control Supervisor; Secretary; Truck Driver. **Educational backgrounds include:** Business Administration; Engineering; Marketing. **Benefits:** Daycare Assistance; Dental Insurance; Disability Coverage; Employee Discounts; Life Insurance; Medical Insurance; Pension Plan; Tuition Assistance. **Special Programs:** Internships. **Operations at this facility include:** Administration; Divisional Headquarters; Manufacturing; Research and Development; Sales. **Number of employees at this location:** 225.

GRANITE KNITWEAR, INC.
P.O. Box 498, Granite Quarry NC 28072-0498. 704/279-5526. **Contact:** Sherry Hess, Personnel Manager. **Description:** A sportswear and fleecewear apparel manufacturer. **Common positions include:** Credit Manager; Customer Service Representative; Human Resources Specialist; Industrial Engineer. **Benefits:** Disability Coverage; Employee Discounts; Life Insurance; Medical Insurance; Profit Sharing; Tuition Assistance. **Corporate headquarters location:** This Location. **Number of employees at this location:** 170.

GUILFORD MILLS, INC.
4023-B West Windover Avenue, Greensboro NC 27407. 910/316-4000. **Contact:** Human Resources. **Description:** Manufactures, processes, and markets warp knit fabrics for the apparel, automotive, home furnishing, swimwear, dress, and sportswear industries. The company operates through 13 manufacturing and distribution centers in the U.S. and three facilities in the U.K. Guilford Mills also has an interest in a warp knit textile factory in Mexico. **Corporate headquarters location:** This Location. **Listed on:** New York Stock Exchange.

HAMPSHIRE HOSIERY, INC.

P.O. Box 528, Spruce Pine NC 28777. 704/765-9011. **Fax:** 704/765-0526. **Contact:** Rick Nichols, Human Resource Manager. **Description:** Manufactures women's sheer hosiery. **Common positions include:** Accountant/Auditor; Blue-Collar Worker Supervisor; Computer Programmer; Electrical/Electronics Engineer; Electrician; General Manager; Human Resources Specialist; Industrial Engineer; Management Trainee; Manufacturer's/Wholesaler's Sales Rep.; Operations/Production Manager; Quality Control Supervisor. **Educational backgrounds include:** Accounting; Business Administration; Computer Science; Economics; Engineering. **Benefits:** 401K; Dental Insurance; Disability Coverage; Life Insurance; Medical Insurance; Savings Plan; Tuition Assistance. **Corporate headquarters location:** This Location. **Parent company:** Hampshire Group, LTD. **Operations at this facility include:** Divisional Headquarters; Manufacturing; Research and Development; Service. **Listed on:** NASDAQ. **Number of employees at this location:** 440. **Number of employees nationwide:** 500.

HAMPTON INDUSTRIES, INC.

P.O. Box 614, Kinston NC 28501-0614. 919/527-8011. **Contact:** Dan McLean. **Description:** Hampton Industries, Inc. manufactures and sells apparel, principally under private or store labels, to national and regional chain and department stores. The company's sales divisions include menswear and activewear, boyswear, womenswear and girlswear, and loungewear. The company's products are sold under the brand names Hampton Private Label, Hampco Apparel, Rawlings, Campus, Le Tigre, Blue Company, Nautica for Boys, Kaynee, Reed St. James, Hampton Loungewear, McGregor Robes, Sloungers, Saylu Loungewear, and Hampton House Loungewear. Sales offices are located at 15 West 34th Street, New York, New York 10001-3060. **Corporate headquarters location:** This Location. **Subsidiaries include:** Angels Flight; Kaynee; Kenbridge Apparel; McGregor for Boys; J.G. Hook for Boys; Prepshirt; Breaking Point; Say-lu; Sergio Big and Tall; Reed St. James for Boys; and Walt Wear Apparel. **Listed on:** American Stock Exchange.

HANES CONVERTING

P.O. Box 457, Conover NC 28613-0457. 704/464-4673. **Contact:** Raeford Smith, Manager of Human Resources. **Description:** Converts fabric and related materials for the bedding and drapery industry.

HOLT MANUFACTURING COMPANY, INC.

P.O. Box 2017, Burlington NC 27216-2017. 910/227-5561. **Fax:** 910/229-7580. **Contact:** Patricia S. Baucom, Director of Personnel. **Description:** An apparel design company, whose disperse dye printing process allows the color and detail of artwork to be transferred to material. Engineered designs using the company's techniques are placed on items such as active wear, swimwear, athletic wear, sleepwear, scarves, rugs, mats, domestics, narrow web elastic, lace trim, labels, ribbons, shoe laces, and other products. **Common positions include:** Accountant/Auditor; Blue-Collar Worker Supervisor; Computer Programmer; Customer Service Representative; Designer; Human Resources Specialist; Industrial Engineer; Industrial Production Manager; Management Trainee; Purchasing Agent and Manager. **Educational backgrounds include:** Accounting; Art/Design; Business Administration; Engineering; Finance; Marketing. **Benefits:** 401K; Dental Insurance; Disability Coverage; Life Insurance; Medical Insurance; Profit Sharing; Savings Plan; Tuition Assistance. **Special Programs:** Internships. **Other U.S. locations:** New York NY. **Operations at this facility include:** Administration; Manufacturing; Research and Development; Sales; Service. **Listed on:** Privately held. **Number of employees at this location:** 200.

HOME INNOVATIONS, INC.

P.O. Box 297, Mooresville NC 28115. 704/664-2711. **Fax:** 704/664-5172. **Contact:** Gerard J. Geier, Jr., Vice President of Human Resources. **Description:** A textile home furnishings company. Home Innovations manufactures curtains, drapery, bed coverings, mattress pads, pillows, comforters, and bedspreads, as well as printed, embroidered, and embellished bath towels and shower curtains. **Common positions include:** Accountant/Auditor; Administrative Services Manager; Blue-Collar Worker Supervisor; Budget Analyst; Chemist; Clerical Supervisor; Computer Programmer; Computer Systems Analyst; Electrician; General Manager; Human Resources Specialist; Industrial Engineer; Management Trainee; Purchasing Agent and Manager; Quality Control Supervisor. **Educational backgrounds include:** Accounting; Business Administration; Communications; Computer Science; Engineering; Finance. **Benefits:** 401K; Dental Insurance; Disability Coverage; Employee Discounts; Life Insurance; Medical Insurance; Pension Plan; Savings Plan. **Corporate headquarters location:** This Location. **Other U.S. locations:** CA; IL; NY; TX. **Operations at this facility include:** Administration; Manufacturing; Regional Headquarters; Sales; Service. **Listed on:**

Privately held. **Number of employees at this location:** 1,800. **Number of employees nationwide:** 2,400.

ITHACA INDUSTRIES, INC.

Highway 268 West, P.O. Box 620, Wilkesboro NC 28697. 910/667-5231. **Contact:** Human Resources. **Description:** Ithaca Industries, Inc. is the largest manufacturer of private label hosiery and underwear products in the United States, offering a broad selection of styles in different quality and price categories to a wide range of customers. The company's principal product lines are hosiery products, such as pantyhose, tights, knee-highs, stockings, men's and boys' underwear, women's and girls' underwear, and T-shirts. Over 90 percent of Ithaca Industries' net sales are from private label products. Ithaca does manufacture some branded products, the most significant of which is the Evan-Piccone line of women's fashion hosiery.

KAYSER-ROTH CORPORATION
CREEDMOOR DISTRIBUTION CENTER

Highway 56 East, Creedmoor NC 27522. 919/528-1891. **Contact:** Jay Brown, Human Resources Manager. **Description:** Distributes sheer hosiery to food and drug stores, mass merchandisers, discount stores, and mom-and-pop stores. **Common positions include:** Accountant/Auditor; Customer Service Representative; Department Manager; General Manager; Human Resources Specialist; Industrial Engineer; Management Trainee; Quality Control Supervisor. **Educational backgrounds include:** Accounting; Business Administration; Computer Science; Engineering. **Benefits:** Disability Coverage; Employee Discounts; Life Insurance; Medical Insurance; Pension Plan; Savings Plan; Tuition Assistance. **Corporate headquarters location:** Greensboro NC. **Other U.S. locations:** Burlington NC; Lumberton NC; Prosperity SC; Dayton TN. **Parent company:** Collins & Aikman Holdings Corporation. **Listed on:** New York Stock Exchange. **Number of employees at this location:** 223.

KIMBERLY-CLARK CORPORATION

32 Smythe Avenue, Hendersonville NC 28792-8503. 704/692-9611. **Contact:** Maureen Ware, Human Resources Director. **Description:** This location is a nonwoven fabrics mill. Mill products are used as component material for the company's products. Overall, Kimberly-Clark Corporation manufactures and markets products for personal, business, and industrial uses throughout the world. Most of the company's products are made from natural and synthetic fibers using advanced technologies in absorbency, fibers, and nonwovens. The name brands of Kimberly-Clark Corporation include: Kleenex facial and bathroom tissue, Huggies diapers and baby wipes, Pull-Ups training pants, Kotex and New Freedom feminine care products, Depend and Poise incontinence care products, Hi-Dri household towels, Kimguard sterile wrap, Kimwipes industrial wipes, and Classic business and correspondence papers. Kimberly-Clark Corporation has extensive operations overseas in Europe and Asia.

LEE INDUSTRIES

P.O. Box 26, Newton NC 28658. 704/464-8318. **Contact:** Ms. Pat Kinkade, Director of Human Resources. **Description:** An upholstery manufacturer.

NATIONAL SPINNING COMPANY INC.

1300 Ward Bridge Road, Warsaw NC 28398. 910/293-7101. **Contact:** Ben Ellenberg, Human Resources Manager. **Description:** Engaged in the manufacture, marketing, and distribution of yarn products to knitwear manufacturers. National Spinning Company also produces hand-knitting yarn and rug kits for distribution to retail chains throughout the United States. **Corporate headquarters location:** New York NY.

PARKDALE MILL

P.O. Drawer 1787, Gastonia NC 28053. 704/864-8761. **Contact:** Beverly Painter, Director of Human Resources. **Description:** A textile manufacturer.

PILLOWTEX CORPORATION

P.O. Box 508, Monroe NC 28111. 704/289-5557. **Contact:** Ms. Peressa Staton, Personnel and Human Resources Manager. **Description:** A broadwoven fabric mill. **Common positions include:** Accountant/Auditor; Administrator; Blue-Collar Worker Supervisor; Customer Service Representative; General Manager; Human Resources Specialist; Operations/Production Manager; Purchasing Agent and Manager; Quality Assurance Engineer. **Benefits:** Life Insurance; Medical Insurance; Savings Plan. **Special Programs:** Training Programs. **Corporate headquarters location:** Dallas TX. **Other U.S. locations:** Lando SC. **Operations at this facility include:** Manufacturing. **Number of employees at this location:** 250.

REGAL MANUFACTURING COMPANY
P.O. Box 2363, Hickory NC 28603. 704/328-5381. **Contact:** Betty Jo Pierce, Personnel Manager. **Description:** Develops, manufactures, and markets elastic yarn for the garment industry. **Common positions include:** Blue-Collar Worker Supervisor; Buyer; Computer Programmer; General Manager; Human Resources Specialist; Industrial Engineer; Operations/Production Manager; Quality Control Supervisor. **Benefits:** 401K; Credit Union; Disability Coverage; Life Insurance; Medical Insurance; Profit Sharing; Savings Plan; Tuition Assistance. **Corporate headquarters location:** This Location. **Parent company:** Worldtex, Inc. **Operations at this facility include:** Administration; Manufacturing; Research and Development; Sales; Service. **Listed on:** New York Stock Exchange.

RHYNE MILLS INC.
P.O. Box 70, Lincolnton NC 28093. 704/732-5560. **Contact:** Renee Reets, Human Resources Director. **Description:** A privately-owned company founded in 1880, Rhyne Mills performs three types of spinning: murata air jet spinning, ring spinning, and parafil spinning. The company runs polyester, acrylic, rayon, and polypropylene.

ROCKY MOUNTAIN CORD COMPANY
419 Gay Street, P.O. Drawer 4304, Rocky Mount NC 27803-0304. 919/977-9130. **Contact:** Kathy Elliott, Human Resources Director. **Description:** Manufactures braided cord and twisted rope. **Benefits:** Disability Coverage; Life Insurance; Medical Insurance. **Special Programs:** Training Programs. **Corporate headquarters location:** This Location. **Operations at this facility include:** Administration; Manufacturing; Research and Development; Sales; Service.

ROYAL HOME FASHIONS INC.
P.O. Box 930, Durham NC 27702. 919/683-8011. **Contact:** Charlene Walter, Director of Human Resources. **Description:** Manufactures home fashion products such as sheets, pillow cases, comforters, and shower curtains. **Common positions include:** Accountant/Auditor; Administrator; Blue-Collar Worker Supervisor; Buyer; Computer Programmer; Credit Manager; Customer Service Representative; Department Manager; Human Resources Specialist; Industrial Engineer; Industrial Production Manager; Instructor/Trainer; Management Trainee; Operations/Production Manager; Purchasing Agent and Manager; Quality Control Supervisor; Teacher. **Educational backgrounds include:** Business Administration; Engineering. **Benefits:** Disability Coverage; Employee Discounts; Life Insurance; Medical Insurance; Pension Plan; Savings Plan; Tuition Assistance. **Special Programs:** Training Programs. **Corporate headquarters location:** This Location. **Other U.S. locations:** Henderson NC; Megame NC. **Parent company:** Croscill Home Fashions. **Operations at this facility include:** Administration; Manufacturing. **Listed on:** Privately held. **Number of employees nationwide:** 1,500.

SHADOWLINE INC.
550 Lenoir Road, Morganton NC 28655. 704/437-3821. **Fax:** 704/437-8423. **Contact:** Judy B. Fisher, Personnel Manager. **Description:** A manufacturer of lingerie. **Common positions include:** Accountant/Auditor; Blue-Collar Worker Supervisor; Clerical Supervisor; Computer Programmer; Computer Systems Analyst; Cost Estimator; Credit Manager; Customer Service Representative; Designer; Human Resources Specialist; Industrial Engineer; Operations/Production Manager; Purchasing Agent and Manager; Quality Control Supervisor; Services Sales Representative. **Educational backgrounds include:** Accounting; Art/Design; Business Administration; Computer Science; Finance; Marketing. **Benefits:** Dental Insurance; Disability Coverage; Employee Discounts; Life Insurance; Medical Insurance; Pension Plan. **Special Programs:** Internships. **Corporate headquarters location:** This Location. **Other U.S. locations:** Boone NC; Fallston NC; Mars Hill NC. **Operations at this facility include:** Administration; Divisional Headquarters; Manufacturing; Research and Development; Sales; Service. **Listed on:** Privately held. **Number of employees at this location:** 200. **Number of employees nationwide:** 500.

SHUFORD MILLS, INC.
1985 Tate Boulevard SE, Hickory NC 28602. 704/328-2131. **Contact:** Mr. Hume Collins, Director of Human Resources. **Description:** Manufactures yarn and tape.

M.J. SOFFE COMPANY, INC.
P.O. Box 2507, Fayetteville NC 28301. 910/483-0032. **Contact:** David Williford, Human Resources Director. **Description:** Manufactures sportswear. All locations of M.J. Soffe Company are in North Carolina. **Common positions include:** Apparel Worker; Computer Operator; Computer Programmer; Computer Systems Analyst; Credit Clerk and Authorizer; Credit Manager; Customer Service Representative; Financial Manager; General Manager; Graphic Artist; Human Resources Specialist;

Industrial Engineer; Inspector/Tester/Grader; Manufacturer's/Wholesaler's Sales Rep.; Marketing/Advertising/PR Manager; Order Clerk; Payroll Clerk; Purchasing Agent and Manager; Secretary; Truck Driver. **Educational backgrounds include:** Art/Design; Engineering. **Benefits:** Dental Insurance; Disability Coverage; Employee Discounts; Life Insurance; Medical Insurance; Pension Plan; Savings Plan. **Operations at this facility include:** Administration; Manufacturing; Regional Headquarters; Sales; Service.

SPANCO YARNS INC.
P.O. Box 547, Raeford NC 28376. 910/875-3711. **Contact:** Lynn McNeil, Human Resources and Training Manager. **Description:** A manufacturer of covered yarn.

SPRAY COTTON MILLS
P.O. Box 3207, Eden NC 27289. 910/623-9181. **Contact:** Bill Jackson, Director of Human Resources. **Description:** A manufacturer of cotton yarns, with two locations in Eden, North Carolina, and one location in Mount Holly, North Carolina.

STONY CREEK KNITTING
P.O. Box 2445, Rocky Mount NC 27802-2445. 919/442-8111. **Fax:** 919/442-8117. **Contact:** Sheila B. Anthony, Human Resources Manager. **Description:** Engaged in the knitting, dyeing, and finishing of yarn. **Common positions include:** Accountant/Auditor. **Educational backgrounds include:** Business Administration; Marketing. **Benefits:** Dental Insurance; Employee Discounts; Life Insurance; Medical Insurance. **Corporate headquarters location:** This Location. **Operations at this facility include:** Sales. **Listed on:** Privately held. **Number of employees at this location:** 320.

SWISS TEXTILES
P.O. Box 759, Erwin NC 28339. 910/897-8111. **Contact:** Larry Spell, Human Resources Director. **Description:** Manufactures broadwoven cotton fabric mills. **Number of employees at this location:** 1,000.

TEXFI INDUSTRIES, INC.
5400 Glenwood Avenue, Suite 215, Raleigh NC 27612. 919/783-4736. **Contact:** Dame Vincent, Vice President of Finance & Treasurer. **Description:** Texfi Industries, Inc. manufactures and markets a diverse line of textile and apparel products from a variety of natural and synthetic fibers and other raw materials. Texfi produces woven finished fabrics, narrow elastic fibers, woven greige fabrics, spun yarns, T-shirts, knitted fleece, and jersey fabrics which are sold throughout the United States and exported to European and Asian markets. The Greige Fabrics Division operates manufacturing facilities at Marion and High Point, North Carolina (there are two plants in High Point) and Jefferson, Georgia. This location is the accounting division. **Common positions include:** Accountant/Auditor; Administrator; Blue-Collar Worker Supervisor; Computer Programmer; Department Manager; Electrical/Electronics Engineer; Financial Analyst; General Manager; Human Resources Specialist; Industrial Engineer; Industrial Production Manager; Instructor/Trainer; Management Trainee; Manufacturer's/Wholesaler's Sales Rep.; Operations/Production Manager; Purchasing Agent and Manager; Quality Control Supervisor; Teacher. **Educational backgrounds include:** Accounting; Business Administration; Engineering; Liberal Arts. **Benefits:** Disability Coverage; Employee Discounts; Life Insurance; Medical Insurance; Pension Plan. **Special Programs:** Training Programs. **Corporate headquarters location:** Spartanburg SC. **Operations at this facility include:** Manufacturing; Service. **Listed on:** New York Stock Exchange. **Number of employees nationwide:** 750.

THOMASVILLE UPHOLSTERY
P.O. Box 500, Hickory NC 28603. 704/528-6630. **Contact:** Sandra Gregory, Personnel Supervisor. **Description:** Manufactures furniture upholstery for the nationwide Thomasville furniture chain and related stores.

UNIFI, INC.
P.O. Box 19109, Greensboro NC 27419-9109. 910/294-4410. **Fax:** 910/316-5422. **Contact:** Raymond Hunt, Human Resources Director. **Description:** The company and its subsidiaries are engaged predominantly in the processing of yarns by texturing synthetic filament polyester and nylon fiber, and in the spinning of cotton and cotton-blend fibers. Sales are both domestic and international, and are mostly to knitters and weavers for the apparel, industrial hosiery, home furnishing, automotive upholstery, and other end-use markets. Ladies' and men's hosiery, high-performance stretch active wear, and medical products, including tape and bandages, are some of the everyday items that contain the company's textured nylon and covered lycra and rubber products. The company maintains manufacturing operations in the United States and Letterkenny, Ireland. Unifi, Inc. exports to over 30 countries from the United States and to more than 20 European countries from Letterkenny. Subsidiaries

include: Vintage Yarns, Inc. and Unifi Spun Yarns, Inc. **Corporate headquarters location:** This Location. **Listed on:** New York Stock Exchange. **Number of employees nationwide:** 6,000.

UNIFI, INC.
P.O. Box 191, Madison NC 27025. 910/427-7120. **Contact:** Raymond Hunt, Human Resources Director. **Description:** The company and its subsidiaries are engaged predominantly in the processing of yarns by texturing synthetic filament polyester and nylon fiber, and in the spinning of cotton and cotton-blend fibers. Sales are both domestic and international, and are mostly to knitters and weavers for the apparel, industrial hosiery, home furnishing, automotive upholstery, and other end-use markets. Ladies' and men's hosiery, high-performance stretch active wear, and medical products, including tape and bandages, are some of the everyday items that contain the company's textured nylon and covered lycra and rubber products. The company maintains manufacturing operations in the United States and Letterkenny, Ireland. Unifi, Inc. exports to over 30 countries from the United States and to more than 20 European countries from Letterkenny. Subsidiaries include: Vintage Yarns, Inc. and Unifi Spun Yarns, Inc. This facility produces ultra-fine to mid-denier textured nylon with various filament counts, including micro-fibers. A portion of these products are package dyed. **NOTE:** Mr. Hunt can be reached at P.O. Box 19109, Greensboro NC 27419-9109. **Corporate headquarters location:** Greensboro NC. **Listed on:** New York Stock Exchange. **Number of employees nationwide:** 6,000.

UNIFI, INC.
P.O. Box 1437, Reidsville NC 27323. 910/342-3361. **Contact:** Raymond Hunt, Human Resources Director. **Description:** The company and its subsidiaries are engaged predominantly in the processing of yarns by texturing synthetic filament polyester and nylon fiber, and in the spinning of cotton and cotton-blend fibers. Sales are both domestic and international, and are mostly to knitters and weavers for the apparel, industrial hosiery, home furnishing, automotive upholstery, and other end-use markets. Ladies' and men's hosiery, high-performance stretch active wear, and medical products, including tape and bandages, are some of the everyday items that contain the company's textured nylon and covered lycra and rubber products. The company maintains manufacturing operations in the United States and Letterkenny, Ireland. Unifi, Inc. exports to over 30 countries from the United States and to more than 20 European countries from Letterkenny. Subsidiaries include: Vintage Yarns, Inc. and Unifi Spun Yarns, Inc. **NOTE:** Mr. Hunt can be reached at P.O. Box 19109, Greensboro NC 27419-9109. **Corporate headquarters location:** Greensboro NC. **Listed on:** New York Stock Exchange. **Number of employees nationwide:** 6,000.

UNIFI, INC.
271 Cardwell Road, Mayodan NC 27027. 910/427-5400. **Contact:** Raymond Hunt, Human Resources Director. **Description:** The company and its subsidiaries are engaged predominantly in the processing of yarns by texturing synthetic filament polyester and nylon fiber, and in the spinning of cotton and cotton-blend fibers. Sales are both domestic and international, and are mostly to knitters and weavers for the apparel, industrial hosiery, home furnishing, automotive upholstery, and other end-use markets. Ladies' and men's hosiery, high-performance stretch active wear, and medical products, including tape and bandages, are some of the everyday items that contain the company's textured nylon and covered lycra and rubber products. The company maintains manufacturing operations in the United States and Letterkenny, Ireland. Unifi, Inc. exports to over 30 countries from the United States and to more than 20 European countries from Letterkenny. Subsidiaries include: Vintage Yarns, Inc. and Unifi Spun Yarns, Inc. **NOTE:** Mr. Hunt can be reached at P.O. Box 19109, Greensboro NC 27419-9109. **Corporate headquarters location:** Greensboro NC. **Listed on:** New York Stock Exchange. **Number of employees nationwide:** 6,000.

UNIFI, INC.
P.O. Box 1188, 13846 NC 87, Eden NC 27288. 910/627-0060. **Contact:** Raymond Hunt, Human Resources Director. **Description:** The company and its subsidiaries are engaged predominantly in the processing of yarns by texturing synthetic filament polyester and nylon fiber, and in the spinning of cotton and cotton-blend fibers. Sales are both domestic and international, and are mostly to knitters and weavers for the apparel, industrial hosiery, home furnishing, automotive upholstery, and other end-use markets. Ladies' and men's hosiery, high-performance stretch active wear, and medical products, including tape and bandages, are some of the everyday items that contain the company's textured nylon and covered lycra and rubber products. The company maintains manufacturing operations in the United States and Letterkenny, Ireland. Unifi, Inc. exports to over 30 countries from the United States and to more than 20 European countries from Letterkenny. Subsidiaries include: Vintage Yarns, Inc.

and Unifi Spun Yarns, Inc. **NOTE:** Mr. Hunt can be reached at P.O. Box 19109, Greensboro NC 27419-9109. **Corporate headquarters location:** Greensboro NC. **Listed on:** New York Stock Exchange. **Number of employees nationwide:** 6,000.

UNIFI, INC.
P.O. Box 737, Madison NC 27025. 910/427-4051. **Contact:** Raymond Hunt, Human Resources Director. **Description:** The company and its subsidiaries are engaged predominantly in the processing of yarns by texturing synthetic filament polyester and nylon fiber, and in the spinning of cotton and cotton-blend fibers. Sales are both domestic and international, and are mostly to knitters and weavers for the apparel, industrial hosiery, home furnishing, automotive upholstery, and other end-use markets. Ladies' and men's hosiery, high-performance stretch active wear, and medical products, including tape and bandages, are some of the everyday items that contain the company's textured nylon and covered lycra and rubber products. The company maintains manufacturing operations in the United States and Letterkenny, Ireland. Unifi, Inc. exports to over 30 countries from the United States and to more than 20 European countries from Letterkenny. Subsidiaries include: Vintage Yarns, Inc. and Unifi Spun Yarns, Inc. **NOTE:** Mr. Hunt can be reached at P.O. Box 19109, Greensboro NC 27419-9109. **Corporate headquarters location:** Greensboro NC. **Listed on:** New York Stock Exchange. **Number of employees nationwide:** 6,000.

UNITY KNITTING MILLS INC.
P.O. Box 827, Wadesboro NC 28170. 704/694-6544. **Contact:** Tonia Diggs, Human Resources Director. **Description:** An apparel manufacturer. **Common positions include:** Accountant/Auditor; Computer Programmer; Operations/Production Manager; Purchasing Agent and Manager; Quality Control Supervisor. **Educational backgrounds include:** Accounting; Business Administration; Communications; Finance; Mathematics. **Benefits:** Disability Coverage; Employee Discounts; Life Insurance; Medical Insurance.

WESTPOINT STEVENS
P.O. Box 1347, Lumberton NC 28359. 910/618-2200. **Contact:** Jay Humphrey, Human Resources Director. **Description:** Manufactures knit fabrics.

Note: Because addresses and telephone numbers of smaller companies change rapidly, we recommend you call each company to verify the information below before inquiring about job opportunities. Mass mailings are not recommended.

Additional employers with under 250 employees:

BROADWOVEN FABRIC MILLS

Carolina Mills Inc.
301 E 2nd St, Newton NC 28658. 704/464-1901.

Carolina Narrow Fabric Co.
604 Memorial Park Dr, Sparta NC 28675. 910/372-2491.

Carthage Fabrics Corp.
261 Niagara Carthage Rd, Carthage NC 28327-9005. 910/947-2211.

Chatham Mills Inc.
480 Hillsboro St, Pittsboro NC 27312. 910/542-3142.

Facemate Corporation
920 Tate Blvd SE, Hickory NC 28602. 704/328-2349.

Langenthal Corp.
1300 Langenthal Dr, Rural Hall NC 27045. 910/969-9551.

Phillips Weaving
325 N Sutherland Ave, Monroe NC 28110-3603. 704/283-8134.

Springs Industries Inc.
10781 Gibson Rd, Laurel Hill NC 28351-8971. 910/462-3930.

Asheboro Elastics Corp.
150 N Park St, Asheboro NC 27203-5455. 910/629-2626.

Blackwelder Textiles Co.
314 S Pink St, Cherryville NC 28021-3504. 704/435-5520.

Doran Textiles
503 N Mountain St, Cherryville NC 28021-2419. 704/487-2031.

Fabric Solutions
201 E 1st St, Lumberton NC 28358-5603. 910/738-9500.

Fieldcrest Cannon Inc.
5101 Terminal St, Charlotte NC 28208-1247. 704/393-8413.

Innovative Yarn
621A Boone Rd, Eden NC 27288-4907. 910/627-8990.

Lexington Industries Inc.
205 Albemarle St, Lexington NC 27292-5239. 704/243-1903.

Liberty Fabrics Inc.
28333 US Highway 64, Jamesville NC 27846-9625. 919/792-8167.

Ly Corp. Manufacturing
703B Concord Rd, Albemarle NC 28001-9301. 704/982-7622.

Premier Quilting Corp.
720 W Industry Dr, Oxford
NC 27565-3501. 919/693-
1151.

**RL Stowe Mill Central
Warehouse**
602 Eagle Rd, Belmont NC
28012-3749. 704/825-
6640.

Van Lathem
1925 W Innes St, Salisbury
NC 28144-2432. 704/642-
1623.

Porritts & Spencer Inc.
P.O. Box 1411, Wilson NC
27894-1411. 919/291-
3800.

**NARROW FABRIC AND
OTHER SMALLWARES
MILLS**

Olympic Narrow Fabrics Co.
900 Gant Rd, Graham NC
27253-3523. 910/227-
8841.

Paxar ASL Group
100 Service Rd, Canton NC
28716-9700. 704/648-
5752.

Shelby Elastics Inc.
639 N Post Rd, Shelby NC
28150-4965. 704/487-
4301.

Southern Webbing Mills
P.O. Box 13919, Greensboro
NC 27415-3919. 910/375-
3103.

Texfi Elastics
328 W Central Ave,
Asheboro NC 27203-3204.
910/672-3821.

Texfi Elastics
327 E Elm St, Graham NC
27253-3023. 910/222-
8075.

Torque Elastics Inc.
3720 S Church St,
Burlington NC 27215-9107.
910/584-0134.

KNITTING MILLS

Adams-Millis Hosiery
118 Burke St, Kernersville
NC 27284. 910/996-4646.

B&J Hosiery Inc.
1317 Boggs Dr, Mount Airy
NC 27030. 910/789-2651.

Baker Heritage Inc.
946 9th St NE, Hickory NC
28601-4062. 704/327-
8000.

Bossong Hosiery Mills
840 W Salisbury St,
Asheboro NC 27203-4327.
910/625-2175.

Catawba Sox Inc.
P.O. Box 517, Conover NC
28613-0517. 704/464-
1690.

Clayson Knitting Co.
Industrial Dr, Red Springs NC
28377. 910/843-5137.

Holiday Hosiery Inc.
1905 International Blvd,
Hudson NC 28638-2734.
704/728-5025.

Holt Hosiery Mills Inc.
3950 Hwy 11, Willard NC
28478. 910/285-2136.

Kathy Hosiery Co. Inc.
309 Colombo St SW,
Valdese NC 28690-2751.
704/879-8121.

Lemco Mills Inc.
766 Koury Dr, Burlington NC
27215-6721. 910/226-
5548.

LJ Russell Hosiery Inc.
105 Poole Rd, Troy NC
27371-9300. 910/576-
0744.

Ridgeview Inc.
2101 N Main Ave, Newton
NC 28658-2737. 704/464-
2972.

Robinson Hosiery Mill
113 Robinson St SE, Valdese
NC 28690-8813. 704/874-
2228.

Robinson Manufacturing Co.
Hughes Blvd, Elizabeth City
NC 27909. 919/335-2985.

Runnymede Mills Inc.
1004 Fountain St, Tarboro
NC 27886-2847. 919/823-
2141.

Sue-Lynn Textiles Inc.
Hwy 49 N, Haw River NC
27258. 910/578-0871.

US Hosiery Corp.
980 3rd Ave SE, Hickory NC
28602-4009. 704/322-
2710.

Willis Hosiery Mills
184 Academy Ave NW,
Concord NC 28025-4850.
704/782-4155.

Ballston Knitting Co.
1553 Carter St, Mount Airy
NC 27030. 910/789-5041.

Brown Wooten Mills Inc.
1400 Carter St, Mount Airy
NC 27030. 910/786-8379.

Candor Hosiery Mill Inc.
602 E Hwy 211, Candor NC
27229. 910/974-4124.

Carolina Hosiery Mills
Tucker St Ext, Burlington NC
27215. 910/226-5581.

Classic Hosiery Inc.
694 County Home Rd,
Yanceyville NC 27379.
910/694-4115.

Eco Knit Inc.
461 N South St, Mount Airy
NC 27030-3533. 910/786-
4044.

Edelweiss Manufacturing Co.
1631 Main Avenue Dr NW,
Hickory NC 28601-5834.
704/324-4612.

Great American Knitting Mills
312 E 9th St, Scotland Neck
NC 27874-1512. 919/826-
4131.

Hole-In-None Hosiery Mill
1247 W Webb Ave,
Burlington NC 27217-1150.
910/228-1758.

Johnson Hosiery Mills
2808 Main Ave NW, Hickory
NC 28601-5659. 704/322-
6185.

Kentucky Derby Hosiery Co.
925 Old Lenoir Rd, Hickory
NC 28601-3446. 704/328-
2634.

Kings Mountain Hosiery Mill
Charles St, Kings Mountain
NC 28086. 704/739-7155.

Mayo Knitting Mills Inc.
2204 W Austin St, Tarboro
NC 27886-2467. 919/823-
3101.

Montgomery Hosiery Mill
451 N Main St, Star NC
27356. 910/428-2191.

Parker Hosiery Co. Inc.
Catawba Ave, Old Fort NC
28762. 704/668-7628.

Paul Lavitt Mills Inc.
1517 F Ave SE, Hickory NC
28602-1358. 704/328-
2463.

Pickett Hosiery Mills Inc.
741 E Webb Ave, Burlington
NC 27217-5971. 910/227-
2716.

Pilot Hosiery Mills Inc.
P.O. Box 608, Pilot Mountain
NC 27041-0608. 910/368-
2291.

Pine Hosiery Mill Inc.
208 S Main St, Star NC
27356. 910/428-2185.

Red Hill Hosiery Mill Inc.
796 20th St NE, Hickory NC
28601-4316. 704/327-
4663.

Ruppe Hosiery Inc.
312 E Gold St, Kings
Mountain NC 28086-3436.
704/739-4537.

Russell-Harvelle Hosiery Mills
103 Industry Ave, Mount
Gilead NC 27306. 910/439-
6116.

Southern Hosiery Mills
P.O. Box 789, Hickory NC
28603-0789. 704/328-
5201.

Thor-Lo Inc.
319 Link St, Rockwell NC
28138-7500. 704/279-
7247.

Thor-Lo Inc.
2210 Newton Dr, Statesville
NC 28677-4850. 704/872-
6522.

Twin City Co.
710 1st St E, Conover NC
28613-1700. 704/464-
4830.

**Willwear Hosiery
Manufacturing Co. Inc.**
Blue Ridge St, Marion NC
28752. 704/652-3626.

Candor Hosiery Mill Inc.
Biscoe Industrial Park, Biscoe
NC 27209. 910/428-1242.

LaBelle Manufacturing Corp.
600 Broome St, Monroe NC
28110-3947. 704/283-
1559.

Pellamy Manufacturing Co.
301 E Franck St, Richlands
NC 28574. 910/324-2701.

ABC Manufacturing
1609 Newton Dr, Statesville
NC 28677-5042. 704/871-
9226.

Burlington Industries Equity
1056 Bombay Rd, Denton
NC 27239. 704/869-4511.

Fairystone Fabrics Inc.
2247 Park Road Ext,
Burlington NC 27215-1924.
910/228-1771.

Jockey International
P.O. Box 8, Cooleemee NC
27014-0008. 704/284-
4088.

Kings Mountain Knit Fabrics
Corner of Oak & Railroad,
Kings Mountain NC 28086.
704/739-6418.

Kingstree Knits
105 Stone St, Haw River NC
27258 910/578-5061.

Knitcraft Inc.
McAdenville Rd, Belmont NC
28012. 704/825-5183.

Ramseur Interlock Knitting
244 State Hwy 22 N,
Ramseur NC 27316.
910/824-2375.

Scott Mills Inc.
2224 Plastics Dr, Gastonia
NC 28054-3442. 704/865-
7447.

Tower Mills Inc.
110 N Broad St, Burlington
NC 27217-3918. 910/227-
6221.

Wales Fabric
214 Superior Stainless Rd,
Gastonia NC 28052-8746.
704/864-3201.

TEXTILE FINISHING

Best Textile Printing Corp.
518 S Pearl St, Rocky Mount
NC 27804-5847. 919/977
0631.

Bloomsburg Mills Inc.
3000 Stitt St, Monroe NC
28110-3953. 704/289-
2536.

Burlington Industries
500 Airport Rd, Rocky
Mount NC 27804-2005.
919/972-6302.

Champion Finishing Co.
200 Bingham Rd, Asheville
NC 28806-3902. 704/252-
0261.

Collins & Aikman Corp.
312 Office St, Concord NC
28027-6373. 704/786-
2181.

Cone Mills Corp.
122 E Main St, Haw River
NC 27258-9625. 910/578-
1212.

Craftsmen Fabrics Industries
280 Manor Ave SW,
Concord NC 28025-5712.
704/786-1157.

Down East Fabrics Inc.
2001 W Vernon Ave,
Kinston NC 28501-3329.
919/523-2112.

EJ Snyder & Co. Inc.
221 Snuggs Rd, Albemarle
NC 28001-2617. 704/982-
9105.

Flynt Fabrics & Finishing
505 Eno St, Hillsborough NC
27278-2357. 919/732-
1600.

Flynt Fabrics Inc.
1902 Tucker St, Burlington
NC 27215-6733. 910/229-
6691.

Goldtex Inc.
401 Patetown Rd, Goldsboro
NC 27530. 919/736-7411.

Graham Dyeing & Finishing
240 Hawkins St, Burlington
NC 27217. 910/228-9981.

Monroe Prints
2501 Ashcraft Ave, Monroe
NC 28110-6822. 704/283-
2135.

Sanford Finishing
Hwy 1 Bypass, Sanford NC
27330. 919/776-4321.

Textile Printing & Processing
P.O. Box 1620, Rocky Mount
NC 27802-1620. 919/977-
0381.

**Deep River Dyeing &
Finishing**
225 Poplar St, Randleman
NC 27317-1546. 910/498-
4181.

Burlington Industries Equity
345 Eastwood Dr, Cramerton
NC 28032. 704/825-3075.

Creative Dyeing
5400 Hovis Rd, Charlotte NC
28208-1244. 704/393-
0190.

Danalex Inc.
1709 Industrial Park,
Gastonia NC 28052-8434.
704/333-1063.

J&C Dyeing Inc.
1000 Grove St, Shelby NC
28152-6852. 704/487-
2322.

Oxford Printing & Finishing
604 W Industry Dr, Oxford
NC 27565-3592. 919/693-
6111.

Precision Fabrics Group
301 E Meadowview Rd,
Greensboro NC 27406-4522.
910/379-3100.

Precision Fabrics Group
6012 High Point Rd,
Greensboro NC 27407-7009.
910/454-3144.

Royal Carolina Corp.
7305 Old Friendly Rd,
Greensboro NC 27410-6236.
910/292-8845.

Shelby Dyeing & Finishing
1038 Sam Lattimore Rd,
Shelby NC 28152-0536.
704/487-0641.

Walker-Rice Inc.
600 Green Valley Rd,
Greensboro NC 27408-7722.
910/297-1300.

CARPETS AND RUGS

Collins & Aikman Corp.
Glenn Rd, Troy NC 27371.
910/572-3721.

Janesville Products
Lackey Town Rd, Old Fort
NC 28762. 704/668-9251.

Karastan-Bigelow
335 Summit Rd, Eden NC
27288-2829. 910/627-
7200.

Karastan-Bigelow
P.O. Box 27050, Greensboro
NC 27425-7050. 910/665-
4000.

Shaw Industries Inc.
10901 Texland Blvd,
Charlotte NC 28273-6217.
704/588-1272.

YARN AND THREAD MILLS

American & Efird Corp.
401 Grover St, Gastonia NC
28054-3231. 704/867-
3664.

Artee Industries Inc.
Blanton Industrial Park, Artee
Rd, Shelby NC 28150.
704/482-3826.

Atlantic Spinners Inc.
212 E Virginia Ave,
Bessemer City NC 28016-
2344. 704/629-6263.

Burlington Industries Equity
514 N Bright Leaf Blvd,
Smithfield NC 27577-4407.
910/934-2166.

Burlington Industries Equity
1627 Spencer Mountain Rd,
Gastonia NC 28054-3047.
704/824-2581.

Burlington Industries Equity
905 W Charlotte Ave, Mount
Holly NC 28120-1207.
704/827-2441.

Carolina Mills Inc.
119 N Oakland Ave,
Statesville NC 28677-3870.
704/872-2726.

Carolina Mills Inc.
935 N Main Ave, Newton NC
28658-3051. 704/464-
1801.

Carolina Mills Inc.
569 S Groze St Ext,
Lincolnton NC 28092.
704/735-2591.

**Chatham Manufacturing
Co./Yarn Division**
Woodruff Rd, Boonville NC
27011. 910/367-7213.

Collins & Aikman Corp.
Hwy 52, Norwood NC
28128. 704/474-3131.

Crescent Spinning Co.
621 Catawba St, Belmont
NC 28012-3352. 704/825-
9611.

Delta Mills Marketing Co.
W Finger St, Maiden NC
28650. 704/428-3261.

Dixie Yarns Inc.
101 E 11th St, Newton NC
28658-2253. 704/464-
4662.

Dominion Yarn Corp.
840 Plantation Dr, Burlington
NC 27215-6711. 910/222-
8554.

Eastern Manufacturing Co.
24 Millbrooke St, Selma NC
27576. 919/965-3162.

Galey & Lord Inc.
1910 Hunt St, Gastonia NC
28054-7421. 704/864-
5797.

Glen Raven Mills Inc.
Hwy 1 S, Norlina NC 27563.
919/456-4141.

Glen Raven Mills Inc.
800 Manning St, Kinston NC
28501-4112. 919/527-
9036.

Globe Manufacturing Co.
3145 Northwest Blvd,
Gastonia NC 28052-1168.
704/864-5495.

**Hadley Peoples
Manufacturing Co.**
P.O. Box 1049, Laurinburg
NC 28353-1049. 910/663-
3030.

Howell Manufacturing Co.
Wert St, Cherryville NC
28021. 704/435-3259.

Milliken & Co.
Hwy 226, Bostic NC 28018.
704/248-3212.

North Carolina Spinning Mills
P.O. Box 818, Lincolnton NC
28093-0818. 704/732-
1171.

Oakdale Cotton Mills
710 Oakdale Rd, Jamestown
NC 27282-9220. 910/454-
1144.

Parkdale Mills Inc.
2701 S Main St, Salisbury
NC 28147-7901. 704/633-
8115.

Parkdale Mills Inc.
100 Mill St, Lexington NC
27292-1624. 704/243-
2141.

Peck Manufacturing Co.
500 Harper St, Warrenton
NC 27589-1617. 919/257-
3191.

Richmond Yarns Inc.
Hwy 220 N, Ellerbe NC
28338. 910/652-5554.

RL Stowe Mills Inc.
710 Catawba St, Belmont
NC 28012-3504. 704/825-
6615.

RL Stowe Mills Inc.
96 Catawba St, Belmont NC
28012-3349. 704/825-
6610.

SCT Yarns Inc.
1100 E Main St, Cherryville
NC 28021-3661. 704/435-
6881.

Shuford Mills Inc.
290 Pleasant Hill Rd, Hudson
NC 28638-2244. 704/728-
3212.

Shuford Mills Inc.
12 Falls Ave, Granite Falls
NC 28630-1508. 704/496-
3234.

Spanco Yarns Inc.
219 W Harden St, Graham
NC 27253-2827. 910/570-
5950.

Spanco Yarns Inc.
215 Bonview Ave,
Lincolnton NC 28092-2127.
704/735-6532.

Stonecutter Mills Corp.
Hwy 108, Mill Spring NC
28756. 704/894-8201.

Tolaram Fibers Inc.
749 Pineview Rd, Randleman
NC 27317-7585. 910/672-
2600.

Tuscarora Yarns Inc.
406 N Main St, China Grove
NC 28023-2534. 704/857-
0173.

American & Efird Inc.
511 Union St, Maiden NC
28650-1400. 704/428-
8690.

COATED FABRICS

**Lumberton Dyeing &
Finishing**
610 E 1st St, Lumberton NC
28358-5838. 910/738-
3705.

Shuford Mills Inc.
447 Main St, Hudson NC
28638-2399. 704/728-
3211.

TIRE CORD AND FABRICS

Rogosin Converters Inc.
10461 Old Wire Rd, Laurel
Hill NC 28351-9387.
910/462-2051.

NONWOVEN FABRICS

Hendrix Batting Co.
2310 Surrett Dr, High Point
NC 27263. 910/431-1181.

Lydall Inc./Westex Division
I-77 & Hwy 421,
Hamptonville NC 27020.
910/468-8522.

CORDAGE AND TWINE

Hickory Industries
429 27th St NW, Hickory NC
28601-4549. 704/322-
2600.

Wall Industries Inc.
Rowan & Oak Sts, Granite
Quarry NC 28072. 704/279-
7901.

Wellington Leisure Products
Nelson St, Pilot Mountain NC
27041. 910/368-4701.

TEXTILE GOODS

Carolina Yarn Processors
P.O. Box A, Tryon NC
28782-2001. 704/859-
5891.

GS Industries Inc.
901 N Ashe Ave, Newton
NC 28658-3048. 704/465-
3800.

Lida Manufacturing Co.
1709 Industrial Park,
Gastonia NC 28052-8434.
704/861-1535.

OMS Textiles
340 Morgan St SE, Valdese
NC 28690-2930. 704/874-
4126.

STI Inc.
Marie St, Kings Mountain NC
28086. 704/739-4503.

MEN'S AND BOYS' CLOTHING

Lions Manufacturing Inc.
1208 Industrial Ave,
Gastonia NC 28054-4629.
704/864-6744.

Pioneer Manufacturing
804 Julian Rd, Salisbury NC
28147-9080. 704/637-
1303.

Accent Apparel Inc.
1204 W Swanzy St,
Elizabethtown NC 28337-
9008. 910/862-2640.

Bassett-Walker Inc.
Hwy 220 Bypass, Stoneville
NC 27048. 910/573-9816.

Bassett-Walker Inc.
Atwood St, Sparta NC
28675. 910/372-4244.

Bassett-Walker Inc.
Globe Ln, Bakersville NC
28705. 704/688-2178.

Encore Textiles Inc.
2317 Stafford St, Monroe
NC 28110-9673. 704/283-
8546.

Hugger Inc.
1443 Gaston St, Lincolnton
NC 28092-4401. 704/735-
7422.

Jasper Textiles Inc.
Hwy 210 W, Angier NC
27501. 919/639-4007.

Jasper Textiles Inc.
P.O. Box 1106, Fremont NC
27830-1006. 919/242-
6182.

Jasper Textiles Inc.
103 Outer Banks Dr,
Havelock NC 28532-1614.
919/444-3400.

Kinston Apparel Manufacturing
3717 W Vernon Ave,
Kinston NC 28501-3201.
919/522-0771.

Lincolnton Manufacturing
Salem Church Rd, Lincolnton
NC 28092. 704/732-1818.

Springford Knitting Co.
501 Spindale St, Spindale
NC 28160-1609. 704/286-
3611.

Whisper Knits Inc.
315 Industrial Dr, Clinton NC
28328-9739. 910/592-
8180.

Indera Mills Co.
400 S Marshall St, Winston-
Salem NC 27101-5282.
910/723-7311.

Devil Dog Manufacturing Co.
RR 1, Box A-37, Newton
Grove NC 28366-9801.
910/594-0247.

Jonbil Inc.
Dabney Dr, Henderson NC
27536. 919/492-8724.

Royals Inc.
325 Fraley Rd, High Point NC
27263-1753. 910/885-
0195.

W&J Rives Inc.
1040 E Springfield Rd, High
Point NC 27263-2158.
910/434-4181.

Ace Sportswear
700 Quality Rd, Fayetteville
NC 28306-2097. 910/323-
1223.

Belvoir Manufacturing
RR 4, Box 69, Greenville NC
27834-9498. 919/758-
9710.

Southern Apparel Co.
E 3rd St Ext, Robersonville
NC 27871. 919/795-3031.

Ashley Co.
10 Harold St, Sylva NC
28779-2612. 704/586-
6376.

Capstar Corp.
600 Park Dr, Statesville NC
28677-4937. 704/878-
2007.

Pluma Inc.
801 Fieldcrest Rd, Eden NC
27288-3632. 910/635-
4000.

Roseboro Manufacturing Co.
Hwy 24, Roseboro NC
28382. 910/525-5118.

Sunrise Apparel
455 Spring St NW, Concord
NC 28025-4569. 704/786-
4191.

WOMEN'S AND MISSES' CLOTHING

Carolina Dress Corp.
1000 Qualla Rd, Hayesville
NC 28904. 704/389-8888.

Hudson Manufacturing Co.
RR 1, Box 181A, New Bern
NC 28560-9191. 919/745-
3711.

Oxford of Burgaw
1090 W Wilmington St,
Burgaw NC 28425-5556.
910/259-5794.

Apricot Co.
Don Juan Rd, Hertford NC
27944. 919/426-5257.

Beulaville Garment Co.
Hwy 41, Beulaville NC
28518. 910/298-3130.

Claco Manufacturing Inc.
US Hwy 64 Bypass,
Hayesville NC 28904.
704/389-6321.

Elkin Valley Apparel Co.
Hwy 268 W, Elkin NC
28621. 910/835-6406.

Four Seasons Apparel Co.
4602 Dundas Dr #110,
Greensboro NC 27407-1612.
910/299-3121.

Gigi of Carolina Inc.
201 N Sweet Tree St,
Cherryville NC 28021.
704/435-3741.

Hemco Inc.
Hwy 13 N, Newton Grove
NC 28366. 910/594-1968.

Len How Corp.
103 E Blue St, Saint Pauls
NC 28384-1811. 910/865-
4058.

Marithe & Francois Girbaud
1801 Stanley Rd, Suite 400,
Greensboro NC 27407-2644.
910/547-7700.

Pierpoint Sportswear Inc.
4111 Romaine St, Suite
206, Greensboro NC 27407-
4211. 910/855-8680.

PT Apparel Inc.
410 N Ashe Ave, Dunn NC
28334-3608. 910/892-
1138.

Tultex Apparel
104 E Roosevelt St,
Mayodan NC 27027-2927.
910/427-5131.

Carolina Underwear Co.
110 W Guilford St,
Thomasville NC 27360-3919. 910/472-7788.

Cassie Cotillion Inc.
2026 Kingsley Dr, Albemarle
NC 28001-4472. 704/983-1136.

Cassie Cotillion Inc.
181 College St, Norwood NC
28128-8441. 704/474-3177.

Glenwood Manufacturing Co.
520 Moore St, Clayton NC
27520-2224. 919/553-7181.

Mylcraft Manufacturing Co.
111 N Main St, Rich Square
NC 27869. 919/539-4151.

**Paul Bruce Manufacturing
Co. Inc.**
Hwy 903 S, Scotland Neck
NC 27874. 919/826-4125.

Sara Lee Intimates
1620 Crawford Rd,
Statesville NC 28677-8501.
704/872-4222.

Shadowline Inc.
241 Shadowline Dr, Boone
NC 28607-4937. 704/264-8828.

HEAD WEAR

NC Garment Co.
512 Townsend Ave, High
Point NC 27263-2046.
910/861-1122.

Stanly Knitting Mills Inc.
12104 E 5th St, Oakboro NC
28129. 704/485-8525.

**CHILDREN'S AND INFANTS'
CLOTHING**

Dixie Kidds Inc.
120 Tom Starling Rd,
Fayetteville NC 28306-9545.
910/423-2000.

Nash Garment Co.
300 Washington St Ext,
Nashville NC 27856.
919/459-7106.

Patsy Aiken Designs Inc.
4812 Hargrove Rd, Raleigh
NC 27604. 919/872-8789.

Tom Togs Inc.
Nassau St, Youngsville NC
27596. 919/556-5132.

Ahoskie Apparel Co. Inc.
Hwy 42 W, Ahoskie NC
27910. 919/332-6158.

Bladen Sportswear Inc.
404 Ben St, Elizabethtown
NC 28337-9304. 910/862-4583.

Devil Dog Manufacturing Co.
Hwy 301 S, Kenly NC
27542. 919/284-4739.

Devil Dog Manufacturing Co.
628 S Pine St, Spring Hope
NC 27882. 919/478-3181.

Devil Dog Manufacturing Co.
2301 Old Stantonsburg Rd,
Wilson NC 27893-8409.
919/291-4495.

K&R Sportswear
602 W Branch St, Spring
Hope NC 27882. 919/478-3173.

Lakedale Manufacturing
700 Quality Rd, Fayetteville
NC 28306-2049. 910/483-9541.

Little Stitches Manufacturing
Oak Hill Rd, Lenoir NC
28645. 704/758-8725.

May Apparel Group Inc.
101 W Nash St, Whitakers
NC 27891. 919/437-3311.

Murfreesboro Manufacturing
310 W Broad St,
Murfreesboro NC 27855-1432. 919/398-3194.

Plymouth Garment Co.
100 Jean St, Plymouth NC
27962-9533. 919/793-5151.

Princeton Manufacturing Co.
507 Pearl St, Princeton NC
27569. 910/936-6211.

Springdale Fashions
605 E Railroad St, Clinton
NC 28328-4305. 910/592-6101.

GLOVES

Carolina Glove Co.
1637 Buffalo Shoals Rd,
Catawba NC 28609-8026.
704/241-3716.

Carolina Glove Co.
RR 7, Box 87, Taylorsville
NC 28681-8911. 704/632-2107.

Carolina Glove Co.
1000 Ridge St, Wilkesboro
NC 28697. 910/667-7187.

North Safety Products
1845 Withers Rd, Maiden NC
28650-9654. 704/428-9291.

Tom Thumb Gloves
Indl Park Rd, Wilkesboro NC
28697. 910/667-1281.

**ROBES AND DRESSING
GOWNS**

Kings Creek Manufacturing
Hwy 268 W, Ferguson NC
28624. 910/973-4870.

BELTS

Gem-Dandy Inc.
200 W Academy St,
Madison NC 27025-2002.
910/548-9624.

**MISC. APPAREL AND
ACCESSORIES**

**Royal Park Uniform
Manufacturing Co.**
Hwy 86 N, Prospect Hill NC
27314. 910/562-3345.

CURTAINS AND DRAPERIES

Dorothy's Ruffled Originals
6721 Market St, Wilmington
NC 28405-3703. 910/686-8000.

Royal Home Fashions
7320 Oakwood Street Ext,
Mebane NC 27302-9211.
910/563-6333.

Toltec Fabrics Inc.
5644 Hornaday Rd #A,
Greensboro NC 27409-2908.
910/292-5008.

TEXTILE BAGS

HBD Inc.
3901 Riverdale Dr,
Greensboro NC 27406-7505.
910/275-4800.

CANVAS PRODUCTS

Dize Co.
1512 S Main St, Winston-Salem NC 27127-2707.
910/722-5181.

Hatteras Group
1104 S Clark St, Greenville
NC 27834-4052. 919/758-9533.

John Boyle & Co. Inc.
Salisbury Rd Box 791,
Statesville NC 28677-6207.
704/872-6303.

STITCHING AND TUCKING

Precision Embroidery Corp.
1419 N Rocky River Rd,
Monroe NC 28110-2102.
704/283-7999.

**TRIMMINGS, APPAREL
FINDINGS, AND RELATED
PRODUCTS**

**Dyeing & Printing of
Lumberton**
1519 Carthage Rd,
Lumberton NC 28358-3411.
910/671-9077.

HH Cutler Co.
10 N Summit Ave, Granite Falls NC 28630-1333. 704/396-1155.

International Screen Printing
309 Anderson Ave, Farmville NC 27828. 919/753-7115.

Nike Sport Graphics
234 W Dudley St, Greenville NC 27834-1467. 919/757-0483.

Ribbon Textiles Inc.
150 Industrial Park Dr, Boone NC 28607-3973. 704/264-6444.

United Screen Printers
13875 Brown Hill Rd, Locust NC 28097. 704/888-6145.

FABRICATED TEXTILE PRODUCTS

Avondale Mills Inc.
Hwy 421 N, Sanford NC 27330. 919/774-7600.

Cortina Fabrics Separating
802 S Graham Hopedale Rd, Burlington NC 27217-4328. 910/570-9739.

Dicey Fabrics Inc.
430 Neisler St, Shelby NC 28152-5000. 704/487-6324.

Graniteville Trading
324 W Wendover Ave, Suite 210, Greensboro NC 27408-8439. 910/275-8518.

New Cherokee Corp.
Jack McKinney Rd, Harris NC 28074. 704/247-2000.

No Nonsense Fashions
Hwy 56 E, Creedmoor NC 27522. 919/528-1891.

QST Industries Inc.
140 Lionheart Dr, Mocksville NC 27028-9440. 704/634-1000.

Robetex Inc.
Hwy 72, Lumberton NC 28358. 910/671-8787.

Swift Textiles
2102 N Elm St, Greensboro NC 27408-5100. 910/272-4293.

Town & Country Linen
599 Raleigh Rd, Henderson NC 27536-5364. 910/431-0551.

APPAREL WHOLESALE

Doe Spun
750 N Pine St, Rocky Mount NC 27804-4627. 919/977-6353.

Down East Togs
1600 Bridges St, Morehead City NC 28557-3650. 919/247-6091.

Hoffman Hosiery Mills
P.O. Box 170, Granite Falls NC 28630-0170. 704/396-2031.

Monarch Hosiery Mills
P.O. Box 1205, Burlington NC 27216-1205. 910/584-0361.

Kingstree Knits
11121 Carmel Commons Blvd, Charlotte NC 28226-3919. 704/543-0002.

Spring Hope Manufacturing
Railroad, Spring Hope NC 27882. 919/478-3181.

Kentucky Derby Hosiery
314 S South St, Mount Airy NC 27030-4450. 910/786-4134.

Belmont Hosiery Mills
117 Chronicle St, Belmont NC 28012-3316. 704/825-8413.

Candor Hosiery
105 Poole Rd, Troy NC 27371-9300. 910/576-3565.

FGR Manufacturers
Bunn Ln, Spring Hope NC 27882. 919/478-7819.

Gerson & Gerson Inc.
Hwy 264, Bailey NC 27807. 919/235-2441.

Quality Textiles Inc.
RR 1, Spring Hope NC 27882. 919/237-3809.

Shana Knitwear
1215 Shana Ln, Asheboro NC 27203. 910/626-0307.

South Carolina

ALLIEDSIGNAL, INC.
FIBERS DIVISION
P.O. Box 1788, Columbia SC 29202. 803/772-2700. **Contact:** Nancy Harrel, Personnel Manager. **Description:** This location produces nylon textile yarns and related products. **Parent company:** AlliedSignal Corporation serves a broad spectrum of industries through its more than 40 strategic businesses, which are grouped into three sectors: Aerospace; Automotive; and Engineered Materials. AlliedSignal Corporation is one of the nation's largest industrial organizations.

AMERICAN FIBER AND FINISHING
P.O. Box 379, Newberry SC 29108. 803/276-2843. **Contact:** Tom Perry, Human Resources Manager. **Description:** A broadwoven textile fabric mill. American Fiber and Finishing manufactures cloth from cotton. The company wholesales this material to other companies that make finished apparel and textile products.

AMOCO FABRICS AND FIBERS COMPANY
P.O. Box 1197, Seneca SC 29679. 864/882-5660. **Contact:** Human Resources. **Description:** Amoco Fabrics and Fibers Company is part of Amoco Corporation's conversion and specialty chemicals division, converting polypropylene into woven carpet-backing and fabrics and yarns for home, automotive, industrial, and medical applications. The company's products include nonwoven fabrics, multifilament yarns, and fibers. In 1993, Amoco Fabrics and Fibers Company acquired Phillips Fibers Corporation. **Parent company:** Amoco Corporation is a worldwide integrated petroleum and chemical company with locations in the United States, China, Mexico, Russia, Egypt, Argentina, Trinidad, the United Kingdom, and other countries. Amoco Corporation's operations include exploration and production; refining, marketing, and transportation; commodity and industrial chemicals; and conversion and specialty chemicals.

BASF CORPORATION
FIBER DIVISION
P.O. Drawer 3025, Anderson SC 29624. 864/260-7000. **Contact:** Human Resources.
Description: BASF Corporation is engaged in the manufacture and marketing of
industrial chemicals, yarns, and man-made fibers. As a whole, BASF Corporation is an
international chemical products organization, doing business in five operating groups:
Agricultural Chemicals; Chemicals; Colors and Auxiliaries; Pigments and Organic
Specialties; and Polymers. **Corporate headquarters location:** Mount Olive NJ. **Number
of employees worldwide:** 125,000.

CLINTON MILLS, INC.
P.O. Drawer 1215, Clinton SC 29325. 864/833-5500. **Contact:** James Buchanan,
Personnel Director. **Description:** A textile manufacturing facility. Clinton Mills, Inc.
produces unfinished fabric.

COATS & CLARK, INC.
30 Patewood Drive, Greenville SC 29615. 864/234-0331. **Contact:** Human
Resources. **Description:** Coats & Clark, Inc. is a producer of thread, trim, and other
textiles. **Parent company:** Coats North American in Charlotte NC is engaged in the
manufacturing of cotton and synthetic thread and yarn; metal and coil slide fasteners,
tapes, trimmings, and small die castings; wood turnings and novelties; and special
machinery spools, nylon travelers, and other plastic injection moldings, as well as
associated products for the industrial and consumer products markets. **Other U.S.
locations:** GA; NY; RI. **Number of employees nationwide:** 6,700.

CONSO PRODUCTS COMPANY
P.O. Box 326, Union SC 29379-0326. 864/427-9004. **Contact:** Sharon O'Dell,
Human Resources Manager. **Description:** Conso Products Company manufactures
decorative products and trimmings including tassels, braids, and fringe.

DELTA WOODSIDE INDUSTRIES, INC.
233 North Main Street, Suite 200, Greenville SC 29601. 864/232-8301. **Contact:**
Jane Greer, Corporate Vice President. **Description:** Delta Woodside Industries, Inc.
produces a wide selection of textiles, fabrics, apparel, and fitness equipment, and also
spins yarn. The fabrics segment produces finished and unfinished woven and knit
fabrics for clothing and home furnishings. The apparel segment makes and sells Duck
Head clothing, T-shirts, and sweatsuits; and operates 37 outlet stores which sell
irregular clothing items throughout the Southeast. Delta Woodside Industries, Inc.
acquired Nautilus International in 1993 and has since manufactured and marketed
physical fitness clothing under the Nautilus name. **Subsidiaries include:** Apparel
Marketing Corporation; Alchem Capital Corporation; Delta Merchandising, Inc. **Listed
on:** New York Stock Exchange. **Number of employees nationwide:** 8,500.

EMERGENT GROUP, INC.
P.O. Box 17526, Greenville SC 29606. 864/235-8056. **Contact:** Human Resources.
Description: A diversified holding company which manufactures and markets children's
clothing; operates a short-line railroad; repairs, operates, and leases railcars; and offers
residential mortgage and construction loans. **Corporate headquarters location:** This
Location. **Subsidiaries include:** Carolina Investors, Inc.; Premier Financial Services, Inc.;
Pickens Railroad Company; Emergent Financial Corporation; Loan Pros, Inc.; Emergent
Business Capital, Inc.; and Young Generations, Inc. **Number of employees nationwide:**
250.

GREENWOOD MILLS, INC.
P.O. Box 1017, Greenwood SC 29648-1017. 864/229-2571. **Contact:** Director of
Personnel. **Description:** Greenwood Mills, Inc. is a textile manufacturer.

HAMPSHIRE GROUP, LIMITED
215 Commerce Boulevard, Anderson SC 29621. 864/225-6232. **Contact:** Bill
Kennedy, Human Resources Manager. **Description:** Hampshire Group, Limited
manufactures branded and private-label sweaters and private-label women's hosiery
through two wholly-owned subsidiaries, Hampshire Designers, Inc. and Hampshire
Hosiery, Inc. Hampshire Designers is one of the largest manufacturers of full-fashion
sweaters in the United States. The company designs, manufactures, and markets its
own classically-styled sweaters under the brand name of Designers Originals and also
manufactures private label sweaters for a number of retailers and apparel companies.
Hampshire Designers operates its distribution segment at this location and has
manufacturing plants in Chilhowie, VA and Quedbradillas, Puerto Rico. Hampshire
Hosiery is engaged in providing customized private label hosiery programs for chains

and mass merchandisers and other large customers. The company operates manufacturing and distribution plants in Spruce Pine, North Carolina. In 1995, Hampshire Group acquired San Francisco Knitworks, Inc., which operates a plant in San Francisco, CA. Sales offices of Hampshire Group are located in New York, NY; Plainville, MA; and Los Angeles, CA. **Corporate headquarters location:** This Location. **Listed on:** NASDAQ. **Number of employees nationwide:** 1,735.

HOECHST CELANESE CORPORATION
P.O. Box 5887, Spartanburg SC 29304. 864/579-5750. **Contact:** Brian Cliff, Human Resources Manager. **Description:** This location manufactures polyester. Overall, Hoechst Celanese Corporation is a science-based, market-driven, international company which produces and markets a variety of products including: chemicals; manufactured fibers for textile and industrial uses; engineering plastics and other high performance advanced materials; polyester; film; printing plates; dyes and pigments; pharmaceuticals; and animal-health and crop-protection products. The company ranks as one of the largest United States chemical companies. Hoechst Celanese Corporation is the largest and fastest-growing member of the international Hoechst Group, which operates 250 companies in 120 countries. **Corporate headquarters location:** Somerville NJ. **Parent company:** Hoechst Group. **Listed on:** New York Stock Exchange. **Number of employees worldwide:** 23,000.

IVA MANUFACTURING COMPANY
Elberton Highway 184 South, P.O. Box 148, Iva SC 29655. 864/348-6151. **Contact:** Personnel Director. **Description:** Iva Manufacturing Company manufactures and retails women's apparel. **Common positions include:** Accountant/Auditor; Administrator; Computer Programmer; Credit Manager; Department Manager; Financial Analyst; Industrial Engineer; Mechanical Engineer; Operations/Production Manager; Purchasing Agent and Manager; Quality Control Supervisor; Transportation/Traffic Specialist. **Educational backgrounds include:** Accounting; Business Administration; Computer Science; Engineering; Marketing. **Benefits:** Employee Discounts; Life Insurance; Medical Insurance; Profit Sharing; Savings Plan; Tuition Assistance. **Operations at this facility include:** Administration; Manufacturing; Regional Headquarters.

JPS TEXTILE GROUP INC.
555 North Pleasantburg Drive, Greenville SC 29607. 864/239-3900. **Contact:** Monnie Broome, Human Resources Manager. **Description:** JPS Textile Group Inc. is a holding company whose companies are engaged in the following areas of business: manufacturing and marketing a broad range of unfinished fabrics used in men's, women's, and children's apparel; automotive products; home furnishings; and residential and commercial carpets. **Corporate headquarters location:** This Location. **Number of employees nationwide:** 6,000.

KLEAR KNIT, INC.
510 Sunset Drive, P.O. Box 236, Clover SC 29710. 803/222-3011. **Contact:** Ms. Jackie George, Human Resources Manager. **Description:** Klear Knit, Inc. manufactures knitted outwear, specializing in men's and boys' clothing.

LA FRANCE INDUSTRIES
P.O. Box 500, La France SC 29656. 864/646-3213. **Contact:** Jane Owens, Human Resources Director. **Description:** Manufactures upholstery material. **Common positions include:** Accountant/Auditor; Blue-Collar Worker Supervisor; Branch Manager; Chemist; Credit Manager; Customer Service Representative; Department Manager; General Manager; Human Resources Specialist; Industrial Engineer; Management Trainee; Manufacturer's/Wholesaler's Sales Rep.; Marketing Specialist; Mechanical Engineer; Operations/Production Manager; Public Relations Specialist; Purchasing Agent and Manager; Quality Control Supervisor; Reporter; Writer. **Benefits:** Dental Insurance; Disability Coverage; Employee Discounts; Life Insurance; Medical Insurance; Pension Plan; Profit Sharing; Savings Plan; Tuition Assistance. **Corporate headquarters location:** Greenville SC. **Operations at this facility include:** Manufacturing; Sales. **Listed on:** New York Stock Exchange.

MILLIKEN & COMPANY
P.O. Box 1926, Spartanburg SC 29304. 864/503-2020. **Contact:** Bob Colaninger, Human Resources Director. **Description:** A privately-controlled, high-technology textile manufacturer with 60 manufacturing locations in the Carolinas and Georgia. Milliken's textile products include clothing, interior furnishings, and commercial and industrial applications. These products are sold nationwide and internationally. **Common positions include:** Chemical Engineer; Electrical/Electronics Engineer; Industrial Engineer; Management Trainee; Manufacturer's/Wholesaler's Sales Rep.; Mechanical Engineer; Operations/Production Manager; Process Engineer. **Educational backgrounds**

include: Business Administration; Chemistry; Engineering; Marketing; Mathematics. **Benefits:** Disability Coverage; Employee Discounts; Life Insurance; Medical Insurance; Pension Plan; Savings Plan; Tuition Assistance. **Corporate headquarters location:** This Location. **Operations at this facility include:** Administration; Research and Development; Service.

ONEITA INDUSTRIES, INC.
P.O. Drawer 24, Andrews SC 29510. 803/264-5225. **Fax:** 803/264-6220. **Contact:** Michele Deese, Director of Human Resources. **Description:** A manufacturer of knit outerwear and underwear. **Common positions include:** Adjuster; Clerical Supervisor; Computer Programmer; Computer Systems Analyst; Credit Manager; Customer Service Representative; Financial Analyst; Health Services Manager; Human Resources Specialist; Operations/Production Manager; Purchasing Agent and Manager; Quality Control Supervisor. **Educational backgrounds include:** Accounting; Business Administration; Engineering; Finance; Marketing. **Benefits:** 401K; Dental Insurance; Disability Coverage; Employee Discounts; Life Insurance; Medical Insurance; Profit Sharing; Savings Plan; Tuition Assistance. **Corporate headquarters location:** This Location. **Operations at this facility include:** Administration; Divisional Headquarters; Manufacturing; Research and Development; Sales. **Listed on:** New York Stock Exchange. **Number of employees at this location:** 360.

SPRINGS INDUSTRIES, INC.
205 North White Street, Fort Mill SC 29715. 803/547-1500. **Contact:** Ms. Robin Harkett, Human Resources Assistant. **Description:** Springs Industries is a producer of home furnishings, finished fabrics, and other fabrics for industrial uses. Products include bedroom accessories, bath products, novelties, window treatments, and specialty fabrics for the clothes manufacturing, home furnishing, home sewing, sporting goods, and fire-retardant industries. **Corporate headquarters location:** This Location. **Listed on:** New York Stock Exchange.

T.N.S. MILLS INC.
210 Henson Road, Blacksburg SC 29702. 864/839-6255. **Contact:** Sid Landers, Personnel Manager. **Description:** A textile manufacturer whose products include yarn and both woven and nonwoven fabric.

TIETEX CORPORATION
3010 North White Stock Road, Spartanburg SC 29304. 864/574-0500. **Fax:** 864/574-9440. **Contact:** Ms. Gean Gilreach, Director of Human Resources. **Description:** One of the largest manufacturers of stitchbonded fabrics in the world. Tietex Corporation uses a patented process to produce fabrics that simulate woven fabrics, but cost substantially less. Other services provided by the company include warp knitting and textile finishing. Finishing processes include flexographic printing, dyeing, acrylic foam coating, heat transfer printing, napping, hot melt adhesive laminating, and embossing. New uses for innovative fabric finishes including flame retardants, antimicrobial, moisture mover, and soil release continue to be developed. Tietex markets include mattress ticking (printed tickings, box spring filler cloth, and commercial tickings with flame retardants); vertical blinds (custom and ready-made vertical and pleated shade fabrics); bedding (prints and solids for comforters, bedspreads, pillow shams, and dust ruffles); upholstery (prints, faux leathers, and faux suedes); outdoor furniture (cushion and umbrella prints); drapery and curtains (prints and solids that can be napped, latex foam-backed, or flame-retarded); industrial fabrics; vacuum cleaner bags (unique foam-backed filter media for outside bags on residential and commercial uprights and stick brooms); roofing (reinforcement for cold process roofing and modified bitumen membranes); shoes (shoe lining and innersole fabrics); medical (fabrics for orthopedic soft goods, arm slings, and restraint vests); sleeping bags (shells and linings for sleeping bags); and home furnishings (Tietex's largest area of business).

UNIBLEND SPINNERS, INC.
201 North Enterprise Street, Union SC 29379. 864/427-7681. **Fax:** 864/427-4212. **Contact:** Kathy McCoy, Director of Human Resources. **Description:** Uniblend Spinners is engaged in spinning yarn. **Common positions include:** Accountant/Auditor; Budget Analyst; Buyer; Computer Programmer; Computer Systems Analyst; Customer Service Representative; Electrician; Human Resources Specialist; Industrial Engineer; Industrial Production Manager; Purchasing Agent and Manager; Quality Control Supervisor. **Educational backgrounds include:** Accounting; Business Administration; Computer Science; Marketing. **Benefits:** 401K; Dental Insurance; Disability Coverage; Life Insurance; Medical Insurance; Savings Plan; Tuition Assistance. **Subsidiaries include:** Elk Spinner, Inc. **Operations at this facility include:** Administration; Divisional

Headquarters; Manufacturing; Sales; Service. **Listed on:** Privately held. **Number of employees at this location:** 425.

WELLINGTON LEISURE PRODUCTS

P.O. Box 129, Jonesville SC 29353. 864/674-5504. **Contact:** Ms. Patti Dennis, Plant Manager. **Description:** Wellington Leisure Products manufactures hammocks, nylon ropes, anchor and dock lines, and plant hangers. **Other U.S. locations:** Madison GA; Paterson NJ.

Note: Because addresses and telephone numbers of smaller companies change rapidly, we recommend you call each company to verify the information below before inquiring about job opportunities. Mass mailings are not recommended.

Additional employers with under 250 employees:

BROADWOVEN FABRIC MILLS

Alice Manufacturing Co.
1006 Rice Rd, Easley SC
29640-7810. 864/859-
6323.

Delta Woodside Industries
710 N Woods Dr, Fountain
Inn SC 29644-9789.
864/967-7111.

Fabric Resources International
RR 2, Mullins SC 29574-
9802. 803/464-2826.

Fabric Resources International
245 Stewart Ave, Rock Hill
SC 29730-3550. 803/324-
7636.

Letters Home Fashions
201D Old Boiling Springs Rd,
Greer SC 29650-4227.
864/675-9960.

Milliken & Co.
225 Bob Little Rd, Jonesville
SC 29353-2202. 864/429-
2743.

Milliken & Co.
138 Broad St, Union SC
29379-2903. 864/427-
4624.

Milliken & Co.
512 Pumpkintown Rd,
Marietta SC 29661-9526.
864/836-1250.

Mount Vernon Mills Inc.
15 Broad St, Williamston SC
29697-1807. 864/847-
7346.

Rosemont Mill
Highway 18, Jonesville SC
29353. 864/674-5544.

Springs Industries Inc.
7748 Kershaw Camden
Hwy, Kershaw SC 29067-
8124. 803/475-0100.

Sullivan-Carson Inc.
503 Kings Mountain St, York
SC 29745-1105. 803/684-
4201.

Delta Mills Marketing Co.
100 Augusta St, Greenville
SC 29601-3504. 864/255-
4122.

Hartwell Industries
Highway 391, Leesville SC
29070. 803/532-3871.

Mellotone
108 E Church St, Blacksburg
SC 29702-1648. 864/839-
6341.

Milliken & Co.
700 Recycle Rd, Kingstree
SC 29556. 803/354-6164.

Milliken & Co.
100 Dalton Dr, Pendleton SC
29670-9178. 864/646-
3263.

Milliken & Co.
Highway 23, Johnston SC
29832. 803/275-2516.

Tartan Textiles
325 Old Greenville Rd,
Spartanburg SC 29301-
4755. 864/576-2896.

Wateree Textile Corp.
412 Groves St, Lugoff SC
29078. 803/438-3416.

KNITTING MILLS

Glenco Hosiery Mills Inc.
Hwy 29, Cowpens Industrial
Pk, Cowpens SC 29330.
864/463-3295.

Fun-Tees Inc.
5308 Liberty Chapel Rd,
Florence SC 29506-5615.
803/665-4339.

TEXTILE FINISHING

Cheraw Dyeing & Finishing
Jersey & W Greene Sts,
Cheraw SC 29520.
803/537-2138.

Greenville Finishing Co.
100 Mill St, Greenville SC
29609-1972. 864/292-
3200.

Phoenix Finishing Corp.
16 Commerce Dr, Gaffney
SC 29340-4506. 864/487-
3594.

Rockland-Bamberg Industries
Calhoun & Church Sts,
Bamberg SC 29003.
803/245-2486.

Specialty Shearing & Dyeing
20 Odom Cir, Greenville SC
29611-2956. 864/233-
1255.

Cherokee Finishing Co.
310 Chandler Dr, Gaffney SC
29340-3900. 864/585-
8123.

CARPETS AND RUGS

Winchester & Son
210 S 2nd St, Easley SC
29640-2906. 864/859-
3203.

Wunda Weve Carpets
2200 Poinsett Hwy,
Greenville SC 29609-2451.
864/298-9100.

Wunda Weve Carpets
1221 S Batesville Rd, Greer
SC 29650-4701. 864/879-
8000.

Avondale Mills Inc.
201 S John St, Walhalla SC
29691. 864/638-5853.

Charles Craft Inc.
Highway 301 N, Hamer SC
29547. 803/774-7341.

Delta Mills Marketing Co.
1728 N Old River Rd,
Pamplico SC 29583-6010.
803/493-2111.

Image Industries Inc.
Highway 9 W, Dillon SC
29536. 803/774-2775.

Multitex Corp. of America
Highway 301, Ulmer SC
29849. 803/584-3458.

Queen Carpet Corp.
Hwy 278 E, Allendale SC
29810. 803/584-3877.

Randolph Yarns Inc.
175 Celriver Rd, Rock Hill SC
29730-7409. 803/366-
4136.

Reeves Brothers Inc.
509 Gray St, Woodruff SC
29388-1757. 864/476-
8151.

**United Merchants &
Manufacturers**
4701 Adrian Hwy, Conway
SC 29526-5827. 803/365-
5571.

WS Libbey Co.
401 Dearborn St #148,
Great Falls SC 29055-1644.
803/482-6688.

Milliken & Co.
Highway 378, Saluda SC
29138. 864/445-2136.

Shakespeare Co.
6111 Shakespeare Rd,
Columbia SC 29223-7323.
803/754-7011.

NONWOVEN FABRICS

Milliken & Co.
1108 Church St, Laurens SC
29360-1610. 864/682-
3115.

Milliken-Sommer
2805 Kemet Way,
Simpsonville SC 29681-
2457. 864/967-9200.

TEXTILE GOODS

EL Mansure Co.
Highway 76, Clinton SC
29325. 864/833-3953.

Forest Fiber Products
1 Fernandina Ct, Columbia
SC 29212-2345. 803/732-
3620.

**MEN'S AND BOYS'
CLOTHING**

Kingstree Knits Inc.
RR 4, Box 356B, Kingstree
SC 29556-9449. 803/382-
5562.

Kingstree/Texfi Knits Inc.
RR 3, Andrews SC 29510-
9803. 803/221-5405.

Owenby Co.
669 Saluda St, Chester SC
29706-1586. 803/385-
5930.

Sir Shirtmakers
140 N Homestead Rd,
Pickens SC 29671-9201.
864/878-2424.

B&H Apparel
Highway 76 W, Mullins SC
29574. 803/464-8744.

Stone Apparel
3452 Main St, Columbia SC
29203-6435. 803/252-
4450.

Stone Manufacturing Co.
Wrenn Dr, Johnston SC
29832. 803/275-4992.

Calvin Klein Jeans Wear
Haigler Street Ext, Abbeville
SC 29620. 864/459-2168.

Greenwood Industries
410 Park Ave, Greenwood
SC 29646-2659. 864/223-
3322.

Estill Manufacturing Co.
221 Grayson St E, Estill SC
29918-9609. 803/625-
2631.

Abbeville Shirtmakers
206 Barnett St, Abbeville SC
29620-2606. 864/459-
5437.

Quality Stitching Co.
300 Greenwood Hwy, Saluda
SC 29138-1008. 864/445-
2126.

Swansea Manufacturing Co.
800 S Brecon St, Swansea
SC 29160. 803/568-3851.

**Williamson-Dickie
Manufacturing Co.**
RR 2, Box 476, Prosperity
SC 29127-9802. 803/364-
2695.

Yopp & Co.
Bannockburn Rd, Florence SC
29505. 803/669-3161.

**WOMEN'S AND MISSES'
CLOTHING**

C&T Manufacturing Co.
100 Bryson Rd, Fountain Inn
SC 29644-9352. 864/963-
3669.

Oxford of Belton Inc.
O'Neal St, Belton SC 29627.
864/338-5221.

Oxford of Camden Inc.
1555 Bradley Rd, Camden
SC 29020-9532. 803/432-
5197.

**Towne & Country
Manufacturing**
601 Bypass, Lugoff SC
29078. 803/438-1561.

Ayers Manufacturing Co.
Highway 52, Coward SC
29530. 803/389-2751.

Carolina Blouse Co.
2836 Laurens Rd, Greenville
SC 29607-5226. 864/288-
0311.

Knight Industries Inc.
Highways 121 & 34,
Newberry SC 29108.
803/321-0421.

Talmadge Manufacturing Co.
RR 2, Box 1, Mc Cormick SC
29835-9601. 864/465-
2193.

Upstate Apparel
223 Kenneth St, Walhalla SC
29691-2443. 864/638-
5803.

Upstate Apparel/River Side
125 Tate Rd, Norris SC
29667-9738. 864/639-
6672.

Victory Sports Inc.
400 Victor Ave Ext, Greer
SC 29651. 864/879-3874.

Hemingway Apparel Inc.
Highway 41 N, Hemingway
SC 29554. 803/558-2525.

Palmetto Garment Co.
P.O. Box 1107, Travelers
Rest SC 29690-1107.
864/834-4125.

**CHILDREN'S AND INFANTS'
CLOTHING**

Kay Cee
1618 Jefferson Davis Hwy,
Camden SC 29020-3335.
803/432-4357.

**Santee Apparel
Manufacturing**
625 Spencer St, Manning SC
29102-2125. 803/435-
8873.

Stepping Stones Capital City
1651 Holland St, West
Columbia SC 29169-5740.
803/794-6850.

WATERPROOF OUTERWEAR

Falcon Industries
750 Wilcox Rd, Estill SC
29918-9776. 803/625-
3165.

**MISC. APPAREL AND
ACCESSORIES**

Carolina Fashions
714 Fairview Rd, Greer SC
29651-9595. 864/877-
4516.

CURTAINS AND DRAPERIES

Curtron Curtains Inc.
Hwy 25 N, Travelers Rest SC
29690. 864/834-7217.

RST&B Curtain & Drapery
325 S Greer Rd, Florence SC
29506-3909. 803/669-
7474.

Richloom Home Fashions
Cork St, Ware Shoals SC
29692. 864/456-7456.

STITCHING AND TUCKING

Cambrai Inc.
3251 Abbeville Hwy,
Anderson SC 29624-4371.
864/296-0043.

David Geoffrey Associates
10 Slazenger Dr, Greenville
SC 29605-3441. 864/422-
0200.

Jubilee Embroidery Co.
411 Highway 601 S, Lugoff
SC 29078. 803/438-2934.

Krieger Corp.
19 Page Ct, Travelers Rest
SC 29690. 864/834-8081.

**TRIMMINGS, APPAREL
FINDINGS, AND RELATED
PRODUCTS**

Four Seasons Screen Printing
101 Bulk Plant Rd, Conway
SC 29526. 803/365-0760.

Pageland Screen Printers
512 S Pine St, Pageland SC
29728-2279. 803/672-
6123.

Screen Prints Inc.
1071 Main St, Smyrna SC
29743-9798. 803/925-
2197.

Silkworm Inc.
654 Coleman Blvd, Mount
Pleasant SC 29464-4018.
803/884-8296.

**FABRICATED TEXTILE
PRODUCTS**

Arcade Textile Inc.
7 Blackwell St, Rock Hill SC
29730-4318. 803/327-
6697.

Asten Inc.
Highway 15 N, Walterboro
SC 29488. 803/549-6333.

**Doran Textiles Dover Yarn
Plant**
401 Guinn St, Clover SC
29710-1064. 803/222-
2343.

Elizabeth Weaving Inc.
404 Elm Rd, Blacksburg SC
29702-9392. 803/936-
7676.

Hartwell Industries
832 Summerland Ave,
Batesburg SC 29006-1412.
803/532-3871.

JB Martin & Co.
P.O. Box 607, Leesville SC
29070-0607. 803/532-
6277.

Peerless Mill Milliken & Co.
110 Milliken Dr, Belton SC
29627-8980. 864/338-
7711.

**Woodside Mills Inc.
Haynsworth**
2115 S McDuffie St,
Anderson SC 29624-3357.
864/224-0251.

APPAREL WHOLESALE

Williston Manufacturing
110 Kelly St, Williston SC
29853-1446. 803/266-
7441.

Carolina Apparel Inc.
Bypass 321, Winnsboro SC
29180. 803/635-1194.

Thomas & Howard Co.
2913 White Horse Rd,
Greenville SC 29611-6120.
864/269-7804.

Thomas & Howard Co.
P.O. Box 6250, Spartanburg
SC 29304-6250. 864/439-
4434.

Thomas & Howard Co.
Interstate 26 & Hwy 34,
Newberry SC 29108.
803/276-0510.

For more information on career opportunities in the apparel and textiles industries:

Associations

**AMERICAN APPAREL MANUFACTURERS
ASSOCIATION**
2500 Wilson Boulevard, Suite 301,
Arlington VA 22201. 703/524-1864.
Publishes numerous magazines,
newsletters, and bulletins for the benefit of
employees in the apparel manufacturing
industry.

**AMERICAN TEXTILE MANUFACTURERS
INSTITUTE**
Office of the Chief Economist, 1801 K
Street NW, Suite 900, Washington DC
20006-1301. 202/862-0500. Fax:
202/862-0570. The national trade
association for the domestic textile
industry. Members are corporations only.

THE FASHION GROUP
597 5th Avenue, 8th Floor, New York NY
10017. 212/593-1715. A nonprofit
organization for professional women in the
fashion industries (apparel, accessories,
beauty, and home). Offers career counseling
workshops 18 times per year.

**INTERNATIONAL ASSOCIATION OF
CLOTHING DESIGNERS**
475 Park Avenue South, 17th Floor, New
York NY 10016. 212/685-6602. Fax:
212/545-1709.

Directories

AAMA DIRECTORY
American Apparel Manufacturers
Association, 2500 Wilson Boulevard, Suite
301, Arlington VA 22201. 703/524-1864.
A directory of publications distributed by
the American Apparel Manufacturers
Association.

APPAREL TRADES BOOK
Dun & Bradstreet Inc., 430 Mountain
Avenue, New Providence NJ 07974.
908/665-5000.

**FAIRCHILD'S MARKET DIRECTORY OF
WOMEN'S AND CHILDREN'S APPAREL**
Fairchild Publications, 7 West 34th Street,
New York NY 10001. 212/630-4000.

Magazines

ACCESSORIES
Business Journals, 50 Day Street, P.O. Box
5550, Norwalk CT 06856. 203/853-6015.

AMERICA'S TEXTILES
Billiam Publishing, 37 Villa Road, Suite 111,
P.O. Box 103, Greenville SC 29615.
864/242-5300.

APPAREL INDUSTRY MAGAZINE
Shore Communications Inc., 6255 Barfield
Road, Suite 200, Atlanta GA 30328-4893.
404/252-8831.

BOBBIN
Bobbin Publications, P.O. Box 1986, 1110
Shop Road, Columbia SC 29202. 803/771-
7500.

TEXTILE HILIGHTS
American Textile Manufacturers Institute,
Office of the Chief Economist, 1801 K
Street NW, Suite 900, Washington DC
20006.

WOMEN'S WEAR DAILY (WWD)
Fairchild Publications, 7 West 34th Street,
New York NY 10001. 212/630-4000.

ARCHITECTURE, CONSTRUCTION, AND ENGINEERING

 *The U.S. Department of Labor has estimated 1.2 million new construction jobs from 1992 through 2005, due to the need to replace aging experienced workers. Residential construction will grow slowly, as a result of the expected decline in population growth. Industrial construction, however, will be stronger because of an increase in exports by manufacturers. Heavy construction is growing faster than the industry average, with much activity in highway, bridge, and street construction.*

Job prospects for engineers have been good for a number of years, and will continue to improve into the next century. Employers will need more engineers as they increase investment in equipment in order to expand output. In addition, engineers will find work improving the nation's deteriorating infrastructure.

North Carolina

AMERICAN MODULAR TECHNOLOGIES (AMT)
P.O. Box 21687, Greensboro NC 27420. 910/622-6200. **Contact:** Allen Fisher, Director of Human Resources. **Description:** American Modular Technologies constructs modular buildings. The company operates nationwide. **Common positions include:** Architect; CADD Operator; Construction and Building Inspector; Construction Contractor and Manager; Cost Estimator; Draftsperson; Industrial Production Manager. **Educational backgrounds include:** Engineering. **Benefits:** 401K; Disability Coverage; Life Insurance; Medical Insurance; Pension Plan; Profit Sharing; Tuition Assistance. **Other U.S. locations:** California; South Carolina; Texas. **Operations at this facility include:** Administration; Divisional Headquarters; Manufacturing; Sales; Service. **Number of employees at this location:** 284.

BARRUS CONSTRUCTION COMPANY
P.O. Box 905, Jacksonville NC 28540. 910/346-3224. **Contact:** Eddie Brailey, Vice President. **Description:** A construction contracting company handling a variety of projects and activities including: asphalt; concrete; curbing; gutters; and the construction of highways, streets, and parking lots.

BARRUS CONSTRUCTION COMPANY
P.O. Box 399, Kinston NC 28502. 919/527-8021. **Contact:** Chet Harrison, Human Resources Manager. **Description:** A construction contracting company handling a variety of projects and activities including: asphalt; concrete; curbing; gutters; and the construction of highways, streets, and parking lots.

BLYTHE CONSTRUCTION
P.O. Box 31635, Charlotte NC 28231. 704/375-8474. **Contact:** Judy Sellers, Human Resources Manager. **Description:** A general residential construction contractor. **Number of employees at this location:** 500.

FACTORY MUTUAL ASSOCIATION
5445-77 Center Drive, Suite 60, Charlotte NC 28217. 704/525-9000. **Contact:** Judy Smith, Personnel. **Description:** A loss control service organization owned by Allendale Insurance, Arkwright, and Protection Mutual Insurance, with 17 district offices strategically located throughout the United States and Canada. Research facilities are located in Norwood, MA, and West Gloucester, RI. Factory Mutual Association's primary objective is to help owner company policyholders to protect their properties and occupancies from damage due to fire, wind, flood, and explosion; boiler, pressure vessel, and machinery accidents; and many other insured hazards. To accomplish this objective, a wide range of engineering, research, and consulting services are provided,

primarily in the field of loss control. **Common positions include:** Chemical Engineer; Civil Engineer; Electrical/Electronics Engineer; Fire Science Engineer; Mechanical Engineer. **Benefits:** Dental Insurance; Disability Coverage; Employee Discounts; Life Insurance; Medical Insurance; Pension Plan; Savings Plan; Tuition Assistance. **Corporate headquarters location:** Norwood MA.

J.A. JONES CONSTRUCTION COMPANY
J.A. Jones Drive, Charlotte NC 28287. 704/553-3000. **Contact:** Jay Fuss, Employment Manager. **Description:** A general contractor involved in the construction of commercial and institutional facilities, heavy and marine structures, process and industrial facilities, and energy facilities both domestically and internationally. Philipp Holzmann USA is the holding company for the American construction and engineering operations of The Holzmann Group of Germany. Holzmann acquired J.A. Jones in 1979. The Holzmann Group operates in three segments: General Construction, Construction of Transportation Systems, and Energy and Environmental Technology. Holzmann is involved in engineering, construction, management services, and maintenance projects throughout the world with operations in Europe, Asia, Africa, North America and the Middle East. **Common positions include:** Civil Engineer; Electrical/Electronics Engineer; Mechanical Engineer. **Educational backgrounds include:** Engineering. **Benefits:** Dental Insurance; Disability Coverage; Employee Discounts; Life Insurance; Medical Insurance; Pension Plan; Profit Sharing; Savings Plan; Tuition Assistance. **Corporate headquarters location:** This Location. **Parent company:** Philipp Holzmann USA, Inc.

OAKWOOD HOMES
P.O. Box 7386, Greensboro NC 27417. 910/855-2400. **Fax:** 910/855-2370. **Contact:** Tom Brinkley, Director of Human Resources. **Description:** Manufactures and sells fabricated housing, under the Oakwood and Freedom brand names. Oakwood Homes also finances a portion of its installment contracts through its finance unit, and acts as an agent on homeowners and credit life insurance written for buyers of its manufactured housing. **Common positions include:** Accountant/Auditor; Credit Manager; Customer Service Representative; Management Trainee; Operations/Production Manager; Sales Representative. **Educational backgrounds include:** Accounting; Finance; Liberal Arts. **Benefits:** 401K; Dental Insurance; Disability Coverage; Life Insurance; Medical Insurance; Pension Plan; Profit Sharing; Tuition Assistance. **Special Programs:** Internships. **Corporate headquarters location:** This Location. **Other U.S. locations:** Nationwide. **Operations at this facility include:** Administration.

SOUTHERN INDUSTRIAL CONSTRUCTORS, INC.
6101 Triangle Drive, Raleigh NC 27613. 919/782-4600. **Contact:** Carl Grimm, Vice President of Finance. **Description:** An industrial construction firm specializing in installing manufacturing processes and equipment. The company operates in 33 states. **Listed on:** Privately held.

THOMPSON-ARTHUR PAVING COMPANY
300 South Benbow Road, Greensboro NC 27401. 910/274-5413. **Contact:** Bill Compton, Personnel Manager. **Description:** An asphalt paving company.

UNDERWRITERS LABORATORIES
12 Laboratory Drive, Research Triangle Park NC 27709. 919/549-1400. **Contact:** Steve Cohan, Human Resources Director. **Description:** An independent, not-for-profit corporation established to help reduce or prevent bodily injury, loss of life, and property damage. The organization is engaged in the scientific investigation of various materials, devices, equipment, construction, methods, and systems, and by the publication of standards, classifications, specifications, and other information. The company's engineering functions are divided among six departments including electrical; burglary protection and signaling; casualty and chemical hazards; fire protection; heating, air-conditioning, and refrigeration; and marine. Underwriters Laboratories also provides a factory inspection service through offices located throughout the United States and in 54 other countries. More than 1,000 employees worldwide are engaged in engineering work. **Number of employees worldwide:** 2,600.

UNITED DOMINION INDUSTRIES LIMITED
2300 One First Union Center, Charlotte NC 28202-6039. 704/347-6800. **Contact:** Timothy Verhagen, Vice President of Human Resources. **Description:** United Dominion Industries Limited, founded in 1882 as Dominion Bridge Company, is an industrial enterprise consisting of market-leader businesses that provide proprietary, manufactured products and engineering for customers worldwide. The company operates in three segments: building products, engineering, and industrial products.

The building products segment manufactures complementary products that encompass architectural metal roofing; side-hinged and rolling steel doors; residential garage doors; pre-engineered metal buildings; loading dock systems and related equipment; and wall, roof, floor and window systems. This segment also provides general and specialized contractor services. The Litwin Companies provide worldwide engineering and construction services for the refining and petrochemical, polymers, specialty chemicals, and environmental control markets. Litwin also provides advanced process control and instrumentation capabilities. The industrial products segment produces sanitary pumps for the food and industrial processing industries; submersible water and petroleum pumps; petroleum leak detection equipment; compaction equipment for soil, asphalt and refuse applications; cooling towers for power generation, industrial, and heating and cooling applications; cast-iron boilers and electrical resistance heaters for industrial and residential customers; industrial machinery and process equipment; and aerospace components. **Corporate headquarters location:** This Location. **Listed on:** New York Stock Exchange. **Number of employees nationwide:** 12,000.

VSL CORPORATION
2840 Plaza Place, Suite 200, Raleigh NC 27612. 919/781-6272. **Fax:** 919/781-6892. **Contact:** Terri Cooley, Human Resources Manager. **Description:** A worldwide contractor specializing in the field of post-tensioning and related engineering. VSL Corporation provides optimized design and erection solutions to construction industry customers. **Common positions include:** Accountant/Auditor; Blue-Collar Worker Supervisor; Branch Manager; Civil Engineer; Claim Representative; Computer Systems Analyst; Construction Contractor and Manager; Cost Estimator; Draftsperson; Structural Engineer. **Benefits:** 401K; Dental Insurance; Disability Coverage; Life Insurance; Medical Insurance; Tuition Assistance. **Corporate headquarters location:** This Location. **Other U.S. locations:** San Jose CA; Washington DC; Miami FL; Las Vegas NV; Dallas TX. **Number of employees at this location:** 220.

WESTMINSTER HOMES
2706 North Church Street, Greensboro NC 27405. 910/375-6200. **Fax:** 910/375-6355. **Contact:** Mr. Cameron Ross, President. **Description:** A real estate and construction company. Westminster Homes specializes in single-family home development and sales in North Carolina. **Common positions include:** Accountant/Auditor; Computer Programmer; Customer Service Representative; Draftsperson; Human Resources Specialist; Manufacturer's/Wholesaler's Sales Rep.; Marketing Specialist; Operations/Production Manager; Purchasing Agent and Manager; Quality Control Supervisor. **Educational backgrounds include:** Accounting; Business Administration; Computer Science; Marketing. **Benefits:** Dental Insurance; Disability Coverage; Employee Discounts; Life Insurance; Medical Insurance; Pension Plan; Profit Sharing; Savings Plan; Stock Option; Tuition Assistance. **Special Programs:** Training Programs. **Corporate headquarters location:** This Location. **Other U.S. locations:** Cary NC. **Parent company:** Weyerhaeuser Company. **Operations at this facility include:** Administration; Sales; Service. **Listed on:** New York Stock Exchange. **Number of employees at this location:** 60. **Number of employees nationwide:** 100.

Note: Because addresses and telephone numbers of smaller companies change rapidly, we recommend you call each company to verify the information below before inquiring about job opportunities. Mass mailings are not recommended.

Additional employers with under 250 employees:

GENERAL CONTRACTORS

Armada Hoffler Construction
4000 Westchase Blvd, Suite 110, Raleigh NC 27607-3939. 919/832-2626.

Beam Construction Co.
601 E Main St, Cherryville NC 28021-3416. 704/435-3206.

Becon Construction Co.
5950 Fairview Rd, Suite 808, Charlotte NC 28210-3104. 704/552-0268.

Bill Clark Construction Co.
1430 Commonwealth Dr, Wilmington NC 28403-0351. 910/256-0885.

C. Richard Dobson Builders
5601 Roanne Way, Suite 314, Greensboro NC 27409-2932. 910/547-8553.

Clancy & Theys Construction
516 W Cabarrus St, Raleigh NC 27603. 919/834-3601.

CP Buckner Steel Erection
P.O. Box 598, Graham NC 27253. 910/376-8888.

David M. Sidbury Inc.
224 W 32nd St, Charlotte NC 28206. 704/332-3513.

Distribution Construction Co.
4806 Old Pineville Rd, Charlotte NC 28217-2157. 704/525-4588.

Donohoe Construction Co.
2809 Highwoods Blvd, Raleigh NC 27604-1000. 919/872-0077.

Duke Builders
3702 Cline School Rd, Concord NC 28025-7347. 704/784-3623.

Floyd King & Sons Inc.
3300 Gribble Rd, Matthews
NC 28105-8104. 704/821-9273.

Life Style Builders & Developers
875 Washington St, Suite 2,
Raleigh NC 27605-3252.
919/755-1991.

LP Cox Co.
1801 Douglas Dr, Sanford
NC 27330-9447. 919/774-4000.

Myrick Construction Inc.
3216 Rehobeth Church Rd,
Greensboro NC 27406-4817.
910/854-1155.

Parker Lancaster Carpenters
5000 Birnamwood Trl,
Greensboro NC 27407-5855.
910/292-7214.

Peek Construction Co.
70 Woodfin Pl, Suite 134,
Asheville NC 28801-2441.
704/252-6462.

Pizzagalli Construction Co.
2000 Aerial Center Pky,
Morrisville NC 27560-9294.
919/481-3323.

Showalter Construction Co.
1925 Bancroft St, Charlotte
NC 28206-3040. 704/376-6372.

Taylor & Murphy Construction Co.
1121 Brevard Rd, Asheville
NC 28806-9555. 704/667-4526.

Willis Home Improvement & Repairs
1500 New Bern Ave, Raleigh
NC 27610-2536. 919/365-4924.

WT Cox Development Co.
726 Liberty St, Ramseur NC
27316-9464. 910/824-8646.

American Disaster Restoration
3813 Beryl Rd, Raleigh NC
27607-5244. 919/832-5581.

Centex Crosland Homes
145 Scaleybark Rd, Charlotte
NC 28209-2608. 704/523-8111.

J&W Enterprises
4819 Aaron Rd, Concord NC
28025-7930. 704/784-8463.

Trent's Construction
RR 3, Roxboro NC 27573-9803. 910/599-6203.

UDC Homes Inc.
Brownes Ferry, Charlotte NC
28227. 704/598-6167.

UDC Homes Inc.
2331 Crown Point Exec Dr,
Suite L, Charlotte NC 28227.
704/847-8402.

Bassett Construction Co.
310 E Main St, Jefferson NC
28640-9703. 910/246-4857.

Buildings Unlimited
803 S Cherry St, Kernersville
NC 27284-8118. 910/993-4991.

H&R Building Contractors
871 Hebler Ln, Randleman
NC 27317-7782. 910/495-1647.

Superior Homes Inc.
80411 Arrowridge Blvd,
Charlotte NC 28273-5604.
704/521-9719.

Homes by George Steele
13024-F Idlewild Rd,
Matthews NC 28105.
704/845-4663.

Jim Walter Homes Inc.
3850 New Bern Ave, Raleigh
NC 27610-1335. 919/231-6225.

Lifetime Homes
3215 Guess Rd, Suite 210,
Durham NC 27705-2669.
919/479-5510.

Ryan Homes Inc.
7139 Badenoch Ct, Charlotte
NC 28217-3483. 704/525-6078.

Super Homes Inc.
12012 Stainsby Ln,
Charlotte NC 28273-6760.
704/588-0559.

GENERAL INDUSTRIAL CONTRACTORS

John Smith & Sons Inc.
515 S Kennedy St, Eden NC
27288. 910/623-2111.

Rodgers Builders Inc.
5701 N Sharon Amity Rd,
Charlotte NC 28215-3984.
704/537-6044.

DJ Rose & Son Inc.
216 S Mayo St, Rocky
Mount NC 27804-5113.
919/442-6105.

CT Wilson Construction Co.
P.O. Box 2011, Durham NC
27702. 919/383-2535.

JH Hudson Construction Co.
US 264 East, Greenville NC
27834. 919/758-2138.

ROAD CONSTRUCTION

Barrus Construction Co.
502 S Glenburnie Rd, New
Bern NC 28560-2776.
919/637-2533.

Champion Contracting Co.
Oak Grove Rd, Kings
Mountain NC 28086.
704/334-0602.

Orville W. Dills Backhoe Service
6676 Tom Ball Rd,
Randleman NC 27317-7290.
910/431-6979.

Sunland Development & Construction Inc.
Hwy 24, Cape Carteret NC
28584. 910/393-2504.

Highway Constructors
US 1 Hwy, Marston NC
28363. 910/582-2600.

BRIDGE, TUNNEL, AND HIGHWAY CONSTRUCTION

Lee Construction Co.
800 Culp Rd, Pineville NC
28134-9469. 704/588-5272.

HEAVY CONSTRUCTION

Hall Contracting Corp.
6415 Lakeview Rd, Charlotte
NC 28269-2602. 704/598-0818.

P&H Pipeline Industries
P.O. Box 875, Kinston NC
28502-0875. 919/527-7725.

Baker Digging
7009 Riley Hill Rd, Wendell
NC 27591-9294. 919/365-4666.

Distribution Construction Co.
4526 Drummond Rd,
Greensboro NC 27406-9510.
910/294-9487.

PLUMBING, HEATING, AND A/C

Eakes Corp.
1216 Perry St, Greensboro
NC 27403-2621. 910/294-2852.

Industrial Piping Inc.
11301 Downs Rd #518,
Pineville NC 28134-8441.
704/588-1100.

JJ Barnes Inc.
118 Drake St, Fayetteville
NC 28301. 910/483-7171.

SPC Service Company
8201 Brownleigh Dr, Raleigh
NC 27612. 919/571-2936.

Custom Plumbing & Heating
1850 Tate Blvd SE, Hickory
NC 28602-4299. 704/322-
1673.

TD Industries
841 Baxter St, Charlotte NC
28202-2720. 704/332-
3207.

**Hockaday Heating & Air
Conditioning Co.**
825 Purser Dr, Raleigh NC
27603-4152. 919/851-
0408.

**Love Plumbing & Air
Conditioning Co.**
2602 Old Charlotte Hwy,
Charlotte NC 28244.
704/377-4076.

Milner Airco Inc.
10039 Industrial Dr, Pineville
NC 28134-8384. 704/552-
9414.

Newcomb and Company
725 Pershing Rd, Raleigh NC
27608-2711. 919/832-
6644.

**Trent Heating & Air
Conditioning**
1201 US Highway 70 E,
New Bern NC 28560-6615.
919/633-2200.

**PAINTING AND PAPER
HANGING**

**Stanly Industrial Painting
Service**
353 Harwood St, Albemarle
NC 28001-4707. 704/983-
1185.

ELECTRICAL WORK

McCarter Electrical Co.
516 Hillside Ave, Laurinburg
NC 28352-3052. 910/276-
2055.

Tics
3900 Barrett Dr, Raleigh NC
27609-6614. 919/571-
9920.

**Floyd S. Pike Electrical
Contracting Inc.**
800 Corporation Pky, Raleigh
NC 27610-1361. 919/231-
3522.

**Floyd S. Pike Electrical
Contracting Inc.**
4130 New Bern Ave, Raleigh
NC 27610-1329. 919/231-
6134.

**Johnsons Modern Electric
Company**
Old Highway 421, East Bend
NC 27018. 910/721-1027.

King Electric Fayetteville
128 S Broad St, Fayetteville
NC 28301. 910/483-4627.

Overcash Electric Inc.
P.O. Box 539, Mooresville
NC 28115-0539. 704/664-
3113.

Port City Electric Co.
P.O. Box 1218, Mooresville
NC 28115-1218. 704/663-
4215.

T&H Electrical Corp.
Hwy 301 S, Wilson NC
27893. 919/291-7132.

**Watson Electrical
Construction Co.**
604 E Gilbreath St, Graham
NC 27253-3748. 910/226-
4441.

**Watson Electrical
Construction Co.**
6517 Hilburn Rd, Raleigh NC
27613-1908. 919/781-
4651.

**MASONRY, STONEWORK,
AND PLASTERING**

Nu-Stone Surfacing Inc.
4301 Stuart Andrew Blvd,
Charlotte NC 28217-1587.
704/523-2242.

Pyramid Masonry Contracting
5104 N I-85, Charlotte NC
28206. 704/597-8998.

Puckett Tile
2735 Layden St, Raleigh NC
27603-2513. 919/832-
9371.

**CARPENTRY AND FLOOR
WORK**

Craftmade Cabinet Co.
4542-A Raeford Rd,
Fayetteville NC 28304.
910/483-6061.

David Stallings Floors
1460 Diggs Dr, Suite B,
Raleigh NC 27603-2771.
919/828-8855.

**ROOFING, SIDING, AND
SHEET METAL WORK**

Centimark Corporation
2981 Interstate St, Charlotte
NC 28208-3607. 704/399-
4626.

Worthington Associates
323 W Morgan St, Raleigh
NC 27601. 919/828-5090.

**MISC. SPECIAL TRADE
CONTRACTORS**

General Industries Inc.
714 S John St, Goldsboro
NC 27530. 919/735-2882.

McGee Corporation
12701 E Independence Blvd,
Matthews NC 28105-4103.
704/882-1500.

Brinley's Grading Service
318 N Dixon St, Cary NC
27513-4427. 919/469-
8903.

Schindler Elevator Corp.
130 Penmarc Dr, Suite 103,
Raleigh NC 27603-2470.
919/834-5424.

Schindler Elevator Corp.
1900 Center Park Dr,
Charlotte NC 28217-2901.
704/329-1470.

Century Contractors Inc.
5100 Smith Farm Rd,
Matthews NC 28105-8132.
704/821-8050.

TR Tucker Construction Co.
1300 Matthews Mint Hill Rd,
Matthews NC 28105-2306.
704/846-4340.

Jim Walter Homes
2400 S Interstate 85,
Charlotte NC 28208-2715.
704/399-8317.

Longley Supply Co.
2018 Oleander Dr,
Wilmington NC 28403-2336.
910/762-7793.

MOBILE HOMES

Brigadier Homes of NC
Hwy 64 E, Nashville NC
27856. 919/459-7026.

Champion Home Builders Co.
Old River Rd, Lillington NC
27546. 910/893-5713.

**Clayton Homes/Fisher
Richfield**
44073 Hwy 52 N, Richfield
NC 28137. 704/463-1341.

Crestline Homes
5880 Crestline Rd,
Laurinburg NC 28352-1780.
910/276-0195.

Fleetwood Homes of NC
600 Lucy Garrett Rd,
Roxboro NC 27573-9794.
910/597-3602.

Fleetwood Homes of NC
E Railroad St, Pembroke NC
28372. 910/521-9731.

Henderson Homes
RR 4, Box 482, Henderson
NC 27536-9504. 919/492-
1300.

Homes by Oakwood
7025 Albert Pick Rd, Suite
301, Greensboro NC 27409-
9519. 910/292-7061.

Homes by Oakwood
508 Palmer Rd, Rockwell NC
28138-9318. 704/279-
4659.

Imperial Homes
2100 Sterling Dr, Albemarle
NC 28001-5390. 704/983-
5292.

Liberty Homes Inc.
RR 1, Box 632, Statesville
NC 28677-9801. 704/878-
2001.

Mansion Homes Inc.
2863 Plank Rd, Robbins NC
27325-7335. 910/948-
2141.

Palm Harbor Homes Inc.
45 Siler City Industrial Park,
Siler City NC 27344.
910/663-2182.

Redman Homes Inc.
2509 Cox Mill Rd, Sanford
NC 27330-9727. 919/258-
3321.

Redman Homes Inc.
16620 Airbase Rd, Maxton
NC 28364. 910/844-5055.

Skyline Corp.
Bethel Church Rd, Mocksville
NC 27028. 704/634-3511.

Titan Homes
Hwy 401 S, Lillington NC
27546. 910/893-2121.

**PREFABRICATED WOOD
BUILDINGS AND
COMPONENTS**

All American Homes of NC
Webb Rd, Ellenboro NC
28040. 704/453-0711.

**CONSTRUCTION
MATERIALS WHOLESALE**

APAC
Old US 29 Hwy, Pelham NC
27311. 910/388-2340.

Best Distributing Co. Raleigh
1711 Lake Wheeler Rd,
Raleigh NC 27603-2329.
919/832-2003.

Amoco Foam Products Co.
6525 Morrison Blvd, Suite
108, Charlotte NC 28211-
3532. 704/366-3218.

Insul-Pads Inc.
9200 US Hwy 220 Business
N, Randleman NC 27317.
910/498-4119.

ACI Glass
3646 N Graham St,
Charlotte NC 28206-1627.
704/333-4433.

Alliance Products Co.
1319 Atando Ave, Charlotte
NC 28206. 704/347-8850.

Carolina Builders Corp.
2410 Binford St, Greensboro
NC 27407. 910/294-2120.

Triad Masonry Burlington
1637 W Webb Ave,
Burlington NC 27217-1139.
910/226-4443.

Interior Distributors Inc.
1105 New Hope Rd, Raleigh
NC 27610-1415. 919/231-
6355.

**PLUMBING, HEATING, AND
A/C EQUIPMENT
WHOLESALE**

Usco Inc.
P.O. Box 1160, Monroe NC
28111-1160. 704/289-
5406.

Usco Inc.
S William St, Henderson NC
27536. 919/492-9193.

Thulman Eastern Corp.
1411 Boulder Ct, Greensboro
NC 27409-8906. 910/218-
0200.

Noland Company
Hwy 301 N, Wilson NC
27893. 919/243-6146.

Davis Meter & Supply
130 Roberts St, Asheville NC
28801-3129. 704/253-
6717.

Piping and Equipment Co.
600 Tom Sadler Rd,
Charlotte NC 28214-9486.
704/394-8200.

RE Michel Company Inc.
4141 Barringer Dr, Suite E,
Charlotte NC 28217-1574.
704/523-5515.

Thermo Industries Inc.
237 Haywood St, Asheville
NC 28801-2618. 704/251-
5191.

Thermo Industries Inc.
1424 S Bloodworth St,
Raleigh NC 27610-3902.
919/829-0155.

Thermo Industries Inc.
4300 Golf Acres Dr,
Charlotte NC 28208-5861.
704/394-7311.

Baker Brothers Inc.
901 Norwalk St, Greensboro
NC 27407. 910/632-9941.

Brady Trane
127 Fayette St, Winston-
Salem NC 27101-3665.
910/725-6050.

CC Dickson Company
507 Yadkin St, Henderson
NC 27536. 919/492-0313.

McCall's Supply Inc.
104 S Chestnut St,
Lumberton NC 28358-6538.
910/618-9000.

ENGINEERING SERVICES

D&Z Inc. Southeast
6324 Fairview Rd, Charlotte
NC 28210-3236. 704/364-
8431.

Duke Fluor Daniel
P.O. Box 1011, Charlotte NC
28201-1011. 704/357-
3271.

McKim & Creed Engineers
243 N Front St, Wilmington
NC 28401-3907. 910/343-
1048.

Perigon
P.O. Box 470928, Charlotte
NC 28247-0928. 704/847-
6346.

CTL Engineering Inc.
6301 Angus Dr, Suite A,
Raleigh NC 27613-4701.
919/782-9895.

Duke Engineering & Service
230 S Tryon St Rm 400,
Charlotte NC 28202-3215.
704/382-9800.

JBM Engineers & Planners
4917 Waters Edge Dr,
Raleigh NC 27606-2459.
919/233-8125.

McKim & Creed Engineers
310 E Johnston St,
Smithfield NC 27577-4518.
910/934-7154.

Dewberry & Davis
8601 Six Forks Rd, Raleigh
NC 27615-2965. 919/847-
0418.

HW Lochner Inc.
3725 National Dr, Suite 123,
Raleigh NC 27612-4879.
919/571-7111.

Presnell Associates Inc.
7508 Independence Blvd,
Suite 102, Charlotte NC
28227-9409. 704/532-
9544.

Wilbur Smith Associates
5 W Hargett St, Rm 910,
Raleigh NC 27601-1348.
919/755-0583.

Mantech Field Engineer Corp.
6th St, Fort Bragg NC
28307. 910/436-5930.

Nus Division
3125 Poplarwood Ct, Raleigh
NC 27604-1020. 919/850-
0080.

ARCHITECTURAL SERVICES

The LPA Group
900 Ridgefield Dr, Raleigh
NC 27609-8505. 919/954-
1244.

SURVEYING SERVICES

DS Atlantic Corporation
7820 N Point Blvd, Winston-
Salem NC 27106-3299.
910/759-7400.

Kimball & Associates
302 Jefferson St, Suite 250,
Raleigh NC 27605-1274.
919/828-8673.

Quadrant Surveying Inc.
River Court Plaza,
Jacksonville NC 28540.
910/346-2067.

South Carolina

DAVIS ELECTRICAL CONSTRUCTORS
P.O. Box 1907, Greenville SC 29602. 864/250-2500. **Contact:** Bill Dyer, Director of
Human Resources. **Description:** Davis Electrical Constructors is an electrical and
instrumentation contractor for power plants, textile manufacturers, and chemical
producers, as well as companies in other industries. **Other U.S. locations:** Baton Rogue
LA; Midland MI.

ENVIRONMENTAL MONITORING & TESTING CORPORATION
825 Main Street South, New Ellenton SC 29809. 803/652-2718. **Contact:** Human
Resources. **Description:** Environmental Monitoring & Testing Corporation is a
diversified drilling company with expertise in environmental drilling; industrial water
wells; recovery wells as related to environmental requirements; construction drilling
and grouting for piling; and stabilization drilling and grouting core drilling as well as
angle coring drilling and grouting for dams and other similar structures. The company
operates as a subcontractor within the construction industry rather than a prime or
general contractor. In 1994, Environmental Monitoring & Testing Corporation moved
all of its operations to this location. **Corporate headquarters location:** This Location.
Number of employees at this location: 21.

FLUOR DANIEL, INC.
100 Fluor Daniel Drive, Greenville SC 29607-2762. 864/281-4400. **Contact:** Jack
Neal, Personnel Director. **Description:** A full-service engineering and construction
company serving the power, industrial, hydrocarbon, and process industries as well as
the federal government. **Other U.S. locations:** Chicago IL; Kansas City MO; Cincinnati
OH; Philadelphia PA; Houston TX; Richmond VA. **Parent company:** Fluor Corporation,
located in Irvine, CA, primarily engages in engineering and construction, as well as the
production of various natural resources. Fluor Corporation provides its services to
energy, natural resource, industrial, commercial, utility, and government clients.
Natural resources produced are principally gold, silver, lead, zinc, iron ore, coal, oil,
and gas. The corporation also provides contract drilling services. **Listed on:** New York
Stock Exchange. **Number of employees worldwide:** 20,000.

HARBERT-YEARGIN
P.O. Box 6508, Greenville SC 29606. 864/242-6960. **Fax:** 864/370-4210. **Contact:**
Mr. Roby Miller, Human Resources Manager. **Description:** A construction company
operating as a division of the Raytheon Engineers and Constructors organization,
which is part of the Raytheon Company. Harbert-Yeargin was formed through the
merger of Yeargin Construction Company, Inc., which was acquired in 1986, with
Harbert Construction, which was purchased in 1993. Raytheon Engineers and
Constructors oversees projects through the following stages: technology development
and evaluation, master planning, environmental assessment, engineering and design,
procurement, fabrication, construction and construction management, startup,
operation, and contract maintenance. Raytheon Engineers and Constructors serves a
variety of industries, ranging from transportation infrastructure and metals to
government services and biotechnology. **Parent company:** Raytheon Company, located
in Lexington, MA, is a diversified, international, multi-industry technology-based
company ranked among the largest U.S. industrial corporations. Raytheon Company
has 110 facilities in 28 states and the District of Columbia. Overseas facilities and
representative offices are located in 26 countries, principally in Europe, the Middle
East, and the Pacific Rim. The company has four business segments: Electronics;
Major Appliances; Aircraft Products; and Energy and Environmental. **Number of
employees worldwide:** 17,000.

JACOBS APPLIED TECHNOLOGY
P.O. Box 1327, Orangeburg SC 29116. 803/534-2424. **Fax:** 803/534-2457. **Contact:**
Jerry Brezeale, Human Resources Manager. **Description:** Jacobs Applied Technology
designs, fabricates, and constructs propane-air gas plants and process plants for the
following industries: chemical, petrochemical, fine chemical, specialty chemical, food
and beverage, pharmaceutical, and consumer. **Common positions include:** Designer;
Draftsperson; Electrical/Electronics Engineer; Mechanical Engineer; Structural Engineer.
Educational backgrounds include: Engineering. **Benefits:** 401K; Dental Insurance;

Disability Coverage; Life Insurance; Medical Insurance; Tuition Assistance. **Parent company:** Jacobs Engineering Group, Inc. (Pasadena CA) is one of the largest engineering and construction companies in the United States. Jacobs Engineering Group, Inc. provides engineering, procurement, construction, and maintenance services to selected clients and industries. These industries include the following: Chemicals and Polymers; Federal Programs; Pulp and Paper; Semiconductor; Petroleum Refining; Facilities and Transportation; Food and Consumer Products; Pharmaceuticals and Biotechnologies; and Basic Resources. Through Jacobs College and other site-specific programs, the company trains more than 5,000 employees per year. **Operations at this facility include:** Administration; Manufacturing; Sales. **Number of employees at this location:** 300. **Number of employees nationwide:** 12,000.

JACOBS SIRRINE ENGINEERS, INC.
P.O. Box 5456, Greenville SC 29606. 864/676-6000. **Contact:** Mary Johnson, Human Resources Representative. **Description:** Jacobs Sirrine Engineers, Inc. provides architectural, engineering, and construction management consulting services. **Common positions include:** Civil Engineer; Draftsperson; Electrical/Electronics Engineer; Mechanical Engineer; Transportation/Traffic Specialist. **Educational backgrounds include:** Engineering. **Benefits:** Dental Insurance; Disability Coverage; Employee Discounts; Life Insurance; Medical Insurance; Profit Sharing; Savings Plan. **Special Programs:** Internships; Training Programs. **Parent company:** Jacobs Engineering Group, Inc. (Pasadena, CA) is one of the largest engineering and construction companies in the United States. Jacobs Engineering Group, Inc. provides engineering, procurement, construction, and maintenance services to selected clients and industries. These industries include the following: Chemicals and Polymers; Federal Programs; Pulp and Paper; Semiconductor; Petroleum Refining; Facilities and Transportation; Food and Consumer Products; Pharmaceuticals and Biotechnologies; and Basic Resources. Through Jacobs College and other site-specific programs, the company trains more than 5,000 employees per year in project management, managing money, health and safety, and numerous other performance enhancing topics. **Operations at this facility include:** Service. **Listed on:** New York Stock Exchange.

LOCKWOOD-GREENE ENGINEERS INC.
P.O. Box 491, Spartanburg SC 29304. 864/578-2000. **Contact:** Scott Madding, Personnel Manager. **Description:** A consulting firm providing engineering and architectural design for industrial and commercial clients. Specifically, the company is involved in the planning and project management of industrial plants and production facilities. Philipp Holzmann USA, which acquired Lockwood-Greene Engineers in 1981, is the holding company of the American design and construction operations of The Holzmann Group of Germany. The group operates in three segments: General Construction, Construction of Transportation Systems, and Energy and Environmental Technology. Holzmann has operations around the world, including a presence in Europe, Asia, Africa, North America, and the Middle East. **Common positions include:** Architect; Architectural Engineer; Chemical Engineer; Civil Engineer; Computer Programmer; Draftsperson; Electrical/Electronics Engineer; Industrial Engineer; Mechanical Engineer; Systems Analyst. **Educational backgrounds include:** Architecture; Computer Science; Engineering. **Benefits:** Dental Insurance; Disability Coverage; Life Insurance; Medical Insurance; Pension Plan; Profit Sharing. **Corporate headquarters location:** This Location. **Parent company:** Philipp Holzmann USA Ltd. **Operations at this facility include:** Service.

SLOAN CONSTRUCTION COMPANY
P.O. Box 2008, Greenville SC 29602. 864/271-9090. **Contact:** Peggy Moore, Director of Human Resources. **Description:** A paving company. Sloan Construction also manufactures their own asphalt.

SUITT CONSTRUCTION COMPANY INC.
1400 Cleveland Street, Greenville SC 29607-2410. 864/250-5000. **Contact:** Louis Mims, Human Resources Director. **Description:** A single-family housing contractor.

Note: Because addresses and telephone numbers of smaller companies change rapidly, we recommend you call each company to verify the information below before inquiring about job opportunities. Mass mailings are not recommended.

Additional employers with under 250 employees:

GENERAL CONTRACTORS

Republic Contracting Corp.
3501 Rawlinson Rd,
Columbia SC 29209-3324.
803/783-3290.

Squires Homes Inc.
132 Stonehurst Dr, Goose
Creek SC 29445-7041.
803/572-7582.

**Argo/Division of MB Kahn
Construction**
112 Old Standing Springs
Rd, Greenville SC 29605-
5914. 864/277-9105.

Centex Homes
101 Brassfield Ct, Irmo SC
29063-8468. 803/781-
0057.

Galaxy Remodeling Inc.
582 W Main St, Spartanburg
SC 29301-2162. 864/573-
8610.

Iron City Construction Co.
RR 3, Manning SC 29102-
9803. 803/473-4873.

**New Carolina Construction
Company**
346 White Horse Rd,
Greenville SC 29605-3657.
864/277-1885.

John Wieland Designs
2736 Gaston Gate, Mount
Pleasant SC 29464-7925.
803/881-1516.

York Construction Co.
1164 Woodruff Rd,
Greenville SC 29607-4127.
864/297-9700.

MB Kahn Construction
RR 2, Ridgeland SC 29936-
9802. 803/726-6660.

Metromont Materials Corp.
P.O. Box 5690, Anderson SC
29623. 864/225-5184.

Pine Valley Construction
112 Valerie Dr, Gaffney SC
29340. 864/487-7973.

Tyger Construction Co.
120 Heywood Ave,
Spartanburg SC 29302-
1208. 864/585-8381.

**The Original Log Cabin
Homes**
2001 Leadenwah Dr,
Wadmalaw Island SC 29487-
6958. 803/559-2444.

Livingston Builders Inc.
1152 Walter Price St, Cayce
SC 29033-3525. 803/739-
0123.

Manning Lynch Inc.
401 Lucerne Dr, Spartanburg
SC 29302-3275. 864/573-
9481.

The Home Place
3468 Cinema Ave, Anderson
SC 29621-4141. 864/225-
7011.

Carolina Builders of SC
3730 S Highway 14,
Greenville SC 29615-6134.
864/458-9575.

American Dream Builders
7 Northway Dr, Taylors SC
29687-2836. 864/292-
1130.

American Family Homes
108 Bruce Rd, Greenville SC
29605-2268. 864/277-
1098.

GENERAL INDUSTRIAL CONTRACTORS

**Loveless Commercial
Contracting Inc.**
1821 State St, Cayce SC
29033-3952. 803/796-
5551.

McCrory Construction Co.
1280 Assembly St #145,
Columbia SC 29201-3122.
803/799-8100.

ROAD CONSTRUCTION

H&H Backhoe Service
158 Marked Beech Rd,
Marietta SC 29661-9543.
864/836-8844.

REA Construction Co.
3176 Charleston Hwy, West
Columbia SC 29172-2712.
803/791-1295.

A&L Underground Inc.
2908 Pelzer Hwy, Easley SC
29642-8756. 864/850-
0754.

Nocuts
1200 Woodruff Rd,
Greenville SC 29607-5730.
864/676-0860.

GE Moore Co.
1042 Reynolds Ave,
Greenwood SC 29649-2734.
864/229-7411.

PLUMBING, HEATING, AND A/C

Carrier Corp.
720 Gracern Rd, Suite 101,
Columbia SC 29210-7657.
803/798-6850.

Thermo-Kinetics Industries
P.O. Box 6747, Greenville
SC 29606-6747. 864/277-
8080.

McIntosh Mechanical Co.
879 S Guignard Dr #2317,
Sumter SC 29150-7468.
803/773-1511.

WO Blackstone Company
425 Huger St, Columbia SC
29201-5223. 803/252-
8222.

**Piedmont Mechanical
Spartanburg**
Old John Dodd Rd, Inman SC
29349. 864/233-8995.

Freeman Mechanical Inc.
1017 Woodruff Rd,
Greenville SC 29607-4108.
864/288-3530.

Hoffman & Hoffman
95 Marcus Dr, Greenville SC
29615-4817. 864/676-
1888.

ELECTRICAL WORK

Gregory Electric Co. Inc.
2124 College St, Columbia
SC 29205-1023. 803/748-
1122.

Ivey Electric Company
344 E Main St, Spartanburg
SC 29302-1943. 864/585-
6286.

Walker & Whiteside Inc.
1400 Lowndes Hill Rd,
Greenville SC 29607-2715.
864/242-4820.

Edwards Electric
P.O. Box 698, Piedmont SC
29673-0698. 864/277-
1517.

Brock Electric Technology
3511 Delree St, West
Columbia SC 29170-2042.
803/796-7069.

Bryant Electric
1530 Bushy Park Rd, Goose
Creek SC 29445-6326.
803/863-9201.

Lorenz Electric Inc.
922 Reddick St, Charleston
SC 29412-5216. 803/762-
7083.

General Power Corp.
1569 Sam Rittenberg Blvd,
Charleston SC 29407-4145.
803/556-1066.

ROOFING, SIDING, AND SHEET METAL WORK

Murton Roofing
2430 Morningside Dr, West
Columbia SC 29169-4658.
803/939-8300.

Merchants' Metals
1101 Pasture Ln, Columbia
SC 29201-4958. 803/254-
6916.

Joyner Home Improvements
263 Dock Rd, Cordova SC
29039-9581. 803/536-
5160.

CONCRETE WORK

Ballenger Paving Company
900 W Lee Rd, Taylors SC
29687-2555. 864/292-
9550.

WATER WELL DRILLING

AE Drilling Services Inc.
102 Pilgrim Rd, Greenville SC
29607-5702. 864/288-
1986.

MISC. SPECIAL TRADE CONTRACTORS

Rogers & Son Construction Company
320 Shady Ln, Summerville
SC 29485-4554. 803/723-
1349.

Glenn Installation Service
1113 Glenn St #C, West
Columbia SC 29169-5053.
803/794-2380.

Otis Elevator Company
3561 Oscar Johnson Dr,
Charleston SC 29405-6875.
803/529-9502.

DR Hembree General Contractor
113 Overbrook Cir,
Greenville SC 29607-1325.
864/235-3264.

JD Smith Co. Inc.
501 La Mesa Rd Unit E,
Mount Pleasant SC 29464-
8404. 803/747-6755.

Window Tinting Plus
1232 Five Chop Rd SE,
Orangeburg SC 29115-7047.
803/531-0720.

PREFABRICATED WOOD BUILDINGS AND COMPONENTS

Mascot Homes Inc.
P.O. Box 127, Gramling SC
29348-0127. 864/472-
2041.

CONSTRUCTION MATERIALS WHOLESALE

Sanders Brothers Construction
4970 Lacross Rd, N
Charleston SC 29406.
803/747-5058.

Blythe Construction Inc.
150 Executive Cntr Dr, Suite
212, Greenville SC 29615-
4505. 864/288-6145.

JF Cleckley & Co.
Highway 17, Ridgeland SC
29936. 803/726-5344.

Dal-Tile Corporation
565 Woodruff Rd, Greenville
SC 29607-3533. 864/288-
8090.

Diamond Hill Plywood Co.
311 Arcadia Dr, Greenville
SC 29609-3860. 864/232-
8788.

Industrial Acoustics Co.
Hwy 52, Moncks Corner SC
29461. 803/761-6430.

Dargan Lybrand Fencing
1683 Old Dunbar Rd, West
Columbia SC 29172-1934.
803/822-3747.

PLUMBING, HEATING, AND A/C EQUIPMENT WHOLESALE

Riley Stoker Corp.
750 Executive Center Dr,
Greenville SC 29615-4521.
864/288-3487.

Gateway Supply Co. Inc.
1312 Hamrick St, Columbia
SC 29201-4517. 803/771-
7160.

Baker Brothers Inc.
515 Fair St, Anderson SC
29625. 864/231-0111.

Baker Brothers Inc.
1220 Asheville Hwy,
Spartanburg SC 29303-
2108. 864/583-5498.

Climatic Corporation
4460 Tile Dr, Charleston SC
29405. 803/554-0651.

McCalls Supply Inc.
612 Atomic Rd, North
Augusta SC 29841-4255.
803/279-3824.

Climatic Corporation
2321 S Pine St, Spartanburg
SC 29302-4337. 864/582-
7206.

Trane Co. Commercial Systems Group
1006 Bankton Dr, Hanahan
SC 29406. 803/747-1901.

ENGINEERING SERVICES

Virogroup Inc. - ETR Division
1445 Pisgah Church Rd,
Lexington SC 29072-8937.
803/957-6270.

Congaree Construction Co.
P.O. Box 90446, Columbia
SC 29290-1446. 803/783-
7812.

Gay Hussey Bell & DeYoung
749 Johnnie Dodds Blvd,
Mount Pleasant SC 29464-
3021. 803/849-7500.

Martin Engineering
P.O. Box 368, White Rock
SC 29177. 803/781-1930.

Black & Veatch
545 N Pleasantburg Dr, Suite
101, Greenville SC 29607-
2183. 864/232-6432.

Bechtel Corporation
1801 Charleston Hwy, Suite
T, Cayce SC 29033-2019.
803/739-2001.

Simons-Eastern
400 Executive Center Dr,
Greenville SC 29615-4510.
864/458-3600.

O'Neal Engineering Inc.
850 S Pleasantburg Dr, Fl 3,
Greenville SC 29607-2456.
864/232-7392.

Post Buckley Schuh & Jernigan
301 21st Ave S, N Myrtle
Beach SC 29582-4203.
803/272-1339.

The L Group Inc.
1109 48th Ave N, Suite
112, Myrtle Beach SC
29577. 803/497-0321.

Sonalysts Inc.
35 Varden Dr, Aiken SC
29803. 803/641-6705.

M. Rosenblatt & Son Inc.
2000 McMillan Ave, Suite T,
N Charleston SC 29405-
7794. 803/744-1686.

John Brown Engineers & Constructors
252 S Pleasantburg Dr,
Greenville SC 29607-2547.
864/467-2500.

ARCHITECTURAL SERVICES

Anderson-Debartolo Pan
145 N Church St,
Spartanburg SC 29306-
5163. 864/591-0018.

GMK Associates Inc.
1333 Main St, Columbia SC
29201-3201. 803/779-
5630.

For more information on career opportunities in architecture, construction, and engineering:

Associations

AACE INTERNATIONAL: THE ASSOCIATION FOR TOTAL COST MANAGEMENT
209 Prairie Avenue, Suite 100, P.O. Box 1557, Morgantown WV 26507-1557. 304/296-8444. 800/858-2678. Toll-free number provides information on scholarships for undergraduates. Fax: 304/291-5728. A membership organization which offers *Cost Engineering,* a monthly magazine; employment referral services; technical reference information and assistance; insurance; and a certification program accredited by the Council of Engineering Specialty Boards.

AMERICAN ASSOCIATION OF ENGINEERING SOCIETIES
1111 19th Street NW, Suite 608, Washington DC 20036-3690. 202/296-2237. A multi-disciplinary organization of professional engineering societies. Publishes reference works, including *Who's Who in Engineering Directory of Engineering Societies and Related Organizations,* and the *Thesaurus of Engineering and Scientific Terms,* as well as statistical reports from studies conducted by the Engineering Workforce Commission.

AMERICAN CONSULTING ENGINEERS COUNCIL
1015 15th Street NW, Suite 802, Washington DC 20005. 202/347-7474. Fax: 202/898-0068. A national organization of more than 5,000 member firms. Offers *Last Word,* a weekly newsletter; *American Consulting Engineer* magazine; life and health insurance programs; books, manuals, video and audiotapes, and contract documents; conferences and seminars; and voluntary peer reviews.

AMERICAN INSTITUTE OF ARCHITECTS
1735 New York Avenue NW, Washington DC 20006. 202/626-7300. 800/365-2724. Contact toll-free number for brochures.

AMERICAN SOCIETY FOR ENGINEERING EDUCATION
1818 N Street NW, Suite 600, Washington DC 20036. 202/331-3500. Promotes engineering education. Publishes monthly magazines.

AMERICAN SOCIETY OF CIVIL ENGINEERS
345 East 47th Street, New York NY 10017. 212/705-7496. Toll-free number: 800/548-2723. A membership organization which offers subscriptions to *Civil Engineering* magazine and *ASCE News,* discounts on various other publications, seminars, audio and videotapes, specialty conferences, an annual convention, group insurance programs, and pension plans.

AMERICAN SOCIETY OF HEATING, REFRIGERATING AND AIR CONDITIONING ENGINEERS
1791 Tullie Circle NE, Atlanta GA 30329. 404/636-8400. Fax: 404/321-5478. A society of 50,000 members which offers handbooks, a monthly journal, a monthly newspaper, discounts on other publications, group insurance, continuing education, and registration discounts for meetings, conferences, seminars, and expositions.

AMERICAN SOCIETY OF LANDSCAPE ARCHITECTS
4401 Connecticut Avenue NW, Washington DC 20008. 202/686-2752. World Wide Web address: http://www.asla.org. Look for Joblink for employment listings.

AMERICAN SOCIETY OF MECHANICAL ENGINEERS
345 East 47th Street, New York NY 10017. 212/705-7722. Handles educational materials for certified engineers, as well as scholarships.

AMERICAN SOCIETY OF NAVAL ENGINEERS
1452 Duke Street, Alexandria VA 22314. 703/836-6727. Holds symposiums based on technical papers. Publishes a journal and newsletter bimonthly.

AMERICAN SOCIETY OF PLUMBING ENGINEERS
3617 Thousand Oaks Boulevard, Suite 210, Westlake CA 91362-3694. 805/495-7120. Provides technical and educational information.

AMERICAN SOCIETY OF SAFETY ENGINEERS
1800 East Oakton Street, Des Plaines IL 60018-2187. 847/692-4121. Jobline service available at ext. 243. Fax: 708/296-3769. A membership organization offering *Professional Safety,* a monthly journal; educational seminars; an annual professional development conference and exposition; technical publications; certification preparation programs; career placement services; and group and liability insurance programs.

ASSOCIATED BUILDERS AND CONTRACTORS
1300 North 17th Street, Rosslyn VA 22209. 703/812-2000. Sponsors annual career fair. Currently in the process of creating a service to find workers for construction companies.

ASSOCIATED GENERAL CONTRACTORS OF AMERICA, INC.
1957 E Street NW, Washington DC 20006. 202/393-2040. A full-service construction association of subcontractors, specialty contractors, suppliers, equipment manufacturers, and professional firms.

Services include government relations, education and training, jobsite services, legal services, and information services.

ILLUMINATING ENGINEERING SOCIETY OF NORTH AMERICA

120 Wall Street, 17th Floor, New York NY 10005-4001. 212/248-5000. An organization for industry professionals involved in the manufacturing, design, specification, and maintenance of lighting systems. Conference held annually. Offers a Technical Knowledge Examination.

JUNIOR ENGINEERING TECHNICAL SOCIETY

1420 King Street, Suite 405, Alexandria VA 22314-2794. 703/548-JETS. Fax: 703/548-0769. E-mail address: jets@nas.edu. A nonprofit, educational society promoting interest in engineering, technology, mathematics, and science. Provides information to high school students and teachers regarding careers in engineering and technology.

NATIONAL ACTION COUNCIL FOR MINORITIES IN ENGINEERING

3 West 35th Street, New York NY 10001. 212/279-2626. Offers scholarship programs for students.

NATIONAL ASSOCIATION OF HOME BUILDERS

1201 15th Street NW, Washington DC 20005. 202/822-0200. A trade association promoting safe and affordable housing. Provides management services and education for members.

NATIONAL ASSOCIATION OF MINORITY ENGINEERING

1133 West Morse Boulevard, Suite 201, Winter Park FL 32789. 407/647-8839.

NATIONAL SOCIETY OF BLACK ENGINEERS

1454 Duke Street, Alexandria VA 22314. 703/549-2207. A nonprofit organization run by college students. Offers scholarships, editorials, and magazines.

NATIONAL SOCIETY OF PROFESSIONAL ENGINEERS

1420 King Street, Alexandria VA 22314-2794. 703/684-2800. Call 703/684-2830 for scholarship information for students. Fax: 703/836-4875. A society of over 73,000 engineers. Membership includes the monthly magazine *Engineering Times;* continuing education; scholarships and fellowships; discounts on publications; health and life insurance programs; and employment service programs.

SOCIETY OF FIRE PROTECTION ENGINEERS

One Liberty Square, Boston MA 02109-4825. 617/482-0686. Fax: 617/482-8184. A professional society which offers members reports, newsletters, *Journal of Fire Protecting Engineering,* insurance programs, short courses, symposiums, tutorials, an annual meeting, and engineering seminars.

Directories

DIRECTORY OF ENGINEERING SOCIETIES

American Association of Engineering Societies, 1111 19th Street NW, Suite 608, Washington DC 20036. 202/296-2237. $185.00. Lists other engineering association members, publications, and convention exhibits.

DIRECTORY OF ENGINEERS IN PRIVATE PRACTICE

National Society of Professional Engineers, 1420 King Street, Alexandria VA 22314. 703/684-2800. $50.00. Lists members and companies.

Magazines

THE CAREER ENGINEER

National Society of Black Engineers, 1454 Duke Street, Alexandria VA 22314. 703/549-2207.

CAREERS AND THE ENGINEER

Adams Media Corporation, 260 Center Street, Holbrook MA 02343. 617/767-8100.

CHEMICAL & ENGINEERING NEWS

American Chemical Society 1155 16th Street NW, Washington DC 20036. 202/872-4600.

COMPUTER-AIDED ENGINEERING

Penton Publishing, 1100 Superior Avenue, Cleveland OH 44114. 216/696-7000.

EDN CAREER NEWS

Cahners Publishing Company, 275 Washington Street, Newton MA 02158. 617/964-3030.

ENGINEERING TIMES

National Society of Professional Engineers, 1420 King Street, Alexandria VA 22314. 703/684-2800.

NAVAL ENGINEERS JOURNAL

American Society of Naval Engineers, 1452 Duke Street, Alexandria VA 22314. 703/836-6727. Subscription: $48.00.

ARTS AND ENTERTAINMENT/RECREATION

 Job opportunities in the entertainment and recreation industries are projected to increase 39 percent through the year 2005, faster than the average for all industries. Higher incomes, growth of leisure time due to a growing population of retirees, and increasing awareness of the health benefits of physical fitness will affect employment growth.

The market for leisure activities is changing. In the past, amusement and recreation services catered to those in their '20s and '30s who had steadily growing incomes. Now that those baby boomers have grown up, companies are targeting adults between 50 and 75 years old.

In Hollywood, the past several years have been marked by mergers: Disney and ABC/Capital Cities, Westinghouse and CBS, Turner Broadcasting and Time Warner, and Seagram and MCA, to name a few of the biggest headline-stealers. And then there's the growing alliance between Hollywood and Silicon Valley. Microsoft, for example, has joined forces with NBC to create an online news station.

North Carolina

THE BILTMORE COMPANY/BILTMORE HOUSE
1 North Pack Square, Asheville NC 28801. 704/274-6270. **Fax:** 704/274-6269. **Contact:** Mr. Terry Clark, Human Resources Manager. **Description:** The Biltmore Company is an organization dedicated to the preservation of the largest privately-owned historic house in America (Biltmore House) and its 50,000-object collection. The Biltmore Company was established in 1986.

BRADY DISTRIBUTING
P.O. Box 19269, Charlotte NC 28219. 704/357-6284. **Contact:** Sue Ballard, Human Resources Manager. **Description:** Distributes and manages coin-operated vending machines and arcade games.

CHARLOTTE SYMPHONY ORCHESTRA
214 North Church Street, Suite 100, Charlotte NC 28202. 704/332-0468. **Contact:** Human Resources. **Description:** A symphony orchestra production company. **Common positions include:** Accountant/Auditor; Computer Programmer; Computer Systems Analyst; Operations/Production Manager. **Educational backgrounds include:** Computer Science; Finance; Liberal Arts; Management/Planning; Marketing. **Benefits:** 401K; Dental Insurance; Medical Insurance. **Operations at this facility include:** Administration; Sales; Service.

SALEM COLLEGE FINE ART CENTER
P.O. Box 10548, Winston-Salem NC 27108. 910/721-2600. **Fax:** 910/721-2683. **Contact:** Jackie Kaylor, Student Developmental Services. **Description:** Music, visual arts, and drama facilities for a women's liberal arts college. **Common positions include:** General Manager; Librarian; Technician. **Educational backgrounds include:** Art/Design; Business Administration; Liberal Arts; Music; Theatre. **Benefits:** Dental Insurance; Life Insurance; Medical Insurance; Pension Plan; Tuition Assistance. **Corporate headquarters location:** This Location. **Operations at this facility include:** Administration; Service. **Listed on:** Privately held.

SPEEDWAY MOTORSPORTS, INC.
US Highway 29 North, P.O. Box 600, Concord NC 28026-0600. 704/455-3239. **Contact:** Marcia Perrell, Administrative Assistant. **Description:** Speedway Motorsports, Inc. is the owner and operator of Charlotte Motor Speedway and Atlanta Motor Speedway. The company promotes, markets and sponsors motorsports activities including eight racing events annually sanctioned by NASCAR, five of which are

associated with the Winston Cup professional stock car racing circuit and three races associated with the Busch Grand National circuit. The company also operates, sanctions, and promotes its "Legends Cars," 5/8-scale modified cars, modeled after those driven by legendary early NASCAR racers, for use on its Legends Car Racing Circuit, which is an entry-level stock car racing series. Other motorsports operations include two ARCA annual stock car races. **NOTE:** The company also hires temporary employees to assist during periods of peak attendance at its events. **Corporate headquarters location:** This Location. **Listed on:** New York Stock Exchange. **Number of full-time employees:** 166. **Number of part-time employees:** 173.

Note: Because addresses and telephone numbers of smaller companies change rapidly, we recommend you call each company to verify the information below before inquiring about job opportunities. Mass mailings are not recommended.

Additional employers with under 250 employees:

MOTION PICTURE AND VIDEO TAPE PRODUCTION AND DISTRIBUTION

AMI Video/Post
3167 Tucker Street Ext,
Burlington NC 27215-8906.
910/227-0171.

Creatavision Inc.
8349-P Arrowridge Blvd,
Charlotte NC 28273.
704/525-1284.

Search Productions
100 Hunters Ln, Youngsville
NC 27596. 919/554-0111.

Cable Adnet
7029 Albert Pick Rd, Suite
204, Greensboro NC 27409-
9521. 910/668-3800.

MOTION PICTURE THEATERS

Church Street Theatres
1809 S Church St,
Burlington NC 27215-5553.
910/229-7469.

Northwoods Theatre
2445 Onslow Dr,
Jacksonville NC 28540-
5607. 910/346-8273.

RACING AND TRACK OPERATION

600 Racing Inc.
5245 NC Highway 49 South,
Harrisburg NC 28075.
704/455-3896.

PHYSICAL FITNESS FACILITIES

Imperial Athletic Club
4700 Emperor Blvd,
Morrisville NC 27560-9759.
919/941-9010.

Gold's Gym Aerobics & Fitness
3576 Yadkinville Rd,
Winston-Salem NC 27106-
2500. 910/924-2600.

Raleigh Athletic Club
7339 Six Forks Rd, Raleigh
NC 27615-7804. 919/847-
8189.

Spa Health Club
30 Westgate Pky, Asheville
NC 28806-3835. 704/254-
4946.

Spa Health Club
Greenwood Commons
Shopping Cen, Durham NC
27713. 919/544-6360.

PUBLIC GOLF COURSES

Gates Four Golf & Country Club
6775 Irongate Dr,
Fayetteville NC 28306-2505.
910/425-2176.

Renaissance Park Golf Club
1525 W Tyvola Rd, Charlotte
NC 28217. 704/357-3373.

MEMBERSHIP SPORTS AND RECREATION CLUBS

Landfall Club
1550 Landfall Dr, Wilmington
NC 28405. 910/256-7641.

Personalities Night Club
1016 Ward Blvd S, Wilson
NC 27893. 919/243-6250.

Providence Square Racquet Club
100 Providence Square Dr,
Charlotte NC 28270-6527.
704/364-8189.

Raintree Country Club
8600 Raintree Ln, Charlotte
NC 28277. 704/542-0800.

AMUSEMENT AND RECREATION SERVICES

Heritage Park
416 Dorothea Dr, Raleigh NC
27601. 919/831-6174.

Club Development Association
Hwy 15-501 S, Aberdeen NC
28315. 910/944-8838.

ZOOLOGICAL GARDENS

North Carolina Zoological Park
4401 Zoo Pky, Asheboro NC
27203. 910/879-7000.

South Carolina

ALABAMA THEATER
4750 Highway 17 South, North Myrtle Beach SC 29582. 803/272-5758. **Contact:** Scarlett Ferguson, Controller. **Description:** A performing arts showcase featuring country music and other contemporary music.

CHARLESTON MUSEUM
360 Meeting, Charleston SC 29402. 803/722-2996. **Contact:** Faith Brownley, Director of Human Resources. **Description:** The Charleston Museum, the oldest municipal museum in the United States, features collections of arts, crafts, textiles, and furniture, with an emphasis on South Carolina history.

SEA PINES ASSOCIATES, INC.
P.O. Box 7000, Hilton Head Island SC 29928. 803/785-3333. **Fax:** 803/842-1927.
Contact: Monika Nash, Director of Human Resources. **Description:** Sea Pines
Associates, Inc. is a holding company with three subsidiaries including Sea Pines
Company, Inc., (also at this address) which operates all of the resort assets including
three resort golf courses, a 28 court racquet club, a home and villa rental management
business, retail sales outlets, food services operations and other resort recreational
facilities. Sea Pines Real Estate Company, Inc. is an independent real estate brokerage
firm with 11 offices serving Island residents. Sea Pines Country Club, Inc. owns and
operates a full-service private country club providing golf, tennis, and clubhouse
facilities for approximately 1,500 equity and associate club members. The company,
through its wholly-owned subsidiary, Sea Pines/TidePointe, Inc., has a general
partnership interest in TidePointe Partners. TidePointe Partners develops and
constructs a continuing care retirement community with a variety of living units and
amenities on Hilton Head Island, South Carolina. **Corporate headquarters location:** This
Location. **Number of employees at this location:** 247.

SEA PINES COMPANY, INC.
P.O. Box 7000, Hilton Head Island SC 29938. 803/842-1882. **Contact:** Monika Nash,
Director of Human Resources. **Description:** Sea Pines Company, Inc. operates resort
assets including three resort golf courses, a 28 court racquet club, a home and villa
rental management business, retail sales outlets, food services operations and other
resort recreational facilities. Parent company, Sea Pines Associates, Inc. is a holding
company with two other subsidiaries including Sea Pines Real Estate Company, Inc.,
an independent real estate brokerage firm with 11 offices serving Island residents; and
Sea Pines Country Club, Inc., which owns and operates a full-service private country
club providing golf, tennis, and clubhouse facilities for approximately 1,500 equity and
associate club members. The company, through its wholly-owned subsidiary, Sea
Pines/TidePointe, Inc., has a general partnership interest in TidePointe Partners.
TidePointe Partners develops and constructs a continuing care retirement community
with a variety of living units and amenities on Hilton Head Island, South Carolina. The
parent company, Sea Pines Associates, Inc. is also located at this address. 803/785-
3333. **Common positions include:** Accountant/Auditor; Administrative Worker/Clerk;
Assistant Manager; Buyer; Cashier; Chef/Cook/Kitchen Worker; Clerical Supervisor;
Computer Operator; Computer Programmer; Computer Systems Analyst; Customer
Service Representative; Department Manager; Dispatcher; Employment Interviewer;
Food and Beverage Service Worker; General Manager; Hotel Manager/Assistant
Manager; Hotel/Motel Clerk; Management Trainee; Marketing/Advertising/PR Manager;
Paralegal; Payroll Clerk; Property and Real Estate Manager; Public Relations Specialist;
Purchasing Agent and Manager; Real Estate Agent; Receptionist; Recreation Worker;
Reservationist; Retail Sales Worker; Secretary; Truck Driver; Typist/Word Processor;
Wholesale and Retail Buyer. **Educational backgrounds include:** Accounting; Business
Administration; Communications; Computer Science; Finance; Liberal Arts; Marketing.
Benefits: 401K; Dental Insurance; Disability Coverage; Employee Discounts; Life
Insurance; Medical Insurance. **Parent company:** Sea Pines Associates, Inc. **Operations
at this facility include:** Administration; Sales; Service. **Number of employees at this
location:** 450.

SOUTH CAROLINA STATE MUSEUM
P.O. Box 100107, Columbia SC 29202-3107. 803/737-4921. **Contact:** Joan McBride,
Director of Human Resources. **Description:** A museum featuring art, history, natural
history, and science and technology. **Corporate headquarters location:** This Location.

*Note: Because addresses and telephone numbers of smaller companies change rapidly,
we recommend you call each company to verify the information below before inquiring
about job opportunities. Mass mailings are not recommended.*

Additional employers with under 250 employees:

TRAILER PARKS/CAMPSITES

Outdoor Resorts of America
19 Arrow Rd, Hilton Head SC
29928. 803/785-7699.

Nosoca Pines Ranch
2990 Singleton Creek Rd,
Heath Springs SC 29058.
803/273-8200.

**MOTION PICTURE AND
VIDEO TAPE PRODUCTION
AND DISTRIBUTION**

Flying Ace Productions
250 International Dr,
Spartanburg SC 29301-
4600. 864/587-4430.

ID Property Protection
8291 Winnsboro Rd,
Blythewood SC 29016-
8878. 803/735-4898.

PUBLIC GOLF COURSES

Cane Patch Par
72nd Av N, Myrtle Beach SC
29572. 803/449-6085.

Coosaw Creek Country Club
8610 Dorchester Rd,
Charleston SC 29420-7302.
803/767-9000.

**Crowfield Golf & Country
Club**
303 Hamlet Cir, Goose Creek
SC 29445-7119. 803/764-
4702.

Midway Driving Range
29th Av S, Myrtle Beach SC
29577. 803/448-6137.

River Club
Pine Dr, Pawleys Island SC
29585. 803/237-8880.

Villas Foxwood Hills Kinston
300 Brighton Dr,
Westminster SC 29693-
5745. 864/647-9503.

**AMUSEMENT PARKS AND
RECREATION CENTERS**

**Charleston Co. Parks &
Recreation**
861 Riverland Dr, Charleston
SC 29412-3107. 803/762-
2172.

Family Kingdom
P.O. Box 2548, Myrtle Beach
SC 29578. 803/626-3447.

Tilt
225 S Pleasantburg Dr, Suite
B10, Greenville SC 29607-
2533. 864/233-9223.

**MEMBERSHIP SPORTS AND
RECREATION CLUBS**

Plantation Club at Longcreek
730 Longtown Rd, Columbia
SC 29223. 803/754-1715.

Long Bay Club
Hwy 9, Longs SC 29568.
803/249-5510.

Thornblade Club
1275 Thornblade Blvd, Greer
SC 29650. 864/234-5100.

For more information on career opportunities in arts, entertainment and recreation:

Associations

AMERICAN ASSOCIATION OF MUSEUMS
1225 I Street NW, Suite 200, Washington
DC 20005. 202/289-1818. Fax: 202/289-
6578. Publishes *AVISO,* a monthly
newsletter containing employment listings
for the entire country.

AMERICAN COUNCIL FOR THE ARTS
1 East 53rd Street, New York NY 10022.
212/223-2787. Fax: 212/980-4857. Visual
Artist Information Hotline: 800/232-2789.
A nonprofit organization for the literary,
visual, and performing arts. Supports K-12
education and promotes public policy
through meetings, forums, and seminars.

AMERICAN CRAFTS COUNCIL
72 Spring Street, New York NY 10012.
212/274-0630. Operates a research library.
Publishes *American Crafts* magazine.

AMERICAN DANCE GUILD
31 West 21st Street, New York NY 10010.
212/627-3790. Holds an annual conference
with panels, performances, and workshops.
Operates a job listings service (available at a
discount to members.)

AMERICAN FEDERATION OF MUSICIANS
1501 Broadway, Suite 600, New York NY
10036. 212/869-1330. Membership
required.

**AMERICAN FEDERATION OF TELEVISION
AND RADIO ARTISTS**
260 Madison Avenue, New York NY
10016. 212/532-0800. Membership
required.

AMERICAN FILM INSTITUTE
John F. Kennedy Center for the Performing
Arts, Washington DC 20566. 202/828-
4000.

AMERICAN GUILD OF MUSICAL ARTISTS
1727 Broadway, New York NY 10019.
212/265-3687.

AMERICAN MUSIC CENTER
30 West 26th Street, Suite 1001, New
York NY 10010-2011. 212/366-5260. Fax:
212/366-5265. A nonprofit research and
information center for contemporary music
and jazz. Provides information services and
grant programs. World Wide Web address:
http://www.amc.net/amc/.

**AMERICAN SOCIETY OF COMPOSERS,
AUTHORS, AND PUBLISHERS (ASCAP)**
One Lincoln Plaza, New York NY 10023.
212/621-6000. Fax: 212/724-9064. A
membership association which licenses
members' work and pays members
royalties. Offers showcases and educational
seminars and workshops.

**AMERICAN SYMPHONY ORCHESTRA
LEAGUE**
1156 15th Street NW, Suite 4800,
Washington DC 20005. 202/628-0099.

**AMERICAN ZOO AND AQUARIUM
ASSOCIATION**
Oglebay Park, Wheeling WV 26003.
304/242-2160. Produces a monthly
newspaper.

**ASSOCIATION OF INDEPENDENT VIDEO
AND FILMMAKERS**
625 Broadway, 9th Floor, New York NY
10012. 212/473-3400.

**NATIONAL ARTISTS' EQUITY
ASSOCIATION**
P.O. Box 28068, Central Station,
Washington DC 20038-8068. 202/628-
9633. A national, nonprofit organization
dedicated to improving economic, health,
and legal conditions for visual artists.

NATIONAL DANCE ASSOCIATION
1900 Association Drive, Reston VA 22091.
703/476-3436. Fax: 703/476-9527.
Promotes the development and
implementation of philosophies and policies
in all forms of dance and in dance education
at all levels.

NATIONAL ENDOWMENT FOR THE ARTS
1100 Pennsylvania Avenue NW,
Washington DC 20506. 202/682-5400.

**NATIONAL RECREATION AND PARK
ASSOCIATION**
2775 South Quincy Street, Suite 300,
Arlington VA 22206. 703/820-4940. Fax:
703/671-6772. A national, nonprofit
service organization. Offers professional
development and training opportunities in
recreation, parks, and leisure services.
Publishes a newsletter and magazine.

PRODUCERS GUILD OF AMERICA
400 South Beverly Drive, Suite 211,
Beverly Hills CA 90212. 310/557-0807.

SCREEN ACTORS GUILD
5757 Wilshire Boulevard, Los Angeles CA
90036-3600. 213/954-1600.

THEATRE COMMUNICATIONS GROUP
355 Lexington Avenue, New York NY
10017. 212/697-5230.

WOMEN'S CAUCUS FOR ART
Moore College of Art, 20th & The Parkway,
Philadelphia PA 19103. 215/854-0922.
Fax: 215/854-0915. A national organization
of professionals in the visual arts. Over
3,700 members. Membership includes an
annual conference; participation in juried
shows; local chapter meetings and regional
conferences; publications including an
annual exhibition catalog of honors awards
and a quarterly newsletter; and insurance
programs.

Directories

ARTIST'S MARKET
Writer's Digest Books, 1507 Dana Avenue,
Cincinnati OH 45207. 513/531-2222.

CREATIVE BLACK BOOK
866 3rd Avenue, 3rd Floor, New York NY
10022. 212/254-1330.

PLAYERS GUIDE
165 West 46th Street, New York NY
10036. 212/869-3570.

ROSS REPORTS TELEVISION
Television Index, Inc., 40-29 27th Street,
Long Island City NY 11101. 718/937-
3990.

Magazines

AMERICAN ARTIST
One Astor Place, 1515 Broadway, New
York NY 10036. 212/764-7300. 800/346-
0085, ext. 477.

AMERICAN CINEMATOGRAPHER
American Society of Cinematographers,
P.O. Box 2230, Hollywood CA 90028.
213/969-4333.

ART BUSINESS NEWS
Myers Publishing Company, 19 Old Kings
Highway South, Darien CT 06820.
203/656-3402.

ART DIRECTION
10 East 39th Street, 6th Floor, New York
NY 10016. 212/889-6500.

ARTFORUM
65 Bleecker Street, New York NY 10012.
212/475-4000.

ARTWEEK
12 South First Street, Suite 520, San Jose
CA 95113. 408/279-2293.

AVISO
American Association of Museums, 1225 I
Street NW, Suite 200, Washington DC
20005. 202/289-1818.

BACK STAGE
1515 Broadway, New York NY 10036.
212/764-7300.

BILLBOARD
Billboard Publications, Inc., 1515 Broadway,
New York NY 10036. 212/764-7300.

CASHBOX
157 West 57th Street, Suite 503, New
York NY 10019. 212/245-4224.

CRAFTS REPORT
300 Water Street, Wilmington DE 19801.
302/656-2209.

DRAMA-LOGUE
P.O. Box 38771, Los Angeles CA 90038.
213/464-5079.

HOLLYWOOD REPORTER
5055 Wilshire Boulevard, 6th Floor, Los
Angeles CA 90036. 213/525-2000.

VARIETY
249 West 17th Street, New York NY
10011. 212/779-1100. 800/323-4345.

WOMEN ARTIST NEWS
300 Riverside Drive, New York NY 10025.
212/666-6990.

AUTOMOTIVE

 *The automotive industry saw a big turnaround in 1994, with sales of new cars and trucks reaching a six-year high. Unfortunately, the boom didn't last. Rising interest rates in early 1995 put the brakes on auto sales. Although the year can't be classified as truly weak, 1995 sales dropped 2.6 percent off 1994's pace. Rising steel prices have also put pressure on the Big Three automakers to cut costs and boost productivity, so don't look for job opportunities to grow very rapidly in '96. Even so, analysts are predicting a 2 percent sales gain in 1996, spurred in part by dropping interest rates.*

Jobseekers should look to auto parts suppliers in addition to the Big Three. While Detroit is using fewer suppliers than in the past, the suppliers that are under contract are being asked to supply more of the finished product. Look for large employers with financial backing and superior skills.

North Carolina

AP PARTS COMPANY
300 Dixie Trail, Building O, Goldsboro NC 27530. 919/735-2030. **Contact:** David Mehl, Human Resources Manager. **Description:** This location has a complex of buildings which include the corporate offices and a manufacturing facility, as well as the distribution center. AP Parts Company is a motor vehicle parts and accessories manufacturer, specializing in mufflers. **Corporate headquarters location:** This Location.

ALLIEDSIGNAL TTBS
701 North Interstate 85, Charlotte NC 28216. 704/391-5500. **Fax:** 704/391-5595. **Contact:** Mark Hart, Manager of Human Resources. **Description:** This location manufactures heavy-duty air brake systems and components for tractor trailer trucks. Overall, AlliedSignal Corporation serves a broad spectrum of industries through its more than 40 strategic businesses, which are grouped into three sectors: Aerospace, Automotive, and Engineered Materials. AlliedSignal Corporation is one of the nation's largest industrial organizations. **Common positions include:** Accountant/Auditor; Buyer; Electrical/Electronics Engineer; Human Resources Specialist; Industrial Engineer; Mechanical Engineer; Purchasing Agent and Manager. **Educational backgrounds include:** Accounting; Business Administration; Engineering; Finance. **Benefits:** Dental Insurance; Disability Coverage; Employee Discounts; Life Insurance; Medical Insurance; Pension Plan; Profit Sharing; Savings Plan; Tuition Assistance; Vision Insurance. **Special Programs:** Internships; Training Programs. **Corporate headquarters location:** Franklin IN. **Parent company:** AlliedSignal Corporation. **Operations at this facility include:** Manufacturing. **Listed on:** New York Stock Exchange. **Number of employees at this location:** 365. **Number of employees nationwide:** 90,000.

G.K.N. AUTO
4901 Womack Road, Sanford NC 27330. 919/776-7561. **Contact:** Joe Jackson, Director of Human Resources. **Description:** Manufactures front-wheel drives for automobiles.

HACKNEY AND SONS INC.
P.O. Box 880, Washington NC 27889. 919/946-6521x213. **Fax:** 919/975-8340. **Contact:** Lloyd Koehler, Director of Human Resources. **Description:** One of the world's largest manufacturers of trucks and trailers for the beverage industry. Hackney and Sons also manufactures emergency service vehicles. **Common positions include:** Accountant/Auditor; Buyer; Computer Programmer; Credit Manager; Draftsperson; Electrical/Electronics Engineer; Electrician; Financial Analyst; General Manager; Industrial Engineer; Industrial Production Manager; Mechanical Engineer; Operations/Production Manager; Purchasing Agent and Manager. **Educational backgrounds include:** Business Administration; Engineering; Management/Planning. **Benefits:** 401K; Dental Insurance; Disability Coverage; Life Insurance; Medical Insurance; Tuition Assistance. **Corporate headquarters location:** This Location. **Other U.S. locations:** KS; NV. **Operations at this facility include:** Administration;

Manufacturing; Regional Headquarters; Sales. **Listed on:** Privately held. **Number of employees at this location:** 250. **Number of employees nationwide:** 500.

BRAD RAGAN, INC.
4404G Stuart Andrew Boulevard, Charlotte NC 28217-9990. 704/521-2100. **Contact:** Phil Jones, Director of Human Resources. **Description:** Brad Ragan, Inc. provides products and services to retail and commercial North American markets and selected South American markets. Through its retail division, Brad Ragan, Inc. offers tires, auto service, and home products to individual consumers in small- to mid-sized southeastern United States markets. The retail facilities and associates provide customer convenience, selection assistance, and competent automotive service. The commercial division sells over- and off-the-road new tires, manufactures and sells over-the-road truck and off-the-road retreading and repairs, and provides related services on and off-site. The commercial facilities and plant and equipment provide capital resource support for the people trained in the skills necessary to effectively fulfill a broad range of tire and service customer requirements, involving the smallest to the very largest over- and off-the-road vehicles and equipment. **Corporate headquarters location:** This Location. **Listed on:** American Stock Exchange. **Number of employees nationwide:** 1,700.

STANADYNE AUTOMOTIVE CORPORATION
POWER PRODUCTS DIVISION
P.O. Box 1105, Washington NC 27889. 919/975-2553. **Contact:** Joe Jernigan, Human Resources Manager. **Description:** Manufactures fuel injection systems for diesel engines. **Common positions include:** Accountant/Auditor; Administrator; Blue-Collar Worker Supervisor; Industrial Engineer; Mechanical Engineer; Operations/Production Manager; Purchasing Agent and Manager; Quality Control Supervisor; Transportation/Traffic Specialist. **Educational backgrounds include:** Accounting; Business Administration; Engineering. **Benefits:** 401K; Dental Insurance; Disability Coverage; Life Insurance; Medical Insurance; Pension Plan; Profit Sharing; Tuition Assistance. **Special Programs:** Training Programs. **Corporate headquarters location:** Windsor CT. **Other U.S. locations:** Tallahassee FL; Jacksonville NC. **Operations at this facility include:** Manufacturing. **Number of employees at this location:** 350.

THOMAS BUILT BUSES, INC.
P.O. Box 2450, High Point NC 27261-2450. 910/889-4871. **Contact:** Rick Holbert, Human Resources Director. **Description:** Manufactures motor vehicles and passenger car bodies.

Note: Because addresses and telephone numbers of smaller companies change rapidly, we recommend you call each company to verify the information below before inquiring about job opportunities. Mass mailings are not recommended.

Additional employers with under 250 employees:

INTERNAL COMBUSTION ENGINES

Simpson Industries Inc.
220 Industrial Blvd, Greenville NC 27834-9003. 919/758-2526.

INDUSTRIAL VEHICLES AND MOVING EQUIPMENT

Kinston Neuse Corp.
2000 Dobbs Farm Rd, Kinston NC 28501-8992. 919/522-3088.

MOTOR VEHICLES AND EQUIPMENT

Bepco Inc.
2475 S Stratford Rd, Winston-Salem NC 27103-6225. 910/760-0740.

Fontaine Modification Co.
9827 Mount Holly Rd, Charlotte NC 28214-9214. 704/391-1355.

Hackney Brothers Inc.
P.O. Box 2728, Wilson NC 27894-2728. 919/237-8171.

Ravens Metal Products
351 White St, Jacksonville NC 28546-6729. 910/577-7778.

Supreme/Murphy Truck Bodies
4000 Airport Dr NW, Wilson NC 27896. 919/291-2191.

WF Mickey Body Co. Inc.
1305 Trinity Ave, High Point NC 27260. 910/882-6806.

Hastings Company
P.O. Box 445, King NC 27021. 910/983-5101.

MGM Brakes
Park Ave, Murphy NC 28906. 704/837-2117.

Midland Brake Inc.
Hwy 221 S, Marion NC 28752. 704/652-9308.

Rockwell International Corp.
5275 Skyway Church Rd, Maxton NC 28364. 910/844-9401.

MOTOR VEHICLE EQUIPMENT WHOLESALE

High Point Auto Auction
6643 Auction Rd, Archdale NC 27263. 910/886-7091.

Great Dane Trailers
3800 N I-85, Charlotte NC
28206. 704/596-3721.

Fruehauf Trailers
7045 Albert Pick Rd,
Greensboro NC 27409-9654.
910/668-2441.

Abex Inc.
P.O. Box 335, Salisbury NC
28145-0335. 704/637-
2010.

Barnes Motor & Parts Co.
315 Barnes St S, Wilson NC
27893-5001. 919/243-
2161.

Genuine Parts Company
516 Rigsbee Ave, Durham
NC 27701-2135. 919/682-
6105.

TRW Replacement Division
805 Pressley Rd, Suite 105,
Charlotte NC 28217-0972.
704/522-9000.

**Universal Auto Radiator
Manufacturing Co.**
1106 N Ohenry Blvd,
Greensboro NC 27405-7120.
910/271-3239.

**Leonard Buildings & Truck
Accessories**
4239 Capital Blvd, Raleigh
NC 27604-4310. 919/872-
4442.

American Eagle Wheel
1660 Sullivan St, Greensboro
NC 27405-7212. 910/230-
1166.

Motor Bearings & Parts Co.
1515 US Highway 1 S,
Southern Pines NC 28387-
7036. 910/692-3343.

American Tire Distributors
1309 E Geer St, Durham NC
27704-5028. 919/596-
1002.

**Brad Ragan Commercial Tire
Center**
6205 Swing Ct, Greensboro
NC 27409-2003. 910/294-
4685.

Heafner Tires & Products
702 E Main St, Lincolnton
NC 28092-3445. 704/735-
8204.

Jonsey Auto Parts
5472 US Highway 264,
Wilson NC 27896-9714.
919/237-5304.

Perfection Hy-Test Co.
426 Maple Ave, Burlington
NC 27215-5934. 910/226-
5501.

**AUTOMOTIVE REPAIR
SHOPS**

Crown Paint and Body Centre
719 Camann St, Greensboro
NC 27407-1501. 910/547-
0120.

**Econo Auto Painting North
Carolina Inc.**
2710 N Tryon St, Charlotte
NC 28206-2757. 704/342-
9788.

Scheib Auto Painters
708 Ramsey St, Fayetteville
NC 28301-4738. 910/323-
2013.

Snider Tire
330 E Lindsay St,
Greensboro NC 27401-2924.
910/275-8641.

**Tri Bandag Recapping
Division**
900 N Miami Blvd, Durham
NC 27703-2228. 919/682-
5508.

**Sentinel Automotive
Distribution Inc.**
1640 S Saunders St, Raleigh
NC 27603-2312. 919/832-
9600.

**Goodyear Auto Service
Centers**
1819 Poole Rd, Raleigh NC
27610. 919/836-2230.

**Goodyear Auto Service
Centers**
Crabtree Valley Shopping
Cntr, Raleigh NC 27612.
919/782-6901.

**Mountaineer Auto & Truck
Service**
2810 Rosemont St,
Charlotte NC 28208-5513.
704/394-5082.

Perry Brothers Tire Service
512 E Market St, Smithfield
NC 27577. 910/934-8123.

Precision Tune
1104 Hwy 210 N, Spring
Lake NC 28390. 910/436-
4400.

Quality Service Center
720 McAdenville Rd, Lowell
NC 28098. 704/824-5748.

Quick 10 Oil Change Center
7210 Six Forks Rd, Raleigh
NC 27615-6159. 919/848-
2226.

Carolina Engine
9000 Statesville Rd,
Charlotte NC 28269-7680.
704/598-2200.

AEA Republic Automotive
2448 Battleground Ave,
Greensboro NC 27408-4002.
910/288-7794.

BP Procare
825 E Arrowood Rd,
Charlotte NC 28217-5810.
704/525-2479.

Asheville Powertrain
1 Wells Ave, Asheville NC
28806. 704/258-3277.

Meineke Discount Mufflers
5300 N Tryon St, Charlotte
NC 28213. 704/596-3093.

South Carolina

AMBAC INTERNATIONAL CORPORATION
P.O. Box 85, Columbia SC 29202. 803/735-1400. **Contact:** Kelvin Ham, Human
Resources Manager. **Description:** Ambac International Corporation manufactures diesel
fuel injection components and systems.

ARROW AUTOMOTIVE INDUSTRIES, INC.
P.O. Box 1748, Spartanburg SC 29304. 864/583-7281. **Contact:** Jerry Fowler,
Human Resources Manager. **Description:** A national precision remanufacturer of
replacement parts for domestic and imported passenger cars, light and heavy trucks,
farm vehicles, and heavy-duty industrial and construction equipment. Arrow's
operations headquarters are in Conway, Arkansas. Operating facilities are located in
Morrilton, Arkansas; Santa Maria, California; Hammond, Indiana; and this location.
Corporate headquarters location: Framingham MA.

BMW OF NORTH AMERICA, INC.
P.O. Box 11000, Spartanburg SC 29304-1100. 864/968-6000. **Contact:** Human
Resources Director. **Description:** A wholly-owned subsidiary of the West German

automobile and motorcycle manufacturer. BMW of North America, Inc. is responsible for United States marketing operations for the company's extensive line of motorcycles and automobiles. **Other U.S. locations:** Westwood NJ. **Parent company:** Bayerische Motoren Werke AG (Munich, Germany).

CHAMPION PARTS INC.
CHAMPION LABORATORIES INC.
P.O. Box 1049, York SC 29745. 803/684-3205. **Contact:** Jeff Smith, Human Resources Manager. **Description:** This location remanufactures and ships replacement automotive filters. Champion Laboratories Inc. operates as a division of Champion Parts Inc. **Corporate headquarters location:** Oak Brook IL. **Parent company:** Cooper Industries Inc., located in Houston, TX, is engaged in diversified business segments including electrical products, electrical power equipment, tools, hardware, automotive products, and petroleum and industrial equipment. Cooper Industries Inc.'s automotive products segment produces Anco windshield wiper products, Belden automotive wire and cable, Champion spark plugs and igniters, Everco and Murray heating and air conditioning parts, Moog steering and suspension components, Precision universal joints, General Driveshaft driveline products, and Wagner brakes and lighting products, among others. These products are geared toward the automotive repair and production, aviation, and industrial markets. **Listed on:** New York Stock Exchange. **Number of employees nationwide:** 45,000.

JPS AUTOMOTIVE PRODUCTS CORPORATION
P.O. Box 567, Greenville SC 29602-0567. 864/239-2320. **Contact:** Bob Cauble, Director of Human Resources. **Description:** Manufactures automotive products including carpet and trunk liners for automobiles. JPS Automotive Products Corporation operates as a subsidiary of JPS Textile Group Inc., a holding company whose companies are engaged in the following areas of business: manufacturing and marketing a broad range of unfinished fabrics used in men's, women's, and children's apparel; automotive products; home furnishings; and residential and commercial carpets. **Parent company:** JPS Textile Group Inc. (Greenville SC).

MACK TRUCKS INC.
One Bulldog Boulevard, Winnsboro SC 29180. 803/635-7100. **Contact:** Dave Frueauf, Director of Human Resources. **Description:** Manufactures and sells heavy-duty trucks, truck tractors, and truck replacement parts; and provides repair and maintenance service for these products. Mack Trucks is one of the largest producers of oversize (over 33,000 pounds) trucks in the United States.

THE TORRINGTON COMPANY
P.O. Box 565, Honea Path SC 29654. 864/369-7395. **Contact:** Fred Norris, Human Resources Manager. **Description:** The Torrington Company designs, develops, manufactures, and markets anti-friction bearings and produces universal joints and precision metal components and assemblies for the automotive industry. The company operates from locations throughout the United States, Germany, Australia, Brazil, Canada, England, and Japan. **Common positions include:** Blue-Collar Worker Supervisor; Buyer; Draftsperson; Electrical/Electronics Engineer; Industrial Engineer; Mechanical Engineer; Metallurgical Engineer; Purchasing Agent and Manager; Quality Control Supervisor. **Educational backgrounds include:** Engineering. **Benefits:** Dental Insurance; Disability Coverage; Life Insurance; Medical Insurance; Pension Plan; Savings Plan; Tuition Assistance. **Corporate headquarters location:** Torrington CT. **Parent company:** Ingersoll Rand Company (Woodcliff Lake, NJ). **Operations at this facility include:** Manufacturing. **Listed on:** New York Stock Exchange. **Number of employees nationwide:** 10,500.

Note: Because addresses and telephone numbers of smaller companies change rapidly, we recommend you call each company to verify the information below before inquiring about job opportunities. Mass mailings are not recommended.

Additional employers with under 250 employees:

INTERNAL COMBUSTION ENGINES

Caterpillar Inc.
107 Southchase Blvd,
Fountain Inn SC 29644-9019. 864/862-8300.

INDUSTRIAL VEHICLES AND MOVING EQUIPMENT

Baker Material Handling
2450 W 5th North St,
Summerville SC 29483-9695. 803/875-8000.

Cascade Corp.
7040 S Highway 11,
Westminster SC 29693-3915. 864/647-1119.

MOTOR VEHICLES AND EQUIPMENT

**Oshkosh Truck Corp./
Chassis Division**
552 Hyatt St, Gaffney SC
29341. 864/487-1700.

Sunex International Inc.
P.O. Box 4215, Greenville
SC 29608. 864/834-8759.

**Lake Shore Radiator &
Specialty Auto**
2050 Mabelene Rd, N
Charleston SC 29406-4654.
803/764-0994.

MOTOR VEHICLE EQUIPMENT WHOLESALE

Carolina International Trucks
1619 Bluff Rd, Columbia SC
29201-4913. 803/799-
4923.

AUTOMOTIVE REPAIR SHOPS

Goodyear Tire & Rubber Co.
1095 Simuel Rd,
Spartanburg SC 29301-
4340. 864/587-5160.

Harmon Auto Glass Co.
4922 Rivers Ave, N
Charleston SC 29406-6375.
803/566-0244.

Western Auto
404 McCravy Dr,
Spartanburg SC 29303-
3178. 864/582-1311.

**Muffler Xpress & Brake
Center**
558 Johnnie Dodds Blvd,
Mount Pleasant SC 29464-
3029. 803/881-4800.

For more information on career opportunities in the automotive industry:

Associations

**AMERICAN AUTOMOBILE
MANUFACTURERS ASSOCIATION**
1401 H Street NW, Suite 900, Washington
DC 20005. 202/326-5500. Fax: 202/326-
5567. A trade association consisting of the
Big Three U.S. automakers: Chrysler, Ford,
and General Motors. Sponsors research
projects, distributes publications, and
reviews social and public policies pertaining
to the motor vehicle industry and its
customers.

**ASSOCIATION OF INTERNATIONAL
AUTOMOBILE MANUFACTURERS**
1001 19th Street North, Suite 1200,
Arlington VA 22209. 703/525-7788.

AUTOMOTIVE SERVICE ASSOCIATION
1901 Airport Freeway, Suite 100, P.O. Box
929, Bedford TX 76095. 817/283-6205.
Works with shops to find workers.
Publishes a monthly magazine with
classified advertisements.

**AUTOMOTIVE SERVICE INDUSTRY
ASSOCIATION**
25 Northwest Point Boulevard, Suite 425,
Elk Grove Village IL 60007-1035. 708/228-
1310. Members are manufacturers and
distributors of automobile replacement
parts. Sponsors a trade show. Publishes
educational guidebooks and training
manuals.

Directories

**AUTOMOTIVE NEWS MARKET DATA
BOOK**
Crain Communications, Automotive News,
1400 Woodbridge Avenue, Detroit MI
48207-3187. 313/446-6000.

WARD'S AUTOMOTIVE YEARBOOK
Ward's Communications, 3000 Town
Center, Suite 2750, Southville MI 48075.
810/357-0800.

Magazines

AUTOMOTIVE INDUSTRIES
Chilton Book Company, 201 King of Prussia
Road, Radnor PA 19089. 800/695-1214.

AUTOMOTIVE NEWS
1400 Woodbridge Avenue, Detroit MI
48207. 313/446-6000.

WARD'S AUTO WORLD
Ward's Communications, Inc., 3000 Town
Center, Suite 2750, Southville MI 48075.
810/357-0800.

WARD'S AUTOMOTIVE REPORTS
Ward's Communications, Inc., 3000 Town
Center, Suite 2750, Southville MI 48075.
810/357-0800.

BANKING/SAVINGS AND LOANS

The banking industry has fared well over the past few years. Banks reported record earnings from 1992 to 1995. Low interest rates have decreased the number of bad loans and have increased investment profits. The early '90s were also a good time for banking professionals, who, despite numerous mergers and consolidations throughout the industry, avoided the large layoffs that hit workers in other industries. As a result of rising interest rates in early 1995, times have begun to change. Analysts argue that there are simply too many banks clogging the market. This glut of banks (over 10,000 in the United States as compared to 60 in Canada), the emphasis on multi-branch banking, and the decline in traditional transactions, has forced banks to consolidate and close branches. This has led to shrinking employment with dramatic layoffs of tellers, bank office workers, and managers. This trend will continue to take place into the next century.

North Carolina

BB&T-SOUTHERN NATIONAL BANK OF NORTH CAROLINA
500 North Chestnut Street, Lumberton NC 28358. 910/671-2000. **Contact:** Robert Williams, Human Resources Director. **Description:** A bank engaged in commercial banking, mortgages, discount brokerage, mutual funds, leasing, insurance, retail banking, trust services, annuities, international banking, cash management, and sales finance. **Parent company:** BB&T Southern National Corporation (Winston-Salem) is a holding company formed by the 1994 merger of Southern National Corporation (a multibank and savings and loan holding company with seven bank subsidiaries performing commercial and mortgage banking and insurance services) and Branch Banking & Trust Financial Corporation. Its subsidiaries form a network of hundreds of branches in cities and communities across the Carolinas and Virginia. Other subsidiaries of BB&T-Southern National Corporation include: BB&T-Southern National Bank of South Carolina; Branch Banking & Trust (BB&T-NC); Lexington State Bank; Community Bank of South Carolina; BB&T-Southern National Bank Savings Bank, Inc.; and Commerce Bank of Virginia Beach.

BB&T-SOUTHERN NATIONAL CORPORATION
P.O. Box 1215, Winston-Salem NC 27102-1215. 910/773-7200. **Fax:** 910/773-7466. **Contact:** Brenda Redmond, Employment Specialist. **Description:** A holding company formed by the 1994 merger of Southern National Corporation (a multibank and savings and loan holding company with seven bank subsidiaries performing commercial and mortgage banking and insurance services) and Branch Banking & Trust Financial Corporation. Its subsidiaries form a network of hundreds of branches in cities and communities across the Carolinas and Virginia. **Common positions include:** Accountant/Auditor; Adjuster; Administrative Services Manager; Attorney; Bank Officer/Manager; Branch Manager; Budget Analyst; Collector; Computer Programmer; Computer Systems Analyst; Credit Manager; Customer Service Representative; Economist/Market Research Analyst; Human Resources Specialist; Investigator; Management Trainee; Purchasing Agent and Manager; Quality Control Supervisor; Securities Sales Rep.; Underwriter/Assistant Underwriter. **Educational backgrounds include:** Accounting; Business Administration; Computer Science; Economics; Finance; Marketing. **Benefits:** 401K; Daycare Assistance; Dental Insurance; Disability Coverage; Employee Discounts; Life Insurance; Medical Insurance; Pension Plan; Tuition Assistance. **Special Programs:** Internships. **Corporate headquarters location:** This Location. **Other U.S. locations:** South Carolina. **Subsidiaries include:** BB&T-Southern National Bank of North Carolina; BB&T-Southern National Bank of South Carolina; Branch Banking & Trust (BB&T-NC); Lexington State Bank; Community Bank of South Carolina; BB&T-Southern National Bank Savings Bank, Inc.; Commerce Bank of Virginia Beach. **Operations at this facility include:** Administration; Divisional

Headquarters; Regional Headquarters; Sales; Service. **Listed on:** New York Stock Exchange. **Number of employees nationwide:** 3,850.

BRANCH BANKING & TRUST COMPANY (BB&T-NC)
P.O. Box 1847, 223 West Nash Street, Wilson NC 27894. 919/399-4229. **Contact:** Sandra Blanton, Human Resources Manager. **Description:** A savings bank. Branch Banking & Trust Company is a wholly-owned subsidiary of Southern National Corporation. BB&T-NC operates 319 branch offices in 161 cities in North Carolina. **Common positions include:** Accountant/Auditor; Bank Officer/Manager; Branch Manager; Computer Programmer; Financial Analyst; Insurance Agent/Broker; Management Trainee. **Educational backgrounds include:** Accounting; Business Administration; Computer Science; Economics; Finance; Marketing. **Benefits:** Disability Coverage; Employee Discounts; Life Insurance; Medical Insurance; Pension Plan; Profit Sharing; Savings Plan; Tuition Assistance. **Parent company:** BB&T Southern National Corporation (headquartered in Winston-Salem NC) is a holding company formed by the 1994 merger of Southern National Corporation (a multibank and savings and loan holding company with seven bank subsidiaries performing commercial and mortgage banking and insurance services) and Branch Banking & Trust Financial Corporation. The company's subsidiaries form a network of hundreds of branches in cities and communities across the Carolinas and Virginia. Other subsidiaries of BB&T-Southern National Corporation include: BB&T-Sourth National Bank of North Carolina; BB&T-Southern National Bank of South Carolina; Lexington State Bank; Community Bank of South Carolina; BB&T-Southern National Bank Savings Bank, Inc.; and Commerce Bank of Virginia Beach. **Listed on:** New York Stock Exchange. **Number of employees nationwide:** 3,850.

CABARRUS BANK OF NORTH CAROLINA
P.O. Box 328, Concord NC 28026. 704/782-1193. **Contact:** Judy Hartis, Human Resources Director. **Description:** The primary business of Cabarrus Bank of North Carolina includes retail and commercial banking, insurance agency activities, and mortgage lending. Cabarrus Bank also has a wholly-owned subsidiary, Cabco, Inc., whose principal business activities consist of the winding-down and disposition of investments in real estate joint ventures that were initiated prior to the company's acquisition of it. The parent company, Carolina First BancShares, Inc., is a bank holding company formed in 1989. The company also owns all of the common stock of Lincoln Bank of North Carolina, a commercial bank; and in 1994, the company purchased 18 percent of First Gaston Bank of North Carolina's common stock. Lincoln Bank has a wholly-owned subsidiary, North State Insurance Agency, Inc., which originates and services property, casualty, commercial, life, and health insurance products. Jointly, Lincoln Bank and Cabarrus Bank own a mortgage company, Carolina First Mortgage Corporation, which originates mortgage loans for resale in the secondary market; and a financial services company, Carolina First Financial Services Corporation, which offers as agent for its customers, mutual funds, and annuity products. **Corporate headquarters location:** This Location. **Other U.S. locations:** Kannapolis NC. **Parent company:** Carolina First BancShares, Inc. (Lincolnton, NC).

CAROLINA FIRST BANCSHARES, INC.
P.O. Box 657, Lincolnton NC 28093. **Contact:** Joy Keever, Human Resources Manager. **Description:** Carolina First BancShares, Inc. is a bank holding company formed in 1989. The company owns all of the common stock of two commercial banks, Lincoln Bank of North Carolina and Cabarrus Bank of North Carolina. The primary business of these banks includes retail and commercial banking, insurance agency activities, and mortgage lending. Lincoln Bank has a wholly-owned subsidiary, North State Insurance Agency, Inc., which originates and services property, casualty, commercial, life, and health insurance products. Cabarrus Bank also has a wholly-owned subsidiary, Cabco, Inc., whose principal business activities consist of the winding-down and disposition of investments in real estate joint ventures that were initiated prior to the company's acquisition of it. Jointly, Lincoln Bank and Cabarrus Bank own a mortgage company, Carolina First Mortgage Corporation, which originates mortgage loans for resale in the secondary market, and a financial services company, Carolina First Financial Services Corporation, which offers as agent for its customers, mutual funds and annuity products. In 1994, the company purchased 18 percent of First Gaston Bank of North Carolina's common stock. **Corporate headquarters location:** This Location. **Subsidiaries include:** North State Insurance Agency, Inc.; Carolina First Financial Services Corporation; Carolina First Mortgage Corporation; Cabarrus Bank; Lincoln Bank.

CENTRAL CAROLINA BANK/CCB FINANCIAL CORPORATION
P.O. Box 931, Durham NC 27702. 919/683-7777. **Contact:** John K. Fawcett, Human Resources Manager. **Description:** CCB Financial Corporation is a bank holding company

whose principal subsidiaries are Central Carolina Bank and Trust Company; CCB Savings Bank of Lenoir, Inc., SSB; and Graham Savings Bank, Inc., SSB. CCB Financial Corporation offers a wide variety of retail, commercial, and trust banking services through its 112 offices located primarily in the Piedmont section of North Carolina. **Corporate headquarters location:** This Location.

CENTURA BANKS, INC.
134 North Church Street, P.O. Box 1220, Rocky Mount NC 27802. 919/977-4400, **Contact:** Human Resources. **Description:** A bank holding company which provides a full range of banking, investment, and insurance services for individuals and businesses. The company's subsidiary, Centura Bank, is a full-service commercial banking institution. In 1994, the company acquired Cleveland Federal Bank of Shelby, North Carolina and First Southern Bancorp Inc. of Asheboro, North Carolina. The company introduced its service "Centura Highway" in 1994, which permits customers to conduct any non-cash transaction via telephone, including opening new accounts, applying for loans, ordering checks, and transferring money between accounts. The company also introduced Centura Securities, a full-service brokerage firm, added a new family of proprietary mutual finds, and began offering property and casualty insurance in 1994. **Corporate headquarters location:** This Location. **Listed on:** New York Stock Exchange. **Number of employees nationwide:** 1,869.

COOPERATIVE BANKSHARES, INC.
201 Market Street, P.O. Box 60028401, Wilmington NC 28402. 910/343-0181. **Contact:** Ms. Dare Rhodes, Human Resources. **Description:** Cooperative Bankshares, Inc. is a savings bank holding company with one subsidiary, Cooperative Bank For Savings, Inc., SSB, which is engaged in general banking activities. The bank offers a wide range of retail banking services including deposit services, banking cards, and alternative investment products. These funds are used for the extension of credit through mortgage loans, savings account loans, and other installment credit such as home equity, auto, and boat loans, and check reserve. The bank operates 16 offices throughout the coastal and inland communities of eastern North Carolina from Corolla to Tabor City. **Corporate headquarters location:** This Location. **Other U.S. locations:** Beaufort NC; Belhaven NC; Corolla NC; Elizabethtown NC; Jacksonville (2) NC; Kill Devil Hills NC; Morehead City NC; Tabor City NC; Robersonville NC; Wallace NC; Washington (2) NC. **Listed on:** NASDAQ.

FEDERAL RESERVE BANK OF RICHMOND
CHARLOTTE BRANCH
P.O. Box 30248, Charlotte NC 28230. 704/358-2100. **Contact:** Gail Ervin, Personnel Manager. **Description:** One of 12 regional Federal Reserve banks that, along with the Federal Reserve Board of Governors in Washington, D.C., and the Federal Open Market Committee (FOMC), comprise the Federal Reserve System, the nation's central bank. As the nation's central bank, the Federal Reserve is charged with three major responsibilities: monetary policy, banking supervision and regulation, and processing payments.

FIRST BANCORP
FIRST BANK
P.O. Box 508, Troy NC 27371. 910/576-6171. **Fax:** 910/576-1070. **Contact:** Patricia McCormick, Human Resources Director. **Description:** First Bancorp is a one-bank holding company. The principal activity of the company is the ownership and operation of First Bank, which is also headquartered at this location. The company also owns and operates two nonbank subsidiaries, Montgomery Data Services, Inc., which provides data processing services to financial institutions; and First Bancorp Financial Services, Inc. (formerly First Recovery, Inc.), which owns and operates various real estate properties. The company also controls First Bank Insurance Services, Inc., an insurance agency acquired in 1994 as a subsidiary. First Bancorp was founded in 1983 as Montgomery Bancorp, and changed its name in 1986. First Bank acquired Central State Bank in 1994 and operates from 28 branches located within a 60-mile radius of Troy, North Carolina. The bank provides a full range of banking services, including the accepting of demand and time deposits, the making of secured and unsecured loans to individuals and businesses, trust services, discount brokerage services, and self-directed IRAs. **Corporate headquarters location:** This Location. **Listed on:** NASDAQ.

FIRST CITIZENS BANCORPORATION OF NORTH CAROLINA, INC.
239 Fayetteville Street Mall, P.O. Box 29550, Raleigh NC 27626-0550. 919/755-7000. **Recorded Jobline:** 919/755-2070. **Contact:** Human Resources. **Description:** A bank holding company with statewide subsidiaries engaged in commercial banking, credit card services, and mortgage banking. **NOTE:** First Citizens Bancorporation only

accepts resumes for positions advertised on their jobline. Please call for a list of available jobs and instructions on how to apply. **Corporate headquarters location:** This Location. **Subsidiaries include:** First Citizens Bank & Trust Company; Bank of Marlinton; Pace America Bank.

FIRST UNION CORPORATION
1600 One First Union Center, Charlotte NC 28288-0953. 704/374-6565. **Contact:** Human Resources. **E-mail address:** comments@firstunion.com. **World Wide Web Address:** http://www.firstunion.com/. **Description:** First Union Corporation is one of the nation's largest bank holding companies with subsidiaries which operate over 1,330 full-service bank branches in the South Atlantic states. These subsidiaries provide retail banking, retail investment, and commercial banking services. The corporation provides other financial services including mortgage banking, home equity lending, leasing, and insurance and securities brokerage services from 222 branch locations. The corporation also operates one of the nation's largest ATM networks. The company has foreign offices in Nassau, the Bahamas and the Cayman Islands. Wholly-owned subsidiary, First Union Mortgage Corporation (704/374-6161), which offers a variety of mortgage banking and insurance services through 18 offices in nine state, is also at this location. **Corporate headquarters location:** This Location. **Subsidiaries include:** First Union National Bank of Florida; First Union National Bank of North Carolina; First Union National Bank of Georgia; First Union National Bank of Virginia; First Union National Bank of South Carolina; First Union National Bank of Tennessee; First Union National Bank of Washington, DC; First Union National Bank of Maryland; First Union Brokerage Services Inc.; First Union Capital Markets Corporation; First Union Home Equity Bank, N.A.; First Union Mortgage Corporation. **Listed on:** New York Stock Exchange. **Number of employees nationwide:** 31,858.

FIRST UNION NATIONAL BANK OF NORTH CAROLINA
One First Union Center, Charlotte NC 28288. 704/374-6161. **Contact:** Personnel. **E-mail address:** comments@firstunion.com. **World Wide Web Address:** http://www.firstunion.com. **Description:** A full-service commercial bank providing corporate and consumer services. First Union National Bank of North Carolina operates 276 offices. The parent company, First Union Corporation, is one of the nation's largest bank holding companies with subsidiaries which operate over 1,330 full-service bank branches in the South Atlantic states. These subsidiaries provide retail banking, retail investment, and commercial banking services. The corporation provides other financial services including mortgage banking, home equity lending, leasing, and insurance and securities brokerage services from 222 branch locations. The corporation also operates one of the nation's largest ATM networks. Wholly-owned subsidiaries of the parent company, First Union Corporation, include First Union Brokerage Services (704/374-6927), which is a securities brokerage firm; and First Union Capital Markets Corporation (704/383-8757), which provides a wide range of securities services, are also at this location. **Common positions include:** Bank Officer/Manager; Branch Manager; Department Manager; Financial Analyst; General Manager; Loan Officer; Management Trainee. **Educational backgrounds include:** Business Administration; Economics; Finance; Liberal Arts. **Benefits:** Dental Insurance; Disability Coverage; Employee Discounts; Life Insurance; Medical Insurance; Pension Plan; Profit Sharing; Savings Plan; Tuition Assistance. **Corporate headquarters location:** This Location. **Parent company:** First Union Corporation (1600 One First Union Center, Charlotte NC). **Listed on:** New York Stock Exchange. **Number of employees nationwide:** 31,858.

LEXINGTON STATE BANK
P.O. Box 867, Lexington NC 27293-0867. 704/246-6500. **Contact:** Ron Sink, Vice President of Personnel. **Description:** A commercial bank also engaged in insurance and financial activities through its subsidiaries. **Common positions include:** Administrator; Bank Officer/Manager; Branch Manager; Customer Service Representative; Department Manager; Insurance Agent/Broker. **Educational backgrounds include:** Business Administration. **Benefits:** 401K; Disability Coverage; Life Insurance; Medical Insurance; Pension Plan; Tuition Assistance. **Corporate headquarters location:** This Location. **Parent company:** BB&T Southern National Corporation (Winston-Salem NC) is a holding company formed by the 1994 merger of Southern National Corporation (a multibank and savings and loan holding company with seven bank subsidiaries performing commercial and mortgage banking and insurance services) and Branch Banking & Trust Financial Corporation. Its subsidiaries form a network of hundreds of branches in cities and communities across the Carolinas and Virginia. Other subsidiaries of BB&T-Southern National Corporation include: BB&T-Sourth National Bank of North Carolina; BB&T-Southern National Bank of South Carolina; Lexington State Bank; Community Bank of South Carolina; BB&T-Southern National Bank Savings Bank, Inc.; and Commerce Bank of Virginia Beach.

LINCOLN BANK OF NORTH CAROLINA
P.O. Box 657, Lincolnton NC 28093. 704/732-2222. **Contact:** Joy Keever, Director of Human Resources. **Description:** The primary business of Lincoln Bank of North Carolina includes retail and commercial banking, insurance agency activities, and mortgage lending. Lincoln Bank has a wholly-owned subsidiary, North State Insurance Agency, Inc., which originates and services property, casualty, commercial, life, and health insurance products. The parent company, Carolina First BancShares, Inc., is a bank holding company formed in 1989. The company also owns all of the common stock of Cabarrus Bank of North Carolina, a commercial bank; and in 1994, the company purchased 18 percent of First Gaston Bank of North Carolina's common stock. Cabarrus Bank also has a wholly-owned subsidiary, Cabco, Inc., whose principal business activities consist of the winding-down and disposition of investments in real estate joint ventures that were initiated prior to the company's acquisition of it. Jointly, Lincoln Bank and Cabarrus Bank own a mortgage company, Carolina First Mortgage Corporation, which originates mortgage loans for resale in the secondary market; and a financial services company, Carolina First Financial Services Corporation, which offers as agent for its customers, mutual funds, and annuity products. **Corporate headquarters location:** This Location. **Other U.S. locations:** Charlotte NC; Cornelius NC; Denver NC; Huntersville NC; Mooresville NC. **Parent company:** Carolina First BancShares, Inc. (Lincolnton, NC).

NATIONSBANK CORPORATION
NationsBank Corporate Center, NC1-007-2108, Charlotte NC 28255. 704/386-8996. **Fax:** 704/335-2269. **Recorded Jobline:** 704/386-8996. **Contact:** Mark Brown, Manager, College Recruiting. **Description:** A financial services firm engaged in commercial lending, consumer banking, trust accounts, mortgage banking, corporate banking, sales, trading, investment banking, operations and systems, audit services, control services, dealer financial services, and bank cards. **NOTE:** Applications are encouraged from graduates with related work experience. **Common positions include:** Accountant/Auditor; Bank Officer/Manager; Branch Manager; Computer Programmer; Computer Systems Analyst; Financial Analyst; Management Trainee; Operations/Production Manager; Services Sales Representative. **Educational backgrounds include:** Accounting; Business Administration; Economics; Finance; Liberal Arts; Management/Planning; Social Science. **Special Programs:** Internships; Training Programs. **Corporate headquarters location:** This Location. **Other U.S. locations:** DC; FL; GA; MD; SC; TN; TX; VA. **Operations at this facility include:** Administration; Divisional Headquarters; Regional Headquarters; Sales; Service. **Listed on:** New York Stock Exchange. **Number of employees nationwide:** 55,000.

UNITED CAROLINA BANCSHARES CORPORATION
127 West Webster Street, Whiteville NC 28472-4041. 910/642-5131. **Contact:** Ms. Jerry Ann Sutton, Employment Development. **Description:** United Carolina Bancshares Corporation is a bank holding company with principal subsidiaries including United Carolina Bank and United Carolina Bank of South Carolina. The banks offer a wide variety of financial services to both the retail and business sectors of North and South Carolina. In 1994, the corporation acquired two insurance agencies in mergers including Sanford Real Estate, Loan & Insurance Company, which is a general insurance agency with three offices in North Carolina; and Executive Insurance Group, Inc., a general insurance agency in Charlotte, North Carolina. In 1994, the corporation also acquired the Bank of Iredell, headquartered in Statesville, North Carolina. **Corporate headquarters location:** This Location. **Listed on:** NASDAQ. **Number of employees nationwide:** 1,829.

WACHOVIA CORPORATION
WACHOVIA BANK OF NORTH CAROLINA
P.O. Box 3099, Winston-Salem NC 27150. 910/770-5195. **Fax:** 910/770-5226. **Contact:** Veronica C. Black, Senior Vice President. **Description:** Wachovia Bank of North Carolina operates commercial banks throughout the state. **Parent company:** Wachovia Corporation is a bank holding company with over 490 branches in North Carolina, Georgia, and South Carolina. The company engages in banking services including trust banking, credit card operations, deposit banking, and corporate banking. Nonbanking subsidiaries are involved in mortgage banking, brokerage services, and management information systems. **Common positions include:** Accountant/Auditor; Bank Officer/Manager; Computer Programmer; Computer Systems Analyst; Credit Manager; Management Trainee. **Educational backgrounds include:** Accounting; Business Administration; Computer Science; Economics; Finance. **Benefits:** Disability Coverage; Life Insurance; Medical Insurance; Pension Plan; Savings Plan; Tuition Assistance. **Corporate headquarters location:** This Location. **Other U.S. locations:** GA; SC. **Operations at this facility include:** Administration; Divisional

Headquarters; Regional Headquarters. **Listed on:** New York Stock Exchange. **Number of employees at this location:** 3,500. **Number of employees nationwide:** 16,000.

Note: Because addresses and telephone numbers of smaller companies change rapidly, we recommend you call each company to verify the information below before inquiring about job opportunities. Mass mailings are not recommended.

Additional employers with under 250 employees:

COMMERCIAL BANKS

BB&T
1617 E Broad St, Statesville
NC 28677-4303. 704/878-3680.

BB&T
625 Green Valley Rd,
Greensboro NC 27408-7721.
910/547-6775.

BB&T
6200 Falls of Neuse Rd,
Raleigh NC 27609-3563.
919/713-4335.

BB&T
2601 Wake Forest Rd,
Raleigh NC 27609-7837.
919/856-3100.

BB&T Center
2520 Sardis Rd N, Charlotte
NC 28227-6744. 704/847-9155.

Central Carolina Bank & Trust Co.
New Market Plaza-Hwy 150
S, Kernersville NC 27284.
910/996-8600.

Central Carolina Bank & Trust Co.
444 N Elm St, Greensboro
NC 27401-2142. 910/373-5000.

Central Carolina Bank & Trust Co.
230 S Tryon St, Suite 100,
Charlotte NC 28202-3215.
704/347-6181.

Centura Bank
1521 E 3rd St, Charlotte NC
28204-3200. 704/377-8923.

First National Bank of Shelby
106 S Lafayette St, Shelby
NC 28150. 704/484-6200.

First Union
6137 Hickory Grove Rd,
Charlotte NC 28215-4207.
704/383-8866.

NationsBank Commercial Corp.
101 N McDowell St, Suite
214, Charlotte NC 28204-2261. 704/375-7820.

NationsBank of North Carolina National Association
508 S Kings Dr, Charlotte
NC 28204-3044. 704/386-5386.

Piedmont Federal Savings & Loan Association
3501 Patterson Ave,
Winston-Salem NC 27105-3628. 910/770-1020.

Southtrust Bank
317 Oak Street, Spindale NC
28160. 704/286-3459.

United Carolina Bank
6659 Falls of Neuse Rd,
Raleigh NC 27615-6816.
919/571-6470.

Wachovia
201 S College St, Charlotte
NC 28244-0002. 704/347-1770.

Bank of Granite
707 College Ave SW, Lenoir
NC 28645-5405. 704/758-9181.

Bank of Granite Corp.
23 N Main St #128, Granite
Falls NC 28630-1401.
704/496-2000.

Branch Banking and Trust Company
6454 Shallowford Rd,
Lewisville NC 27023-9603.
910/945-3795.

Branch Banking and Trust Company
1120 Randolph St,
Thomasville NC 27360-5759. 910/475-7151.

Branch Banking and Trust Company
101 S Caswell St, La Grange
NC 28551-1707. 919/566-3175.

Centura Bank
2150 Country Club Rd, Suite
245, Winston-Salem NC
27104-4241. 910/631-5630.

Centura Bank
4 Palmer Street Cir, Franklin
NC 28734-3337. 704/524-8425.

East Carolina Bank
P.O. Box 337, Engelhard NC
27824-0337. 919/925-9411.

First American Federal Savings Bank
P.O. Box 26984, Greensboro
NC 27419-6984. 910/852-8410.

First Charter National Bank
22 Union St N, Concord NC
28025-4727. 704/786-3300.

First Citizens Bank & Trust Company
416 S Main St, Walnut Cove
NC 27052-8308. 910/591-7127.

First Citizens Bank & Trust Company
123 Grandville St, Windsor
NC 27983. 919/794-9103.

First Citizens Bank & Trust Company
206 Carthage St, Sanford
NC 27330-4205. 919/775-3501.

First Union National Bank North Carolina
300 N Greene St,
Greensboro NC 27401-2167.
910/378-4011.

First Union National Bank North Carolina
Highway 67-A, East Bend NC
27018. 910/699-3914.

High Point Bank Corp.
P.O. Box 2276, High Point
NC 27261-2276. 910/889-3300.

Home Federal Savings Bank
500 E Broad St, Statesville
NC 28677-5331. 704/873-4363.

Mid-South Bank & Trust Company
1750 US Highway 1 S,
Southern Pines NC 28387-7039. 910/692-6111.

NationsBank of North Carolina National Association
P.O. Box 46, Hertford NC
27944. 919/426-5723.

NationsBank of North Carolina National Association
2604 E Main St, Boger City NC 28092. 704/735-8009.

Pioneer Savings Bank
3532 Sunset Ave, Rocky Mount NC 27804-3408. 919/443-5048.

Robeson Savings Bank
301 S Main St, Red Springs NC 28377. 910/843-5171.

Southern National Bank North Carolina
1106 Sunset Ave, Clinton NC 28328. 910/592-9898.

United Carolina Bank
P.O. Box 479, Parkton NC 28371. 910/858-3916.

United Carolina Bank
185 W Morganton Rd, Southern Pines NC 28387-5915. 910/692-7283.

United Carolina Bank
113 Village Rd NE, Leland NC 28451-7413. 910/371-6474.

Wachovia Bank North Carolina National Association
804 Randolph St, Thomasville NC 27360-5715. 910/472-6710.

SAVINGS INSTITUTIONS

CK Federal Savings Bank
40 Cabarrus Ave E, Concord NC 28025-3452. 704/788-3193.

Clyde Savings Bank
Broadway & Woodlin, Asheville NC 28801. 704/254-8144.

Home Federal Savings & Loan Association
139 S Tryon St, Charlotte NC 28202. 704/373-0400.

Home Savings Bank
604 E Ehringhaus St, Elizabeth City NC 27909-4950. 919/335-0848.

Home Savings Bank
3208 Sunset Ave, Rocky Mount NC 27804-3505. 919/937-1863.

Home Savings Bank
115 S Mustian St, Kill Devil Hills NC 27948-8450. 919/480-1877.

Home Savings Bank
1725 S Glenburnie Rd, New Bern NC 28562-5208. 919/636-2997.

CREDIT UNIONS

AT&T Family Federal Credit Union
585 Waughtown St, Suite 2A, Winston-Salem NC 27107. 910/725-1955.

AT&T Family Federal Credit Union
1510 E Dixie Dr, Asheboro NC 27203-8893. 910/625-6500.

Marine Federal Credit Union
1101 Gum Branch Rd, Jacksonville NC 28540-5742. 910/577-7333.

State Employees Credit Union
633 Blowing Rock Rd, Boone NC 28607-4830. 704/264-0206.

Bricks Community Credit Union
RR 1, Box 153, Whitakers NC 27891-9605. 919/445-5710.

Cafe Credit Union
P.O. Box 19185, Charlotte NC 28219-9185. 704/391-4186.

Carlyle & Co. Credit Union
P.O. Box 21768, Greensboro NC 27420-1768. 910/294-2450.

Caswell Credit Union
P.O. Box 241, Yanceyville NC 27379-0241. 910/694-4661.

Citizen-Times Credit Union
P.O. Box 2386, Asheville NC 28802-2386. 704/252-5611.

Goldsboro Firemens Credit Union
204 S Center St, Goldsboro NC 27530-4805. 919/731-2742.

Jack Armstrong Credit Union
P.O. Box 887, Henderson NC 27536-0887. 919/492-1131.

MMC Credit Union
1305 Old Highway 70 W, Black Mountain NC 28711-2523. 704/669-6467.

Wellco Credit Union
131 N Pine St, Hazelwood NC 28738-2016. 704/456-5769.

OFFICES OF BANK HOLDING COMPANIES

American Bancshares
201 E Windsor St, Monroe NC 28112-4841. 704/283-2176.

Atlantic Community Bancorp
450 N Winstead Ave, Rocky Mount NC 27804-2229. 919/937-1900.

Southern Bancshares
121 E Main St #629, Mount Olive NC 28365-2112. 919/658-7000.

South Carolina

AGFIRST FARM CREDIT BANK
P.O. Box 1499, Columbia SC 29202. **Contact:** Beth Sears, Recruiter. **Description:** Agfirst Farm Credit Bank is an agricultural money lender. This bank lends money and offers services only for farmers. Agfirst Farm Credit Bank does not offer banking services to the general public. **Common positions include:** Accountant/Auditor; Computer Programmer; Systems Analyst. **Educational backgrounds include:** Accounting; Agricultural Science; Business Administration; Computer Science; Economics; Finance. **Benefits:** Dental Insurance; Disability Coverage; Life Insurance; Medical Insurance; Pension Plan; Thrift Plan. **Corporate headquarters location:** This Location. **Operations at this facility include:** Administration; Divisional Headquarters.

AMERICAN FEDERAL BANK FSB
P.O. Box 1268, Greenville SC 29602. 864/255-7000. **Contact:** John Hailley, Human Resources Manager. **Description:** A national commercial bank.

BRANCH BANKING & TRUST COMPANY OF SOUTH CAROLINA (BB&T)
P.O. Box 408, Greenville SC 29602. 864/458-2000. **Contact:** Mr. Pat Mitchell, Human Resources Department Manager. **Description:** A savings bank. Branch Banking

& Trust Company of South Carolina is a wholly-owned subsidiary of Southern National Corporation. A savings bank. Branch Banking & Trust Company is a wholly-owned subsidiary of Southern National Corporation. Branch Banking & Trust Company of South Carolina operates 110 branch offices in 51 cities in South Carolina. **Common positions include:** Accountant/Auditor; Bank Officer/Manager; Computer Programmer; Customer Service Representative; Department Manager; Financial Analyst; Underwriter/Assistant Underwriter. **Educational backgrounds include:** Accounting; Finance; Mathematics. **Benefits:** Dental Insurance; Disability Coverage; Life Insurance; Medical Insurance; Pension Plan; Tuition Assistance. **Special Programs:** Training Programs. **Corporate headquarters location:** This Location. **Parent company:** BB&T Southern National Corporation (Winston-Salem) is a holding company formed by the 1994 merger of Southern National Corporation (a multibank and savings and loan holding company with seven bank subsidiaries performing commercial and mortgage banking and insurance services) and Branch Banking & Trust Financial Corporation. Its subsidiaries form a network of hundreds of branches in cities and communities across the Carolinas and Virginia. Other subsidiaries of BB&T-Southern National Corporation include: BB&T-Southern National Bank of South Carolina; Branch Banking & Trust (BB&T-NC); Lexington State Bank; Community Bank of South Carolina; BB&T-Southern National Bank Savings Bank, Inc.; and Commerce Bank of Virginia Beach. **Operations at this facility include:** Administration; Divisional Headquarters; Regional Headquarters. **Listed on:** New York Stock Exchange.

COMMUNITY BANKSHARES, INC.
1820 Columbia Road NE, P.O. Box 2166, Orangeburg SC 29115. 803/535-1060. **Contact:** Human Resources. **Description:** Community Bankshares, Inc. is a one bank holding company. The company began operations in 1993 when it acquired Orangeburg National Bank as a wholly-owned subsidiary. Orangeburg National Bank offers a full array of commercial banking services. Deposit services include business and personal checking accounts, NOW accounts, savings accounts, money market accounts, various term certificates of deposit, IRA accounts, and other deposit services. The bank also offers loans for commercial and consumer purposes. Other services include safe deposit boxes, VISA and Master Card charge cards, tax deposits, bonds, and automated tellers. **Corporate headquarters location:** This Location. **Number of employees at this location:** 34.

FIRST CITIZENS BANCORPORATION OF SOUTH CAROLINA, INC.
P.O. Box 29, Columbia SC 29202. 803/771-8700. **Contact:** Human Resources. **Description:** First Citizens Bancorporation of South Carolina, Inc. is a bank holding company with statewide subsidiaries engaged in commercial banking, credit card services, and mortgage banking. **Corporate headquarters location:** This Location. **Subsidiaries include:** First Citizens Bank & Trust Company of South Carolina; First Citizens Mortgage Corporation; and Waters Enterprises, Inc. **Number of employees nationwide:** 1,000.

FIRST FINANCIAL HOLDINGS, INC.
P.O. Box 118068, Charleston SC 29423-8068. 803/529-5800. **Contact:** Mr. Jerry Gazes, Human Resources Manager. **Description:** First Financial Holdings, Inc. is a multiple thrift holding company serving retail banking markets. Until 1992, First Federal Savings and Loan Association of Charleston, acquired in 1988, was its only subsidiary. In October 1992, First Financial Holdings, Inc. acquired Peoples Federal Savings and Loan Association in Conway, SC as a second subsidiary. **Corporate headquarters location:** This Location. **Listed on:** NASDAQ. **Number of employees at this location:** 564.

FIRST NATIONAL CORPORATION
P.O. Box 1287, Orangeburg SC 29116-1287. 803/534-2175. **Contact:** Allen Hay, Human Resources Manager. **Description:** First National Corporation is a bank holding company whose subsidiaries perform commercial banking operations and provide other financial services. The company's primary wholly-owned subsidiary is First National Bank. In 1992, First National Corporation acquired Santee Cooper State Bank. **Corporate headquarters location:** This Location. **Number of employees at this location:** 256.

FIRST UNION NATIONAL BANK OF SOUTH CAROLINA
P.O. Box 1329, Greenville SC 29602. 864/255-8000. **Contact:** Julie Sizer, Human Resources Manager. **E-mail address:** comments@firstunion.com. **World Wide Web Address:** http://www.firstunion.com/. **Description:** A full-service commercial bank providing corporate and consumer services. First Union National Bank of South Carolina operates 66 offices. **Corporate headquarters location:** This Location. **Parent company:** First Union Corporation (Charlotte, NC) is one of the nation's largest bank

holding companies. First Union Corporation's subsidiaries operate over 1,330 full-service bank branches in the South Atlantic states. These subsidiaries provide retail banking, retail investment, and commercial banking services. The corporation provides other financial services including mortgage banking, home equity lending, leasing, and insurance and securities brokerage services from 222 branch locations. The corporation also operates one of the nation's largest ATM networks. **Listed on:** New York Stock Exchange. **Number of employees nationwide:** 31,858.

WACHOVIA BANK OF SOUTH CAROLINA

101 Greystone Boulevard, Columbia SC 29226. 803/765-3000. **Contact:** Jeff Scott, Personnel Director. **Description:** Wachovia Bank of South Carolina operates commercial banks throughout the state. The parent company, Wachovia Corporation, is a bank holding company with subsidiaries including Wachovia Bank of North Carolina and Wachovia Bank of Georgia. Wachovia Corporation operates over 490 branches in the three southeastern states. The company engages in banking services including trust banking, credit card operations, deposit banking, and corporate banking. Nonbanking subsidiaries are involved in mortgage banking, brokerage services, and management information systems. **Corporate headquarters location:** This Location. **Other U.S. locations:** Statewide. **Parent company:** Wachovia Corporation (Winston-Salem, NC). **Listed on:** New York Stock Exchange. **Number of employees nationwide:** 16,000.

Note: Because addresses and telephone numbers of smaller companies change rapidly, we recommend you call each company to verify the information below before inquiring about job opportunities. Mass mailings are not recommended.

Additional employers with under 250 employees:

COMMERCIAL BANKS

First Piedmont Federal
1516 Reidville Rd,
Spartanburg SC 29301-3837. 864/576-4466.

Palmetto Federal Savings Bank SC
432 West Ave, North Augusta SC 29841-3620. 803/279-6250.

Peoples Federal Savings & Loan
4242 Main St, Loris SC 29569. 803/756-1000.

Lexington State Bank
126 E Main St, Lexington SC 29072-3461. 803/359-5111.

Carolina Bank & Trust Co.
P.O. Box 326, Lamar SC 29069-0326. 803/393-5472.

Carolina First Savings FSB
South Morgan Ave, Andrews SC 29510. 803/264-5833.

Coastal Federal Savings Bank
310 Hwy 378, Conway SC 29526. 803/248-6336.

Coastal Federal Savings Bank
112 Hwy 17 S & Glens Bay Rd, Surfside Beach SC 29575. 803/238-1671.

Cooper River Federal Savings Association
3356 Rivers Ave, Charleston SC 29405-7725. 803/572-4600.

First Palmetto Savings Bank
2480 Main St, Elgin SC 29045-8999. 803/438-6236.

First Palmetto Savings Bank
206 Cashua St, Darlington SC 29532-3302. 803/393-4051.

First Palmetto Savings Bank
101 Hampton St, Kershaw SC 29067. 803/475-2370.

First Palmetto Savings Bank
P.O. Box 148, Winnsboro SC 29180-0148. 803/635-5589.

First Palmetto Savings Bank
618 N Main St, Marion SC 29571-3034. 803/423-3400.

NationsBank of SC
1325 Saint Matthews Rd NE, Orangeburg SC 29115-3421. 803/531-3446.

NationsBank of SC
7420 Rivers Ave, N Charleston SC 29406-4659. 803/720-2244.

NationsBank of SC
2411 Oak St, Myrtle Beach SC 29577. 803/946-3209.

NationsBank of SC
301 N Main St, Anderson SC 29621. 864/260-5500.

National Bank of SC
501 Dekalb St, Camden SC 29020-4313. 803/929-2070.

Southern National
1900 Assembly St, Columbia SC 29201-2404. 803/748-7100.

The First Savings Bank
P.O. Box 672, Clemson SC 29633-0672. 864/654-5574.

First Citizens Bank & Trust
500 Main St, Elgin SC 29045. 803/733-3610.

First Federal Savings & Loan Association
1025 Church St, Georgetown SC 29440-3513. 803/546-8500.

First Federal Savings & Loan Association
822 Coleman Blvd, Mount Pleasant SC 29464-4036. 803/884-8526.

First Federal Savings & Loan Association
1960 Old Trolley Rd, Summerville SC 29485-8207. 803/875-2260.

SAVINGS INSTITUTIONS

Cooper River Federal
136 St James Av, Charleston SC 29412. 803/553-1519.

Heritage Federal Savings & Loan Association
81 N Greenwood Ave, Ware Shoals SC 29692-1227. 864/456-7471.

Palmetto Federal Savings Bank SC
Jacob Smart Blvd, Ridgeland SC 29936. 803/726-8186.

Peoples Federal Savings & Loan Association
P.O. Box 1740, Conway SC 29526-1740. 803/248-7550.

CREDIT UNIONS

SRP Federal Credit Union
1913 Ellenton St, Barnwell SC 29812-1424. 803/259-2781.

Federal Credit Union Dentsville
7227 Parklane Rd, Columbia SC 29223-7653. 803/736-3110.

Darlington County Teacher Credit Union
P.O. Box 820, Darlington SC 29532-0820. 803/393-2580.

Pepto Makers Credit Union
P.O. Box 2468, Greenville SC 29602-2468. 864/277-7110.

OFFICES OF BANK HOLDING COMPANIES

Anchor Financial Corp.
2002 Oak St, Myrtle Beach SC 29577-3145. 803/448-1411.

CNB Corp.
1400 3rd Ave #820, Conway SC 29526-5004. 803/248-5721.

Coastal Financial Corp.
2619 Oak St, Myrtle Beach SC 29577-3129. 803/448-5151.

For more information on career opportunities in the banking/savings and loans industry:

Associations

AMERICA'S COMMUNITY BANKERS
900 19th Street NW, Suite 400, Washington DC 20006. 202/857-3100. A trade association representing the expanded thrift industry. Members are institutions (not individuals).

AMERICAN BANKERS ASSOCIATION
1120 Connecticut Avenue NW, Washington DC 20036. 202/663-5221. Provides banking education and training services, sponsors industry programs and conventions, and publishes articles, newsletters, and the ABA Service Member Directory.

Directories

AMERICAN BANK DIRECTORY
Thomson Financial Publications, 6195 Crooked Creek Road, Norcross GA 30092. 770/448-1011.

AMERICAN SAVINGS DIRECTORY
McFadden Business Publications, 6195 Crooked Creek Road, Norcross GA 30092. 770/448-1011.

BUSINESS WEEK/TOP 200 BANKING INSTITUTIONS ISSUE
McGraw-Hill, Inc., 1221 Avenue of the Americas, 39th Floor, New York NY 10020. 212/512-4776.

MOODY'S BANK AND FINANCE MANUAL
Moody's Investors Service, Inc., 99 Church Street, First Floor, New York NY 10007. 212/553-0300.

POLK'S BANK DIRECTORY
R.L. Polk & Co., P.O. Box 305100, Nashville TN 37320-5100. 615/889-3350.

RANKING THE BANKS/THE TOP NUMBERS
American Banker, Inc., 1 State Street Plaza, New York NY 10004. 212/943-6700.

Magazines

ABA BANKING JOURNAL
American Bankers Association, 1120 Connecticut Avenue NW, Washington DC 20036. 202/663-5221.

BANK ADMINISTRATION
1 North Franklin, Chicago IL 60606. 800/323-8552.

BANKERS MAGAZINE
Warren, Gorham & Lamont, Park Square Building, 31 St. James Avenue, Boston MA 02116-4112. 617/423-2020.

JOURNAL OF COMMERCIAL BANK LENDING
Robert Morris Associates, P.O. Box 8500 S-1140, Philadelphia PA 19178. 215/851-9100.

BIOTECHNOLOGY, PHARMACEUTICALS, AND SCIENTIFIC R&D

During the early '90s, the pharmaceutical industry was characterized by a mass of mergers and acquisitions, with drug companies concentrating on cutting costs to boost profit margins.

While more mergers may be on the way, most of the big staff cuts are history, and profitability is up. Even so, industry watchers don't expect the arrival of many big-selling new products in the near future, and many companies have slashed research and development budgets. According to the Pharmaceutical Research and Manufacturers of America, the 8 percent growth in R&D spending was the lowest in 20 years.

As more drug patents continue to expire, the impact will be felt by large pharmaceutical companies. There will be a negative impact on their sales growth. Conversely, the expired patents mean more opportunities for generic drug manufacturers, who should continue to gain market share through 1996.

North Carolina

AJINOMOTO USA INC.
4020 Ajinomoto Drive, Raleigh NC 27610. 919/231-0100. **Contact:** Stewart Adams, Personnel Administrator. **Description:** Produces amino acids using a high-tech fermentation process. Ajinomoto USA Inc.'s final product is sold to pharmaceutical companies for nutritional additives in intravenous solutions. The company also provides amino acids used in the health food market. **Common positions include:** Biological Scientist/Biochemist; Blue-Collar Worker Supervisor; Chemical Engineer; Chemist; Department Manager; Engineering Technician; Laboratory Technician; Microbiologist; Production Technician; Quality Control Supervisor. **Educational backgrounds include:** Biology; Chemistry; Engineering; Microbiology; Pharmacology. **Benefits:** Dental Insurance; Disability Coverage; Life Insurance; Medical Insurance; Pension Plan; Tuition Assistance. **Corporate headquarters location:** Tokyo, Japan.

BRISTOL-MYERS SQUIBB COMPANY
9707 Chapel Hill Road, P.O. Box 300, Morrisville NC 27560. 919/319-7800. **Contact:** Human Resources. **Description:** Bristol-Myers Squibb is a manufacturer of pharmaceuticals, medical devices, nonprescription drugs, and toiletries and beauty aids. The company's pharmaceutical products include cardiovasculars, anti-infectives, anti-cancer agents, AIDS therapy treatments, central nervous system drugs, diagnostic agents, and other drugs. Its line of nonprescription products includes formulas, vitamins, analgesics, remedies, and skin care products sold under brand names Bufferin, Excedrin, Nuprin, and Comtrex. Beauty aids include Clairol and Ultress hair care, Nice n' Easy and Clairesse hair colorings, hair sprays, gels, and deodorants. **Listed on:** New York Stock Exchange.

CHEMICAL INDUSTRY INSTITUTE OF TOXICOLOGY (CIIT)
P.O. Box 12137, Research Triangle Park NC 27709. 919/558-1200. **Contact:** Beth Royals, Personnel Director. **Description:** Chemical Industry Institute of Toxicology is an independent, nonprofit research corporation dedicated to the scientific, objective study of toxicological issues involved in the manufacture, handling, use, and disposal of commodity chemicals, and to the training of toxicologists. **Common positions include:** Research Scientist. **Educational backgrounds include:** Ph.D.; Toxicology. **Benefits:** Medical Insurance.

EMBREX INC.
1035 Swabia Court, P.O. Box 13989, Research Triangle Park NC 27703. 919/941-5185. **Fax:** 919/941-5186. **Contact:** Helen Makarczyk, Human Resources. **Description:** Embrex, Inc. develops and commercializes the "in ovo" (in the egg)

automated egg injection system, which eliminates the need for manual vaccination of newly hatched broiler chicks. Its patented INOVOJECT system inoculates 100 percent of chicks three days prior to hatch versus the post-hatch manual injection method. This controlled, sanitized injection system inoculates 20,000 to 30,000 chicks per hour. The company's product line and research also include viral neutralizing factors, immunomodulators, gene vaccines, and performance enhancement products which alters bird physiology for early delivery. **Corporate headquarters location:** This Location. **Listed on:** NASDAQ. **Number of employees nationwide:** 100.

GLAXO WELLCOME INC.
5 Moore Drive, Research Triangle Park NC 27709. 919/248-2100. **Recorded Jobline:** 919/315-8347. **Contact:** Steve Sons, Director of Human Resources Operations. **Description:** A pharmaceutical preparations company which develops AZT, an AIDS treatment drug. **Common positions include:** Accountant/Auditor; Biological Scientist/Biochemist; Chemist; Clinical Lab Technician; Computer Programmer; Computer Systems Analyst; Data Processor; Pharmacist; Research Scientist. **Educational backgrounds include:** Biology; Chemistry; Computer Science. **Benefits:** 401K; Daycare Assistance; Dental Insurance; Disability Coverage; Employee Discounts; Life Insurance; Medical Insurance; Pension Plan; Profit Sharing; Savings Plan; Tuition Assistance. **Special Programs:** Internships. **Other U.S. locations:** Greenville NC. **Operations at this facility include:** Administration; Research and Development. **Listed on:** New York Stock Exchange.

MALLINCKRODT CHEMICAL, INC.
8801 Capital Boulevard, P.O. Box 17627, Raleigh NC 27619. 919/878-2800. **Contact:** Glen Pritchett, Personnel Supervisor. **Description:** Mallinckrodt Chemical is a producer of pharmaceutical and specialty industrial chemicals. It is also a joint venture partner in a worldwide flavors business. The company is the world's largest producer of acetominophen and a major producer of medicinal narcotics and laboratory chemicals. **Parent company:** Mallinckrodt Group Inc. is a provider of specialty chemicals and human and animal health products worldwide through Mallinckrodt Chemical and two other technology-based businesses: Mallinckrodt Medical, Inc., and Mallinckrodt Veterinary, Inc. Mallinckrodt Medical is a provider of technologically advanced, cost effective products and services to five medical specialties: anesthesiology, cardiology, critical care, nuclear medicine, and radiology. The company has a leadership position in many global markets. Mallinckrodt Veterinary is one of the world's leading animal health and nutrition companies, with approximately 1,000 products sold in more than 100 countries. Products include pharmaceuticals, livestock and pet vaccines, pesticides, surgical supplies, anesthetics and mineral feed ingredients. Headquartered in St. Louis, Missouri, Mallinckrodt Group has 10,300 employees worldwide.

MERCK & COMPANY, INC.
4633 Merck Road, Wilson NC 27893. 919/243-2011. **Contact:** Ms. Gaye Newton, Personnel Director. **Description:** Merck is a worldwide organization engaged primarily in the business of discovering, developing, producing, and marketing products for the maintenance of health and the environment. Products include human and animal pharmaceuticals and chemicals sold to the health care, oil exploration, food processing, textile, paper, and other industries. The company has joint ventures with Johnson & Johnson, DuPont, and AB Astra. Merck also runs an ethical drug mail order marketing business. **Corporate headquarters location:** Whitehouse Station NJ. **Listed on:** New York Stock Exchange.

RESEARCH TRIANGLE INSTITUTE (RTI)
P.O. Box 12194, Research Triangle Park NC 27709. 919/541-6200. **Fax:** 919/541-7004. **Contact:** Gerard Collins, Human Resources. **World Wide Web Address:** crm@rti.org. **Description:** A nonprofit independent research organization involved in many scientific fields, under contract to business, industry, federal, state, and local governments, industrial associations, and public service agencies. The institute was created as a separately-operated entity by the joint action of North Carolina State University, Duke University, and the University of North Carolina at Chapel Hill, however, close ties are maintained with the universities' scientists, both through the active research community of the Research Triangle region and through collaborative research for government and industry clients. RTI responds to national priorities in health, the environment, advanced technology, and social policy with contract research for the U.S. government including applications in statistics, social sciences, chemistry, life sciences, environmental sciences, engineering, and electronics. In conducting research and development, the institute applies the knowledge, experience, and technology created in its government-funded research. The institute operates a 180-acre campus in the center of Research Triangle Park, which includes

laboratory and office facilities for all technical programs. In addition, fully-staffed research facilities are maintained at sites in Florida, Virginia, and Washington, DC. **Common positions include:** Biological Scientist/Biochemist; Biomedical Engineer; Chemical Engineer; Chemist; Computer Programmer; Economist/Market Research Analyst; Electrical/Electronics Engineer; Geologist/Geophysicist; Human Resources Specialist; Statistician; Systems Analyst. **Educational backgrounds include:** Biology; Chemistry; Computer Science; Engineering; Mathematics. **Benefits:** Daycare Assistance; Dental Insurance; Disability Coverage; Life Insurance; Medical Insurance; Pension Plan; Tuition Assistance. **Corporate headquarters location:** This Location. **Other U.S. locations:** Washington DC; Cocoa Beach FL; Hampton VA. **Operations at this facility include:** Administration; Research and Development. **Number of employees nationwide:** 1,500.

RHONE, POULENC & COMPANY
Two T.W. Alexander Drive, P.O. Box 12014, Durham NC 27709. 919/549-2000. **Contact:** Fred Sefcovic, Human Resources Director. **Description:** A commercial, physical, and biological research firm. **Number of employees at this location:** 500.

ROCHE BIOMEDICAL LABORATORIES, INC.
P.O. Box 2230, Burlington NC 27215. 910/229-1127. **Contact:** Natalie Pierce, National Staffing Specialist. **Description:** Corporate headquarters for a number of medical laboratories. **Common positions include:** Biological Scientist/Biochemist; Chemist; Manufacturer's/Wholesaler's Sales Rep.; Technician. **Educational backgrounds include:** Biology; Chemistry; Medical Technology; Sales. **Benefits:** Dental Insurance; Disability Coverage; Life Insurance; Medical Insurance; Pension Plan; Savings Plan; Tuition Assistance. **Special Programs:** Internships; Training Programs. **Corporate headquarters location:** This Location. **Parent company:** Hoffman-LaRoche. **Operations at this facility include:** Administration; Regional Headquarters; Research and Development; Sales; Service. **Number of employees nationwide:** 9,108.

Note: Because addresses and telephone numbers of smaller companies change rapidly, we recommend you call each company to verify the information below before inquiring about job opportunities. Mass mailings are not recommended.

Additional employers with under 250 employees:

PHARMACEUTICAL PREPARATIONS

Barre-National Inc.
1877 Kawai Rd, Lincolnton NC 28092-5905. 704/735-5700.

Chelsea Labs
2021 E Roosevelt Blvd, Monroe NC 28112-4133. 704/289-5531.

Clinipad Corp.
7101 McFarlane Blvd, Charlotte NC 28262-3363. 704/596-1522.

Lederle-Praxis Biologicals
4300 Oak Park Rd, Sanford NC 27330-9550. 919/775-7100.

Pharmacia Inc.
P.O. Box 597, Clayton NC 27520-0597. 919/553-3831.

ID Russell Co.
Hwy 74, Marshville NC 28103. 704/624-6635.

Strickland Distributors
2121 S Jefferson Davis Hwy, Sanford NC 27330-8912. 919/776-8600.

BIOLOGICAL PRODUCTS

Greer Laboratories Inc.
639 Nuway Cir NE, Lenoir NC 28645-3647. 704/754-5327.

DRUGS, DRUG PROPRIETARIES, AND DRUGGISTS' SUNDRIES

North Carolina Mutual Wholesale Drug
816 Ellis Rd, Durham NC 27703-6019. 919/596-2151.

MEDICAL AND DENTAL LABORATORIES

Medical Center Diagnostic Imaging
624 Quaker Ln, Suite 104C, High Point NC 27262-3832. 910/887-2609.

National Health Labs Inc.
1301 Medical Dr, Fayetteville NC 28304-4425. 910/484-6770.

National Health Labs Inc.
529 Brookdale Dr, Statesville NC 28677-4107. 704/878-0948.

Neil Diagnostic
301 J J Dr, Greensboro NC 27406. 910/370-1137.

Roche Biomedical Labs
Chestnut St, Weaverville NC 28787. 704/689-2426.

Roche Biomedical Labs
226 Ashville Ave, Suite 10, Cary NC 27511-6660. 919/233-0787.

Roche Biomedical Labs
8430 University Executive Park, Charlotte NC 28262. 704/549-8647.

Roche Biomedical Labs
445K Western Blvd, Jacksonville NC 28546-6870. 910/455-1080.

Roche Biomedical Labs
750 Hartness Rd, Statesville NC 28677. 704/878-0092.

Smithkline Beecham Clinic Labs
3325 Executive Dr, Suite 220, Raleigh NC 27609-7449. 919/872-0185.

Associated Laboratories
425 SW Conover Blvd, Conover NC 28613. 704/464-3070.

South Carolina

CORNING CLINICAL LABS
1843 Ashley River Road, Suite B, Charleston SC 29407. 803/763-1380. **Contact:** Human Resources. **Description:** A medical lab that primarily draws blood.

PERRIGO COMPANY
4615 Dairy Drive, Greenville SC 29607. 864/288-5521. **Contact:** Jimmie Fannell, Personnel Manager. **Description:** Manufactures and sells pharmaceuticals, vitamins, and personal care products for the store brand market, nationally and internationally. **Benefits:** 401K; Dental Insurance; Disability Coverage; Employee Discounts; Life Insurance; Medical Insurance; Profit Sharing; Savings Plan; Tuition Assistance. **Corporate headquarters location:** Allegan MI. **Listed on:** NASDAQ. **Number of employees nationwide:** 3,171.

ROCHE BIOMEDICAL LABORATORIES
874 North Church Street, Spartanburg SC 29303. 864/582-8551. **Contact:** Human Resources. **Description:** A medical laboratory.

SMITHKLINE BEECHAM CORPORATION
65 Windham Boulevard, Aiken SC 29801. 803/649-3471. **Contact:** Human Resources Manager. **Description:** A health care company engaged in the research, development, manufacture, and marketing of ethical pharmaceuticals, animal health products, ethical and proprietary medicines, and ethical and proprietary eye care products. The company's principal divisions include SmithKline Beecham Pharmaceuticals, SmithKline Beecham Animal Health, SmithKline Beecham Consumer Healthcare, and SmithKline Beecham Clinical Laboratories. The company is also engaged in many other aspects of the health care field, including the production of medical instruments and electronic instruments used in the health care field. SmithKline Beecham manufactures proprietary medicines through its subsidiary, Menley & James Laboratories (same address), including such nationally known products as Contac Cold Capsules, Sine-Off sinus medicine, Love cosmetics, and Sea & Ski outdoor products. **Corporate headquarters location:** Philadelphia PA. **Number of employees nationwide:** 20,000.

For more information on career opportunities in biotechnology, pharmaceuticals, and scientific R&D:

Associations

AMERICAN ASSOCIATION FOR CLINICAL CHEMISTRY
2101 L Street NW, Suite 202, Washington DC 20037-1526. 202/857-0717 or 800/892-1400. International scientific/medical society of individuals involved with clinical chemistry and other clinical labscience-related disciplines.

AMERICAN ASSOCIATION OF COLLEGES OF PHARMACY
1426 Prince Street, Alexandria VA 22314-2841. 703/739-2330. An organization composed of all U.S. pharmacy colleges and over 2,000 school administrators and faculty members. Career publications include: *Shall I Study Pharmacy?*, *Pharmacy: A Caring Profession*, and *A Graduate Degree in the Pharmaceutical Sciences: An Option For You?*

AMERICAN COLLEGE OF CLINICAL PHARMACY (ACCP)
3101 Broadway, Suite 380, Kansas City MO 64111. 816/531-2177. Operates ClinNet jobline at 412/648-7893 for both members and nonmembers, for a fee.

AMERICAN PHARMACEUTICAL ASSOCIATION
2215 Constitution Avenue NW, Washington DC 20037. 202/628-4410. Operates a resume referral service for all members.

AMERICAN SOCIETY FOR BIOCHEMISTRY AND MOLECULAR BIOLOGY
9650 Rockville Pike, Bethesda MD 20814-3996. 301/530-7145. A nonprofit scientific and educational organization whose primary scientific activities are in the publication of the *Journal of Biological Chemistry* and holding an annual scientific meeting. Also publishes a career brochure entitled *Unlocking Life's Secrets: Biochemistry and Molecular Biology*.

AMERICAN SOCIETY OF HEALTH SYSTEM PHARMACISTS
7272 Wisconsin Avenue, Bethesda MD 20814. 301/657-3000. Provides pharmaceutical education. Updates pharmacies on current medical developments. Offers a service for jobseekers for a fee.

BIOMEDICAL RESEARCH INSTITUTE
355 K Street, Chula Vista CA 91911-1209. 619/427-9940. Fax: 619/427-2634. A nonprofit organization which promotes scientific research and education and provides annual scholarships to students. Maintains a national Institutional Review Board.

BIOTECHNOLOGY INDUSTRY ORGANIZATION
1625 K Street NW, Suite 1100, Washington DC 20006-1604. 202/857-0244. Fax: 202/857-0237. Represents

agriculture, biomedical, diagnostic, food, energy, and environmental companies.

NATIONAL PHARMACEUTICAL COUNCIL
1894 Preston White Drive, Reston VA 22091. 703/620-6390. Fax: 703/476-0904. An organization of research-based pharmaceutical companies. Fax requests to the attention of Pat Adams, Vice President of Finance and Administration.

Directories

DRUG TOPICS RED BOOK
Medical Economics Company, 5 Paragon Drive, Montvale, NJ 07645. 201/358-7200.

Magazines

DRUG TOPICS
Medical Economics Company, 5 Paragon Drive, Montvale NJ 07645. 201/358-7200.

PHARMACEUTICAL ENGINEERING
International Society of Pharmaceutical Engineers, 3816 West Linebaugh Avenue, Suite 412, Tampa FL 33624. 813/960-2105.

BUSINESS SERVICES AND NON-SCIENTIFIC RESEARCH

 *The business services sector, which includes 16 of the 20 fastest growing industries, covers a broad spectrum of careers, including everything from adjustment and collection services to data processing companies. While the job outlook varies upon which service is being discussed, in general, the business services sector is among the fastest-growing in the nation. Increasingly, American companies are "outsourcing" functions like data processing to outside firms. Often large organizations will go so far as to hand over the management of their entire data center to an outside service provider. This trend is expected to boost opportunities for those who work for data processing services.*

Other types of services that benefit from this trend include security firms and personnel services firms. Many businesses are using temporary workers instead of hiring new permanent staffers, thus avoiding the much higher overhead costs such as health insurance. Companies that supply these temporary workers, as well as those that place permanent workers, are among the fastest-growing in the nation. While one-third of the jobs available are administrative support occupations, there is a growing trend toward specialization which will open up more positions for highly skilled workers, such as engineers or managers.

North Carolina

A CLEANER WORLD
611 North Main Street, Kernersville NC 27284. 910/996-3896. **Contact:** Joe Flores, Store Manager. **Description:** A Cleaner World offers garment pressing services.

BURNS INTERNATIONAL SECURITY
4000G Spring Garden Street, Greensboro NC 27407. 910/292-9825. **Contact:** Larry Holder, Manager. **Description:** Offers a wide range of protective services and contract security guard programs to businesses and government. Burns International Security Services also provides electronic security systems and security planning consultation. **Listed on:** New York Stock Exchange. **Number of employees nationwide:** 20,000.

W.F. ISLEY & COMPANY
322 East Lindsay, Greensboro NC 27401. 910/272-5519. **Contact:** Human Resources. **Description:** W.F. Isley & Company sharpens paper cutting blades and knives for printing presses.

ORKIN LAWN CARE
5031 West Harris Boulevard, Charlotte NC 28213. 704/596-8878. **Contact:** Human Resources. **Description:** Orkin Lawn Care offers landscape and tree services.

PRIME EQUIPMENT
P.O. Box 36217, Charlotte NC 28236. 704/332-5171. **Fax:** 704/335-1138. **Contact:** Jim Stroupe, Branch Manager. **Description:** Engaged in equipment rental and sale to the industrial and construction industries. **Common positions include:** Sales Associate; Sales Representative. **Educational backgrounds include:** Business Administration. **Benefits:** 401K; Dental Insurance; Life Insurance; Medical Insurance; Pension Plan; Profit Sharing; Savings Plan. **Corporate headquarters location:** Houston TX. **Parent company:** Investcorp International, Inc. **Operations at this facility include:** Sales; Service. **Listed on:** Privately held. **Number of employees at this location:** 18. **Number of employees nationwide:** 1,200.

SHORES DRY CLEANERS
804 Westchester Drive, High Point NC 27262. 910/886-4009. **Contact:** Allan Peatrous, Manager. **Description:** Shores Dry Cleaners offers garment pressing services.

TEXTILEASE CORPORATION
4700 Dwight Evans Road, Charlotte NC 28217. 704/523-9593. **Contact:** Laurie Howard, Office Manager. **Description:** Textilease Corporation offers laundry rental, including uniforms, and cleaning services to the hotel and restaurant industry.

Note: Because addresses and telephone numbers of smaller companies change rapidly, we recommend you call each company to verify the information below before inquiring about job opportunities. Mass mailings are not recommended.

Additional employers with under 250 employees:

LINEN SUPPLY

Business Linen Supply
702 E 5th St, Lumberton NC 28358-5812. 910/739-2732.

National Linen & Uniform Service
365 Dalton Ave, Charlotte NC 28206-3117. 704/332-8156.

Rus of Burlington
840 Trollingwood Hawfields Rd, Mebane NC 27302-8170. 910/578-1491.

Unifirst
1901 Equitable Pl, Charlotte NC 28213-6535. 704/597-1970.

ADJUSTMENT AND COLLECTION SERVICES

Assetcare
2 Centerview Dr, Greensboro NC 27407-3708. 910/299-9720.

JRT Services
350 Henderson Dr #A, Jacksonville NC 28540-5606. 910/938-1899.

Milliken and Michaels
1126 Blowing Rock Rd, Boone NC 28607. 704/264-0454.

Credit Bureau Systems
100 W Morgan St, Durham NC 27701-. 919/683-1055.

PHOTOCOPYING AND DUPLICATING SERVICES

McRae Graphics
3101 Stoneybrook Dr, Suite 124, Raleigh NC 27604-3786. 919/790-0525.

CLEANING AND MAINTENANCE SERVICES

Clegg's Termite & Pest Control Inc.
2401 Reichard St, Durham NC 27705-. 919/968-8304.

Clegg's Termite & Pest Control Inc.
4205 Stuart Andrew Blvd, Suite F, Charlotte NC 28217-1584. 704/529-6388.

Cleggs Termite & Pest Control Inc.
101 Woodwinds Industrial Ct, Cary NC 27511-6203. 919/469-9975.

Cleggs Termite & Pest Control Inc.
3322 Neuse Blvd, New Bern NC 28560-4110. 919/636-2345.

Dodson Brothers Exterminating
8307 University Exec Park Dr, Charlotte NC 28262-3358. 704/548-8883.

Dodson Brothers Exterminating
P.O. Box 18525, Charlotte NC 28218-0525. 704/375-2581.

Orkin Exterminating Co.
107 Bonita Dr, Greensboro NC 27405-7601. 910/275-3314.

Orkin Exterminating Co.
609 Mercury St, Raleigh NC 27603-2343. 919/828-3221.

Prism
2008 Gateway Blvd, Charlotte NC 28208-2734. 704/392-2995.

Sears Authorized Termite & Pest Control
4324 Barringer Dr, Suite 108, Charlotte NC 28217-1500. 704/522-8585.

Smith Exterminating Co.
5507 Hillsborough St, Raleigh NC 27606-1535. 919/851-0220.

Steritech Pest Elimination
830 Tyvola Rd, Charlotte NC 28217-3537. 704/527-0089.

Terminix Termite & Pest Control
3313 US Highway 64 E, Asheboro NC 27203-8457. 910/629-7887.

Terminix Termite & Pest Control
1609 S York Rd, Gastonia NC 28052-6159. 704/867-6364.

Terminix Termite & Pest Control
6020 Oak Forest Dr, Raleigh NC 27604-1802. 919/790-0995.

Terminix Termite & Pest Control
208 W 3rd St, Washington NC 27889-4904. 919/946-1582.

Tilley Pest Control Service
2915 Pink Hill Rd, Kinston NC 28501-6265. 919/527-3749.

Wilson Pest Control Co.
521 W Kings Hwy, Eden NC 27288-4962. 910/627-4221.

Wilson Pest Control Co.
401 W End Blvd, Winston-Salem NC 27101-1120. 910/722-1193.

All-Star Maintenance
3614 Ashley Cir, Wilmington NC 28403-2608. 910/452-0508.

Timmons Janitorial
648 S Peace Haven Rd, Winston-Salem NC 27103-7038. 910/768-2087.

Extra Touch House Cleaning
7604 Ladden Ct, Raleigh NC 27615-5013. 919/846-9664.

Hazel Company
1950 S College Ave, Charlotte NC 28203. 704/342-9600.

Magicbroom Maintenance Service
7510 Wellesley Park S, Raleigh NC 27615-5713. 919/870-1880.

Southern Building Maintenance Co. Inc.
1520 Brookside Dr, Raleigh NC 27604-2058. 919/828-5400.

BC Maintenance
3607 Calvin St, Greensboro NC 27405. 910/282-9746.

MISC. EQUIPMENT RENTAL AND LEASING

JW Burress Inc.
6511 Statesville Rd, Charlotte NC 28269-1763. 704/597-0500.

COMPUTER PROCESSING AND DATA PREPARATION SERVICES

Sungard Trust Systems
P.O. Box 240882, Charlotte NC 28224-0882. 704/527-6300.

Metavision Corporation
4900 Waters Edge Dr, Raleigh NC 27606-2465. 919/859-9205.

Computer Horizons Corp.
5511 Capital Center Dr, Raleigh NC 27606-3365. 919/859-0500.

EDS Federal Corp.
4905 Waters Edge Dr, Raleigh NC 27606-2463. 919/851-8888.

Wesson Taylor Wells & Associates
2300 Yorkmont Rd, Charlotte NC 28217-4522. 704/357-0895.

DETECTIVE, GUARD, AND ARMORED CAR SERVICES

National Security Service
515 Cornelius Harnett Dr, Wilmington NC 28401-2856. 910/762-2880.

Pinkerton Security & Investigation Service
2216 W Meadowview Rd, Suite 110, Greensboro NC 27407-3401. 910/547-0337.

Pinkerton Security & Investigation Service
4020 West Chase Blvd, Raleigh NC 27607. 919/833-1390.

Pinkerton Security & Investigation Service
5501 Executive Center Dr, Suite 1, Charlotte NC 28212-. 704/535-5244.

Advance Security Inc.
5601 Roanne Way, Suite 203C, Greensboro NC 27409-2933. 910/854-2193.

Allied Security Forces
4101 West Blvd, Charlotte NC 28208-6423. 704/399-4980.

Allied Security Inc.
500 E Morehead St, Charlotte NC 28202-2606. 704/372-8050.

American Protective Service
2500 Gateway Centre Blvd, Morrisville NC 27560-9121. 919/469-4717.

Corporate Intelligence Associates
230 Oak Summit Rd, Winston-Salem NC 27105-1625. 910/661-0180.

Employers Security Co.
230 Oak Summit Rd, Winston-Salem NC 27105-1625. 910/661-0178.

Globe Security Systems
Raleigh-Durham Airport, Morrisville NC 27560. 919/840-0917.

Industrial Loss Prevention
P.O. Box 35622, Fayetteville NC 28303-0622. 910/483-9330.

Security Forces Inc.
6320 Angus Dr, Raleigh NC 27613-4756. 919/787-0749.

August Investigations
27 1st Ave NE, Suite 101, Hickory NC 28601-6219. 704/328-4036.

Brinsons Private Investigating
1702 US Highway 70 E, New Bern NC 28560-6829. 919/638-2149.

RGC Investigations
P.O. Box 1190, Winston-Salem NC 27102-1190. 910/765-7444.

SECURITY SYSTEMS SERVICES

National Security Services
4324 Barringer Dr, Suite 112, Charlotte NC 28217-1500. 704/525-7985.

Yale Security
1902 Airport Rd, Monroe NC 28110-7396. 704/375-1734.

ADT Security Systems
1900 Scott Ave, Charlotte NC 28203-6046. 704/864-7511.

Emergency Networks
7504 Independence Blvd, Suite 109, Charlotte NC 28227-9407. 704/567-2529.

National Guardian Security Service Corp.
130 Penmarc Dr, Raleigh NC 27603-2470. 919/828-0216.

Safeway Security Systems
408 S Iredell Ave, Spencer NC 28159-2229. 704/633-4063.

MISC. BUSINESS SERVICES

A Ventures Inc.
4043B Sentry Post Rd, Charlotte NC 28208-6471. 704/399-2290.

Async-Voice Message Service
4601 Charlotte Park Dr, Suite 185, Charlotte NC 28217-1900. 704/529-0450.

Design Interiors Etc.
3231 Sussex Rd, Raleigh NC 27607-6638. 919/783-8450.

Muzak
3100 Highwoods Blvd, Suite 102, Raleigh NC 27604-1033. 919/872-2004.

UNCG Office of Information Service
1716B Spring Garden St, Greensboro NC 27403-2742. 910/334-5371.

PR Newswire
801 Oberlin Rd, Suite 330, Raleigh NC 27605-1172. 919/821-4048.

PR Newswire
212 S Tryon St, Suite 1060, Charlotte NC 28281-0001. 704/338-9366.

Jones & Frank
4720 Old Poole Rd, Raleigh NC 27610-3037. 919/231-1998.

Asset Management & Marketing Inc.
1615 S Lake Park Blvd, Carolina Beach NC 28428-5724. 910/458-6494.

Office Interiors Inc.
1100 Central Ave, Charlotte NC 28204-2104. 704/332-2661.

Interior Accents by Susan
120 W Lexington Ave, High Point NC 27262-2532. 910/887-5378.

Interior Visions
6122 Falls of Neuse Rd,
Raleigh NC 27609-3528.
919/872-6155.

A-Plus Communications Center
2221 Edge Lake Dr,
Charlotte NC 28217-4509.
704/357-0848.

Commercial Courier Express
5700 Chapel Hill Rd, Raleigh
NC 27607-5104. 919/859-2949.

Pony Express Courier Corp.
Davis St, Whiteville NC
28472. 910/642-5376.

RGIS Inventory Specialists
1142 Executive Cir, Suite E,
Cary NC 27511-4570.
919/481-1574.

Bowman Enterprises Inc.
402 W Martin St, Benson NC
27504-1148. 910/894-3662.

Ladd Imaging Services
312 W Church St, Benson
NC 27504-1334. 910/894-7060.

Relocation Center
6620 Fairview Rd, Charlotte
NC 28210-3322. 704/365-6900.

Grace Dearborn
8929 J M Keynes Dr, Suite
360, Charlotte NC 28262-8406. 704/548-0108.

LABOR ORGANIZATIONS

IBEW Local 379
5825 Old Concord Rd,
Charlotte NC 28213-7111.
704/596-2091.

Iron Workers Local 843
325 J J Dr, Suite 109,
Greensboro NC 27406-4425.
910/274-9856.

NALC Branch 459
709 W Johnson St, Raleigh
NC 27603-1229. 919/856-0446.

South Carolina

DEFENDER SERVICES
P.O. Box 1775, Columbia SC 29202-1775. 803/776-4220. **Contact:** Mr. Keary Chrisley, Vice President of Personnel. **Description:** A maintenance engineering company. Defender Services offers cleaning, painting, floor sanding, maintenance, yard work, grounds work, relighting, housekeeping, trash removal, security, and general manpower provision. **Corporate headquarters location:** This Location.

DIVERSCO INC.
P.O. Box 5527, Spartanburg SC 29304. 864/579-3420. **Contact:** Rick Van Vleet, Human Resources Manager. **Description:** Diversco Inc. provides contract cleaning and maintenance services for a variety of industrial companies.

EDUCATIONAL SOLUTIONS
22 South Main Street, P.O. Box 8186, Greenville SC 29604. **Contact:** Human Resources. **Description:** Provides consulting services, as well as setting up learning centers at industrial companies for those companies' employees. The company operates across the southeastern United States.

GENERAL PHYSICS CORPORATION
1555 Whiskey Road, Aiken SC 29803. 803/649-0515. **Contact:** Susan Eichstedt, Human Resources Manager. **Description:** Provides training, engineering, and technical services to hundreds of clients in the aerospace, automotive, defense, government, manufacturing, utility, independent power, pharmaceutical, and process industries. Subsidiaries include GP Environmental and GP Technologies. **Benefits:** 401K; Dental Insurance; Disability Coverage; Life Insurance; Medical Insurance; Tuition Assistance. **Corporate headquarters location:** Columbia MD. **Parent company:** National Patent Development Corporation. **Listed on:** New York Stock Exchange. **Number of employees nationwide:** 1,300.

TERMINIX SERVICE INC.
P.O. Box 2627, Columbia SC 29202. 803/772-1783. **Contact:** Rebecca Sellers, Director of Human Resources. **Description:** A pest control service.

Note: Because addresses and telephone numbers of smaller companies change rapidly, we recommend you call each company to verify the information below before inquiring about job opportunities. Mass mailings are not recommended.

Additional employers with under 250 employees:

LINEN SUPPLY

National Linen Service
125 Hillside Dr, Greenville
SC 29607. 864/232-8795.

Servitex Linen Services
219 Strand Industrial Dr,
Little River SC 29566-7887.
803/399-2610.

Cintas-The Uniform People
1722 Airport Blvd, Cayce SC
29033-1806. 803/794-4774.

Apparelmaster/A Division of Yeamans
1306 Yeamans Hall Rd, Charleston SC 29406-2759. 803/554-0424.

Aratex Services Inc.
2210 Technical Pky #B, Charleston SC 29406-4930. 803/767-0759.

Standard Uniform Services
190 Old Mill Rd, Greenville SC 29607-5339. 864/297-5427.

ADJUSTMENT AND COLLECTION SERVICES

Medaphis Physician Services
8085 Rivers Ave, Charleston SC 29406-9239. 803/554-7072.

CREDIT REPORTING SERVICES

ARC Inc.
2154 N Center St, Suite B202, Charleston SC 29406-4056. 803/797-8738.

Trans Union
145 King St, Charleston SC 29401-2213. 803/720-8546.

CLEANING AND MAINTENANCE SERVICES

Orkin Pest Control Services
1278 Wolfe Trl SW, Orangeburg SC 29115-7341. 803/534-5710.

Ferreira II Pest Control Co.
1548 Remount Rd, N Charleston SC 29406-3272. 803/744-1994.

System II Pest Control
122 Seneca Ct, Spartanburg SC 29301-4863. 864/576-3435.

Terminix Service
818 Saint Andrews Blvd, Charleston SC 29407-7148. 803/556-3230.

Terminix Service
1409 S Irby St, Florence SC 29505-2759. 803/669-1892.

Terminix Service
1503 Montague Avenue Ext, Greenwood SC 29649-9015. 864/229-4999.

Terminix Service
508 Highway 38 S, Bennettsville SC 29512-4636. 803/774-7051.

Terminix Service
1010 W Main St, Pickens SC 29671-2122. 864/878-6509.

Helena Chemical Co.
Hwy 176, Cameron SC 29030. 803/536-9493.

Diversco Inc.
109 Mill St, Union SC 29379-9308. 864/429-3935.

Diversco Inc.
2304 S Main St, Greenwood SC 29646-4523. 864/227-2223.

Diversco Inc.
4802 Ninety Six Hwy, Ninety Six SC 29666-8951. 864/543-3344.

IH Services Inc.
Rice Rd, Easley SC 29640. 864/859-0270.

Industrial Housekeeping
Mills Av, Liberty SC 29657. 864/843-9192.

Swisher Service Co. Inc.
2805 Wade Hampton Blvd #B, Taylors SC 29687-2750. 864/292-9327.

MISC. EQUIPMENT RENTAL AND LEASING

Don Williams Inc.
11107 Broad River Rd, Irmo SC 29063-9673. 803/781-7899.

DETECTIVE, GUARD, AND ARMORED CAR SERVICES

Anderson Armored Car Service
115 N Manning St, Anderson SC 29621-5616. 864/224-5353.

American Security Greenville
100 Murray Dr, Cheraw SC 29520-1630. 803/537-4817.

Atlas Security
200 Farrs Bridge Rd, Greenville SC 29611-1932. 864/246-2457.

Burns International Security Service
84 Villa Rd, Greenville SC 29615-3016. 864/241-0977.

Crowe's Inc.
1319 Manse Jolly Rd, Anderson SC 29621-3426. 864/261-6113.

Murray Guard Inc.
8740 Northpark Blvd, Suite 225, Charleston SC 29406-9262. 803/553-8076.

Nationwide Security Inc.
440 Knox Abbott Dr, Cayce SC 29033-4353. 803/739-9254.

Wells Fargo Guard Services
2840 W Palmetto St, Florence SC 29501-5932. 803/662-9943.

Confidential Investigative Service
3706 E North St, Greenville SC 29615-2395. 864/292-0185.

SECURITY SYSTEMS SERVICES

National Guardian Security Service
1519 Trade St, Myrtle Beach SC 29577-6536. 803/626-2203.

MISC. BUSINESS SERVICES

Underground Utility Locating
2808 2nd Loop Rd, Florence SC 29501-5462. 803/669-7182.

Carolina Designs
1450 Calhoun St, Newberry SC 29108-2846. 803/276-1949.

Executive Answering Center
P.O. Box 2892, Sumter SC 29151-2892. 803/469-4100.

Telesales USA Inc.
145 N Church St, Spartanburg SC 29306-5163. 864/597-0801.

Tag & Label Corp.
16 Berryhill Rd, Suite 100, Columbia SC 29210-6433. 803/731-8462.

Trust Associates
852 Orleans Rd, Charleston SC 29407-4844. 803/571-1654.

Revels Auction
2301 Adelaide St, Newberry SC 29108-4501. 803/321-9109.

International Barter Group
2231 Technical Pky, N Charleston SC 29406-4963. 803/824-1435.

Speedy-Pak Inc.
919 Lucas St N, West Columbia SC 29169-7004. 803/796-4536.

Jack Gray Transport
2700 Nazareth Rd, Wellford SC 29385-9106. 864/433-7555.

Graham Distribution Center
3150 Charleston Hwy, West Columbia SC 29172-2712. 803/926-3081.

Corporate Developmint
19 Exchange St, Charleston SC 29401. 803/853-9999.

Lanier Worldwide Inc.
3820 Faber Place Dr,
Charleston SC 29405-8548.
803/745-6266.

Rainsoft
7360 Cross County Rd, N

Charleston SC 29418-8473.
803/552-0003.

Southeastern Estimating
Highway 153 at I-85,
Greenville SC 29614.
864/220-5954.

LABOR ORGANIZATIONS

**National Association of
Letter Carriers**
3314 W Montague Ave,
Charleston SC 29418-5937.
803/747-8897.

For more information on career opportunities in miscellaneous business services and non-scientific research:

Associations

AMERICAN SOCIETY OF APPRAISERS
P.O. Box 17265, Washington DC 20041.
703/478-2228. Toll-free number: 800/ASA-VALU. Fax: 703/742-8471. An
international, nonprofit, independent
appraisal organization. ASA teaches, tests,
and awards designations.

EQUIPMENT LEASING ASSOCIATION OF AMERICA
1300 17th Street, Suite 1010, North
Arlington VA 22209. 703/527-8655.

NATIONAL ASSOCIATION OF PERSONNEL SERVICES
3133 Mt. Vernon Avenue, Alexandria VA
22305. 703/684-0180. Fax: 703/684-0071. Provides federal legislative
protection, education, certification, and
business products and services to its
member employment service agencies.

CHARITIES AND SOCIAL SERVICES

The outlook for social service workers is better than average. In fact, opportunities for qualified applicants are expected to be excellent, partly due to the rapid turnover in the industry as a result of lower wages offered.

Note: Because of the high turnover rate and the continuous need for social services, the outlook for this industry has remained constant over the past few years.

North Carolina

AMERICAN RED CROSS
601F Country Club Drive, Greenville NC 27834. 919/355-3800. **Contact:** Raquel Morris, Chapter Manager. **Description:** Nationwide, services include disaster relief, CPR training, and blood donations. **Corporate headquarters location:** Washington DC.

CUMBERLAND SHELTERED WORKSHOP
815 Washington Drive, Fayetteville NC 28301. 910/485-4131. **Contact:** Human Resources. **Description:** Provides job training and vocational rehabilitation services.

DURHAM EXCHANGE CLUB INDUSTRY, INC.
1717 East Lawson Street, Durham NC 27703. 919/596-1341. **Contact:** Human Resources. **Description:** Provides individual and family social services. **Number of employees nationwide:** 250.

WAVERLY MILLS COMMUNITY CENTER
23 Third Street, Laurinburg NC 28352. 910/276-1441. **Contact:** Ms. Ravonda John, Personnel Director. **Description:** A community center offering social services.

WINSTON-SALEM INDUSTRIES FOR THE BLIND
7730 North Point Drive, Winston-Salem NC 27106-3310. 910/759-0551. **Contact:** Laura C. Spain, Manager of Human Resources. **Description:** A shelter workshop for the blind. **Corporate headquarters location:** This Location. **Operations at this facility include:** Manufacturing.

Note: Because addresses and telephone numbers of smaller companies change rapidly, we recommend you call each company to verify the information below before inquiring about job opportunities. Mass mailings are not recommended.

Additional employers with under 250 employees:

JOB TRAINING AND VOCATIONAL REHABILITATION SERVICES

Orange Enterprises Inc.
500 Valley Forge Rd, Hillsborough NC 27278-9502. 919/732-8124.

Telamon Corporation
801 E Broad Ave, Rockingham NC 28379-4382. 910/997-5541.

MISC. SOCIAL SERVICES

Foster Grandparents Program
1700 Fisher St, Morehead City NC 28557-3658. 919/726-5219.

Spectrum House
401 E Whitaker Mill Rd Rm 102, Raleigh NC 27608-2631. 919/856-6420.

Goodwill Industries
1337 E Dixie Dr, Asheboro NC 27203-8889. 910/629-5955.

American Cancer Society
500 E Morehead St, Charlotte NC 28202-2606. 704/376-1659.

American Cancer Society
620 W Morgan St, Raleigh NC 27603-1830. 919/834-1636.

American Cancer Society
11 S Boylan Ave, Raleigh NC 27603-1850. 919/834-8463.

American Friends Service Committee
606 E Springfield Rd, High Point NC 27263-1846. 910/885-6921.

Four County Community Service Head Start
RR 1 Box 226B, Whiteville NC 28472. 910/648-4111.

Host Homes
621 W 2nd St, Winston-Salem NC 27101-3717. 910/725-4678.

Senior Citizens Service
Pender Inc.
312 W Williams St, Burgaw
NC 28425. 910/259-9119.

Wake County Opportunities
567 E Hargett St, Raleigh NC
27601-1517. 919/833-
2885.

South Carolina

BERKELEY CITIZENS
1301 Old Highway 52, P.O. Drawer 429, Moncks Corner SC 29461. **Contact:** Human
Resources. **Description:** Provides support services for people with mental retardation,
head and spinal cord injuries, autism, and other related disabilities.

HABITAT FOR HUMANITY
P.O. Box 11502, Columbia SC 29211. 803/252-3570. **Contact:** Jim Nichols, Director.
Description: Habitat for Humanity is a social services organization that builds homes
for the homeless. The majority of this organization's staff consists of volunteers.
Special Programs: Internships. **Corporate headquarters location:** Americus GA. **Other
U.S. locations:** Nationwide.

MUSCULAR DYSTROPHY ASSOCIATION
2711 Middleburgh, Suite 107, Columbia SC 29204. 803/799-7435. **Contact:** Susan
Beach, Human Resources. **Description:** A social services organization which provides
funding for research to cure neuromuscular diseases. The group also provides support
groups, summer camps, and educational programs. Other area locations include
Greenville NC and Charleston SC. **Corporate headquarters location:** Tuscon AZ. **Other
U.S. locations:** Nationwide.

*Note: Because addresses and telephone numbers of smaller companies change rapidly,
we recommend you call each company to verify the information below before inquiring
about job opportunities. Mass mailings are not recommended.*

Additional employers with under 250 employees:

MISC. SOCIAL SERVICES

Community Services
309 Pridmore St, Laurens SC
29360-3339. 864/984-
5123.

Wateree Community Actions
637 Rutledge St, Camden SC
29020-4237. 803/432-
3411.

Salvation Army
103 E 1st Ave, Easley SC
29640-3036. 864/855-
6408.

Salvation Army
4248 Dorchester Rd,
Charleston SC 29405-7433.
803/747-5271.

**Anderson Community
Residence**
1705 S Holly St, Anderson
SC 29625-3552. 864/225-
9941.

**Orangeburg Area Mental
Health Center**
700 Gilway, Holly Hill SC
29059. 803/496-3410.

**Life Abilities Greenville
County**
113 Mills Ave, Greenville SC
29605. 864/232-4185.

United Way Service Center
360 W Church St, Batesburg
SC 29006. 803/532-0820.

Ronald McDonald House
706 Grove Rd, Greenville SC
29605-4211. 864/235-
0506.

Wateree Community Actions
3 W Boyce St, Manning SC
29102. 803/435-4337.

For more information on career opportunities in charities and social services:

<u>Associations</u>

AMERICAN COUNCIL OF THE BLIND
1155 15th Street NW, Suite 720,
Washington DC 20005. 202/467-5081.
Membership. Offers an annual conference, a
monthly magazine, and scholarships.

CATHOLIC CHARITIES USA
1731 King Street, Suite 200, Alexandria VA
22314. 703/549-1390. Membership.

**FAMILY SERVICE ASSOCIATION OF
AMERICA**
11700 West Lake Park Drive, Park Place,
Milwaukee WI 53224. 414/359-1040.
Membership.

**NATIONAL COUNCIL ON FAMILY
RELATIONS**
3989 Central Avenue NE, Suite 550,
Minneapolis MN 55421. 612/781-9331.
Fax: 612/781-9348. Membership. Publishes
two quarterly journals. Offers an annual
conference and newsletters.

**NATIONAL FEDERATION OF SOCIETIES
FOR CLINICAL SOCIAL WORK, INC.**
P.O. Box 3740, Arlington VA 22203.
703/522-3866. A lobbying organization.
Offers newsletters and a conference every
two years to membership organizations.

NATIONAL FEDERATION OF THE BLIND
1800 Johnson Street, Baltimore MD
21230. 410/659-9314. Membership of
50,000 in 600 local chapters. Publishes a
monthly magazine.

NATIONAL MULTIPLE SCLEROSIS SOCIETY
733 Third Avenue, New York NY 10017.
212/986-3240. Toll-free: 800/344-4867.
Publishes a quarterly magazine.

CHEMICALS/RUBBER AND PLASTICS

 *First the good news: Overall growth in the chemical industry is on the upswing. Chemical products and services are currently in high demand, thus creating a need for more workers, and recent price increases are holding steady.*

Now the bad news: Costs for pollution reduction are rising. Factories are running at 85 percent capacity, and if companies increase spending on plant and equipment, an oversupply could result if economic growth slows too quickly.

Growth prospects for the domestic synthetic rubber industry remain mixed, reflecting the industry's dependence on tire manufacturing. The tire industry shows signs of stabilizing after undergoing a period characterized by massive restructuring, the effects of recession in the domestic market, and consistently high levels of imports.

In the plastics industry, greater reliance on computer-aided design and manufacturing is expected in the last half of the 1990s, as production is streamlined. These measures will be aimed at strengthening the industry's competitiveness in the areas of quality control and improved client relations.

North Carolina

BASF CORPORATION
4824 Parkway Plaza Boulevard, Suite 300, Charlotte NC 28217-9730. 704/423-2000. **Contact:** Manager/Human Resources. **Description:** This location is engaged in the manufacture and marketing of industrial chemicals, yarns, and man-made fibers. **Corporate headquarters location:** This Location. **Parent company:** BASF America Inc.

FLAMBEAU AIRMOLD CORPORATION
P.O. Box 610, Roanoke Rapids NC 27870. 919/536-2171. **Fax:** 919/536-2201. **Contact:** Dawn Quimby, Human Resources Manager. **Description:** A manufacturer of rigid plastic doublewall cases through a blow-molding process. **Common positions include:** Electrical/Electronics Engineer; Electrician; Industrial Engineer; Mechanical Engineer. **Educational backgrounds include:** Engineering; Marketing. **Benefits:** 401K; Dental Insurance; Disability Coverage; Medical Insurance; Pension Plan; Savings Plan; Tuition Assistance. **Corporate headquarters location:** Baraboo WI. **Other U.S. locations:** Middlefield OH. **Operations at this facility include:** Administration; Divisional Headquarters; Manufacturing; Sales. **Number of employees at this location:** 200.

FOAM DESIGN, INC.
2425 South Alston Avenue, Durham NC 27713. 919/596-0668. **Fax:** 919/598-1761. **Contact:** Bryant Morton. **Description:** A producer of foam and foam products. Manufactures cushioning products made of polyethylene, polyurethane, and polystyrene foams for the protection of products such as typewriters, printed circuit boards, medical instruments, and electronic components. When creating foam cushioning for a specific product, the design and engineering staff analyze factors such as size, weight, fragility, center of gravity, and structural and component strengths and weaknesses of the products. Shock measuring equipment performs monitored testing for cushion packaging applications. Cushioning products are used to package consumer goods, for the transport of aerospace and military missile components and related hardware, for the handling and shipping of automotive parts, and in the packaging of electronics components and assemblies. Foam Design also manufacturers consumer products such as camping pads, bodyboards, and archery targets.

GOODYEAR TIRE & RUBBER COMPANY
890 Pineview Road, Randleman NC 27317. 910/495-2201. **Contact:** Dean Anderson, Human Resources Manager. **Description:** Goodyear Tire & Rubber Company's principal business is the development, manufacture, distribution, and sale of tires for most applications worldwide. Goodyear also manufactures and sells a broad spectrum of rubber products and rubber-related chemicals for various industrial and consumer markets and provides auto repair services. The company operates 32 plants in the United States, 42 plants in 29 other countries, and more than 1,800 retail tire and service centers and other distribution facilities around the globe. Strategic business units of Goodyear Tire & Rubber include: North American Tire; Kelly-Springfield; Goodyear Europe; Goodyear Latin America; Goodyear Asia; Engineered Products; Chemicals; Celeron; and Goodyear Racing. **Corporate headquarters location:** Akron OH. **Listed on:** New York Stock Exchange.

HOECHST CELANESE CORPORATION
P.O. Box 32414, Charlotte NC 28232. 704/554-2000. **Contact:** Elizabeth Dickey, Human Resources Manager. **Description:** The research and development facility for Hoechst Celanese Corporation. Overall, Hoechst Celanese Corporation is a science-based, market-driven, international company dedicated to producing and marketing chemicals, manufactured fibers for textile and industrial uses, plastics and high-performance advanced materials, polyester, film, printing plates, dyes and pigments, pharmaceuticals, and animal-health and crop-protection products. Hoechst Celanese ranks as one of the largest U.S. chemical companies, and is the largest and fastest-growing member of the international Hoechst Group. The Hoechst Group operates 250 companies in 120 countries. **Corporate headquarters location:** Somerville NJ. **Parent company:** Hoechst Group. **Number of employees worldwide:** 23,000.

HOECHST CELANESE CORPORATION
P.O. Box 327, Wilmington NC 28402. 910/341-5500. **Contact:** Blanche Anthony, Human Resources Secretary. **Description:** Overall, the Hoechst Celanese Corporation is a science-based, market-driven, international company which produces and markets chemicals, manufactured fibers for textile and industrial uses, plastics and high-performance advanced materials, polyester, film, printing plates, dyes and pigments, pharmaceuticals, and animal-health and crop-protection products. Hoechst Celanese ranks as one of the largest U.S. chemical companies, and is the largest and fastest-growing member of the international Hoechst Group. The Hoechst Group operates 250 companies in 120 countries. **Corporate headquarters location:** Somerville NJ. **Parent company:** Hoechst Group. **Number of employees worldwide:** 23,000.

NORCOMP LIMITED PARTNERSHIP
P.O. Box 3867, 2633 Plastics Drive, Gastonia NC 28054-0020. 704/866-9161. **Contact:** Brenda Goins, Administrative Assistant. **Description:** Engaged in the production and distribution of proprietary and custom-molded plastics for original equipment manufacturer markets. Also produces and distributes interconnect devices. **Common positions include:** Accountant/Auditor; Administrative Services Manager; Blue-Collar Worker Supervisor; Computer Systems Analyst; General Manager; Industrial Engineer; Mechanical Engineer; Operations/Production Manager; Purchasing Agent and Manager; Quality Control Supervisor; Transportation/Traffic Specialist. **Educational backgrounds include:** Accounting; Business Administration; Engineering. **Benefits:** Disability Coverage; Life Insurance; Medical Insurance; Pension Plan; Tuition Assistance. **Corporate headquarters location:** Minneapolis MN. **Operations at this facility include:** Administration; Manufacturing. **Listed on:** Privately held. **Number of employees at this location:** 70.

OLYMPIC PRODUCTS COMPANY
4100 Pleasant Garden Road, Greensboro NC 27406. 910/378-9620. **Contact:** Gene Knight, Personnel Manager. **Description:** A manufacturer of urethane foam for the furniture, bedding, and automotive industries. **Common positions include:** Blue-Collar Worker Supervisor; Customer Service Representative. **Educational backgrounds include:** Liberal Arts. **Benefits:** Dental Insurance; Disability Coverage; Life Insurance; Medical Insurance; Stock Option. **Operations at this facility include:** Administration; Manufacturing; Sales; Service. **Number of employees at this location:** 310.

RESISTOFLEX COMPANY
A CRANE COMPANY
P.O. Box 1449, Marion NC 28752. 704/724-9524. **Contact:** Kevin Hall, Human Resources Director. **Description:** Resistoflex Company, which operates as a division of the Crane Company, manufactures thermoplastic products, including thermoplastic line pipe and flexible hoses. The Crane Company is a maker and wholesaler of a diverse number of engineered products for a variety of industries. Its industrial production unit

manufactures products and systems for the defense, aerospace, construction, and transportation markets. Products include fiberglass-reinforced panels, vending machines, water filtration and conditioning systems, pumps, valves, and coin machines. A subsidiary, Hydro-Aire, develops and manufactures brake systems, fuel pumps, and other products primarily for the aerospace industry. Crane Company's wholesaling activities are conducted through a subsidiary, Huttig Sash & Door, which operates 47 branch warehouses across the United States. This business is mostly concentrated on doors, molding, trim, windows, and other construction products, and sells mostly to contractors and other larger wholesalers. **Common positions include:** Accountant/Auditor; Administrator; Blue-Collar Worker Supervisor; Buyer; Customer Service Representative; Draftsperson; Financial Analyst; Human Resources Specialist; Industrial Engineer; Marketing Specialist; Mechanical Engineer; Operations/Production Manager; Purchasing Agent and Manager; Quality Control Supervisor; Systems Analyst. **Educational backgrounds include:** Accounting; Business Administration; Computer Science; Engineering; Finance; Marketing; Mathematics. **Benefits:** Dental Insurance; Disability Coverage; Life Insurance; Medical Insurance; Pension Plan; Savings Plan; Tuition Assistance. **Corporate headquarters location:** New York NY. **Operations at this facility include:** Administration; Manufacturing; Research and Development; Sales.

REXHAM INDUSTRIAL GROUP
P.O. Box 368, Matthews NC 28106. 704/847-9171. **Contact:** Brenda Sawyer, Human Resources Director. **Description:** Specializes in custom, roll-to-roll coating and laminating of films, foils, and papers used in high-performance products. The company provides technical, pilot, and production services for companies worldwide.

SANDOZ CHEMICALS CORPORATION
P.O. Box 18278, Charlotte NC 28218. 704/331-7000. **Contact:** Patricia Marlowe, Human Resources Director. **Description:** A dye and special chemical manufacturer. **Corporate headquarters location:** This Location.

SANDOZ CHEMICALS CORPORATION
MOUNT HOLLY PLANT
P.O. Box 669246, Charlotte NC 28266. **Contact:** Patricia Marlowe, Human Resources Director. **Description:** A dye and special chemical manufacturer. **NOTE:** Ms. Marlowe can be reached at the corporate headquarters location at P.O. Box 18278, Charlotte NC 28218. 704/331-7000.

U.S. PACKAGING INC.
P.O. Box 608, Maxton NC 28364. 910/844-5293. **Contact:** Susan Hill, Human Resources Director. **Description:** Manufactures cellulose products.

VITAFOAM INC.
2222 Surret Drive, High Point NC 27263. 910/431-1171. **Fax:** 910/431-7747. **Contact:** Kim Flowers, Personnel. **Description:** Vitafoam is an international leader in the application of science, technology, and engineering with the production of specialized polymer, fiber, and fabric components for the furnishing, transportation, apparel, packaging, and engineering industries.

Note: Because addresses and telephone numbers of smaller companies change rapidly, we recommend you call each company to verify the information below before inquiring about job opportunities. Mass mailings are not recommended.

Additional employers with under 250 employees:

INDUSTRIAL INORGANIC CHEMICALS

Occidental Chemical Corp.
5408 Holly Shelter Rd,
Castle Hayne NC 28429-6350. 910/675-7200.

PLASTICS MATERIALS, SYNTHETICS, AND ELASTOMERS

Dow Corning Corp.
2914 Patterson St,
Greensboro NC 27407-3337.
910/547-7100.

Ferro Corp.
526 Dog Eye Rd, Benson NC
27504. 919/894-7837.

ICI Americas Inc./Films
Division
Cedar Creek Rd, Fayetteville
NC 28301. 910/433-8200.

Polychem Alloy Inc.
4245 US Highway 321 S,
Granite Falls NC 28630-
8585. 704/396-1799.

Wellman Inc.
Cedar Creek Rd, Fayetteville
NC 28301. 910/323-3535.

MANMADE FIBERS

GS Fibers Inc.
104 S Oxford St, Claremont
NC 28610. 704/459-7645.

Cameo Fibers Inc.
2010 Breana Rd, Conover
NC 28613-7825. 704/459-
7064.

**SOAP AND OTHER
DETERGENTS**

Kay Chemical Co.
8300 Capital Dr, Greensboro
NC 27409-9790. 910/668-
7290.

**CLEANING, POLISHING, AND
SANITATION
PREPARATIONS**

Pioneer Eclipse Corp.
Hwy 18 N & Eclipse Rd,
Sparta NC 28675. 910/372-
8080.

Southchem Inc.
2000 E Pettigrew St,
Durham NC 27703-4049.
919/596-0681.

**PAINTS, VARNISHES, AND
RELATED PRODUCTS**

BASF Corp.
1110 Carbon City Rd,
Morganton NC 28655-7271.
704/584-1771.

Guardsman Products Inc.
2147 Brevard Rd, High Point
NC 27263-1703. 910/889-
6344.

**INDUSTRIAL ORGANIC
CHEMICALS**

Colurtex Exports Pvt Ltd.
7804 Waterford Lakes Dr,
Charlotte NC 28210-7441.
704/552-7623.

Borden Chemical
1411 Industrial Dr,
Fayetteville NC 28301-6396.
910/483-1311.

Novo Nordisk Biochemical
Hwy 56 E, Franklinton NC
27525. 919/494-2014.

**AGRICULTURAL
CHEMICALS**

BASF Corp.
P.O. Box 13528, Durham NC
27709-3528. 919/361-
5300.

ADHESIVES AND SEALANTS

Patch Rubber Co. Inc.
P.O. Box H, Roanoke Rapid
NC 27870-8082. 919/536-
2574.

PRINTING INK

Sun Chemical Corp.
1701 Westinghouse Blvd,
Charlotte NC 28273-6328.
704/587-8300.

Zeneca Specialty Inks
7830 N Point Blvd, Suite
101, Winston-Salem NC
27106-3261. 910/759-
0354.

**CHEMICALS AND
CHEMICAL PREPARATIONS**

BASF Corp.
4330 Chesapeake Dr,
Charlotte NC 28216-3411.
704/392-4313.

Camco Manufacturing
121 Landmark Dr,
Greensboro NC 27409-9626.
910/668-7661.

Digichem Inc.
8539 Monroe Rd, Suite 6,
Charlotte NC 28212-7510.
704/536-0677.

High Point Chemical Corp.
243 Woodbine St, High Point
NC 27260-8339. 910/884-
2214.

Nationwide Industries
P.O. Box 131, Durham NC
27702-0131. 919/286-
4446.

**MISC. RUBBER AND
PLASTICS PRODUCTS**

Imperial Fire Hose Co.
11325 Nations Ford Rd,
Pineville NC 28134-8393.
704/588-4862.

Lawrence Industries
P.O. Box 1838, Burlington
NC 27216-1838. 910/578-
2161.

RUBBER PRODUCTS

Oliver Rubber Co.
408 Telephone Ave,
Asheboro NC 27203-6800.
910/629-1436.

Bandag Inc.
505 W Industry Dr, Oxford
NC 27565-3591. 919/693-
8855.

Gates Rubber Co.
101 Gates Ln, Jefferson NC
28640. 910/246-7185.

Halstead Industrial Products
1004 Keisler Rd, Conover NC
28613. 704/464-5880.

HBD Industries Inc.
1801 S Railroad St, Salisbury
NC 28144-6751. 704/636-
0121.

Neptco Inc.
Hwy 321 S, Lenoir NC
28645. 704/728-5951.

**North Carolina Foam
Industries**
511 Carter St, Mount Airy
NC 27030. 910/789-9161.

**UNSUPPORTED PLASTICS
PRODUCTS**

Alpha Plastics
Hwy 177 S, Hamlet NC
28345. 910/582-4602.

Armin Plastics
1921 Freedom Dr, Charlotte
NC 28208-5250. 704/331-
9921.

Printpack Inc.
3510 Asheville Hwy,
Hendersonvlle NC 28791-
0703. 704/693-1723.

Rex-Rosenlew International
1308 Blair St, Thomasville
NC 27360-3249. 910/476-
3131.

Rexham Packaging
2600 Phoenix Dr,
Greensboro NC 27406-6321.
910/292-9911.

Southern Film Extruders
P.O. Box 2104, High Point
NC 27261-2104. 910/885-
8091.

PLASTICS PRODUCTS

Azdel Inc.
925 Washburn Switch Rd,
Shelby NC 28150-7008.
704/434-2271.

Funder America Inc.
200 Funder Rd, Mocksville
NC 27028-2886. 704/634-
3501.

Constar International
4915 Hovis Rd, Charlotte NC
28208-1512. 704/392-
8174.

Amoco Foam Products Co.
520 Radar Rd, Greensboro
NC 27410. 910/292-2798.

Foam Tech Inc.
117 Cedar Lane Dr,
Lexington NC 27292-5709.
704/352-7121.

Foamex LP
Hwy 115 & Bailey Rd,
Cornelius NC 28031.
704/892-8081.

Plastic Packaging Inc.
1246 Main Ave SE, Hickory
NC 28602. 704/328-2466.

A&E Products Group
RR 3 Box 1141, Bostic NC
28018-9514. 704/245-
1281.

AEP Industries Inc.
Stallings Industrial Park,
Matthews NC 28105.
704/821-9233.

AFA Corp.
135 Pine St, Forest City NC
28043-4590. 704/245-
1160.

Americhem Inc.
723 Commerce Dr, Concord
NC 28025-7746. 704/782-
6411.

Bonny Products Inc.
350 Page Rd, Washington
NC 27889-8753. 919/975-
6669.

Cambridge Industries Inc.
1400 Burris Rd, Newton NC
28658-1753. 704/465-
5759.

Cashiers Plastic
Hwy 64 W, Cashiers NC
28717. 704/743-3461.

CPM Inc.
New Cut Rd Box 1328,
Lexington NC 27292-0200.
704/243-2131.

Crellin Inc.
25 Pine St, Forest City NC
28043-4516. 704/245-
0118.

Dart Container Corp.
3219 Wesleyan Rd,
Randleman NC 27317-7667.
910/495-1101.

Eslon Thermoplastics
10100 Rodney Blvd, Pineville
NC 28134-7538. 704/889-
2431.

IEM Plastics
606 Walters St, Reidsville
NC 27320-2615. 910/342-
0356.

Kerr Plastic Products
Johhny Mitchell Rd, Ahoskie
NC 27910. 919/332-5151.

Mack Molding Co. Inc.
RR 16 Box 353-F, Statesville
NC 28677-9816. 704/878-
9641.

Mid-State Plastics Inc.
Hwy 220 N, Seagrove NC
27341. 910/873-7221.

Norandex Inc.
402 Penny Rd, Claremont NC
28610. 704/459-2200.

Nypro Carolina Inc.
3260 Nova Ln, Burlington NC
27215-8877. 910/227-
1470.

Otto Industries
12700 General Dr, Charlotte
NC 28273-6415. 704/588-
9191.

Owens-Illinois Inc.
1015 County Home Rd,
Hamlet NC 28345-4390.
910/582-7301.

Quality Molded Products
920 E Raleigh St, Siler City
NC 27344-2708. 910/663-
3141.

Rexham Laminex Inc.
P.O. Box 240655, Charlotte
NC 28224-0655. 704/588-
4700.

Rutland Plastics Technologies
10021 Rodney Blvd, Pineville
NC 28134-8574. 704/553-
0046.

Southern Case
2728 Capital Blvd, Raleigh
NC 27604-1510. 919/832-
0877.

Tri-Plas Inc.
Wesley Chapel, Indian Trail
NC 28079. 704/289-1526.

United Plastics Corp.
511 Hay St, Mount Airy NC
27030-5629. 910/786-
2127.

United Southern Industry
3 Duke St, Forest City NC
28043-2541. 704/245-
6453.

Fawn Industries Plastic Division
410 Jeffries Cv, Rocky
Mount NC 27804-6620.
919/977-7664.

Nolu Plastics Inc.
11817 Harris Pointe Dr,
Charlotte NC 28269-1235.
704/598-1174.

PLASTICS MATERIALS WHOLESALE

Piedmont Plastics Inc.
2606 Phoenix Dr,
Greensboro NC 27406-6347.
910/218-0128.

CHEMICALS AND ALLIED PRODUCTS WHOLESALE

Benco Division Livingston & Haven
11616 Wilmar Blvd,
Charlotte NC 28273-6409.
704/588-6297.

Burlington Chemical Co.
615 Huffman Mill Rd,
Burlington NC 27215-5167.
910/584-0111.

Litton Industries Inc. Airtron
1201 Continental Blvd,
Charlotte NC 28273-6320.
704/588-2340.

National Starch & Chemical
P.O. Box 399, Salisbury NC
28145-0399. 704/633-
1731.

Prillman Chemical Corp.
334 Worth St, Fayetteville
NC 28301-5632. 910/483-
2106.

Texaco Chemical Co.
2229 Park Rd, Charlotte NC
28203. 704/376-5768.

Austin Powder Co.
4411 Oakcliffe Rd,
Greensboro NC 27406-8671.
910/373-8976.

PAINTS, VARNISHES, AND SUPPLIES WHOLESALE

Lilly Industries Inc.
1717 English Rd, High Point
NC 27262. 910/889-2157.

South Carolina

COMPOSITE MATERIALS INC.
P.O. Box 3060, Rock Hill SC 29732. 803/327-8071. **Contact:** Allan B. Wolf, Vice President and Operations Manager. **Description:** Composite Materials Inc. (formerly Clark-Schwebel Distribution Corporation) is a wholesale distributor of fiberglass and related chemicals. **Common positions include:** Credit Manager; Customer Service Representative; General Manager; Operations/Production Manager; Purchasing Agent and Manager; Sales Associate; Warehouse Manager. **Educational backgrounds include:** Business Administration; Economics; Liberal Arts. **Benefits:** Dental Insurance; Disability Coverage; Life Insurance; Medical Insurance; Profit Sharing; Savings Plan. **Special Programs:** Training Programs. **Corporate headquarters location:** This Location. **Other U.S. locations:** Van Buren AR; Lakeland FL; Miami FL; Elkhart IN. **Operations at this facility include:** Administration; Regional Headquarters; Sales; Service.

DAYCO PRODUCTS INC.
P.O. Box 500, Williston SC 29853. 803/266-7046. **Contact:** David Hayes, Human Resources Manager. **Description:** A worldwide manufacturer and distributor of a wide range of highly-engineered rubber and plastic products, many of which are used for replacement purposes. Principal markets include the agricultural, automotive, construction, energy, printing, mining, textile, and transportation industries. **Corporate headquarters location:** Dayton OH. **Parent company:** Mark IV Industries. **Listed on:** New York Stock Exchange.

ENGELHARD CORPORATION
554 Engelhard Drive, Seneca SC 29678. 864/882-9841. **Contact:** Human Resources. **Description:** Engelhard Corporation's products include precious metal catalysts and refining operations for the petrochemicals and fine chemicals industries; base metal catalysts for specialty chemical producers; catalysts for the hydrogenation of fats and oils, with the high activity, selectivity, and poison-resistance the industry needs in achieving consistent performance from variable feedstocks; and separation products encompassing a wide variety of treated natural minerals for the enhancement, purification, and bleaching of chemical products. Engelhard Corporation has some of the most advanced catalyst manufacturing and research and development facilities in the world, coupled with unsurpassed resources for technical support and custom product development on a global scale. **Other U.S. locations:** MS; NJ; Elyria OH; TX.

MARTIN COLOR-FI, INC.
320 Neeley Street, Sumter SC 29150. 803/436-4200. **Fax:** 803/436-4220. **Contact:** Hope Dunn, Personnel Director. **Description:** Martin Color-fi, Inc. produces polyester fiber and pellets from recycled plastic materials such as soft drink bottles, polyester fiber waste, and film waste. The company uses low-cost waste materials to produce polyester fibers for a wide range of markets, including automotive fabrics, carpet, home furnishings, industrial materials and construction reinforcement materials, and pelletized plastics for injection molding and thermoforming processes. The company also produces carpet and rug yarns and specialty carpets for the recreational vehicle and manufactured housing markets. The company's common stock is traded under the symbol MRCF. **Common positions include:** Blue-Collar Worker Supervisor; Computer Programmer; Computer Systems Analyst; Draftsperson; Electrician; General Manager; Human Resources Specialist; Industrial Production Manager; Management Trainee; Operations/Production Manager; Purchasing Agent and Manager; Quality Control Supervisor; Registered Nurse; Transportation/Traffic Specialist. **Educational backgrounds include:** Accounting; Business Administration; Engineering; Finance. **Benefits:** 401K; Dental Insurance; Disability Coverage; Employee Discounts; Life Insurance; Medical Insurance; Pension Plan; Profit Sharing; Savings Plan; Tuition Assistance. **Corporate headquarters location:** Edgefield SC. **Other U.S. locations:** Pensacola FL; Dalton GA; Laurens SC; Trenton SC. **Listed on:** NASDAQ. **Number of employees at this location:** 400. **Number of employees nationwide:** 850.

MILES, INC.
P.O. Box 118088, Charleston SC 29423-8088. 803/820-6000. **Contact:** Valerie Harvin, Director of Human Resources. **Description:** Miles, Inc. produces polyurethane raw materials and polymer thermoplastics resins and blends, coatings, and industrial chemicals and other related products. **Other U.S. locations:** Pittsburgh PA.

NAN YA PLASTICS CORPORATION AMERICA
P.O. Box 939, Lake City SC 29560-0939. 803/389-7800. **Contact:** Robert Moore, Human Resources Manager. **Description:** This plant was established in 1990, and is engaged in producing polyester fiber, chip, and filament. Nan Ya Plastics Corporation America's products include PVC rigid film; PET sheet; PVC panel and pipe; electronic-related products (printed circuit boards, copper-clad laminates, copper foil, epoxy, BPA, and glass fiber and cloth); PP synthetic paper (a newly developed product similar in quality to wood pulp paper); and polyester fiber. **Parent company:** Formosa Plastics Group (Taipei, Taiwan, ROC), has more than a dozen other affiliated companies. Taiwanese subsidiaries of the Formosa Plastics Group include: Sunrise Plywood Company, Ltd.; Tai Shih Textile Industry Corporation; Yung Chia Chemical Industries Corporation; Formosa Taffeta Company, Ltd.; Tairay Garments Manufacturing Company, Ltd.; Weng Fung Industrial Company, Ltd.; Tah Shin Spinning Corporation; Formosa Transport Corporation; Formosa Fairway Corporation; Pei Jen Company, Ltd.; FPG Fiber Glass Corporation; Formosa Heavy Industries Corporation; Formosa Petrochemical Corporation. Other subsidiaries of the Formosa Plastics Group include: Formosa Plastics Corporation, USA; Nan Ya Plastics Corporation, U.S.A.; J-M Manufacturing Corporation; Formosa Hydrocarbon Group, Formosa Plastics Corporation, America; Formosa Chemicals & Fibre Corporation, America; and P.T.

Indonesia Nana Ya Indah Plastics Corporation. **Number of employees at this location:** 600.

SPAN-AMERICA MEDICAL SYSTEMS, INC.
P.O. Box 5231, Greenville SC 29606. 864/288-8877. **Contact:** Melinda Gage, Director of Human Resources. **Description:** Span-America Medical Systems, Inc., founded in 1970, manufactures and distributes a variety of polyurethane foam products and contract packaging for the health care, consumer, and industrial markets. The company's principal health care products consist of polyurethane foam mattress overlays including its Geo-Matt overlay, therapeutic replacement mattresses, patient positioners, and single-use flexible packaging products. These products are marketed primarily to hospitals but are also marketed to long-term care facilities in the United States. The company also sells these products on a limited basis in Canada. Span-America's foam mattress overlays include convoluted and lapidus foam pads which are designed to provide patients with greater comfort and assist in treating patients suffering from burns or pressure ulcers. The company's replacement mattresses consist of its PressureGuard mattresses, a line of therapeutic replacement mattresses, obtained through the acquisition of Healthflex in 1992. PressureGuard mattresses are designed to replace existing hospital or long-term care mattresses to eliminate the need for mattress overlays. Span-America's specialty line of patient positioners is sold primarily under the trademark Span-Aids, which consists of over 300 different foam items which aid in relieving the basic patient positioning problems of elevation, immobilization, muscle contracture, foot drop, and foot or leg rotation. The majority of the company's health care foam products are sold to Baxter Healthcare Corporation (formerly American Hospital Supply), which distributes the products. Span-America's consumer foam products consist primarily of convoluted mattress overlays and specially designed pillows for the consumer bedding market. The company's industrial products consist primarily of foam packaging and cushioning materials. **Corporate headquarters location:** This Location. **Listed on:** NASDAQ. **Number of employees nationwide:** 4,000.

UNIROYAL GOODRICH TIRE COMPANY
199 Maple Street, Winnsboro SC 29180. 803/635-4651x252. **Contact:** Tom England, Director of Human Resources. **Description:** A tire manufacturer. Parent company, Michelin, has operations in the United States, Canada, Mexico, Asia, Europe, Brazil, Nigeria, and Algeria. The company emphasizes research and development to improve both products (specifically, by increasing mechanical and acoustical comfort, improving wet adhesion and handling, and reducing rolling resistance) and manufacturing processes (improving product quality and increasing equipment productivity, particularly through greater flexibility). **Parent company:** Michelin.

WESTINGHOUSE ELECTRIC CORPORATION
P.O. Drawer R, Columbia SC 29250. 803/776-2610. **Contact:** Mr. Clayton Jennings, Director of Human Resources. **Description:** This location of the company manufactures industrial chemicals and other products. Overall, Westinghouse Electric Corporation is a diversified manufacturing company with interests in defense electronics, environmental services, broadcasting, mobile refrigeration units, office furniture, energy systems, and power generation. The company conducts operations through 791 locations in the U.S. and over 30 other countries. **Corporate headquarters location:** Pittsburgh PA. **Subsidiaries include:** Thermo King; The Knoll Group; Westinghouse Broadcasting. **Listed on:** New York Stock Exchange. **Number of employees nationwide:** 120,000.

Note: *Because addresses and telephone numbers of smaller companies change rapidly, we recommend you call each company to verify the information below before inquiring about job opportunities. Mass mailings are not recommended.*

Additional employers with under 250 employees:

INDUSTRIAL GASES

Carotane Propane Gas
403 N Main St, Marion SC 29571-3029. 803/423-4732.

INDUSTRIAL INORGANIC CHEMICALS

Halocarbon Products Corp.
1100 Dittman Rd, North Augusta SC 29841. 803/278-3500.

Sybron Chemicals Inc.
P.O. Box 125, Wellford SC 29385-0125. 864/439-6333.

PLASTICS MATERIALS, SYNTHETICS, AND ELASTOMERS

DLH Inc.
5515 Charter Oaks Ln, York SC 29745. 803/831-1375.

EMS-American Grilon
P.O. Box 1717, Sumter SC 29151. 803/481-3172.

Exchange Plastics Corp.
109 Live Oak Way, Taylors SC 29687-3551. 864/268-2963.

Morton International Inc.
130 Mountain Creek Church Rd, Greenville SC 29609-6929. 864/292-5700.

MANMADE FIBERS

Teepak Inc.
P.O. Box 159, Swansea SC 29160-0159. 803/796-9730.

Teepak-Summerville Inc.
2755 W 5th North St, Summerville SC 29483-9605. 803/871-9677.

Star Fibers Inc.
P.O. Box 588, Edgefield SC 29824-0588. 803/637-3153.

CHEMICAL AGENTS, SULFONATED OILS, AND RELATED PRODUCTS

Henkel Corp.
2 W Golden Strip Dr, Mauldin SC 29662-2604. 864/963-4031.

PAINTS, VARNISHES, AND RELATED PRODUCTS

Southern Coatings Inc.
730 Fulton St, Sumter SC 29150. 803/775-6351.

INDUSTRIAL ORGANIC CHEMICALS

Ibis Ltd.
Highway 52 N, Kingstree SC 29556. 803/382-8485.

Milliken Chemical Co.
P.O. Box 817, Inman SC 29349. 864/472-9041.

MTM Hardwicke Inc.
2114 Larry Jeffers Rd, Elgin SC 29045. 803/438-3471.

AGRICULTURAL CHEMICALS

Scotts Co.
830 N Highway 25, Travelers Rest SC 29690-8990. 864/834-7273.

ADHESIVES AND SEALANTS

Para-Chem Southern Inc.
863 Highway 14, Simpsonville SC 29681-5837. 864/967-7691.

PRINTING INK

Wikoff Color Corp.
1886 Merritt Rd, Fort Mill SC 29715-7707. 803/548-2210.

CHEMICALS AND CHEMICAL PREPARATIONS

ABCO Industries Ltd.
200 Railroad St, Roebuck SC 29376-3121. 864/576-6821.

Calgon Corp.
603 High Tech Ct, Greer SC 29650-4801. 864/879-7100.

Sequa Chemicals Inc.
1 Sequa Ln, Chester SC 29706-2174. 803/385-5181.

Westvaco Corp.
P.O. Box 70848, Charleston SC 29415-0848. 803/740-2300.

MISC. RUBBER AND PLASTICS PRODUCTS

Dayco Products Inc.
Recold Rd Industrial Pk, Walterboro SC 29488. 803/538-5941.

HBD Industries Inc.
2400 Highway 1 S, Elgin SC 29045-9053. 803/438-3431.

RUBBER PRODUCTS

Parker-Hannifin Corp.
3025 W Croft Cir, Spartanburg SC 29302-4801. 864/573-7332.

UNSUPPORTED PLASTICS PRODUCTS

Armin Plastics
609 Worley Rd, Greenville SC 29609-3849. 864/235-3853.

Paragon Plastics Inc.
945 Rice Avenue Ext, Union SC 29379-8642. 864/427-0371.

PLASTICS PRODUCTS

Amoco Foam Products Co.
Old Highway 28, Beech Island SC 29841. 803/827-0116.

Carlisle Geauga Co.
601 E Wise St, Trenton SC 29847. 803/275-4486.

Cryovac
150 Cryovac Blvd, Seneca SC 29678-0900. 864/885-6200.

DFI
131 Frey Rd, Spartanburg SC 29301-1008. 864/574-2697.

Dispoz-O Plastics Inc.
Old Laurens Rd, Fountain Inn SC 29644. 864/862-4004.

Fabri-Kal Corp.
1321 Highway 20, Piedmont SC 29673. 864/299-1720.

Precision Southeast Inc.
4900 Highway 501, Myrtle Beach SC 29577-9447. 803/347-4218.

Pretech
111 Krieger Dr, Travelers Rest SC 29690-8099. 864/834-8061.

SPM Seneca
1642 Blue Ridge Blvd, Seneca SC 29672-6602. 864/882-5652.

CARBON AND GRAPHITE PRODUCTS

Showa Denko/Carbon
478 Ridge Rd, Ridgeville SC 29472-7830. 803/875-3200.

PLASTICS MATERIALS WHOLESALE

Composite Technology
777 John C. Calhoun Dr SE, Orangeburg SC 29115-6113. 803/534-5769.

CHEMICALS AND ALLIED PRODUCTS WHOLESALE

GA Ag Chem Inc.
N Highway 301, Hamer SC 29547. 803/774-2562.

GA Ag Chem-Distribution
815 E Church St, Bishopville SC 29010-2019. 803/484-9426.

PAINTS, VARNISHES, AND SUPPLIES WHOLESALE

Olney Paint Company
P.O. Box 1172, Spartanburg SC 29304. 864/585-2431.

United Paint Decorating Center
324 Wade Hampton Blvd, Greenville SC 29609-5739. 864/232-8169.

For more information on career opportunities in the chemicals/rubber and plastics industries:

Associations

AMERICAN ASSOCIATION FOR CLINICAL CHEMISTRY
2101 L Street NW, Suite 202, Washington DC 20037-1526. 202/857-0717 or 800/892-1400. International scientific/medical society of individuals involved with clinical chemistry and other clinical lab science-related disciplines.

AMERICAN CHEMICAL SOCIETY
Career Services, 1155 16th Street NW, Washington DC 20036. 202/872-4600.

AMERICAN INSTITUTE OF CHEMICAL ENGINEERS
345 East 47th Street, New York NY 10017. 212/705-7338 or 800/242-4363. Provides leadership in advancing the chemical engineering profession as it meets the needs of society.

AMERICAN INSTITUTE OF CHEMISTS, INC.
7315 Wisconsin Avenue, Suite 502 E, Bethesda MD 20814. 301/652-2447. A professional organization supporting the social, economic, and career objectives of the individual scientist.

CHEMICAL MANAGEMENT & RESOURCES ASSOCIATION
60 Bay Street, Suite 702, Staten Island NY 10301. 718/876-8800. Fax: 718/720-4666. Engaged in marketing, marketing research, business development, and planning for the chemical and allied process industries. Provides technical meetings, educational programs, and publications to members.

CHEMICAL MANUFACTURERS ASSOCIATION
2501 M Street NW, Washington DC 20037. 202/887-1100. A trade association that develops and implements programs and services and advocates public policy that benefits the industry and society.

THE ELECTROCHEMICAL SOCIETY
10 South Main Street, Pennington NJ 08534-2896. An international educational society dealing with electrochemical issues. Also publishes monthly journals.

SOAP AND DETERGENT ASSOCIATION
475 Park Avenue South, 27th Floor, New York NY 10016. 212/725-1262. A trade association and research center.

SOCIETY OF PLASTICS ENGINEERS
14 Fairfield Drive, P.O. Box 403, Brookfield CT 06804-0403. 203/775-0471. Dedicated to helping members attain higher professional status through increased scientific, engineering, and technical knowledge.

THE SOCIETY OF THE PLASTICS INDUSTRY, INC.
1275 K Street NW, Suite 400, Washington DC 20005. 202/371-5200. Promotes the development of the plastics industry and enhances public understanding of its contributions while meeting the needs of society.

Directories

CHEMICAL INDUSTRY DIRECTORY
State Mutual Book and Periodical Service, Order Department, 17th Floor, 521 5th Avenue, New York NY 10175. 516/537-1104.

CHEMICALS DIRECTORY
Cahners Publishing, 275 Washington Street, Newton MA 02158. 617/964-3030.

DIRECTORY OF CHEMICAL ENGINEERING CONSULTANTS
American Institute of Chemical Engineering, 345 East 47th Street, New York NY 10017. 212/705-7338.

DIRECTORY OF CHEMICAL PRODUCERS
SRI International, 333 Ravenswood Avenue, Menlo Park CA 94025. 415/326-6200.

Magazines

CHEMICAL & ENGINEERING NEWS
American Chemical Society 1155 16th Street NW, Washington DC 20036. 202/872-4600.

CHEMICAL MARKETING REPORTER
Schnell Publishing Company, 80 Brot Street, 23rd Floor, New York NY 10004. 212/248-4177.

CHEMICAL PROCESSING
Putnam Publishing Company, 301 East Erie Street, Chicago IL 60611. 312/644-2020.

CHEMICAL WEEK
888 7th Avenue, 26th Floor, New York NY 10106. 212/621-4900.

COMMUNICATIONS: TELECOMMUNICATIONS AND BROADCASTING

The telecommunications and broadcasting industries are poised on the edge of a revolution. At long last, Congress has finally deregulated the telecommunications industry, allowing long-distance carriers, local phone companies, and cable TV operators to get into each other's businesses. For the first time, consumers will be able to choose their local phone company, and that company will probably also provide them with their cable hookups.

Business in the telecommunications industry has been booming even without deregulation. The industry continues to break new ground and reach more customers, especially in wireless phone service. However, the industry has been shaken by recent layoffs at AT&T.

In broadcasting, competition is high, especially for high-profile positions such as newscasters and DJs. In television, the hottest industry is cable. Cable companies are rapidly expanding, and opportunities for technical workers are growing. In radio, syndicated radio shows are tearing up the airwaves. Larger stations with more money, more experience, and bigger names are producing shows which smaller stations are picking up to save money. This increase in syndication will lead to continued competition in the radio industry.

North Carolina

AT&T (AMERICAN TELEPHONE & TELEGRAPH)
P.O. Box 20046, Greensboro NC 27420. 910/279-7000. **Contact:** Steve Mascia, Human Resources Manager. **Description:** This location is an administrative facility. AT&T (American Telephone & Telegraph) is a long-distance telephone company which provides domestic and international voice and data communications and management services; telecommunications products; computer products; switching and transmission equipment; and components. **Other area locations:** There are several business units for AT&T located in the Greensboro area. **Other U.S. locations:** Dublin NC; Mesquite TX.

ALCATEL NETWORK SYSTEMS
2912 Wake Forest Road, Raleigh NC 27609. 919/850-6000. **Contact:** Human Resources Department. **Description:** This location provides engineering design and also manufactures circuit boards. Overall, Alcatel Network Systems is an international telecommunications systems company. **Common positions include:** Electrical/Electronics Engineer; Software Engineer. **Educational backgrounds include:** Computer Science. **Special Programs:** Internships. **Corporate headquarters location:** Richardson TX. **Other U.S. locations:** St. Louis MO. **Operations at this facility include:** Administration; Manufacturing; Research and Development; Service.

ALCATEL TELECOMMUNICATIONS CABLE
P.O. Box 39, Claremont NC 28610. 704/459-9821. **Contact:** Wayne Cole, Vice President of Human Resources. **Description:** Alcatel Telecommunications Cable manufactures optical fiber and the telecommunications cable that houses optical fiber. The company's customers include cable television companies and other companies that use fiber optic cable. **Common positions include:** Chemical Engineer; Electrical/Electronics Engineer; Materials Engineer; Mechanical Engineer. **Educational backgrounds include:** Engineering. **Benefits:** 401K; Dental Insurance; Disability Coverage; Life Insurance; Medical Insurance; Pension Plan; Tuition Assistance.

Corporate headquarters location: Hickory NC. **Other U.S. locations:** Elisabethtown KY; Tarboro NC; Roanoke VA. **Parent company:** Alcatel Network Systems. **Operations at this facility include:** Divisional Headquarters; Manufacturing; Research and Development; Sales. **Number of employees at this location:** 500. **Number of employees nationwide:** 2,000.

GTE SOUTH INC.
4100 Roxboro Road, P.O. Box 1412, Durham NC 27702. 919/471-5000. **Contact:** Human Resources. **Description:** As part of GTE Telephone Operations, GTE South provides a wide variety of communications services ranging from local telephone services for the home and office to highly complex voice and data services for industry. GTE is the fourth-largest publicly held telecommunications company in the world, the largest U.S.-based local telephone company, and the second-largest cellular-service provider in the United States. GTE is spread across 28 states, with large concentrations of customers in suburban and rural areas. In the U.S., Telephone Operations served 17.4 million access lines in 28 states at the end of 1994. In addition, GTE's affiliated telephone companies in Canada, the Dominican Republic, and Venezuela served 5.5 million access lines. Telephone Operations is presently undergoing a three-year re-engineering program. By the end of 1994, Telephone Operations had reduced its U.S. workforce to approximately 69,000 employees, a 23 percent reduction over the number of employees four years previous. This reduction is expected to continue as additional re-engineering programs are implemented. **Corporate headquarters location:** Stamford CT. **Other U.S. locations:** Nationwide.

GLENAYRE TECHNOLOGIES, INC.
5935 Carnegie Boulevard, Charlotte NC 28209. 704/553-0038. **Contact:** Beverly Cox, Vice President of Human Resources. **Description:** Glenayre, which was originally involved in the real estate development business, acquired the GEMS Business from GEL in 1992. The GEMS Business designs, manufactures, markets, and services switches, transmitters, controls, and related software used in personal communications systems including its paging, voice messaging, and message management and mobile data systems; transit communications systems; and mobile telephone systems. The GEMS Business accounts for all of the company's continuing business operations. In 1995, the company entered into an agreement to acquire MUX, located in Belmont, California. MUX designs, manufactures, and markets products for use in point-to-point microwave communication systems. **Corporate headquarters location:** This Location. **Listed on:** NASDAQ. **Number of employees nationwide:** 1,000.

JEFFERSON PILOT COMMUNICATIONS
One Julian Price Place, Charlotte NC 28208. 704/374-3500. **Contact:** Ms. Terry Mace, Vice President of Human Resources. **Description:** A television and radio broadcasting company. Parent company, Jefferson Pilot Corporation, is a holding company whose other holdings include life annuity, accident and health, property and casualty, and title insurance operations.

NORTHERN TELECOM, INC.
Department 6611, P.O. Box 13010, Research Triangle Park NC 27709. 919/992-5000. **Toll-free phone:** 800/377-6790. **Contact:** Director of Personnel. **Description:** Designs, develops, manufactures, markets, sells, installs, and services central office switching equipment, integrated business systems, terminals transmission equipment, cable and outside plant products, and other telecommunications products and services. **Corporate headquarters location:** This Location. **Other U.S. locations:** San Ramon CA; Stone Mountain GA; Morton Grove IL; Nashville TN. **Number of employees nationwide:** 30,000.

SPRINT MID-ATLANTIC TELECOM
14111 Capital Boulevard, Wake Forest NC 27587-5900. 919/554-7900. **Contact:** William L. Ricks, Manager of Professional Recruiting. **Description:** Sprint Mid-Atlantic Telecom provides telephone service to North Carolina, South Carolina, Tennessee, and Virginia using 1.66 million access lines. The company operates three divisions, Sprint United Telephone-Southeast, Sprint Carolina Telephone, and Sprint Centel properties in Virginia and North Carolina. Combined, Sprint Mid-Atlantic Telecom is the largest unit in Sprint's Local Telecommunications Division (LTD). Sprint Carolina Telephone provides local telephone service to 50 counties in eastern and central North Carolina. Overall, Sprint is a diversified telecommunications company, with a nationwide, all-digital, fiber optic network. Sprint's divisions provide global long-distance voice, data, and video products and services; local telephone services in 19 states; and cellular operations that serve 42 metropolitan markets and more than 50 rural service areas. Sprint's Staff Associate Program is a two- to three-year developmental program

designed to ensure an influx of highly competent individuals who have the capability to assume middle- to upper-level management positions within the corporation. Each candidate should have the opportunity to experience at least three of the following departments: Finance, Information Systems, Marketing, Network Operations, Customer Service, and International. Rotational assignments are challenging and allow the individual to be an immediate contributor while gaining a broad understanding of industry issues and operations. The program incorporates formal training and individual development, including periodical assessment of leadership skills. In order to provide a meaningful experience for the participants and meet the business needs of the corporation, Staff Associates are hired into one of three specific tracks: Financial, Technological, or General Management. Each track builds upon the strength and interest of the individual. Students should contact their placement offices regarding on-campus interviews. **Common positions include:** Accountant/Auditor; Computer Programmer; Economist/Market Research Analyst; Electrical/Electronics Engineer; Human Resources Specialist; Instructor/Trainer; Management Trainee. **Educational backgrounds include:** Accounting; Business Administration; Communications; Computer Science; Economics; Engineering; Finance. **Benefits:** Dental Insurance; Disability Coverage; Life Insurance; Medical Insurance; Pension Plan; Savings Plan; Stock Option; Tuition Assistance. **Corporate headquarters location:** Westwood KS. **Other U.S. locations:** Nationwide. **Parent company:** Sprint Corporation. **Operations at this facility include:** Administration; Sales; Service. **Listed on:** New York Stock Exchange. **Number of employees nationwide:** 55,000.

TDP ELECTRONICS
111 Old Bee Tree Road, Swannanoa NC 28778-3410. 704/298-6990. **Contact:** Jane McMahan, Director of Human Resources. **Description:** Manufactures radio and television broadcasting equipment.

VANGUARD CELLULAR
2002 Pisgah Church Road, Suite 300, Greensboro NC 27455-3314. 910/282-3690. **Contact:** Tina Stanley, Recruiter. **Description:** Sells and services cellular telephones. **Common positions include:** Accountant/Auditor; Adjuster; Administrative Assistant; Administrative Services Manager; Attorney; Branch Manager; Budget Analyst; Computer Programmer; Computer Systems Analyst; Credit Manager; Customer Service Representative; Electrical/Electronics Engineer; Financial Analyst; Human Resources Specialist; Marketing Specialist; Mathematician; Microwave Engineer; Operations/Production Manager; Paralegal; Purchasing Agent and Manager; Services Sales Representative; Statistician; Systems Analyst; Technical Writer/Editor. **Benefits:** 401K; Cafeteria Plan; Dental Insurance; Disability Coverage; Life Insurance; Medical Insurance; Stock Option; Tuition Assistance. **Special Programs:** Internships. **Corporate headquarters location:** This Location. **Operations at this facility include:** Accounting/Auditing; Administration; Customer Service; Engineering and Design; Financial Offices; Research and Development; Sales. **Listed on:** NASDAQ. **Number of employees at this location:** 400. **Number of employees nationwide:** 1,100.

Note: Because addresses and telephone numbers of smaller companies change rapidly, we recommend you call each company to verify the information below before inquiring about job opportunities. Mass mailings are not recommended.

Additional employers with under 250 employees:

COMMUNICATIONS EQUIPMENT

Alcatel Network Systems
510 Commerce St, Clinton NC 28328-4326. 910/592-3134.

Newton Instrument Co.
111 E A St #727, Butner NC 27509-2426. 919/575-6426.

Aer-Aerotron Inc.
4901 Capital Blvd, Raleigh NC 27604-4414. 919/872-4400.

AT&T Network Systems
2606 Phoenix Dr, Suite 600, Greensboro NC 27406-6347. 910/632-3540.

Century Cable
222 N Wilkinson Dr, Laurinburg NC 28352-2927. 910/276-1001.

MacKay Communications
4901B Capital Blvd, Raleigh NC 27604-4414. 919/850-3000.

Mark IV Industries Inc.
P.O. Box 33, High Point NC 27261. 910/887-2611.

Mac's Satellite Systems
530 McDonald Ave, Hamlet NC 28345-3136. 910/582-5316.

TELEPHONE COMMUNICATIONS

Page Net
4000 Westchase Blvd, Suite 190, Raleigh NC 27607-3958. 919/833-7243.

Page South
4205 Old Wake Forest Rd 201, Raleigh NC 27609. 919/286-3777.

AT&T
4600 Marriott Dr, Suite 510,
Raleigh NC 27612-3307.
919/783-8635.

AT&T
3200 Northline Ave, Suite
501R, Greensboro NC
27408-7611. 910/294-
4906.

AT&T
10000 Twin Lakes Pky,
Charlotte NC 28269-7653.
704/875-7300.

AT&T Network Systems
100 S Eugene St,
Greensboro NC 27401-2236.
910/378-4531.

**Carolina Telephone &
Telegraph Co.**
300 New Bridge St,
Jacksonville NC 28540-
4756. 910/347-9011.

MCI
105A Creek Ridge Rd,
Greensboro NC 27406-4424.
910/274-5058.

**South Bell Phone &
Telegraph Co. Inc.**
128 W Hargett St, Raleigh
NC 27601-1314. 919/821-
8367.

**Southern Bell Administrative
Office**
2200 Pinecroft Rd,
Greensboro NC 27407-4703.
910/855-4533.

**Southern Bell Business
Communications**
4651 Charlotte Park Dr,
Suite 230, Charlotte NC
28217-1911. 704/522-
4000.

Southern Bell
24 O Henry Ave, Asheville
NC 28801-2604. 704/258-
7005.

Southern Bell
3219 Glenwood Ave, Raleigh
NC 27612-5008. 919/821-
6126.

**Southern Bell Phone &
Telegraph Co.**
3222 Summit Ave,
Greensboro NC 27405-3742.
910/378-7006.

**Southern Bell Phone &
Telegraph Co.**
155 E Glendale Ave, Mount
Holly NC 28120-2121.
704/827-7005.

**Southern Bell Phone &
Telegraph Co.**
412 S Broad St, Gastonia NC
28054-4304. 704/861-
2801.

Alltel Carolina Inc.
236 W Center Ave,
Mooresville NC 28115-3119.
704/664-5666.

Cable & Wireless Inc.
3733 National Dr, Suite 222,
Raleigh NC 27612-4845.
919/787-4411.

Citizens Telephone Co.
P.O. Box 1137, Brevard NC
28712-1137. 704/884-
9011.

LCI International
8720 Red Oak Blvd,
Charlotte NC 28217-3990.
704/527-7706.

LCI International
1 W Pack Sq #525, Asheville
NC 28801-3402. 704/252-
0688.

Lexington Telephone Co.
200 N State St, Lexington
NC 27292-3428. 704/249-
9901.

**MCI Telecom Corp.
Information & Sales**
22 Pack Sq, Asheville NC
28801. 704/253-3481.

Sprint
3605 Glenwood Ave, Suite
250, Raleigh NC 27612-
4956. 919/783-2300.

Sprint
280 N Bridge St, Elkin NC
28621-3405. 910/526-
3310.

Sprint/Centel-North Carolina
320 1st Ave NW, Hickory
NC 28601-6123. 704/328-
0101.

Telemanagement Consultants
1510 Battleground Ave,
Greensboro NC 27408-8000.
910/691-8145.

**Trans National
Communications**
7004 Chaftain Pl,
Greensboro NC 27410-8656.
910/393-0006.

BTI
1 W Pack Sq #507, Asheville
NC 28801-3402. 704/251-
1422.

Carriage Technologies
5972 Rathlin Ln, Concord NC
28027-8800. 704/784-
5834.

Crown Cellular Inc.
1101 Tyvola Rd, Charlotte
NC 28217-3500. 704/525-
2356.

Excel
3712 Old Battleground Rd,
Greensboro NC 27410-2314.
910/282-3070.

LDDS
20 Battery Park Flat Iron
Building, Asheville NC
28801. 704/254-3212.

Sky One Communications
1301 E Millbrook Rd, Raleigh
NC 27609-5481. 919/790-
8800.

Telecomm/America Group
5807 High Point Rd,
Greensboro NC 27407-7004.
910/855-7224.

Accu-Call
5870 Faringdon Pl, Raleigh
NC 27609-3931. 919/872-
9242.

CMY Associates
11 Stone St, Writsvlle Beach
NC 28480-2851. 910/256-
5248.

Corley Communications
627 Minuet Ln, Charlotte NC
28217-2704. 704/525-
4004.

DSI Telecom
72 Biltmore Ave, Asheville
NC 28801-3624. 704/259-
9019.

Insync Communications
1301 King Cross Ct, Raleigh
NC 27614-9026. 919/872-
6100.

PST Inc.
205 Regency Executive Park
Dr, Charlotte NC 28217-
3989. 704/525-8000.

RP Teletrends
5000 Falls of Neuse Rd,
Raleigh NC 27609-5480.
919/850-0611.

Universal Communication
7516 Manford Ct, Charlotte
NC 28217-7979. 704/523-
4034.

**RADIO BROADCASTING
STATIONS**

WBXB FM
1001 Paradise Rd, Edenton
NC 27932. 919/482-3200.

WFTK AM
211 W C St, Butner NC
27509-2329. 919/781-
1030.

**TELEVISION
BROADCASTING STATIONS**

WBTV
1 Julian Price Pl, Charlotte
NC 28208-5211. 704/374-
3500.

WCCB
One TV Pl, Charlotte NC
28205. 704/372-1800.

WCNC TV
1001 Wood Ridge Center Dr,
Charlotte NC 28217.
704/329-3636.

WLOS
288 Macon Ave, Asheville
NC 28804-3798. 704/255-
0013.

WLXI TV
2109 Patterson St,
Greensboro NC 27407-2531.
910/855-5610.

WSOC TV
1901 N Tryon St, Charlotte
NC 28206-2733. 704/335-
4999.

WUNF TV
P.O. Box 14900, Durham NC
27709-4900. 919/549-
7000.

WTVD
16 W Martin St, Raleigh NC
27601. 919/899-3610.

**CABLE/PAY TELEVISION
SERVICES**

CATV Subscribers Service
808 Summit Ave,
Greensboro NC 27405-7834.
910/273-5553.

Cablevision
400 Old Belmont Mt Holly
Rd, Belmont NC 28012.
704/827-7507.

Cablevision
501 Hwy 210 N, Spring Lake
NC 28390. 910/497-7851.

**Cablevision High Point
Jamestown**
118 State St, Greensboro NC

27408-5920. 910/271-
2660.

**Direct Broadcast Cable
Service**
30 Shoreline Dr, New Bern
NC 28562-8957. 919/638-
3438.

**McDowell County
Cablevision**
12 S Garden St, Marion NC
28752-4051. 704/652-
3818.

Tele Media Company
104 S 4th St, Mebane NC
27302-2652. 910/622-
3096.

TW Programing Company
801 E Broad Ave,
Rockingham NC 28379-
4382. 910/895-4912.

South Carolina

COSMOS BROADCASTING CORPORATION
P.O. Box 19023, Greenville SC 29602. **Contact:** Personnel. **Description:** Cosmos Broadcasting Corporation owns eight television broadcasting stations in eight different states.

PIRELLI CABLE CORPORATION
700 Industrial Drive, Lexington SC 29072. 803/951-4800. **Contact:** Jerome F. Monteith, Vice President of Human Resources. **Description:** A manufacturer of a broad range of energy cables, fiber optic telecommunications cables, optical-electronic devices, systems for the telecommunications market, and associated accessories and services. **Common positions include:** Accountant/Auditor; Blue-Collar Worker Supervisor; Budget Analyst; Buyer; Chemical Engineer; Computer Programmer; Computer Systems Analyst; Credit Manager; Customer Service Representative; Designer; Electrical/Electronics Engineer; Electrician; Financial Analyst; General Manager; Human Resources Specialist; Industrial Engineer; Industrial Production Manager; Manufacturer's/Wholesaler's Sales Rep.; Materials Engineer; Mechanical Engineer; Operations/Production Manager; Purchasing Agent and Manager; Quality Control Supervisor; Technical Writer/Editor. **Educational backgrounds include:** Accounting; Computer Science; Engineering; Marketing. **Benefits:** 401K; Dental Insurance; Disability Coverage; Life Insurance; Medical Insurance; Pension Plan; Savings Plan; Tuition Assistance. **Corporate headquarters location:** This Location. **Other U.S. locations:** Colusa CA; Abbeville SC; Lexington SC. **Operations at this facility include:** Administration; Divisional Headquarters; Manufacturing; Regional Headquarters; Research and Development; Sales; Service. **Number of employees at this location:** 100. **Number of employees nationwide:** 1,250.

ROCK HILL TELEPHONE COMPANY
P.O. Box 470, Rock Hill SC 29731. 803/324-9011. **Contact:** Judy Comer, Director of Personnel. **Description:** A telephone company.

Note: Because addresses and telephone numbers of smaller companies change rapidly, we recommend you call each company to verify the information below before inquiring about job opportunities. Mass mailings are not recommended.

Additional employers with under 250 employees:

**TELEPHONE
COMMUNICATIONS**

Dial Page
810 Dutch Square Blvd,
Suite 105, Columbia SC
29210. 803/731-9191.

**AT&T General Business
Systems Marketing**
1201 Main St, Suite 2100,
Columbia SC 29201-3230.
803/765-0400.

MCI
2 Hampton Ave, Greenville
SC 29601-1945. 864/235-
5303.

MCI Consumer Customer Service
50 International Dr, Greenville SC 29615-4832. 864/676-1000.

Pittman Industries Inc.
3307 Broad River Rd, Columbia SC 29210-5424. 803/731-5551.

SC Loop Assignment Center
1600 Hampton St, Columbia SC 29201. 803/733-5180.

Southern Bell Telephone Co.
1731 Bush River Rd, Columbia SC 29210-6811. 803/731-3255.

Southern Bell Telephone Co.
218 College St, Greenville SC 29601-2013. 864/298-1771.

Southern Bell Telephone Co.
201 E Broad St, Suite 201, Spartanburg SC 29306-3289. 864/573-4047.

Commonwealth Communications Group
1201 48th Ave N, Myrtle Beach SC 29577-5424. 803/449-6200.

Farmers Telephone Co-op
1101 E Main St, Kingstree SC 29556. 803/382-2333.

Econocall Communications
1301 Pridgen Rd, Myrtle Beach SC 29577-4222. 803/626-4411.

MCI
1401 Main St, Columbia SC 29201. 803/733-9000.

Corporate Telemanagement Group
712 Richland St, Suite H, Columbia SC 29201-2300. 803/779-8800.

Summit Teleservices Inc.
3650 Claypond Rd, Myrtle Beach SC 29577-7326. 803/236-4100.

Voice-Tel of Western Carolinas
145 N Church St Unit 105, Spartanburg SC 29306-5146. 864/573-6844.

Sandhills Enterprises
3243 Bagnal Dr, Columbia SC 29204-3421. 803/787-5160.

Ken-Net-Com
4740 Ohear Ave, Charleston SC 29405-4935. 803/745-0870.

Bell Atlantic Metro Mobile
80 International Dr, Suite 500, Greenville SC 29615-4844. 864/676-2300.

California Tel Communications
3 Terminal St, Myrtle Beach SC 29577-3595. 803/444-0448.

Fidelity Communications
3734 Elberta St, Columbia SC 29210-4680. 803/561-0808.

RADIO BROADCASTING STATIONS

WAVF FM
1964 Ashley River Rd,

Charleston SC 29407-4782. 803/554-4401.

WEPR FM
1101 George Rogers Blvd, Columbia SC 29201-4761. 803/737-3420.

WLFJ FM
2420 Wade Hampton Blvd, Greenville SC 29615-1146. 864/292-6040.

WTCB FM
1801 Charleston Hwy, Cayce SC 29033-2019. 803/796-7600.

TELEVISION BROADCASTING STATIONS

WCSC Inc.
P.O. Box 186, Charleston SC 29402-0186. 803/723-8371.

WLOS TV 13 Television
10 Verdae Blvd, Greenville SC 29607-3805. 864/297-1313.

WYFF TV
505 Rutherford St, Greenville SC 29609-5385. 864/224-3842.

CABLE/PAY TELEVISION SERVICES

Telecable of Greenville
17 Lindsay Ave, Greenville SC 29607. 864/271-8526.

Carolina Cable Inc.
8438 Savannah Hwy, Norway SC 29113. 803/263-4600.

For more information on career opportunities in the communications industries:

Associations

ACADEMY OF TELEVISION ARTS & SCIENCES
5220 Lankershim Boulevard, North Hollywood CA 91601. 818/754-2800.

AMERICAN WOMEN IN RADIO AND TELEVISION, INC.
1650 Tysons Boulevard, Suite 200, McLean VA 22102. 703/506-3290. A national, nonprofit professional organization of women and men who work in electronic media and related fields. Services include News and Views, a fax newsletter transmitted biweekly to members; Careerline, a national listing of job openings available to members only; and the AWRT Foundation, which supports charitable and educational programs and annual awards.

BROADCAST PROMOTION AND MARKETING EXECUTIVES
2029 Century Park East, Suite 555, Los Angeles CA 90028. 310/788-7600. Fax: 310/788-7616.

INTERACTIVE SERVICES ASSOCIATION
Suite 865, 8403 Colesville Road, Silver Springs MD 20910. 301/495-4955.

INTERNATIONAL TELEVISION ASSOCIATION
6311 North O'Connor Road, Suite 230, Irving TX 75309. 214/869-1112. Membership required.

NATIONAL ASSOCIATION OF BROADCASTERS
1771 N Street NW, Washington DC 20036. 202/429-5300, ext. 5490. Fax: 202/429-5343. Provides employment information.

NATIONAL CABLE TELEVISION ASSOCIATION
1724 Massachusetts Avenue NW, Washington DC 20036-1969. 202/775-3651. Fax: 202/775-3695. A trade association. Publications include Cable Television Developments, Secure Signals, Kids and Cable, Linking Up, Only on Cable, and Producers' Sourcebook: A Guide to Program Buyers.

U.S. TELEPHONE ASSOCIATION
1401 H Street NW, Suite 600, Washington
DC 20005-2136. 202/326-7300.

<u>Magazines</u>

BROADCASTING AND CABLE
Broadcasting Publications Inc., 1705 DeSales Street NW, Washington DC 20036.
202/659-2340.

ELECTRONIC MEDIA
Crain Communications, 220 East 42nd
Street, New York NY 10017. 212/210-
0100.

COMPUTER HARDWARE, SOFTWARE, AND SERVICES

Hardware and software: Companies are starting to invest more in corporate technology after several years of lean spending. Network servers have been the hot business product recently, and that trend will continue through 1996. Expect the boom in big machines -- parallel computers, mainframes, and minicomputers -- to support a growing interest in online databases, accessing the Internet, and e-mail. PCs will remain the strongest part of the hardware market. The composition of the software industry is shrinking with many firms merging or acquiring others. Despite consolidation in the industry, and despite the crisis at Apple Computer, the overall number of software jobs is still rising.

What's hot on the market? Although it still accounts for a tiny percentage of software sales, Internet-related software -- and World Wide Web browsing software in particular -- is quickly transforming the industry. Analysts predict that sales of Internet software will double every year through at least 2000, and by then sales could hit $4 billion a year.

Services: Computer services professionals perform three activities: systems integration, custom programming, and consulting/training. Consulting and integration are the fastest-growing segments in computing due to the demand for networking. With more computer power available, more computer support will be needed.

North Carolina

ANALYSTS INTERNATIONAL CORPORATION (AiC)
2500 Gateway Center Boulevard, Suite 575, Morrisville NC 27560-9121. 919/460-6141. **Contact:** Recruiting Department. **Description:** Analysts International Corporation (AiC) is an international computer consulting firm with 2,700 employees worldwide. The company assists clients in developing systems in a variety of industries using different programming languages and software. This involves systems analysis, design, and development. **Corporate headquarters location:** Minneapolis MN.

AVANT!
P.O. Box 13665, Research Triangle Park NC 27709. 919/941-6600. **Contact:** Emma Parker, Director of Human Resources. **Description:** Avant! develops, markets, and supports software products that assist IC designing engineers in performing automated design, layout, and physical verification and analysis of advanced integrated circuits. The company's proprietary hierarchical physical verification software enables design engineers to improve time to market, reduce design risk, and obtain complete and fast verification of integrated circuits. The company's VeriCheck family of design verification software was introduced in 1992 and includes hierarchical products addressing geometric and electrical verification and parasitic extraction for resistance and capacitance analysis. The company also produces a family layout products which execute under UNIX or MS-DOS operating systems and run on platforms including DEC, HP, IBM, and Sun workstations and on 386/486-based PCs. **Corporate headquarters location:** This Location. **Listed on:** NASDAQ. **Number of employees at this location:** 97.

BROADWAY & SEYMOUR, INC.
128 South Tryon Street, Charlotte NC 28202-5050. 704/372-4281. **Contact:** Mark Hazzard, Recruiting Manager. **Description:** Develops information technology systems

and software. **Common positions include:** Computer Engineer; Computer Programmer; Computer Scientist; Computer Systems Analyst; Customer Service Representative; Software Engineer; Technical Writer/Editor. **Educational backgrounds include:** Computer Science. **Benefits:** 401K; Dental Insurance; Disability Coverage; Employee Discounts; Life Insurance; Medical Insurance; Stock Option; Tuition Assistance. **Corporate headquarters location:** This Location. **Other U.S. locations:** Boston MA; St. Paul MN; Raleigh NC; Worthington OH; Houston TX. **Operations at this facility include:** Administration; Research and Development; Sales; Service.

COMPUTER IDENTICS CORPORATION
11735 Man-O-War Trail, Raleigh NC 27613. 919/676-1938. **Fax:** 919/676-4161. **Contact:** Steven P. Archer, Human Resources. **Description:** Computer Identics Corporation is dedicated to providing data collection integrators with complete solutions, including scanning components, networking, software tools, and support services. Customers are primarily involved in materials handling and factory automation environments, and include systems integrators, original equipment manufacturers, value added resellers, and end users performing in-house system integration. Products and related services fall into four major categories: omnidirectional scanning systems, intelligent fixed position line scanners, data collection terminals, and networking products. Computer Identics Corporation's foreign subsidiaries are located in Canada, Belgium, England, France, and Germany. **Benefits:** 401K. **Corporate headquarters location:** Canton MA. **Other U.S. locations:** Mission Viejo CA; San Jose CA; West Hartford CT; Roswell GA; Schaumburg IL; Southfield MI; Cincinnati OH; Irving TX. **Listed on:** NASDAQ.

DATA GENERAL CORPORATION
62 T.W. Alexander Drive, Research Triangle Park NC 27709. 919/248-5970. **Contact:** Lynne Hall, Human Resources. **Description:** Designs, manufactures, and markets general purpose computer systems and related products and services, including peripheral equipment, software services, training, and maintenance. Data General markets directly to end-users and OEM's and offers six product families whose applications include: industrial manufacturing for controlling discrete assembly line operations, monitoring continuous production processes, testing, production planning, inventory management, and environmental surveillance. The company's products are also used in business data systems.

DATASOUTH COMPUTER CORPORATION
4216 Stuart Andrew Boulevard, P.O. Box 240947, Charlotte NC 28224. 704/523-8500. **Toll-free phone:** 800/476-2120. **Fax:** 704/525-6104. **Contact:** Tina Johnson, Personnel Manager. **Description:** Datasouth Computer Corporation designs, manufactures, and markets heavy-duty dot matrix and thermal printers used primarily with multi-user micro, mini, and mainframe computers for high volume, print-intensive applications. The company's three printer product lines include Performax, an alternative to the line printer for high speed report printing; XL series, for medium volume forms printing applications; and Documas, which was the company's first narrow carriage printer offering dual tractor allowing automatic switching from one form to another. The company also manufactures a portable thermal printer, Freeliner, which is used primarily for printing one packing or shipping label at a time. The company sells its products through a network of nearly 100 distributors worldwide and direct to high volume major accounts primarily in the transportation and travel, health care, and manufacturing and distribution industries. In 1994, Datasouth merged into Bull Run Corporation and operates as its wholly-owned subsidiary. The parent company also owns Gray Communication Systems, Inc., a newspaper publisher and television station operator; and Host Communications, Inc. a media and marketing services company. Bull Run Corporation, which was originally a mining resource company incorporated under the name of Bull Run Gold Mines, Ltd., sold its mining interests in 1990 and has since become a diversified holding company. **Corporate headquarters location:** This Location. **Parent company:** Bull Run Corporation (Atlanta GA). **Listed on:** NASDAQ. **Number of employees nationwide:** 125.

IBM CORPORATION
8501 IBM Drive, Charlotte NC 28262-8563. 704/594-1000. **Recorded Jobline:** 800/964-4473. **Contact:** Central Employment. **Description:** International Business Machines (IBM) is a developer, manufacturer, and marketer of advanced information processing products, including computers and microelectronics technology, software, networking systems, and information technology-related services. The company strives to offer value through its United States, Canada, Europe/Middle East/Africa, Latin America, and Asia Pacific business units, by providing comprehensive and complete product choices. **NOTE:** Send resumes to Staffing Services Center, IBM Corporation, 3808 Six Fork Road, Raleigh NC, 27609. Fax: 919/301-2787. **Common**

positions include: Chemical Engineer; Computer Operator; Computer Programmer; Data Entry Clerk; Electrical/Electronics Engineer; Manufacturing Engineer; Mechanical Engineer; Sales Representative; Secretary; Software Engineer; Systems Analyst; Technical Writer/Editor; Technician.

IBM CORPORATION
3808 Six Fork Road, Raleigh NC 27609. **Toll-free phone:** 800/426-3333. **Fax:** 919/301-2787. **Recorded Jobline:** 800/964-4473. **Contact:** Staffing Services Center. **Description:** International Business Machines (IBM) is a developer, manufacturer, and marketer of advanced information processing products, including computers and microelectronics technology, software, networking systems, and information technology-related services. The company strives to offer value through its United States, Canada, Europe/Middle East/Africa, Latin America, and Asia Pacific business units, by providing comprehensive and complete product choices.

IBM CORPORATION
WORKFORCE SOLUTIONS COMPANY
P.O. Box 12195, Research Triangle Park NC 27709. 919/543-5221. **Recorded Jobline:** 800/964-4473. **Contact:** Jenny Mays, Hiring Manager. **Description:** International Business Machines (IBM) is a developer, manufacturer, and marketer of advanced information processing products, including computers and microelectronics technology, software, networking systems, and information technology-related services. The company strives to offer value through its United States, Canada, Europe/Middle East/Africa, Latin America, and Asia Pacific business units, by providing comprehensive and complete product choices. **Common positions include:** Chemical Engineer; Computer Operator; Computer Programmer; Data Entry Clerk; Electrical/Electronics Engineer; Manufacturing Engineer; Mechanical Engineer; Sales Representative; Secretary; Software Engineer; Systems Analyst; Technical Writer/Editor; Technician.

MEDIC COMPUTER SYSTEMS
8601 Six Forks Road, Suite 300, Raleigh NC 27615. 919/847-8102. **Contact:** Jan Guy, Human Resources Director. **Description:** The company manufactures computer hardware and software systems for use in medical practices and hospitals.

MEMOREX TELEX
3301 Terminal Drive, Human Resources Department, Raleigh NC 27604. 919/250-6370. **Fax:** 919/250-6349. **Contact:** Ms. Terry Bymum, Manager of Staffing. **Description:** Researches, develops, and manufactures computer peripheral devices. **Common positions include:** Accountant/Auditor; Bindery Worker; Blue-Collar Worker Supervisor; Buyer; Commercial Artist; Computer Operator; Customer Service Representative; Electrical/Electronics Engineer; Electrician; Heating/AC/Refrigeration Technician; Printing Press Operator. **Educational backgrounds include:** Accounting; Computer Science; Engineering; Marketing. **Benefits:** Dental Insurance; Disability Coverage; Life Insurance; Medical Insurance; Pension Plan; Savings Plan; Tuition Assistance. **Corporate headquarters location:** Dallas TX. **Operations at this facility include:** Divisional Headquarters; Manufacturing; Regional Headquarters; Research and Development. **Listed on:** NASDAQ. **Number of employees at this location:** 500. **Number of employees nationwide:** 5,000.

NDC AUTOMATION
3101 Latrobe Drive, Charlotte NC 28211-4849. 704/362-1115. **Contact:** Gail Hentz, Director of Human Resources. **Description:** NDC Automation acquires, develops, and markets hardware, software, and engineering services that are incorporated into and used to control automatic guided vehicle systems (AGVS), which are used by customers to transport materials between various locations within a manufacturing or distribution facility.

NOVELL, INC.
5250 Seventy Seven Center Drive, Suite 350, Charlotte NC 28217. 704/527-0045. **Contact:** Joe Tiblier, Office Manager. **Description:** Charlotte sales office of Novell, the only major company that is singularly focused on network software. The company sets and adheres to open standards, develops new tools and systems, works in partnership with other companies, and makes computer networks easy to use and manage. Novell has grown to become the third-largest software company in the world by building software that spans from operating systems, network infrastructure, and services to network applications and information access products. A $2 billion software company, Novell employs approximately 7,900 worldwide with major development sites in California, Utah, and New Jersey. Novell's leading products include NetWare 4, UnixWare 2, PerfectOffice 3, and GroupWise 4. Novell is built

around four business units that develop complementary system software components and applications used to deploy advanced network-based information systems: the NetWare Systems Group; the UNIX Systems Group; the Information Access and Management Group; and the Applications Group.

RECOGNITION SYSTEMS DIVISION
Taggart Creek Road, Suite 110, Charlotte NC 28208. 704/392-1424. **Contact:** Jim Shropshire, Branch Manager. **Description:** Designs, manufactures, and sells image-enable processing computer systems throughout the world. **Number of employees nationwide:** 500.

STRATEGIC TECHNOLOGIES
301 Gregson Drive, Cary NC 27511. 919/481-9797. **Contact:** Gail Davis, Human Resources Director. **Description:** A company that sells and integrates corporate information systems.

Note: Because addresses and telephone numbers of smaller companies change rapidly, we recommend you call each company to verify the information below before inquiring about job opportunities. Mass mailings are not recommended.

Additional employers with under 250 employees:

COMPUTERS AND RELATED EQUIPMENT

Ammdahl
227 W Trade St, Suite 1900, Charlotte NC 28202-1675. 704/333-2131.

Broadband Technologies
P.O. Box 13737, Research Triangle Park NC 27709-3737. 919/544-0015.

COMPUTERS AND COMPUTER EQUIPMENT WHOLESALE

Cisco Systems Inc.
3100 Smoketree Ct, Raleigh NC 27604-1057. 919/878-6800.

Rodan Inc.
3305 16th Ave SE, Conover NC 28613-9213. 704/464-2816.

COMPUTER SOFTWARE, PROGRAMMING, AND SYSTEMS DESIGN

Datawatch Corp.
3700-B Lyckan Pkwy, Durham NC 27707. 919/490-1277.

Global Software Inc.
1009 Spring Forest Rd, Raleigh NC 27615-5833. 919/872-7800.

Management Systems Associates Inc.
5580 Centerview Dr, Raleigh NC 27606-3364. 919/851-6177.

Creative Systems & Consulting Co.
1133 Cliff Rd, Asheboro NC 27203-6950. 910/625-3555.

Information Systems of North Carolina Inc.
7500 E Independence Blvd, Charlotte NC 28227-9450. 704/535-7180.

Cost Containment Inc.
308 Sherwee Dr, Raleigh NC 27603-3522. 919/779-7219.

CSC Compusource
114 MacKenan Dr, Cary NC 27511-7921. 919/469-3325.

Early Cloud & Company
6211 Carmel Rd, Charlotte NC 28226. 704/544-0461.

SDRC
1319 Kingscross Dr, Charlotte NC 28211-3971. 704/366-8073.

Softest Inc.
605 Stokesbury Ct, Raleigh NC 27606-2652. 919/851-7449.

Sysplus Inc.
508 Foxhall St, Raleigh NC 27609. 919/781-2900.

COMPUTER RENTAL AND LEASING

Comdisco Inc.
13801 Reese Blvd W, Suite 280, Huntersville NC 28078-6308. 704/875-9290.

COMPUTER MAINTENANCE AND REPAIR

Norand Corporation
9711A Southern Pines Blvd, Charlotte NC 28273-5560. 704/523-8605.

Back It Up
70 Main St, Canton NC 28716. 704/648-9893.

Coeco Office Systems
205 E Arlington Blvd, Greenville NC 27858-5015. 919/321-2400.

Data I/O
3709 Alliance Dr, Greensboro NC 27407-2059. 910/632-0404.

Data Systems of Lumberton
324 E 24th St, Lumberton NC 28358. 910/738-2444.

Safelab Systems Inc.
7225 Circlebank Dr, Raleigh NC 27615. 919/876-6142.

South Carolina

AT&T GLOBAL INFORMATION SOLUTIONS
3325 Platt Springs Road, West Columbia SC 29169. 803/796-9740. **Contact:** Julie Godshall, Staffing Specialist. **Description:** An office location of the national company that develops, manufactures, markets, installs, and services business information processing systems for worldwide markets. Generally, AT&T Global Information Solutions' products and services may be grouped by the following categories: general

purpose computer systems, which range from small business systems to large mainframe processors; industry-specific occupation workstations, which include application specific workstations for retail, financial, manufacturing, and other markets; general purpose workstations; software at both the software and application levels; support services, which include software and hardware maintenance, consulting services, customer training, and documentation; data processing and telecommunications services, including a worldwide network of data processing centers; components, including semiconductor products and component sub-assemblies marketed to other manufacturers; and other business forms and supplies, marketed to both NCR and non-NCR users. Operates through the following divisions: Direct Marketing and Customer Support; Systemedia Group; Independent Marketing Organization; Development and Production Group; NCR Comten, Inc.; and Applied Digital Data Systems, Inc. **Common positions include:** Computer Programmer; Computer Systems Analyst; Customer Service Representative; Electrical/Electronics Engineer; Financial Analyst; General Manager; Human Resources Specialist; Industrial Engineer; Management Analyst/Consultant; Management Trainee; Quality Control Supervisor; Software Engineer; Technical Writer/Editor. **Educational backgrounds include:** Business Administration; Computer Science; Electronics; Engineering; Finance; Marketing; Mathematics. **Benefits:** 401K; Dental Insurance; Disability Coverage; Employee Discounts; Life Insurance; Medical Insurance; Pension Plan; Salary Continuation; Tuition Assistance; Wellness Program. **Special Programs:** Internships. **Corporate headquarters location:** Dayton OH. **Other U.S. locations:** Nationwide. **Parent company:** AT&T (American Telephone & Telegraph). **Operations at this facility include:** Administration; Divisional Headquarters; Manufacturing; Research and Development; Service. **Listed on:** New York Stock Exchange. **Number of employees at this location:** 1,300. **Number of employees nationwide:** 52,000.

AT&T GLOBAL INFORMATION SOLUTIONS
WORKSTATION PRODUCTS DIVISION
7240 Moorefield Highway, Liberty SC 29657. 864/843-1500. **Contact:** Ms. Pat Kay, Human Resources Representative. **Description:** An office location of the national company that develops, manufactures, markets, installs, and services business information processing systems for worldwide markets. Generally, AT&T Global Information Solutions' products and services may be grouped by the following categories: general purpose computer systems, which range from small business systems to large mainframe processors; industry-specific occupation workstations, which include application specific workstations for retail, financial, manufacturing, and other markets; general purpose workstations; software at both the software and application levels; support services, which include software and hardware maintenance, consulting services, customer training, and documentation; data processing and telecommunications services, including a worldwide network of data processing centers; components, including semiconductor products and component sub-assemblies marketed to other manufacturers; and other business forms and supplies, marketed to both NCR and non-NCR users. Operates through the following divisions: Direct Marketing and Customer Support; Systemedia Group; Independent Marketing Organization; Development and Production Group; NCR Comten, Inc.; and Applied Digital Data Systems, Inc. **Common positions include:** Computer Programmer; Electrical/Electronics Engineer; Software Engineer. **Educational backgrounds include:** Computer Science; Engineering. **Benefits:** 401K; Dental Insurance; Disability Coverage; Employee Discounts; Life Insurance; Medical Insurance; Pension Plan; Profit Sharing; Savings Plan; Stock Option; Tuition Assistance. **Special Programs:** Internships. **Corporate headquarters location:** Dayton OH. **Other U.S. locations:** Nationwide. **Operations at this facility include:** Manufacturing. **Listed on:** New York Stock Exchange. **Number of employees at this location:** 1,200. **Number of employees nationwide:** 52,000.

BLACKBAUD INC.
4401 Belle Oaks Drive, Charleston SC 29405-8530. 803/740-5400. **Contact:** Ms. Kathy Culvern, Personnel Coordinator. **Description:** Blackbaud Inc. offers computer programming services for all types of non-profit companies. Blackbaud Inc.'s software is designed to help these companies with a wide variety of activities including fundraising, administration, and organization.

COMPUTER PROFESSIONALS (CPI)
River Hill Conference Center, 54 Marina Road, Lake Wylie SC 29710. 803/831-9111. **Contact:** Human Resources. **Description:** Computer Professionals is a provider of information systems, as well as consulting and integration services. **Number of employees at this location:** 350.

DIGITAL EQUIPMENT CORPORATION
30 Patewood Drive, Greenville SC 29607. 864/675-5000. **Contact:** Human Resources. **Description:** Digital Equipment Corporation designs, manufactures, sells, and services computers and associated peripheral equipment, as well as related software and supplies. Applications and programs include scientific research, computation, communications, education, data analysis, industrial control, time sharing, commercial data processing, graphic arts, word processing, health care, instrumentation, engineering, and simulation. **Corporate headquarters location:** Maynard MA. **Listed on:** New York Stock Exchange. **Number of employees worldwide:** 77,800.

GRC INTERNATIONAL INC./SWL DIVISION
7410 Northside Drive, Suite 105, North Charleston SC 29420. 803/569-2888. **Fax:** 803/572-0150. **Contact:** Human Resources. **Description:** An international provider of knowledge-based professional services and technology-based product solutions to government and commercial customers. GRC International Inc.'s activities encompass sophisticated telecommunications products, network systems analysis, and network software development operations for the commercial market. The company is involved in creating large-scale decision-support systems and software engineering environments; applying operations research and mathematical modeling to business and management systems; and implementing advanced database technology. GRC International Inc. also provides studies and analysis capabilities for policy development and planning; modeling and simulation of hardware and software used in real-time testing of sensor, weapon, and battlefield management command, control, and communication systems; and testing and evaluation. **Corporate headquarters location:** Vienna VA. **Other U.S. locations:** Nationwide. **Listed on:** New York Stock Exchange. **Number of employees worldwide:** 1,245.

GATES/FA DISTRIBUTING INC.
39 Pelham Ridge Drive, Greenville SC 29615. 864/234-0736. **Contact:** Lois McNamara, Human Resources Director. **Description:** Gates/FA Distributing Inc. distributes microcomputers, networking software, and computer peripheral equipment including monitors, hard-disk drives, modems, and other related equipment. The company also packages computer systems, offers systems integration services, and provides technical support services. **Common positions include:** Buyer; Computer Operator; Computer Programmer; Credit Clerk and Authorizer; Credit Manager; Customer Service Representative; Human Resources Specialist; Marketing/Advertising/PR Manager; Payroll Clerk; Services Sales Representative. **Educational backgrounds include:** Accounting; Business Administration; Computer Science; Marketing. **Benefits:** 401K; Credit Union; Dental Insurance; Disability Coverage; Life Insurance; Medical Insurance. **Corporate headquarters location:** This Location. **Operations at this facility include:** Administration; Regional Headquarters; Sales. **Number of employees at this location:** 285. **Number of employees nationwide:** 385.

POLICY MANAGEMENT SYSTEMS CORPORATION
P.O. Box 10, Columbia SC 29202. 803/735-4000. **Contact:** Roger Hall, Recruiter. **Description:** Policy Management Systems Corporation licenses to customers its standardized insurance software systems and provides automation and administrative support and information services to the worldwide insurance industry. The company also provides professional support services, which include implementation and integration assistance, consulting and education services, information and outsourcing services ranging from making available software licensed from the company on a remote processing basis from the company's data centers to complete systems management, processing, administration support and automated information services through the company's nationwide telecommunications network using the company's database products. **Corporate headquarters location:** This Location. **Listed on:** New York Stock Exchange.

Note: Because addresses and telephone numbers of smaller companies change rapidly, we recommend you call each company to verify the information below before inquiring about job opportunities. Mass mailings are not recommended.

Additional employers with under 250 employees:

COMPUTERS AND RELATED EQUIPMENT

NCR Corp. Cooperative Computing Systems
3245 Platt Springs Rd, West Columbia SC 29170-2503. 803/796-9740.

COMPUTER SOFTWARE, PROGRAMMING, AND SYSTEMS DESIGN

Digital Equipment Corp.
4055 Faber Place Dr, Charleston SC 29405-8514. 803/744-4114.

Financial Management Accounting
44 Bow Cir, Hilton Head SC 29928. 803/686-6909.

SCT Utility Systems Inc.
2700 Middleburg Dr, Suite 101, Columbia SC 29204-2416. 803/799-4094.

Advanced Computer Systems
617 Riverwalk Way, Irmo SC 29063-9336. 803/732-3212.

Omni Analysis Inc.
107 Abbey Ln, Summerville SC 29485-8007. 803/875-9074.

Paradigm Technologies
443 Meeting St, West Columbia SC 29169-7532. 803/739-9390.

Computer Consulting Group
84 Villa Rd, Greenville SC 29615-3016. 864/232-7940.

COMPUTER MAINTENANCE AND REPAIR

Newer Systems
1013 Pine Log Rd, Aiken SC 29803-7311. 803/642-0007.

Solution Computers
2860 Joyce St, Sumter SC 29154-4669. 803/775-4310.

Universal Financial
104 Corporate Blvd, West Columbia SC 29169-4600. 803/796-9702.

For more information on career opportunities in the computer industry:

Associations

ASSOCIATION FOR COMPUTING MACHINERY
1515 Broadway, 17th Floor, New York NY 10036. 212/869-7440. Membership required.

INFORMATION TECHNOLOGY ASSOCIATION OF AMERICA
1616 North Fort Myer Drive, Suite 1300, Arlington VA 22209. 703/522-5055.

MULTIMEDIA DEVELOPMENT GROUP
2601 Mariposa Street, San Francisco CA 94110. 415/553-2300. Fax: 415/553-2403. Internet: info@mdg.org. A nonprofit trade association dedicated to the business and market development of multimedia companies.

Magazines

COMPUTER-AIDED ENGINEERING
Penton Publishing, 1100 Superior Avenue, Cleveland OH 44114. 216/696-7000.

COMPUTERWORLD
IDG, 375 Cochituate Road, P.O. Box 9171, Framingham MA 01701-9171. 508/879-0700.

DATA COMMUNICATIONS
McGraw-Hill, 1221 Avenue of the Americas, New York NY 10020. 212/512-2000.

DATAMATION
Cahners Publishing, 275 Washington Street, Newton MA 02158. 617/964-3030.

IDC REPORT
International Data Corporation, Five Speen Street, Framingham MA 01701. 508/872-8200.

EDUCATIONAL SERVICES

Job prospects for college and university faculty, elementary school teachers, counselors, and education administrators should show moderate improvement throughout the '90s, although most of the openings will result from retirements. Among kindergarten and elementary school teachers, the best opportunities await those with training in special education. The employment outlook is also good for teacher aides, as many assist special education teachers, as school reforms call for more individual attention to students, and as the number of students who speak English as a second language rises. Adult education and secondary school teachers, and sports and physical fitness instructors and coaches are other occupations expected to grow faster than average.

North Carolina

ALLEGHANY EDUCATIONAL OFFICES
ALLEGHANY COUNTY SCHOOL DISTRICT
One Peachtree Street, Sparta NC 28675. 910/372-4345. **Contact:** Duane Davis, Director of Personnel. **Description:** Administrative offices of the public school district.

APPALACHIAN STATE UNIVERSITY
Office of Personnel Services, 504 Dauph Blan Street, Boone NC 28608. 704/262-3186. **Fax:** 704/262-6489. **Contact:** Doris Greer, Staff Placement Officer. **Description:** A state university offering four-year programs for undergraduates. Appalachian State University offers a variety of areas of study for its students, including: business, applied arts, education, and arts and sciences. **Common positions include:** Accountant/Auditor; Administrative Services Manager; Architectural Engineer; Blue-Collar Worker Supervisor; Civil Engineer; Clerical Supervisor; Computer Programmer; Electrical/Electronics Engineer; Electrician; Health Services Manager; Hotel Manager/Assistant Manager; Human Resources Specialist; Industrial Engineer; Landscape Architect; Librarian; Library Technician; Mechanical Engineer; Pharmacist; Physician; Preschool Worker; Public Relations Specialist; Purchasing Agent and Manager; Registered Nurse; Restaurant/Food Service Manager; Social Worker; Technical Writer/Editor. **Educational backgrounds include:** Accounting; Business Administration; Communications; Computer Science; Engineering; Marketing. **Benefits:** 401K; Daycare Assistance; Dental Insurance; Disability Coverage; Life Insurance; Medical Insurance; Pension Plan; Savings Plan; Tuition Assistance. **Special Programs:** Internships; Training Programs. **Operations at this facility include:** Administration; Research and Development; Service. **Number of employees at this location:** 1,100.

ASHEBORO CITY SCHOOLS
P.O. Box 1103, Asheboro NC 27204. 910/625-5104. **Contact:** Gary Jarrett, Director of Personnel. **Description:** Administrative offices for the public school system.

CALDWELL COUNTY SCHOOL DISTRICT
1914 Hickory Boulevard, Lenoir NC 28645. 704/728-8407. **Contact:** Helen P. Hall, Personnel Director. **Description:** Administrative offices of the public school district. **Common positions include:** Counselor; Education Administrator; Preschool Worker; Psychologist; Social Worker; Speech-Language Pathologist; Teacher.

CHARLOTTE-MECKLENBURG SCHOOL SYSTEM
701 East 2nd Street, Charlotte NC 28202. 704/379-7000. **Contact:** Human Resources. **Description:** Administrative offices of the public school system.

DUKE UNIVERSITY
705 Broad Street, Box 90496, Durham NC 27708-0496. 919/684-2015. **Contact:** Employment Office. **Description:** A research university founded in 1892 which operates four campuses: West and East are both main campuses with academic buildings, administrative offices, libraries, residence halls, recreational facilities and dining halls; North includes residence halls and dining facilities; and Central Campus consists of Duke-owned apartments. Duke enrolls 5,000 undergraduates in its Trinity

College of Arts and Sciences and 900 students in its School of Engineering, along with 4,100 graduate and professional students in arts and sciences, business, divinity, engineering, the environment, law, medicine, and nursing. The university also operates the Duke University Art Museum, the Duke University Marine Laboratory and the Duke Primate Center. In 1990, the university established the Duke University Community Service Center (CSC) which provides support to various groups including the Duke Cancer Patient Support Group and the Durham County Youth Home. **NOTE:** Jobseekers must fill out an employment application. Please call to receive one. Number of faculty members: 1,900. **Common positions include:** Clinical Lab Technician; Computer Programmer; Computer Systems Analyst; EEG Technologist; EKG Technician; Medical Records Technician; Physical Therapist; Physician Assistant; Registered Nurse; Respiratory Therapist; Social Worker; Speech-Language Pathologist.

EAST CAROLINA UNIVERSITY
Human Resources Department, 210 East First Street, Greenville NC 27858. 919/328-6352. **Fax:** 919/328-4191. **Contact:** Joan Taylor, Employment Supervisor. **Description:** A university. **Common positions include:** Accountant/Auditor; Administrative Services Manager; Bindery Worker; Cashier; Clerical Supervisor; Computer Operator; Computer Programmer; Computer Systems Analyst; Construction Contractor and Manager; Customer Service Representative; Dietician/Nutritionist; Electrician; Employment Interviewer; General Manager; Graphic Artist; Health Services Worker; Heating/AC/Refrigeration Technician; Human Resources Specialist; Librarian; Library Technician; Licensed Practical Nurse; Line Installer/Cable Splicer; Medical Records Technician; Occupational Therapist; Payroll Clerk; Pharmacist; Physical Therapist; Physician Assistant; Printing Press Operator; Receptionist; Recreation Worker; Registered Nurse; Secretary; Social Worker; Speech-Language Pathologist; Stenographer; Stock Clerk; Surgical Technician; Systems Analyst; Typist/Word Processor. **Educational backgrounds include:** Accounting; Biology; Business Administration; Computer Science; Engineering; Finance; Marketing. **Benefits:** Disability Coverage; Life Insurance; Medical Insurance; Pension Plan; Tuition Assistance. **Special Programs:** Training Programs.

ELIZABETH CITY BOARD OF EDUCATION
P.O. Box 2247, Elizabeth City NC 27906-2247. 919/335-2981. **Contact:** Personnel Department. **Description:** A public school system.

FORSYTH TECHNICAL COMMUNITY COLLEGE
2100 Silas Creek Parkway, Winston-Salem NC 27103. 910/723-0371. **Fax:** 910/761-2399. **Contact:** Mr. Larry V. Weaver, Assistant to the Executive Vice President. **Description:** An educational institution. **Common positions include:** Automotive Mechanic/Body Repairer; Computer Programmer; Computer Systems Analyst; Counselor; Electrical/Electronics Engineer; Electrician; Emergency Medical Technician; Librarian; Library Technician; Mathematician; Mechanical Engineer; Paralegal; Radiologic Technologist; Respiratory Therapist; Teacher. **Educational backgrounds include:** Accounting; Art/Design; Biology; Business Administration; Chemistry; Computer Science; Engineering; Finance; Liberal Arts; Marketing; Mathematics; Physics. **Benefits:** 401K; Dental Insurance; Disability Coverage; Medical Insurance; Tuition Assistance. **Operations at this facility include:** Administration; Research and Development. **Number of employees at this location:** 310.

HALIFAX COUNTY SCHOOLS
P.O. Box 468, Halifax NC 27839. 919/583-5111. **Contact:** Human Resources. **Description:** A public school system.

McDOWELL COUNTY BOARD OF EDUCATION
P.O. Box 130, Marion NC 28752. 704/652-4535. **Contact:** Cynthia Davis, Director of Health Program. **Description:** A public school board.

MONTGOMERY COUNTY SCHOOLS
P.O. Box 427, Troy NC 27371. 910/576-6511. **Contact:** Mr. Currie Whitley, Auxiliary Services. **Description:** A public school system.

NORTH CAROLINA A&T STATE UNIVERSITY
1601 East Market Street, Department of Human, Resources, Suite 200, Dowdy Building, Greensboro NC 27411. 910/334-7862. **Contact:** Lillian Couch, Director of Human Resources. **Description:** A state university.

NORTH CAROLINA CENTRAL UNIVERSITY
P.O. Box 19714, Durham NC 27707. 919/560-6253. **Contact:** Mavis Lewis, Director of Human Resources. **Description:** A university.

NORTH CAROLINA SCHOOL OF ART
200 Waughtown Street, Winston-Salem NC 27127-2189. 910/770-3399. **Contact:** Brenda McGinn, Human Resources Director. **Description:** An art college. **Number of employees at this location:** 500.

NORTH CAROLINA STATE UNIVERSITY
Human Resources Department, Box 7210, Raleigh NC 27695-7210. 919/515-2135. **Contact:** Ms. Terri Yardley, Director of Human Resources. **Description:** A state university. **Common positions include:** Administrative Assistant; Administrative Services Manager; Data Processor; Research Technician. **Educational backgrounds include:** Biology; Chemistry; Computer Science; Engineering; Physics. **Benefits:** Dental Insurance; Employee Discounts; Life Insurance; Medical Insurance; Pension Plan; Savings Plan; Tuition Assistance. **Number of employees at this location:** 7,000.

RUTHERFORD COUNTY SCHOOLS
219 Fairground Road, Spindale NC 28160. 704/286-2757. **Contact:** Thomas L. Porter Jr., Personnel Director. **Description:** A public school system.

UNIVERSITY OF NORTH CAROLINA AT CHAPEL HILL
Office of Human Resources, Employment Department, Campus Box 1045, 725 Airport Road, Chapel Hill NC 27599-1045. 919/962-2211. **Contact:** Jack Stone, Director of Employment. **Description:** A campus of the University of North Carolina. **NOTE:** Send an application with your resume. **Common positions include:** Biological Scientist/Biochemist; Computer Programmer; Customer Service Representative; Statistician; Systems Analyst. **Educational backgrounds include:** Biology; Computer Science; Liberal Arts. **Benefits:** 403B; Dental Insurance; Disability Coverage; Employee Discounts; Life Insurance; Medical Insurance; Pension Plan; Tuition Assistance. **Special Programs:** Training Programs. **Number of employees at this location:** 8,000.

UNIVERSITY OF NORTH CAROLINA AT CHARLOTTE
Personnel Department, 9201 University City Boulevard, Charlotte NC 28223. 704/547-2000. **Fax:** 704/547-3239. **Contact:** Leonard Covington, Associate Director of Human Resources. **Description:** UNC Charlotte is a growing comprehensive institution serving an area that includes nearly 1.6 million people. The university employs almost 2,000 full-time faculty and staff and has an enrollment of approximately 15,600 students. Campus facilities include over 50 academic/administrative buildings and residence halls located on approximately 1,000 acres. **Common positions include:** Accountant/Auditor; Administrative Services Manager; Automotive Mechanic/Body Repairer; Civil Engineer; Clerical Supervisor; Computer Programmer; Computer Systems Analyst; Electrical/Electronics Engineer; Electrician; Human Resources Specialist; Library Technician; Registered Nurse; Software Engineer. **Educational backgrounds include:** Accounting; Business Administration; Communications; Computer Science; Finance. **Benefits:** 401K; Dental Insurance; Disability Coverage; Medical Insurance; Pension Plan; Savings Plan; Tuition Assistance. **Operations at this facility include:** Administration. **Number of employees at this location:** 2,500.

UNIVERSITY OF NORTH CAROLINA AT GREENSBORO
1100 Spring Garden Street, Greensboro NC 27412-5001. 910/334-5000. **Contact:** Robert Allen Bridge, Vice Chancellor of Human Resources. **Description:** A campus of the state university.

UNIVERSITY OF NORTH CAROLINA AT WILMINGTON
University Center, 601 South College Road, Wilmington NC 28403. 910/395-3000. **Contact:** Sam Connally, Human Resources Director. **Description:** A campus of the state university.

VANCE COUNTY SCHOOLS
P.O. Box 7001, Henderson NC 27536. 919/492-2127. **Contact:** Will McLean, Personnel Manager. **Description:** A public school system.

WARREN COUNTY SCHOOLS
P.O. Box 110, Warrenton NC 27589. 919/257-3184. **Contact:** Ms. Princine Jefferies, Personnel Director. **Description:** A public school system.

WATTS SCHOOL OF NURSING
3643 North Roxboro Street, Durham NC 27704. 919/470-7346. **Contact:** Cynthia Jones, Recruiter & Student Affairs Coordinator. **Description:** A nursing school.

WAYNE COUNTY PUBLIC SCHOOLS
P.O. Drawer 1797, Goldsboro NC 27533-1797. 919/731-5900. **Contact:** Dr. Steven Taylor, Personnel Director. **Description:** A public school district.

WELDON CITY SCHOOL DISTRICT
301 Mulberry Street, Weldon NC 27890. 919/536-4821. **Contact:** Debra Lanham, Director of Human Resources. **Description:** A public school district.

WESTERN CAROLINA UNIVERSITY
Office of Human Resources, Cullowhee NC 28723. 704/227-7211. **Contact:** Kathy Wong, Director of Human Resources. **Description:** A university.

Note: Because addresses and telephone numbers of smaller companies change rapidly, we recommend you call each company to verify the information below before inquiring about job opportunities. Mass mailings are not recommended.

Additional employers with under 250 employees:

ELEMENTARY AND SECONDARY SCHOOLS

Charlotte Latin School
P.O. Box 6143, Charlotte NC 28207-0001. 704/846-1100.

Providence Day School
5800 Sardis Rd, Charlotte NC 28270-5365. 704/364-6848.

Guilford Middle School
401 College Rd, Greensboro NC 27410-5199. 910/316-5833.

Kiser Middle School
716 Benjamin Pky, Greensboro NC 27408-8218. 910/370-8240.

Northwest Guilford Middle School
5300 NW School Rd, Greensboro NC 27409-9613. 910/605-3333.

Andrews High School
1920 McGuinn Dr, High Point NC 27265-3332. 910/819-2800.

Asheville High School
419 McDowell St, Asheville NC 28803-2690. 704/255-5352.

Broughton High School
723 Saint Marys St, Raleigh NC 27605. 919/856-7810.

Chapel Hill High School
1709 High School Rd, Chapel Hill NC 27516-9243. 919/929-2106.

Dudley High School
1200 Lincoln St, Greensboro NC 27401. 910/370-8130.

East Burke High School
P.O. Box 515, Icard NC 28666. 704/397-5541.

East Mecklenburg High School
6800 Monroe Rd, Charlotte NC 28212-6821. 704/343-6430.

Eastern Guilford High School
415 Peeden Dr, Gibsonville NC 27249-9218. 910/274-8461.

Enka High School
P.O. Box 579, Enka NC 28728-0579. 704/667-5421.

Enloe High School
128 Clarendon Cres, Raleigh NC 27610-2408. 919/856-7860.

Freedom High School
511 Independence Blvd, Morganton NC 28655-5500. 704/433-1310.

Garinger High School
1100 Eastway Dr, Charlotte NC 28205-1498. 704/343-6450.

Goldsboro High School
P.O. Box 1757, Goldsboro NC 27533-1757. 919/731-5930.

Grimsley High School
801 Westover Ter, Greensboro NC 27408-8207. 910/370-8180.

High Point Central High School
801 Ferndale Blvd, High Point NC 27262-4713. 910/819-2825.

Hoggard High School
4305 Shipyard Blvd, Wilmington NC 28403-6193. 910/350-2072.

Independence High School
1967 Patriot Dr, Charlotte NC 28227. 704/343-6900.

Jordan High School
6806 Garrett Rd, Durham NC 27707-5699. 919/560-3912.

Kinston High School
2601 N Queen St, Kinston NC 28501-1799. 919/527-8067.

Laney High School
2700 N College Rd, Wilmington NC 28405-8816. 910/350-2089.

Lee Senior High School
1708 Nash St, Sanford NC 27330-5899. 919/776-7541.

McDowell High School
Highway 70 W, Marion NC 28752. 704/652-7920.

Millbrook High School
2201 Spring Forest Rd, Raleigh NC 27615-7500. 919/850-8787.

Myers Park High School
2400 Colony Rd, Charlotte NC 28209-1743. 704/343-5800.

New Hanover High School
1307 Market St, Wilmington NC 28401-4399. 910/251-6100.

North Forsyth High School
5705 Shattalon Dr, Winston-Salem NC 27105-1332. 910/661-4880.

Northeast Guilford High School
6700 McLeansville Rd, McLeansville NC 27301-9716. 910/376-2500.

Northern High School
117 Massey Rd, Durham NC 27712-1499. 919/560-3956.

Northwest Guilford High School
5240 NW School Rd,
Greensboro NC 27409-9611.
910/605-3300.

Page High School
201 Alma Pinnix Dr,
Greensboro NC 27405-4398.
910/370-8200.

Ragsdale High School
602 High Point Rd,
Jamestown NC 27282-
8572. 910/819-2960.

Reynolds High School
1 Rocket Dr, Asheville NC
28803. 704/298-2500.

Reynolds High School
301 N Hawthorne Rd,
Winston-Salem NC 27104-
3299. 910/727-2061.

Richmond Senior High School
Highway 1 North,
Rockingham NC 28379.
910/895-6371.

Sanderson High School
5500 Dixon Dr, Raleigh NC
27609-4200. 919/881-
4800.

Scotland High School
1000 W Church St,
Laurinburg NC 28352-3565.
910/276-7370.

Smith High School
2407 S Holden Rd,
Greensboro NC 27407-5799.
910/294-7300.

Smithfield Selma High School
P.O. Box 1497, Smithfield
NC 27577-1497. 910/934-
5191.

South Mecklenburg High School
8900 Park Rd, Charlotte NC
28210-7699. 704/343-
3600.

Southern Guilford High School
5700 Drake Rd, Greensboro
NC 27406. 910/674-4250.

Southwest High School
4364 Barrow Rd, High Point
NC 27265. 910/272-1104.

West Charlotte High School
2219 Senior Dr, Charlotte
NC 28216. 704/343-6060.

West Forsyth High School
1735 Lewisville Clemmons
Rd, Clemmons NC 27012-
8374. 910/766-6467.

West Mecklenburg High School
7400 Tuckaseegee Rd,
Charlotte NC 28214-2621.
704/343-6080.

Western Guilford High School
409 Friendway Rd,
Greensboro NC 27410-4998.
910/316-5800.

Gateway Education Center
3205 E Wendover Ave,
Greensboro NC 27405-6433.
910/375-2575.

McIver Education Center
1401 Summit Ave,
Greensboro NC 27405-6763.
910/370-8260.

Elkin City School District
P.O. Box 310, Elkin NC
28621-0310. 910/835-
3135.

COLLEGES, UNIVERSITIES, AND PROFESSIONAL SCHOOLS

Barber Scotia College
145 Cabarrus Ave W,
Concord NC 28025-5187.
704/793-4900.

Belmont Abbey College
Belmont Ave, Belmont NC
28012. 704/825-6700.

Bennett College
900 E Washington St,
Greensboro NC 27401-3298.
910/273-4431.

Catawba College
2300 W Innes St, Salisbury
NC 28144-2488. 704/637-
4111.

Chowan College
P.O. Box 37, Murfreesboro
NC 27855. 919/398-4101.

Greensboro College
815 W Market St,
Greensboro NC 27401-1875.
910/272-7102.

Johnson C. Smith University
100-152 Beatties Ford Rd,
Charlotte NC 28216.
704/378-1000.

Lees McRae College
P.O. Box 128, Banner Elk NC
28604-0128. 704/898-
5241.

Pfeiffer College
P.O. Box 960, Misenheimer
NC 28109-0960. 704/463-
1360.

St. Andrews Presbyterian College
1700 Dogwood Mile St,
Laurinburg NC 28352-5521.
910/277-5000.

Warren Wilson College
P.O. Box 9000, Asheville NC
28802-9000. 704/298-
3325.

JUNIOR COLLEGES AND TECHNICAL INSTITUTES

Alamance Community College
P.O. Box 8000, Graham NC
27253-8000. 910/578-
2002.

Asheville Buncombe Tech Community
340 Victoria Rd, Asheville
NC 28801-4897. 704/254-
1921.

Catawba Valley Community College
2550 US Highway 70 SE,
Hickory NC 28602-8302.
704/327-7000.

Coastal Carolina Community College
444 Western Blvd,
Jacksonville NC 28546-
6899. 910/455-1221.

College of the Albemarle
P.O. Box 2327, Elizabeth
City NC 27906-2327.
919/335-0821.

Craven Community College
P.O. Box 885, New Bern NC
28563-0885. 919/638-
4131.

Davidson County Community College
P.O. Box 1287, Lexington
NC 27293-1287. 704/249-
8186.

Durham Technical Community College
1637 E Lawson St, Durham
NC 27703-5023. 919/598-
9222.

Edgecombe Community College
2009 W Wilson St, Tarboro
NC 27886-9361. 919/823-
5166.

Gaston College
201 Highway 321 S, Dallas
NC 28034-1499. 704/922-
6200.

Johnston Community College
P.O. Box 2350, Smithfield
NC 27577. 910/934-3051.

Lenoir Community College
P.O. Box 188, Kinston NC
28502-0188. 919/527-
6223.

Pitt Community College
P.O. Box 7007, Greenville
NC 27835-7007. 919/321-
4200.

Rockingham Community College
P.O. Box 38, Wentworth NC
27375. 910/342-4261.

Rowan Cabarrus Community College
P.O. Box 1595, Salisbury NC 28145-1595. 704/637-0760.

Sandhills Community College
2200 Airport Rd, Pinehurst NC 28374-8283. 910/692-6185.

Surry Community College
P.O. Box 304, Dobson NC 27017-0304. 910/386-8121.

Vance-Granville Community College
P.O. Box 917, Henderson NC 27536. 919/492-2061.

Wayne Community College
P.O. Box 8002, Goldsboro NC 27533-8002. 919/735-5151.

Western Piedmont Community College
1001 Burkemont Ave, Morganton NC 28655-4511. 704/438-6000.

Wilkes Community College
Collegiate Drive, Wilkesboro NC 28697. 910/651-8600.

VOCATIONAL SCHOOLS

ECPI College of Technology
7015 Albert Pick Rd, Greensboro NC 27409-9654. 910/665-1400.

MISC. SCHOOLS AND EDUCATIONAL SERVICES

John Casablancas Modeling
830 Tyvola Rd, Charlotte NC 28217-3537. 704/523-6966.

CHILD DAYCARE SERVICES

Alexander YWCA Day Care
910 N Alexander St, Charlotte NC 28206-3330. 704/372-6317.

Bright Horizons Child Center
1551 Arrow Point Ln, Charlotte NC 28273-8112. 704/523-5192.

Children First Learning Center
1004 Palmer Plaza Ln, Charlotte NC 28211-1185. 704/365-4550.

Children's Academy Day Care
101 Oceana Pl, Cary NC 27513-5273. 919/481-0666.

Creative Day School
1021 W Clemmonsville Rd, Winston-Salem NC 27127-4914. 910/784-8697.

Creative World 2 Day Care
2411 Flint Dr, Wilmington NC 28401-7711. 910/799-5195.

Dorothy's Child Development Day Center
315 E Pilot St, Durham NC 27707-3032. 919/688-6525.

Emma School Age Day Care Center
175 Bingham Rd, Asheville NC 28806-3800. 704/255-7760.

Four County Community Service Inc.
Cnty Rd 1006, Tabor City NC 28463. 910/653-5403.

Glen Arden Elementary School Age
175 Bingham Rd, Asheville NC 28806-3800. 704/684-7894.

Happy Kids Day Care
521 Kelly Rd, Wilmington NC 28409-3159. 910/395-5286.

Highland Preschool & Afterschool
1901 Ridge Rd, Raleigh NC 27607-3143. 919/787-2182.

Kiddie Kollege Knowledge 2
12 Berkshire Pl, Smithfield NC 27577-4734. 910/934-9837.

Kinder Care Learning Center
1700 Providence Rd, Charlotte NC 28207-2632. 704/366-7180.

Kinder Care Learning Center
5508 W Friendly Ave, Greensboro NC 27410-4212. 910/294-0580.

Kinder Care Learning Center
6601 E Wt Harris Blvd, Charlotte NC 28215-5102. 704/536-0830.

Kinder Elder Care Center
P.O. Box 2001, Southern Pines NC 28388-2001. 910/692-0364.

La Petite Academy
917 E Wt Harris Blvd, Charlotte NC 28213-5145. 704/548-0304.

La Petite Academy
P.O. Box 1069, Huntersville NC 28078-1069. 704/875-0399.

Little Angels Daycare
500 Kinard Dr, Winston-Salem NC 27101-3512. 910/725-2972.

Little Friends Learning Centers
787 Village Rd NE, Leland NC 28451-8469. 910/371-1818.

Matthews After School Center
200 McDowell Ave, Charlotte NC 28204. 704/343-3940.

Northwest Child Development Council
1208 Hattie Ave, Winston-Salem NC 27101-1842. 910/748-9200.

Pisgah Elementary School Age Program
175 Bingham Rd, Asheville NC 28806-3800. 704/255-5924.

PJ's Overnight Child Care
1212 Fenimore St, Winston-Salem NC 27103-5004. 910/727-1093.

Rocking Horse Child Care Center
2200 W Vandalia Rd, Greensboro NC 27407-7622. 910/854-0111.

Sharon After School Day Care
P.O. Box 30035, Charlotte NC 28230-0035. 704/343-6725.

St. Marks Center Developmental Day Program
601 N Graham St, Charlotte NC 28202-1400. 704/333-7107.

UCP Developmental Day Care Center
314 Chapanoke Rd, Raleigh NC 27603-3400. 919/851-5705.

United Day Care Services
1200 Arlington St, Greensboro NC 27406-1421. 910/378-7700.

Woodland Christian Day Care
3665 Patterson Ave, Winston-Salem NC 27105-3537. 910/767-6170.

Yadkinville Migrant Head Start
Hwy 601, Yadkinville NC 27055. 910/463-5993.

YMCA of Greensboro
1015 W Market St, Greensboro NC 27401-1816. 910/272-4146.

Garner Head Start Center
568 E Lenoir St, Raleigh NC 27601-2483. 919/779-1535.

South Carolina

ANDERSON COUNTY SCHOOL DISTRICT 1
P.O. Box 99, Williamston SC 29697. 864/847-7344. **Contact:** Human Resources. **Description:** Administrative offices for the public school district.

ANDERSON COUNTY SCHOOL DISTRICT 5
P.O. Box 439, Anderson SC 29622. 864/260-5000. **Contact:** Mrs. Pat Buckner, Human Resources. **Description:** Administrative offices for the public school district.

BOWMAN SCHOOL DISTRICT 2
P.O. Box 36, Bowman SC 29018. 803/829-2541. **Contact:** Human Resources. **Description:** Administrative offices of a public school district.

CLARENDON SCHOOL DISTRICT 3
P.O. Box 270, Turbeville SC 29162. 803/659-2188. **Contact:** Human Resources. **Description:** Administrative offices of the public school district. **Common positions include:** Teacher.

MEDICAL UNIVERSITY OF SOUTH CAROLINA (M.U.S.C.)
171 Ashley Avenue, Charleston SC 29425-1055. 803/792-2071. **Contact:** Ms. Rese Porter-Wolf, Employment Manager. **Description:** Engaged in educating health professionals, treating patients, and performing research. The university includes a children's hospital; the Institute of Psychiatry; Hollings Oncology Center; the Biomedical Research Center; heart and liver transplant programs; and a student population of over 3,000 enrolled in the six colleges. **Common positions include:** Accountant/Auditor; Architect; Biological Scientist/Biochemist; Biomedical Engineer; Blue-Collar Worker Supervisor; Buyer; Chemist; Civil Engineer; Commercial Artist; Computer Programmer; Department Manager; Dietician/Nutritionist; Draftsperson; Electrical/Electronics Engineer; Financial Analyst; Health Care Administrator; Human Resources Specialist; Marketing Specialist; Mechanical Engineer; Operations/Production Manager; Physicist/Astronomer; Statistician; Systems Analyst; Technical Writer/Editor; Transportation/Traffic Specialist. **Educational backgrounds include:** Accounting; Biology; Business Administration; Chemistry; Computer Science; Engineering; Finance; Marketing; Mathematics; Physics. **Benefits:** Dental Insurance; Disability Coverage; Life Insurance; Medical Insurance; Pension Plan; Savings Plan; Tuition Assistance. **Special Programs:** Internships. **Corporate headquarters location:** This Location. **Operations at this facility include:** Administration; Research and Development.

NORTH SCHOOL DISTRICT
P.O. Box 640, North SC 29112. 803/247-2163. **Contact:** Bernita Guess, Interim Superintendent. **Description:** A public school district.

SALUDA SCHOOL DISTRICT 1
404 North Wise Road, Saluda SC 29138. 864/445-8441. **Contact:** Patricia Ward, Director of Human Resources. **Description:** A public school district.

SCHOOL DISTRICT 17
P.O. Box 1180, Sumter SC 29151. 803/469-8536. **Contact:** Human Resources. **Description:** Administrative offices for a public school district.

SCHOOL DISTRICT 6
1493 W.O. Ezell Boulevard, Spartanburg SC 29301. 864/576-4212. **Contact:** Ms. Monty King, Human Resources Director. **Description:** Administrative offices for a public school district.

UNION COUNTY SCHOOLS
P.O. Box 907, Union SC 29379. 864/429-1740. **Contact:** Dr. Richard Baldwin, Director of Human Resources. **Description:** A public school system.

UNIVERSITY OF SOUTH CAROLINA
508 Assembly Street, Columbia SC 29208. 803/777-3821. **Contact:** Ms. Barbara Clark, Employment Manager. **Description:** A four-year state university founded in 1801. The university awards bachelor's, master's, and doctoral degrees and enrolls over 25,000 students per year. The University of South Carolina also has campuses in Spartanburg and Aiken. **Common positions include:** Accountant/Auditor; Administrator; Biological Scientist/Biochemist; Blue-Collar Worker Supervisor; Buyer; Chemist; Commercial Artist; Computer Programmer; Department Manager; Economist/Market Research Analyst; General Manager; Geographer;

Geologist/Geophysicist; Management Trainee; Physicist/Astronomer; Systems Analyst; Technical Writer/Editor. **Educational backgrounds include:** Accounting; Art/Design; Biology; Business Administration; Chemistry; Communications; Computer Science; Economics; Engineering; Finance; Geology; Liberal Arts; Marketing; Mathematics; Physics. **Benefits:** Dental Insurance; Disability Coverage; Life Insurance; Medical Insurance; Pension Plan. **Operations at this facility include:** Administration; Research and Development; Service. **Number of employees at this location:** 1,400.

WARE SHOALS SCHOOL DISTRICT 51
42 Sparks Avenue, Ware Shoals SC 29692. 864/456-7496. **Contact:** Wanda Collins, Director of Human Resources. **Description:** A public school district.

WILLIAMSBURG COUNTY SCHOOL DISTRICT
423 School Street, Kingstree SC 29556. 803/354-5571. **Fax:** 803/354-3213. **Contact:** Mr. Francis Burrows, Director of Human Resources. **Description:** A public school district. **Common positions include:** Accountant/Auditor; Clerical Supervisor; Computer Operator; Computer Programmer; Computer Systems Analyst; Education Administrator; Human Resources Specialist; Librarian; Payroll Clerk; Preschool Worker; Psychologist; Public Relations Specialist; Purchasing Agent and Manager; Receptionist; Registered Nurse; Restaurant/Food Service Manager; Secretary; Social Worker; Speech-Language Pathologist; Teacher; Teacher Aide; Transportation/Traffic Specialist; Typist/Word Processor. **Educational backgrounds include:** Accounting; Art/Design; Biology; Business Administration; Chemistry; Communications; Computer Science; Economics; Finance; Mathematics; Physics; Special Education. **Benefits:** Credit Union; Dental Insurance; Disability Coverage; Life Insurance; Medical Insurance; Pension Plan; Tuition Assistance. **Corporate headquarters location:** This Location. **Operations at this facility include:** Administration. **Number of employees at this location:** 1,003.

WINTHROP COLLEGE
303 Tillman Hall, Rock Hill SC 29733. 803/323-2273. **Contact:** Gail O'Steen, Employment Coordinator. **Description:** Winthrop College is a four-year state college offering bachelor's degrees and master's degrees. The college was founded in 1886 and has an enrollment of approximately 5,100 students.

Note: Because addresses and telephone numbers of smaller companies change rapidly, we recommend you call each company to verify the information below before inquiring about job opportunities. Mass mailings are not recommended.

Additional employers with under 250 employees:

ELEMENTARY AND SECONDARY SCHOOLS

Bob Jones Elementary School
1700 Wade Hampton Blvd, Greenville SC 29614-1000. 864/242-5100.

Sullivan Middle School
1825 Eden Ter, Rock Hill SC 29730. 803/366-8181.

Irmo Middle School Campus
6051 Wescott Rd, Columbia SC 29212. 803/732-8200.

Conway High School
2201 Church St, Conway SC 29526-2975. 803/248-6321.

Dorman High School
1491 W O Ezell Blvd, Spartanburg SC 29301-1590. 864/576-4202.

South Florence High School
3200 S Irby St, Florence SC 29505-5029. 803/664-8190.

Greenwood High School
1710 Cokesbury Rd, Greenwood SC 29649-8971. 864/229-2528.

Hartsville Senior High School
701 Lewellyn Dr, Hartsville SC 29550-5298. 803/383-3130.

Airport High School
1315 Boston Ave, West Columbia SC 29170-2192. 803/822-5600.

Spartanburg Senior High School
500 Dupre Dr, Spartanburg SC 29307-2978. 864/594-4410.

Lake City High School
P.O. Box 1157, Lake City SC 29560-1157. 803/394-3321.

Lexington High School
2463 Augusta Hwy, Lexington SC 29072-2296. 803/359-5565.

Lower Richland High School
2615 Lower Richland Blvd, Hopkins SC 29061-8641. 803/695-3000.

Marlboro County High School
951 Fayetteville Avenue Ext, Bennettsville SC 29512-4100. 803/479-5900.

North Charleston High School
1087 E Montague Ave, Charleston SC 29405-4826. 803/745-7140.

Stratford High School
951 Crowfield Blvd, Goose Creek SC 29445-7124. 803/820-4000.

Irmo High School
6671 Saint Andrews Rd, Columbia SC 29212-2198. 803/732-8100.

Orangeburg-Wilkinson High School
601 Bruin Parkway, Orangeburg SC 29118-1460. 803/534-6180.

Socastee High School
4900 Socastee Blvd,
Surfside Beach SC 29575-
7221. 803/293-2513.

Sumter High School
2580 McCrays Mill Rd,
Sumter SC 29154-6098.
803/481-4480.

St. John's High School
545 Spring St, Darlington SC
29532. 803/398-5140.

Wando High School
1560 Mathis Ferry Rd,
Mount Pleasant SC 29464-
9703. 803/849-2830.

Dillon County School District
P.O. Box 644, Lake View SC
29563-0644. 803/759-
3001.

Orangeburg County School District 2
P.O. Box 36, Bowman SC
29018. 803/829-2541.

Orangeburg County School District 7
P.O. Box 820, Elloree SC
29047-0820. 803/897-
2211.

Greenwood County School District 50
P.O. Box 248, Greenwood
SC 29648. 864/223-4348.

Spartanburg County School District 6
1493 W O Ezell Blvd,
Spartanburg SC 29301-
2615. 864/576-4212.

COLLEGES, UNIVERSITIES, AND PROFESSIONAL SCHOOLS

Anderson College
316 Boulevard, Anderson SC
29621-4035. 864/231-
2000.

Central Wesleyan College
P.O. Box 102, Central SC
29630-0102. 864/639-
2453.

Claflin College
700 College St NE,
Orangeburg SC 29115-4477.
803/534-2710.

Coker College
East College Ave, Hartsville
SC 29550. 803/383-8000.

Columbia College
1301 Columbia College Dr,
Columbia SC 29203-5998.
803/786-3012.

Converse College
580 E Main St, Spartanburg
SC 29302. 864/596-9000.

Erskine College
P.O. Box 176, Due West SC
29639. 864/379-2131.

Limestone College
1115 College Dr, Gaffney SC
29340. 864/489-7151.

Morris College
100 W College St, Sumter
SC 29150-3599. 803/775-
9371.

Newberry College
2100 College St, Newberry
SC 29108-2197. 803/276-
5010.

Presbyterian College
503 S Broad St, Clinton SC
29325-2865. 864/833-
2820.

Voorhees College
Voorhees Rd, Denmark SC
29042. 803/793-3351.

Wofford College
429 N Church St,
Spartanburg SC 29303-
3663. 864/597-4000.

JUNIOR COLLEGES AND TECHNICAL INSTITUTES

Central Carolina Technical College
506 N Guignard Dr, Sumter
SC 29150-2468. 803/778-
1961.

Florence Darlington Technical College
P.O. Box 100548, Florence
SC 29501-0548. 803/661-
8324.

Horry Georgetown Technical College
P.O. Box 1966, Conway SC
29526. 803/347-3186.

Piedmont Technical College
1467 Emerald Rd,
Greenwood SC 29646-9559.
864/941-8324.

Spartanburg Technical College
P.O. Box 4386, Spartanburg
SC 29305-4386. 864/591-
3600.

Tri County Technical College
P.O. Box 587, Pendleton SC
29670-0587. 864/646-
8361.

York Technical College
452 S Anderson Rd, Rock
Hill SC 29730-3395.
803/327-8000.

BUSINESS, SECRETARIAL, AND DATA PROCESSING SCHOOLS

Computer Source Connecting Point
2435 E North St, Suite
1213D, Greenville SC
29615-1442. 864/268-
0461.

MISC. SCHOOLS AND EDUCATIONAL SERVICES

Trident Literacy Association
6296 Rivers Ave, Suite 310,
Charleston SC 29406-4973.
803/747-2223.

CHILD DAYCARE SERVICES

ABC Child Development
E Main, Moncks Corner SC
29461. 803/761-8620.

Child's World Sunshine House
1801 Bypass 72 NE,
Greenwood SC 29649-1612.
864/223-5665.

Rocking Horse Child Care Centers
4109 E North St, Greenville
SC 29615-2350. 864/268-
9163.

Tender Loving Care
1218 N Main St, Fountain
Inn SC 29644-1323.
864/963-2838.

For more information on career opportunities in educational services:

Associations

AMERICAN ASSOCIATION OF SCHOOL ADMINISTRATORS
1801 North Moore Street, Arlington VA
22209-9988. 703/528-0700. Fax:
703/841-1543. An organization of school
system leaders. Membership includes a
national conference on education; programs
and seminars; *The School Administrator,* a
monthly magazine; *Leadership News,* a bimonthly newspaper; *The AASA Professor,* a

quarterly publication; and a catalog of other
publications and audiovisuals.

AMERICAN FEDERATION OF TEACHERS
555 New Jersey Avenue NW, Washington
DC 20001. 202/879-4400.

COLLEGE AND UNIVERSITY PERSONNEL ASSOCIATION
1233 20th Street NW, Suite 301,
Washington DC 20036. 202/429-0311.
Membership required.

NATIONAL ASSOCIATION OF BIOLOGY TEACHERS
11250 Roger Bacon Drive #19, Reston VA 22090-5202. 703/471-1134. Toll-free number: 800/406-0775. Fax: 703/435-5582. A professional organization for biology and life science educators. E-mail address: nabter@aol.com.

NATIONAL ASSOCIATION OF COLLEGE ADMISSION COUNSELORS
1631 Prince Street, Alexandria VA 22314. 703/836-2222. An education association of secondary school counselors, college and university admission officers, and related individuals who work with students as they make the transition from high school to post-secondary education.

NATIONAL ASSOCIATION OF COLLEGE AND UNIVERSITY BUSINESS OFFICERS
1 DuPont Circle, Suite 500, Washington DC 20036. 202/861-2500. Association for those involved in the financial administration and management of higher education. Membership required.

NATIONAL SCIENCE TEACHERS ASSOCIATION
1840 Wilson Boulevard, Arlington VA 22201-3000. 703/243-7100. Organization committed to the improvement of science education at all levels, preschool through college. Publishes five journals, a newspaper, and a number of special publications. Also conducts national and regional conventions.

Books

ACADEMIC LABOR MARKETS
Falmer Press, Taylor & Francis, Inc., 1900 Frost Road, Suite 101, Bristol PA 19007. 800/821-8312.

HOW TO GET A JOB IN EDUCATION
Adams Media Corporation, 260 Center Street, Holbrook MA 02343. 617/767-8100.

Directories

WASHINGTON HIGHER EDUCATION ASSOCIATION DIRECTORY
Council for Advancement and Support of Education, 11 DuPont Circle NW, Suite 400, Washington DC 20036 202/328-5900.

ELECTRONIC/INDUSTRIAL ELECTRICAL EQUIPMENT

Heading into 1996, industry analysts expect productivity in the fast-paced electronics industry to continue to spiral downward, even as the number of production workers in the industry levels off. Intense competition from overseas has companies cutting costs by sending labor-intensive operations to low-wage regions like the Far East and Mexico. On the other hand, the increased computerization of the industry is fueling the demand for highly-trained, knowledgeable workers.

Semiconductor manufacturers, in particular, are growing steadily. Starting out the year, the Semiconductor Industry Association forecasted a growth rate of about 15 percent. The year actually came in at 26 percent. Factors spawning a high demand for semiconductors: a surging PC market, new information highway markets, and a stronger telecommunications and consumer electronics market.

North Carolina

ACME ELECTRIC CORPORATION
4815 West Fifth Street, Lumberton NC 28358-0499. 910/738-4251. **Fax:** 910/739-0024. **Contact:** Cavin D. Clapp, Administrative Manager. **Description:** Acme Electric Corporation manufactures dry-type industrial distribution transformers and related products. **Common positions include:** Administrative Services Manager; Buyer; Customer Service Representative; Designer; Draftsperson; Electrical/Electronics Engineer; Electrician; Financial Analyst; General Manager; Industrial Engineer; Industrial Production Manager; Mechanical Engineer; Operations/Production Manager; Purchasing Agent and Manager; Quality Control Supervisor; Transportation/Traffic Specialist. **Benefits:** 401K; Dental Insurance; Disability Coverage; Life Insurance; Medical Insurance; Pension Plan; Profit Sharing; Savings Plan; Tuition Assistance. **Corporate headquarters location:** Amherst NY. **Operations at this facility include:** Administration; Divisional Headquarters; Management Consulting; Sales. **Listed on:** New York Stock Exchange. **Number of employees at this location:** 280. **Number of employees nationwide:** 1,000.

AMETEK, INC.
704 Myrtle Drive, Graham NC 27253. 910/229-5591. **Contact:** Barbara Winkler, Human Resource Manager. **Description:** This location is an electrical fractural horsepower motor assembly plant. Overall, AMETEK, Inc. is a global manufacturing company which has grown, through a combination of acquisitions and internal growth, into a diversified company which serves a variety of industrial and commercial markets. The company produces and sells its products through its Electromechanical, Precision Instruments, and Industrial Materials groups. The Electromechanical Group has a leading market share in the production of electric motors for vacuum cleaners and floor care products, while technical motor products for computer, medical, and other markets is a growing business. The company employs more than 6,000 people worldwide and operates 32 manufacturing facilities in 12 states as well as in Italy, Denmark, England, and Mexico. **Common positions include:** Blue-Collar Worker Supervisor; Computer Systems Analyst; Electrical/Electronics Engineer; Electrician; Human Resources Specialist; Industrial Engineer; Mechanical Engineer. **Educational backgrounds include:** Business Administration; Engineering; Liberal Arts. **Benefits:** 401K; Dental Insurance; Disability Coverage; Employee Discounts; Life Insurance; Medical Insurance; Pension Plan; Savings Plan; Tuition Assistance. **Corporate headquarters location:** Kent OH. **Operations at this facility include:** Administration; Manufacturing. **Number of employees at this location:** 250.

ANALOG DEVICES, INC.
7910 Triad Center Drive, Greensboro NC 27409. 910/668-9511. **Contact:** Gail Bechard, Human Resources Manager. **Description:** Analog Devices, Inc. is a *Fortune* 500 company that designs, manufactures, and markets a broad line of high-performance linear, mixed-signal, and digital integrated circuits (ICs) that address a wide range of real-world signal processing applications. The company's principal products include system-level ICs and general purpose, standard linear ICs. Other products include devices manufactured using assembled product technology, such as hybrids, which combine unpackaged IC chips and other chip-level components in a single package. ICs represent approximately 90 percent of total revenues. System-level ICs include special purpose linear and mixed-signal ICs and digital signal processing (DSP) ICs. Some mixed-signal ICs contain a DSP core. Analog's system-level ICs are used primarily in communications and computer applications. The company's largest communications application is the pan-European GSM (Global System for Mobile Communications) digital cellular telephone system. Analog's core technologies are required for all of the emerging communications standards, providing the company numerous new product opportunities for ICs used in the wireless, fiber optic, coaxial cable, and twisted pair applications that will be part of the new information infrastructure. Analog sells its products worldwide through a direct sales force, third-party industrial distributors, and independent sales representatives. The company has direct sales offices in 17 countries, including the U.S. Analog meets most of its needs for wafers fabricated on linear and mixed-signal processes with wafers fabricated at company-owned production facilities, and uses third-party wafer fabricators for most wafers that can be fabricated on industry standard digital processes.

CEM CORPORATION
P.O. Box 200, Matthews NC 28106. 704/821-7015. **Fax:** 704/821-7894. **Contact:** Steve Spradlint, Human Resources Manager. **Description:** CEM Corporation develops, manufactures, markets, and services microwave-based instrumentation for testing and analysis in industrial and analytical laboratory markets. The company's products include: microwave digestion systems; moisture/solids analyzers; fat analyzer systems; microwave extraction systems; microwave ashing systems; and SpectroPrep systems. **Corporate headquarters location:** This Location. **Subsidiaries include:** CEM (Microwave Technology) Ltd. (Buckingham, UK); CEM GmbH (Kamp-Linfort, Germany); CEM S.r.l. (Cologno al Serio, Italy). **Listed on:** NASDAQ. **Number of employees nationwide:** 175.

COOPER INDUSTRIES INC.
BUSSMANN DIVISION
1000 Craigmont Road, Black Mountain NC 28711. 704/669-6482. **Contact:** Don Koppenhaver, Human Resources Manager. **Description:** The Bussmann Division of Cooper Industries manufactures electrical protection devices, such as fuses, fuse holders, and fuse boxes. The division's major markets include secondary electrical power distribution, construction, and electronic signal transmission and control. Its products are distributed for use in general construction, plant maintenance, utilities, process and energy applications, shopping centers, parking lots, sports facilities, and data processing and telecommunications systems; through distributors and direct to manufacturers for use in electronic equipment for consumer, industrial, government, and military applications; and directly to original equipment manufacturers of appliances, tools, machinery, and electronic equipment. Overall, Cooper Industries Inc. is a diversified company engaged in three primary areas of manufacturing: tools and hardware, electrical and electronic products, and automotive products. **Corporate headquarters location:** Houston TX. **Other U.S. locations:** Goldsboro NC. **Listed on:** New York Stock Exchange. **Number of employees at this location:** 500. **Number of employees nationwide:** 45,000.

COOPER INDUSTRIES INC.
BUSSMANN DIVISION
210 Dixie Trail, Goldsboro NC 27530. 919/734-3900. **Contact:** David Hunter, Human Resources Manager. **Description:** The Bussmann Division of Cooper Industries manufactures electrical protection devices, such as fuses, fuse holders, and fuse boxes. The division's major markets include secondary electrical power distribution, construction, and electronic signal transmission and control. Its products are distributed for use in general construction, plant maintenance, utilities, process and energy applications, shopping centers, parking lots, sports facilities, and data processing and telecommunications systems; through distributors and direct to manufacturers for use in electronic equipment for consumer, industrial, government, and military applications; and directly to original equipment manufacturers of appliances, tools, machinery, and electronic equipment. Overall, Cooper Industries Inc. is a diversified company engaged in three primary areas of manufacturing: tools and

hardware, electrical and electronic products, and automotive products. **Corporate headquarters location:** Houston TX. **Other U.S. locations:** Black Mountain NC. **Listed on:** New York Stock Exchange. **Number of employees nationwide:** 45,000.

CREE RESEARCH INC.
2810 Meridian Parkway, Durham NC 27713. 919/361-5709. **Fax:** 919/361-4630. **Contact:** Connie Gruenwald, Human Resources Manager. **Description:** Cree Research, Inc. develops, manufactures, and markets electronic devices made from silicon carbide (SiC), a semiconductor material that is superior to other semiconductor materials for certain applications. The company manufactures a commercialized super bright blue light-emitting diode based on a combination of SiC and gallium nitride. In addition, Cree Research, Inc. markets its SiC wafers to corporate, government, and university research laboratories. Other devices are under development, including SiC radio frequency and microwave power devices and high-temperature semiconductors. In 1994, the company acquired Real Color Displays, Inc., which serves the moving message display market. **Corporate headquarters location:** This Location. **Listed on:** NASDAQ. **Number of employees nationwide:** 100.

CROUSE-HINDS MOLDED PRODUCTS
Route 4, P.O. Box 156, La Grange NC 28551. 919/566-0225. **Contact:** Jim McDermid, Employee Relations Manager. **Description:** A manufacturer of electrical plugs and receptacles.

CUTLER-HAMMER, INC.
P.O. Box 5715, Asheville NC 28813. 704/684-2381. **Contact:** David King, Human Resources Manager. **Description:** This location operates as part of the Cutler-Hammer business unit of Eaton Corporation. Cutler-Hammer is in Eaton's electrical and electronic controls segment, which produces industrial and commercial controls (electromechanical and electronic controls; motor starters, contactors, overloads, and electric drives; programmable controllers, counters, man/machine interface panels and pushbuttons; photoelectric, proximity, temperature, and pressure sensors; circuit breakers; load centers; safety switches; panelboards; switchboards; dry type transformers; busway; meter centers; portable tool switches; commercial switches; relays; illuminated panels; annunciator panels; and electrically actuated valves and actuators); automotive and appliance controls (electromechanical and electronic controls; convenience, stalk, and concealed switches; knock sensors; climate control components; speed controls; timers; pressure switches; water valves; range controls; thermostats; gas valves; infinite switches; and temperature and humidity sensors); and specialty controls (automated material handling systems, automated guided vehicles, stacker cranes, ion implanters, engineered fasteners, golf grips, and industrial clutches and brakes). These products are sold, either directly by the company or indirectly through distributors and manufacturers' representatives, to industrial, commercial, automotive, appliance, aerospace, and government customers. Parent company also has operations in vehicle components (truck components, passenger car components, and off-highway vehicle components, which are usually sold directly from the company's plants to original equipment manufacturers of trucks, passenger cars, and off-highway vehicles) and defense systems (strategic countermeasures, tactical jamming systems, electronic intelligence, and electronic support measures for the federal government). **Corporate headquarters location:** Pittsburgh PA. **Parent company:** Eaton Corporation (Cleveland, OH). **Listed on:** London Stock Exchange; Midwest Stock Exchange; New York Stock Exchange; Pacific Exchange. **Number of employees nationwide:** 51,000.

DOUGLAS BATTERY MANUFACTURING COMPANY
P.O. Box 12159, Winston-Salem NC 27117. 910/650-7000. **Fax:** 910/650-7057. **Contact:** Linda Niblock, Assistant Manager of Human Resources. **Description:** A manufacturer of lead-acid batteries for industrial, automotive, lawn and garden, marine, and specialty applications. **Common positions include:** Automotive Mechanic/Body Repairer; Buyer; Chemical Engineer; Computer Programmer; Computer Systems Analyst; Customer Service Representative; Electrical/Electronics Engineer; Electrician; General Manager; Human Resources Specialist; Industrial Engineer; Management Trainee; Mechanical Engineer; Operations/Production Manager; Purchasing Agent and Manager; Quality Control Supervisor; Registered Nurse. **Educational backgrounds include:** Business Administration; Engineering; Finance; Liberal Arts. **Benefits:** 401K; Dental Insurance; Disability Coverage; Employee Discounts; Life Insurance; Medical Insurance; Profit Sharing; Savings Plan; Tuition Assistance. **Corporate headquarters location:** This Location. **Other U.S. locations:** CO; CT; FL; GA; IA; IN; KS; KY; MO; MS; PA; TX. **Operations at this facility include:** Administration; Divisional Headquarters; Manufacturing; Regional Headquarters;

Research and Development; Sales; Service. **Listed on:** Privately held. **Number of employees at this location:** 550. **Number of employees nationwide:** 850.

EXIDE ELECTRONICS
8609 Six Forks Road, Raleigh NC 27615. 919/870-3305. **Contact:** M. Paul Rousseau, Human Resources Manager. **Description:** An electronics company. **Common positions include:** Accountant/Auditor; Advertising Clerk; Computer Programmer; Computer Systems Analyst; Customer Service Representative; Designer; Electrical/Electronics Engineer; Financial Analyst; Human Resources Specialist; Manufacturer's/Wholesaler's Sales Rep.; Marketing Specialist; Mechanical Engineer; Public Relations Specialist; Purchasing Agent and Manager; Quality Control Supervisor; Services Sales Representative; Software Engineer; Systems Analyst; Technical Writer/Editor; Transportation/Traffic Specialist. **Educational backgrounds include:** Accounting; Computer Science; Finance; Marketing. **Benefits:** 401K; Dental Insurance; Disability Coverage; Employee Discounts; Life Insurance; Medical Insurance; Profit Sharing; Savings Plan; Stock Option; Tuition Assistance. **Special Programs:** Internships. **Corporate headquarters location:** This Location. **Operations at this facility include:** Administration; Divisional Headquarters; Manufacturing; Regional Headquarters; Research and Development; Sales; Service. **Listed on:** NASDAQ. **Number of employees at this location:** 1,000. **Number of employees nationwide:** 1,050.

GENERAL ELECTRIC COMPANY
P.O. Box 2188, Hickory NC 28603-2188. 704/462-3000. **Contact:** Bruce Crawford, Director of Human Resources. **Description:** This location manufactures transformers. General Electric is a diversified company operating in the following areas: aircraft engines (jet engines, replacement parts, and repair services for commercial, military, executive, and commuter aircraft); appliances; broadcasting (NBC); industrial (lighting products, electrical distribution and control equipment, transportation systems products, electric motors, and electrical and electronic industrial automation products); materials (plastics, ABS resins, silicones, super-abrasives, and laminates); power systems (products for the generation, transmission, and distribution of electricity); technical products and services (medical systems and equipment, as well as computer-based information and data interchange services for both internal use and external commercial and industrial customers); and capital services (consumer services, financing, specialty insurance; and Kidder, Peabody securities broker/investment bank). **Corporate headquarters location:** Fairfield CT.

KEARFOTT GUIDANCE AND NAVIGATION CORPORATION
Route 70, Black Mountain NC 28711. 704/686-3811. **Contact:** Ken Clymer, Employment Supervisor. **Description:** Manufactures precision electromechanical and electronic components used to generate, sense, control, and display motion such as synchros, resolvers, cant angle sensors, servo motors, pulse generators, and similar equipment. **Common positions include:** Accountant/Auditor; Blue-Collar Worker Supervisor; Buyer; Computer Programmer; Department Manager; Electrical/Electronics Engineer; Human Resources Specialist; Industrial Engineer; Manufacturer's/Wholesaler's Sales Rep.; Manufacturing Engineer; Material Control Specialist; Materials Engineer; Mechanical Engineer; Purchasing Agent and Manager; Quality Control Supervisor. **Educational backgrounds include:** Accounting; Business Administration; Computer Science; Engineering; Finance; Mathematics; Physics. **Benefits:** Dental Insurance; Disability Coverage; Employee Discounts; Life Insurance; Medical Insurance; Pension Plan; Savings Plan; Tuition Assistance. **Corporate headquarters location:** Stamford CT. **Other U.S. locations:** Little Falls NJ. **Listed on:** New York Stock Exchange.

KEMET ELECTRONIC CORPORATION
P.O. Box 2428, Shelby NC 28151. 704/484-8181. **Contact:** Gilda Pruitt, Human Resources Manager. **Description:** Manufactures electronic capacitors.

LITTON CLIFTON PRECISION
P.O. Box 160, Murphy NC 28906. 704/837-5115. **Fax:** 704/837-3343. **Contact:** William Wallace, Human Resources Manager. **Description:** Manufactures rotating electromechanical components, such as synchros, subfractional and horsepower motors. **Common positions include:** Electrical/Electronics Engineer. **Corporate headquarters location:** Woodland Hills CA. **Other U.S. locations:** Springfield PA; Blacksburg VA. **Parent company:** Litton Industries, Inc. **Listed on:** New York Stock Exchange. **Number of employees at this location:** 400.

MATSUSHITA COMPRESSOR CORPORATION OF AMERICA
One Panasonic Way, Mooresville NC 28115. 704/664-6700. **Fax:** 704/664-7707. **Contact:** Tina Robertson, Human Resources Director. **Description:** A manufacturer of

compressors for room air-conditioners. **Common positions include:** Accountant/Auditor; Blue-Collar Worker Supervisor; Buyer; Computer Programmer; Computer Systems Analyst; Electrical/Electronics Engineer; Electrician; Human Resources Specialist; Mechanical Engineer; Purchasing Agent and Manager; Quality Control Supervisor. **Benefits:** 401K; Dental Insurance; Disability Coverage; Employee Discounts; Life Insurance; Medical Insurance; Tuition Assistance. **Corporate headquarters location:** Secaucus NJ. **Other U.S. locations:** Columbus GA; Franklin Park IL; Danville TN; Knoxville TN. **Parent company:** MEI, Japan. **Operations at this facility include:** Administration; Manufacturing. **Listed on:** New York Stock Exchange. **Number of employees at this location:** 600. **Number of employees nationwide:** 250,000.

PROCTOR SILEX
261 Yadkin Road, Southern Pines NC 28387. 910/692-7676. **Contact:** Cecila Weston, Human Resources Administrator. **Description:** Manufactures electronic products.

SOLA/HEVI-DUTY
A UNIT OF GENERAL SIGNAL
P.O. Box 268, U.S. Highway 117 South, Goldsboro NC 27530. 919/734-8900. **Toll-free phone:** 800/377-4384. **Fax:** 919/580-3245. **Contact:** Ms. Aubrey Jones, Human Resources Director. **Description:** Founded in 1930. Sola/Hevi-Duty is a worldwide manufacturer of power protection, conversion, and transformer products. Sola/Hevi-Duty manufactures a complete line of UPS (uninterruptible power systems), power supplies, power conditioners, and voltage regulators. These products are designed to protect systems and data from the voltage surges, dips, spikes, brownouts, blackouts, frequency errors, and noise that are the commonplace results of lightning storms, nearby machinery cycling on and off (machine tools, elevators, air conditioners, etc.), and other causes. Sola's wide range of power protection equipment is designed to stand guard between the "real world" and customers' critical equipment. Depending on the desired degree of protection, the power can be filtered, regulated, or backed-up with batteries. Products are available in a wide range of VA sizes, design styles, application types, and feature options. Sola holds over 100 patents in UPS and power conditioning products. **Corporate headquarters location:** Elk Grove Village IL. **Other U.S. locations:** Australia; England; Italy; Mexico; Switzerland; Toronto, Canada; Elk Grove Village IL.

TRION, INC.
P.O. Box 760, Sanford NC 27330. 919/775-2201. **Contact:** Mike Womble, Director of Human Resources. **Description:** Manufactures electronic indoor air cleaners for home, office, and industrial use. **Common positions include:** Advertising Clerk; Buyer; Computer Programmer; Credit Manager; Customer Service Representative; Designer; Draftsperson; Electrical/Electronics Engineer; Electrician; Mechanical Engineer; Quality Control Supervisor. **Educational backgrounds include:** Business Administration; Engineering; Marketing. **Benefits:** 401K; Disability Coverage; Life Insurance; Medical Insurance; Pension Plan; Savings Plan; Tuition Assistance. **Corporate headquarters location:** This Location. **Operations at this facility include:** Administration; Engineering and Design; Manufacturing; Research and Development; Sales. **Listed on:** NASDAQ. **Number of employees at this location:** 300.

Note: Because addresses and telephone numbers of smaller companies change rapidly, we recommend you call each company to verify the information below before inquiring about job opportunities. Mass mailings are not recommended.

Additional employers with under 250 employees:

TRANSFORMERS

ABB Power T&D Co. Inc.
Hwy 43 N, Pinetops NC
27864. 919/827-2121.

SWITCHGEAR AND SWITCHBOARD APPARATUS

Pass & Seymour Legrand
6511 Franz Warner Pky,
Whitsett NC 27377-9215.
910/449-3500.

ELECTRICAL INDUSTRIAL APPARATUS

Burcliff Industries
Ulco Dr, Franklin NC 28734.
704/369-9541.

Escod Industries Inc.
Hwy 90 E, Taylorsville NC
28681. 704/632-4663.

ELECTRIC LIGHTING AND WIRING EQUIPMENT

GE Co.
900 N George St, Goldsboro
NC 27530-2432. 919/731-5100.

GE Co.
1114 Old Concord Rd,
Salisbury NC 28146-1353.
704/637-5200.

Preformed Line Products Co.
1700 Woodhurst Ln,
Albemarle NC 28001-5376.
704/983-6161.

Robert Abbey Inc.
3166 Main Ave SE, Hickory
NC 28602-8374. 704/322-
3480.

Regent Lighting Corp.
2611 Lavista Dr, Burlington
NC 27215-7550. 910/226-
2411.

Ray-O-Vac
P.O. Box 900, Kinston NC
28502-0900. 919/522-
1400.

**ELECTRONIC COMPONENTS
AND ACCESSORIES**

RCL Shallcross Inc.
Highway 70 E, Smithfield NC
27577. 910/934-5181.

Bitron Inc.
638 Instrument Dr, Rocky
Mount NC 27804-8628.
919/977-1075.

C&K Components Inc.
8182 US Highway 70 W,
Clayton NC 27520-9463.
919/553-3131.

Dialight Corp.
265 Industrial Dr, Roxboro
NC 27573-6028. 910/597-
2291.

Electroswitch
2010 Yonkers Rd, Raleigh
NC 27604-2258. 919/833-
0707.

MCR Inc.
1400 Dogwood Way,
Mebane NC 27302-9115.
910/563-5005.

Neptco Inc.
3908 Hickory Blvd, Granite
Falls NC 28630. 704/396-
2121.

Premier Circuit Assembly
RR 3, Spring Hope NC
27882-9803. 919/478-
4111.

**ELECTRICAL EQUIPMENT,
MACHINERY, AND SUPPLIES**

Austin Co.
Hwy 421 W, Yadkinville NC
27055. 910/468-2851.

Belden Wire & Cable
385 Georgia Hwy, Franklin
NC 28734. 704/524-2181.

GE Company
604 Green Valley Rd,
Greensboro NC 27408-7719.
910/854-9350.

General Cable Co.
131 Johnston Pky, Kenly NC
27542. 919/284-5144.

Reliance Electric Co.
2311 W Cone Blvd,
Greensboro NC 27408-4029.
910/282-8700.

**AEROSPACE AND/OR
NAUTICAL SYSTEMS AND
INSTRUMENTS**

Sturdy Corp.
1822 Carolina Beach Rd,
Wilmington NC 28401-6504.
910/763-8261.

**ELECTRICAL EQUIPMENT
WHOLESALE**

Bryant Electric Supply
605 E Franklin Blvd, Gastonia
NC 28054-7150. 704/866-
6000.

Specialty Lighting Inc.
639 Washburn Switch Rd,
Shelby NC 28150-7712.
704/482-3416.

Walker & Associates Inc.
P.O. Box 1029, Welcome NC
27374-1029. 704/731-
6394.

Cameron & Barkley Co.
75 Fairview Rd, Asheville NC
28803-2305. 704/274-
4774.

James McGraw Inc.
820 Winston St, Greensboro
NC 27405-7236. 910/272-
4557.

Control Design Supply
458 Crompton St, Charlotte
NC 28273-6215. 704/588-
4410.

Eaton Corporation
3020 Lee Ave, Sanford NC
27330-6241. 919/776-
8451.

GE Company
1409 Mill St, Greensboro NC
27408-8012. 910/274-
4109.

Graybar Electric Company
1200 Grecade St,
Greensboro NC 27408-8416.
910/275-9441.

Ligon Electric Supply Co.
2709 Patterson St,

Greensboro NC 27407-2316.
910/855-8200.

Minarik Electric Co.
608 Matthews Mint Hill Rd,
Matthews NC 28105-2797.
704/841-4088.

Rittal Corp.
1510 Fallen Tree Ct,
Charlotte NC 28262-3100.
704/597-7210.

Wilmington Electric
1112 Chestnut St,
Wilmington NC 28401-4320.
910/763-7381.

Siemens
3200 Northline Ave,
Greensboro NC 27408-7611.
910/852-1758.

Houston Wire & Cable
200 Forsyth Hall Dr,
Charlotte NC 28273-5815.
704/588-5940.

Charlotte Light Bulb Supply
4311 South Blvd, Charlotte
NC 28209-2622. 704/527-
1393.

Gregory Poole Power System
701 Blue Ridge Rd, Raleigh
NC 27606-6310. 919/890-
4321.

Power Control Services
1220 S Washington St,
Rocky Mount NC 27801-
5700. 919/972-3400.

**Marathon Electric
Manufacturing Corp.**
101 Gannaway Dr,
Jamestown NC 27282-
9775. 910/454-3687.

**Piedmont Motor Control
Ltd.**
8100 Arrowridge Blvd,
Charlotte NC 28273-5600.
704/523-7121.

**ELECTRONIC PARTS AND
EQUIPMENT WHOLESALE**

Emsco
2923 Pacific Ave,
Greensboro NC 27406-4512.
910/275-8776.

Hammond Electronics
2923 Pacific Ave,
Greensboro NC 27406-4548.
910/275-6391.

Cray Communications
52 Cub Dr, Thomasville NC
27360-9261. 910/885-
2228.

South Carolina

ABB POWER DISTRIBUTION, INC.
P.O. Box 100524, Florence SC 29501-0524. 803/665-4144. **Contact:** Jill Heiden,
Human Resources Manager. **Description:** ABB Power Distribution, Inc. manufactures

medium and low voltage circuit breakers and kirk lock (interlock) systems. **Common positions include:** Accountant/Auditor; Advertising Sales; Budget Analyst; Buyer; Computer Programmer; Computer Systems Analyst; Customer Service Representative; Draftsperson; Economist/Market Research Analyst; Electrical/Electronics Engineer; Electrician; General Manager; Industrial Engineer; Industrial Production Manager; Mechanical Engineer; Public Relations Specialist; Quality Control Supervisor; Software Engineer. **Educational backgrounds include:** Accounting; Business Administration; Communications; Computer Science; Economics; Engineering; Finance; Liberal Arts; Marketing; Mathematics. **Benefits:** 401K; Dental Insurance; Disability Coverage; Life Insurance; Medical Insurance; Pension Plan; Tuition Assistance. **Corporate headquarters location:** Norwalk CT. **Other U.S. locations:** Nationwide. **Parent company:** Asea Brown Boveri, Inc. is a supplier of industrial equipment and services for industries such as electric power generation, oil and gas exploration, and chemical production and refinement. **Operations at this facility include:** Manufacturing; Research and Development; Sales. **Listed on:** Privately held. **Number of employees at this location:** 139. **Number of employees nationwide:** 35,500.

AVX CORPORATION
P.O. Box 867, Myrtle Beach SC 29578. 803/448-9411. **Contact:** Kathryn Byrd, Human Resources Manager. **Description:** AVX Corporation is a worldwide manufacturer and supplier of a broad line of passive electronic components and related products. The company's primary passive electronic component sales are of ceramic and tantalum capacitors, both in leaded and surface-mount versions. AVX Corporation's customers include original equipment manufacturers (OEMs) in such industries as telecommunications, computers, automotive electronics, medical devices and instrumentation, industrial instrumentation, military and aerospace electronic systems, and consumer electronics. Sales of company products are made by independent manufacturer's representatives, company-employed direct sales personnel, and independent electronic component distributors. The company also manufactures and sells electronic connectors and distributes and sells certain passive components and connectors manufactured by its parent company. **Parent company:** Kyocera, a Japanese public company, principally engaged in the worldwide manufacture and distribution of ceramic and related products including fine ceramic parts, semiconductor parts, electronic components, and consumer-related products; electronic equipment; and optical instruments. **Corporate headquarters location:** This Location. **Listed on:** New York Stock Exchange.

ALSIMAG TECHNICAL CERAMICS INC.
One Technology Place, Highway 14, Laurens SC 29360-0089. 864/682-3215. **Contact:** Ann Harris, Human Resources. **Description:** Alsimag Technical Ceramics Inc. manufactures porcelain electrical supplies. The company operates through several work groups: Structural Ceramics, Textiles, and Electrical. Alsimag Technical Ceramics also offers some contract services.

CUTLER-HAMMER, INC.
P.O. Box 1406, Greenwood SC 29648. 864/229-3006. **Contact:** Bob Pridemore, Human Resources Manager. **Description:** This location operates as part of Eaton Corporation's Cutler-Hammer business unit. Cutler-Hammer, Inc. is in the electrical and electronic controls segment, which produces industrial and commercial controls (electromechanical and electronic controls; motor starters, contactors, overloads, and electric drives; programmable controllers, counter, man-to-machine interface panels, and pushbuttons; photoelectric, proximity, temperature, and pressure sensors; circuit breakers; load centers; safety switches; panelboards; switchboards; dry tape transformers; busway; meter centers; portable tool switches; commercial switches; relays; illuminated panels; annunciator panels; and electrically actuated valves and actuators); automotive and appliance controls (electromechanical and electronic controls; convenience, stalk, and concealed switches; knock sensors; climate control components; speed controls; timers; pressure switches; water valves; range controls; thermostats; gas valves; infinite switches; and temperature and humidity sensors); and specialty controls (automated material handling systems, automated guided vehicles, stacker cranes, ion implanters, engineered fasteners, golf grips, and industrial clutches and brakes). These products are sold directly by the company or indirectly through distributors and manufacturers' representatives to industrial, commercial, automotive, appliance, aerospace, and government customers. **Corporate headquarters location:** Pittsburgh PA. **Parent company:** Eaton Corporation (Cleveland OH) also has operations in vehicle components and defense systems. Vehicle components are usually sold directly from the company's plants to original equipment manufacturers of trucks, passenger cars, and off-highway vehicles, and include truck components, passenger car components, and off-highway vehicle components. Defense systems provide strategic countermeasures, tactical jamming systems, electronic intelligence, and

electronic support measures for the federal government. **Listed on:** London Stock Exchange; Midwest Stock Exchange; New York Stock Exchange; Pacific Exchange. **Number of employees nationwide:** 51,000.

ESSEX GROUP, INC.
P.O. Box 640, Chester SC 29706. 803/581-9200. **Contact:** Glen Craig, Human Resources Manager. **Description:** A manufacturer and distributor of electrical wire and cable and electrical insulation products, including magnetic wire, building wire, telephone cable, and other related products. **Benefits:** 401K; Dental Insurance; Disability Coverage; Life Insurance; Medical Insurance; Pension Plan; Savings Plan; Tuition Assistance. **Corporate headquarters location:** Fort Wayne IN. **Listed on:** Privately held.

MEMC ELECTRONIC MATERIALS INC.
P.O. Box 5397, Spartanburg SC 29304. 864/576-6630. **Contact:** Larry Norman, Director of Human Resources. **Description:** Manufactures electronic components. MEMC Electronic Materials, Inc. was established in April, 1989. The company is owned by Huls AG, a chemical company in Marl, Germany who is part of the VEBA Group, headquartered in Dusseldorf. The company is the second largest silicon wafer company and the largest supplier in North America and Europe, as well as the largest Western supplier to Japan. The company plays a prominent role as a producer of polished silicon wafers and CMOS Epi worldwide. Company operations are international in scope, with manufacturing and technical research located in all major semiconductor producing regions, including three U.S. locations, two European locations, one Japanese location, one Malaysian location, one Korean location (affiliate: PHC), and one Taiwanese location (affiliate: TEM). Products include Czochralaski-grown silicon wafers, sold as polished or with an epitaxial layer in diameter ranges from 4 to 6 inches. The number of individually specified parameters leads to hundreds of unique products. Applications use ranges from discrete diodes to complex micro-processors and DRAM memories. Another affiliate of MEMC is SiBond, LLC, which manufactures silicon-on-insulator wafers (SOI) used for the next generation of high speed microprocessors, very high density memory, and low power applications. Silicon wafers form the base substrate for integrated circuits serving the electronic industry's $95 billion semiconductor market. MEMC employs 5000 worldwide.

NEWARK ELECTRONICS
217 Wilcox Avenue, Gaffney SC 29341. 864/487-1900. **Contact:** John Sanders, Director of Human Resources. **Description:** Newark Electronics is a distribution company that distributes electronics parts and products through sales offices in North America and Europe. **Other U.S. locations:** Nationwide. **Parent company:** Premier Industrial Corporation (Cleveland, OH) is a broad line distributor of electronic components used in the production and maintenance of equipment; a supplier of maintenance products for industrial, commercial, and institutional applications; and a manufacturer of fire-fighting equipment. **Listed on:** New York Stock Exchange.

PHILIPS COMPONENTS
PHILIPS ELECTRONICS NORTH AMERICA CORPORATION
6071 Saint Andrews, Columbia SC 29212. 803/772-2500. **Contact:** Human Resources. **Description:** This facility manufactures electronic capacitors. Overall, Philips Components is a manufacturer of electronic components for industrial, telecommunications, and computer companies. **Corporate headquarters location:** New York NY. **Parent company:** Philips Electronics NV is one of the larger industrial companies in the United States and a multimarket manufacturing organization with nationwide locations and various subsidiaries. The company concentrates its efforts primarily in the fields of consumer electronics, consumer products, electrical and electronics components, and professional equipment.

PROGRESS LIGHTING, INC./COWPENS MANUFACTURING PLANT
P.O. Box 989, Cowpens SC 29330. 864/463-3274. **Contact:** Human Resources. **Description:** This location is a manufacturing plant. Progress Lighting, Inc. is a manufacturer of home and commercial lighting systems and fixtures. **Common positions include:** Accountant/Auditor; Blue-Collar Worker Supervisor; Buyer; Claim Representative; Computer Programmer; Credit Manager; Customer Service Representative; Department Manager; Draftsperson; Electrical/Electronics Engineer; General Manager; Human Resources Specialist; Industrial Designer; Industrial Engineer; Management Trainee; Manufacturer's/Wholesaler's Sales Rep.; Marketing Specialist; Mechanical Engineer; Operations/Production Manager; Purchasing Agent and Manager; Quality Control Supervisor; Systems Analyst; Transportation/Traffic Specialist. **Educational backgrounds include:** Accounting; Art/Design; Business Administration;

Computer Science; Engineering; Finance; Liberal Arts; Marketing. **Benefits:** Dental Insurance; Employee Discounts; Life Insurance; Medical Insurance; Pension Plan; Savings Plan. **Corporate headquarters location:** This Location. **Operations at this facility include:** Administration; Divisional Headquarters; Manufacturing; Regional Headquarters; Research and Development; Sales; Service.

SCHLUMBERGER INDUSTRIES
313B North Highway, West Union SC 29696. 864/638-8300. **Contact:** David Dunn, Employment Manager. **Description:** This location of the company is engaged in the manufacture of electro-mechanical watt-per-hour meters. The parent company, Schlumberger Ltd., manufactures measurement, electronics, and testing products; and provides well site exploration and computer aided design. **Corporate headquarters location:** Greenwood SC. **Parent company:** Schlumberger Ltd. (The Netherlands). **Listed on:** New York Stock Exchange.

SQUARE D COMPANY
1990 Sandifer Boulevard, Seneca SC 29678. 864/882-2414. **Contact:** Russ Karpick, Human Resources Director. **Description:** A manufacturer of electrical distribution products for the construction industry. The company's products are used in commercial and residential construction, industrial facilities, and machinery and original equipment manufacturers products. Residential building products feature circuit breakers with an exclusive quick-open mechanism that isolates potential dangers quickly; a complete home wiring system connecting multiple telephone lines, audio signals, and VCR, cable, or closed circuit television. Owners can transfer different audio or video signals to different rooms, monitor callers at entrances, monitor children from another room, broadcast music, or leave wake-up calls. Square D also manufactures a Home Power System which reduces installation times and cuts labor costs. In office developments, hotels and restaurants, retail shops, and other businesses, Square D Company provides products ranging from parking lot gate controls and uninterrupted power systems for personal computers to space-saving remote-controlled lighting and custom circuit breaker panel boards. Square D Company also equips public buildings such as schools, stadiums, museums, hospitals, prisons, military bases, and wastewater treatment plants with electrical distribution systems. **Common positions include:** Accountant/Auditor; Buyer; Electrical/Electronics Engineer; Financial Analyst; Human Resources Specialist; Industrial Engineer; Mechanical Engineer. **Educational backgrounds include:** Accounting; Business Administration; Engineering; Finance. **Benefits:** Dental Insurance; Disability Coverage; Employee Discounts; Life Insurance; Medical Insurance; Pension Plan; Savings Plan; Tuition Assistance. **Corporate headquarters location:** Palatine IL. **Other U.S. locations:** AZ; CA; KY; MO; NE; OH; TN. **Parent company:** Groupe Schneider. **Operations at this facility include:** Manufacturing.

Note: Because addresses and telephone numbers of smaller companies change rapidly, we recommend you call each company to verify the information below before inquiring about job opportunities. Mass mailings are not recommended.

Additional employers with under 250 employees:

SWITCHGEAR AND SWITCHBOARD APPARATUS

Carter & Crawley Inc.
P.O. Box 5069, Greenville SC 29606. 864/288-6250.

Century III Inc.
1 Century Pl, Greer SC 29651. 864/848-2505.

Joslyn Clark Controls
2013 W Meeting St, Lancaster SC 29720-8842. 803/286-8491.

ELECTRICAL INDUSTRIAL APPARATUS

MSD Inc.
700 Orange St, Darlington SC 29532. 803/393-5421.

ELECTRIC LIGHTING AND WIRING EQUIPMENT

Supreme Corp.
122 E Laurel St, Mullins SC 29574. 803/464-0554.

Ohio Brass Co.
1850 Richland Ave E, Aiken SC 29801. 803/648-8386.

Amida Industries Inc.
590 Huey Rd, Rock Hill SC 29730. 803/324-3011.

ELECTRONIC COMPONENTS AND ACCESSORIES

Computer Dynamics Inc.
107 S Main St, Greer SC 29650-2018. 864/877-8700.

Cooper Power Systems
1520 Emerald Rd, Greenwood SC 29646-8840. 864/223-2311.

Cornell Dubilier Marketing
140 Technology Pl, Liberty SC 29657-3300. 864/843-2277.

AVX Corp.
2875 Highway 501 W, Conway SC 29526-4454. 803/347-4627.

Autecs
Highway 81 & I-85, Anderson SC 29621. 864/260-8811.

ELECTRICAL ENGINE EQUIPMENT

Carolina Assemblies Inc.
311 Wesley St, Myrtle Beach
SC 29577. 803/236-4006.

Escod Industries Inc.
1024 6th Ave S, N Myrtle
Beach SC 29582-3318.
803/272-6165.

ELECTRICAL EQUIPMENT WHOLESALE

Greenwood Supply Co.
P.O. Box 3069, Greenwood
SC 29648-3069. 864/229-2501.

Shealy Electrical Wholesale
P.O. Box 48, Greenville SC
29602-0048. 864/242-6880.

Exide Corporation
27 West Rd, Travelers Rest
SC 29690-1722. 864/834-5351.

WW Grainger Inc.
550 Chris Dr, West Columbia
SC 29169-4669. 803/926-8100.

For more information on career opportunities in the electronic/industrial electrical equipment industry:

Associations

AMERICAN CERAMIC SOCIETY
735 Ceramic Place, Westerville OH 43081.
614/890-4700. 800/837-1804. Provides
ceramics futures information. Membership
required.

ELECTROCHEMICAL SOCIETY
10 South Main Street, Pennington NJ 08534-2896. 609/737-1902. Fax: 609/737-2743.
An international society which holds bi-annual
meetings internationally and periodic meetings
through local sections. Publications include the
monthly *Journal of the Electrochemical Society*
and the quarterly *Interface*.

ELECTRONIC INDUSTRIES ASSOCIATION
2500 Wilson Boulevard, Arlington VA 22201-3834. 703/907-7500.

ELECTRONICS TECHNICIANS ASSOCIATION
602 North Jackson Street, Greencastle IN
46135. 317/653-8262. Offers published job-hunting advice from the organization's officers
and members. Also offers educational material
and certification programs.

INSTITUTE OF ELECTRICAL AND ELECTRONICS ENGINEERS (IEEE)
345 East 47th Street, New York NY 10017.

212/705-7900. Toll-free customer service line:
800/678-4333.

INSTITUTE OF ELECTRICAL AND ELECTRONICS ENGINEERS (IEEE)
1828 Elm Street NW, Suite 1202, Washington
DC 20036-5104. Professional activities line:
202/785-0017. National information line:
202/785-2180.

INTERNATIONAL BROTHERHOOD OF ELECTRICAL WORKERS
1125 15th Street NW, Washington DC
20005. 202/833-7000. Has over 1,000
apprenticeship programs.

INTERNATIONAL SOCIETY OF CERTIFIED ELECTRONICS TECHNICIANS
2708 West Berry Street, Ft. Worth TX 76109.
817/921-9101.

NATIONAL ELECTRONICS SALES AND SERVICES ASSOCIATION
2708 West Berry, Ft. Worth TX 76109.
817/921-9061. Provides newsletters and
directories to members.

SOCIETY OF MANUFACTURING ENGINEERS (SME)
One SME Drive, P.O. Box 930, Dearborn MI
48121. 313/271-1500. Offers a resume
database for members.

ENVIRONMENTAL AND WASTE MANAGEMENT SERVICES

According to the Environmental Protection Agency, the increase in environmental awareness over recent decades is more than just a trend. State and national legislation, such as the 1990 amendments to the Clean Air Act, has generated a new range of opportunities in skilled administrative, professional, and technical areas. However, the most critical positions need in the industry is for scientists and engineers. These two groups develop new solutions to old problems, and therefore are instrumental in the research and development stages.

On the other hand, the current climate in the Congress is significantly cooler towards environmental regulation than in years past. Many members of Congress argue that American business is already overburdened by the Federal government, and some propose that the Environmental Protection Agency itself be disbanded.

North Carolina

COMPUCHEM ENVIRONMENTAL
3306 Chapel Hill/Nelson Highway, Research Triangle Park NC 27709. 919/406-1600. **Contact:** Human Resources. **Description:** CompuChem Environmental conducts environmental research and offers environmental services.

ENSYS ENVIRONMENTAL PRODUCTS, INC.
P.O. Box 14063, Research Triangle Park NC 27709. 919/941-5509. **Fax:** 919/941-5519. **Contact:** Jim Mapes, Director of Product Development. **Description:** EnSys, founded in 1987, develops and sells immunoassay-based and chemical-based test systems for fast and inexpensive detection of hazardous chemicals in the environment. EnSys products include field test kits and laboratory analytical systems for the detection of fuel products, benzene, PCBs, polyaromatic hydrocarbons, pentachlorophenol, pesticides, and other compounds regulated by the Environmental Protection Agency. EnSys provides its customers with products and support services that reduce the cost of assessment and remediation at contaminated sites. The company sells its test kits and other associated products and services to environmental consulting and engineering firms, hazardous waste processing firms, environmental testing laboratories and various state and federal agencies through distributors and a regionally based direct sales force in the United States. Product names include Aldicarb, Atrazine, Alachlor, Benomyl, Benzene, Chlorothalonil, Cryptosporidium, Crude Oil, Dioxin, Giardia, Imazaquin, Mercury, Metolachlor, Polyaromatic hydrocarbons, Polychlorinated biphenyls, Pentachlorophenol, RDX, Triazine, Trifluralin, Trihalomethanes, Trinitrotoluene, Total petroleum hydrocarbons. The company also markets and sells its products and services in Europe through EnSys (Europe) Limited, a wholly-owned subsidiary of the company. European headquarters: EnSys (Europe) Limited, Suite 17, The Old Power Station, 121 Mortlake High Street, London SW14 8SN, England. **Corporate headquarters location:** This Location. **Listed on:** NASDAQ.

GROUNDWATER TECHNOLOGY
1000 Perimeter Park Drive, Suite I, Morrisville NC 27560. 919/467-2227. **Contact:** Leslie Hart, Human Resources. **Description:** Groundwater Technology develops advanced technologies for the environmental restoration of contaminated sites. One of the largest environmental consulting, engineering, and remediation firms, the company has over 1,500 employees in 70 locations throughout North America, Europe, and Australia. Of these, nearly 1,000 are professional geologists, hydrogeologists, engineers, and environmental scientists. **Corporate headquarters location:** Norwood MA.

QUANTERRA ENVIRONMENTAL SERVICES

8100A Brownleigh Drive, Raleigh NC 27612. 919/510-0228. **Fax:** 919/510-0141. **Contact:** Mr. Alston Sykes, Lab Manager. **Description:** In June 1994, Corning's Enseco division and IT Analytical Services, the two largest commercial environmental analytical companies in the world, merged to become Quanterra, a completely new, independent company. Quanterra provides a complete range of environmental testing services to private industry, engineering consultants, and government agencies in support of major federal and state environmental regulations. The company also possesses a variety of special analytical capabilities, including specialization in the following areas: Air Toxics; Field Analytical Services, Radiochemistry/Mixed Waste; and Advanced Technology. The company is owned jointly by Corning Incorporated and International Technology Corporation. The company's goal is to provide customers with the highest level of service in the environmental analytical testing industry. **Other U.S. locations:** CA; CO; FL; MO; OH; TN; TX; WA.

Note: Because addresses and telephone numbers of smaller companies change rapidly, we recommend you call each company to verify the information below before inquiring about job opportunities. Mass mailings are not recommended.

Additional employers with under 250 employees:

SANITARY SERVICES

GDS Inc.
4062 Section House Rd,
Hickory NC 28601-9393.
704/256-2158.

Wilson County Landfill
RR 5, Wilson NC 27893-
9805. 919/291-7335.

**Laidlaw Environmental
Service**
Watlington Industrial Rd,

Reidsville NC 27320.
910/342-5568.

Recycling of Multi Materials
9100 Deponie Dr, Raleigh NC
27615. 919/870-0506.

South Carolina

ENVIROMETRICS INC.

9229 University Boulevard, Charleston SC 29406. 803/553-9456. **Contact:** Ms. Robin Bowers, Human Resources Manager. **Description:** Envirometrics Inc. is a holding company with subsidiaries which provide the following services: air sampling and industrial hygiene products and services; environmental and industrial hygiene laboratory services; environmental health and occupational safety consulting services; air modeling; air permitting; environmental and civil engineering; surveying and civil site design; land planning; RCRA/CERCLA site management; and wetlands and biological services. The company's ACT cards and electronic readers provide a passive on-site monitoring system for measuring personal exposure to hazardous and toxic chemicals in the air. Since 1988, through subsidiary Envirometrics Products, the company has sold and distributed a variety of products, primarily for the asbestos sampling professional providing on-site asbestos testing and related services. The company also manufactures and sells standard air sampling cassettes and its proprietary Bellmouth cassettes which sample air for the existence of lead, asbestos, and other ceramic or man-made vitreous fibers. The company's subsidiary Azimuth operates a fully accredited Industrial Hygiene laboratory to perform analyses of air samples for asbestos, metals, and organic vapors. **Corporate headquarters location:** This Location. **Subsidiaries include:** Envirometrics Products Company, Azimuth Incorporated, and Trico Envirometrics, Inc. **Listed on:** NASDAQ. **Number of employees at this location:** 92.

ENVIRONMENTAL MONITORING & TESTING CORPORATION

825 Main Street South, New Ellenton SC 29809. 803/652-2718. **Contact:** Human Resources. **Description:** Environmental Monitoring & Testing Corporation is a diversified drilling company with expertise in environmental drilling; industrial water wells; recovery wells as related to environmental requirements; construction drilling and grouting for piling; and stabilization drilling and grouting core drilling as well as angle coring drilling and grouting for dams and other similar structures. The company operates as a subcontractor within the construction industry rather than a prime or general contractor. In 1994, Environmental Monitoring & Testing Corporation moved all of its operations to this location. **Corporate headquarters location:** This Location. **Number of employees at this location:** 21.

INCENDERE
200 Alta Vista Court, Lexington SC 29073. 803/359-8820. **Contact:** Human Resources. **Description:** Incendere gathers and disposes biomedical waste for other companies.

For more information on career opportunities in environmental and waste management services:

Associations

AIR AND WASTE MANAGEMENT ASSOCIATION
One Gateway Center, Third Floor, Pittsburgh PA 15222. 412/232-3444. A nonprofit, technical and educational organization providing a neutral forum where all points of view of an environmental management issue can be addressed.

ASSOCIATION OF STATE & INTERSTATE WATER POLLUTION CONTROL ADMINISTRATORS
750 First Street NE, Suite 910, Washington DC 20002. 202/898-0905. Fax: 202/898-0929. A national, nonpartisan professional organization comprised of government officials. Members implement surface and groundwater protection programs throughout the nation.

ENVIRONMENTAL INDUSTRY ASSOCIATION
4301 Connecticut Avenue N, Suite 300, Washington DC 20008. 202/659-4613. Fax: 202/966-4818.

INSTITUTE OF CLEAN AIR COMPANIES
1707 L Street NW, Suite 570, Washington DC 20036. 202/457-0911-4201. A national association of companies involved in stationary source air pollution control.

U.S. ENVIRONMENTAL PROTECTION AGENCY
401 M Street SW, Washington DC 20460. 202/260-2090. Provides EPA background career information.

WATER ENVIRONMENT FEDERATION
601 Wythe Street, Alexandria VA 22314. 703/684-2400. Subscription to jobs newsletter required for career information.

Magazines

CAREERS AND THE ENGINEER
Adams Media Corporation, 260 Center Street, Holbrook MA 02343. 617/767-8100.

ENVIRONMENTAL CAREER OPPORTUNITIES
1776 I Street NW, Suite 710, Washington DC 20006. A publication that lists career opportunities in the environmental fields. $67 for 12 issues; $127 for 26 issues.

JOURNAL OF AIR AND WASTE MANAGEMENT ASSOCIATION
One Gateway Center, Third Floor, Pittsburgh PA 15222. 412/232-3444.

FABRICATED/PRIMARY METALS AND PRODUCTS

In 1995, the demand for steel dropped from 114 million tons to 110 million tons, and executives in the industry were not expecting a turnaround in 1996. While the price of structural beams rose, the price for flat-rolled steel -- used in automobiles, for example -- plummeted. At the about the same time, in early 1995, the industry was undergoing a boom in minimill-construction -- these new mills are now adding more capacity to an already glutted fabricated metals market.

North Carolina

EASCO ALUMINUM COMPANY
P.O. Box 177, Winton NC 27986. 919/358-5811. **Fax:** 919/358-1141. **Contact:** Gary Purvis, Personnel Supervisor. **Description:** Easco Aluminum Company is engaged in the manufacture of aluminum products, with operations in customized aluminum extrusions. **Common positions include:** Accountant/Auditor; Blue-Collar Worker Supervisor; Draftsperson; Electrical/Electronics Engineer; Electrician; General Manager; Human Resources Specialist; Industrial Production Manager; Manufacturer's/Wholesaler's Sales Rep.; Quality Control Supervisor. **Educational backgrounds include:** Accounting; Business Administration; Engineering. **Benefits:** 401K; Dental Insurance; Disability Coverage; Life Insurance; Medical Insurance; Pension Plan. **Corporate headquarters location:** Girard OH. **Other U.S. locations:** CT; IN; OH. **Operations at this facility include:** Administration; Manufacturing; Sales; Service. **Listed on:** Privately held. **Number of employees at this location:** 400.

EASCO ALUMINUM COMPANY
P.O. Box 2437, Burlington NC 27216. 910/227-8826. **Contact:** Martha M. Shoffner, Administration Manager. **Description:** Easco Aluminum Company is engaged in the manufacture of aluminum products, with operations in customized aluminum extrusions. **Common positions include:** Blue-Collar Worker Supervisor; Department Manager; Manufacturer's/Wholesaler's Sales Rep. **Benefits:** 401K; Dental Insurance; Disability Coverage; Life Insurance; Medical Insurance; Pension Plan. **Corporate headquarters location:** Girard OH. **Other U.S. locations:** CT; IN; OH. **Listed on:** Privately held.

INSTEEL INDUSTRIES, INC.
1373 Boggs Drive, Mount Airy NC 27030. 910/786-2141. **Contact:** Gary Kniskern, Vice President of Administration. **Description:** Insteel Industries, Inc. produces industrial wire, galvanized fencing products, nails, specialty wire fabrics, concrete reinforcing products, and Insteel 3-D. **Common positions include:** Accountant/Auditor; Computer Programmer; Computer Systems Analyst; Credit Manager; Customer Service Representative; Financial Analyst; General Manager; Human Resources Specialist; Industrial Production Manager; Mechanical Engineer; Metallurgical Engineer; Purchasing Agent and Manager; Quality Control Supervisor. **Educational backgrounds include:** Accounting; Engineering. **Benefits:** 401K; Dental Insurance; Disability Coverage; Life Insurance; Medical Insurance; Pension Plan; Profit Sharing; Savings Plan; Tuition Assistance. **Corporate headquarters location:** This Location. **Operations at this facility include:** Administration; Regional Headquarters; Sales. **Listed on:** New York Stock Exchange. **Number of employees at this location:** 1,000.

NATIONAL GYPSUM COMPANY
2001 Rexford Road, Charlotte NC 28211. 704/365-7300. **Contact:** Wayne Juby, Vice President of Human Resources. **Description:** This location of National Gypsum

Company produces structural metal work. Overall, the company manufactures gypsum wallboard and joint compounds, and is an integrated, diversified manufacturer of quality products for the building, construction, and shelter markets.

NUCOR CORPORATION
2100 Rexford Road, Charlotte NC 28211. 704/366-7000. **Contact:** James Coblin, Manager of Personnel Services. **Description:** Nucor Corporation is a steel and steel products manufacturer with mills in many locations including: North and South Carolina, Nebraska, Texas, Utah, and Arizona. The company's products include hot-rolled and cold-finished steel shapes; girders and joists; and beams. **Corporate headquarters location:** This Location. **Listed on:** New York Stock Exchange.

ORO MANUFACTURING COMPANY
P.O. Box 5018, Monroe NC 28111-5018. 704/283-2186. **Contact:** Patricia Engel, Director of Human Resources. **Description:** Oro Manufacturing Company is engaged in light metal fabrication. The company operates complete facilities for fabrication as well as for finishing operations. **Common positions include:** Blue-Collar Worker Supervisor; Buyer; Draftsperson; Human Resources Specialist; Industrial Engineer; Mechanical Engineer; Operations/Production Manager; Purchasing Agent and Manager; Quality Control Supervisor. **Educational backgrounds include:** Engineering. **Benefits:** Disability Coverage; Employee Discounts; Life Insurance; Medical Insurance; Tuition Assistance.

TELEDYNE ALLVAC
2020 Ashcraft Avenue, P.O. Box 5030, Monroe NC 28111. 704/289-4511. **Contact:** Becky Brazell, Personnel Manager. **Description:** Teledyne Allvac is a wholesaler of assorted metal and wire products. **Common positions include:** Accountant/Auditor; Administrator; Aerospace Engineer; Biological Scientist/Biochemist; Blue-Collar Worker Supervisor; Buyer; Chemist; Electrical/Electronics Engineer; Human Resources Specialist; Industrial Engineer; Industrial Production Manager; Manufacturer's/Wholesaler's Sales Rep.; Marketing Specialist; Mechanical Engineer; Metallurgical Engineer; Operations/Production Manager; Public Relations Specialist; Quality Control Supervisor. **Educational backgrounds include:** Accounting; Biology; Business Administration; Chemistry; Engineering; Marketing. **Benefits:** Dental Insurance; Disability Coverage; Employee Discounts; Life Insurance; Medical Insurance; Pension Plan; Savings Plan; Stock Option; Tuition Assistance. **Corporate headquarters location:** Los Angeles CA. **Other U.S. locations:** Paramount CA; Elk Grove Village IL; Agawam MA; Solon OH; Houston TX. **Operations at this facility include:** Administration; Manufacturing; Research and Development; Sales; Service. **Listed on:** New York Stock Exchange.

Note: Because addresses and telephone numbers of smaller companies change rapidly, we recommend you call each company to verify the information below before inquiring about job opportunities. Mass mailings are not recommended.

Additional employers with under 250 employees:

STEEL WORKS, BLAST FURNACES, AND ROLLING MILLS

Queensboro Steel Corporation
P.O. Box 1769, Wilmington NC 28402-1769. 910/763-6237.

STEEL WIRE, NAILS, AND SPIKES

Branford Wire & Manufacturing Company
P.O. Box 677, Mountain Home NC 28758-0677. 704/692-5791.

STEEL PIPE AND TUBES

Romac Metals
129 Honeycutt Road, Troutman NC 28166-7610. 704/528-4531.

IRON AND STEEL FOUNDRIES

Foundry Service Inc.
530 East Main Street. Biscoe NC 27209-9779. 910/428-2111.

NONFERROUS ROLLING AND DRAWING OF METALS

Wolverine Tube Inc.
555 North Park Drive,

Roxboro NC 27573. 910/503-3500.

Victory White Metal Company
3650 Patterson Avenue, Suite C, Winston-Salem NC 27105-3500. 910/744-1388.

DIE-CASTINGS

Allied Die Casting & Manufacturing Company
18 Industrial Park Road, Rutherfordton NC 28139-2933. 704/286-4003.

Consolidated Metco Inc.
780 Patton Avenue, Monroe

NC 28110-2438. 704/289-6491.

Southern Die Castings & Engineering
1800 Albertson Road, High Point NC 27260-8206. 910/882-0186.

NONFERROUS FOUNDRIES

Briggs-Shaffner Company
500 Brookstown Avenue, Winston-Salem NC 27101-5027. 910/722-2571.

PRIMARY METAL PRODUCTS

American Powdered Metals
P.O. Box 915, Conover NC 28613-0915. 704/464-0642.

Evtech
9103 Forsyth Park Drive Charlotte NC 28273-3882. 704/588-2112.

METAL CONTAINERS

American National Can Company
4000 Old Milwaukee Lane, Winston-Salem NC 27107-6103. 910/785-8501.

Reynolds Metals Company
200 Peeler Road, Salisbury NC 28147-8334. 704/638-3202.

FABRICATED STRUCTURAL METAL PRODUCTS

Brenner Company Inc.
3415 North Glenn Avenue, Winston-Salem NC 27105-3822. 910/725-8333.

Southern Engineering Company
3015 Wilkinson Boulevard, Charlotte NC 28208-5625. 704/399-8331.

Cookson Company
800 Tulip Drive, Gastonia NC 28052-1860. 704/866-9146.

Fenestra Corporation
12190 University City Boulevard, Harrisburg NC 28075. 704/455-5171.

Kinco Corporation
150 Westside Drive, Asheville NC 28806-2847. 704/254-2353.

Metal Industries Inc.
2601 Commerce Drive, Concord NC 28025. 704/782-6310.

Moss Supply Company Inc.
5001 North Graham Street, Charlotte NC 28269-4826. 704/596-8717.

Captive-Aire Systems
112 Wheaton Drive, Youngsville NC 27596-9414. 919/554-2410.

Kysor Carolina Metal Products
5019 Hovis Road, Charlotte NC 28208-1233. 704/392-3217.

Amerimark Building Products
Highway 501 South, Roxboro NC 27573. 910/599-2151.

Field Controls Company
2308 Airport Road, Kinston NC 28501-8928. 919/522-3031.

Leslie-Locke Inc.
295 McKoy Road, Burgaw NC 28425-4421. 910/259-6374.

Beaman Corporation
6306 Old 421 Road, Liberty NC 27298-8285. 910/622-6200.

METAL FASTENERS

Penn Engineering & Manufacturing Corporation
200 Kapp Street, Winston-Salem NC 27105-2641. 910/661-1936.

METAL FORGINGS

Boston Gear Operations
3900 Westinghouse Boulevard, Charlotte NC 28273-4517. 704/588-5610.

Rexnord Corporation
1000 Chain Drive, Morganton NC 28655-7239. 704/584-4000.

SMB North America Inc.
500 Oak Tree Drive, Selma NC 27576-3544. 919/965-5555.

METAL STAMPINGS

Precision Concepts Inc.
2701 Boulder Park Court, Suite 100, Winston-Salem NC 27101-4729. 910/761-8572.

Wrico Stamping Company of North Carolina
10240 Industrial Drive, Pineville NC 28134-6517. 704/554-9060.

COATING, ENGRAVING, AND ALLIED SERVICES

Colorworks Inc.
3010 Executive Drive, Greensboro NC 27406-5304. 910/272-8150.

Galvan Industries Inc.
7320 Millbrook Road,

Harrisburg NC 28075. 704/455-5102.

STEEL SPRINGS

Leggett & Platt Inc.
1629 Blandwood Drive, High Point NC 27260-8302. 910/884-4306.

Maryland Precision Spring Company
5600 Executive Center Drive, Suite 1, Charlotte NC 28212-8826. 704/535-4198.

FABRICATED WIRE PRODUCTS

M-B Industires Inc.
U.S. Highway 64 East, Rosman NC 28772. 704/862-4201.

Universal Spring Company
819 Herman Court, High Point NC 27263-2165. 910/434-3485.

Leggett & Platt Inc.
1430 Sherman Court, High Point NC 27260-8200. 910/889-2600.

Merchants Metals Inc.
P.O. Box 1820, Statesville NC 28687-1820. 704/872-7453.

Phelps Dodge Magnet Wire Company
17360 Plant Road, Laurinburg NC 28352. 910/276-0975.

Technibilt
P.O. Box 309, Newton NC 28658-0309. 704/464-7388.

Torpedo Wire & Strip Inc.
R.R. 6, Rocky Mount NC 27804-9806. 919/977-3900.

FABRICATED METAL PRODUCTS

Chace Precision Metals
1704 Barnes Street, Reidsville NC 27320-6406. 910/342-2381.

Owen Steel Company of North Carolina
2528 North Chester Street, Gastonia NC 28052-1808. 704/865-8571.

Quality Metal Products
Edgewood Circle, Gastonia NC 28052. 704/867-3843.

WHOLESALE METALS SERVICE CENTERS AND OFFICES

Jorgensen Steel & Aluminum
4015 Westinghouse Blvd,

Charlotte NC 28273-4518.
704/588-9878.

O'Neal Steel Inc.
301 Standard Drive,

Greensboro NC 27409.
910/668-1100.

South Carolina

ALUMAX, INC.
P.O. Box 1000, Goose Creek SC 29445. 803/572-3700. **Contact:** Human Resources. **Description:** Alumax, Inc. is one of the largest aluminum producers in North America. The company operates more than 90 plants and facilities in the United States, Canada, and Western Europe. Operations can be divided into three major product classes including primary aluminum, semi-fabricated products, and fabricated products. Primary aluminum is produced under the name Alumax Primary Aluminum Corporation. Semi-fabricated products are produced by a range of Alumax companies: Alumax Mill Products, Inc. produces coil, sheet, and plate aluminum; Alumax Extrusions, Inc. supplies soft alloy aluminum extrusion; Alumax Foils, Inc. produces aluminum foil for flexible packaging and food service markets; and Alumax Engineered Metal Processes, Inc. engages in semi-solid metal forming technology. Fabricated products are produced by Kawneer Company, Inc., which manufactures and markets non-residential architectural building products such as storefronts, building entrances, facings, window framing, and curtainwall systems; and Alumax Fabricated Products, Inc., which provides fabricated aluminum and steel products for the building and construction, transportation, and consumer durables markets. The Alumax Technical Center, Inc. operates as a technological entrepreneur, providing product research, development, and technical support. **Corporate headquarters location:** Norcross GA. **Listed on:** New York Stock Exchange.

HOMELITE INC.
P.O. Box 25069, Columbia SC 29224. 803/788-2970. **Contact:** Bonnie M. Heddy, Human Resources Manager. **Description:** Homelite Inc. manufactures saw chain from raw material. The company's manufacturing process includes the punch press, tool and die, heat treating, induction heat treating, chrome plating, and automatic assembly. Homelite Inc. also has an engineering design and development group. **Common positions include:** Accountant/Auditor; Designer; Draftsperson; Electrician; General Manager; Human Resources Specialist; Industrial Engineer; Mechanical Engineer; Operations/Production Manager; Quality Control Supervisor. **Educational backgrounds include:** Accounting; Engineering. **Benefits:** Dental Insurance; Disability Coverage; Life Insurance; Medical Insurance; Pension Plan; Profit Sharing; Tuition Assistance. **Corporate headquarters location:** Charlotte NC. **Parent company:** John Deere & Company (Moline IL) manufactures, distributes, and finances the sale of heavy equipment and machinery for use in the agricultural equipment and industrial equipment industries. The agricultural equipment sector manufactures tractors, soil, seeding, and harvesting equipment. The industrial equipment segment manufactures a variety of earth moving equipment, tractors, loaders, and excavators; while the consumer products division manufactures a variety of tractors and products for the homeowner. Financial services, including personal and commercial lines of insurance, retail, and managed health care services, are also offered by John Deere & Company. . **Operations at this facility include:** Manufacturing. **Number of employees at this location:** 157.

NUCOR STEEL
P.O. Box 525, Darlington SC 29532. 803/393-5841. **Contact:** Ken Barnhill, Personnel Manager. **Description:** This location operates as part of Nucor Corporation's Nucor Steel Division, which produces bars, angles, light structural, sheet, and special steel products. In addition to selling steel on the open market, these mills assure an economical supply of steel for the parent company's other divisions. The parent company, Nucor Corporation, is a manufacturer of steel products, whose other divisions include: Vulcraft, one of the nation's largest producers of steel joists and joist girders; Nucor Cold Finish, which produces cold-finished steel bars used extensively for shafting and machined precision parts; Nucor Grinding Balls, which produces steel grinding balls in Utah for the mining industry; Nucor Fastener, a steel bolt-making facility; Nucor Bearing Products, Inc., which produces steel bearings and machined steel parts; and Nucor Building Systems, which produces metal buildings and components. **Other U.S. locations:** AZ; NE; TX; UT. **Parent company:** Nucor Corporation. **Listed on:** New York Stock Exchange.

SMI OWEN STEEL COMPANY
801 Blossom Street, Columbia SC 29201. 803/251-7505. **Fax:** 803/251-7506. **Contact:** Judi Parsons, Human Resources Assistant. **Description:** SMI Owen Steel Company is engaged in steel fabrication. The company primarily produces structural and reinforcing steel used in large-scale construction. **Common positions include:** Accountant/Auditor; Cost Estimator; Credit Manager; Customer Service Representative; Draftsperson; Electrician; Structural Engineer; Transportation/Traffic Specialist. **Educational backgrounds include:** Business Administration; Engineering. **Benefits:** 401K; Disability Coverage; Life Insurance; Medical Insurance; Tuition Assistance. **Corporate headquarters location:** This Location. **Other U.S. locations:** Lawrenceville GA. **Operations at this facility include:** Administration; Manufacturing; Sales.

B.F. SHAW, INC.
P.O. Box 1199, Laurens SC 29360. 864/682-4000. **Contact:** Jeff Ottoson, Vice President. **Description:** B.F. Shaw, Inc. is a union shop fabricator of piping components for both new construction and the maintenance of existing systems. **Common positions include:** Draftsperson; Pipe Fitter; Welder. **Benefits:** Life Insurance; Medical Insurance; Pension Plan; Tuition Assistance. **Special Programs:** Training Programs. **Corporate headquarters location:** Baton Rouge LA. **Operations at this facility include:** Manufacturing.

SPARTANBURG STEEL PRODUCTS INC.
P.O. Box 6428, Spartanburg SC 29304. 864/585-5211. **Contact:** George Cherpas, Director of Personnel. **Description:** Spartanburg Steel Products Inc. is a metal fabrications firm. The company manufactures a variety of products including automotive stampings, beverage containers, and beer kegs. **Common positions include:** Accountant/Auditor; Blue-Collar Worker Supervisor; Buyer; Computer Programmer; Credit Manager; Customer Service Representative; Draftsperson; Electrical/Electronics Engineer; General Manager; Human Resources Specialist; Industrial Designer; Industrial Engineer; Management Trainee; Manufacturer's/Wholesaler's Sales Rep.; Mechanical Engineer; Metallurgical Engineer; Purchasing Agent and Manager; Quality Control Supervisor. **Educational backgrounds include:** Accounting; Business Administration; Computer Science; Engineering; Finance; Liberal Arts. **Benefits:** Dental Insurance; Disability Coverage; Life Insurance; Medical Insurance; Pension Plan; Profit Sharing; Tuition Assistance. **Corporate headquarters location:** This Location. **Operations at this facility include:** Manufacturing; Research and Development; Sales.

WELLS ALUMINUM INC.
P.O. Box 627, Belton SC 29627. 864/338-8000. **Contact:** David L. McKee, Director of Human Resources. **Description:** Wells Aluminum Inc. is engaged in aluminum extrusion operations. **Common positions include:** Blue-Collar Worker Supervisor; Buyer; Customer Service Representative; Department Manager; Draftsperson; General Manager; Operations/Production Manager; Transportation/Traffic Specialist. **Educational backgrounds include:** Business Administration; Marketing. **Benefits:** Dental Insurance; Disability Coverage; Life Insurance; Medical Insurance; Pension Plan; Savings Plan. **Corporate headquarters location:** Baltimore MD.

Note: Because addresses and telephone numbers of smaller companies change rapidly, we recommend you call each company to verify the information below before inquiring about job opportunities. Mass mailings are not recommended.

Additional employers with under 250 employees:

STEEL WORKS, BLAST FURNACES, AND ROLLING MILLS

Kline Iron & Steel Company
401 Gervais Street,
Columbia SC 29201-3043.
803/251-8000.

Talley Metals Technology
Highway 172, Mc Bee SC
29101. 803/335-7540.

STEEL WIRE, NAILS, AND SPIKES

Insteel Wire Products
East Gapway Road, Andrews
SC 29510. 803/264-5275.

IRON AND STEEL FOUNDRIES

Bahan Machine & Foundry
200 West Warehouse Court,

Taylors SC 29687-2539.
864/244-4220.

Greenwood Foundries
711 West Alexander Avenue,
Greenwood SC 29646-2303.
864/227-1713.

Conbraco Industries Inc.
Highway 501 East, Conway
SC 29526. 803/347-4666.

SMELTING AND REFINING OF NONFERROUS METALS

Kennecott Ridgeway Mining
Smallwood Road & Highway
46, Ridgeway SC 29130.
803/337-3276.

MacAlloy Corporation
1800 Pittsburgh Avenue,
North Charleston SC 29405-
9423. 803/722-8355.

NONFERROUS ROLLING AND DRAWING OF METALS

Briteline Extrusions Inc.
575 Beech Hill Road,
Summerville SC 29485-
7810. 803/873-4410.

Grumman Aircraft Systems
341 Industrial Drive,
Lexington SC 29072-3701.
803/359-1910.

DIE-CASTINGS

Imperial Die Casting Corporation
2249 Old Liberty Road,
Liberty SC 29657-8965.
864/859-0202.

PHB Inc.
168 Parker Drive, Beaufort
SC 29902. 803/846-2201.

COPPER FOUNDRIES

Gorham Bronze
45 Windham Boulevard,
Aiken SC 29801-9384.
803/648-9514.

METAL CONTAINERS

American National Can Corporation
609 Cousar Street,
Bishopville SC 29010-1938.
803/484-5361.

PRIMARY METAL PRODUCTS

NN Ball & Roller Inc.
700 Industrial Road,
Walterboro SC 29488-9374.
803/538-2131.

FABRICATED STRUCTURAL METAL PRODUCTS

SMI Owen Joist Corporation
850 Taylor Street, Cayce SC
29033. 803/796-5910.

Lifetime Doors Inc.
Mayfield Street, Denmark SC
29042. 803/793-3385.

Carolina Tank Corporation
100 Industrial Park, Chester
SC 29706. 803/581-3900.

RECO Industries Inc.
1839 Dunbar Road, Cayce
SC 29033-2217. 803/794-
3360.

Senior Boiler & Tube Company
506 Charlotte Highway,
Lyman SC 29365-1439.
864/439-4489.

Georgia-Pacific Corporation
5260 Cureton Ferry Road,
Catawba SC 29704-8799.
803/324-1100.

METAL FORGINGS

Precision Gear Train
4500 Leeds Avenue, North
Charleston SC 29405-8520.
803/745-1523.

Kaiser Aluminum
1508 Highway 246 South,
Greenwood SC 29646-8411.
864/223-6515.

METAL STAMPINGS

MPI International
5798 North Main Street,
Cowpens SC 29330-9713.
864/463-3251.

Walbar Metals
5502 Highway 25 North,
Hodges SC 29653-9675.
864/374-5050.

FABRICATED WIRE PRODUCTS

Straits Steel & Wire Company
99 Roush Street, Anderson
SC 29625-3113. 864/261-
0792.

WHOLESALE METALS SERVICE CENTERS AND OFFICES

Amico-Greenville
1520 Roper Mountain Road,
Greenville SC 29615-5600.
864/458-7241.

Edgcomb Metals Company
1 White Horse Road
Extension, Greenville SC
29605-3669. 864/277-
6011.

Kline Iron & Steel Company
841 Williams Street, West
Columbia SC 29169-5041.
803/251-6221.

For more information on career opportunities in the fabricated/primary metals and products industries:

Associations

ASM INTERNATIONAL: THE MATERIALS INFORMATION SOCIETY
Materials Park OH 44073. 800/336-5152.
Gathers, processes, and disseminates
technical information to foster the
understanding and application of engineered
materials.

AMERICAN FOUNDRYMEN'S SOCIETY
505 State Street, Des Plaines IL 60016-
847/824-0181.

AMERICAN WELDING SOCIETY
550 LeJeune Road NW, Miami FL 33126.
305/443-9353.

Directories

DIRECTORY OF STEEL FOUNDRIES IN THE UNITED STATES, CANADA, AND MEXICO
Steel Founder's Society of America, 455
State Street, Des Plaines IL 60016.
847/299-9160.

Magazines

AMERICAN METAL MARKET
25 7th Avenue, New York NY 10019.
212/887-8580.

IRON AGE NEW STEEL
191 South Gary, Carol Stream IL 60188.
708/462-2285.

IRON & STEEL ENGINEER
Association of Iron and Steel Engineers,
Three Gateway Center, Suite 2350,
Pittsburgh PA 15222. 412/281-6323.

MODERN METALS
625 North Michigan Avenue, Suite 2500,
Chicago IL 60611. 312/654-2300.

FINANCIAL SERVICES

You can't get much better than 1995. The stock market soared throughout the year, boosting business at brokerage houses. And, although the market isn't expected to be as hot in '96, it appears likely that the Federal Reserve will lower interest rates, putting the pieces into place for another solid year.

Jobseekers who have experience with mergers and acquisitions should benefit. At the same time, expect more consolidation among brokerage houses themselves. Analysts believe that the largest houses will get larger and the small boutique firms will continue to prosper, but the firms in the middle may get crunched.

North Carolina

AMERICAN GENERAL FINANCE
1724 Winkler Street, Wilkesboro NC 28697. 910/838-5157. **Contact:** Human Resources. **Description:** American General Finance was founded in 1920 and has grown to become a large consumer lending company with over 1,300 branches in 41 states. American General Finance has assets of more than $9 billion. The company's subsidiaries are engaged in the consumer finance, credit card, and insurance businesses. In 1982, American General Finance became part of the American General Corporation family as an operating subsidiary. **NOTE:** Jobseekers should send resumes to the corporate headquarters location: 601 NW 2nd Street, P.O. Box 59, Evansville, IN 47701. **Corporate headquarters location:** Evansville IN. **Parent company:** American General Corporation. **Number of employees nationwide:** 8,700.

FARM CREDIT SERVICES
2302 Soabar Avenue, Greensboro NC 27416-6510. **Toll-free phone:** 800/228-2185. **Contact:** Tommy Emerson, President. **Description:** Farm Credit Services provides financial services through 46 branch offices in the United States. FCS offers long-, intermediate-, and short-term financing to agricultural producers, farm-related businesses, fisherman, part-time farmers, and country home owners. The banks and related associations provide credit and credit-related services to, or for the benefit of, eligible borrowers for qualified agricultural purposes.

FIRST BANCORP FINANCIAL SERVICES, INC.
Highway 24/27 West, Troy NC 27371-0552. **Contact:** Human Resources. **Description:** First Bancorp Financial Services, Inc. (formerly First Recovery, Inc.), which currently owns and operates various real estate as a subsidiary of First Bancorp, which was founded in 1983, as Montgomery Bancorp. First Bancorp is a one-bank holding company whose principal activity is the ownership and operation of First Bank, which is headquartered in Troy, North Carolina. First Bank acquired Central State Bank in 1994 and conducts business from 28 branches located within a 60-mile radius of Troy, North Carolina. The bank provides a full range of banking services, including the accepting of demand and time deposits, the making of secured and unsecured loans to individuals and businesses, trust services, discount brokerage services, and self-directed IRAs. The parent company, First Bancorp, also owns and operates subsidiaries including Montgomery Data Services, Inc., which provides data processing services to financial institutions; and First Bank Insurance Services, Inc. **Corporate headquarters location:** This Location. **Parent company:** First Bancorp (Troy, NC). **Listed on:** NASDAQ.

FIRST UNION HOME EQUITY BANK, N.A.
1000 Louis Rose Place, Charlotte NC 28262-8546. 704/593-9300. **Contact:** Mary Jones, Vice President of Human Resources. **E-mail address:** comments@firstunion.com. **World Wide Web Address:** http://www.firstunion.com/. **Description:** Offers home equity loans through 184 offices in 42 states. The parent company, First Union Corporation, is one of the nation's largest bank holding companies with subsidiaries which operate over 1,330 full-service bank branches in the South Atlantic states. These subsidiaries provide retail banking, retail investment,

and commercial banking services. The corporation provides other financial services including mortgage banking, home equity lending, leasing, insurance and securities brokerage services from 222 branch locations. The corporation also operates one of the nation's largest ATM networks. **Corporate headquarters location:** This Location. **Parent company:** First Union Corporation (Charlotte, NC). **Listed on:** New York Stock Exchange. **Number of employees nationwide:** 31,858.

INTERSTATE/JOHNSON LANE
121 West Trade Street, #1100, Charlotte NC 28202. 704/379-9000. **Contact:** Gloria Gibson, Human Resources Director. **Description:** A securities brokerage firm.

SCOTT & STRINGFELLOW, INC.
2626 Glenwood Avenue, Suite 100, Raleigh NC 27608. 919/571-1893. **Toll-free phone:** 800/763-1893. **Contact:** James C. Hill, Jeff O'Quinn, Co-Managers. **Description:** A full-service regional brokerage and investment banking firm. Services of Scott & Stringfellow include investment advice and brokerage for individual and institutional clients, investment banking and securities underwriting for corporations and municipalities, and a wide array of other investment-related financial services including investment advisory services through its affiliate, Scott & Stringfellow Capital Management, Inc. Scott & Stringfellow has 27 offices located in Virginia (19), North Carolina (Charlotte, Greensboro, Kinston, North Wilkesboro, Wilmington, Winston-Salem, and this location), and West Virginia (1). **Corporate headquarters location:** Richmond VA. **Parent company:** Scott & Stringfellow Financial, Inc. (Richmond VA). **Listed on:** New York Stock Exchange. **Number of employees nationwide:** 475.

Note: Because addresses and telephone numbers of smaller companies change rapidly, we recommend you call each company to verify the information below before inquiring about job opportunities. Mass mailings are not recommended.

Additional employers with under 250 employees:

CREDIT AGENCIES AND INSTITUTIONS

First Greensboro Home Equity Inc.
1912 Eastchester Dr, High Point NC 27265-1405. 910/889-0700.

American General Finance
1506 W Innes St, Salisbury NC 28144-2504. 704/633-4311.

American General Finance
49 Plaza Pky, Lexington NC 27292. 704/243-7970.

American General Finance
1544 E Broad St, Statesville NC 28677. 704/873-1916.

American General Finance
4330 Fayetteville Rd, Lumberton NC 28358-2677. 910/739-7593.

Associates Financial Services
1939 E Main St, Albemarle NC 28001. 704/983-1114.

Banc One Mortgage Corp.
2115 Rexford Rd, Charlotte NC 28211. 704/367-3900.

Banc Plus Mortgage Inc.
4020 Oleander Dr, Suite 1, Wilmington NC 28403-6813. 910/799-9500.

Commercial Credit Corp. NC
2300 High Point Rd, Greensboro NC 27403-2644. 910/294-0211.

Commercial Credit Corp. NC
2602 Eric Ln, Burlington NC 27215-5475. 910/222-9994.

Commercial Credit Corp. NC
1500 Atkinson St, Laurinburg NC 28352-5010. 910/277-0021.

Commercial Credit Corp. NC
205 E Main St, Whiteville NC 28472-4225. 910/642-1818.

Commercial Credit Corp. NC
618 N Eugene St, Greensboro NC 27401-2022. 910/275-9191.

Green Tree Financial
3101 Poplarwood Ct, Suite 127, Raleigh NC 27604-1045. 919/872-8010.

Machine Tool Finance Corp.
5501 Executive Center Dr, Suite 2, Charlotte NC 28212. 704/535-9141.

Mercury Finance Company
1111A Lejeune Blvd, Jacksonville NC 28540-6392. 910/455-0332.

Mountain Farm Credit
231 Haywood St, Asheville NC 28801-2618. 704/258-8996.

Nationscredit Financial Service Corp.
3646 Capital Blvd, Raleigh NC 27604-3328. 919/876-5865.

Regional Acceptance Corp.
3004 S Memorial Dr, Greenville NC 27834-6207. 919/756-2148.

Safeway Finance Corp.
1235 S Scales St, Reidsville NC 27320-5630. 910/349-8452.

Safeway Finance Corp.
2000 Avondale Dr, Suite P, Durham NC 27704-4357. 919/220-2545.

Security Pacific Financial Service Inc.
232 Summit Square Blvd, Rural Hall NC 27045. 910/377-3131.

Spring Financial Services
1706 Winkler Mill Rd, Wilkesboro NC 28697-8355. 910/667-9539.

Transouth Financial Corp.
359 S Cox St, Asheboro NC
27203. 910/626-4004.

Transouth Financial Corp.
906 E Ash St, Goldsboro NC
27530-3806. 919/735-
1841.

Blazer Financial Services
6404 Falls of Neuse Rd,
Raleigh NC 27615-6811.
919/876-9300.

Chrysler Credit Corp.
3605 Glenwood Ave, Raleigh
NC 27612-4954. 919/783-
9300.

National City Mortgage Co.
802 Green Valley Rd,
Greensboro NC 27408-7020.
910/274-1196.

United Financial Services
854 S Fayetteville St,
Asheboro NC 27203-6456.
910/629-8020.

Avco Financial Services
4701 Wrightsville Ave, Suite
D3, Wilmington NC 28403-
6916. 910/392-2052.

First Factors Corporation
101 S Main St, Suite 200,
High Point NC 27260-5239.
910/889-2929.

MORTGAGE BANKERS

**Barclays American Mortgage
Corp.**
3608 W Friendly Ave, Suite
212, Greensboro NC 27410-
4833. 910/852-8805.

**First Greensboro Home
Equity Inc.**
1500 Pinecroft Rd, Suite
100, Greensboro NC 27407-
3808. 910/854-7071.

ICM Mortgage Corp.
6747 Fairview Rd, Charlotte
NC 28210-3361. 704/365-
1530.

National City Mortgage Co.
5510 Six Forks Rd, Raleigh
NC 27609. 919/848-2117.

National City Mortgage Co.
7401 Carmel Executive Park,
Charlotte NC 28226.
704/543-1314.

SNMC National Mortgage
1 Centerview Dr, Suite 104,
Greensboro NC 27407-3712.
910/299-3100.

Wendover Funding Inc.
725 N Regional Rd,
Greensboro NC 27409-9016.
910/668-7000.

SECURITY BROKERS AND DEALERS

Cogun Industries Inc.
Pineville Matthews Rd, Suite
155, Matthews NC 28105-
9153. 704/541-1671.

AG Edwards & Sons Inc.
324 W Wendover Ave, Suite
110, Greensboro NC 27408-
8438. 910/272-0523.

Alex Brown & Sons Inc.
One Triad Park Blvd,
Winston-Salem NC 27101.
910/724-6921.

Barney Smith Shearson
Tallywood Shopping Cntr,
Fayetteville NC 28303.
910/483-6181.

Edward D. Jones & Co.
111-D Davis St, Asheboro
NC 27203. 910/625-5250.

Edward D. Jones & Co.
408 Holly Hill Ln, Burlington
NC 27215-5200. 910/584-
7788.

Edward D. Jones & Co.
11 Salem St, Thomasville NC
27360-3903. 910/475-
9191.

Edward D. Jones & Co.
119 W Chatham St, Cary NC
27511-3331. 919/469-
0045.

Edward D. Jones & Co.
205 Lenmore Dr SE, Concord
NC 28025-2631. 704/786-
0040.

Edward D. Jones & Co.
1608 Godwin Ave,
Lumberton NC 28358-4208.
910/738-7666.

Edward D. Jones & Co.
115 N Haywood St,
Waynesville NC 28786-
3745. 704/452-0635.

Interstate/Johnson Lane
203 Queen St, Morganton
NC 28655-3341. 704/437-
6673.

JC Bradford & Co.
3008 S Church St,
Burlington NC 27215-5153.
910/584-1308.

JC Bradford & Co.
1415 Freeway Dr, Reidsville
NC 27320-7105. 910/342-
5911.

JC Bradford & Co.
2102-A N Elm St,
Greensboro NC 27408.
910/275-9676.

Paine Webber Inc.
2200 W Main St, Durham
NC 27705-4640. 919/286-
8600.

PD Edward Jones Co.
1600 Sherwood Dr,
Reidsville NC 27320-4200.
910/634-1380.

Scott & Stringfellow Inc.
400 W Market St,
Greensboro NC 27401-2241.
910/378-1824.

Scott & Stringfellow Inc.
311 9th St, N Wilkesboro NC
28659-4105. 910/838-
7769.

INVESTMENT ADVISORS

IDS Financial Services
7300 Carmel Executive Park,
Charlotte NC 28226.
704/541-9292.

Fidelity Financial Inc.
1003 Dresser Ct, Raleigh NC
27609-7323. 919/876-
9130.

South Carolina

AMERICAN GENERAL FINANCE
321 Bells Highway, Unit D, Walterboro SC 29488. 803/549-5536. **Contact:** Human
Resources. **Description:** American General Finance was founded in 1920 and has
grown to become a large consumer lending company with over 1,300 branches in 41
states. American General Finance has assets of more than $9 billion. The company's
subsidiaries are engaged in the consumer finance, credit card, and insurance
businesses. In 1982, American General Finance became part of the American General
Corporation family as an operating subsidiary. **NOTE:** Jobseekers should send resumes
to the corporate headquarters location: 601 NW 2nd Street, P.O. Box 59, Evansville,
IN 47701. **Corporate headquarters location:** Evansville IN. **Parent company:** American
General Corporation. **Number of employees nationwide:** 8,700.

EMERGENT GROUP, INC.
P.O. Box 17526, Greenville SC 29606. 864/235-8056. **Contact:** Human Resources. **Description:** A diversified holding company which offers residential mortgage and construction loans; operates a short-line railroad; repairs, operates, and leases railcars; and manufactures and markets children's clothing. **Corporate headquarters location:** This Location. **Subsidiaries include:** Carolina Investors, Inc.; Premier Financial Services, Inc.; Pickens Railroad Company; Emergent Financial Corporation; Loan Pros, Inc.; Emergent Business Capital, Inc.; and Young Generations, Inc. **Number of employees nationwide:** 250.

FLEET MORTGAGE GROUP INC.
1333 Main Street, Columbia SC 29211. 803/929-7900. **Contact:** Human Resources Department. **Description:** A large servicer of single-family residential mortgages and one of the largest originators of home loans. **Corporate headquarters location:** This Location. **Parent company:** Fleet Financial Group, founded in 1791, is a diversified financial services company with approximately 1,200 offices nationwide. Based in Providence, RI, Fleet Financial Group has 21,500 employees that work at six banks, with branches throughout New England; New York; London, England; and at more than 10 major financial services companies located throughout the United States including Atlanta, GA; Long Beach, CA; and New York, NY. Affiliated banking companies include: Fleet Bank, N.A.; Fleet Bank of Maine; Fleet Bank of Massachusetts, N.A.; Fleet Bank-NH; Fleet Bank; Fleet Bank-RI. Affiliated financial services companies include: AFSA Data Corp.; Fleet Brokerage Securities; Fleet Capital, Inc.; Fleet Credit Corp.; Fleet Private Equity; Fleet Finance, Inc.; Fleet Investment Advisors; Fleet Investment Services; Fleet Securities, Inc.; Fleet Services Corp.; and RECOLL Management Corp. **NOTE:** Fleet also acquired Shawmut Banks in 1995. **Listed on:** New York Stock Exchange. **Number of employees at this location:** 4,340.

MERRILL LYNCH
One Chamber of Commerce Drive, P.O. Box 5607, Hilton Head SC 29938. 803/785-9620. **Contact:** Human Resources. **Description:** One of the largest securities brokerage firms in the world, Merrill Lynch provides financial services in securities, financial planning, insurance, estate planning, mortgages, and related areas. The company also brokers commodity futures and options, is a major underwriter of new securities issues, and is a dealer in corporate and municipal securities. **Benefits:** 401K; Dental Insurance; Disability Coverage; Employee Discounts; Life Insurance; Medical Insurance; Pension Plan; Tuition Assistance. **Corporate headquarters location:** New York NY. **Listed on:** New York Stock Exchange.

SECURITY GROUP INC.
P.O. Box 811, Spartanburg SC 29301. 864/582-8193. **Contact:** Heidi Bolton, Human Resources Director. **Description:** A credit institution. **Corporate headquarters location:** This Location.

SMITH BARNEY
551 East Main Street, Spartanburg SC 29302. 864/585-7761. **Contact:** Fran Godshall, Operations Manager. **Description:** An investment banking and securities broker. Smith Barney also provides related financial services.

WORLD ACCEPTANCE CORPORATION
P.O. Box 6429, 1251 South Pleasantburg Drive, Greenville SC 29605. 864/277-4570. **Contact:** Richard Myers, Supervisor. **Description:** World Acceptance Corporation provides small loan consumer financial services. **Corporate headquarters location:** This Location. **Listed on:** NASDAQ. **Number of employees nationwide:** 800.

Note: Because addresses and telephone numbers of smaller companies change rapidly, we recommend you call each company to verify the information below before inquiring about job opportunities. Mass mailings are not recommended.

Additional employers with under 250 employees:

CREDIT AGENCIES AND INSTITUTIONS

Aiken Credit Co.
218 Park Ave SE, Aiken SC 29801. 803/642-5670.

American General Finance
513 S Main St, Bishopville SC 29010-1519. 803/484-4133.

American General Finance
1356 Grove Park NE, Orangeburg SC 29115-2455. 803/534-0346.

Atlantic Savings Bank
2 Gillon St, Charleston SC
29401. 803/853-0878.

Avco Financial Services
4122 Clemson Blvd, Suite 2
A, Anderson SC 29621-
1100. 864/260-0097.

Blazer Financial Services
331 By Pass 123, Seneca
SC 29678-0819. 864/882-
2754.

World Finance Corp.
707 Bay St, Beaufort SC
29902-5504. 803/524-
1600.

Colonial Finance Co.
2000 McMillan Ave,
Charleston SC 29405-7794.
803/554-1252.

Commercial Credit Corp.
975 Bacons Bridge Rd Unit
162, Summerville SC 29485-
4189. 803/875-9185.

Commercial Credit Corp.
205 Columbia Ave,
Lexington SC 29072-2662.
803/957-5115.

Compass Mortgage Inc.
1350 Ashley River Rd,
Charleston SC 29407-5347.
803/763-1101.

Covington Credit Corp.
102 Broughton St SW,
Orangeburg SC 29115-5907.
803/533-0050.

Delta Loans
509 12th St, West Columbia
SC 29169-6334. 803/939-
0223.

Delta Loans
321 N Parler Ave, Saint
George SC 29477-2225.
803/563-9275.

Delta Loans
403 E Washington St,
Walterboro SC 29488-4073.
803/549-1877.

Delta Loans
221 N Main St, Marion SC
29571. 803/423-7342.

Equicredit Corp. of SC
100 Executive Cntr Dr, Suite
106, Greenville SC 29615-
4508. 864/675-9836.

Equity One Inc.
N Hwy 52, Moncks Corner
SC 29461. 803/899-1060.

Finance South
1735 Reidville Rd,
Spartanburg SC 29301-
5460. 864/587-2118.

Finance South
700 E Main St, Duncan SC
29334. 864/949-6635.

First Family Financial Service
1671 Springdale Dr, Camden
SC 29020-2079. 803/425-
5568.

First Security Mortgage Corp.
109 Laurens Rd, Suite 115,
Greenville SC 29607-1860.
864/374-9123.

First Union Mortgage Corp.
1517 Sam Rittenberg Blvd,
Charleston SC 29407-4191.
803/571-2200.

Gold Key Lease
650 Executive Center Dr,
Greenville SC 29615-4520.
864/288-0781.

Kentucky Finance Co.
115 E Blackstock Rd,
Spartanburg SC 29301-
2604. 864/574-5301.

Lenders Loans
2010 Main St, Barnwell SC
29812-2070. 803/541-
4600.

Mercury Finance Co.
946 Orleans Rd, Charleston
SC 29407-4889. 803/766-
7603.

National Finance Company
469 King St, Charleston SC
29403-6231. 803/722-
2637.

National Finance Company
107 E Memorial Blvd, Saint
George SC 29477-2239.
803/563-9211.

Norwest Financial
107 S Highway 52, Moncks
Corner SC 29461-3953.
803/899-7241.

Peoples Savings & Loan Co.
215 S Main St, Anderson SC
29624-1620. 864/224-
5681.

Prime Lending Inc.
553 Georgia Ave, North
Augusta SC 29841-3701.
803/442-9674.

Quick Credit Corp.
1104 12th St, Cayce SC
29033-3305. 803/791-
3700.

Regional Finance Company
141 Laurens St SW, Aiken
SC 29801-3847. 803/649-
0040.

Regional Finance Company
528 Knox Abbott Dr, Suite
1, Cayce SC 29033-4160.
803/794-0034.

Regional Finance Company
417 King St, Charleston SC
29403-6407. 803/723-
5105.

Ridge Loan Co.
137C N Oak St, Batesburg
SC 29006-1733. 803/532-
2398.

Safeway Finance Corp.
1848 Wilson Rd, Newberry
SC 29108-2922. 803/276-
2813.

Safeway Finance Corp.
Woodruff Plaza, Woodruff
SC 29388. 864/476-3104.

Safeway Finance Corp.
1705 N Main St, Anderson
SC 29621-4761. 864/226-
5770.

Security Finance
2721 Cleveland St, Elloree
SC 29047. 803/897-2126.

Security Finance
350 Washington Sq,
Walterboro SC 29488-4720.
803/549-9428.

Security Finance Corp.
201 W Pitts St, Clinton SC
29325-2318. 864/833-
3600.

Southern Finance
359 W Evans St, Florence
SC 29501-3429. 803/667-
6012.

United Financial Services
916 Chesterfield Hwy,
Cheraw SC 29520-7008.
803/537-6215.

Sunbelt Credit
5114 Fairfield Rd, Columbia
SC 29203-4314. 803/786-
1100.

Sunbelt Credit
208 E Main St, Spartanburg
SC 29306-5127. 864/582-
5421.

TICO Credit
Chester Crossing, Chester
SC 29706. 803/581-0875.

World Finance Corp.
620 12th St, West Columbia
SC 29169-6337. 803/791-
4381.

Transamerica Financial Service
1836 Ashley River Rd Unit 5,
Charleston SC 29407-4781.
803/763-6610.

Transamerica Financial Service
408 N Pleasantburg Dr,
Greenville SC 29607-2128.
864/232-3988.

Transouth Financial Corp.
1400 Reidville Rd,
Spartanburg SC 29306-
3927. 864/574-9100.

Transsouth Financial Corp.
1014 Dekalb St, Camden SC
29020-4117. 803/432-
6161.

Transsouth Financial Corp.
104 Central Ave #A, Goose
Creek SC 29445-2949.
803/572-5500.

Transsouth Financial Corp.
102 Old Trolley Rd,
Summerville SC 29485-
4909. 803/875-9660.

Transsouth Financial Corp.
215 Kelley St, Lake City SC
29560-2415. 803/394-
2000.

Transsouth Financial Corp.
112 W Cherokee Rd,
Florence SC 29501-5246.
803/669-4111.

Transsouth Financial Corp.
321 By Pass, Winnsboro SC
29180. 803/635-1467.

World Finance Corp.
1405 Main St, Newberry SC
29108-3431. 803/276-
5880.

United Carolina Bank
401 W Butler Rd, Mauldin
SC 29662-2532. 864/297-
3800.

World Fin Corp. Bennettsville
112 Broad St, Bennettsville
SC 29512-4002. 803/479-
8351.

United Companies Lending
250 Executive Center Dr #B-
27, Greenville SC 29615-
4518. 864/281-9836.

World Finance Corp.
106 NE Main St,
Simpsonville SC 29681-
2656. 864/228-0034.

World Finance Corp.
122 N Main St, Anderson SC
29621-5609. 864/226-
2444.

World Finance Corp.
198 Russell St NW,
Orangeburg SC 29115-5934.
803/536-5494.

World Finance Corp.
7 N Congress St, York SC
29745-1528. 803/628-
1554.

World Finance Corp.
104 S Pendleton St, Easley
SC 29640-3046. 864/859-
7534.

World Finance Corp.
Charleston
370 King St, Charleston SC
29401. 803/722-2966.

Mercury Finance Co.
2102 Laurens Rd, Greenville
SC 29607-3222. 864/297-
0044.

Southern Finance Co.
516 N Main St, Marion SC
29571-3032. 803/423-
1529.

Security Finance
415 Rutledge St, Camden SC
29020-4422. 803/432-
1247.

The Finance Co.
56 Bridgetown Rd #J, Hilton
Head SC 29928-3365.
803/785-2542.

Century Car Mart
504 N Main St, Mauldin SC
29662-2308. 864/234-
4904.

MORTGAGE BANKERS

Banc One Mortgage Corp.
251 S Pine St, Spartanburg
SC 29302-2626. 864/542-
8646.

CTX Mortgage Company
2430 Mall Dr, Suite 18O,
Charleston SC 29406-6546.
803/740-7171.

Equity One
610 Highway 1 S, Lugoff SC
29078-9414. 803/438-
0455.

Equity One
402 N Pleasantburg Dr,
Greenville SC 29607-2128.
864/467-1049.

Equity One
1807 N Cherry Rd, Suite
173, Rock Hill SC 29732-
2657. 803/366-7182.

First Federal of Spartanburg
1488 W O Ezell Blvd,
Spartanburg SC 29301-
1553. 864/596-8384.

NationsBanc Mortgage Corp.
116 S Pleasantburg Dr,
Greenville SC 29607-2520.
864/241-2124.

**Resource Bancshares
Mortgage Group**
3600 Forest Dr, Columbia
SC 29204-4033. 803/790-
4500.

Ryland Mortgage Co.
950 Houston Northcutt Blvd,
Mount Pleasant SC 29464-
3482. 803/856-9222.

**Southern National Mortgage
Service**
100 Miracle Mile Dr,
Anderson SC 29621-1300.
864/261-4000.

Anchor Bank
11 Pope Ave, Hilton Head SC
29928-4701. 803/785-
4848.

The Loan Pros Inc.
6185 Rivers Ave, N
Charleston SC 29406-4999.
803/863-9100.

Transsouth Financial Corp.
307 W Main St, Kingstree
SC 29556-3234. 803/354-
7478.

SECURITY BROKERS AND DEALERS

AG Edwards & Sons Inc.
896 N Walnut St, Seneca SC
29678-2735. 864/882-
4924.

Carolina Securities Corp.
309 Columbia Ave,
Lexington SC 29072-2664.
803/359-1820.

Cohig & Associates Inc.
7 Charlotte St, 1st Flr,
Charleston SC 29403-6307.
803/577-7653.

Edward D. Jones & Co.
2043 W Dekalb St, Camden
SC 29020-2057. 803/432-
6998.

Edward D. Jones & Co.
1226 Yeamans Hall Rd,
Hanahan SC 29406-2750.
803/566-1247.

Edward D. Jones & Co.
723-A St Andrews Blvd,
Charleston SC 29407.
803/763-3555.

Edward D. Jones & Co.
354 Folly Rd, Charleston SC
29412-2549. 803/795-
7957.

Edward D. Jones & Co.
210 S Cedar St, Summerville
SC 29483-6063. 803/851-
1840.

Edward D. Jones & Co.
915 3rd Ave, Conway SC
29526-5144. 803/248-
7292.

Edward D. Jones & Co.
630 E Washington St,
Greenville SC 29601-2963.
864/232-5880.

JC Bradford & Co.
4975 Lacross Rd, Suite 101,
Charleston SC 29406-6524.
803/744-1180.

JC Bradford & Co.
12 Miller Rd, Sumter SC
29150-2403. 803/775-
9228.

Legg Mason
200 Meeting St Unit 11,
Charleston SC 29401-3156.
803/722-4557.

Sunamerica Securities
1735 Wilson Rd, Newberry

SC 29108-2919. 803/321-
3211.

Wheat First Butcher Singer
401 N Main St, Greenville SC
29601-2026. 864/467-
9800.

INVESTMENT ADVISORS

Consolidated Planning
845 Lowcountry Blvd, Mount
Pleasant SC 29464-3041.
803/884-2071.

For more information on career opportunities in financial services:

Associations

FINANCIAL EXECUTIVES INSTITUTE
P.O. Box 1938, Morristown NJ 07962-
1938. 201/898-4600. Fee and membership
required. Publishes biennial member
directory. Provides member referral service.

INSTITUTE OF FINANCIAL EDUCATION
111 East Wacker Drive, Chicago IL 60601.
312/946-8800. Offers career development
program.

**NATIONAL ASSOCIATION OF BUSINESS
ECONOMISTS**
1233 20th Street NW, Suite 505,
Washington DC 20036. 202/463-6223.
Bulletin board number: 216/241-6254.
Newsletter and electronic bulletin board list
job openings. Members can upload resumes
and listed positions desired to bulletin
board.

**NATIONAL ASSOCIATION OF CREDIT
MANAGEMENT**
8815 Centre Park Drive, Suite 200,
Columbia MD 21045-2158. 410/740-5560.
Contact: Delores Richman. Publishes a
business credit magazine.

**NATIONAL ASSOCIATION OF REAL
ESTATE INVESTMENT TRUSTS**
1129 20th Street NW, Suite 305,
Washington DC 20036. 202/785-8717.
Contact: Donna Smith, Membership.

PUBLIC SECURITIES ASSOCIATION
40 Broad Street, 12th Floor, New York NY
10004. 212/809-7000. Contact: Caroline
Binn x427. Publishes an annual report and
several newsletters.

SECURITIES INDUSTRY ASSOCIATION
120 Broadway, 35th Floor New York NY
10271. 212/608-1500. Contact: Phil

Williams/Membership. Publishes a security
industry yearbook.

TREASURY MANAGEMENT ASSOCIATION
7315 Wisconsin Avenue, Suite 1250-W,
Bethesda MD 20814. 301/907-2862.

Directories

**DIRECTORY OF AMERICAN FINANCIAL
INSTITUTIONS**
Thomson Business Publications, 6195
Crooked Creek Road, Norcross GA 30092.
770/448-1011. Sales 800/321-3373.

MOODY'S BANK AND FINANCE MANUAL
Moody's Investor Service, 99 Church
Street, New York NY 10007. 212/553-
0300.

Magazines

**BARRON'S: NATIONAL BUSINESS AND
FINANCIAL WEEKLY**
Dow Jones & Co., 200 Liberty Street, New
York NY 10281. 212/416-2700.

FINANCIAL PLANNING
40 West 57th Street, 11th Floor, New York
NY 10019. 212/765-5311.

FINANCIAL WORLD
Financial World Partners, 1328 Broadway,
3rd Floor, New York NY 10001. 212/594-
5030.

**FUTURES: THE MAGAZINE OF
COMMODITIES AND OPTIONS**
250 South Wacker Drive, Suite 1150,
Chicago IL 60606. 312/977-0999.

INSTITUTIONAL INVESTOR
488 Madison Avenue, 12th Floor, New
York NY 10022. 212/303-3300.

FOOD AND BEVERAGES/AGRICULTURE

 *Employment in food processing is expected to fall slightly through 2005. Although the industry's output should grow, increasing automation and productivity will mean food can be produced with fewer workers. However, some food processing industries are likely to remain fairly labor intensive. For example, meat packing and poultry processing are difficult to fully automate because each animal processed is different. Professional specialty occupations, although small in number, are also expected to grow. The growth of these occupations -- including engineers, systems analysts, and food scientists -- reflects the industry's emphasis on scientific research to improve food products and production processes. Demand for food scientists will also grow in response to expanding government inspection and regulation of food production.*

Several factors may slow the decline in food processing employment. As consumers increasingly seek 'ready-to-heat' foods, the food processing industry has introduced many new products. Many of these new goods, which require more processing than the items they are replacing, will help maintain the demand for food processors in the future. In addition, the food processing industry is taking advantage of new technology to perform much of the processing formerly done by retailers. One other factor that may help stem employment decline is growing international trade in food products. Food processing firms expect growing trade to provide new markets for their products. The emerging field of biotechnology and other new food science technologies may also provide new jobs.

North Carolina

CAROLINA TURKEYS
P.O. Box 589, Mt. Olive NC 28365. 919/658-6743. **Contact:** Human Resources. **Description:** Carolina Turkeys is a turkey processing company. The company was formed when two of North Carolina's largest family-run turkey processing operations merged in 1986. Carolina Turkeys' operations now run 24 hours per day, processing more than 22 million birds annually. The company is a fully integrated operation that includes diagnostic labs, research and breeder farms, hatcheries, and feed mills. The company's line of turkey meats is distributed across the country to restaurants and delis, hospitals, schools, and retail markets. Products include: Just Perfect Turkey Breast, Premium Turkey Breasts, Classic and Legend Turkey Breasts, Deluxe and Deli Turkey Breasts, and Cured Deli Meats & Franks.

CASE FARMS, INC.
P.O. Box 308, Morganton NC 28680. 704/438-6900. **Contact:** Human Resources. **Description:** Case Farms, Inc. processes chicken for sale to retailers. The company also sells chicken parts to manufacturers of pet foods.

COCA-COLA BOTTLING COMPANY CONSOLIDATED
1900 Rexford Road, Charlotte NC 28211-3481. 704/551-4400. **Contact:** Bob Pettus, Human Resources Manager. **Description:** Coca-Cola Bottling Company Consolidated bottles, cans, and markets soft drinks, primarily products of the Coca-Cola Company, and operates franchise bottling operations. The company conducts operations in 11 southeastern states. **Listed on:** NASDAQ. **Number of employees at this location:** 3,900.

EAGLE SNACKS, INC.
200 East 3rd Street, P.O. Box 535, Robersonville NC 27871. 919/795-5141. **Contact:** Sam Taylor, Employee Relations Manager. **Description:** Eagle Snacks, Inc., which began operations in 1979, produces and distributes a line of snack food items. The line of snack and nut items is distributed through a network of Anheuser-Busch wholesalers and independent distributors throughout the United States. The company produces a broad line of snack items including Thins and Ripples Potato Chips, Crispy Cooked Potato Chips, Nacho Cheese and Ranch flavored Tortilla Thins, Restaurant Style and El Grande Style Tortilla Chips, Eagle Salsa and Bean Dip, and several other products. Eagle also markets nuts, including Honey Roast and Lightly Salted Peanuts, Mixed Nuts, Fancy Cashews, and others. **Corporate headquarters location:** St. Louis MO. **Parent company:** Anheuser-Busch Companies Inc.

FAST FOOD MERCHANDISERS, INC.
801 East Main Street, Forest City NC 28043. 704/245-3515. **Contact:** Cheryl Hamrick, Personnel Manager. **Description:** A fast-food distribution company serving Hardee's Food Systems. Established in 1962, Fast Food Merchandisers was formed by Hardee's to keep up with the growing demand for the restaurant's products. The manufacturing and distribution group services nearly all of Hardee's restaurants from its three plants and ten distribution facilities, which are located across the country. Hardee's Food Systems, Inc. is one of the largest fast-food hamburger restaurant companies in the world, operating over 4,000 restaurants in 40 states and 10 foreign countries. **Corporate headquarters location:** Rocky Mount NC.

FLOWERS BAKING COMPANY
801 Main Street, Jamestown NC 27282. 910/841-8840. **Contact:** Director of Human Resources. **Description:** Operates more than 20 bakeries which produce a wide variety of products, including bread, buns, rolls, and donuts for retail sale to food stores, restaurants, institutions, and more than 200 company-owned stores nationally. This location of Flowers Baking Company produces sandwich bread and hot dog buns. **Corporate headquarters location:** Chicago IL.

FRITO-LAY INC.
900 North Long Street, Salisbury NC 28144. 704/633-8100. **Contact:** Employment Manager, Personnel. **Description:** Other area locations: 2911 Nevada Boulevard, Charlotte, NC 28217. **NOTE:** Frito-Lay Inc. accepts mailed inquiries only. Frito-Lay Inc. is a worldwide manufacturer and wholesaler of snack products, including Fritos Corn Chips, Lays Potato Chips, Doritos Tortilla Chips, Ruffles Potato Chips, Cheetos, and a wide range of other snack foods. The parent company, PepsiCo, also operates on a worldwide basis within three industry segments: beverages, snack foods, and restaurants. The beverage segment primarily markets its brands worldwide and manufactures concentrates for its brands for sale to franchised bottlers worldwide. The segment also operates bottling plants and distribution facilities of its own located in the U.S. and key international markets, and distributes ready-to-drink Lipton tea products under a joint venture agreement. In addition, under separate distribution and joint-venture agreements, the segment distributes certain previously existing, as well as jointly developed Ocean Spray juice products. The international snack food business includes major operations in Mexico, the United Kingdom, and Canada. The restaurant segment consists primarily of the operations of the worldwide Pizza Hut, Taco Bell, and KFC chains. PFS, PepsiCo's restaurant distribution operation, supplies company-owned and company franchised restaurants principally in the United States. **Common positions include:** Accountant/Auditor; Blue-Collar Worker Supervisor; Electrical/Electronics Engineer; Food Scientist/Technologist; Human Resources Specialist; Industrial Engineer; Mechanical Engineer; Operations/Production Manager; Purchasing Agent and Manager; Quality Control Supervisor. **Educational backgrounds include:** Biology; Business Administration; Engineering. **Benefits:** Dental Insurance; Disability Coverage; Employee Discounts; Life Insurance; Medical Insurance; Pension Plan; Savings Plan; Tuition Assistance. **Corporate headquarters location:** Plano TX. **Listed on:** New York Stock Exchange.

GOLDEN POULTRY COMPANY, INC.
P.O. Box 3668, Sanford NC 27330. 919/774-7333. **Contact:** Human Resources. **Description:** A processing plant for the poultry producer and marketer. Golden Poultry Company processes and markets chickens for the food service and retail industries. Retail products are marketed under the Young 'n Tender label or under customers' private labels and sold primarily in Florida, Georgia, the Mid-Atlantic states, the Northeast, and the Midwest. The company also purchases and resells processed chicken, turkey, beef, pork, seafood, dairy, and other food products. Customers include a fast-growing retail chain in the Southeast, major fast-food companies, and many other retail, institutional, and restaurant accounts east of the Rockies. Golden

Poultry is a subsidiary of Gold Kist, Inc., which owns 71 percent of the company. Plans for 1995 include a $6 million project that will increase Carolina Golden Products' capability to produce individual quick frozen chicken products. **Corporate headquarters location:** Atlanta GA. **Parent company:** Gold Kist, Inc.

GOODMARK FOODS, INC.
6131 Falls of Neuse Road, Raleigh NC 27609. 919/790-9940. **Contact:** Clint Neal, Director of Human Resources. **Description:** A producer and marketer of meat snacks. GoodMark Foods' principal meat snack brands include Slim Jim, Penrose, Pemmican, and Smokey Mountain. The company also produces an extruded grain snack under the Andy Capp's brand name. The company also produces and packages and sells packaged meats under the Jesse Jones brand. **Corporate headquarters location:** This Location. **Listed on:** NASDAQ. **Number of employees nationwide:** 1,000.

GUARDIAN CORPORATION
P.O. Box 7397, Rocky Mount NC 27804. 919/443-4101. **Contact:** Stan Figlewski, Senior Vice President of Human Resources and Administration. **Description:** A food services company. **Number of employees nationwide:** 1,000.

HOUSE OF RAEFORD FARMS
P.O. Box 40, Rose Hill NC 28458. 910/289-3191. **Toll-free phone:** 800/768-5879. **Fax:** 910/289-4555. **Contact:** Laura Blanton, Personnel Manager. **Description:** A poultry processing plant. **Common positions include:** Accountant/Auditor; Credit Manager; Electrician; General Manager; Human Resources Specialist; Registered Nurse. **Educational backgrounds include:** Business Administration. **Benefits:** 401K; Dental Insurance; Employee Discounts; Life Insurance; Medical Insurance; Savings Plan. **Corporate headquarters location:** Raeford NC. **Other U.S. locations:** Natawa MI; Hemingway SC. **Operations at this facility include:** Manufacturing; Sales. **Listed on:** Privately held. **Number of employees at this location:** 600. **Number of employees nationwide:** 3,900.

LANCE, INC.
P.O. Box 32368, Charlotte NC 28232. 704/554-1421. **Contact:** Randy Godfried, Human Resources Director. **Description:** LANCE, Inc., founded in 1913, produces snack products primarily including various crackers sold in individual-size packages. In 1980, the company introduced the Home-pak line of products for sale in supermarkets. The company also introduced the Club-pak line of products which are packaged in eighteen count units for sale at mass merchandiser 'clubs.' In the late 1980s, the company began its Snack-Right program which includes a reformulated entire product line, eliminating animal fats and tropical oils. The company also sells products under private labels and cookies under the Vista brand name, which are produced at the Vista Bakery in Columbia, South Carolina. The company also operates Midwest Biscuit in Burlington, Iowa and Caronuts in Boykins, Virginia. **Corporate headquarters location:** This Location. **Listed on:** NASDAQ.

LUNDY PACKING COMPANY
P.O. Box 49, Clinton NC 28329. 910/592-2104. **Contact:** David Moore, Human Resources Manager. **Description:** A meat packing plant. **Number of employees nationwide:** 1,000.

MERCHANTS DISTRIBUTORS INC. (MDI)
P.O. Box 2148, Hickory NC 28601. 704/323-4100. **Fax:** 704/323-4341. **Contact:** Rod Dooley, Director of Human Resources. **Description:** A wholesale grocery company. **Common positions include:** Accountant/Auditor; Automotive Mechanic/Body Repairer; Buyer; Computer Programmer; Computer Systems Analyst; Customer Service Representative; Manufacturer's/Wholesaler's Sales Rep.; Operations/Production Manager; Transportation/Traffic Specialist; Wholesale and Retail Buyer. **Educational backgrounds include:** Accounting; Business Administration; Computer Science; Finance; Marketing. **Benefits:** 401K; Credit Union; Dental Insurance; Disability Coverage; Life Insurance; Medical Insurance; Pension Plan; Tuition Assistance. **Special Programs:** Internships. **Operations at this facility include:** Administration; Sales. **Listed on:** Privately held. **Number of employees at this location:** 1,260.

MILLER BREWING COMPANY
1900 Barnes Street, Reidsville NC 27320. 910/342-7225. **Contact:** Jim Grant, Human Resources Manager. **Description:** Miller Brewing Company produces and distributes beer and other malt beverages. Principal beer brands include Miller Lite, Lite Ice, Miller Genuine Draft, Miller Genuine Draft Light, Miller High Life, Miller Reserve, Lowenbrau, Milwaukee's Best, and Meister Brau, and Red Dog and Icehouse from the Plank Road Brewery. Miller also produces Sharp's, a non-alcoholic brew. A subsidiary, the Jacob

Leinenkugel Brewing Company of Chippewa Falls, Wisconsin, brews Leinenkugel's Original Premium, Leinenkugel's Light, Leinie's Ice, Leinenkugel's Limited, Leinenkugel's Red Lager, and four seasonal beers: Leinenkugel's Genuine Bock, Leinenkugel's Honey Weiss, Leinenkugel's Autumn Gold, and Leinenkugel's Winter Lager. Miller owns and operates the second largest beer importer in the United States, Molson Breweries U.S.A., Inc., based in Reston, Virginia, which imports the Molson beers from Canada as well as Foster's Lager and many other brands. Miller is also majority owner of Celis Brewery Inc. in Austin, Texas. **Corporate headquarters location:** Milwaukee WI. **Parent company:** Philip Morris Companies Inc. (New York). **Number of employees nationwide:** 155,000.

PERDUE FARMS, INC.
P.O. Box 1180, Robbins NC 27325. 910/948-2223. **Contact:** Human Resources. **Description:** This location houses a poultry processing plant. Perdue Farms is one of the largest suppliers of fresh poultry products in the United States. The company's products are sold in supermarkets, small groceries, and quality butcher shops from Maine to Georgia and as far west as Chicago, Illinois. It is a fully integrated operation, from breeding and hatching to delivering packaged goods to market. The company was originally a supplier of table eggs, later selling chicken to large companies like Swift and Armour. In 1968 the company began to sell its own brand of chicken. The company operated under the name A.W. Perdue & Son until 1971. **Corporate headquarters location:** Salisbury MD. **Number of employees nationwide:** 18,000.

PERDUE FARMS, INC.
P.O. Box 1357, 416 South Long Drive, Rockingham NC 28379. 910/895-5284. **Contact:** John Vivvens, Plant Manager. **Description:** This location houses a poultry processing plant. Perdue Farms is one of the largest suppliers of fresh poultry products in the United States. The company's products are sold in supermarkets, small groceries, and quality butcher shops from Maine to Georgia and as far west as Chicago, Illinois. It is a fully integrated operation, from breeding and hatching to delivering packaged goods to market. The company was originally a supplier of table eggs, later selling chicken to large companies like Swift and Armour. In 1968 the company began to sell its own brand of chicken. The company operated under the name A.W. Perdue & Son until 1971. **Corporate headquarters location:** Salisbury MD. **Number of employees nationwide:** 18,000.

PERDUE FARMS, INC.
P.O. Box 428, Robersonville NC 27871. 919/795-4151. **Contact:** Bill Coradetti, Human Resources Manager. **Description:** This location houses a poultry processing plant. Perdue Farms is one of the largest suppliers of fresh poultry products in the United States. The company's products are sold in supermarkets, small groceries, and quality butcher shops from Maine to Georgia and as far west as Chicago, Illinois. It is a fully integrated operation, from breeding and hatching to delivering packaged goods to market. The company was originally a supplier of table eggs, later selling chicken to large companies like Swift and Armour. In 1968 the company began to sell its own brand of chicken. The company operated under the name A.W. Perdue & Son until 1971. **Corporate headquarters location:** Salisbury MD. **Number of employees nationwide:** 18,000.

PERDUE FARMS, INC.
P.O. Box 460, Lewiston NC 27849. 919/348-2001. **Contact:** Bob Bullock, Human Resources Manager. **Description:** This location houses a poultry processing plant. Perdue Farms is one of the largest suppliers of fresh poultry products in the United States. The company's products are sold in supermarkets, small groceries, and quality butcher shops from Maine to Georgia and as far west as Chicago, Illinois. It is a fully integrated operation, from breeding and hatching to delivering packaged goods to market. The company was originally a supplier of table eggs, later selling chicken to large companies like Swift and Armour. In 1968 the company began to sell its own brand of chicken. The company operated under the name A.W. Perdue & Son until 1971. **Corporate headquarters location:** Salisbury MD. **Number of employees nationwide:** 18,000.

PIEDMONT POULTRY PROCESSING, INC.
P.O. Box 129, Lumber Bridge NC 28357. 910/843-5942. **Contact:** Otto Lange, Director of Human Resources. **Description:** A chicken processing plant.

SMITHFIELD PACKING COMPANY, INC.
2602 West Vernon Avenue, Kinston NC 28501. 919/522-4777. **Contact:** Pamela Nobles, Personnel Director. **Description:** Smithfield Packing Company, Inc. processes

and sells ham under the retail name Smithfield Hams. The company's products are distributed nationwide.

STANDARD COMMERCIAL CORPORATION
P.O. Box 450, Wilson NC 27894. 919/291-5507. **Fax:** 919/237-1109. **Contact:** Nancy Hanes, Human Resources Director. **Description:** A large dealer of leaf tobacco for clients in 85 countries. The company buys and processes a variety of tobaccos for sale to domestic and international makers of cigarettes, cigars, and pipe tobaccos. Standard Commercial Corporation also purchases, processes, and markets wool to international customers. The company operates three tobacco processing plants in the United States and 17 other plants throughout the world, and eight wool manufacturing and storage plants in eight countries. The company is also involved in importing-exporting in Eastern Europe and operates a building supply company. **Corporate headquarters location:** This Location. **Listed on:** New York Stock Exchange.

THE STROH BREWERY COMPANY
4791 Schlitz Avenue, Winston-Salem NC 27107. 910/788-6710. **Contact:** E. Paul Hoeing, Manager of Industrial Relations. **Description:** Brews malt beverages. **Common positions include:** Accountant/Auditor; Administrator; Biological Scientist/Biochemist; Blue-Collar Worker Supervisor; Department Manager; Electrical/Electronics Engineer; Industrial Engineer; Industrial Production Manager; Mechanical Engineer; Plant Manager; Production Manager; Quality Control Supervisor. **Educational backgrounds include:** Accounting; Business Administration; Chemistry; Engineering; Finance. **Benefits:** Dental Insurance; Disability Coverage; Employee Discounts; Life Insurance; Medical Insurance; Pension Plan; Thrift Plan; Tuition Assistance. **Corporate headquarters location:** Detroit MI. **Other U.S. locations:** FL; MN; PA; TX. **Operations at this facility include:** Administration; Manufacturing; Research and Development. **Number of employees at this location:** 502.

TYSON FOODS INC.
1600 River Road, P.O. Box 88, Wilkesboro NC 28697. 910/838-2171. **Contact:** Gerald Lankford, Division Personnel Manager. **Description:** This location is engaged in poultry slaughtering, processing, and packaging. Overall, Tyson Foods Inc. is one of the world's largest fully integrated producers, processors, and marketers of poultry-based food products. The company also produces other center-of-the-plate and convenience food items. Chicken continues to account for 75 percent of sales, and Tyson Foods Inc.'s poultry production capacity is projected by the company to increase to approximately 37 million heads per week by the end of 1997. Familiar Tyson products include: Tyson Holly Farms Fresh Chicken, Weaver, Louis Kemp Crab, Lobster Delights, Healthy Portion, Beef Stir Fry, Crab Delights Stir Fry, Chicken Fried Rice Kits, Pork Chops with Cinnamon Apples, Salmon Grill Kits, Fish'n Chips Kits, and Rotisserie Chicken. **Common positions include:** Blue-Collar Worker Supervisor; Food Scientist/Technologist; Human Resources Specialist; Industrial Production Manager; Management Trainee; Operations/Production Manager; Quality Control Supervisor. **Educational backgrounds include:** Biology; Business Administration. **Benefits:** Dental Insurance; Disability Coverage; Employee Discounts; Life Insurance; Medical Insurance; Pension Plan; Savings Plan. **Special Programs:** Training Programs. **Corporate headquarters location:** Springsdale AR. **Operations at this facility include:** Divisional Headquarters.

U.S. FOOD SERVICE/BIGGERS BROTHERS, INC.
920 Black Satchel Drive, Charlotte NC 28216. 704/394-7121. **Fax:** 704/392-9713. **Contact:** Ms. Kelly Griggs, Human Resources Administrator. **Description:** U.S. Food Service is the parent company of Biggers Brothers, Inc., a wholesale food distributor. **Common positions include:** Accountant/Auditor; Buyer; Computer Programmer; Computer Systems Analyst; Dietician/Nutritionist; Human Resources Specialist; Services Sales Representative. **Educational backgrounds include:** Accounting; Business Administration; Computer Science. **Benefits:** 401K; Dental Insurance; Disability Coverage; Employee Discounts; Life Insurance; Medical Insurance; Profit Sharing; Tuition Assistance. **Corporate headquarters location:** Wilkes Barre PA. **Operations at this facility include:** Administration. **Listed on:** Privately held. **Number of employees at this location:** 850.

Note: Because addresses and telephone numbers of smaller companies change rapidly, we recommend you call each company to verify the information below before inquiring about job opportunities. Mass mailings are not recommended.

Additional employers with under 250 employees:

CORN

Ciba Seeds
P.O. Box 18300, Greensboro
NC 27419-8300. 910/547-
1000.

CROP FARMS

BAZ Farms Inc.
RR 2, Rose Hill NC 28458-
9802. 910/289-3659.

Carroll's Foods Inc.
RR 2, Warsaw NC 28398-
9802. 910/293-7371.

Murphy Farms Inc.
RR 1, White Oak NC 28399-
9801. 910/866-4741.

TDM Farm
RR 2, Newton Grove NC
28366-9802. 910/567-
6155.

BEEF

Carrolls Foods Inc.
325 McKay St, Laurinburg
NC 28352-3837. 910/276-
0648.

DAIRY FARMS

Maola Milk & Ice Cream
RR 2, Cameron NC 28326-
9802. 919/499-5134.

Pine State Creamery Co.
201 Raleigh Rd, Henderson
NC 27536-4977. 919/438-
7155.

POULTRY AND EGGS

Golden Poultry Hatchery
222 W Raleigh St, Siler City
NC 27344-3420. 910/742-
4747.

Perdue Farms Inc.
Old Hwy 211 W, West End
NC 27376. 910/673-4148.

Diamond Poultry Farms
Arrington Bridge Rd, Seven
Springs NC 28578.
919/658-6093.

Hudson Foods
3347 Old 421 Rd, Liberty
NC 27298-8292. 910/622-
2505.

MEAT AND POULTRY PROCESSING

Carolina Packers
2999 Hwy 301 S, Smithfield
NC 27577. 910/934-2181.

Curtis Packing Co.
2416 Randolph Ave,
Greensboro NC 27406-2910.
910/275-7684.

Boneless Hams Inc.
2001 Susan Park Rd, Dunn
NC 28334. 910/892-6157.

Stadlers Country Ham
2921 Rt 100, Elon College
NC 27244. 910/584-1396.

Wampler-Longacre Inc.
2000 Thrift Rd, Charlotte NC
28208-4451. 704/342-
9300.

Cal-Maine Foods Inc.
State Route 1708, Greenville
NC 27834. 919/756-4187.

Perdue Farms Inc.
820 Tom Starling Rd,
Fayetteville NC 28306-8100.
910/484-2729.

Prestige Farms
7120 Orr Rd, Charlotte NC
28213-6447. 704/596-
2824.

DAIRY PRODUCTS

Coastal Dairy Products
400 Douglas St S, Wilson
NC 27893-4918. 919/243-
6161.

Flav-O-Rich
3939 W Market St,
Greensboro NC 27407-1303.
910/299-0221.

Land-O-Sun Dairies Inc.
461 US Highway 70 SW,
Hickory NC 28602-5019.
704/322-3730.

Carolina Dairies Corp.
800 W Vernon Ave, Kinston
NC 28501-3610. 919/523-
1101.

Dairy Fresh Inc.
2221 Patterson Ave,
Winston-Salem NC 27105-
6036. 910/723-0311.

Flav-O-Rich
103 N Cherry St, Wilkesboro
NC 28697-2319. 910/838-
3125.

Milkco Inc.
220 Deaverview Rd,
Asheville NC 28806-1710.
704/254-9560.

Pine State Creamery Co.
500 Glenwood Ave, Raleigh
NC 27603-1286. 919/828-
7401.

PRESERVED FRUITS AND VEGETABLES

Dunbar Foods Corp.
1000 S Fayetteville Ave,
Dunn NC 28334-6213.
910/892-3175.

Luck's Inc.
798 State Hwy 705,
Seagrove NC 27341.
910/873-7211.

Knorr Best Foods
2525 Bank St, Asheboro NC
27203-3087. 910/672-
5024.

B&H Foods Inc.
2122 Thrift Rd, Charlotte NC
28208-4449. 704/332-
4106.

GRAIN MILL PRODUCTS

Mid State Mills Inc.
324 E A St, Newton NC
28658-2304. 704/464-
1611.

Best Foods Baking Group
1029 Cox Rd, Gastonia NC
28054-3484. 704/867-
3631.

Corn Products
4501 Overdale Rd, Winston-
Salem NC 27107-6145.
910/785-0100.

DOG AND CAT FOOD

Friskies Pet Care Products
502 W Broad St, Elizabeth
City NC 27909-3527.
919/335-2885.

PREPARED FEEDS AND INGREDIENTS FOR ANIMALS

Cape Fear Feed Products
1309 Industrial Dr,
Fayetteville NC 28301-6323.
910/483-0473.

Purina Mills Inc.
1710 N Tryon St, Charlotte
NC 28206-2730. 704/377-
7240.

BAKERY PRODUCTS

Carolina Foods Inc.
1807 S Tryon St, Charlotte
NC 28203. 704/333-9812.

Interstate Brands Corp.
Hwy 301, Rocky Mount NC
27801. 919/977-3400.

Krispy Kreme Doughnut Corp.
1814 Ivy Ave, Winston-
Salem NC 27105-5216.
910/725-2981.

Krispy Kreme Doughnut Corp.
3401 Wilkinson Blvd,
Charlotte NC 28208-5633.
704/394-6375.

Nabisco Inc.
1130 Tarrant Rd, Greensboro
NC 27409. 910/272-6209.

President Baking Co.
933 Louise Ave, Charlotte
NC 28204-2131. 704/334-
7611.

**SUGAR AND
CONFECTIONERY
PRODUCTS**

Beacon Sweets Inc.
288 Mazeppa Rd,
Mooresville NC 28115-7928.
704/664-4300.

Lance Inc.
2300 W Meadowview Rd,
Suite 217, Greensboro NC
27407-3711. 910/854-
8400.

COOKED NUTS AND SEEDS

Seabrook Enterprises
1 Peanut Dr, Edenton NC
27932. 919/482-2112.

FATS AND OILS

CBP Resources Inc.
5533 York Hwy, Gastonia
NC 28052-8729. 704/864-
9941.

BEVERAGES

Canada Dry of Charlotte
3639 N I 85, Charlotte NC
28269. 704/596-7333.

Cheerwine Bottling Co.
1515 Lewisville Clemmons
Rd, Clemmons NC 27012-
8373. 910/766-4781.

Coca-Cola Bottling Co.
230 S Morgan St, Roxboro
NC 27573-5222. 910/599-
9204.

Coca-Cola Bottling Works
218 W Lewis St, Whiteville
NC 28472-4032. 910/642-
3002.

Coca-Cola USA
3759 Jamestown Cir,
Raleigh NC 27609-7160.
919/781-7616.

Independent Beverage Corp.
3936 Corporation Cir,
Charlotte NC 28216-3421.
704/399-2504.

Long Beverage Inc.
10405 Chapel Hill Rd,
Morrisville NC 27560-8710.
919/596-9395.

Pepsi-Cola Bottling Co.
1402 E Washington St,
Rockingham NC 28379-
3941. 910/895-9085.

Pepsi-Cola Bottling Co.
2245 N Church St, Rocky
Mount NC 27804-2028.
919/446-7181.

Pepsi-Cola Bottling Co.
2820 South Blvd, Charlotte
NC 28209-1802. 704/523-
6761.

Pepsi-Cola Bottling Co.
400 S Chippewa St,
Lumberton NC 28358-5918.
910/738-6266.

Pepsi-Cola Bottling Co.
N Park Dr, Goldsboro NC
27530. 919/778-8300.

SEAFOOD

Sea Safari Limited Inc.
314 Water St, Belhaven NC
27810-1538. 919/943-
3590.

CHIPS AND SNACKS

**Frito-Lay Inc. Sales
Department**
217 Stetson Dr, Charlotte
NC 28262-3364. 704/597-
9001.

FOOD PREPARATIONS

Best Bagels in Town
2403 Battleground Ave,
Greensboro NC 27408-4035.
910/288-6004.

Made Rite Foods
2414 Battleground Ave,
Greensboro NC 27408-4002.
910/288-6646.

Sunburst Foods Inc.
1002 Sunburst Dr, Goldsboro
NC 27534-8667. 919/778-
2151.

TOBACCO PRODUCTS

American Tobacco Co.
5500 Executive Center Dr,
Suite 2, Charlotte NC
28212-8821. 704/568-
2901.

**Brown & Williamson Tobacco
Corp.**
Pineville Matthews Rd, Suite
110, Matthews NC 28105-
9152. 704/545-7760.

**Brown & Williamson Tobacco
Corp.**
11111 Carmel Commons
Blvd, Charlotte NC 28226-
3919. 704/543-7760.

**Brown & Williamson Tobacco
Corp.**
600 N Chestnut St, Winston-
Salem NC 27101-3052.
910/722-5125.

Gold Leaf Keatec Inc.
RR 3, Kinston NC 28501-
9803. 919/523-0337.

Japan Tobacco
212 Loft Ln, Apt 118,
Raleigh NC 27609-3867.
919/846-6093.

Japan Tobacco
4700 Homewood Ct, Suite
240, Raleigh NC 27609-
5732. 919/782-1076.

Lorillard Inc.
5819 Ramsey St,
Fayetteville NC 28311-3416.
910/822-0882.

**New Planters Tobacco
Warehouse**
1111 Goshen St, Oxford NC
27565-9314. 919/693-
2298.

Old Belt Farmers Co-Op
P.O. Box 821, Rural Hall NC
27045-0821. 910/969-
6891.

Phillip Morris
2640N Yonkers Rd, Raleigh
NC 27604-3228. 919/833-
0575.

Taylor Brothers
2415 S Stratford Rd,
Winston-Salem NC 27103-
6225. 910/768-4630.

Carolina Leaf Tobacco Co.
P.O. Box 796, Greenville NC
27835-0796. 919/752-
2144.

General Processors Inc.
217 W Industry Dr, Oxford
NC 27565-3565. 919/693-
1116.

**Thorp Greenville Export
Tobacco**
P.O. Box 267, Rocky Mount
NC 27802-0267. 919/977-
3161.

Top Tobacco International
2451 S College Rd,
Wilmington NC 28412-6811.
910/392-7070.

FOOD WHOLESALE

American Home Food
5601 Roanne Way, Suite
108, Greensboro NC 27409-
2915. 910/852-7841.

**Biggers Brothers Greensboro
Sales**
1109 S Holden Rd,
Greensboro NC 27407-2306.
910/855-0319.

Campbell Sales Co. Regional
7421 Carmel Executive Park,
Charlotte NC 28226.
704/542-6039.

Forrest E G Co.
1023 N Chestnut St,
Winston-Salem NC 27101-
1519. 910/723-9151.

Golden State Foods Corp.
8416 Triad Dr, Greensboro
NC 27409-9018. 910/668-
0011.

Maxwell's Gourmet Food
3209 Gresham Lake Rd,
Raleigh NC 27615-4131.
919/878-4321.

Nash Finch Co.
P.O. Box 1709, Lumberton
NC 28359-1709. 910/739-
4161.

Nash Finch Co.
3051 N Church St, Rocky
Mount NC 27804-6609.
919/446-6151.

Nestle Brands Food Service
Forum VI, Suite 501,
Greensboro NC 27408.
910/852-8300.

Piedmont Plastics Inc.
P.O. Box 26006, Charlotte
NC 28221-6006. 704/597-
8200.

Sam's Club
7100 Forest Point Blvd,
Charlotte NC 28217-8000.
704/522-6200.

Unijax Sloan
1000 N Hoskins Rd,
Charlotte NC 28216-3435.
704/392-9341.

**Mello Buttercup Ice Cream
Co.**
3301C Cessna Rd, Charlotte
NC 28208. 704/357-6028.

Golden Poultry Co. Inc.
P.O. Box 1452, Durham NC
27702. 919/683-1371.

Frito Lay
1014 White Jenkins Rd,
Bessemer City NC 28016-
8751. 704/922-1223.

Bell/Sysco Food Service
116 Woodfin Ave, Asheville
NC 28804-2038. 704/255-
7676.

Merita Warehouse
1021 Chapel Hill Rd,
Burlington NC 27215-6716.
910/226-9547.

**FARM PRODUCT RAW
MATERIALS WHOLESALE**

Eastern Processors Inc.
P.O. Box 1506, Greenville
NC 27835-1506. 919/752-
8600.

ALCOHOL WHOLESALE

RH Barringer Distributing Co.
1620 Fairfax Rd, Greensboro
NC 27407-4139. 910/854-
0555.

Sullivan Wholesale
P.O. Box 35087, Fayetteville
NC 28303-0087. 910/488-
6126.

**FARM SUPPLIES
WHOLESALE**

Mac-Page Inc.
1600 S Wilson Ave, Dunn
NC 28334. 910/892-1103.

**Meherrin Agricultural &
Chemical Co.**
P.O. Box 200, Severn NC
27877-0200. 919/585-
1744.

**Swift Agricultural Chemicals
Corp.**
S Front, Warsaw NC 28398.
910/293-4435.

CA Perry & Son Inc.
Cross Roads Division, Tyner
NC 27980. 919/221-8765.

IMC Fertilizer Inc.
Airport Rd, Shelby NC
28150. 704/487-4661.

Lebanon Agricorp
8858 NC 96 S, Benson NC
27504. 910/894-2922.

Residex Corp.
1800A Associates Ln,
Charlotte NC 28217-2805.
704/357-6047.

Purina Mills Inc.
7949 S NC 87 Hwy, Graham
NC 27253. 910/376-9328.

**FLOWERS AND FLORAL
PRODUCTS WHOLESALE**

Metrolina Greenhouses
16400 Huntersville,
Huntersville NC 28078.
704/875-1371.

Van Wingerden International
556 Jeffress Rd, Fletcher NC
28732. 704/891-4116.

South Carolina

CAROLINA GOLDEN PRODUCTS COMPANY
2050 Highway 15 South, Sumter SC 29150. 803/481-8555. **Contact:** Darryl Davids,
Manager/Human Resources Department. **Description:** Carolina Golden Products
Company processes and markets whole and cut chicken. The company is a
partnership between two subsidiaries of Gold Kist, Inc.: wholly-owned AgriGolden, and
majority-owned Golden Poultry. This location is a poultry processing plant, and has
been named a key plant in increasing Golden Poultry's production. Customers include
retailers, restaurants, and institutional accounts. In retail stores, Golden Poultry
markets chicken under the Young 'n Tender label or under the customer's private
label. The company has facilities in Florida, Georgia, and the Mid-Atlantic states; and
also sells to accounts in the Northeast and the Midwestern states. **Other U.S.
locations:** FL. **Parent company:** Gold Kist, Inc. (Atlanta GA). **Listed on:** NASDAQ.
Number of employees nationwide: 14,000.

COLUMBIA FARMS
P.O. Box 577, Leesville SC 29070. 803/532-4488. **Contact:** Keith Lampkin, Director
of Human Resources. **Description:** A fully-integrated poultry processing and food
distribution company. **Common positions include:** Accountant/Auditor; Food
Scientist/Technologist; Human Resources Specialist; Management Trainee; Quality
Control Supervisor. **Educational backgrounds include:** Business Administration.
Benefits: Life Insurance; Medical Insurance. **Corporate headquarters location:** This
Location. **Other U.S. locations:** Columbia SC; Greenville SC. **Operations at this facility
include:** Manufacturing. **Number of employees nationwide:** 1,300.

COLUMBIA FARMS
P.O. Box 4767, Greenville SC 29608. 864/268-6917. **Contact:** Curtis Lewis, Human
Resources Manager. **Description:** This location is a processing plant and supplies
chicken to fast-food restaurants. Overall, Columbia Farms is a fully-integrated poultry

processing and food distribution company. **Corporate headquarters location:** Leesville SC. **Number of employees nationwide:** 1,300.

COLUMBIA FARMS
P.O. Box 168, Columbia SC 29202. 803/794-8440. **Contact:** Mrs. Patsy Elmore, Human Resources Manager. **Description:** A fully-integrated poultry processing and food distribution company. **Corporate headquarters location:** Leesville SC. **Number of employees nationwide:** 1,300.

FLOWERS BAKING COMPANY
P.O. Box 4367, Spartanburg SC 29305. 864/503-9101. **Contact:** Mr. Jessie Hobby, Human Resources. **Description:** Operates more than 20 bakeries which produce a wide variety of products, including bread, buns, rolls, and donuts for retail sale to food stores, restaurants, institutions, and more than 200 company-owned stores nationally. This location of Flowers Baking Company produces snack cakes. **Corporate headquarters location:** Chicago IL.

GREENWOOD PACKING PLANT
P.O. Box 188, Greenwood SC 29648. 864/229-5611. **Contact:** Jim Brabham, Human Resources Director. **Description:** A pork packing plant.

LOUIS RICH COMPANY
P.O. Box 640, Newberry SC 29100. 803/276-5015. **Contact:** Dennis Weeks, Human Resources Manager. **Description:** A poultry processor.

NESTLE CORPORATION
P.O. Box 1419, Gaffney SC 29342. 864/487-7111. **Contact:** Ron Gilmer, Human Resources Director. **Description:** Manufactures frozen food products such as lasagna and macaroni and cheese.

PYA MONARCH
P.O. Box 1328, Greenville SC 29602. 864/676-8600. **Contact:** Dan Gibson, Vice President of Human Resources. **Description:** PYA Monarch is engaged in food service distribution activities, with operations in institutional foods. The parent company, Sara Lee Corporation, is a diversified consumer products firm. **Corporate headquarters location:** This Location. **Parent company:** Sara Lee Corporation (Chicago, IL).

SASIB BEVERAGE AND FOOD NORTH AMERICA INC.
P.O. Box 108008, Charleston SC 29423. 803/572-6640. **Contact:** Bill Pehling, Director of Human Resources. **Description:** Sasib Beverage and Food manufactures beverage processing products including drink dispensers.

Note: Because addresses and telephone numbers of smaller companies change rapidly, we recommend you call each company to verify the information below before inquiring about job opportunities. Mass mailings are not recommended.

Additional employers with under 250 employees:

CROP FARMS

Bonnie Plant Farm
RR 1, Alcolu SC 29001-9801. 803/473-3144.

DAIRY FARMS

Flav-O-Rich Dairy
9559 Highway 78, Ladson SC 29456-3912. 803/863-1567.

MEAT AND POULTRY PROCESSING

Brown Packing Co. Inc.
227 Boyd St, Gaffney SC 29341-1502. 864/489-5723.

Teepak
P.O. Box 11925, Columbia SC 29211. 803/796-9730.

Cal-Maine Foods Inc.
State Route 42, Bethune SC 29009. 803/334-6233.

Gentry's Poultry Co. Inc.
Highway 39, Ward SC 29166. 864/445-2161.

House of Raeford Farms
Lakewood Plantation Rd, Hemingway SC 29554. 803/558-9461.

ISE America Inc.
2063 Alexander St, Newberry SC 29108-2456. 803/276-5803.

DAIRY PRODUCTS

Peeler Jersey Farms Inc.
706 Leadmine St, Gaffney SC 29340-3636. 864/489-1108.

Regis Milk Co.
578 Meeting St, Charleston SC 29403-4537. 803/723-3418.

PRESERVED FRUITS AND VEGETABLES

Pontiac Foods
813 Bookman Rd, Elgin SC 29045-9609. 803/699-1600.

BAKERY PRODUCTS

Bradshaw Distributing
1221 Edwards Dr, Moncks
Corner SC 29461-9276.
803/761-8175.

Kroger Co.
433 Sayre St, Anderson SC
29624-2603. 864/226-
9135.

Merita Bread Bakery
1153 E Day St, Florence SC
29506-2722. 803/662-
3203.

Palmetto Baking Co.
272 Broughton St SW,
Orangeburg SC 29115-5908.
803/534-3535.

Pepperidge Farm Inc.
10 Windham Blvd, Aiken SC
29801-9385. 803/649-
7901.

Piemonte Foods Inc.
400 Augusta St #9239,
Greenville SC 29601-3510.
864/242-0424.

Sara Lee Bakery
1916 Piedmont Hwy,
Greenville SC 29605-4830.
864/299-0604.

SUGAR AND CONFECTIONERY PRODUCTS

JF Johnson Inc.
225 Summerland Ave,
Batesburg SC 29006-1348.
803/532-6341.

FATS AND OILS

Hartsville Oil Mill
P.O. Box 124, Darlington SC
29532-0124. 803/393-
1501.

BEVERAGES

A&L Foods Inc.
2370 Levels Church Rd,
Aiken SC 29801-9600.
803/649-2900.

Coca-Cola Consolidated
50 International Dr, Suite
101, Greenville SC 29615-
4832. 864/234-5200.

Pepsi-Cola Distributing Co.
1009 S Main St, Marion SC
29571. 803/423-5511.

CHIPS AND SNACKS

Borden Inc.
15 Ash St, Spartanburg SC
29303. 864/585-9011.

TOBACCO PRODUCTS

TS Ragsdale Co. Inc.
213 S Church St #215, Lake
City SC 29560-2617.
803/394-8567.

ALCOHOL WHOLESALE

The Oasis
810 Market St, Cheraw SC
29520-2645. 803/537-
0709.

Capital Wine & Beverage Distributors
3150 Charleston Hwy, West
Columbia SC 29172-2712.
803/739-0188.

Southern Wine & Spirits
1004 Catawba Ave,
Columbia SC 29201-4206.
803/799-5353.

FARM SUPPLIES WHOLESALE

GA Ag Chemical
Whitman St Ext SE,
Orangeburg SC 29115.
803/536-3201.

Gold Kist Inc.
100 Woodtrail Dr, Gaston SC
29053-9168. 803/796-
4672.

For more information on career opportunities in the food and beverage, and agriculture industries:

Associations

AMERICAN ASSOCIATION OF CEREAL CHEMISTS (AACC)
3340 Pilot Knob Road, St. Paul MN 55121.
612/454-7250. Contact: Marla Meyers.
Dedicated to the dissemination of technical
information and continuing education in
cereal science.

AMERICAN FROZEN FOOD INSTITUTE
1764 Old Meadow Lane, Suite 350.
McLean VA 22102. 703/821-0770. A
national trade association representing the
interests of the frozen food industry.

AMERICAN SOCIETY OF AGRICULTURAL ENGINEERS
2950 Niles Road, St. Joseph MI 49085.
616/429-0300. Contact: Julie Swim.

AMERICAN SOCIETY OF BREWING CHEMISTS ASSOCIATION
3340 Pilot Knob Road, St. Paul MN 55121.
612/454-7250. Founded in 1934 to
improve and bring uniformity to the brewing
industry on a technical level.

CIES - THE FOOD BUSINESS FORUM
3800 Moore Plaza, Alexandria VA 22305.
703/549-4525. A global food business
network. Membership is on a company
basis. Members learn how to manage their
businesses more effectively and gain access
to information and contacts.

DAIRY AND FOOD INDUSTRIES SUPPLY ASSOCIATION (DFISA)
1451 Dolly Madison Boulevard, McLean VA
22101-3850. 703/761-2600. Contact:
Dorothy Brady. A trade association whose
members are suppliers to the food, dairy,
liquid processing, and related industries.

MASTER BREWERS ASSOCIATION OF THE AMERICAS (MBAA)
2421 North Mayfair Road, Suite 310,
Wauwatosa, WI 53226. 414/774-8558.
Promotes, advances, improves, and protects
the professional interests of brew and malt
house production and technical personnel.
Disseminates technical and practical
information.

NATIONAL AGRICULTURAL CHEMICALS ASSOCIATION
1156 15th Street NW, Suite 900,
Washington DC 20005. 202/296-1585.

NATIONAL BEER WHOLESALERS' ASSOCIATION
1100 South Washington Street, Alexandria
VA 22314-4494. 703/683-4300. Fax:
703/683-8965. Contact: Karen Craig.

NATIONAL FOOD PROCESSORS ASSOCIATION
1401 New York Avenue NW, Suite 400,
Washington DC 20005. 202/639-5900.
Contact: Ned Endler.

NATIONAL SOFT DRINK ASSOCIATION
1101 16th Street NW, Washington DC
20036. 202/463-6732.

**UNITED DAIRY INDUSTRY ASSOCIATION
(UDIA)**
10255 West Higgins Road, Suite 900,
Rosemont IL 60018. 847/803-2000. A
federation of state and regional dairy
promotion organizations that develop and
execute effective programs to increase
consumer demand for U.S.-produced milk
and dairy products.

Directories

**FOOD ENGINEERING'S DIRECTORY OF U.S.
FOOD PLANTS**
Chilton Book Company, Chilton Way,
Radnor PA 19089. 800/695-1214.

THOMAS FOOD INDUSTRY REGISTER
Thomas Publishing Company, Five Penn

Plaza, New York NY 10001. 212/695-
0500.

Magazines

BEVERAGE WORLD
Keller International Publishing Corporation.
150 Great Neck Road, Great Neck NY
11021. 516/829-9210.

FOOD PROCESSING
301 East Erie Street, Chicago IL 60611.
312/644-2020.

FROZEN FOOD AGE
Maclean Hunter Media, #4 Stamford Forum,
Stamford CT 06901. 203/325-3500.

PREPARED FOODS
Gorman Publishing Company, 8750 West
Bryn Mawr, Chicago IL 60631. 312/693-
3200.

GOVERNMENT

 *While the federal government is still the nation's largest employer, the number of federal jobs is rapidly on the decline. Adding to this instability was the federal government's shutdown on more than one occasion while the President and Congress were in budgetary deadlock. The decrease in Department of Defense employment that started with the collapse of the Soviet Union has only increased due to federal deficits. The Defense Department is expected to reduce its workforce through attrition over the next decade.*

Employment in other executive agencies is also expected to fall. Many workers are being offered buyouts, early retirement, and other incentives to leave the federal government. Demand remains strong, however, for nurses and engineers.

The outlook for state and local government workers is somewhat better. While opportunities vary from one state to the next, the Bureau of Labor Statistics forecasts a 16 percent job rise through 2005. Adding to the demand is the rising need for services. Since the early '80s, the government has decentralized and states have assumed more responsibility for providing services. Many policy decisions have been shifted to individual state governments, which are increasingly dealing with transportation problems, health care issues, energy policies, and poverty.

Even so, future job growth may be slowed by budgetary constraints. Local governments are struggling to meet the demand for services because tax revenues and federal aid are declining. Many states have cut their workforces to reduce spending and keep budgets balanced.

In North Carolina, government workers form a large portion of the job market. The state of North Carolina itself is one of the largest employers, and unlike most states around the country, it employed more people in December 1995 than it did a year earlier. The number of state workers rose by about 370 workers during that time. On the local level, about 890 new hires were made, with almost 600 of those for new teachers and school administrators. Even the federal government added employees in North Carolina in 1995, adding 490 during the year.

In South Carolina, the job prospects for government workers are mixed. In total, about 6,000 government jobs were lost, with state workers taking the biggest hit. They lost over 5,000 jobs during 1995. About 2,000 federal workers were also laid off. Some of these losses were made up on the local level, where the local teachers and administrators gained about 1,400 jobs and non-education workers gained about 1,800.

North Carolina

CARY, CITY OF
P.O. Box 8005, Cary NC 27512-8005. 919/469-4070. **Contact:** John Brooks, Personnel Director. **Description:** Administrative offices of the city of Cary, NC. **Common positions include:** Accountant/Auditor; Architect; Attorney; Automotive Mechanic/Body Repairer; Budget Analyst; Buyer; Chemist; Civil Engineer; Clerical Supervisor; Computer Programmer; Computer Systems Analyst; Construction and Building Inspector; Customer Service Representative; Draftsperson; Electrician; Human Resources Specialist; Surveyor; Urban/Regional Planner. **Benefits:** 401K; Dental Insurance; Disability Coverage; Life Insurance; Medical Insurance; Pension Plan; Tuition Assistance.

CHARLOTTE, CITY OF
600 East Fourth Street, Charlotte NC 28202. 704/336-2285. **Fax:** 704/336-6588. **Contact:** William Wilder, Human Resources Consulting Manager. **Description:** Administrative offices for the city of Charlotte, NC. **Common positions include:** Accountant/Auditor; Attorney; Automotive Mechanic/Body Repairer; Blue-Collar Worker Supervisor; Budget Analyst; Buyer; Civil Engineer; Claim Representative; Clerical Supervisor; Computer Programmer; Computer Systems Analyst; Construction and Building Inspector; Customer Service Representative; Draftsperson; Electrician; Human Resources Specialist; Human Service Worker; Management Analyst/Consultant; Public Relations Specialist; Purchasing Agent and Manager; Real Estate Agent; Social Worker; Surveyor; Transportation/Traffic Specialist; Urban/Regional Planner. **Educational backgrounds include:** Accounting; Business Administration; Communications; Computer Science; Economics; Engineering; Finance; Liberal Arts; Marketing. **Benefits:** 401K; Dental Insurance; Disability Coverage; Life Insurance; Medical Insurance; Pension Plan; Tuition Assistance. **Corporate headquarters location:** This Location. **Operations at this facility include:** Administration; Divisional Headquarters; Service. **Number of employees at this location:** 4,500.

FAYETTEVILLE CITY MANAGER'S OFFICE
433 Hay Street, Fayetteville NC 28301. 910/433-1990. **Contact:** Lois Jircitano, Director of Neighborhood Services. **Description:** The offices of Fayetteville's city manager. **Operations at this facility include:** Administration; Financial Offices. **Number of employees at this location:** 1,000.

RALEIGH, CITY OF
Municipal Complex, P.O. Box 590, Raleigh NC 27602. 919/890-3315. **Contact:** Suzon Jervis, Personnel Recruitment. **Description:** Administrative offices for the city of Raleigh. **Common positions include:** Attorney; Automotive Mechanic/Body Repairer; Budget Analyst; Buyer; Clerical Supervisor; Computer Systems Analyst; Customer Service Representative; Draftsperson; Human Resources Specialist; Landscape Architect; Public Relations Specialist. **Educational backgrounds include:** Accounting; Business Administration; Finance. **Benefits:** 401K; Dental Insurance; Disability Coverage; Life Insurance; Medical Insurance; Pension Plan; Tuition Assistance. **Operations at this facility include:** Administration. **Number of employees at this location:** 2,450.

U.S. ENVIRONMENTAL PROTECTION AGENCY
Human Resources Management Division(MD-29), 79 Alexander Drive, Research Triangle Park NC 27711. 919/541-3014. **Fax:** 919/541-1360. **Contact:** Randy Brady, Human Resources Director. **Description:** The Environmental Protection Agency was created in 1970 through an executive reorganization plan designed to consolidate the environmental activities of the federal government into a single agency. The EPA is dedicated to improving and preserving the quality of the environment, both national and global, and protecting human health and the productivity of natural resources. The agency is committed to ensuring that: federal environmental laws are implemented and enforced effectively; U.S. policy, both foreign and domestic, fosters the integration of economic development and environmental protection so that economic growth can be sustained over the long term; and public and private decisions affecting energy, transportation, agriculture, industry, international trade, and natural resources fully integrate considerations of environmental quality. This location of the EPA is a research and development laboratory. **Common positions include:** Accountant/Auditor; Biological Scientist/Biochemist; Biomedical Engineer; Chemical Engineer; Chemist; Civil Engineer; Electrical/Electronics Engineer; Industrial Engineer; Mathematician; Mechanical Engineer; Meteorologist. **Corporate headquarters location:** Washington DC. **Other U.S. locations:** San Francisco CA; Denver CO; Atlanta GA; Chicago IL; Kansas City KS; Boston MA; New York NY; Philadelphia PA; Dallas TX; Seattle WA.

Operations at this facility include: Divisional Headquarters; Research and Development. **Number of employees nationwide:** 19,000.

Note: Because addresses and telephone numbers of smaller companies change rapidly, we recommend you call each company to verify the information below before inquiring about job opportunities. Mass mailings are not recommended.

Additional employers with under 250 employees:

UNITED STATES POSTAL SERVICE

Henderson Main Post Office
905 S Garnett St, Henderson NC 27536. 919/438-4343.

PUBLIC ORDER AND SAFETY

City Police Neighborhood Resource Center
801A Moton Dr, Greensboro NC 27401. 910/370-9067.

ADMINISTRATION OF PUBLIC HEALTH PROGRAMS

Halifax County Health Department
Dobbs, Halifax NC 27839. 919/583-5021.

HOUSING AND URBAN DEVELOPMENT PROGRAMS

Housing Authority Administration
901 N Cleveland Ave, Winston-Salem NC 27101-3102. 910/727-8500.

Housing Developments Cleveland
1135 E 15th St, Winston-Salem NC 27105-6134. 910/727-8565.

NATIONAL SECURITY AND INTERNATIONAL AFFAIRS

Air National Guard Recruiting
5225 Morris Field Dr, Charlotte NC 28208-5704. 704/391-4100.

South Carolina

CHARLESTON AIR FORCE BASE
437SVS/SVXH, 101 West Hill Boulevard, Building 221, Charleston SC 29404. 803/566-2953. **Contact:** Ms. Rene Sharp, Human Resources Office Chief. **Description:** A U.S. Air Force base.

CHARLESTON COUNTY GOVERNMENT
Personnel, County Office Building, Two Court House Square, Room 409-A, Charleston SC 29401-2265. 803/723-6716. **Fax:** 803/723-6725. **Contact:** Mrs. Bai Serrano, Employment Specialist. **Description:** Charleston County Government, which operates under a Council-Administrator form of government, provides a broad range of services. These services include public safety (law enforcement, emergency medical services, emergency preparedness, detention facilities, and fire protection); engineering services; economic development; street and drainage maintenance; waste disposal; recycling; planning and zoning administration; grants administration; criminal prosecution services; criminal, civil, probate, and family court administration; document recording services; tax assessment; collection and dispersal; alcohol and other drug abuse services; library services; veteran's assistance; and voter registration. **NOTE:** Department worksites may be in different locations within Charleston County. **Common positions include:** Accountant/Auditor; Administrative Services Manager; Attorney; Buyer; Civil Engineer; Clerical Supervisor; Construction and Building Inspector; Counselor; Draftsperson; Emergency Medical Technician; Equipment Operator; Human Resources Specialist; Librarian; Licensed Practical Nurse; Paralegal; Police/Law Enforcement Officer; Purchasing Agent and Manager; Registered Nurse. **Educational backgrounds include:** Accounting; Business Administration; Economics; Engineering; Marketing. **Benefits:** 401K; Dental Insurance; Disability Coverage; Life Insurance; Medical Insurance; Sick Days. **Corporate headquarters location:** This Location. **Operations at this facility include:** Administration. **Number of employees nationwide:** 2,000.

CHARLESTON NAVAL BASE
1635 Second Street West, Charleston SC 29408-1962. 803/743-4185. **Contact:** Human Resources Office. **Description:** A naval base employing military personnel as well as civilians.

Note: Because addresses and telephone numbers of smaller companies change rapidly, we recommend you call each company to verify the information below before inquiring about job opportunities. Mass mailings are not recommended.

Additional employers with under 250 employees:

EXECUTIVE, LEGISLATIVE, AND GENERAL GOVERNMENT

USPO Vehicle Maintenance Division
250 S Church St Rear, Spartanburg SC 29306-3418. 864/585-0301.

JTPA
2010 Pageland Hwy, Lancaster SC 29720-7608. 803/285-2034.

PUBLIC ORDER AND SAFETY

Sheriffs Department Administration
2001 Duke St, Beaufort SC 29902-4405. 803/525-7256.

ADMINISTRATION OF SOCIAL AND MANPOWER PROGRAMS

York County Social Services
18 W Liberty St, York SC 29745-1454. 803/684-2315.

For more information about career opportunities in the government:

Directories

ACCESS...FCO ON-LINE
Federal Research Service, Inc., P.O. Box 1059, 243 Church Street, Vienna VA 22183-1059. 703/281-0200. This is the online service of the *Federal Career Opportunities* publication. To join online, the cost is $25 for the set-up and $45 for one hour, payable by credit card over the phone.

HEALTH CARE: SERVICES, EQUIPMENT, AND PRODUCTS

 *With no time to worry about the failure of government-proposed health care reforms, the health care industry is surging ahead with its own solutions, pressured by a competitive marketplace to cut costs. HMOs and insurance providers are looking to nursing homes and home care companies as an alternative to long-term hospital stays, and shifting from inpatient to less expensive outpatient care. Hospitals are streamlining operations and consolidating, with cutback efforts targeting staff, as well as unnecessary tests and laboratory fees. Hospital cost-cutting has also hurt medical equipment suppliers, as many hospitals form networks to share expensive equipment.*

Even so, from 1990 to 1995, the number of health care workers in the United States grew from 8.86 million 10.5 million. Despite pressure to cut back, the health care industry remains a growth area. As the elderly population continues to grow faster than the population as a whole and the survival rate of the severely ill continues to improve, the need for new workers will continue to increase, and the large employment base will create replacement needs.

North Carolina

AMSCO INTERNATIONAL, INC.
10002 Lufkin Road, P.O. Box 747, Apex NC 27502. 919/362-0842. **Contact:** Human Resources. **Description:** AMSCO International, Inc. develops, manufactures, distributes, and services control, decontamination, and surgical products. The company's products are used primarily in the health care industry and by certain research, scientific, and industrial customers. Infection control and decontamination products include sterilizers, washing equipment, accessories, and related consumable items which are used to prevent the spread of infectious diseases and biological contamination in the processing of pharmaceuticals, chemicals, research materials, and food. The company's surgical product line of general surgical tables, lights, and stainless steel cabinets are used by health care providers in both hospital and outpatient surgical settings. **Corporate headquarters location:** Pittsburgh PA. **Subsidiaries include:** American Sterilizer Company (Pittsburgh, PA); AMSCO Finn-Aqua Oy (Finland); AMSCO Asia Pacific, Inc. (Pittsburgh, PA); AMSCO Latin America (Pittsburgh, PA). **Other U.S. locations:** Montgomery AL; Wilson NY; Erie PA. **Operations at this facility include:** Manufacturing. **Listed on:** New York Stock Exchange. **Number of employees worldwide:** 3,100.

CENTRAL PRISON HOSPITAL
1300 Western Boulevard, Raleigh NC 27606. 919/733-0800x411. **Fax:** 919/733-1089. **Contact:** Hospital Administrator. **Description:** A prison hospital. **Common positions include:** Corrections Officer; Dental Assistant/Dental Hygienist; Dentist; Electrician; Financial Manager; Health Services Worker; Human Service Worker; Licensed Practical Nurse; Nursing Psychiatric Aide; Payroll Clerk; Pharmacist; Physical Therapist; Physician; Physician Assistant; Podiatrist; Psychologist; Recreation Worker; Registered Nurse; Secretary; Social Worker; Stock Clerk; Teacher; Welder. **Benefits:** Disability Coverage; Life Insurance; Medical Insurance; Pension Plan; Tuition Assistance. **Operations at this facility include:** Service. **Number of employees at this location:** 500.

COASTAL HEALTHCARE GROUP, INC.
2828 Croasdaile Drive, Durham NC 27705. 919/383-0355. **Contact:** Bob Elder, Director of Human Resources. **Description:** Coastal Healthcare Group, Inc. is a national

provider of physician practice management services to hospitals, government entities, managed care organizations, and other health care institutions. Under contract with its clients, the company identifies and organizes physician practices for credentialing and privileging, and coordinates the ongoing scheduling of health care professionals who provide clinical coverage in designated areas of primary care, mainly in the areas of emergency care. Coastal Healthcare Group, Inc. also assists clients' administrative and medical staff in such areas as quality assurance, risk management, practice accreditation, and marketing, as well as in the documentation, billing, and collection of professional charges. **Number of employees nationwide:** 3,825.

DAVIS COMMUNITY HOSPITAL
P.O. Box 1823, Statesville NC 28687. 704/873-0281. **Fax:** 704/878-2563. **Contact:** Jim Cline, Human Resources Director. **Description:** A 149-bed, state-of-the-art, acute care facility. **Common positions include:** Accountant/Auditor; Biomedical Engineer; Clerical Supervisor; Dietician/Nutritionist; EEG Technologist; EKG Technician; Food Scientist/Technologist; Human Resources Specialist; Licensed Practical Nurse; Medical Records Technician; Nuclear Medicine Technologist; Occupational Therapist; Pharmacist; Physical Therapist; Psychologist; Public Relations Specialist; Radiologic Technologist; Recreational Therapist; Registered Nurse; Respiratory Therapist; Social Worker; Surgical Technician. **Educational backgrounds include:** Accounting; Business Administration; Finance; Marketing. **Benefits:** 401K; Dental Insurance; Disability Coverage; Life Insurance; Medical Insurance; Profit Sharing; Savings Plan. **Special Programs:** Internships. **Corporate headquarters location:** Nashville TN. **Other U.S. locations:** Southeastern U.S. **Parent company:** Health Trust, Inc. **Operations at this facility include:** Administration; Service. **Listed on:** New York Stock Exchange. **Number of employees at this location:** 540.

DUKE UNIVERSITY MEDICAL CENTER
Duke University, 705 Broad Street, Durham NC 27708. 919/684-5557. **Contact:** Employment Office. **Description:** A medical care facility.

DURHAM REGIONAL HOSPITAL
3643 North Roxboro Street, Durham NC 27704. 919/470-4000. **Contact:** Susan Jernigan, Director of Human Resources. **Description:** A hospital.

MALLINCKRODT MEDICAL INC.
P.O. Box 61038, Raleigh NC 27661. 919/878-2930. **Contact:** Coleen Hoyle, or Millicent Henderson, Human Resources. **Description:** Mallinckrodt Medical is a provider of technologically advanced, cost effective products and services to five medical specialties: anesthesiology, cardiology, critical care, nuclear medicine, and radiology. The company has a leadership position in many global markets. **Parent company:** Mallinckrodt Group Inc. (St. Louis MO) is a provider of specialty chemicals and human and animal health products worldwide through Mallinckrodt Medical and two other technology-based businesses: Mallinckrodt Chemical, Inc. and Mallinckrodt Veterinary, Inc. Mallinckrodt Chemical is a producer of pharmaceutical and specialty industrial chemicals. It is also a joint venture partner in a worldwide flavors business. The company is the world's largest producer of acetaminophen and a major producer of medicinal narcotics and laboratory chemicals. Mallinckrodt Veterinary is one of the world's leading animal health and nutrition companies, with approximately 1,000 products sold in more than 100 countries. Products include pharmaceuticals, livestock and pet vaccines, pesticides, surgical supplies, anesthetics and mineral feed ingredients. Mallinckrodt Group has 10,300 employees worldwide. **Number of employees at this location:** 160.

MALLINCKRODT VETERINARY, INC.
8900 Capital Boulevard, Raleigh NC 27604-3116. 919/878-1503. **Contact:** Jim Edens, Manager of Human Resources. **Description:** Mallinckrodt Veterinary is one of the world's leading animal health and nutrition companies, with approximately 1,000 products sold in more than 100 countries. Products include pharmaceuticals, livestock and pet vaccines, pesticides, surgical supplies, anesthetics and mineral feed ingredients. **Parent company:** Mallinckrodt Group Inc. (St. Louis MO) is a provider of specialty chemicals and human and animal health products worldwide through Mallinckrodt Veterinary and two other technology-based businesses: Mallinckrodt Chemical, Inc., and Mallinckrodt Medical, Inc. Mallinckrodt Chemical is a producer of pharmaceutical and specialty industrial chemicals. It is also a joint venture partner in a worldwide flavors business. The company is the world's largest producer of acetaminophen and a major producer of medicinal narcotics and laboratory chemicals. Mallinckrodt Medical is a provider of technologically advanced, cost effective products and services to five medical specialties: anesthesiology, cardiology, critical care,

nuclear medicine, and radiology. The company has a leadership position in many global markets. Mallinckrodt Group has 10,300 employees worldwide.

MARGARET R. PARDEE MEMORIAL HOSPITAL
715 Fleming Street, Hendersonville NC 28791. 704/696-4209. **Fax:** 704/696-1208. **Contact:** W.T. Bullard, Director of Human Resources. **Description:** A 262-bed acute care hospital. **Common positions include:** Dietician/Nutritionist; Licensed Practical Nurse; Occupational Therapist; Pharmacist; Physical Therapist; Radiologic Technologist; Registered Nurse; Respiratory Therapist; Surgical Technician. **Benefits:** Daycare Assistance; Dental Insurance; Disability Coverage; Life Insurance; Medical Insurance; Pension Plan; Tuition Assistance. **Corporate headquarters location:** This Location. **Number of employees at this location:** 925.

MOSES CONE MEMORIAL HOSPITAL
1200 North Elm Street, Greensboro NC 27401-1020. **Toll free phone for human resources:** 800/476-6737. **Contact:** Diane Everhart, Recruitment Manager. **Description:** Moses Cone Memorial Hospital is the largest medical center in Greensboro. Moses Cone Memorial is also a Level II Trauma Center as well as a teaching hospital and referral center. The hospital operates five centers specializing in neuroscience, cardiology, cancer, rehabilitation, and trauma. Laboratories and radiology facilities at Moses Cone Memorial are equipped with advanced technology. The hospital's pharmacists actively participate in drug therapies. The Moses Cone Health System is continuing to invest in updating and expanding its facility. New plans call for the expansion of clinical program space, critical care capacity, and support services by the turn of the century. **Common positions include:** Accountant/Auditor; Blue-Collar Worker Supervisor; Claim Representative; Clerical Supervisor; Clinical Lab Technician; Computer Programmer; Computer Systems Analyst; Dental Assistant/Dental Hygienist; Dentist; Dietician/Nutritionist; EEG Technologist; EKG Technician; Electrician; Emergency Medical Technician; Financial Analyst; Human Resources Specialist; Librarian; Library Technician; Mechanical Engineer; Medical Records Technician; Nuclear Medicine Technologist; Occupational Therapist; Pharmacist; Physical Therapist; Physician; Preschool Worker; Psychologist; Public Relations Specialist; Purchasing Agent and Manager; Radiologic Technologist; Recreational Therapist; Registered Nurse; Respiratory Therapist; Restaurant/Food Service Manager; Social Worker; Speech-Language Pathologist; Surgical Technician; Teacher. **Educational backgrounds include:** Accounting; Biology; Computer Science; Finance; Marketing. **Benefits:** 403B; Daycare Assistance; Dental Insurance; Disability Coverage; Employee Discounts; Life Insurance; Medical Insurance; Pension Plan; Tuition Assistance. **Corporate headquarters location:** This Location. **Parent company:** Moses Cone Health System is comprised of Moses Cone Memorial Hospital (547 beds), the Women's Hospital of Greensboro (115 beds), and the Health Services Division including the Extended Care Center, a 150 bed long-term care facility. **Operations at this facility include:** Administration. **Number of employees at this location:** 4,000.

THE NORTH CAROLINA BAPTIST HOSPITALS, INC.
Medical Center Boulevard, Winston-Salem NC 27157-1185. 910/716-4717. **Contact:** Steven Haynes, Director of Human Resources. **Description:** A hospital system. **Common positions include:** Accountant/Auditor; Adjuster; Clinical Lab Technician; Computer Systems Analyst; Dietician/Nutritionist; EEG Technologist; EKG Technician; Food and Beverage Service Worker; Health Services Worker; Licensed Practical Nurse; Nuclear Medicine Technologist; Physical Therapist; Registered Nurse. **Educational backgrounds include:** Business Administration; Computer Science. **Benefits:** Daycare Assistance; Dental Insurance; Disability Coverage; Employee Discounts; Life Insurance; Medical Insurance; Pension Plan; Tuition Assistance. **Corporate headquarters location:** This Location. **Number of employees at this location:** 5,500.

NORTH CAROLINA EYE AND EAR HOSPITAL
1110 West Main Street, Durham NC 27701. 919/682-9341. **Contact:** Jane Green, Director of Human Resources. **Description:** A hospital specializing in eye and ear care.

NORTHERN HOSPITAL HOME CARE
933 Rockford Street, P.O. Box 1605, Mount Airy NC 27030. 910/719-7434. **Fax:** 910/719-7435. **Contact:** Lynn Lambert, Nursing Manager. **Description:** A hospital specializing in home health care. **Common positions include:** Occupational Therapist; Physical Therapist; Registered Nurse; Social Worker; Speech-Language Pathologist. **Educational backgrounds include:** Health Care. **Benefits:** Dental Insurance; Disability Coverage; Employee Discounts; Life Insurance; Medical Insurance; Pension Plan; Savings Plan; Tuition Assistance. **Corporate headquarters location:** This Location.

Other U.S. locations: Cana VA. **Listed on:** Privately held. **Number of employees at this location:** 200.

ONSLOW MEMORIAL HOSPITAL
P.O. Box 1358, 317 Western Boulevard, Jacksonville NC 28541-1358. 910/577-2250. **Contact:** Dawn Wenrich, Vice President of Human Resources. **Description:** A hospital. **Common positions include:** Chef/Cook/Kitchen Worker; Claim Representative; Clinical Lab Technician; Department Manager; Dietician/Nutritionist; EEG Technologist; EKG Technician; Licensed Practical Nurse; Medical Records Technician; Nuclear Medicine Technologist; Payroll Clerk; Pharmacist; Physical Therapist; Physician; Registered Nurse; Respiratory Therapist; Secretary; Social Worker. **Benefits:** Dental Insurance; Disability Coverage; Employee Discounts; Life Insurance; Medical Insurance; Pension Plan; Savings Plan.

PITT COUNTY MEMORIAL HOSPITAL
UNIVERSITY MEDICAL CENTER OF EASTERN CAROLINA
Employment, P.O. Box 6028, Greenville NC 27835. 919/816-4556. **Fax:** 919/816-8776. **Recorded Jobline:** 919/816-4900. **Contact:** Ms. Jan Kimble, Manager of Employment. **Description:** A 725-bed Level I regional medical center and constituent of the University Medical Center of Eastern Carolina in Pitt County. This location also serves as the teaching facility for the East Carolina University School of Medicine, Nursing, and Allied Health programs. **Common positions include:** Nuclear Medicine Technologist; Occupational Therapist; Pharmacist; Physical Therapist; Registered Nurse; Respiratory Therapist; Speech-Language Pathologist. **Educational backgrounds include:** Health Care. **Benefits:** 401K; Daycare Assistance; Dental Insurance; Disability Coverage; Employee Discounts; Life Insurance; Medical Insurance; Pension Plan; Tuition Assistance. **Corporate headquarters location:** This Location. **Number of employees at this location:** 4,000.

PRESBYTERIAN HOSPITAL FOUNDATION
P.O. Box 33549, Human Resources, Charlotte NC 28233. 704/384-4048. **Contact:** Roger Simpson, Vice President of Human Resources. **Description:** A medical membership organization.

RANDOLPH HOSPITAL, INC.
P.O. Box 1048, Asheboro NC 27204. 910/625-5151x271. **Fax:** 910/625-0414. **Contact:** Vicky Cox, Director of Employee Relations and Staffing. **Description:** A health care facility. **Common positions include:** Clinical Lab Technician; Dietician/Nutritionist; EEG Technologist; EKG Technician; Health Services Manager; Human Resources Specialist; Medical Records Technician; Nuclear Medicine Technologist; Pharmacist; Physical Therapist; Physician; Public Relations Specialist; Purchasing Agent and Manager; Radiologic Technologist; Registered Nurse; Respiratory Therapist; Social Worker; Surgical Technician. **Benefits:** Dental Insurance; Disability Coverage; Life Insurance; Medical Insurance; Pension Plan; Savings Plan. **Corporate headquarters location:** This Location. **Number of employees at this location:** 560.

SAINT JOSEPH'S HOSPITAL
428 Biltmore Avenue, Asheville NC 28801. 704/255-3864. **Fax:** 704/255-3972. **Contact:** Ruby Monteath, Personnel Specialist. **Description:** A hospital. **Common positions include:** Clinical Lab Technician; Dietician/Nutritionist; EEG Technologist; EKG Technician; Electrician; Medical Records Technician; Nuclear Medicine Technologist; Occupational Therapist; Pharmacist; Physical Therapist; Radiologic Technologist; Registered Nurse; Respiratory Therapist; Social Worker; Speech-Language Pathologist; Surgical Technician. **Benefits:** Dental Insurance; Disability Coverage; Employee Discounts; Life Insurance; Medical Insurance; Pension Plan; Tuition Assistance. **Corporate headquarters location:** This Location. **Number of employees at this location:** 1,400.

U.S. DEPARTMENT OF VETERANS AFFAIRS MEDICAL CENTER
508 Fulton Street, Durham NC 27705. 919/286-0411. **Contact:** Gary Doll, Chief of Personnel. **Description:** The U.S. Department of Veterans Affairs (VA) was established March 15, 1989 to resume responsibility for providing federal benefits to veterans and their dependents. Headed by the Secretary of Veterans Affairs, VA is the second largest of the 14 cabinet departments and operates nationwide programs of health care, assistance services, and national cemeteries. The most visible of all VA benefits and services is VA's health care system, the largest in the nation. From 54 hospitals in 1930, the VA health care system has grown to include 171 medical centers; more than 364 outpatient, community, and outreach clinics; 130 nursing home care units; and 37 domiciliaries. VA operates at least one medical center in each of the 48 contiguous states, Puerto Rico, and the District of Columbia. With approximately

76,000 medical center beds, VA treats nearly 1 million patients in VA hospitals; 75,000 in nursing home care units; and 25,000 in domiciliaries. VA's outpatient clinics register approximately 24 million visits per year.

THE WOMEN'S HOSPITAL OF GREENSBORO

801 Green Valley Road, Greensboro NC 27408. 910/574-6523. **Contact:** Becky Hunnycutt, Personnel Director. **Description:** Founded in 1990, the Women's Hospital of Greensboro is a family-centered, 115-bed facility, and the only North Carolina hospital dedicated exclusively to the care of women and newborns. Particular attention has been paid to giving this facility a homelike environment. The hospital also offers additional women's services including ultrasound, mammography, surgery, and outpatient treatment. In addition, an entire floor is dedicated to a Level III neonatal intensive care unit. This unit combines the highest level of technology with concentrated, attentive care for high-risk newborns from a three county region. The hospital also specializes in the area of perinatology. **Common positions include:** Accountant/Auditor; Blue-Collar Worker Supervisor; Claim Representative; Clerical Supervisor; Clinical Lab Technician; Computer Programmer; Computer Systems Analyst; Dental Assistant/Dental Hygienist; Dentist; Dietician/Nutritionist; EEG Technologist; EKG Technician; Electrician; Emergency Medical Technician; Financial Analyst; Human Resources Specialist; Librarian; Library Technician; Licensed Practical Nurse; Mechanical Engineer; Medical Records Technician; Occupational Therapist; Pharmacist; Physical Therapist; Physician; Preschool Worker; Psychologist; Public Relations Specialist; Purchasing Agent and Manager; Radiologic Technologist; Recreational Therapist; Registered Nurse; Respiratory Therapist; Restaurant/Food Service Manager; Social Worker; Speech-Language Pathologist; Surgical Technician; Teacher. **Educational backgrounds include:** Accounting; Biology; Business Administration; Computer Science; Finance; Marketing. **Benefits:** 401K; Daycare Assistance; Dental Insurance; Disability Coverage; Employee Discounts; Life Insurance; Medical Insurance; Pension Plan; Tuition Assistance. **Parent company:** The Moses Cone Health System. **Operations at this facility include:** Administration.

Note: Because addresses and telephone numbers of smaller companies change rapidly, we recommend you call each company to verify the information below before inquiring about job opportunities. Mass mailings are not recommended.

Additional employers with under 250 employees:

MEDICAL EQUIPMENT

Acme United Corp.
Hwy 117, Fremont NC
27830. 919/242-5182.

Acme United Corp.
106 Industry Ct, Goldsboro
NC 27530-9124. 919/734-
0064.

Arrow International Inc.
312 Commerce Pl,
Randleman NC 27317-7442.
910/498-4153.

Ivac
100 Ivac Way, Creedmoor
NC 27522-9651. 919/528-
1861.

Wilson-Cook Medical
4900 Bethania Station Rd,
Winston-Salem NC 27105-
1203. 910/744-0157.

Asheville Orthotic Prosthetic
2 Jean Dr, Asheville NC
28803-9548. 704/274-
0023.

CPP
1200 E Sunrise Ave,
Thomasville NC 27360-
4952. 910/472-3400.

HW Andersen Products
3944 Hwy 54, Haw River
NC 27258. 910/376-3000.

Qualex Inc.
241 Tillinghast St,
Fayetteville NC 28301-4747.
910/483-4658.

Rocky Mount Instruments
653 Instrument Dr, Rocky
Mount NC 27804. 919/442-
8068.

MEDICAL EQUIPMENT AND SUPPLIES WHOLESALE

National Medical Care
10701W S Commerce Blvd,
Charlotte NC 28273-6321.
704/588-7900.

Philips Medical Systems
9801 Southern Pines Blvd,
Suite G, Charlotte NC
28273. 704/527-9420.

Southeastern Hospital Supply
205 Forsythe St, Fayetteville
NC 28303-5498. 910/484-
2186.

Thompson Dental Co.
117 S Westgate Dr,
Greensboro NC 27407-1623.
910/294-1951.

DOCTORS' OFFICES AND CLINICS

Nalle Clinic
1918 Randolph Rd, Charlotte
NC 28207-1102. 704/342-
8000.

Carolinas Medical Group
501 Billingsley Rd, Charlotte
NC 28211-1009. 704/358-
2744.

Rex Hospital Radiology Department
Rex Hospital, Raleigh NC
27607. 919/783-3023.

DENTISTS' OFFICES AND CLINICS

Edwards & Henson II
3401 Brookshire Blvd,
Charlotte NC 28216-4003.
704/399-4531.

OFFICES AND CLINICS OF HEALTH PRACTITIONERS

Optometric Eye Care Center
410-G Westinghouse Blvd,
Charlotte NC 28273.
704/588-5210.

Thomas/House & Associates
3219 Pineville Matthews Rd,
Charlotte NC 28226-9301.
704/541-0468.

Physical Therapy Service
Mebane
206 S 5th St, Mebane NC
27302-2704. 910/563-
4900.

Presbyterian Orthopaedic
Hospital
1960 Randolph Rd, Charlotte
NC 28207-1102. 704/347-
2664.

Rehability Center
4301 Lake Boone Trl, Raleigh
NC 27607-7507. 919/782-
4184.

Rehability Center
853 B Wake Forest Business
Park, Wake Forest NC
27587-7185. 919/556-
5123.

Therasport
110 S Park Ter, Eden NC
27288-5351. 910/627-
7778.

Favorite Nurses
7520 E Independence Blvd,
Charlotte NC 28227-9405.
704/531-9315.

Research Triangle
Occupational Health
2609 N Duke St, Suite 301,
Durham NC 27704-3048.
919/220-5558.

NURSING AND PERSONAL
CARE FACILITIES

Heritage Hospital
111 Hospital Dr, Tarboro NC
27886-2011. 919/641-
7700.

AMH Segraves Care Center
200 Hospital Ave, Jefferson
NC 28640-9244. 910/246-
7101.

Autumn Care of Biscoe
Lambert Rd, Biscoe NC
27209. 910/428-2117.

Autumn Care of Mocksville
1007 Howard St, Mocksville
NC 27028-2574. 704/634-
3535.

Autumn Care of Raeford
1206 N Fulton St, Raeford
NC 28376-1926. 910/875-
4280.

Autumn Care of Saluda
Esseola Circle, Saluda NC
28773. 704/749-2261.

Brantwood Nursing &
Retirement Center
1038 College St, Oxford NC
27565-2507. 919/690-
3334.

Brentwood Hills Nursing
Center
500 Beaverdam Rd, Asheville
NC 28804-1806. 704/254-
8833.

Brian Center Health &
Retirement
6000 Bethabara Park Blvd,
Winston-Salem NC 27106-
2740. 910/744-5674.

Brian Center Health &
Retirement Wilson
P.O. Box 3566, Wilson NC
27895-3566. 919/237-
6300.

Brian Center Health &
Rehabilitation
1700 Wayne Memorial Dr,
Goldsboro NC 27534-2240.
919/731-2805.

Brian Center Health &
Retirement
629 SE Railroad St, Wallace
NC 28466-2091. 910/285-
6646.

Brian Center Health &
Retirement
816 S Aspen St, Lincolnton
NC 28092-3106. 704/735-
8065.

Brian Center Health &
Retirement
250 Bishop Ln, Concord NC
28025-2888. 704/788-
6400.

Brian Center Health &
Retirement
1306 S King St, Windsor NC
27983-9663. 919/794-
5146.

Brian Center Health &
Retirement
204 Dairy Rd, Clayton NC
27520-7216. 919/553-
8232.

Brian Center Health &
Retirement
204 Old Highway 74,
Monroe NC 28112-8122.
704/283-3066.

Brian Center Nurse Care
700 N Wall St, Waynesville
NC 28786. 704/452-3154.

Brian Center Nurse Care
RR 2, Hertford NC 27944-
9802. 919/426-5391.

Brian Center Nurse Care
29-70 N, Lexington NC
27292. 704/249-7521.

Brightmoor Nursing Center
615 W Fisher St, Salisbury
NC 28144. 704/633-2781.

Brighton Manor
415 Sunset Dr, Fuquay
Varina NC 27526-2147.
919/552-5609.

Britthaven of Clyde
30 Morgan St, Clyde NC
28721-9467. 704/627-
2789.

Britthaven of Kernersville
738 Piney Grove Rd,
Kernersville NC 27284-2314.
910/996-4038.

Britthaven of Morganton
107 Magnolia Dr, Morganton
NC 28655-4505. 704/437-
8760.

Britthaven of Onslow
1839 Onslow Dr,
Jacksonville NC 28540-
5906. 910/455-3610.

Britthaven of Pamlico
Keel Rd, Grantsboro NC
28529. 919/745-5005.

Britthaven of Piedmont
33426 Old Salisbury Rd,
Albemarle NC 28001-8342.
704/983-1195.

Britthaven of Snow Hill
1304 SE 2nd St, Snow Hill
NC 28580-2014. 919/747-
8126.

Britthaven of Washington
205 Lovers Ln, Washington
NC 27889-3437. 919/975-
1636.

Britthaven of Wilmington
5429 Oleander Dr,
Wilmington NC 28403-5811.
910/791-3451.

Britthaven of Wilson
403 Crestview Ave SW,
Wilson NC 27893-4505.
919/237-0724.

Britthaven of Wrightsville
221 Summer Rest Rd,
Wilmington NC 28405-4135.
910/256-3733.

Brunswick Cove Nursing
Center
NC 133 Hwy, Leland NC
28451. 910/371-9894.

Buena Vista Nursing Center
877 Hill Everhart Rd,
Lexington NC 27292-7102.
704/246-6644.

Carol Woods Retirement
Community
750 Weaver Dairy Rd,
Chapel Hill NC 27514-1438.
919/968-4511.

Carrington Place Nursing
Home
600 Fullwood Rd, Matthews
NC 28105-2659. 704/841-
4920.

Carrolton Nursing Center
1170 Linkhaw Rd,
Lumberton NC 28358-2524.
910/671-1163.

Carrolton of Fayetteville
2743 Legion Rd, Fayetteville
NC 28306-3222. 910/424-
9417.

**Central Continuing Care
Nurse**
1287 Newsome St, Mount
Airy NC 27030-5427.
910/786-2133.

Century Care Center Inc.
316 W Burkhead St,
Whiteville NC 28472-3102.
910/642-7139.

Century Care Center Inc.
8900 Hasty Rd, Laurinburg
NC 28352-0706. 910/276-
8400.

Cherry Oaks Nursing Center
700 Self St, Cherryville NC
28021-2735. 704/435-
6029.

**Convalescent Center of
Halifax**
101 Carolina St, Weldon NC
27890. 919/536-4817.

Countryside Manor
7700 US Highway 158,
Stokesdale NC 27357-9398.
910/643-6301.

Courtland Terrace
2300 Aberdeen Blvd,
Gastonia NC 28054-0613.
704/834-4800.

Emerald Health Care
539 3rd St SW, Taylorsville
NC 28681-3005. 704/632-
8146.

Evangeline of Gatesville
RR 1, Box 238, Gatesville
NC 27938-9801. 919/357-
2124.

Evergreens Inc.
206 Greensboro Rd, High
Point NC 27260-3456.
910/886-4121.

**Glenn Forest Health Care
Center**
1101 Hartwell St, Garner NC
27529-3675. 919/772-
8888.

Grace Heights
109 Foothills Dr, Morganton
NC 28655-5152. 704/433-
7160.

**Graybrier Nursing &
Retirement Center**
116 Lane Ave, High Point NC
27260. 910/431-8888.

Greentree Ridge
70 Sweeten Creek Rd,
Asheville NC 28803-2318.
704/274-7646.

Guardian Care of Burgaw
810 S Walker St, Burgaw NC
28425. 910/259-2149.

Guardian Care of Farmville
Hwy 258 S, Farmville NC
27828. 919/753-5547.

Guardian Care of Henderson
280 S Beckford Dr,
Henderson NC 27536-2564.
919/438-6141.

**Guardian Care of Scotland
Neck**
920 Junior High School Rd,
Scotland Neck NC 27874.
919/826-5146.

Guardian Care of Zebulon
509 W Gannon Ave, Zebulon
NC 27597. 919/269-9621.

Hallmark Center
1403 Conner St, Windsor NC
27983. 919/794-4441.

**Highland Farms Retirement
Community**
200 Tabernacle Rd, Black
Mountain NC 28711-2592.
704/669-6473.

**High Country Healthcare &
Rehabilitation**
301 Combs St, Sparta NC
28675. 910/372-2441.

Hillcrest Nursing Center
2680 Hwy 66 South,
Kernersville NC 27284.
910/869-4114.

**Home Health Hospice Service
Craven County**
2818 Neuse Blvd, New Bern
NC 28562-2839. 919/636-
4930.

Hospice of Macon County
Roller Mill Rd, Franklin NC
28734. 704/369-6641.

**Huntington Health Care &
Retirement**
311 S Campbell St, Burgaw
NC 28425. 910/259-6007.

Lakeview Living Center
1010 Lakeview Dr, Pineville
NC 28134-7567. 704/889-
2273.

**Len Care Nurse &
Convalescent Center**
Hwy 701 S, Elizabethtown
NC 28337. 910/862-8100.

**Life Care Center of Banner
Elk**
Norwood Hollow Rd, Banner
Elk NC 28604. 704/898-
5136.

**Life Care Center
Hendersonville**
400 Thompson St,
Hendersonvlle NC 28792-
2811. 704/697-4348.

Lutheran Homes
1265 21st St NE, Hickory
NC 28601-2911. 704/328-
2006.

Lutheran Homes
24724 US 52 Hwy S,
Albemarle NC 28001-8179.
704/982-8191.

**Madison Manor Nursing
Center**
50 Manor Rd, Mars Hill NC
28754-9778. 704/252-
3646.

Maxim Healthcare
3020 Pickett Rd, Durham NC
27705-6000. 919/419-
1484.

Medela Inc.
2636 Cottage Pl, Greensboro
NC 27455-2917. 910/288-
1828.

Morehead Nursing Center
Penny Ln, Morehead City NC
28557. 919/726-0031.

Mountain Vista Health Park
106 Mount Vista Rd, Denton
NC 27239-8793. 704/869-
2181.

**Ocean Trail Convalescent
Center**
430 N Fodale Ave, Southport
NC 28461-3699. 910/457-
9581.

**Pemberton Place Nursing
Center**
310 E Wardell Dr, Pembroke
NC 28372. 910/521-1273.

**Pine Haven Convalescent
Center Henderson**
1245 Park Ave, Henderson
NC 27536-4025. 919/492-
7021.

Pinehurst Nursing Center
2092 Blake Blvd, Pinehurst
NC 28374. 910/295-6158.

Prince Nursing Care Unit
1199 Hayes Forest Dr,
Winston-Salem NC 27106.
910/759-1044.

Rest Haven Nursing Home
1769 Dunn Rd, Fayetteville
NC 28301-8912. 910/483-
5027.

Roanoke Valley Nurse Home
115 N Main, Rich Square NC
27869. 919/539-4161.

Saint Joseph of the Pines
590 Central Dr, Southern
Pines NC 28387-2812.
910/692-2212.

**Sealevel Extended Care
Facility**
468 US Highway 70
Sealevel, Sealevel NC
28577. 919/225-4611.

**Sentara Nursing Center
Currituck**
Hwy 168, Barco NC 27917.
919/453-8072.

Shoreland Health Care & Retirement
Flowers Pridgen Dr, Whiteville NC 28472. 910/642-4300.

Silas Creek Manor
3350 Silas Creek Pky, Winston-Salem NC 27103-3014. 910/765-0550.

Spencer Health Care Center
1404 S Salisbury Ave, Spencer NC 28159-1921. 704/633-3892.

Senior Citizens Home Henderson Inc.
Ruin Creek Rd, Henderson NC 27536. 919/492-0066.

Stanly Manor
625 Bethany Rd, Albemarle NC 28001-8523. 704/982-0770.

Transitional Health Service
931 N Aspen St, Lincolnton NC 28092-2113. 704/732-7055.

Transitional Health Service
1825 Concord Lake Rd, Kannapolis NC 28083-6447. 704/933-3781.

Twin Lakes Health Care Center
100 Wade Coble Dr, Burlington NC 27215-9756. 910/538-1400.

Village Care of King
440 Ingram Dr, King NC 27021-8208. 910/983-4900.

Wadesboro Nursing Home
2000 Country Club Rd, Wadesboro NC 28170-3204. 704/694-4106.

Wesley Pines
1000 Wesley Pines Rd, Lumberton NC 28358. 910/738-9691.

Wesleyan Arms Inc.
1901 N Centennial St, High Point NC 27262-7602. 910/884-2222.

White Oak Manor-Kings Mountain
716 Sipes St, Kings Mountain NC 28086-2716. 704/739-8132.

White Oak Manor-Tryon
200 Oak St, Tryon NC 28782. 704/859-9161.

Wilkes Senior Village Inc.
Brickyard Rd, N Wilkesboro NC 28659. 910/667-2020.

Alamance Memorial Hospital
730 Hermitage Rd, Burlington NC 27215-3512. 910/570-5130.

Albemarle
200 Trade St, Tarboro NC 27886-5029. 919/823-2799.

Autumn Care of Marion
610 Airport Rd, Marion NC 28752-3106. 704/652-6701.

Black Mountain Center Alzheimers Unit
Old Hwy 70, Black Mountain NC 28711. 704/669-3100.

Carolina Village
600 Carolina Village Rd, Hendersonvlle NC 28792-2828. 704/692-6275.

Carrolton of Dunn
P.O. Box 948, Dunn NC 28335-0948. 910/892-8843.

Centerclair
185 Yountz Rd, Lexington NC 27292-0607. 704/249-7057.

Clapps Nursing Center
4558 Pleasant Garden Rd, Pleasant Garden NC 27313-9208. 910/674-2252.

Countryside Villa of Duplin
214 Lanefield Rd, Warsaw NC 28398-8719. 910/293-3144.

Evangeline of Andrews
59 Kent St, Andrews NC 28901-9772. 704/321-3075.

Fair Haven Home
RR 1, Box 398, Bostic NC 28018-9657. 704/245-9095.

Golden Age
201 Cow Palace Rd, Lexington NC 27292-7869. 704/956-1132.

Guardian Care of Kenansville
P.O. Box 478, Kenansville NC 28349-0478. 910/296-1561.

Louisburg Nursing Center
202 Smoketree Way, Louisburg NC 27549-2165. 919/496-2188.

McDowell Nursing Center
RR 3, Box 270, Nebo NC 28761-9750. 704/652-3032.

Meadowbrook Terrace Clemmons
P.O. Box 987, Clemmons NC 27012. 910/766-9186.

Meadowbrook Terrace Greensboro
1915 Boulevard St, Greensboro NC 27407-4513. 910/299-9945.

Meadowbrook Terrace of Davie
RR 6, Box 300, Advance NC 27006-9321. 910/998-0240.

Montgomery Memorial Hospital
520 Allen St, Troy NC 27371-2802. 910/572-1301.

Mountain Trace Nursing Center
50 Mountain Trace Rd, Sylva NC 28779-9564. 704/586-9130.

Park Ridge Living Center
P.O. Box 5339, Fletcher NC 28732-5339. 704/684-4857.

Penick Memorial Home
P.O. Box 2001, Southern Pines NC 28388-2001. 910/692-0300.

Pinelake Healthcare
801 Pinehurst Ave, Carthage NC 28327-9338. 910/947-5155.

Plantation Estates Medical
701 Plantation Estates Dr, Matthews NC 28105-6550. 704/845-6220.

Presbyterian Home of High Point
201 Greensboro Rd, High Point NC 27260-3482. 910/883-9111.

Saint Joseph Pines East Campus
2660 Camp Easter Rd, Southern Pines NC 28387-2200. 910/692-1644.

Sandhills Hospice Inc.
5 Aviemore Dr, Pinehurst NC 28374-9797. 910/295-2220.

Scotia Village
2200 Elm Ave, Laurinburg NC 28352-8035. 910/277-2000.

Silver Bluff
RR 5, Box 102, Canton NC 28716-9376. 704/648-2044.

Skyland Care Center
21 Skyland Dr, Sylva NC 28779-2694. 704/586-8935.

Trent Village Nursing Homes
P.O. Box 369, Pollocksville NC 28573-0369. 919/224-0112.

Triangle East Nursing Care Center
1705 Tarboro St SW, Wilson NC 27893-3428. 919/399-8998.

Vencor Hospital-Greensboro
P.O. Box 16132, Greensboro
NC 27416-0132. 910/271-
2800.

**Whispering Pines Nursing
Home**
523 Country Club Dr,
Fayetteville NC 28301-7613.
910/488-0711.

Yancey Nursing Center
310 Pensacola Rd, Burnsville
NC 28714-3318. 704/682-
9759.

McDowell Hospital
P.O. Box 730, Marion NC
28752-0730. 704/659-
5000.

**Spruce Pine Community
Hospital**
P.O. Box 9, Spruce Pine NC
28777-0009. 704/765-
4201.

Washington County Hospital
1 Medical Plz, Plymouth NC
27962-9500. 919/793-
4135.

Evangeline of Woodfin
135 Weaverville Rd,
Weaverville NC 28787.
704/645-6619.

Graham Care Center
222 Milltown Rd,
Robbinsville NC 28771.
704/479-8421.

**HOSPITALS AND MEDICAL
CENTERS**

Chatham Hospital
P.O. Box 649, Siler City NC
27344-0649. 910/663-
2113.

**Community Hospital of
Rocky Mount**
1031 Noell Lane, Rocky
Mount NC 27804. 919/937-
5100.

Crawley Memorial Hospital
315 W College Ave, Boiling
Spgs NC 28017. 704/434-
9466.

District Memorial Hospital
1 Whitaker Ln, Andrews NC
28901-9229. 704/321-
1291.

Hamlet Hospital
P.O. Box 1109, Hamlet NC
28345-1109. 910/582-
3611.

Hoots Memorial Hospital
P.O. Box 68, Yadkinville NC
27055-0068. 910/679-
2041.

McCain Correctional Hospital
P.O. Box 5118, McCain NC
28361-9798. 910/944-
2351.

**Memorial Hospital
Greensboro**
P.O. Box 16167, Greensboro
NC 27416-0167. 910/275-
9741.

Our Community Hospital
P.O. Box 405, Scotland Neck
NC 27874-0405. 919/826-
4144.

**Person County Memorial
Hospital**
615 Ridge Rd, Roxboro NC
27573-4629. 910/599-
2121.

Pungo District Hospital
210 Front St, Belhaven NC
27810-1408. 919/943-
2111.

Saint Luke's Hospital
220 Hospital Dr, Columbus
NC 28722-9473. 704/894-
3311.

Swain County Hospital
45 Plateau St, Bryson City
NC 28713. 704/488-2155.

Ten Broeck Hospital
1 3rd Ave NW, Hickory NC
28601-5017. 704/328-
2226.

**HOME HEALTH CARE
SERVICES**

**Caswell County Home Health
Agency**
P.O. Box H, Yanceyville NC
27379-2002. 910/694-
9592.

**Cleveland Home Health
Agency Inc.**
719 E Grover St, Shelby NC
28150-4035. 704/487-
5225.

**Columbus In Home Health
Service**
110 W Main St #900,
Whiteville NC 28472-4012.
910/640-1965.

Community Care
2579 Eric Ln, Suite E,
Burlington NC 27215-5416.
910/229-6919.

Coram Healthcare
3909 Westpoint Blvd,
Winston-Salem NC 27103-
6728. 910/765-3680.

Health Services Personnel
111 Railroad St N, Ahoskie
NC 27910. 919/332-4900.

HHA of Chapel Hill
101 Ephesus Church Rd,
Chapel Hill NC 27514-2534.
919/929-7149.

Home Health & Hospice Care
101 W Greene St, Snow Hill
NC 28580-1431. 919/747-
4106.

Infusion Specialists Inc.
915 Kildaire Farm Rd, Suite
2, Cary NC 27511-3936.
919/467-4755.

Interim Healthcare
2635 Sunset Ave, Rocky
Mount NC 27804-3748.
919/443-7222.

Maxim Healthcare Services
3200 Wake Forest Rd,
Raleigh NC 27609-7451.
919/981-0887.

Medvisit Inc.
1111 Huffman Mill Rd,
Burlington NC 27215-8862.
910/538-0670.

Olsten Home Healthcare
406 S Fayetteville St,
Asheboro NC 27203-5772.
910/629-3178.

Olsten Kimberly Quality Care
6 Forks Rd, Twin Forks
Office Park, Raleigh NC
27609. 919/848-8020.

Pediatric Services of America
2101 Sardis Rd N, Charlotte
NC 28227-7711. 704/845-
5611.

Quantum Health Resources
4180 Piedmont Pky,
Greensboro NC 27410-8109.
910/316-0080.

**St. Joseph Pines Home
Health Agency**
945 E 4th Ave, Red Springs
NC 28377-1641. 910/843-
3324.

**St. Joseph Pines Home
Health Agency**
403 Chatham St, Pittsboro
NC 27312. 910/542-4746.

Total Care Inc.
2591 E Main St, Unit 107,
Lincolnton NC 28092-4154.
704/732-4939.

Total Care Inc.
1200 E Morehead St, Suite
290, Charlotte NC 28204-
2850. 704/334-9562.

Well Care & Nursing Service
2424 S 17th St, Wilmington
NC 28401-7904. 910/452-
1555.

**SPECIALTY OUTPATIENT
FACILITIES**

Detox Center
1308 Highland Dr,
Washington NC 27889-
3424. 919/946-1978.

Lancaster Recovery Center
9800 Southern Pines Blvd,
Charlotte NC 28273-5522.
704/527-1491.

Surry Yadkin Area Mental Health
Shack Town Road,
Yadkinville NC 27055.
910/679-8805.

Alliance For Mentally Ill
300 Hawthorne Ln, Charlotte
NC 28204-2434. 704/333-8218.

Carolina Residential Care
1505 W Friendly Ave,
Greensboro NC 27403-1206.
910/273-1782.

RESIDENTIAL CARE

Will-O-Haven Rest Home
510 Banner Ave, Greensboro
NC 27401-4374. 910/273-9496.

Belair Health Care Center
2065 Lyon St, Gastonia NC
28052-6230. 704/867-7300.

Brentwood Chateau
502 Beaverdam Rd, Asheville
NC 28804-1806. 704/254-5313.

Crescent View Retirement Community
2533 Hendersonville Rd,
Arden NC 28704-8538.
704/687-0068.

Mount Olive Retirement Village Inc.
600 Smith Chapel Rd, Mount
Olive NC 28365-2632.
919/658-6501.

Salemtowne Moravian Retirement
5401 Indiana Ave, Winston-Salem NC 27106-2832.
910/767-8130.

The Pines at Davidson
400 Avinger Ln, Davidson
NC 28036. 704/896-1100.

Well Spring Retirement Community
4100 Well Spring Dr,
Greensboro NC 27410-8800.
910/545-5350.

HEALTH AND ALLIED SERVICES

American Cancer Society
1114 Magnolia St,
Greensboro NC 27401-1426.
910/273-2102.

Hearing Health Care Service
905 W Main St, Suite 21F,
Durham NC 27701-2076.
919/489-0995.

NABI Biomedical Center North America
102 S 17th St, Wilmington
NC 28401. 910/763-0224.

Portamedic Services
820 Benson Rd, Garner NC
27529-4205. 919/779-5454.

Robeson Health Care Corp.
Breece St, Pembroke NC
28372. 910/521-1521.

Alpha Plasma Center
731 Central Ave, Charlotte
NC 28204-2023. 704/332-1510.

Alpha Plasma Center
129 Franklin St, Fayetteville
NC 28301-5641. 910/483-2280.

Community Bio-Resources
224 N Elm St, Greensboro
NC 27401-2402. 910/273-3429.

Plasma Alliance
1511 Central Ave, Charlotte
NC 28205-5013. 704/333-0335.

Mooresville Rescue Squad
204 E Iredell Ave,
Mooresville NC 28115-2419.
704/663-3660.

Med Tech Services Group
6209 Sandy Forks Rd,
Raleigh NC 27615-7207.
919/847-7365.

South Carolina

ANDERSON AREA MEDICAL CENTER
800 North Fant Street, Anderson SC 29621. 864/261-1162. **Fax:** 864/261-1952. **Recorded Jobline:** 864/261-1588. **Contact:** Linda McFall, Employment Manager. **Description:** Anderson Area Medical Center is a 567-bed acute care regional medical center. **NOTE:** The medical center's recorded jobline is available 24 hours per day and is updated every Monday by 5 p.m. **Common positions include:** Clinical Lab Technician; Physical Therapist. **Educational backgrounds include:** Medical Technology; Physical Therapy. **Benefits:** Dental Insurance; Disability Coverage; Employee Discounts; Flexible Benefits; Life Insurance; Medical Insurance; Pension Plan; Tuition Assistance. **Operations at this facility include:** Administration. **Number of employees at this location:** 2,500.

BAPTIST MEDICAL CENTER
P.O. Box 2129, Easley SC 29641-2129. 864/855-7623. **Fax:** 864/855-7521. **Recorded Jobline:** 864/855-7562. **Contact:** Jeff Payne, Director of Human Resources. **Description:** An acute care community medical center. Baptist Medical Center is a division of SC Healthcare Systems, Inc., headed by the 550-bed Baptist Medical Center in Columbia, SC. **Common positions include:** Accountant/Auditor; Buyer; Claim Representative; Clerical Supervisor; Clinical Lab Technician; Computer Programmer; Computer Systems Analyst; Counselor; Customer Service Representative; Dietician/Nutritionist; Education Administrator; EKG Technician; Financial Analyst; Health Services Manager; Licensed Practical Nurse; Medical Records Technician; Nuclear Medicine Technologist; Pharmacist; Physical Therapist; Physician; Public Relations Specialist; Purchasing Agent and Manager; Quality Control Supervisor; Radiologic Technologist; Registered Nurse; Respiratory Therapist; Restaurant/Food Service Manager; Science Technologist; Speech-Language Pathologist; Surgical Technician. **Educational backgrounds include:** Accounting; Biology; Business Administration; Chemistry; Computer Science. **Benefits:** 401K; Dental Insurance; Disability Coverage; Employee Discounts; Life Insurance; Medical Insurance; Tuition Assistance. **Corporate headquarters location:** Columbia SC. **Operations at this facility include:** Administration. **Listed on:** Privately held. **Number of employees at this location:** 550. **Number of employees nationwide:** 3,200.

BAPTIST MEDICAL CENTER
Taylor at Marion Street, Columbia SC 29220. 803/771-5678. **Contact:** Trip Gregory, Director of Human Resources. **Description:** A 550-bed acute care community medical center. **Parent company:** SC Healthcare Systems Inc.

BAUSCH & LOMB
8507 Pelham Road, Greenville SC 29615. 864/297-5500. **Contact:** Cheryl Snyder, Human Resources Manager. **Description:** Bausch & Lomb competes in selected segments of the global health care and optical markets. The Healthcare Segment consists of three sectors: Personal Health, Medical, and Biomedical. The Personal Health Sector is comprised of branded products purchased directly by consumers in health and beauty aid sections of pharmacies, food stores, and mass merchandise outlets. Products include lens care solutions; oral, eye, and skin care products; and nonprescription medications. The Medical Sector consists of contact lenses, ophthalmic pharmaceuticals, hearing aids, dental implants, and other products sold to health care professionals, or which are obtained by consumers through a prescription. The Biomedical Sector includes products and services supplied to customers engaged in the research and development of pharmaceuticals and the production of genetically engineered materials. These include purpose-bred research animals, bioprocessing services, and products derived from specific pathogen-free eggs. The Optics Segment consists primarily of premium-priced sunglasses sold under such brand names Ray-Ban and Revo. The company's manufacturing or marketing organizations have been established in 34 countries, and the company's products are distributed in more than 70 other nations. As part of the Personal Health Sector, this location of Bausch & Lomb manufactures eye care solutions for contact lens wearers. **Corporate headquarters location:** Rochester NY. **Number of employees worldwide:** 14,400.

BECTON DICKINSON
P.O. Box 2128, Sumter SC 29151-2128. 803/469-8010. **Contact:** Human Resources Department. **Description:** A medical and pharmaceutical company engaged in the manufacture of health care products, medical instrumentation, a line of diagnostic products, and industrial safety equipment. Becton Dickinson's major product lines for medical equipment include hypodermics, intravenous equipment, operating room products, thermometers, gloves, and specialty needles. The company also offers contract packaging services. **Common positions include:** Accountant/Auditor; Department Manager; Electrical/Electronics Engineer; Industrial Engineer; Mechanical Engineer; Operations/Production Manager. **Educational backgrounds include:** Accounting; Business Administration; Economics; Engineering. **Benefits:** Dental Insurance; Disability Coverage; Life Insurance; Medical Insurance; Pension Plan; Savings Plan; Tuition Assistance. **Special Programs:** Internships; Training Programs. **Corporate headquarters location:** Franklin Lakes NJ. **Listed on:** New York Stock Exchange.

GE MEDICAL SYSTEMS
3001 West Radio Drive, P.O. Box 100539, Florence SC 29501-0539. **Contact:** Mark Reilly, Human Resources Representative. **Description:** GE Medical Systems is a manufacturer of superconducting magnets for magnetic resonance imaging (MRI). **Common positions include:** Electrical/Electronics Engineer; Mechanical Engineer; Physicist/Astronomer. **Educational backgrounds include:** Engineering; Physics. **Benefits:** Dental Insurance; Disability Coverage; Employee Discounts; Life Insurance; Medical Insurance; Pension Plan; Savings Plan; Tuition Assistance. **Special Programs:** Training Programs. **Other U.S. locations:** Milwaukee WI. **Parent company:** General Electric Company, located in Fairfield, CT, is a diversified manufacturer operating in the following areas: aircraft engines (jet engines, replacement parts, and repair services for commercial, military, executive, and commuter aircraft); appliances; broadcasting (NBC); industrial (lighting products, electrical distribution and control equipment, transportation systems products, electric motors and related products, a broad range of electrical and electronic industrial automation products, and a network of electrical supply houses); materials (plastics, ABS resins, silicones, superabrasives, and laminates); power systems (products for the generation, transmission, and distribution of electricity); technical products and systems (medical systems and equipment, as well as a full range of computer-based information and data interchange services for both internal use and external commercial and industrial customers); and capital services (consumer services; financing; specialty insurance; and Kidder, Peabody investment bank and securities broker). **NOTE:** Resumes should be sent to: P.O. Box 55250, Bridgeport CT 06610. General Electric Company employs over 230,000 worldwide. **Operations at this facility include:** Manufacturing; Research and Development. **Listed on:** New York Stock Exchange.

GREENVILLE HOSPITAL SYSTEM
701 Grove Road, Greenville SC 29605. 864/455-8976. **Fax:** 864/455-5959. **Recorded Jobline:** 864/455-8799. **Contact:** Human Resources. **Description:** Greenville Hospital System is a multi-hospital system in South Carolina which provides health care services for several communities and major tertiary referral services for the upstate area. It is the second-largest employer in the county employing over 5,000 people, with approximately 1,100 beds providing multiple levels of care. **Common positions include:** Administrative Worker/Clerk; EEG Technologist; EKG Technician; Licensed Practical Nurse; Management; Nuclear Medicine Technologist; Occupational Therapist; Pharmacist; Physical Therapist; Physician; Registered Nurse; Respiratory Therapist; Speech-Language Pathologist; Surgical Technician. **Educational backgrounds include:** Health Care. **Benefits:** 403B; Dental Insurance; Disability Coverage; Life Insurance; Medical Insurance; Pension Plan; Savings Plan; Tuition Assistance. **Corporate headquarters location:** This Location.

KERSHAW COUNTY MEDICAL CENTER
P.O. Box 7003, Camden SC 29020. 803/432-4311. **Fax:** 803/425-6369. **Recorded Jobline:** 803/424-5426. **Contact:** Desiree Berry, Employment Coordinator. **Description:** A medical center. **NOTE:** Kershaw County Medical Center hires for both full- and part-time positions. **Common positions include:** Chef/Cook/Kitchen Worker; Dietician/Nutritionist; EKG Technician; Electrician; Emergency Medical Technician; Medical Records Technician; Nuclear Medicine Technologist; Occupational Therapist; Office Manager; Physical Therapist; Radiologic Technologist; Registered Nurse; Respiratory Therapist; Secretary; Social Worker; Surgical Technician. **Educational backgrounds include:** Health Care. **Benefits:** Dental Insurance; Disability Coverage; Employee Discounts; Life Insurance; Medical Insurance; Pension Plan; Savings Plan; Tuition Assistance. **Corporate headquarters location:** This Location. **Number of employees at this location:** 600.

LEXINGTON MEDICAL CENTER
2720 Sunset Boulevard, West Columbia SC 29169. 803/791-2131. **Contact:** Tom Hecker, Director of Human Resources. **Description:** A medical center. **Common positions include:** Accountant/Auditor; Customer Service Representative; Dietician/Nutritionist; EKG Technician; Electrician; Food and Beverage Service Worker; Licensed Practical Nurse; Nuclear Medicine Technologist; Occupational Therapist; Pharmacist; Physical Therapist; Preschool Worker; Radiologic Technologist; Registered Nurse; Respiratory Therapist; Secretary; Surgical Technician; Teacher. **Benefits:** Dental Insurance; Employee Discounts; Life Insurance; Medical Insurance. **Corporate headquarters location:** This Location. **Operations at this facility include:** Service. **Number of employees nationwide:** 1,750.

LORIS COMMUNITY HOSPITAL
3655 Mitchell Street, Loris SC 29569. 803/756-9196. **Fax:** 803/756-9195. **Contact:** Theresa McNair, Director of Personnel. **Description:** A general acute care facility. **Common positions include:** Biomedical Engineer; Clerical Supervisor; Clinical Lab Technician; Dietician/Nutritionist; EKG Technician; Licensed Practical Nurse; Medical Records Technician; Nuclear Medicine Technologist; Physical Therapist; Radiologic Technologist; Registered Nurse; Respiratory Therapist; Social Worker; Surgical Technician. **Benefits:** 401K; Dental Insurance; Disability Coverage; Employee Discounts; Life Insurance; Medical Insurance; Pension Plan; Savings Plan; Tuition Assistance. **Corporate headquarters location:** This Location. **Operations at this facility include:** Administration; Service. **Number of employees at this location:** 450.

PHOENIX MEDICAL TECHNOLOGY, INC.
P.O. Box 346, Andrews SC 29510. 803/221-5100. **Fax:** 803/221-5201. **Contact:** Theresa Ranson, Personnel Manager. **Description:** Phoenix Medical Technology, Inc. manufactures and markets medical products, primarily vinyl and latex examination gloves. The company also manufactures and markets gloves for electronics manufacturers, clean room applications, food handlers, and meat processors. Primary customers include hospitals, doctors offices, dentists, medical supply distributors, electronics assembly plants, power plants, and food and meat processing plants. **Common positions include:** Accountant/Auditor; Administrator; Biological Scientist/Biochemist; Blue-Collar Worker Supervisor; Buyer; Chemist; Computer Programmer; Customer Service Representative; General Manager; Industrial Production Manager; Management Trainee; Marketing Specialist; Operations/Production Manager; Quality Control Supervisor. **Educational backgrounds include:** Accounting; Business Administration; Chemistry; Marketing. **Benefits:** Disability Coverage; Life Insurance; Medical Insurance; Pension Plan; Profit Sharing; Tuition Assistance. **Special Programs:** Training Programs. **Corporate headquarters location:** This Location. **Operations at this**

facility include: Administration; Manufacturing; Research and Development; Sales; Service.

PROFESSIONAL MEDICAL PRODUCTS INC.

P.O. Box 3288, Greenwood SC 29648. 864/223-4281. **Contact:** Alice R. Hill, Director of Human Resources. **Description:** Professional Medical Products Inc. manufactures and sells disposable health care products including incontinent care products, wound care products, operating room supplies, urological products, and respiratory care products. The company operates sales offices nationwide, with more than 70 field sales representatives. **Common positions include:** Blue-Collar Worker Supervisor; Clerical Supervisor; Computer Programmer; Computer Systems Analyst; Credit Manager; Customer Service Representative; Designer; Electrician; Financial Analyst; Human Resources Specialist; Industrial Engineer; Industrial Production Manager; Mechanical Engineer; Operations/Production Manager; Purchasing Agent and Manager; Quality Control Supervisor; Registered Nurse; Respiratory Therapist; Sales Representative; Transportation/Traffic Specialist. **Educational backgrounds include:** Accounting; Business Administration; Computer Science; Engineering; Finance; Liberal Arts; Marketing. **Benefits:** 401K; Dental Insurance; Disability Coverage; Life Insurance; Medical Insurance; Savings Plan; Tuition Assistance. **Special Programs:** Internships. **Corporate headquarters location:** This Location. **Other U.S. locations:** Nationwide. **Operations at this facility include:** Administration; Divisional Headquarters; Manufacturing; Sales. **Listed on:** Privately held. **Number of employees at this location:** 620. **Number of employees nationwide:** 1,200.

PROVIDENCE HOSPITAL

2709 Laurel Street, Columbia SC 29204. 803/256-5410. **Fax:** 803/256-5838. **Recorded Jobline:** 803/256-5627. **Contact:** Human Resources. **Description:** An acute care hospital. **Common positions include:** Biomedical Engineer; Buyer; Claim Representative; Clerical Supervisor; Clinical Lab Technician; Computer Programmer; Computer Systems Analyst; Credit Manager; Dietician/Nutritionist; Education Administrator; EKG Technician; Electrician; Food Scientist/Technologist; Human Resources Specialist; Licensed Practical Nurse; Medical Records Technician; Nuclear Medicine Technologist; Pharmacist; Physical Therapist; Public Relations Specialist; Purchasing Agent and Manager; Radiologic Technologist; Registered Nurse; Respiratory Therapist; Restaurant/Food Service Manager; Social Worker; Surgical Technician. **Educational backgrounds include:** Health Care. **Benefits:** 403B; Dental Insurance; Disability Coverage; Employee Discounts; Life Insurance; Medical Insurance; Pension Plan; Tuition Assistance. **Operations at this facility include:** Service. **Number of employees at this location:** 1,200.

RICHLAND MEMORIAL HOSPITAL

15 Medical Park, Columbia SC 29203-6897. 803/434-6271. **Contact:** Employment Services Department. **Description:** A nationally-recognized 626-bed regional community teaching hospital. The Richland Memorial's facilities include a Children's Hospital; the Center for Cancer Treatment and Research; The Heart Center; the Midlands trauma center; and Richland Springs, which is a free-standing psychiatric hospital. As one of South Carolina's largest health care organizations, services are provided to approximately 225,000 out-of-state patients. Specialty services include a partially-matched bone marrow transplantation program, high-risk obstetrics, orthopedics, psychiatry, cardiology, oncology, nephrology, neonatology, neurology, neurosurgery, and medical and surgical services. Richland Memorial Hospital has a 750-member medical and dental staff. The hospital is also affiliated with the University of South Carolina and other universities. **Common positions include:** Accountant/Auditor; Budget Analyst; Buyer; Clinical Lab Technician; Computer Programmer; Computer Systems Analyst; Construction Contractor and Manager; Customer Service Representative; Dental Assistant/Dental Hygienist; Dental Lab Technician; Dentist; Dietician/Nutritionist; Draftsperson; EEG Technologist; EKG Technician; Electrician; Human Resources Specialist; Librarian; Library Technician; Licensed Practical Nurse; Medical Records Technician; Nuclear Medicine Technologist; Occupational Therapist; Pharmacist; Physical Therapist; Physician; Public Relations Specialist; Purchasing Agent and Manager; Radiologic Technologist; Recreational Therapist; Registered Nurse; Respiratory Therapist; Social Worker; Speech-Language Pathologist; Statistician; Surgical Technician. **Educational backgrounds include:** Accounting; Biology; Business Administration; Computer Science; Finance; Health Care; Marketing; Mathematics. **Benefits:** 401K; Dental Insurance; Disability Coverage; Employee Discounts; Life Insurance; Medical Insurance; On-Site Daycare; Tuition Assistance. **Special Programs:** Internships. **Corporate headquarters location:** This Location. **Operations at this facility include:** Administration; Service. **Number of employees at this location:** 4,364.

TUOMEY REGIONAL HOSPITAL
129 North Washington Street, Sumter SC 29150. 803/778-9000. **Contact:** Joey Finley, Employment Supervisor. **Description:** A medical center. **Common positions include:** Occupational Therapist; Pharmacist; Physical Therapist; Registered Nurse; Social Worker; Speech-Language Pathologist. **Benefits:** Dental Insurance; Employee Discounts; Life Insurance; Medical Insurance; Pension Plan; Tuition Assistance.

Note: Because addresses and telephone numbers of smaller companies change rapidly, we recommend you call each company to verify the information below before inquiring about job opportunities. Mass mailings are not recommended.

Additional employers with under 250 employees:

MEDICAL EQUIPMENT

MDT Diagnostic Co.
7371 Spartan Blvd E, N
Charleston SC 29418-8444.
803/552-8652.

Conco Medical Co.
481 Lakeshore Pky, Rock Hill
SC 29730-4205. 803/325-
7600.

MEDICAL EQUIPMENT AND SUPPLIES WHOLESALE

Thompson Dental Co.
1106 Knox Abbott Dr, Cayce
SC 29033. 803/796-3065.

Homedco
1824 E Main St, Easley SC
29640-3878. 864/855-
4413.

Patterson Dental Company
2154 N Center St, Suite
B201, Charleston SC 29406-
4056. 803/797-3409.

DOCTORS' OFFICES AND CLINICS

UCI Medical Affiliates
6168 Saint Andrews Rd,
Columbia SC 29212-3151.
803/772-8840.

Mental Health Center Santee Wateree
215 N Magnolia St, Sumter
SC 29150-4943. 803/775-
9364.

DENTISTS' OFFICES AND CLINICS

Orthodontic Center of Columbia
275 Harbison Blvd, Columbia
SC 29212-2222. 803/749-
4746.

Orthodontic Center of Charleston
2070 Northbrook Blvd, Suite
17A, Charleston SC 29406-
9253. 803/572-9439.

Crowncare
116 Dreher Rd, West
Columbia SC 29169-4502.
803/739-1551.

Palmetto Dental Personnel
210 Plantation Ct, Lugoff SC
29078-9144. 803/438-
3237.

OFFICES AND CLINICS OF HEALTH PRACTITIONERS

Dr. Myron Rones
7801 Rivers Ave, Charleston
SC 29406-4015. 803/572-
1528.

Professional Rehab Center
233 E Blackstock Rd,
Spartanburg SC 29301-
2652. 864/574-7013.

Rehability Center
1400 B St #544, Conway
SC 29526-3621. 803/347-
7141.

Florence Nurse Service
1415 Augusta St, Greenville
SC 29605-4027. 864/233-
0044.

Advance Care Services
2440 Mall Dr, N Charleston
SC 29406-6544. 803/566-
9605.

Visiting Professionals
1404 W Main St, Lexington
SC 29072-2332. 803/432-
2675.

NURSING AND PERSONAL CARE FACILITIES

Colleton Regional Hospital
501 Robertson Blvd,
Walterboro SC 29488-5714.
803/549-6371.

Oakhaven Nursing Home
123 Oak St #85, Darlington
SC 29532-2628. 803/398-
7041.

Midlands Center
8301 Farrow Rd, Columbia
SC 29203. 803/935-7508.

Aiken Nursing Home
123 Dupont Dr, Aiken SC
29801. 803/648-0434.

Harper Nursing Center
301 Liberty St N, Estill SC
29918. 803/625-3852.

Blue Ridge Nursing Center
1800 Crestview Rd, Easley
SC 29642-3528. 864/859-
3236.

Brookside Nursing Center
208 James St, Anderson SC
29625-2942. 864/226-
3427.

Clemson Area Retirement Center
500 Downs Loop, Clemson
SC 29631-2035. 864/654-
1155.

Cypress of Hilton Head
87 Bird Song Way, Hilton
Head SC 29926-1365.
803/689-7077.

Ebenezer Nursing Home
111 Sedgewood Dr, Rock
Hill SC 29732-2315.
803/329-6565.

Edgefield Health Care Center
1 Abel Dr, Edgefield SC
29824-9337. 803/637-
5312.

Emily's Nursing Center
412 Main St S, New Ellenton
SC 29809-1508. 803/652-
3190.

English Park Nursing Center
1305 N Main St, Marion SC
29571-2010. 803/423-
8530.

Florence Convalescent Center
133 W Clarke Rd, Florence
SC 29501-0722. 803/669-
4374.

Fountain Inn Convalescent Home
501 Gulliver St, Fountain Inn
SC 29644-2105. 864/862-
2554.

Golden Acres Nursing Facility
604 Hampton St, Iva SC
29655-8785. 864/348-
7433.

Grand Strand Healthcare
4452 Socastee Blvd, Myrtle
Beach SC 29575-7253.
803/293-1137.

Pines Nursing & Convalescent Home
203 Lakeside Dr, Dillon SC 29536-1911. 803/774-2741.

Greenville Nursing Center
809 Laurens Rd, Greenville SC 29607-1914. 864/232-8196.

Hallmark Health Center
255 Midland Pky, Summerville SC 29485-8104. 803/821-5005.

Saluda Nursing Center
Newberry Hwy, Saluda SC 29138. 864/445-2146.

Harvey's Nursing Home
163 Love & Care Rd, Six Mile SC 29682-9569. 864/868-2307.

Heritage Home of Florence
515 S Warley St, Florence SC 29501-5132. 803/662-4573.

Honorage Nursing Center
1207 N Cashua Dr, Florence SC 29501-6969. 803/665-6172.

Tanglewood Health Care Center
Third Rd 74, Ridgeway SC 29130. 803/337-3211.

Hospice of the Midlands
1400 Pickens St, Columbia SC 29201-3465. 803/376-4090.

JF Hawkins Nursing Home
1330 Kinard St, Newberry SC 29108-3038. 803/276-2601.

Jenkins Nursing Home
401 Murray St, Marion SC 29571-4732. 803/423-6947.

Jolley Acres Nursing Home
1180 Wolfe Trl SW, Orangeburg SC 29115-7339. 803/534-1001.

Jonathon's Nursing Center
138 Rosemond St, Pickens SC 29671-2434. 864/878-9620.

Kingstree Nursing Facility
110 W Mill St, Kingstree SC 29556-3300. 803/354-6116.

Orangeburg Nursing Home
755 Whitman St SE, Orangeburg SC 29115-6163. 803/534-7036.

Laurel Hill Inc.
716 E Cedar Rock St, Pickens SC 29671-2899. 864/878-4739.

Westminster Health Center
1330 India Hook Rd, Rock Hill SC 29732-2412. 803/328-5000.

Magnolia Manor
8020 White Ave, Spartanburg SC 29303-2043. 864/542-8515.

Magnolia Manor
63 Blackstock Rd, Inman SC 29349-1849. 864/472-9055.

Magnolia Manor
1415 Parkway, Greenwood SC 29646-4044. 864/227-9500.

National Healthcare Center
200 Frontage Rd, North Augusta SC 29841-7408. 803/278-4272.

Mariner Health Care
Carolina Av, Sumter SC 29150. 803/775-5394.

Marion County Convalescent Center
Conway Hwy, Marion SC 29571. 803/423-2601.

McCormick Health Care Center
Holiday Rd, McCormick SC 29835. 864/391-2390.

Oakbrook Convalescent Center
920 Travelers Blvd, Summerville SC 29485-8288. 803/875-9053.

Myrtle Beach Manor
9547 Hwy 17 N, Myrtle Beach SC 29572. 803/449-5283.

White Oak Estates Nurse & Retirement Center
400 Webber Rd, Spartanburg SC 29307. 864/579-7004.

Windsor Manor Inc.
RR 5, Manning SC 29102-9805. 803/478-2323.

Sea Isle Comprehensive Health Care
3627 Maybank Hwy, Johns Island SC 29455-4825. 803/559-5505.

Oconee Community Residence
350 Keowee School Rd, Seneca SC 29672-6743. 864/882-7637.

Stroud Memorial
2906 Geer Hwy, Marietta SC 29661. 864/836-6381.

Peachtree Center Cherokee County
1420 N Limestone St, Gaffney SC 29340-4734. 864/487-2717.

Woodruff Health Care
1114 E Georgia Rd, Woodruff SC 29388-9350. 864/476-7092.

White Oak Manor
111 S Congress St, York SC 29745-1836. 803/684-0035.

Rolling Green Village
1 Hoke Smith Blvd, Greenville SC 29615-5399. 864/297-0558.

Magnolia Manor-Spartanburg
P.O. Box 4127, Spartanburg SC 29305-4127. 864/585-0218.

Lila Doyle Nursing Care Facility
101 Lila Doyle Dr #858, Seneca SC 29672-9495. 864/885-7675.

Silver Springs Long Term Care
P.O. Box 250, Williston SC 29853-0250. 803/266-3229.

Lake Marion Nursing Facility
P.O. Box 940, Summerton SC 29148-0940. 803/485-2317.

Hopewell Health Care Center
1761 Pinewood Rd, Sumter SC 29154-9056. 803/481-8591.

Meadow Brook Health Care Center
P.O. Box 33, Blackville SC 29817-0033. 803/284-4313.

Riverside Nursing Center
109 Bentz Rd, Piedmont SC 29673-1412. 864/845-5177.

National Healthcare Center
9405 Highway 17 Byp, Murrells Inlet SC 29576-9301. 803/650-2213.

Barnwell County Hospital
P.O. Box 588, Barnwell SC 29812-0588. 803/259-1000.

Greenbrier Nursing Center
721 W Curtis St, Simpsonville SC 29681-2526. 864/967-7191.

HOSPITALS AND MEDICAL CENTERS

Chestnut Hill Mental Health Center
6243 White Horse Rd, Greenville SC 29611-3800. 864/246-7622.

HOME HEALTH CARE SERVICES

American Homepatient
181 E Evans St, Florence SC 29506-2512. 803/664-2818.

Beaufort Jasper Home Health Service
P.O. Box 357, Ridgeland SC 29936-0357. 803/525-8100.

Carolina Home Health Care
104 Corporate Blvd, Suite 418, West Columbia SC 29169-4600. 803/791-3704.

Community Health PCA's
130 Broad St, Sumter SC 29150-4237. 803/775-2006.

Healthmaster Home Health Care
636 Broughton St NE, Orangeburg SC 29115-4811. 803/534-2022.

Incare Home Health Inc.
4685 Hwy 175 Bypass, Myrtle Beach SC 29577. 803/293-4614.

Pediatric Services of America
704 E Washington St, Greenville SC 29601-3035. 864/242-2209.

Tokos Medical Corp.
1180 Sam Rittenberg Blvd, Charleston SC 29407-3382. 803/769-7677.

Total Care Inc.
2592 N Fraser St, Georgetown SC 29440-6416. 803/546-1313.

Tri County Home Health Care & Service
21 W Calhoun St, Sumter SC 29150-4216. 803/773-8311.

KIDNEY DIALYSIS CENTERS

Georgetown Dialysis Center
712 N Fraser St, Georgetown SC 29440-3353. 803/527-3431.

SPECIALTY OUTPATIENT FACILITIES

Circle Park Associates
601 W Gregg Ave, Florence SC 29501-4316. 803/665-9349.

Circle Park Prevention Center
604 W Gregg Ave, Florence SC 29501. 803/669-8087.

Columbia Metro Treatment Center
421 Capitol Sq, West Columbia SC 29169-7564. 803/791-9422.

Hope New Treatment Center
200 Ermine Rd, West Columbia SC 29170-2024. 803/791-9918.

Kershaw, County of
506 Monroe St, Camden SC 29020-2220. 803/424-0555.

HEALTH AND ALLIED SERVICES

Voyager's Health Source
755 Johnnie Dodds Blvd, Mount Pleasant SC 29464-3026. 803/884-1101.

Safari Corp.
225 Midland Pky, Summerville SC 29485-8104. 803/572-0190.

Alpha Plasma Center
3818 Dorchester Rd, Charleston SC 29405-7565. 803/744-8818.

RESIDENTIAL CARE

Banyan Retirement Services
1106 Woods Crossing Rd, Greenville SC 29607-3514. 864/234-5324.

Switzer Residential Care Center
1817 Jonesville Hwy, Union SC 29379-9793. 864/429-0890.

For more information on career opportunities in the health care industry:

Associations

ACCREDITING COMMISSION ON EDUCATION FOR HEALTH SERVICES ADMINISTRATION
1911 North Fort Myer Drive, Suite 503, Arlington VA 22209. 703/524-0511.

AMERICAN ACADEMY OF FAMILY PHYSICIANS
8880 Ward Parkway, Kansas City MO 64114. 816/333-9700. Promotes continuing education for family physicians.

AMERICAN ACADEMY OF PHYSICIAN ASSISTANTS
950 North Washington Street, Alexandria VA 22314. 703/836-2272. Promotes the use of physician assistants.

AMERICAN ASSOCIATION FOR CLINICAL CHEMISTRY
2101 Lovely Street NW, Suite 202, Washington, DC 20037-1526. 202/857-0717. A nonprofit association for clinical, chemical, medical, and technical doctors.

AMERICAN ASSOCIATION FOR RESPIRATORY CARE
11030 Ables Lane, Dallas TX 75229-4593. 214/243-2272. Promotes the art and science of respiratory care, while focusing on the needs of the patients.

AMERICAN ASSOCIATION OF COLLEGES OF OSTEOPATHIC MEDICINE
6110 Executive Boulevard, Suite 405, Rockville MD 20852. 301/468-2037. Provides applications processing services for colleges of osteopathic medicine.

AMERICAN ASSOCIATION OF COLLEGES OF PODIATRIC MEDICINE
1350 Piccard Drive, Suite 322, Rockville MD 20850. 301/990-7400. Provides applications processing services for colleges of podiatric medicine.

AMERICAN ASSOCIATION OF DENTAL SCHOOLS
1625 Massachusetts Avenue NW, Washington DC 20036-2212. 202/667-9433. Fax: 202/667-0642. E-mail address: aads@aads.jhu.edu. Represents all 54 of the dental schools in the U.S. as well as individual members. Goals of the organization include the expansion of postdoctoral training and increasing the number of women and minorities in the dental field.

AMERICAN ASSOCIATION OF HEALTHCARE CONSULTANTS
11208 Waples Mill Road, Suite 109, Fairfax VA 22030. 703/691-2242.

AMERICAN ASSOCIATION OF HOMES AND SERVICES FOR THE AGING
901 E Street NW, Suite 500, Washington DC 20004-2037. 202/783-2242.

AMERICAN ASSOCIATION OF MEDICAL ASSISTANTS
20 North Wacker Drive, Suite 1575, Chicago IL 60606. 312/899-1500.

AMERICAN ASSOCIATION OF NURSE ANESTHETISTS
222 South Prospect Avenue, Park Ridge IL 60068-4001. 847/692-7050.

AMERICAN CHIROPRACTIC ASSOCIATION
1701 Clarendon Boulevard, Arlington VA 22209. 703/276-8800. A national, nonprofit professional membership organization. Provides educational services (through films, booklets, texts, and kits), regional seminars and workshops, and major health and education activities to provide information on public health, safety, physical fitness, and disease prevention.

AMERICAN COLLEGE OF HEALTHCARE ADMINISTRATORS
325 South Patrick Street, Alexandria VA 22314. 703/549-5822. A professional membership society for individual long-term care professionals. Sponsors educational programs, supports research, and produces a number of publications, including the *Journal of Long-Term Care Administration* and *The Long-Term Care Administrator*.

AMERICAN COLLEGE OF HEALTHCARE EXECUTIVES
One North Franklin, Suite 1700, Chicago IL 60606-3491. 312/424-2800. Offers credentialing and educational programs. Publishes *Hospital & Health Services Administration* (a journal), and *Healthcare Executive* (a magazine).

AMERICAN COLLEGE OF MEDICAL PRACTICE EXECUTIVES
104 Inverness Terrace, East Englewood CO 80112-5306. 303/397-7869.

AMERICAN COLLEGE OF PHYSICIAN EXECUTIVES
4890 West Kennedy Boulevard, Suite 200, Tampa FL 33609-2575. 813/287-2000.

AMERICAN DENTAL ASSOCIATION
211 East Chicago Avenue, Chicago IL 60611. 312/440-2500.

AMERICAN DENTAL HYGIENISTS ASSOCIATION
Division of Professional Development, 444 North Michigan Avenue, Suite 3400, Chicago IL 60611. 312/440-8900.

AMERICAN DIETETIC ASSOCIATION
216 West Jackson Boulevard, Chicago IL 60606-6995. 312/899-0040 or 800/877-1600. Promotes optimal nutrition to improve public health and well-being.

AMERICAN HEALTH INFORMATION MANAGEMENT ASSOCIATION
919 North Michigan Avenue, Suite 1400, Chicago IL 60611. 312/787-2672.

AMERICAN HOSPITAL ASSOCIATION
One North Franklin Street, Suite 2700, Chicago IL 60606. 312/422-3000.

AMERICAN MEDICAL ASSOCIATION
515 North State Street, Chicago IL 60610. 312/464-5000. An organization for medical doctors.

AMERICAN MEDICAL TECHNOLOGISTS
710 Higgins Road, Park Ridge IL 60068. 847/823-5169.

AMERICAN NURSES ASSOCIATION
600 Maryland Avenue SW, Suite 100W, Washington DC 20024-2571. 202/554-4444.

AMERICAN OCCUPATIONAL THERAPY ASSOCIATION
4720 Montgomery Lane, Bethesda MD 20824-1220. 301/652-2682. 800/377-8555. Fax: 301/652-7711.

AMERICAN OPTOMETRIC ASSOCIATION
243 North Lindbergh Boulevard, St. Louis MO 63141. 314/991-4100. Offers publications, discounts, and insurance programs for members.

AMERICAN ORGANIZATION OF NURSE EXECUTIVES
One North Franklin Street, Suite 3400, Chicago IL 60606. 312/422-2800.

AMERICAN PHYSICAL THERAPY ASSOCIATION
1111 North Fairfax Street, Alexandria VA 22314. 703/684-2782. Small fee required for information.

AMERICAN PUBLIC HEALTH ASSOCIATION
1015 15th Street NW, Suite 300, Washington DC 20005. 202/789-5600.

AMERICAN VETERINARY MEDICAL ASSOCIATION
1931 North Meacham Road, Suite 100, Schaumburg IL 60173-4360. 847/925-8070. Provides a forum for the discussion of issues of importance to the veterinary profession, and for the development of official positions.

ASSOCIATION OF MENTAL HEALTH ADMINISTRATORS
60 Revere Drive, Suite 500, Northbrook IL 60062. 847/480-9626.

ASSOCIATION OF UNIVERSITY PROGRAMS IN HEALTH ADMINISTRATION
1911 North Fort Myer Drive, Suite 503, Arlington VA 22209. 703/524-5500.

GROUP HEALTH ASSOCIATION OF AMERICA, INC.
1129 20th Street NW, Suite 600, Washington DC 20036. 202/778-3200.

HEALTHCARE FINANCIAL MANAGEMENT ASSOCIATION
Two Westbrook Corporate Center, Suite 700, Westchester IL 60154. 708/531-9600.

NATIONAL MEDICAL ASSOCIATION
1012 Tenth Street NW, Washington DC 20001. 202/347-1895.

Magazines

AMERICAN JOURNAL OF NURSING
555 West 57th Street, New York NY 10019. Publishes five editions: Hospital, Critical Care, Continuing Care, Regular, and

Nurse Practitioner. Accredited as a provider of continuing education in nursing by the American Nurses Credentialing Center.

AMERICAN MEDICAL NEWS
American Medical Association, 515 North State Street, Chicago IL 60605. 312/464-5000.

CHANGING MEDICAL MARKETS
Theta Corporation, Theta Building, Middlefield CT 06455. 860/349-1054.

HEALTH CARE EXECUTIVE
American College of Health Care Executives, One North Franklin, Suite 1700, Chicago IL 60606. 312/424-2800.

MODERN HEALTHCARE
Crain Communications, 740 North Rush Street, Chicago IL 60611. 312/649-5374.

NURSEFAX
Springhouse Corporation, 1111 Bethlehem Pike, P.O. Box 908, Springhouse PA 19477. 215/646-8700. This is a jobline service designed to be used in conjunction with *Nursing* magazine. Please call to obtain a copy of the magazine or the nursing directory.

HOTELS AND RESTAURANTS

Job opportunities in the restaurant industry are plentiful. A number of trends will boost job growth, including population growth, rising incomes, and more dual-income families. Some demand will be met through labor-saving innovations like salad bars, untended meal stations, automated beverage stations, and central kitchens that serve a number of establishments in the same restaurant chain. In the fast-food sector, use of labor-saving technology is essential to remain competitive. Since the most time consuming transaction at drive-in windows is making change, some restaurants are experimenting with debit and credit cards to reduce transaction time. However, despite labor-saving innovations, the increased demand for services will increase the need for workers.

Jobs in hotels, motels, and other lodging places will be plentiful throughout the next decade. Driving the growth will be many of the same trends affecting the restaurant industry, as well as low-cost airfares and foreign tourism in the U.S. Another hot trend: legalized gambling. The hotel and motel industry invests heavily in the gaming industry, and that has further fueled job growth. This growth will continue as hotels increasingly attract families by offering relatively inexpensive casino vacation packages.

The greatest growth is in all-suite properties and budget motels. Since they don't have restaurants, dining rooms, lounges, or kitchens, these properties offer few jobs for food and beverage workers, but jobs should be available for managers and assistant managers. The trend toward chain-affiliated lodging places should provide managers with opportunities for advancement into general manager positions and corporate administrative jobs.

North Carolina

CHARLOTTE MARRIOTT CITY CENTER
100 West Trade Street, Charlotte NC 28202. 704/333-9000. **Contact:** Diane Bolling Director of Human Resources. **Description:** A 421-guest room hotel, featuring an indoor pool, a health club, and two restaurants. The hotel also has a variety of meeting facilities, including a ballroom, seven conference suites, five meeting rooms, and two board rooms.

GOLDEN CORRAL CORPORATION
5151 Glenwood Avenue, Raleigh NC 27612. 919/781-9310. **Contact:** Susanne Flawinski, Human Resources Coordinator. **Description:** A chain of family steak houses. **Common positions include:** Accountant/Auditor; Adjuster; Attorney; Budget Analyst; Buyer; Computer Operator; Computer Programmer; Computer Systems Analyst; Construction Contractor and Manager; Economist/Market Research Analyst; Editor; Employment Interviewer; General Manager; Human Resources Specialist; Interviewing Clerk; Market Research Analyst; Paralegal; Payroll Clerk; Property and Real Estate Manager; Public Relations Specialist; Purchasing Agent and Manager; Receptionist; Restaurant/Food Service Manager; Secretary; Systems Analyst; Technical Writer/Editor; Typist/Word Processor. **Educational backgrounds include:** Accounting; Business Administration; Communications; Computer Science; Finance; Liberal Arts; Marketing. **Benefits:** Dental Insurance; Disability Coverage; Employee Discounts; Life Insurance; Medical Insurance; Pension Plan; Tuition Assistance. **Corporate headquarters location:** This Location. **Other U.S. locations:** Tampa FL; Kansas City MO; Dallas TX; Houston TX. **Operations at this facility include:** Administration;

Research and Development; Service. **Number of employees at this location:** 200. **Number of employees nationwide:** 11,000.

WINSTON HOTELS, INC.
2209 Century Drive, Raleigh NC 27612. 919/510-6010. **Contact:** LaRuby Joy, Human Resources. **Description:** A real estate investment trust. Winston Hotels owns 16 hotels, including 11 Hampton Inns in Georgia, North Carolina, South Carolina, and Virginia, and five Comfort Inns in North Carolina and Virginia. **Corporate headquarters location:** This Location.

Note: Because addresses and telephone numbers of smaller companies change rapidly, we recommend you call each company to verify the information below before inquiring about job opportunities. Mass mailings are not recommended.

Additional employers with under 250 employees:

EATING PLACES

Acheson's Restaurant
Station Square Mall, Rocky Mount NC 27804. 919/985-3515.

Angus Barn Ltd.
Hwy 70 E, Durham NC 27703. 919/683-1398.

Angus Barn Ltd.
9401 Glenwood Ave, Raleigh NC 27612-7514. 919/781-2444.

Annabelle's Restaurant
335 Cross Creek Mall, Fayetteville NC 28303-7241. 910/864-5434.

Apple House Cafeteria
101 Holly Hill Mall, Burlington NC 27215-5148. 910/584-3314.

Applebees Neighborhood Grill & Bar
2001 N Main St, High Point NC 27262-2133. 910/886-8450.

Applebees Neighborhood Grill & Bar
202 Greenville Blvd SW, Greenville NC 27834-6908. 919/355-2421.

Applebees Neighborhood Grill & Bar
115 Tunnel Rd, Asheville NC 28805-1817. 704/251-9194.

Arby's of Burlington
781 Huffman Mill Rd, Burlington NC 27215-5124. 910/584-5472.

Atlantis Seafood Restaurant
2740 N Church St, Rocky Mount NC 27804-6601. 919/977-2239.

Big Easy
2526 Hillsborough St, Raleigh NC 27607-7266. 919/755-0041.

Biscuitville
2336 Randleman Rd, Greensboro NC 27406-3604. 910/273-8025.

Biscuitville
114 W Kings Hwy, Eden NC 27288-5008. 910/627-0267.

Bojangles Famous Chicken & Biscuits
2315 S Elm Eugene St, Greensboro NC 27406-3616. 910/272-5607.

Bojangles Famous Chicken & Biscuits
3737 High Point Rd, Greensboro NC 27407-4627. 910/299-4419.

Bojangles Famous Chicken & Biscuits
2929 Freedom Dr, Charlotte NC 28208-3857. 704/394-3655.

Bojangles Famous Chicken & Biscuits
513 Curtis Bridge Rd, Wilkesboro NC 28697-2211. 910/838-8668.

Brintles Homestyle Restaurant
3630 W Pine St, Mount Airy NC 27030-9004. 910/352-3165.

Bullard Restaurant Inc. Executive Office
1901 N Pine St, Lumberton NC 28358. 910/738-7183.

Burger King
3003 High Point Rd, Greensboro NC 27403-3637. 910/292-7782.

Burger King
2421 Randleman Rd, Greensboro NC 27406-4309. 910/274-8487.

Burger King
3700 S Holden Rd, Greensboro NC 27406-9587. 910/316-0328.

Burger King
5275 N Roxboro Rd, Durham NC 27712-2830. 919/477-9796.

Burger King
Hwy 74, Wingate NC 28174. 704/233-4077.

Burger King
3709 N Tryon St, Charlotte NC 28206-2058. 704/372-0616.

Burger King
720 S Main St, Burlington NC 27215-5845. 910/570-1115.

Burger King
7102 US Highway 64 E, Knightdale NC 27545-9265. 919/266-5966.

Calabash West
501 New Leicester Hwy, Asheville NC 28806-2122. 704/252-0264.

Captain D's
123 Eastway Dr, Charlotte NC 28213-7101. 704/598-7555.

Captain D's
722 Pressley Rd, Charlotte NC 28217-4614. 704/527-1745.

Captain's Galley
105-J Statesville Rd, Huntersville NC 28078. 704/875-6038.

Carolina Country BBQ Restaurant
838 Tyvola Rd, Charlotte NC 28217-3510. 704/525-0337.

Charburger
1906 Clarendon Blvd, New Bern NC 28560-4590. 919/633-4067.

Charley's Restaurant
Southpark, Charlotte NC 28211. 704/364-7475.

Checkers Drive In Restaurant
3244 Capital Blvd, Raleigh
NC 27604-3338. 919/878-
9050.

Chick-Fil-A
3102 Garden Rd, Burlington
NC 27215-9784. 910/584-
3050.

Chili's Grill & Bar
4600 Durham-Chapel Hill
Blvd, Durham NC 27707.
919/489-6699.

Cooker Bar & Grille
4516 Falls of Neuse Rd,
Raleigh NC 27609-6204.
919/981-7400.

**Crowley's Old Favorites
Restaurant**
3071 Medlin Dr, Raleigh NC
27607-6627. 919/787-
3431.

Damon's Clubhouse
3019 Auto Drive, Durham
NC 27707. 919/493-2574.

Darryl's Restaurant & Bar
501 N McPherson Church
Rd, Fayetteville NC 28303-
4409. 910/864-1914.

Darryl's Restaurant & Bar
2101 N Church St,
Greensboro NC 27405-5671.
910/378-1808.

Denny's Restaurant
55 Jr Rd, Smithfield NC
27577. 919/965-3275.

Domino's Pizza
312 Ames Rd, Matthews NC
28105. 704/847-3030.

**El Cancun Mexican
Restaurant**
303 S Dekalb St, Shelby NC
28150-5403. 704/480-
0089.

Fearrington House
Fearrington Village Cntr,
Pittsboro NC 27312.
910/542-2121.

Frullati Restaurant
Four Seasons Mall,
Greensboro NC 27407.
910/854-5881.

**Gardners Barbecue &
Catering Service**
West Ridge Shopping Cntr,
Rocky Mount NC 27804.
919/443-3996.

Giluigi's Pasta & Pizza
4721 Atlantic Ave, Raleigh
NC 27604-1856. 919/954-
9900.

**Golden Corral Family
Restaurant**
2909 E Millbrook Rd, Raleigh
NC 27604-2815. 919/872-
0500.

**Golden Corral Family Steak
House**
3108 Garden Rd, Burlington
NC 27215-9784. 910/584-
3890.

**Golden Corral Family Steak
House**
Franklin Plz Cntr, Louisburg
NC 27549. 919/496-6836.

Golden Skillet
Plymouth Shopping Cntr,
Plymouth NC 27962.
919/793-9083.

Grady's American Grill
4010 Chapel Hill Blvd,
Durham NC 27707-2501.
919/419-7022.

Grady's American Grill
5546 Albemarle Rd,
Charlotte NC 28212-3683.
704/537-4663.

Gumby's Pizza
3017 Hillsborough St,
Raleigh NC 27607-5434.
919/836-1555.

Haberdasher Pizza & More
621-C N Main St,
Kernersville NC 27284.
910/996-1500.

Ham's Restaurant
Brassfield Shopping Center,
Greensboro NC 27410.
910/288-3334.

Hardee's
1237 Tyvola Rd, Charlotte
NC 28210-3609. 704/525-
3893.

Hardee's
61 Hendersonville Rd,
Asheville NC 28803-2648.
704/274-5544.

Hardee's
2635 Hendersonville Rd,
Arden NC 28704-8527.
704/684-1595.

Hardee's
1250 Fairview Dr, Lexington
NC 27292-5332. 704/249-
2124.

Hardee's
101 Jackson Ct, Lumberton
NC 28358-1102. 910/738-
1477.

Hardee's
1525 N Chester St, Gastonia
NC 28052-1846. 704/866-
8631.

Hardee's
Little River Square Shopping
Center, Goldsboro NC
27530. 919/736-3464.

Hardee's
596 Central St, Lenoir NC
28645. 704/728-3411.

Hardee's
110 Bickett Blvd, Louisburg
NC 27549. 919/496-3015.

Hardee's
501 US Highway 117 N,
Burgaw NC 28425-5105.
910/259-9233.

Hardee's
1035 Bethania-Rural Hall Rd,
Rural Hall NC 27045.
910/924-6894.

Harper's Restaurant
6518 Fairview Rd, Charlotte
NC 28210. 704/366-6688.

Hink's Grill
513 Salisbury Ave,
Albemarle NC 28001-3245.
704/982-7411.

House of Taipei
8933 J M Keynes Dr,
Charlotte NC 28262-8433.
704/549-4038.

J&S Cafeteria
800 Fairview Rd, Asheville
NC 28803-1059. 704/298-
0507.

K&W Cafeteria
4310 Big Tree Way,
Greensboro NC 27409-2733.
910/852-8957.

K&W Cafeteria
3300 Healy Dr, Winston-
Salem NC 27103-1477.
910/768-1066.

K&W Cafeteria
310 Oak Avenue Mall Dr,
Kannapolis NC 28081-4340.
704/938-9116.

K&W Cafeteria
511 Woodburn Rd, Raleigh
NC 27605. 919/832-7505.

Kentucky Fried Chicken
2304 Maple Ave, Burlington
NC 27215. 910/229-6104.

Kentucky Fried Chicken
430 Ramsey St, Suite 106,
Fayetteville NC 28301-4974.
910/323-2211.

Kentucky Fried Chicken
214 N Berkeley Blvd,
Goldsboro NC 27534-4324.
919/751-0874.

Lakeside Restaurant
20210 Henderson Rd,
Davidson NC 28036-9215.
704/896-8985.

Libby Hill Seafood
2561 Peters Creek Pky,
Winston-Salem NC 27127-
5657. 910/785-3469.

Little Caesar's Pizza
Battleground Plaza Shop
Center, Greensboro NC
27410. 910/282-6444.

Little Caesar's Pizza
3214 Randleman Rd,
Greensboro NC 27406-6529.
910/379-7491.

Little Caesar's Pizza
9229A Lawyers Rd,
Charlotte NC 28227-5143.
704/545-3713.

Lone Star Steakhouse &
Saloon
3101 N Sharon Amity Rd,
Charlotte NC 28205-6538.
704/568-2388.

Lone Star Steakhouse &
Saloon
5033 South Blvd, Charlotte
NC 28217-2715. 704/523-
2388.

Lone Star Steakhouse &
Saloon
3707 Battleground Ave,
Greensboro NC 27410-2345.
910/282-9895.

Lone Star Steakhouse &
Saloon
504 Hanes Mall Blvd,
Winston-Salem NC 27103-
5634. 910/760-9720.

Lone Star Steakhouse &
Saloon
3025 High Point Rd,
Greensboro NC 27403-3655.
910/855-1228.

Lone Star Steakhouse &
Saloon
17 Tunnel Rd, Asheville NC
28805-1229. 704/259-
9500.

Lone Star Steakhouse &
Saloon
6515 Glenwood Ave, Raleigh
NC 27612-7157. 919/781-
8400.

Long John Silvers Seafood
306 Blowing Rock Blvd,
Lenoir NC 28645-4406.
704/758-4051.

Long John Silvers Seafood
800 Biltmore Ave, Asheville
NC 28803-2559. 704/258-
2317.

Longhorn Steaks
2518 Sardis Rd N, Charlotte
NC 28227. 704/847-1212.

Longhorn Steaks
2925 Battleground Ave,
Greensboro NC 27408-2705.
910/545-3200.

Lucky 32 Restaurant
1421 Westover Ter,
Greensboro NC 27408-7908.
910/370-0707.

Lucky 32 Restaurant
109 S Stratford Rd, Winston-
Salem NC 27104-4213.
910/724-3232.

Macado's
125 Summit Ave,
Greensboro NC 27401-3003.
910/373-0600.

Main Street Cafe
107 W Main St, Washington
NC 27889-4943. 919/946-
3239.

Mama Mias Inc.
3215 Avent Ferry Rd,
Raleigh NC 27606-2720.
919/851-0043.

McDonald's
2802 Raleigh Rd NW, Wilson
NC 27896-8665. 919/243-
7077.

McDonald's
5005 Sunset Rd, Charlotte
NC 28269-2748. 704/596-
0954.

McDonald's
3810 Lake Boone Trl, Raleigh
NC 27607-2927. 919/781-
0504.

McDonald's
220 Huffman Mill Rd,
Burlington NC 27215-5115.
910/584-7700.

McDonald's
9150 Lawyers Rd, Charlotte
NC 28227-5146. 704/545-
6210.

McDonald's
8305 Creedmoor Rd, Raleigh
NC 27613-1374. 919/847-
8111.

McGuffey's Restaurant
9709 E Independence Blvd,
Matthews NC 28105-4625.
704/845-2522.

McGuffey's Restaurant
13 Kenilworth Knls, Asheville
NC 28805-1846. 704/252-
0956.

Mi Casita Restaurante
703 Grove St, Fayetteville
NC 28301-5111. 910/323-
6181.

Miami Subs Grill
2401 Wake Forest Rd,
Raleigh NC 27608-1709.
919/836-8333.

Morton's of Chicago
227 W Trade St, Charlotte
NC 28202-1675. 704/333-
2602.

Olive Garden Italian
Restaurant
3000 High Point Rd,
Greensboro NC 27403-3638.
910/854-7094.

Olive Garden Italian
Restaurant
1809 Walnut St, Cary NC
27511. 919/233-9714.

Olive Garden Italian
Restaurant
4805 Capital Blvd, Raleigh
NC 27604. 919/954-8557.

Outback Steakhouse
7500 Creedmoor Rd, Raleigh
NC 27613-1641. 919/846-
3848.

Papa John's Pizza
5724 E Wt Harris Blvd,
Charlotte NC 28215-5730.
704/531-0123.

Pargos Restaurant
4512 Falls of Neuse Rd,
Raleigh NC 27609-6204.
919/872-4220.

Pargos Restaurant
400 Greenville Blvd SW,
Greenville NC 27834-6965.
919/756-9977.

PD Quix
Cary Village Shopping
Center, Cary NC 27511.
919/469-5787.

Perkins Family Restaurant &
Bakery
2127 Chapel Hill Rd,
Burlington NC 27215-7142.
910/570-3796.

Piccadilly Cafeteria
3 S Tunnel Rd, Asheville NC
28805-2221. 704/298-
5048.

Pizza City USA
2314 N William St,
Goldsboro NC 27530-1442.
919/734-4000.

Pizza Hut
1618 Spring Garden St,
Greensboro NC 27403-2350.
910/272-9500.

Pizza Hut
2125 S Church St,
Burlington NC 27215-5327.
910/226-4464.

Pizza Hut
593 S Stratford Rd, Winston-
Salem NC 27103-1806.
910/768-9933.

Pizza Hut
3140 Raeford Rd,
Fayetteville NC 28303-5378.
910/484-8127.

Pizza Hut
1153 N Wesleyan Blvd,
Rocky Mount NC 27804-
1840. 919/446-5600.

Pizza Hut
4445 Fayetteville Rd,
Lumberton NC 28358-2674.
910/738-8206.

Pizza Hut
6404 Albemarle Rd,
Charlotte NC 28212-3816.
704/536-3511.

Pizza Hut
4709 Tuckaseegee Rd,
Charlotte NC 28208-2507.
704/393-0099.

Pizza Hut
3203 Yanceyville St #A,
Greensboro NC 27405-4043.
910/621-8500.

Pizza Hut
2505 Battleground Ave,
Greensboro NC 27408-4003.
910/288-3333.

Pizza Hut
Hwy 64 E, Pittsboro NC
27312. 910/542-1057.

Pizza Hut
1200 Sunset Ave, Clinton
NC 28328. 910/592-9333.

Pizza Hut
3735 Battleground Ave,
Greensboro NC 27410-2345.
910/288-4245.

Pizza Hut
3044 Eastway Dr, Charlotte
NC 28205. 704/535-9828.

Pizza Inn
1015 Summit Ave,
Greensboro NC 27405-7007.
910/273-3625.

Pizza Inn
4800 W Market St,
Greensboro NC 27407-1404.
910/852-2020.

Pizza Inn
Tarboro Shp Center, Tarboro
NC 27886. 919/823-1018.

Pizza Inn
4207 High Point Rd,
Greensboro NC 27407-4231.
910/294-1425.

Po' Folks
3015 High Point Rd,
Greensboro NC 27403-3637.
910/292-0962.

Quincy's Family Steak House
2507 Randleman Rd,
Greensboro NC 27406-4311.
910/379-7097.

Rainbow Deli & Cafe
8200 Providence Rd, Suite
400, Charlotte NC 28277-
9702. 704/541-1811.

Red Hot & Blue
6615 Falls of Neuse Rd,
Raleigh NC 27615-6816.
919/846-7427.

Red Lobster Restaurants
2001 N Church St,
Greensboro NC 27405-5633.
910/272-5625.

Roast Grill
7 S West St, Raleigh NC
27603-1831. 919/832-
8292.

Rock-Ola Cafe
1405 Garner Station Blvd,
Garner NC 27529. 919/772-
4555.

Rock-Ola Cafe
103 Muirs Chapel Rd,
Greensboro NC 27410-6112.
910/854-2278.

Rock-Ola Cafe
200 W Woodlawn Rd,
Charlotte NC 28217-2153.
704/529-6564.

Romano's Macaroni Grill
4020 Chapel Hill Blvd,
Durham NC 27707-2501.
919/489-0313.

Ruby Tuesday Restaurant
Cross Creek Plaza,
Fayetteville NC 28303.
910/864-4400.

Ryan's Family Steak House
1415 E Dixie Dr, Asheboro
NC 27203-5080. 910/625-
2441.

Sagebrush of Winston
2905 Reynolda Rd, Winston-
Salem NC 27106-3015.
910/727-1200.

**Sagebrush Steakhouse &
Saloon**
1420 2nd St NE, Hickory NC
28601-2553. 704/322-
1137.

Sal's New York Cafe Inc.
2322 N Church St,
Burlington NC 27217-3175.
910/229-9656.

Sbarro
4325 Glenwood Ave, Suite
P5, Raleigh NC 27612-4504.
919/781-9814.

Sbarro
264 Hanes Mall Blvd,
Winston-Salem NC 27103.
910/768-9724.

**Scoops Famous Hershey's
Ice Cream**
2302 Hillsborough St, #104,
Raleigh NC 27607-7353.
919/821-1833.

Shoney's
2541 Little Rock Rd,
Charlotte NC 28214-2757.
704/392-0713.

Shoney's
25 Fury Dr, Asheville NC
28806-1504. 704/258-
3788.

Skats of Princeton
101 Smith St, Princeton NC
27569. 910/936-2152.

Spaghetti Bowl
1385 N Church St,
Burlington NC 27217-2803.
910/227-2088.

Steak Escape
3320 Silas Creek Pky,
Winston-Salem NC 27103-
3031. 910/659-0005.

**Subway Sandwiches &
Salads**
1426 Carolina Ave,
Washington NC 27889-
3314. 919/946-1645.

Taco Bell
803 NC 24-27 Byp E,
Albemarle NC 28001.
704/982-6394.

Taco Bell
800 Brevard Rd, Asheville
NC 28806-2245. 704/667-
9901.

Tasty Grill
1231 W Lee St, Greensboro
NC 27403-2808. 910/272-
3855.

The Summit Restaurant
3122 Garden Rd, Burlington
NC 27215-9784. 910/584-
1323.

Tiffany's Cabaret
4016 W Wendover Ave,
Greensboro NC 27407-1901.
910/855-9024.

TPI Restaurants
11521C Granite St,
Charlotte NC 28273-6412.
704/588-6470.

Tri Arc Food Systems
901 Jones Franklin Rd, Suite
101, Raleigh NC 27606-
3374. 919/859-1131.

Tripps Restaurant
3286 Silas Creek Pky,
Winston-Salem NC 27103-
3011. 910/659-0080.

Tripps Restaurant
6413 Falls of the Neuse Rd,
Raleigh NC 27615. 919/876-
9183.

Tripps Restaurant
4402 W Wendover Ave,
Greensboro NC 27407-2600.
910/854-9518.

Village Inn Pizza Parlor
Newtowne Plaza Shopping
Center, Statesville NC
28677. 704/873-0256.

Village Tavern
1903 Westridge Rd,
Greensboro NC 27410-2425.
910/282-3063.

Waffle House
2701 Alamance Rd,
Burlington NC 27215-5457.
910/226-3087.

Waffle House
907 E Main St, Benson NC
27504-9399. 910/894-
4188.

Waffle House
551 N McPherson Church
Rd, Fayetteville NC 28303-
4409. 910/864-4773.

**Wendy's Old Fashioned
Hamburgers**
1058 W Club Blvd, Durham
NC 27701-1154. 919/286-
7084.

**Wendy's Old Fashioned
Hamburgers**
2191 N Roberts Ave,
Lumberton NC 28358-2867.
910/739-8701.

**Wendy's Old Fashioned
Hamburgers**
1500 W Lee St, Greensboro
NC 27403-2715. 910/292-
6066.

**Wendy's Old Fashioned
Hamburgers**
3712 Battleground Ave,
Greensboro NC 27410-2344.
910/545-3235.

**Wendy's Old Fashioned
Hamburgers**
1225 W Roosevelt Blvd,
Monroe NC 28110-2819.
704/289-1009.

**Wendy's Old Fashioned
Hamburgers**
501 S Regional Rd,
Greensboro NC 27409-9309.
910/668-2911.

**Western Steer Family Steak
House**
Hwy 221, Jefferson NC
28640. 910/246-3360.

**Western Steer Family Steak
House**
800 S Main St, Burlington
NC 27215-5741. 910/227-
8369.

Dette's Cafe
1671 Hayes Rd, Creedmoor
NC 27522-8739. 919/528-
4790.

Domino's Pizza
2641 Randleman Rd,
Greensboro NC 27406-5159.
910/370-1471.

Domino's Pizza
3223 The Plaza Road,
Charlotte NC 28205.
704/375-8794.

Hot Stuff Pizza
N Main St, Troy NC 27371.
910/576-4710.

Christinne's Fine Dining
207 Greenville Blvd SW,
Greenville NC 27834-6907.
919/355-9500.

Corporate Cafe
Depot Shopping Center,
Matthews NC 28105.
704/845-2121.

Ma Beatty's Kitchen
2000 Avondale Dr, Durham
NC 27704-4359. 919/220-
1442.

DRINKING PLACES

Crossroads Lounge
3206 High Point Rd,
Greensboro NC 27407-4618.
910/299-2742.

Sidetrack Bar & Lounge
232 Main St, Eden NC
27288-3916. 910/635-
0432.

HOTELS AND MOTELS

Comfort Inn
5111 N Interstate 85 Service
R, Charlotte NC 28269-
4894. 704/598-0007.

Days Inn Woodlawn
122 W Woodlawn Rd,
Charlotte NC 28217-2110.
704/527-1620.

Embassy Suites Hotel
4800 S Tryon St, Charlotte
NC 28217-2402. 704/527-
8400.

**Embassy Suites Hotel
Greensboro**
204 Centreport Dr,
Greensboro NC 27409-9510.
910/668-4535.

Fairfield Inn
3361 Lackey St, Lumberton
NC 28358-9044. 910/739-
8444.

**Homewood Suites Hotel
North**
8340 N Tryon St, Charlotte
NC 28262-3417. 704/549-
8800.

Omni Charlotte Hotel
222 E 3rd St, Charlotte NC
28202. 704/377-6664.

Red Roof Inn
5116 N Interstate 85 Service
R, Charlotte NC 28206-
1378. 704/596-8222.

**Country Club Whispering
Pines**
Villas, Whisper Pines NC
28327. 910/949-3777.

Daystop
1101 S Hwy 61, Whitsett
NC 27377. 910/449-7353.

Guest Inn
406 Henderson Blvd, Atlantic
Beach NC 28512-7455.
919/726-5818.

Hampton Inn
715 Sullivan Rd, Statesville
NC 28677-3439. 704/878-
2721.

Holiday Inn
I-95, Rocky Mount NC
27801. 919/937-6300.

Motel 6
1415 Tunnel Rd, Asheville
NC 28805-2803. 704/299-
3040.

**Park Lane Motel at 4
Seasons**
3005 High Point Rd,
Greensboro NC 27403-3637.
910/294-4565.

Red Roof Inn
I-40 & High Point Rd,
Greensboro NC 27403.
910/852-6560.

Red Roof Inn
I-77 & Broad St, Statesville
NC 28677. 704/878-2051.

Shoney's Motor Inn-Charlotte
2541 Little Rock Rd,
Charlotte NC 28214-2757.
704/394-2000.

**Charlotte Marriott Executive
Park**
5700 Westpark Dr, Charlotte
NC 28217-3550. 704/527-
9650.

Holiday Inn Center City
230 N College St, Charlotte
NC 28202-2112. 704/335-
5400.

Ramada Inn Airport Central
515 Clanton Rd, Charlotte
NC 28217-1309. 704/527-
3000.

South Carolina

THE CLUB GROUP, LTD.
P.O. Box 6989, Hilton Head SC 29938. 803/363-5699. **Contact:** Christiana G. Martin,
Director of Administration. **Description:** The Club Group, Ltd. runs a resort operation
and hospitality company. **Common positions include:** Accountant/Auditor;
Chef/Cook/Kitchen Worker; Food and Beverage Service Worker; Hotel
Manager/Assistant Manager; Human Resources Specialist; Restaurant/Food Service
Manager.

FLAGSTAR COMPANIES INC.
203 East Main Street, Spartanburg SC 29319. 864/597-7709. **Toll-free number:** 800/755-2273. **Recorded Jobline:** 800/959-TEAM. **Contact:** Joseph Smith, Director of Human Resources. **Description:** A holding company whose subsidiaries own, operate, and franchise over 2,000 family-style, fast-food, and steakhouse restaurants in 49 states, under the names Hardees, Quincy's, Denny's, and El Pollo Loco. These subsidiaries also provide contract food and vending services; operate food, beverage, and lodging facilities; and provide ancillary food services at national and state parks, sports stadiums, and arenas. **Common positions include:** Accountant/Auditor; Blue-Collar Worker Supervisor; Budget Analyst; Computer Programmer; Computer Systems Analyst; Customer Service Representative; General Manager; Human Service Worker; Management Trainee; Paralegal; Public Relations Specialist; Restaurant/Food Service Manager. **Educational backgrounds include:** Accounting; Business Administration; Computer Science; Food Services; Marketing. **Benefits:** 401K; Dental Insurance; Disability Coverage; Life Insurance; Medical Insurance; Savings Plan; Tuition Assistance. **Special Programs:** Internships. **Corporate headquarters location:** This Location. **Other U.S. locations:** Nationwide. **Operations at this facility include:** Administration; Divisional Headquarters; Manufacturing; Regional Headquarters; Research and Development. **Listed on:** NASDAQ. **Number of employees at this location:** 700. **Number of employees nationwide:** 90,000.

RYAN'S FAMILY STEAKHOUSES, INC.
405 Lancaster Avenue, P.O. Box 100, Greer SC 29652. 864/879-1000. **Contact:** Tim Mayfield, Director of Training and Recruiting. **Description:** Ryan's Family Steakhouses, Inc. owns and franchises over 200 restaurants in 20 states. The company's menu includes steaks, hamburgers, chicken, fish, and a Megabar. **Common positions include:** Restaurant/Food Service Manager. **Benefits:** 401K; Daycare Assistance; Dental Insurance; Disability Coverage; Employee Discounts; Life Insurance; Medical Insurance; Savings Plan. **Special Programs:** Training Programs. **Corporate headquarters location:** This Location. **Listed on:** NASDAQ. **Number of employees nationwide:** 15,000.

SANDS OCEANFRONT RESORTS
P.O. Box 2968, Myrtle Beach SC 29578. 803/449-0880. **Fax:** 803/497-6871. **Contact:** Ms. Sandi Madorno, Assistant Director of Human Resources. **Description:** A corporation that owns and/or manages six resorts in Myrtle Beach and three resorts in North Carolina. **Common positions include:** Accountant/Auditor; Administrative Services Manager; Clerical Supervisor; Customer Service Representative; General Manager; Hotel Manager/Assistant Manager; Human Resources Specialist; Purchasing Agent and Manager; Restaurant/Food Service Manager. **Educational backgrounds include:** Business Administration; Hotel Administration; Liberal Arts; Marketing; Restaurant Management. **Benefits:** 401K; Dental Insurance; Life Insurance; Medical Insurance; Tuition Assistance. **Corporate headquarters location:** This Location. **Listed on:** Privately held. **Number of employees nationwide:** 900.

SEA PINES ASSOCIATES, INC.
P.O. Box 7000, Hilton Head Island SC 29928. 803/785-3333. **Fax:** 803/842-1927. **Contact:** Monika Nash, Director of Human Resources. **Description:** Sea Pines Associates, Inc. is a holding company with three subsidiaries including Sea Pines Company, Inc., (also at this address) which operates all of the resort assets including three resort golf courses, a 28 court racquet club, a home and villa rental management business, retail sales outlets, food services operations and other resort recreational facilities. Sea Pines Real Estate Company, Inc. is an independent real estate brokerage firm with 11 offices serving Island residents. Sea Pines Country Club, Inc. owns and operates a full-service private country club providing golf, tennis, and clubhouse facilities for approximately 1,500 equity and associate club members. The company, through its wholly-owned subsidiary, Sea Pines/TidePointe, Inc., has a general partnership interest in TidePointe Partners. TidePointe Partners develops and constructs a continuing care retirement community with a variety of living units and amenities on Hilton Head Island, South Carolina. **Corporate headquarters location:** This Location. **Number of employees at this location:** 247.

SEA PINES COMPANY, INC.
P.O. Box 7000, Hilton Head Island SC 29938. 803/842-1882. **Contact:** Monika Nash, Director of Human Resources. **Description:** Sea Pines Company, Inc. operates resort assets including three resort golf courses, a 28 court racquet club, a home and villa rental management business, retail sales outlets, food services operations and other resort recreational facilities. Parent company, Sea Pines Associates, Inc. is a holding company with two other subsidiaries including Sea Pines Real Estate Company, Inc., an independent real estate brokerage firm with 11 offices serving Island residents; and Sea Pines Country Club, Inc., which owns and operates a full-service private country

club providing golf, tennis, and clubhouse facilities for approximately 1,500 equity and associate club members. The company, through its wholly-owned subsidiary, Sea Pines/TidePointe, Inc., has a general partnership interest in TidePointe Partners. TidePointe Partners develops and constructs a continuing care retirement community with a variety of living units and amenities on Hilton Head Island, South Carolina. The parent company, Sea Pines Associates, Inc. is also located at this address. 803/785-3333. **Common positions include:** Accountant/Auditor; Administrative Worker/Clerk; Assistant Manager; Buyer; Cashier; Chef/Cook/Kitchen Worker; Clerical Supervisor; Computer Operator; Computer Programmer; Computer Systems Analyst; Customer Service Representative; Department Manager; Dispatcher; Employment Interviewer; Food and Beverage Service Worker; General Manager; Hotel Manager/Assistant Manager; Hotel/Motel Clerk; Management Trainee; Marketing/Advertising/PR Manager; Paralegal; Payroll Clerk; Property and Real Estate Manager; Public Relations Specialist; Purchasing Agent and Manager; Real Estate Agent; Receptionist; Recreation Worker; Reservationist; Retail Sales Worker; Secretary; Truck Driver; Typist/Word Processor; Wholesale and Retail Buyer. **Educational backgrounds include:** Accounting; Business Administration; Communications; Computer Science; Finance; Liberal Arts; Marketing. **Benefits:** 401K; Dental Insurance; Disability Coverage; Employee Discounts; Life Insurance; Medical Insurance. **Parent company:** Sea Pines Associates, Inc. **Operations at this facility include:** Administration; Sales; Service. **Number of employees at this location:** 450.

Note: *Because addresses and telephone numbers of smaller companies change rapidly, we recommend you call each company to verify the information below before inquiring about job opportunities. Mass mailings are not recommended.*

Additional employers with under 250 employees:

EATING PLACES

Alex's Restaurants
3713 Dorchester Rd,
Charleston SC 29405-7566.
803/747-9198.

Applebees Neighborhood Grill & Bar
88 Old Trolley Rd,
Summerville SC 29485-4904. 803/871-0682.

Applebees Neighborhood Grill & Bar
1922 Augusta St, Greenville
SC 29605-2938. 864/233-9006.

Applebees Neighborhood Grill & Bar
430 Congaree Rd, Greenville
SC 29607-2729. 864/288-6642.

Applebees Neighborhood Grill & Bar
3944 Grandview Dr,
Simpsonville SC 29680-3163. 864/228-0461.

Arby's
Rock Hill Galleria, Rock Hill
SC 29730. 803/366-5586.

Arcade Nightclub
5 Liberty St, Charleston SC
29401-1400. 803/722-5656.

Beverage Station Square
2859 Highway 17, Murrells
Inlet SC 29576-7622.
803/359-1100.

Blossom Cafe
171 E Bay St, Charleston SC
29401-2126. 803/722-9200.

Bojangles Famous Chicken N Biscuits
2737 Sunset Blvd, West
Columbia SC 29169-4809.
803/796-4419.

Bojangles Famous Chicken N Biscuits
881 Chesterfield Hwy,
Cheraw SC 29520-7004.
803/537-1636.

Burger King
107 Travis Ave, Saluda SC
29138. 864/445-9018.

Burger King
7 Cherry St, Charleston SC
29403-5744. 803/723-0138.

Burger King
3579 Savannah Hwy, Johns
Island SC 29455-7935.
803/556-9211.

Burger King
5900 S Kings Hwy, Surfside
Beach SC 29575-4968.
803/238-0658.

CD's Hot Fish Shop
1660 Savannah Hwy,
Charleston SC 29407-6257.
803/763-7955.

Chick-Fil-A
1024 Johnnie Dodds Blvd,
Mount Pleasant SC 29464-3107. 803/881-6811.

China
2117 Old Spartanburg Rd,
Greer SC 29650-2704.
864/322-0405.

Chuck E. Cheese's
253 Congaree Rd, Greenville
SC 29607-2707. 864/297-6400.

Cokesbury Cafe
4126 Cokesbury Rd, Hodges
SC 29653-9717. 864/374-7112.

Denny's
2521 Wade Hampton Blvd,
Greenville SC 29615-1147.
864/292-9105.

Quincy's Family Steak House
602 Hearon Cir, Spartanburg
SC 29303-2020. 864/583-6154.

Domino's Pizza Inc.
616 Columbia Ave,
Lexington SC 29072-2620.
803/957-6400.

Dukes Bar-B-Q
118 N Railroad Ave,
Ridgeville SC 29472-8015.
803/871-6507.

Fatz Cafe
225 S Pleasantburg Dr,
Greenville SC 29607-2533.
864/467-9542.

Fatz Cafe
3123 S Highway 14,
Greenville SC 29615-5906.
864/288-1929.

Fatz Cafe
5051 Calhoun Memorial
Hwy, Easley SC 29640-
3859. 864/859-9832.

French Quarter Restaurant
195 E Bay St, Charleston SC
29401-2126. 803/722-
1611.

Garcia's Mexican Restaurant
9600 N Kings Hwy, Myrtle
Beach SC 29572-4006.
803/449-4435.

Garibaldi Cafe
2013 Greene St, Columbia
SC 29205-1638. 803/771-
8888.

**Golden Corral Family Steak
House**
125 Dekalb St, Camden SC
29020-4529. 803/432-
0227.

Grand Strand Pizza Inc.
1706 S Kings Hwy, Myrtle
Beach SC 29577-4602.
803/448-5976.

Hardee's
10 Highway 17 N, Surfside
Beach SC 29575-6035.
803/238-3398.

Hardee's
601 Railroad Ave, Allendale
SC 29810-1056. 803/584-
4200.

Hardee's
502 W Columbia Ave,
Batesburg SC 29006-1845.
803/532-9735.

Hardee's
1425 Chapin Rd, Chapin SC
29036-8874. 803/345-
5499.

Hardee's
300 Lee St, Johnston SC
29832-1438. 803/275-
3926.

Hardee's
516 S Hampton St, Kershaw
SC 29067-1833. 803/475-
3690.

Hardee's
Palmeto Plaza, Sumter SC
29150. 803/775-7494.

Hardee's
209 Spring St, Charleston
SC 29403-5101. 803/577-
7820.

Hardee's
201 Goose Creek Blvd N,
Goose Creek SC 29445-
2966. 803/553-7780.

Hardee's
201 Main St S, New Ellenton
SC 29809-1332. 803/652-
3608.

Hardee's
1397 E Main St, Duncan SC
29334-9138. 864/433-
0264.

Hardee's/Spartan Foods
US 76 & Woody Road,
Pendleton SC 29670.
864/646-4812.

Holmes Boy Grill
319 D S Lafeyette Rd,
Sumter SC 29150. 803/778-
2848.

Huddle House
1302 Meeting Street Rd,
Charleston SC 29405-9332.
803/853-8864.

Huddle House
933 Folly Rd, Charleston SC
29412. 803/762-7404.

J&R Restaurant
610 W Liberty St, Sumter SC
29150-4821. 803/775-
3544.

Jah-Mi's Caribbean Cuisine
4159 Dorchester Rd,
Charleston SC 29405-7426.
803/566-7842.

Josie Joe's
1313 Shrimp Boat Ln, Mount
Pleasant SC 29464-4379.
803/881-8671.

K&W Cafeteria
79th Av, Myrtle Beach SC
29572. 803/449-1442.

K&W Cafeteria
Hwy 17 at 20th Av S, Myrtle
Beach SC 29577. 803/448-
1669.

Ken's Cafe
313 Courthouse Aly, Gaffney
SC 29340-3163. 864/488-
0919.

Kenny Rogers Roasters
1836 Ashley River Rd,
Charleston SC 29407-4781.
803/766 4488.

Kentucky Fried Chicken
101 Dekalb St, Camden SC
29020. 803/432-3651.

Kentucky Fried Chicken
1014 Broad St, Sumter SC
29150. 803/775-4333.

Krystal
6301 Rivers Ave, N
Charleston SC 29406-4802.
803/572-7390.

Little Caesar's Pizza
1140 N Pleasantburg Dr,
Greenville SC 29607-1223.
864/244-4154.

Lizard's Thicket Restaurants
885 Chestnut St NE,
Orangeburg SC 29115-3503.
803/534-1977.

Lizard's Thicket Restaurants
501 Knox Abbott Dr, Cayce
SC 29033-4124. 803/791-
0314.

Lizard's Thicket Restaurants
2234 Sunset Blvd, West
Columbia SC 29169-4714.
803/794-0923.

Louis's Charleston Grill
224 King St, Charleston SC
29401-3102. 803/577-
4522.

Market Place Buffet & Bakery
4973 Rivers Ave, N
Charleston SC 29406-6301.
803/554-8585.

McDonald's
Fairfield Plaza, Winnsboro SC
29180. 803/635-5002.

McDonald's
360 Pinewood Rd, Sumter
SC 29150-5444. 803/775-
1807.

McDonald's
215 Dekalb St, Camden SC
29020-4401. 803/432-
3300.

McDonald's
5510 Rivers Ave, N
Charleston SC 29406-6131.
803/554-7561.

McDonald's
5381 Dorchester Rd,
Charleston SC 29418-5651.
803/552-6904.

McDonald's
1390 E Main St, Duncan SC
29334-9137. 864/433-
9991.

**Monterrey Mexican
Restaurant**
2801 Poinsett Hwy,
Greenville SC 29609-1244.
864/271-3625.

Nathan's Deli
1836 Ashley River Rd ,Unit
7, Charleston SC 29407-
4781. 803/556-3354.

**O'Charleys Restaurant &
Lounge**
775 Haywood Rd, Greenville
SC 29607-2721. 864/297-
6267.

Papa John's Pizza
1836 Ashley River Rd,
Charleston SC 29407-4781.
803/763-6666.

Pizza Hut
2275 Sunset Blvd, West
Columbia SC 29169-4713.
803/791-9999.

Pizza Hut
4397 Dorchester Rd,
Charleston SC 29405-7430.
803/744-2600.

Pizza Hut
1750 Remount Rd, N
Charleston SC 29406-3286.
803/744-1600.

Pizza Hut
7480 Rivers Ave, N
Charleston SC 29406-4659.
803/572-5555.

Pizza Hut
915 Folly Rd, Charleston SC
29412-3907. 803/795-
2244.

Pizza Hut
1621 Augusta St, Greenville
SC 29605-2923. 864/271-
0888.

Pizza Hut
2113 Old Spartanburg Rd,
Suite 10, Greer SC 29650-
2704. 864/292-8100.

Pizza Inn
1000 NE Main St,
Simpsonville SC 29681-
6012. 864/967-0466.

Portabello's Restaurant
1608 Atlantic Ave, Sullivans
Island SC 29482-9725.
803/722-6868.

Prime Sirloin Buffet & Bakery
105 Franklin Ave,
Spartanburg SC 29301-
6556. 864/576-1077.

**Wendy's Old Fashioned
Hamburgers**
1721 Sam Rittenberg Blvd,
Charleston SC 29407-4928.
803/571-4226.

Ronnie's Seafood Restaurant
480 W Coleman Blvd, Mount
Pleasant SC 29464-3433.
803/884-4074.

Ruby Tuesday Restaurant
Magnolia Mall, Florence SC
29501. 803/673-0545.

Rush's
201 Columbia Ave,
Lexington SC 29072-2611.
803/359-8858.

Ryan's Family Steak House
1928 Whiskey Rd, Aiken SC
29803-6176. 803/648-
2629.

Ryan's Family Steak House
1707 Charleston Hwy, West
Columbia SC 29169-5051.
803/796-2728.

S&S Cafeteria
Haywood Mall, Greenville SC
29607-2781. 864/288-
4164.

Sav-Way Food Stores
233 N Coit St, Florence SC
29501-2516. 803/678-
3442.

Schlotzsky's Deli
1208 Saint Matthews Rd NE,
Orangeburg SC 29115-3420.
803/536-5628.

Waffle House
216 Blythewood Rd,
Blythewood SC 29016-
9515. 803/735-1732.

Waffle House
4551 Augusta Rd, Greenville
SC 29605. 864/277-4479.

Shoney's Restaurant
1705 White Horse Rd,
Greenville SC 29605-4825.
864/269-4720.

Shoney's Restaurant
Main St & Hwy 278, Hilton
Head SC 29926-1628.
803/681-7300.

Stax's Grill
850 Woods Crossing Rd,
Greenville SC 29607-2757.
864/288-5546.

Subway
7724 N Kings Hwy, Myrtle
Beach SC 29572-3041.
803/497-9162.

T Bonz Gill & Grill at Barefoot
4732 Highway 17 S, N
Myrtle Beach SC 29582-
5355. 803/272-7111.

Taco Bell
5856 Rivers Ave, N
Charleston SC 29406-6031.
803/744-4563.

Taco Bell
101 Walmart Blvd, Moncks
Corner SC 29461-3966.
803/899-7878.

Taco Bell
615 Fairview Rd,
Simpsonville SC 29680-
6706. 864/967-7135.

The Pantry
701 Mauldin Rd, Greenville
SC 29607. 864/277-1332.

Victory Cafe
Piedmont Hwy at Lakeside
Park, Piedmont SC 29673.
864/422-1234.

Village Grill & Bar
302 W Wade Hampton Blvd,
Greer SC 29650-1535.
864/968-0030.

Waffle House
3695 Saint Matthews Rd,
Orangeburg SC 29118-8411.
803/536-5481.

Waffle House
I-85 Highway 76, Anderson
SC 29621. 864/261-8124.

Waffle House
1119 Woodruff Rd,
Greenville SC 29607-4119.
864/288-9816.

**Wendy's Old Fashioned
Hamburgers**
1405 E Main St, Duncan SC
29334-9219. 864/433-
1301.

**Wendy's Old Fashioned
Hamburgers**
5115 Dorchester Rd,
Charleston SC 29418-5607.
803/552-9467.

**Wendy's Old Fashioned
Hamburgers**
1295 W Dorchester Rd,
Summerville SC 29485.
803/871-3685.

**Wendy's Old Fashioned
Hamburgers**
194 Cannon St, Charleston
SC 29403-5715. 803/577-
0472.

Domino's Pizza
1039 Johnnie Dodds Blvd,
Mount Pleasant SC 29464-
6155. 803/881-7900.

Tony's Pizza Service
278 Main Rd, Johns Island
SC 29455-3404. 803/766-
7133.

Senior Catering Inc.
205 E Market St,
Bennettsville SC 29512-
3128. 803/454-0555.

Slugger's Deli & Dogs
5646 Rivers Ave, N
Charleston SC 29406-6080.
803/554-5689.

**Applebee's Neighborhood
Grill & Bar**
3441 Clemson Blvd,
Anderson SC 29621-1356.
864/225-4752.

Cactus Jack's
507 37th Ave S, N Myrtle
Beach SC 29582-4910.
803/272-7445.

Frank's Sports Bar & Grill
3715 E North St, Greenville
SC 29615-2363. 864/268-
6386.

McGuffey's Restaurant
711 Congaree Rd, Greenville
SC 29607-3519. 864/288-
3116.

DRINKING PLACES

Tucker's Lounge
3381 Ashley Phosphate Rd
#A, Charleston SC 29418-
8416. 803/767-0033.

Classics of Charleston
7910 Dorchester Rd, N
Charleston SC 29418-3106.
803/767-8281.

Music Farm
32 Ann St, Charleston SC
29403. 803/722-8904.

Dudley's
346 King St, Charleston SC
29401-1440. 803/723-
2784.

Skyline Club
100 Lee St, West Columbia
SC 29170. 803/822-8608.

The Ladies Club
1902 Parmley Dr, Conway
SC 29527-4463. 803/248-
6854.

HOTELS AND MOTELS

**Wild Dunes Resort
Accommodations & Golf**
P.O. Box 20575, Charleston
SC 29413-0575. 803/886-
2260.

Quality Suites
5225 N Arco Ln, Charleston
SC 29418-7001. 803/747-
7300.

Ocean Forest Villa Resort
5601 N Ocean Blvd, Myrtle
Beach SC 29577-2394.
803/449-9661.

Seabrook Island Reservations
1001 Landfall Way, Johns
Island SC 29455-6303.
803/768-0880.

Rice Planters Inn
Hwy 63 & I 95, Walterboro
SC 29488. 803/538-8964.

Economy Inns of America
1776 Burning Tree Dr,
Columbia SC 29210-5850.
803/798-9210.

Cricket Inn
1465 S Pleasantburg Dr,
Greenville SC 29605-1332.
864/277-8670.

Holiday Inn-Coliseum
630 Assembly St, Columbia
SC 29201-4029. 803/799-
7800.

**Hilton Myrtle Beach
Oceanfront**
10000 Beach Club Dr, Myrtle
Beach SC 29572. 803/449-
5000.

For more information on career opportunities in hotels and restaurants:

Associations

**AMERICAN HOTEL AND MOTEL
ASSOCIATION**
1201 New York Avenue NW, Suite 600,
Washington DC 20005-3931. 202/289-
3100. Provides lobbying services and
educational programs, maintains and
disseminates industry data, and produces a
variety of publications.

**THE EDUCATIONAL FOUNDATION OF THE
NATIONAL RESTAURANT ASSOCIATION**
250 South Wacker Drive, 14th Floor,
Chicago IL 60606. 312/715-1010. Offers
educational products, including textbooks,
manuals, instruction guides, manager and
employee training programs, videos, and
certification programs.

NATIONAL RESTAURANT ASSOCIATION
1200 17th Street NW, Washington DC
20036. 202/331-5900. Provides a number
of services, including government lobbying,
communications, research, and information,
and operates the Educational Foundation
(see separate address).

Directories

**DIRECTORY OF CHAIN RESTAURANT
OPERATORS**
Business Guides, Inc., Lebhar-Friedman,
Inc., 3922 Coconut Palm Drive, Tampa FL
33619-8321. 813/664-6700.

**DIRECTORY OF HIGH-VOLUME
INDEPENDENT RESTAURANTS**
Lebhar-Friedman, Inc., 3922 Coconut Palm
Drive, Tampa FL 33619-8321. 813/664-
6700.

Magazines

**CORNELL HOTEL AND RESTAURANT
ADMINISTRATION QUARTERLY**
Cornell University School of Hotel
Administration, Statler Hall, Ithaca NY
14853-6902. 607/255-9393.

HOTEL AND MOTEL MANAGEMENT
120 West 2nd Street, Duluth MN 55802.

INNKEEPING WORLD
Box 84108, Seattle WA 98124. 206/362-
7125.

NATION'S RESTAURANT NEWS
Lebhar-Friedman, Inc., 3922 Coconut Palm
Drive, Tampa, FL 33619. 813/664-6700.

INSURANCE

What's the job outlook in insurance? That depends on which industry segment you're looking at. Health insurers, who have avoided any Washington-based reforms, are reaping record profits, while property-casualty and life insurers are still struggling. The industry has been consolidating with major mergers, and that's likely to continue in 1996. Under pressure from low returns, and a growing number of environmental claims, the property-casualty industry needs to cut overhead. In many cases, that also means jobs.

The picture in health insurance is much brighter. By moving more and more consumers into managed care, insurers are benefiting from the economies of scale. Many of the biggest players in the insurance industry have moved into managed care. Metropolitan Life and Travelers Corporation, for example, combined health insurance operations into Metra Health in order to compete with leaders like CIGNA, Aetna, and Prudential.

North Carolina

BLUE CROSS & BLUE SHIELD OF NORTH CAROLINA
P.O. Box 2291, Durham NC 27702. 919/490-2552. **Contact:** Michael Plueddeman, Manager of Employee Relations. **Description:** A non-profit, voluntary prepayment health care plan. Blue Cross & Blue Shield of North Carolina also serves as a fiscal intermediary for various programs of the federal and state government, such as Medicare. **Common positions include:** Accountant/Auditor; Actuary; Administrator; Claim Representative; Computer Programmer; Customer Service Representative; Department Manager; Economist/Market Research Analyst; Human Resources Specialist; Insurance Agent/Broker; Public Relations Specialist; Services Sales Representative; Statistician; Systems Analyst; Underwriter/Assistant Underwriter. **Educational backgrounds include:** Accounting; Business Administration; Computer Science; Economics; Finance; Health Care; Marketing; Mathematics. **Benefits:** Dental Insurance; Disability Coverage; Life Insurance; Medical Insurance; Pension Plan; Savings Plan; Tuition Assistance.

FIRST BANK INSURANCE SERVICES, INC.
1102 North Main Street, High Point NC 27262. 910/802-4000. **Contact:** Michael Gay, President. **Description:** First Bank Insurance Services, Inc. is an insurance agency acquired by First Bancorp in 1994 as a subsidiary. First Bancorp was founded in 1983, as Montgomery Bancorp, and changed its name in 1986. First Bancorp is a one-bank holding company whose principal activity is the ownership and operation of First Bank, which is headquartered in Troy, North Carolina. First Bank acquired Central State Bank in 1994 and conducts business from 28 branches located within a 60-mile radius of Troy, North Carolina. The bank provides a full range of banking services, including the accepting of demand and time deposits, the making of secured and unsecured loans to individuals and businesses, trust services, discount brokerage services, and self-directed IRAs. The parent company, First Bancorp, also owns and operates two nonbank subsidiaries, Montgomery Data Services, Inc., which provides data processing services to financial institutions; and First Bancorp Financial Services, Inc. (formerly First Recovery, Inc.), which owns and operates various real estate. **Corporate headquarters location:** This Location. **Parent company:** First Bancorp (Troy, NC). **Listed on:** NASDAQ.

INTEGON CORPORATION
P.O. Box 3199, Winston-Salem NC 27102-3199. 910/770-2000. **Contact:** John Beattie, Vice President of Human Resources. **Description:** Integon Corporation operates in 22 states through more than 11,000 independent agents. By year-end 1996, the company plans to do business in 30 to 35 states. Integon operates in four divisions. The company's East division, comprised of Alabama, Florida, Georgia, North Carolina, Ohio, and Virginia, primarily underwrites nonstandard auto insurance. The division also

underwrites preferred auto, homeowners, and mobile home insurance in North Carolina. The North Division underwrites nonstandard auto insurance in Connecticut, Illinois, Indiana, Maine, Maryland, New Hampshire, New York, Pennsylvania, Rhode Island, and Vermont. The South Division underwrites nonstandard auto insurance in Kentucky, Louisiana, Mississippi, Tennessee, and Texas. The Specialty Auto division underwrites insurance for business autos and motorcycles and is offered as a complementary product to the agents in the other divisions. **Corporate headquarters location:** This Location. **Listed on:** New York Stock Exchange. **Number of employees nationwide:** 1,750.

INVESTORS TITLE COMPANY
121 North Columbia Street, P.O. Drawer 2687, Chapel Hill NC 27515-2687. 919/968-2200. **Fax:** 919/942-4686. **Contact:** Ms. L. Dawn Martin, Vice President of Human Resources. **Description:** Investors Title Company, through its two title insurance subsidiaries, Investors Title Insurance Company and Northeast Investors Title Insurance Company, writes title insurance in Florida, Georgia, Illinois, Indiana, Kentucky, Nebraska, New York, North Carolina, Pennsylvania, South Carolina, Tennessee, and Virginia. A third subsidiary, Investors Title Exchange Corporation, serves as a qualified intermediary in tax-deferred exchanges of real property. Investors Title Company operates 24 offices throughout North Carolina. **Corporate headquarters location:** This Location. **Listed on:** NASDAQ. **Number of employees nationwide:** 120.

MID-SOUTH INSURANCE COMPANY
4317 Ramsey Street, P.O. Box 2069, Fayetteville NC 28302-2069. 910/822-1020. **Contact:** Human Resources. **Description:** Engaged primarily in the marketing, underwriting, and servicing of health, accident, and life insurance policies. Sales offices of Mid-South Insurance Company are located in Charlotte, Fayetteville, and Greensboro, North Carolina; and Columbia, South Carolina. **Corporate headquarters location:** This Location. **Listed on:** NASDAQ.

NORTH CAROLINA MUTUAL LIFE INSURANCE COMPANY
411 West Chapel Hill Street, Durham NC 27701. 919/682-9201. **Fax:** 919/683-1694. **Contact:** Roger Gregory, Director of Human Resources. **Description:** A life insurance company. **Common positions include:** Accountant/Auditor; Administrative Services Manager; Assistant Manager; Attorney; Budget Analyst; Cashier; Claim Representative; Clerical Supervisor; Computer Operator; Computer Programmer; Computer Systems Analyst; Customer Service Representative; Department Manager; Employment Interviewer; Financial Services Sales Rep.; General Manager; Human Resources Specialist; Insurance Agent/Broker; Marketing/Advertising/PR Manager; Payroll Clerk; Printing Press Operator; Public Relations Specialist; Purchasing Agent and Manager; Real Estate Agent; Receptionist; Secretary; Securities Sales Rep.; Services Sales Representative; Typist/Word Processor; Underwriter/Assistant Underwriter. **Educational backgrounds include:** Accounting; Business Administration; Communications; Computer Science; Finance; Liberal Arts; Marketing; Mathematics. **Benefits:** Dental Insurance; Disability Coverage; Employee Discounts; Legal Services; Medical Insurance; Pension Plan; Profit Sharing; Tuition Assistance. **Corporate headquarters location:** This Location. **Operations at this facility include:** Administration. **Number of employees at this location:** 144. **Number of employees nationwide:** 560.

ROYAL INSURANCE
9300 Arrowpoint Boulevard, Charlotte NC 28273. 704/522-2000. **Contact:** John Cross, Human Resources Administrative Department Manager. **Description:** An insurance holding company. **Common positions include:** Accountant/Auditor; Claim Representative; Human Resources Specialist; Industrial Engineer; Insurance Agent/Broker; Underwriter/Assistant Underwriter. **Educational backgrounds include:** Accounting; Business Administration; Computer Science; Economics; Engineering; Insurance. **Benefits:** 401K; Dental Insurance; Disability Coverage; Employee Discounts; Life Insurance; Medical Insurance; Pension Plan; Profit Sharing; Savings Plan; Tuition Assistance. **Corporate headquarters location:** This Location. **Listed on:** London Stock Exchange. **Number of employees at this location:** 800.

Note: Because addresses and telephone numbers of smaller companies change rapidly, we recommend you call each company to verify the information below before inquiring about job opportunities. Mass mailings are not recommended.

Additional employers with under 250 employees:

INSURANCE COMPANIES

Manulife Financial
227 W Trade St, Suite 2300, Charlotte NC 28202-1675. 704/377-6161.

Triangle Life Insurance Co.
P.O. Box 12637, Raleigh NC 27605-2637. 919/755-7571.

Selective Insurance Co.
9101 Southern Pines Blvd, Charlotte NC 28273-5519. 704/527-8012.

American Professionals Insurance Co.
P.O. Box 27257, Raleigh NC 27611-7257. 919/836-2000.

Century American Casualty
P.O. Box 15879, Durham NC 27704-0879. 919/383-0279.

GE Home Equity Insurance Corp. of NC
P.O. Box 177800, Raleigh NC 27619-1800. 919/846-4100.

INSURANCE AGENTS, BROKERS, AND SERVICES

Metropolitan Life Insurance
6100 Fairview Rd, Suite 525, Charlotte NC 28210-3277. 704/552-6445.

Coresource Inc.
6100 Fairview Rd, Suite 1000, Charlotte NC 28210-3277. 704/552-0900.

State Farm Insurance Co.
9801 Independence Point Pky, Matthews NC 28105-2780. 704/841-6900.

South Carolina

ATLANTIC COAST LIFE INSURANCE COMPANY
P.O. Box 20010, Charleston SC 29413. **Contact:** Department of Interest. **Description:** A life insurance company.

COLONIAL LIFE AND ACCIDENT INSURANCE COMPANY
P.O. Box 1365, Columbia SC 29202. 803/798-7000. **Fax:** 803/731-2618. **Recorded Jobline:** 803/750-0088. **Contact:** Lisa Sanders, Staffing Specialist. **Description:** An accident and health insurance company. **Common positions include:** Accountant/Auditor; Administrative Services Manager; Advertising Clerk; Attorney; Budget Analyst; Claim Representative; Computer Programmer; Computer Systems Analyst; Custodian; Customer Service Representative; Designer; Insurance Agent/Broker; Operations/Production Manager; Public Relations Specialist; Technical Writer/Editor; Underwriter/Assistant Underwriter. **Educational backgrounds include:** Accounting; Art/Design; Business Administration; Communications; Computer Science; Economics; Finance; Liberal Arts; Marketing. **Benefits:** 401K; Daycare Assistance; Dental Insurance; Disability Coverage; Employee Discounts; Life Insurance; Pension Plan; Profit Sharing; Savings Plan; Tuition Assistance. **Corporate headquarters location:** This Location. **Parent company:** Unum Corporation (Portland ME) is an insurance company providing income protection to small- and medium-sized employers through a broad range of life, health, disability, and retirement products. **Operations at this facility include:** Administration; Research and Development; Sales; Service. **Listed on:** New York Stock Exchange. **Number of employees at this location:** 1,200. **Number of employees nationwide:** 4,300.

LIBERTY LIFE INSURANCE COMPANY
THE LIBERTY CORPORATION
Wade Hampton Boulevard, P.O. Box 789, Greenville SC 29602. 864/268-8334. **Contact:** Jan Haubernreich, Director of Employment. **Description:** Liberty Life Insurance Company provides a broad range of insurance services. The parent company, The Liberty Group, is a holding company with subsidiaries engaged in life, accident, and health insurance, as well as television broadcasting. **Common positions include:** Accountant/Auditor; Actuary; Attorney; Computer Programmer; Customer Service Representative; Department Manager; Human Resources Specialist; Insurance Agent/Broker; Marketing Specialist; Systems Analyst; Underwriter/Assistant Underwriter. **Educational backgrounds include:** Accounting; Business Administration; Communications; Computer Science; Finance; Liberal Arts; Marketing; Mathematics. **Benefits:** Dental Insurance; Disability Coverage; Life Insurance; Medical Insurance; Profit Sharing; Savings Plan; Tuition Assistance. **Corporate headquarters location:** This Location. **Listed on:** New York Stock Exchange. **Number of employees nationwide:** 800.

PALMETTO CASUALTY INSURANCE
P.O. Box 2124, West Columbia SC 29171. 803/796-6700x200. **Contact:** George Bailey, Personnel. **Description:** Provides a variety of insurance products, including: automotive, mobile home, homeowner, general liability, and inland marine.

THE SEIBELS BRUCE INSURANCE GROUP, INC.
1501 Lady Street, P.O. Box One, Columbia SC 29202. 803/748-2000. **Contact:** Alexis Stewart, Human Resources. **Description:** The Seibels Bruce Insurance Group, Inc. is the parent company of South Carolina Insurance Company (SCIC) and its wholly-owned subsidiaries. Founded in 1869, South Carolina Insurance performs servicing carrier activities for several large state and federal insurance facilities. MGA services are also performed for a large non-affiliated insurance company. SCIC consists of a group of multiline property and casualty insurance companies and associated companies with headquarters in South Carolina and Kentucky. The underwriting activities are primarily conducted in North Carolina, South Carolina, Kentucky, Georgia and Tennessee by offering insurance products through independent insurance agents. **Corporate headquarters location:** This Location. **Subsidiaries include:** Consolidated American Insurance Company; Catawba Insurance Company; Kentucky Insurance Company; Seibels, Bruce & Company; South Carolina Insurance Company; Agency Specialty of Kentucky, Inc.; Agency Specialty, Inc.; Investors National Life Insurance Company of South Carolina; Policy Finance Company; Forest Lake Travel Service, Inc.; FLT Plus, Inc.; Seibels Bruce Service Corporation. **Listed on:** NASDAQ. **Number of employees at this location:** 423.

For more information on career opportunities in insurance:

Associations

ALLIANCE OF AMERICAN INSURERS
1501 Woodfield Road, Suite 400 West, Schaumburg IL 60173-4980. 847/330-8500.

HEALTH INSURANCE ASSOCIATION OF AMERICA
555 13th Street North, Suite 600E, Washington DC 20004. 202/824-1600.

INSURANCE INFORMATION INSTITUTE
110 William Street, 24th Floor, New York NY 10038. 212/669-9200. Provides informational products on property and casualty insurance.

SOCIETY OF ACTUARIES
475 North Martingale Road, Suite 800, Schaumburg IL 60173-2226. 847/706-3500.

Directories

INSURANCE ALMANAC
Underwriter Printing and Publishing Company, 50 East Palisade Avenue, Englewood NJ 07631. 201/569-8808. Hardcover annual, 639 pages, $115. Available at libraries.

INSURANCE MARKET PLACE
Rough Notes Company, Inc., P.O. Box 564, Indianapolis IN 46206. 317/634-1541.

INSURANCE PHONE BOOK AND DIRECTORY
Reed Reference Publishing, 121 Chanlon Road, New Providence NJ 07974. 800/521-8110. $89.95, new editions available every other year. Also available at libraries.

NATIONAL DIRECTORY OF HEALTH MAINTENANCE ORGANIZATIONS
Group Health Association of America, 1129 20th Street NW, Suite 600, Washington DC 20036. 202/778-3200.

Magazines

BEST'S REVIEW
A.M. Best Company, A.M. Best Road, Oldwick NJ 08858-9988. 908/439-2200. Monthly.

INSURANCE JOURNAL
Wells Publishing, 9191 Towne Centre Drive, Suite 550, San Diego, CA 92122-1231 619/455-7717. A biweekly magazine covering the insurance industry. Subscription: $78 per year, $3 for a single issue.

INSURANCE TIMES
M & S Communications, 20 Park Plaza, Suite 1101, Boston MA 02116. 617/292-7117. A regional biweekly insurance newspaper for insurance professionals.

LEGAL SERVICES

The number of people working in the legal services field has exploded since the early '70s. According to a 1969 survey by the Bureau of Labor Statistics (BLS), there were 387,000 workers in legal services. Today, that number is well over 1 million. The glut of lawyers has led to tremendous competition in the legal profession. Law firms are laying off associates and firing unproductive partners. Graduates of prestigious law schools face tough competition for jobs, but for the top graduates, the offers will be there. According to Jon Sargent, an economist for the Office of Economic Growth at the BLS, some jobseekers looking to break into this industry may need to look outside the mainstream legal services industry: nonprofit companies, government positions, or law firms in smaller communities.

Paralegals have carved out a niche for themselves and continue to be the fastest-growing profession in legal services. "Paralegals have become a cost-effective way to provide legal services in many cases," says Sargent, referring to the realization by many employers that paralegals can do many of the same jobs as associates, at a much lower cost.

North Carolina

BROOKS, PIERCE, McLENDON, HUMPHREY & LEONARD
P.O. Box 2600, Greensboro NC 27420. 910/373-8850. **Contact:** Mr. S.L. Rodenbough, Recruiting. **Description:** Brooks, Pierce, McLendon, Humphrey & Leonard is a corporate law firm. **Common positions include:** Attorney. **Number of employees at this location:** 100.

PARKER POE ADAMS & BERNSTEIN
2500 Charlotte Plaza, Charlotte NC 28244. 704/372-9000. **Contact:** JoAnn Cenon, Personnel Manager. **Description:** A legal services firm. **Corporate headquarters location:** This Location.

PERRY, PERRY AND PERRY
518 Plaza Boulevard, Kinston NC 28501. 919/523-5107. **Contact:** Betty Worthington, Attorney/Office Manager. **Description:** A law firm. **Number of employees at this location:** 500.

Note: Because addresses and telephone numbers of smaller companies change rapidly, we recommend you call each company to verify the information below before inquiring about job opportunities. Mass mailings are not recommended.

Additional employers with under 250 employees:

LEGAL SERVICES

Moore & Van Allen
NationsBank Corporate Center 100, Charlotte NC 28202. 704/331-1000.

Adams Kleemeier Hagan
P.O. Box 3463, Greensboro NC 27402-3463. 910/373-1600.

Smith Anderson Blount
P.O. Box 2611, Raleigh NC 27602-2611. 919/821-1220.

Bell Seltzer Park & Gibson
P.O. Box 34009, Charlotte NC 28234-4009. 704/331-6000.

Kennedy Covington
100 North Street Suite 4200, Charlotte NC 28202. 704/331-7400.

Poyner & Spruill
P.O. Box 10096, Raleigh NC 27605-0096. 919/783-6400.

Petree Stockton LLP
1001 W 4th St, Winston-Salem NC 27101-2410. 910/607-7300.

Petree Stockton LLP
301 S College St, Charlotte
NC 28202-6000. 704/338-
5000.

Hunton & Williams
P.O. Box 109, Raleigh NC

27602-0109. 919/899-
3000.

Cranfill Sumner & Hartzog
225 Hillsborough St, Suite
300, Raleigh NC 27603-
1766. 919/828-5100.

Maupin Taylor Ellis & Adams
P.O. Box 19764, Raleigh NC
27619-9764. 919/981-
4000.

Smith Helms Mulliss
P.O. Box 31247, Charlotte
NC 28231-1247. 704/343-
2000.

South Carolina

NEXSEN PRUET JACOBS & POLLARD
P.O. Drawer 2426, Columbia SC 29202. 803/771-8900. **Contact:** Mr. Barry Keith, Director of Personnel. **Description:** A legal services firm. **Corporate headquarters location:** This Location.

SINKLER & BOYD
P.O. Box 11889, Columbia SC 29211. 803/779-3080. **Contact:** Lisa Palmer, Office Manager. **Description:** A law firm specializing in several areas including bankruptcy and real estate law.

TURNER PADGET GRAHAM & LANEY
P.O. Box 1473, Columbia SC 29202-1473. 803/254-2200. **Contact:** Sylvia Brown, Personnel Manager. **Description:** A legal services firm.

Note: Because addresses and telephone numbers of smaller companies change rapidly, we recommend you call each company to verify the information below before inquiring about job opportunities. Mass mailings are not recommended.

Additional employers with under 250 employees:

LEGAL SERVICES

Holmes & Thomson LLP
P.O. Box 858, Charleston SC
29402 803/723-2000.

Ness Motley Loadholt
2202 Jackson St, Barnwell
SC 29812. 803/259-9900.

Haynsworth Marion McKay
P.O. Box 2048, Greenville
SC 29602-2048. 864/240-
3200.

Young Clement Rivers & Tisdale
P.O. Box 993, Charleston SC

29402-0993. 803/577-
4000.

Leatherwood Walker Todd & Mann
1451 E Main St, Spartanburg
SC 29307-2245. 864/582-
4365.

For more information on career opportunities in legal services:

Associations

AMERICAN BAR ASSOCIATION
750 North Lake Shore Drive, Chicago IL
60611. 312/988-5000.

FEDERAL BAR ASSOCIATION
1815 H. Street NW, Suite 408, Washington
DC 20006-3697. 202/638-0252.

NATIONAL ASSOCIATION OF LEGAL ASSISTANTS
1516 South Boston, Suite 200, Tulsa OK
74119-4013. 918/587-6828. An
educational association. Offers the National

Voluntary Association Exam. Memberships
are available.

NATIONAL FEDERATION OF PARALEGAL ASSOCIATIONS
P.O. Box 33108, Kansas City MO 64114-
0108. 816/941-4000. World Wide Web
address: http://www.paralegals.org. Offers
magazines, seminars, and Internet job
listings.

NATIONAL PARALEGAL ASSOCIATION
P.O. Box 629, 6186 Honey Hollow Road,
Doylestown PA 18901. 215/297-8333.

MANUFACTURING AND WHOLESALING: MISCELLANEOUS CONSUMER

The consumer goods manufacturing industry is more than just one industry. To generally forecast about the entire range of companies that make products for consumers is risky, since so much can differ from one segment to the next. In fact, many consumer manufacturers are listed under more specific categories in this book.

With that said, some general statements can be made about the outlook for this gigantic field. Over the long term, many analysts are optimistic. An improved economy, as well as an aging baby boom generation with growing disposable income, should provide stimulus for increases in personal durables. Continued growth in international trade should also point to a favorable long-term outlook for household consumer durables.

U.S. exports of household durables should also expand as trade barriers drop. The North American Free Trade Agreement (NAFTA), passed in early 1994, will give U.S. manufacturers even greater access to what is already the second-largest export market for U.S. household durables. Other trade agreements may follow with several Latin American countries. Potential markets in Eastern Europe and independent states of the former Soviet Union may also open.

North Carolina

ATHENS FURNITURE COMPANY
P.O. Box 431, Statesville NC 28687. 704/873-6312. **Contact:** Connie Pinion, Human Resources Manager. **Description:** Athen Furniture Company manufactures wood household furniture. **Number of employees at this location:** 500.

BASSETT FURNITURE INDUSTRIES, INC.
P.O. Box 47, Newton NC 28658. 704/464-3354. **Contact:** Human Resources. **Description:** Manufactures and sells a full line of furniture for the home, such as bedroom and dining suites, accent pieces, occasional tables, wall and entertainment units, upholstered sofas, chairs and love seats, recliners, and mattresses and box springs. **Corporate headquarters location:** Bassett VA. **Number of employees nationwide:** 7,800.

C.M./CRAFTMARK
P.O. Box 617, Highway 321 North, Maiden NC 28650. 704/428-9978. **Contact:** Ken Lawing, Human Resources Manager. **Description:** C.M./Craftmark manufactures several types of household furniture with the exception of bedroom and dining room furniture.

CARROWAY COMPANY
7310 U.S. Highway 311 South, Sophia NC 27350. 910/861-4169. **Contact:** Ruth Powell, Personnel. **Description:** A manufacturer of upholstered household furniture. Products include couches and love seats. Carroway Company has three subsidiaries located in Mississippi: Washington Furniture Manufacturing Company, Inc. and National Furniture Manufacturing Company, Inc., which are both furniture manufacturers; and Buckhorn Carriers, Inc., which is a trucking company.

CARSON INC.
P.O. Box 150, High Point NC 27261. 910/887-3544. **Contact:** Kathy Proctor, Human Resources Manager. **Description:** Carson Inc. manufactures upholstered furniture. The company wholesales its furniture to retail stores. **Corporate headquarters location:** This Location.

CARSON INC.
4200 Cheyenne Drive, Archdale NC 27263. 910/431-1101. **Contact:** Human Resources. **Description:** Carson Inc. manufactures upholstered furniture. The company wholesales its furniture to retail stores. **NOTE:** Please send resumes to the corporate headquarters location: Carson Inc., P.O. Box 150, High Point, NC 27261. 910/887-3544. Attention: Kathy Proctor, Human Resources Manager. **Corporate headquarters location:** High Point NC.

CLAYTON MARCUS COMPANY, INC.
P.O. Box 100, Hickory NC 28603. 704/495-2200. **Contact:** Larry Chapman, Director/Human Resources. **Description:** A furniture upholsterer. The parent company, LADD Furniture Corporation, is a residential wood, metal, and upholstered furniture designer and manufacturer, with 26 manufacturing facilities in 10 states and Mexico. LADD markets its broad line of residential and contract furniture under the major brand names American Drew, American of Martinsville, Barclay, Brown Jordan, Clayton Marcus, Daystrom, Design Horizons, Fournier, LADD Home Theatre, Lea, Pennsylvania House, and Pilliod. The company distributes these products both domestically and, through LADD International, worldwide. LADD also owns and operates two support companies, Lea Lumber & Plywood and LADD Transportation. **Common positions include:** Blue-Collar Worker Supervisor; Clerical Supervisor; Computer Operator; Computer Programmer; Cost Estimator; Customer Service Representative; Department Manager; Designer; Draftsperson; Electrical/Electronics Engineer; Human Resources Specialist; Industrial Engineer; Inspector/Tester/Grader; Marketing/Advertising/PR Manager; Order Clerk; Purchasing Agent and Manager; Quality Control Supervisor; Receptionist; Secretary; Services Sales Representative; Stock Clerk; Truck Driver; Typist/Word Processor. **Educational backgrounds include:** Accounting; Art/Design; Business Administration; Computer Science; Engineering; Finance; Liberal Arts; Marketing. **Benefits:** Dental Insurance; Disability Coverage; Employee Discounts; Life Insurance; Medical Insurance; Pension Plan; Savings Plan; Tuition Assistance. **Special Programs:** Internships. **Other U.S. locations:** High Point NC. **Parent company:** LADD Furniture Corporation. **Operations at this facility include:** Administration; Divisional Headquarters; Manufacturing; Research and Development; Sales. **Listed on:** NASDAQ. **Number of employees at this location:** 635.

DREXEL HERITAGE FURNITURE #2
361 Blue Ridge Street, Marion NC 28752. 704/652-2535. **Fax:** 704/652-2535x249. **Contact:** Teresa Pope, Human Resources Manager. **Description:** A furniture manufacturer. **Common positions include:** Computer Operator; Department Manager; Electrical/Electronics Engineer; Electrician; Industrial Engineer; Machinist; Mechanical Engineer; Payroll Clerk; Quality Control Supervisor; Receptionist; Registered Nurse; Secretary; Stock Clerk; Typist/Word Processor. **Educational backgrounds include:** Art/Design; Business Administration; Engineering; Mathematics. **Benefits:** Dental Insurance; Disability Coverage; Employee Discounts; Life Insurance; Medical Insurance; Pension Plan; Profit Sharing; Savings Plan; Tuition Assistance. **Special Programs:** Apprenticeships; Internships; Training Programs. **Corporate headquarters location:** Drexel NC. **Parent company:** Masco Corporation (Taylor, MI). **Operations at this facility include:** Divisional Headquarters; Manufacturing. **Listed on:** New York Stock Exchange. **Number of employees at this location:** 516. **Number of employees nationwide:** 5,000.

DURACELL U.S.A.
305 Highway 64 East, Lexington NC 27292. 704/242-6000. **Contact:** Russ Johnson, Human Resources Manager. **Description:** Duracell is a maker of a line of batteries sold worldwide under the Duracell trademark. The company also markets and distributes its products with extensive operations in the U.S., Europe, Mexico, South America, the Middle East, and the Pacific Rim. Battery types include alkaline (which accounts for most business), zinc, rechargeable, and lithium. The company also manufactures batteries used in hearing aids and photographic and communications equipment. A subsidiary conducts marketing operations for a line of lighting products under the Durabeam name. Manufacturing facilities are located in the United States, Canada, Mexico, the United Kingdom, and Belgium. The company also plans to build manufacturing plants in China and India. **Common positions include:** Accountant/Auditor; Buyer; Chemical Engineer; Chemist; Electrical/Electronics Engineer; Human Resources Specialist; Industrial Engineer; Mechanical Engineer; Purchasing Agent and Manager. **Educational backgrounds include:** Chemistry;

Computer Science; Engineering; Mathematics. **Benefits:** Daycare Assistance; Dental Insurance; Disability Coverage; Employee Discounts; Life Insurance; Medical Insurance; Pension Plan; Savings Plan; Stock Option; Tuition Assistance. **Special Programs:** Internships. **Corporate headquarters location:** Bethel CT. **Other U.S. locations:** La Grange GA; Lancaster SC; Cleveland TN. **Operations at this facility include:** Manufacturing. **Listed on:** New York Stock Exchange. **Number of employees worldwide:** 7,700.

FRIGIDAIRE COMPANY
4411 West Vernon Avenue, Kinston NC 28501. 919/527-5100. **Contact:** Tony Smits, Human Resources. **Description:** Manufactures household appliances, including laundry machines, ranges, dishwashers, refrigerators, freezers, air conditioners, and disposers. AB Electrolux, the parent company, has four business areas: Household Appliances, Commercial Appliances, Outdoor Products, and Industrial Products. The main operation in Household Appliances is white goods, which account for 70 percent of sales. Other operations include floor-care products, absorption refrigerators for caravans and hotel rooms, room air-conditioners, and sewing machines, as well as kitchen and bathroom cabinets. The main operations in Commercial Appliances are food-service equipment for restaurants and institutions, and equipment for such applications as apartment-house laundry rooms and commercial laundries. These product areas account for almost 75 percent of sales. Other operations include refrigeration equipment and freezers for shops and supermarkets, as well as vacuum cleaners and wet/dry cleaners for commercial use. Outdoor Products include garden equipment, chain saws, and other equipment for forestry operations. Garden equipment refers to portable products such as lawn trimmers and leaf blowers, as well as lawn mowers and garden tractors. Industrial Products comprise the group's second largest business area. Over 40 percent of sales consist of profiles and other half-finished goods in aluminum, manufactured by Granges. Other main operations include car safety belts and other products for personal safety in cars as well as materials-handling equipment. **Benefits:** Dental Insurance; Disability Coverage; Employee Discounts; Life Insurance; Medical Insurance; Pension Plan; Retirement Plan; Tuition Assistance. **Corporate headquarters location:** Dublin OH. **Parent company:** AB Electrolux.

HAMMARY FURNITURE COMPANY
P.O. Box 760, Lenoir NC 28645. 704/728-3231. **Contact:** Larry Herman, Director of Human Resources. **Description:** A furniture manufacturer. Products include tables, wall units, couches, love seats, and chairs.

HAWORTH MYRTLE-MUELLER
P.O. Box 2490, High Point NC 27261. 910/885-4021. **Contact:** Bob Allen, Director of Human Resources. **Description:** A manufacturer of desks.

HENREDON FURNITURE INDUSTRIES, INC.
P.O. Box 110, High Point NC 27261. 910/885-9141. **Contact:** Miss Tiki Wittenburg, Manager of Human Resources. **Description:** A furniture manufacturer. **Corporate headquarters location:** Morganton NC. **Number of employees nationwide:** 2,000.

HENREDON FURNITURE INDUSTRIES, INC.
P.O. Box 70, Morganton NC 28680. 704/437-5261. **Contact:** Human Resources. **Description:** A furniture manufacturer. **Common positions include:** Accountant/Auditor; Advertising Clerk; Budget Analyst; Buyer; Computer Programmer; Computer Systems Analyst; Credit Manager; Customer Service Representative; Designer; Draftsperson; Electrical/Electronics Engineer; Electrician; Human Resources Specialist; Industrial Engineer; Industrial Production Manager; Licensed Practical Nurse; Management Trainee; Mechanical Engineer; Operations/Production Manager; Purchasing Agent and Manager; Quality Control Supervisor; Transportation/Traffic Specialist; Travel Agent. **Educational backgrounds include:** Accounting; Art/Design; Business Administration; Engineering; Finance; Marketing. **Benefits:** 401K; Bonus Award/Plan; Dental Insurance; Disability Coverage; Employee Discounts; Life Insurance; Medical Insurance; Pension Plan; Tuition Assistance. **Corporate headquarters location:** This Location. **Parent company:** Masco. **Operations at this facility include:** Administration; Divisional Headquarters; Manufacturing; Research and Development; Sales; Service. **Number of employees at this location:** 750. **Number of employees nationwide:** 2,000.

HICKORY CHAIR COMPANY
P.O. Box 2147, Hickory NC 28603. 704/328-1801. **Contact:** Mr. T.R. Doherty, Human Resources Director. **Description:** A manufacturer of 18th-century style furniture, since 1911. Hickory Chair's parent company is The Lane Company, and The Lane Company's parent company is listed on NYSE as Interco. **Common positions include:** Accountant/Auditor; Administrative Services Manager; Blue-Collar Worker

Supervisor; Budget Analyst; Buyer; Computer Programmer; Computer Systems Analyst; Customer Service Representative; Designer; Draftsperson; Electrician; Emergency Medical Technician; Financial Analyst; General Manager; Human Resources Specialist; Industrial Engineer; Industrial Production Manager; Management Trainee; Mechanical Engineer; Operations/Production Manager; Purchasing Agent and Manager; Quality Control Supervisor; Software Engineer. **Educational backgrounds include:** Accounting; Art/Design; Business Administration; Computer Science; Engineering; Finance; Marketing. **Benefits:** Dental Insurance; Disability Coverage; Employee Discounts; Life Insurance; Medical Insurance; Pension Plan; Profit Sharing; Savings Plan; Tuition Assistance. **Special Programs:** Internships; Training Programs. **Corporate headquarters location:** Altavista VA. **Parent company:** The Lane Company Inc. **Operations at this facility include:** Administration; Divisional Headquarters; Manufacturing; Sales. **Listed on:** New York Stock Exchange. **Number of employees at this location:** 1,000.

HICKORY HILL FURNITURE
501 Hoyle Street SW, Valdese NC 28690. 704/874-2124. **Contact:** John Greene, Manager of Human Resources. **Description:** Manufactures upholstered furniture.

HICKORY WHITE
P.O. Box 1600, High Point NC 27261. 910/885-1200. **Contact:** Jim Murry, Human Resources Manager. **Description:** Manufactures furniture and high-end case goods. **Corporate headquarters location:** Raleigh NC. **Parent company:** Sunstates Corporation.

HIGHLAND HOUSE FURNITURE
207 20th Street Southeast, Hickory NC 28602. 704/323-8600. **Contact:** David Barnes, Personnel Director. **Description:** A furniture manufacturer.

HOME CARE INDUSTRIES, INC.
P.O. Box 1148, Oxford NC 27565. 919/693-1002. **Contact:** Ruth Kozak. **Description:** Manufactures vacuum cleaner bags.

THE HON COMPANY
Route 8, Box 7576, Louisburg NC 27549. 919/496-5701. **Contact:** Larry Burns, Personnel Manager. **Description:** A manufacturer of wooden office furniture. **Common positions include:** Accountant/Auditor; Administrator; Blue-Collar Worker Supervisor; Customer Service Representative; Draftsperson; General Manager; Industrial Engineer; Operations/Production Manager; Purchasing Agent and Manager; Quality Control Supervisor. **Educational backgrounds include:** Business Administration. **Benefits:** Dental Insurance; Life Insurance; Medical Insurance; Pension Plan. **Corporate headquarters location:** Muscatine IA.

JOYNER MANUFACTURING
P.O. Box 688, Louisburg NC 27549. 919/496-5171. **Contact:** Carolyn Files, Personnel Manager. **Description:** A manufacturer of drawer components.

KING HICKORY FURNITURE
P.O. Box 1179, Hickory NC 28603. 704/322-6025. **Contact:** Clarice Spires, Human Resources Director. **Description:** Manufactures sofas, sleepers, love seats, settees, ottomans, and other furniture. All furniture has hardwood frames and hand-tied springs. The company offers over 600 types of fabric to choose from. Products are all produced in North Carolina and sold by dealers across the U.S.

KORN INDUSTRIES, INC.
P.O. Box 100, Sumter SC 29151. 803/778-5444. **Contact:** Human Resources. **Description:** Manufactures wood household furniture. **Number of employees at this location:** 500.

LA-Z-BOY CHAIR COMPANY
P.O. Box 698, Lincolnton NC 28093. 704/735-0441. **Contact:** Gary Deam, Human Resources Manager. **Description:** A manufacturer of upholstered seating and one of the nation's largest overall manufacturers of residential furniture. La-Z-Boy is best known for its upholstered recliner and dominates the marketplace for this class of product. The company has grown into a complete furniture resource for family rooms, living rooms, bedrooms, and dining rooms, usually retailing in a broad middle-price range, although certain products target higher-income purchasers. La-Z-Boy operates 24 plants in the United States and Canada, with its products being sold through over 10,000 retail locations. The company operates in five divisions. La-Z-Boy Residential produces stationary chairs, sofas and love seats, recliners, reclining sofas, sleeper sofas, and modular seating groups, which it sells in a national network of La-Z-Boy

proprietary stores, and in better-quality department stores, furniture stores, and regional furniture chains. La-Z-Boy Canada manufactures residential seating and markets La-Z-Boy Residential products in Canada. The company is also initiating a Canadian network of La-Z-Boy proprietary retail stores. Hammary produces occasional tables, living room cabinets, wall entertainment units, and upholstered furniture sold in quality furniture and department stores, as well as CompaTables occasional tables, which are featured in La-Z-Boy proprietary stores. Kincaid makes solid-wood bedroom, dining room, and occasional furniture sold through in-store Kincaid Galleries, select La-Z-Boy Furniture Galleries stores, and better-quality stores nationally. La-Z-Boy Contract Furniture Group includes La-Z-Boy Business Furniture, La-Z-Boy Healthcare Furniture (hospital chairs, recliners, and special mobile recliners, marketed through contract dealers and medical sales companies), and La-Z-Boy Hospitality Furniture (specially engineered La-Z-Boy recliners that are sold directly to major hotel and motel chains and through hospitality sales companies. **Corporate headquarters location:** Monroe MI. **Number of employees nationwide:** 9,370.

LADD FURNITURE, INC.
One Plaza Center, P.O. Box HP3, High Point NC 27261-1500. 910/889-0333. **Fax:** 910/888-6446. **Contact:** Vic Dyer, Vice President of Human Resources. **Description:** A residential wood, metal, and upholstered furniture designer, manufacturer, and seller, with 26 manufacturing facilities in 10 states and Mexico. LADD markets its broad line of residential and contract furniture under the major brand names American Drew, American of Martinsville, Barclay, Brown Jordan, Clayton Marcus, Daystrom, Design Horizons, Fournier, LADD Home Theatre, Lea, Pennsylvania House, and Pilliod. The company distributes these products both domestically and, through LADD international, worldwide. LADD also owns and operates two support companies, Lea Lumber & Plywood and LADD Transportation. **Corporate headquarters location:** This Location. **Listed on:** NASDAQ. **Number of employees nationwide:** 7,900.

LEVOLOR HOME FASHIONS
4110 Premier Drive, High Point NC 27265. 910/812-8181. **Contact:** Joe Ketter, Human Resources Director. **Description:** Manufactures drapery hardware and window blinds and shades.

LEXINGTON HICKORYCRAFT PLANT
P.O. Box 1733, Hickory NC 28603. 704/322-5995. **Contact:** Bill McBrayer, Director of Human Resources. **Description:** A manufacturer of dining room and bedroom furniture. In 1995, the company began expanding its operations to include upholstery.

MILLER DESK INC.
1212 Lincoln Drive, High Point NC 27261. 910/886-7061. **Contact:** David Pugh, Director of Human Resources. **Description:** A manufacturer of case goods, office furniture, and both ergonomic and traditional seating. The company has three manufacturing plants in High Point, North Carolina, and sales representatives across the United States.

RAUCH INDUSTRIES, INC.
P.O. Box 609, Gastonia NC 28053-0609. 704/867-5333. **Fax:** 704/864-2081. **Contact:** Carolyn Barnes, Personnel Manager. **Description:** Rauch Industries is a manufacturer and importer of Christmas and holiday decorations. **Common positions include:** Blue-Collar Worker Supervisor; Buyer; Customer Service Representative; Electrical/Electronics Engineer. **Educational backgrounds include:** Accounting; Business Administration; Engineering. **Benefits:** 401K; Dental Insurance; Disability Coverage; Life Insurance; Medical Insurance; Profit Sharing; Savings Plan. **Corporate headquarters location:** This Location. **Operations at this facility include:** Administration; Manufacturing; Research and Development; Sales; Service. **Listed on:** American Stock Exchange; NASDAQ; New York Stock Exchange. **Number of employees at this location:** 850. **Number of employees nationwide:** 1,000.

ST. TIMOTHY CHAIR COMPANY
P.O. Box 2427, Hickory NC 28603. 704/322-7125. **Contact:** Jerry Duckworth, Personnel Manager. **Description:** A manufacturer of case goods and chairs. St. Timothy Chair Company is a division of Classic Leather, and produces Classic Leather's residential line.

SOUTHERN FURNITURE COMPANY
1099 Second Avenue Place SE, Conover NC 28613. 704/464-0311. **Contact:** Mr. Gail Hall, Personnel and Human Resources Director. **Description:** A manufacturer of upholstery goods and case goods. The company has plants located throughout North Carolina. This is Southern Furniture's main location.

STEELCASE
P.O. Box 1389, Fletcher NC 28732. 704/684-2241. **Contact:** Dicky Featherstone, Director of Human Resources. **Description:** A manufacturer of wood office furniture. **Corporate headquarters location:** Grand Rapids MI.

STONEVILLE FURNITURE COMPANY
P.O. Box 15, Stoneville NC 27048. 910/573-3751. **Contact:** Ken Langford, Human Resources Director. **Description:** A manufacturer of dining room tables and chairs. Stoneville Furniture Company produces only metal furniture. The company is owned by Intex, which has locations in Michigan, California, and Hong Kong.

ZEMA CORPORATION
P.O. Box 12803, Research Triangle Park NC 27709. 919/851-9494. **Fax:** 919/859-2170. **Contact:** Dorothy Jackson, Human Resources Director. **Description:** Zema Corporation is a formulator, manufacturer, and supplier of Zema brand and Pulvex brand pet health care and grooming products. Major product categories include shampoos, dip concentrates, collars, flea traps, animal and surface sprays, vitamins, and de-wormers. Zema's products are primarily sold under its own brand names and, to a lesser extent, on a private label basis. Zema holds an inventory of 20 EPA product registrations allowing for the sale of most forms of ectoparasite products for the treatment of fleas and ticks on dogs and cats. These registrations, coupled with a 30,000 square foot production plant and distribution center, provide Zema with the ability to offer a complete product line and full-service turn-key program for national retailers. Zema markets its products to approximately 500 accounts. Customers represent the full range of pet product distributors, including specialty pet distributors; mass merchandisers; warehouse clubs; grocery, drug, and discount chains; export accounts; and private label accounts. **Parent company:** Agri-Nutrition Group.

Note: Because addresses and telephone numbers of smaller companies change rapidly, we recommend you call each company to verify the information below before inquiring about job opportunities. Mass mailings are not recommended.

Additional employers with under 250 employees:

WOOD KITCHEN CABINETS

IXL Furniture Co.
1268 Toxey Rd, Elizabeth City NC 27909-2917. 919/338-3322.

Ultra Craft Co.
6163 Old 421 Rd, Liberty NC 27298-8283. 910/622-4281.

HOUSEHOLD FURNITURE

Baker Furniture Co.
521 Milling Rd, Mocksville NC 27028-2855. 704/634-2183.

Bassett Furniture Industries
1010 Salisbury Rd, Statesville NC 28677-6211. 704/872-5691.

Boling Co.
108 W 3rd St, Siler City NC 27344-3454. 910/663-2400.

Bush Industries Inc.
2601 Greengate Dr, Greensboro NC 27406-5244. 910/275-6171.

Chaircraft
Hwy 127 N, Hickory NC 28601. 704/495-8291.

Charleston Forge Inc.
200 Industrial Park Dr, Boone NC 28607-3975. 704/264-0100.

Component Concepts
200 Mason Way, Thomasville NC 27360-4923. 910/475-1331.

Craftique Inc.
Old US Highway 70 W, Mebane NC 27302. 910/563-1212.

CTH-Sherrill Occasional
Hwy 70 S E, Hickory NC 28601. 704/328-5241.

Grand Manor Furniture
929 Harrisburg Dr SW, Lenoir NC 28645-6126. 704/758-5521.

H&H Furniture Co.
State Hwy 220 S, Seagrove NC 27341. 910/873-7520.

Hammary Furniture/Plant 14
175 N Main St, Granite Falls NC 28630-1329. 704/726-3400.

Hickory Chair Co.
1902 Emmanual Church Rd, Conover NC 28613-9132. 704/465-3650.

Kincaid Furniture Co. Inc.
Rocky Rd, Lenoir NC 28645. 704/754-0574.

Kolcraft of NC
10832 State Highway 211 E, Aberdeen NC 28315. 910/944-9345.

L&M Frame Co.
205 5th Ave SW, Taylorsville NC 28681-3024. 704/632-6093.

Lineage Home Furnishings
Altapass Rd, Spruce Pine NC 28777. 704/765-1079.

Lineage Home Furnishings
4000 Lineage Ct, High Point NC 27265-8125. 910/454-6688.

Michael Thomas Furniture
100 E Newberry Ave, Liberty NC 27298. 910/622-3075.

Orbit Industries Inc.
RR 16, Box 349, Statesville NC 28677-9816. 704/872-8953.

Weiman Co.
P.O. Box 217, Ramseur NC 27316-0217. 910/824-2324.

**West Jefferson Wood
Products**
301 Locust St, W Jefferson
NC 28694-9701. 910/246-
7121.

Alexvale Furniture/Plant 3
RR 1, Hickory NC 28602-
9801. 704/462-2011.

Baker Furniture Co.
2219 Shore St, High Point
NC 27263-2511. 910/431-
9115.

Bradington-Young Inc.
920 E 1st St, Cherryville NC
28021-2935. 704/435-
5881.

Bradington-Young Inc.
4040 10th Avenue Dr SW,
Hickory NC 28602-4535.
704/328-9172.

Braxton Culler Inc.
1950 W Green Dr, High Point
NC 27260-1666. 910/885-
9186.

Classic Gallery Inc.
2009 Fulton Pl, High Point
NC 27263-1705. 910/886-
4191.

Claude Gable Co. Inc.
322 Fraley Rd, High Point NC
27263-1714. 910/883-
1351.

Conover Chair Co. Inc.
210 4th St SW, Conover NC
28613-2628. 704/464-
0251.

CR Laine Furniture Co.
2829 US Highway 70 SW,
Hickory NC 28602-4630.
704/328-1831.

**Drexel Heritage
Furniture/Plant 37**
741 W Ward Ave, High Point
NC 27260-1645. 910/812-
4430.

Drexel Heritage Furniture
109 E Fleming Dr, Morganton
NC 28655-3675. 704/438-
5767.

Drexel Heritage Furniture
230 Best St, Shelby NC
28150-3704. 704/482-
3871.

EJ Victor
110 Wamsutta Mill Rd,
Morganton NC 28655-5551.
704/437-1991.

Henredon Furniture Industries
109 Mount View Dr, Mount
Airy NC 27030-2454.
910/789-9141.

J. Royale Furniture Inc.
1610 Debra Herman Rd,
Conover NC 28613-8205.
704/322-1262.

Key City Furniture Co.
503 C St, N Wilkesboro NC
28659-4327. 910/838-
4191.

Klaussner Furniture Industries
8425 Triad Dr, Greensboro
NC 27409-9018. 910/668-
7701.

Lancer Inc.
US Hwy 220 S, Star NC
27356. 910/428-2181.

Leathercraft Inc.
102 Hwy 70, Conover NC
28613. 704/322-3305.

McCreary Modern Inc.
2564 US Highway 321 S,
Newton NC 28658-9349.
704/464-6465.

Motioncraft
I-40 & Bethel Church Rd,
Morganton NC 28655.
704/437-2255.

North Hickory Furniture Co.
P.O. Box 759, Hickory NC
28603-0759. 704/328-
1841.

Pearson Co.
1420 Progress Ave, High
Point NC 27260-8319.
910/882-8135.

Pembrook Chair Corp.
2702 Heart Dr, Claremont
NC 28610. 704/459-2163.

Pilot Furniture Co.
2796 NC Highway 16 S,
Newton NC 28658-8207.
704/464-8780.

Precedent Furniture Inc.
1884 State Rd, Newton NC
28658. 704/465-0844.

Sherrill Furniture
P.O. Box 189, Hickory NC
28603-0189. 704/322-
2640.

Southwood Furniture Corp.
2860 Nathan St, Hickory NC
28602. 704/465-1776.

Spectrum Furniture Co.
2450 Coltrane Mill Rd, High
Point NC 27263-8907.
910/861-5643.

Taylor King Furniture Inc.
RR 3 Box 193, Taylorsville
NC 28681-9317. 704/632-
7731.

Temple Inc.
102 S 7th Avenue Ext,
Maiden NC 28650-1451.
704/428-8031.

Woodmark Originals
1920 Jarrell St, High Point
NC 27260-8812. 910/841-
4900.

Woodmark Originals
4015 Cheyenne Dr, Archdale
NC 27263-3240. 910/861-
5267.

Crown Leisure Products
RR 2 Box 6-6, Maxton NC
28364-9400. 910/844-
3011.

Wellington Hall Ltd.
RR 1, Lexington NC 27292-
9801. 704/249-4931.

MISC. FURNITURE AND FIXTURES

**Alexvale Hickory Fry
Furniture Inc.**
E US 64 Hwy, Taylorsville
NC 28681. 704/632-9404.

**American Martinsville
Casegoods**
101 S Main St, High Point
NC 27260-5239. 910/889-
9181.

BPI Inc.
520 Grace Church Rd,
Salisbury NC 28147-9690.
704/639-1274.

Dixie Furniture
P.O. Box 1008, Lexington
NC 27293-1008. 704/249-
5329.

Doxey Furniture Corp.
Hwy 211 E, Aberdeen NC
28315. 910/944-7101.

Emerson Leather
816 13th St NE, Hickory NC
28601-4100. 704/328-
1701.

King Arthur
401 Meacham Rd, Statesville
NC 28677-2975. 704/872-
0300.

Klaussner Furniture Industries
907 NC Hwy 49 S, Asheboro
NC 27203. 910/625-5100.

Leggett & Platt Inc.
Home Rd, Lexington NC
27292. 704/352-2111.

Lyon-Shaw Inc.
1538 Jake Alexander Blvd
W, Salisbury NC 28147-
1213. 704/636-8270.

Myrtle Desk Co.
801 Millis St, High Point NC
27260-7203. 910/885-
4021.

LAWN AND GARDEN TRACTORS AND RELATED EQUIPMENT

Jacobsen Textron
11524 Wilmar Blvd,
Charlotte NC 28273-6409.
704/588-5120.

POWER-DRIVEN HAND TOOLS

DML Industrial Products
620 23rd St NW, Hickory NC 28601. 704/322-4266.

HOUSEHOLD AUDIO AND VIDEO EQUIPMENT

Fujicone Inc.
100 Industrial Dr, Clinton NC 28328-9704. 910/592-0181.

WHOLESALE FURNITURE AND HOME FURNISHINGS

Custom Frame Work
1402 Prison Camp Rd, Newton NC 28658-9453. 704/464-9651.

Selig Manufacturing Co.
P.O. Box 469, Siler City NC 27344-0469. 910/742-4126.

Thayer Coggin Inc.
230 South Rd, High Point NC 27262-8153. 910/841-6000.

Alfred Williams & Co. Distributing
8541 Glenwood Ave, Raleigh NC 27612. 919/783-7730.

Claudia Home Fashions
13955 Browns Hill Rd, Stanfield NC 28163-8628. 704/888-0078.

Shaw Industries
1128 Old Greensboro Rd, Kernersville NC 27284-8411. 910/996-3943.

Orders Distributing Co.
2521 Noblin Rd, Raleigh NC 27604-2415. 919/878-3990.

PHOTOGRAPHIC EQUIPMENT AND SUPPLIES WHOLESALE

Young-Phillips Sales Co.
1312 Crossbeam Dr, Charlotte NC 28217-2800. 704/357-3093.

Eastman Kodak Co.
9101 Southern Pines Blvd, Charlotte NC 28273-5519. 704/522-7658.

HARDWARE WHOLESALE

Peter Meier Inc.
1215 S Park Dr, Kernersville NC 27284-3179. 910/996-7774.

SPORTING AND RECREATIONAL GOODS AND SUPPLIES WHOLESALE

Henry's Tackle
Highway 24, Morehead City NC 28557. 919/726-6186.

PAPER AND OFFICE SUPPLIES WHOLESALE

Sweet Paper Brokerage
3915 Beryl Rd, Raleigh NC 27607-5212. 919/821-8096.

Data Supplies Inc.
510 Corliss St, Greensboro NC 27406-5216. 910/271-6516.

Shade Allied Inc.
1901 Ashwood Ct, Greensboro NC 27455-3010. 910/282-0065.

Wesley Business Forms
315 S Westgate Dr, Suite B, Greensboro NC 27407-1631. 910/854-8309.

Associated Stationers
1400 Westinghouse Blvd, Charlotte NC 28273-6325. 704/588-3020.

South Carolina

AMERICAN YARD PRODUCTS, INC.
P.O. Box 1687, Orangeburg SC 29116. 803/536-3285. **Contact:** Wanda Hutto, Human Resources Manager. **Description:** American Yard Products, Inc. manufactures lawn- and garden-related equipment, including riding lawnmowers. **Number of employees nationwide:** 1,000.

ANCHOR CONTINENTAL, INC.
P.O. Drawer G, Columbia SC 29250. 803/799-8800. **Fax:** 803/376-5431. **Contact:** Sandra Rivers, Personnel Manager. **Description:** Anchor Continental, Inc. manufactures a variety of pressure-sensitive tape products. The company's products include duct tape and masking tape. **Common positions include:** Accountant/Auditor; Blue-Collar Worker Supervisor; Chemist; Computer Programmer; Controls Engineer; Customer Service Representative; Electrical/Electronics Engineer; Electrician; Human Resources Specialist; Industrial Engineer; Industrial Production Manager; Mechanical Engineer; Operations/Production Manager; Process Engineer; Purchasing Agent and Manager; Quality Control Supervisor; Sales Representative. **Educational backgrounds include:** Accounting; Business Administration; Chemistry; Engineering; Manufacturing Management; Marketing. **Benefits:** 401K; Dental Insurance; Disability Coverage; Employee Discounts; Life Insurance; Medical Insurance; Tuition Assistance. **Corporate headquarters location:** This Location. **Other U.S. locations:** Covington OH; Kingsport TN. **Subsidiaries include:** Three Sigma; Holliston Mills. **Operations at this facility include:** Administration; Manufacturing; Research and Development; Sales; Service. **Listed on:** Privately held. **Number of employees at this location:** 750. **Number of employees nationwide:** 1,400.

DELTA WOODSIDE INDUSTRIES, INC.
233 North Main Street, Suite 200, Greenville SC 29601. 864/232-8301. **Contact:** Jane Greer, Corporate Vice President. **Description:** Delta Woodside Industries, Inc. produces a wide selection of fitness equipment, textiles, fabrics, and apparel, and also spins yarn. The company acquired Nautilus International in 1993. **Subsidiaries include:** Apparel Marketing Corporation; Alchem Capital Corporation; Delta Merchandising, Inc. **Listed on:** New York Stock Exchange. **Number of employees nationwide:** 8,500.

ELLETT BROTHERS
267 Columbia Avenue, Chapin SC 80334-5371. 803/345-3751. **Contact:** Human Resources. **Description:** Ellett Brothers has distribution, product sourcing, and teleservicing operations at this location. Overall, Ellett Brothers is a manufacturer of leisure products whose product-line is focused on natural outdoor sports and related activities including hunting and shooting, marine, camping, and archery. **Corporate headquarters location:** This Location. **Listed on:** NASDAQ. **Number of employees nationwide:** 354.

FRIGIDAIRE COMPANY
101 Masters Boulevard, Anderson SC 29624. 864/224-5264. **Contact:** Rod Blough, Director of Human Resources. **Description:** Manufactures household appliances, including laundry machines, ranges, dishwashers, refrigerators, freezers, air conditioners, and disposers. AB Electrolux, the parent company, has four business areas: Household Appliances, Commercial Appliances, Outdoor Products, and Industrial Products. The main operation in Household Appliances is white goods, which account for 70 percent of sales. Other operations include floor-care products, absorption refrigerators for caravans and hotel rooms, room air-conditioners, and sewing machines, as well as kitchen and bathroom cabinets. The main operations in Commercial Appliances are food-service equipment for restaurants and institutions, and equipment for such applications as apartment-house laundry rooms and commercial laundries. These product areas account for almost 75 percent of sales. Other operations include refrigeration equipment and freezers for shops and supermarkets, as well as vacuum cleaners and wet/dry cleaners for commercial use. Outdoor Products include garden equipment, chain saws, and other equipment for forestry operations. Garden equipment refers to portable products such as lawn trimmers and leaf blowers, as well as lawn mowers and garden tractors. Industrial Products comprise the group's second largest business area. Over 40 percent of sales consist of profiles and other half-finished goods in aluminum, manufactured by Granges. Other main operations include car safety belts and other products for personal safety in cars as well as materials-handling equipment. **Benefits:** Dental Insurance; Disability Coverage; Employee Discounts; Life Insurance; Medical Insurance; Pension Plan; Retirement Plan; Tuition Assistance. **Corporate headquarters location:** Dublin OH. **Parent company:** AB Electrolux.

LA-Z-BOY CHAIR COMPANY
901 North Douglas Street, Florence SC 29501. 803/669-2431. **Contact:** Tommy Casey, Director of Human Resources. **Description:** A manufacturer of upholstered seating and one of the nation's largest overall manufacturers of residential furniture. La-Z-Boy is best known for its upholstered recliner and dominates the marketplace for this class of product. The company has grown into a complete furniture resource for family rooms, living rooms, bedrooms, and dining rooms, usually retailing in a broad middle-price range, although certain products target higher-income purchasers. La-Z-Boy operates 24 plants in the United States and Canada, with its products being sold through over 10,000 retail locations. The company operates in five divisions. La-Z-Boy Residential produces stationary chairs, sofas and love seats, recliners, reclining sofas, sleeper sofas, and modular seating groups, which it sells in a national network of La-Z-Boy proprietary stores, and in better-quality department stores, furniture stores, and regional furniture chains. La-Z-Boy Canada manufactures residential seating and markets La-Z-Boy Residential products in Canada. The company is also initiating a Canadian network of La-Z-Boy proprietary retail stores. Hammary produces occasional tables, living room cabinets, wall entertainment units, and upholstered furniture sold in quality furniture and department stores, as well as CompaTables occasional tables, which are featured in La-Z-Boy proprietary stores. Kincaid makes solid-wood bedroom, dining room, and occasional furniture sold through in-store Kincaid Galleries, select La-Z-Boy Furniture Galleries stores, and better-quality stores nationally. La-Z-Boy Contract Furniture Group includes La-Z-Boy Business Furniture, La-Z-Boy Healthcare Furniture (hospital chairs, recliners, and special mobile recliners, marketed through contract dealers and medical sales companies), and La-Z-Boy Hospitality Furniture (specially engineered La-Z-Boy recliners that are sold directly to major hotel and motel chains and through hospitality sales companies. **Corporate headquarters location:** Monroe MI. **Number of employees nationwide:** 9,370.

3M TAPE MANUFACTURING DIVISION
P.O. Box 6806, Greensville SC 29605. 864/277-8270. **Contact:** Wes Klinkhammer, Director of Human Resources. **Description:** This division manufactures tape. Overall, 3M manufactures products in three sectors: Industrial and Consumer; Information, Imaging, and Electronic; and Life Sciences. The Industrial and Consumer Sector includes a variety of products under brand names including 3M, Scotch, Post-it, Scotch-Brite, and Scotchgard. The Information, Imaging, and Electronic Sector is a

leader in several high-growth global industries, including telecommunications, electronics, electrical, imaging, and memory media. The Life Sciences Sector serves two broad market categories: health care, and traffic and personal safety. In the health care market, 3M is a leading provider of medical and surgical supplies, drug-delivery systems, and dental products; in traffic and personal safety, 3M is a leader in products for transportation safety, worker protection, vehicle and sign graphics, and out-of-home advertising. **Corporate headquarters location:** St. Paul MN. **Listed on:** Amsterdam Stock Exchange; Chicago Stock Exchange; Frankfurt Stock Exchange; New York Stock Exchange; Pacific Exchange; Paris Stock Exchange; Swiss Stock Exchange; Tokyo Stock Exchange. **Number of employees nationwide:** 85,000.

WILSON SPORTING GOODS COMPANY
206 Georgia Street, Fountain Inn SC 29644. 864/862-4416. **Fax:** 864/862-6150. **Contact:** Ken Clardy, Human Resources Manager. **Description:** This location manufactures tennis balls and racquetballs. Overall, Wilson Sporting Goods Company manufactures sports-related products for golf, tennis, and team sports. The company operates eight domestic manufacturing plants and 11 other operations located outside the continental limits of the United States. Wilson Sporting Goods Company has been affiliated with the NFL since 1941, has been the official baseball of the NCAA championships since 1986, and has been the official ball of many of professional baseball's minor leagues. The company also manufactures and supplies uniforms to the NFL, Major League Baseball, and the NBA, as well as many colleges, universities, and high schools throughout the United States. Since 1924, the company has maintained an "Advisory Staff" of famous sports personalities who field-test equipment and offer recommendations and suggestions on equipment improvements and changes to Wilson designers and research specialists. In 1989, Wilson was acquired by Amer Group, Ltd., an international, highly-diversified conglomerate also involved in the marketing of motor vehicles, paper, communications, and tobacco. **Common positions include:** Accountant/Auditor; Blue-Collar Worker Supervisor; Butcher; Chemical Engineer; Chemist; Draftsperson; Electrical/Electronics Engineer; Electrician; Financial Analyst; General Manager; Human Resources Specialist; Industrial Engineer; Mechanical Engineer; Operations/Production Manager; Purchasing Agent and Manager; Quality Control Supervisor. **Educational backgrounds include:** Communications; Liberal Arts. **Benefits:** 401K; Dental Insurance; Disability Coverage; Employee Discounts; Life Insurance; Medical Insurance; Pension Plan; Savings Plan; Tuition Assistance. **Corporate headquarters location:** Chicago IL. **Other U.S. locations:** Nationwide. **Parent company:** Amer Group, Ltd. (Helsinki, Finland). **Operations at this facility include:** Manufacturing. **Listed on:** Privately held. **Number of employees at this location:** 450. **Number of employees nationwide:** 4,500.

Note: Because addresses and telephone numbers of smaller companies change rapidly, we recommend you call each company to verify the information below before inquiring about job opportunities. Mass mailings are not recommended.

Additional employers with under 250 employees:

HOUSEHOLD FURNITURE

Carolina Furniture Works
406 Brooklyn St, Sumter SC 29150-5859. 803/775-6381.

MISC. FURNITURE AND FIXTURES

Kirsch
Highway 21 S, Orangeburg SC 29115. 803/536-5790.

HAND AND EDGE TOOLS

Stanley Tools
100 Stanley Rd, Cheraw SC 29520-3999. 803/537-9311.

SAW BLADES AND HAND SAWS

Ernst Winter & Son Inc.
100 Wilhelm Winter St, Travelers Rest SC 29690-2226. 864/834-4145.

International Knives & Saws Hannaco
P.O. Box 100535, Florence SC 29501-0535. 803/662-6345.

JEWELRY, SILVERWARE, AND PLATED WARE

OC Tanner Co.
125 Woodlands W, Columbia SC 29223-3378. 803/699-9747.

TOYS AND SPORTING GOODS

Dunlop-Slazenger Corp.
728 N Pleasantburg Dr, Greenville SC 29607-1623. 864/241-2200.

True Temper/Sports Division
150 True Temper Dr, Seneca SC 29678. 864/882-5947.

OFFICE AND ART SUPPLIES

Capital Imaging Co.
2745 W 5th North St, Summerville SC 29483-9605. 803/871-6084.

BROOMS AND BRUSHES

O'Dell Mop & Broom Co.
Indian Mound Rd, Ware
Shoals SC 29692. 864/861-
2222.

WHOLESALE FURNITURE AND HOME FURNISHINGS

Wright Line Inc.
16 Glenhawk Loop, Irmo SC
29063-8419. 803/732-
4755.

Carolina Contract Window Coverings
224 Trade St, Greer SC
29651-3447. 864/879-
1925.

Nationwide Flooring
685 Coleman Blvd, Mount
Pleasant SC 29464-4017.
803/884-5238.

Orders Distributing Co.
501 Congaree Rd, Greenville
SC 29607-3515. 864/288-
4220.

PHOTOGRAPHIC EQUIPMENT AND SUPPLIES WHOLESALE

Worldwide Camera
2060 Sam Rittenberg Blvd
Unit, Charleston SC 29407-
4616. 803/766-2752.

WHOLESALE OF ELECTRICAL APPLIANCES, TELEVISIONS, AND RADIOS

Dynair Industries
2532 Oscar Johnson Dr,
Charleston SC 29405-6869.
803/554-8105.

HARDWARE WHOLESALE

Delavan Inc.
P.O. Box 969, Bamberg SC
29003. 803/245-4347.

SLS Systems Ltd. Bolt & Nut
7374 Peppermill Pky,
Charleston SC 29418-7412.
803/552-6800.

Welco Supply
1508 Whitehall Rd, Anderson
SC 29625-1916. 864/225-
2537.

SPORTING AND RECREATIONAL GOODS AND SUPPLIES WHOLESALE

FCS Golf Systems
1 E Main St, Greenville SC
29611-4311. 864/271-
0201.

TOYS AND HOBBY PRODUCTS WHOLESALE

American Importers of SC
P.O. Box 308, Rowesville SC
29133-0308. 803/534-
8221.

PAPER AND OFFICE SUPPLIES WHOLESALE

Paper Stock Dealers Inc.
3800 Forest Dr, Columbia
SC 29204-4146. 803/738-
1900.

McBee Systems
4 Carriage Ln, Suite 400F,
Charleston SC 29407-6051.
803/766-3790.

For more information on career opportunities in consumer manufacturing and wholesaling:

Associations

ASSOCIATION FOR MANUFACTURING TECHNOLOGY
7901 Westpark Drive, McLean VA 22102.
703/893-2900. Offers research services.

ASSOCIATION OF HOME APPLIANCE MANUFACTURERS
20 North Wacker Drive, Chicago IL 60606.
312/984-5800.

NATIONAL ASSOCIATION OF MANUFACTURERS
1331 Pennsylvania Avenue NW, Suite
1500, Washington DC 20004. 202/637-
3000. A lobbying association for
manufacturers.

NATIONAL HOUSEWARES MANUFACTURERS ASSOCIATION
6400 Schafer Court, Suite 650, Rosemont
IL 60018. 847/292-4200. Offers shipping
discounts and other services.

SOCIETY OF MANUFACTURING ENGINEERS
P.O. Box 930, One SME Drive, Dearborn MI
48121. 313/271-1500. Offers educational
events and educational materials on
manufacturing.

Directories

APPLIANCE MANUFACTURER ANNUAL DIRECTORY
Appliance Manufacturer, 5900 Harper Road,
Suite 105, Solon OH 44139. 216/349-
3060. $25.00.

HOUSEHOLD AND PERSONAL PRODUCTS INDUSTRY BUYERS GUIDE
Rodman Publishing Group, 17 South
Franklin Turnpike, Ramsey NJ 07446.
201/825-2552. $12.00.

Magazines

APPLIANCE
1110 Jorie Boulevard, Oak Brook IL 60522-
9019. 708/990-3484. Monthly. $70.00 for
a one-year subscription.

COSMETICS INSIDERS REPORT
Advanstar Communications, 131 West 1st
Street, Duluth MN 55802. 800/346-0085.
$189.00 for a one-year subscription.
Twenty-four issues annually. Features
timely articles on cosmetics marketing and
research.

MANUFACTURING AND WHOLESALING: MISCELLANEOUS INDUSTRIAL

New investments by American businesses have generated much of the U.S. economy's expansion in recent years. That's good news for machinery manufacturers, who have been very busy. Through October 1995, the manufacturing of machinery and equipment was up about 12 percent over the previous year.

Employment in the wholesale trade sector is also closely tied to the growth of the economy. However, industry trends will change a good portion of the composition and nature of wholesale trade employment. Consolidation of the industry into fewer firms and the spread of new technology should slow growth in some occupations, but many new jobs will be created in others as firms provide a growing array of support services. In addition, these trends will change the role of many other workers.

Heightened competition and pressure to lower operating costs should continue to force distributors to merge with or acquire other firms. The resulting consolidation of wholesale trade among fewer, larger firms will reduce the demands for some workers as merged companies eliminate duplicated staff. Consolidation and greater competition among wholesale trade firms, however, will lead more firms to expand customer service, increasing the demand for these types of workers. Clerks or sales workers will advance to many of these new customer service or marketing jobs, and new workers may be needed for financial, logistical, technical, or advertising positions.

North Carolina

A.G. INDUSTRIES INC.
376 Pine Street, Forest City NC 28043. 704/245-9871. **Contact:** Gray Webber, Human Resources Manager. **Description:** A.G. Industries Inc. manufactures display cabinets and display racks for wholesale to stores.

ALTEC INDUSTRIES, INC.
P.O. Box 2000, 1550 Aerial Avenue, Creedmoor NC 27522. 919/528-2535. **Contact:** Karen Hohlefelder, Human Resources Administrator. **Description:** Altec Industries, Inc. manufactures a wide variety of products including utility trucks, overhead traveling cranes, hoists, and monorail systems. **Common positions include:** Accountant/Auditor; Administrator; Blue-Collar Worker Supervisor; Buyer; Computer Programmer; Draftsperson; Environmental Scientist; Human Resources Specialist; Marketing Specialist; Mechanical Engineer; Operations/Production Manager; Purchasing Agent and Manager; Technical Writer/Editor. **Educational backgrounds include:** Accounting; Engineering. **Benefits:** 401K; Dental Insurance; Disability Coverage; Life Insurance; Medical Insurance; Pension Plan; Tuition Assistance. **Special Programs:** Internships. **Corporate headquarters location:** Birmingham AL. **Other U.S. locations:** CA; MO; PA. **Operations at this facility include:** Manufacturing; Service. **Number of employees at this location:** 220.

ATHEY PRODUCTS CORPORATION
P.O. Box 669, Raleigh NC 27602. 919/556-5171. **Fax:** 919/556-7950. **Contact:** Human Resources. **Description:** A manufacturer and seller of heavy duty equipment including twin engine and natural gas powered street sweepers, conveyors, force-feed loaders, and refuse collection products. **Corporate headquarters location:** This Location. **Listed on:** NASDAQ. **Number of employees nationwide:** 325.

BOSTON GEAR
DIVISION OF IMO INDUSTRIES INC.
506 South Bickett Boulevard, Louisburg NC 27549. 919/496-2041. **Contact:** Dona Woodard, Office Manager. **Description:** Boston Gear manufactures speed-reducers used for conveyors such as the conveyors at check-out counters. **Common positions include:** Blue-Collar Worker Supervisor; Buyer; Human Resources Specialist; Industrial Engineer. **Educational backgrounds include:** Engineering. **Benefits:** Dental Insurance; Disability Coverage; Medical Insurance; Tuition Assistance. **Corporate headquarters location:** Lawrenceville NJ. **Operations at this facility include:** Manufacturing. **Listed on:** New York Stock Exchange. **Number of employees at this location:** 115.

COMM SCOPE COMPANY
P.O. Box 199, Catawba NC 28609. 704/241-3142. **Contact:** Jim Wright, Human Resources Manager. **Description:** Comm Scope Company manufactures coaxial cables and fiber cables.

COMMERCIAL INTERTECH
P.O. Box 219, Kings Mountain NC 28086. 704/739-9781. **Contact:** Mrs. Mikie Smith, Human Resources Manager. **Description:** Commercial Intertech manufactures hydraulic pumps and hydraulic pump parts.

COPELAND CORPORATION
4401 East Dixon Boulevard, Shelby NC 28152. 704/484-3011. **Contact:** Ed Shealy, Human Resources Manager. **Description:** A manufacturer of compressors and condensing units for the commercial, industrial, and residential air conditioning and refrigeration industries. **Benefits:** Dental Insurance; Disability Coverage; Life Insurance; Medical Insurance; Pension Plan; Profit Sharing; Savings Plan; Tuition Assistance. **Corporate headquarters location:** Sidney OH. **Parent company:** Emerson Electric.

DANA CORPORATION
WIX DIVISION
P.O. Box 1967, Gastonia NC 28053-1967. 704/864-6711. **Contact:** Glenn Parrish, Director of Human Resources. **Description:** This location manufactures air, oil, and specialty filters. Dana Corporation, founded in 1905, is a global leader in engineering, manufacturing, and marketing of products and systems for the worldwide vehicular, industrial, and mobile off-highway original equipment markets and is a major supplier to the related aftermarkets. Dana is also a leading provider of lease financing services in selected markets. The company's products include: drivetrain components, such as axles, driveshafts, clutches, and transmissions; engine parts, such as gaskets, piston rings, seals, pistons, and filters; chassis products, such as vehicular frames and cradles and heavy duty side rails; fluid power components, such as pumps, motors, and control valves; and industrial products, such as electrical and mechanical brakes and clutches, drives, and motion control devices. Dana's vehicular components and parts are used on automobiles, pickup trucks, vans, minivans, sport utility vehicles, medium and heavy trucks, and off-highway vehicles. The company's industrial products include mobile off-highway and stationary equipment applications. Dana Corporation has over 55,000 employees worldwide at almost 700 facilities in 27 countries. **Common positions include:** Accountant/Auditor; Administrator; Advertising Clerk; Buyer; Chemical Engineer; Computer Programmer; Customer Service Representative; Draftsperson; Electrical/Electronics Engineer; Human Resources Specialist; Industrial Engineer; Machine Operator; Manufacturing Engineer; Metallurgical Engineer. **Educational backgrounds include:** Accounting; Business Administration; Computer Science; Engineering; Liberal Arts; Marketing. **Benefits:** Dental Insurance; Disability Coverage; Employee Discounts; Life Insurance; Medical Insurance; Pension Plan; Savings Plan; Tuition Assistance. **Special Programs:** Internships; Training Programs. **Corporate headquarters location:** Toledo OH. **Operations at this facility include:** Administration; Manufacturing; Research and Development; Sales; Service. **Listed on:** New York Stock Exchange.

E.I. DuPONT de NEMOURS & COMPANY
6324 Fairview Road, Charlotte NC 28210. 704/362-7400. **Contact:** Linda Robinson, Site Administrator. **Description:** This location of E.I. DuPont manufactures fibers, markets polymers, and performs engineering services. Overall, DuPont manufactures specialty chemicals, such as titanium dioxide, fluorochemicals, and polymer intermediates, used in coatings, paper, plastic, textile, and other industries; manufactures specialty fibers for textile, apparel, and other markets; produces engineering polymers, elastomers, fluoropolymers, ethylene polymers, and other polymers for packaging, construction, electrical, paper, and other industries; explores for, produces, refines, markets, supplies, and transports crude oil; produces and transports natural gas and natural gas products; produces agricultural chemicals; and

owns and operates refineries. **Corporate headquarters location:** Wilmington DE. **Other U.S. locations:** LaPorte TX. **Operations at this facility include:** Marketing.

EATON CORPORATION
FLUID POWER DIVISION
P.O. Box 1509, Fletcher NC 28732. 704/684-3501x157. **Fax:** 704/687-5348. **Contact:** Anthony Allen, Human Resources Administrator. **Description:** A manufacturer of viscous fan drives. **Common positions include:** Accountant/Auditor; Computer Systems Analyst; Human Resources Specialist; Industrial Engineer; Management Trainee; Mechanical Engineer. **Educational backgrounds include:** Accounting; Business Administration; Engineering. **Benefits:** 401K; Dental Insurance; Disability Coverage; Employee Discounts; Life Insurance; Medical Insurance; Pension Plan; Profit Sharing; Tuition Assistance. **Special Programs:** Internships. **Corporate headquarters location:** Cleveland OH. **Number of employees at this location:** 500. **Number of employees nationwide:** 50,000.

FMC CORPORATION
LITHIUM DIVISION
P.O. Box 3925, Gastonia NC 28016. 704/868-5300. **Fax:** 704/868-5370. **Contact:** Mark McDonald, Human Resources Manager. **Description:** This location manufactures lithium-based compounds including metals and carbonates. FMC Corporation is an industrial conglomerate. The company's industrial chemicals sector includes natural soda ash and derivatives, peroxides, lithium compounds, phosphorous, and specialty chemicals. Performance chemicals includes insecticides, fungicides and herbicides, pharmaceutical ingredients, food additives, stabilizers, and thickeners. The United Defense Sector includes tracked military and combat vehicles, naval gun and missile launching systems and steel components for U.S. and foreign governments. The machinery and equipment sector includes food machinery, petroleum equipment, and transportation equipment.

FASCO CONTROLS CORPORATION
1100 Airport Road, Shelby NC 28150. 704/482-9582. **Contact:** Bill Noblitt, Employee Relations Manager. **Description:** Supplies components to the automotive, truck, appliance, heating, aerospace, and other markets. **Common positions include:** Accountant/Auditor; Blue-Collar Worker Supervisor; Buyer; Computer Programmer; Customer Service Representative; Department Manager; Draftsperson; Electrical/Electronics Engineer; General Manager; Human Resources Specialist; Industrial Engineer; Management Trainee; Manufacturer's/Wholesaler's Sales Rep.; Marketing Specialist; Mechanical Engineer; Metallurgical Engineer; Operations/Production Manager; Purchasing Agent and Manager; Quality Control Supervisor; Systems Analyst. **Educational backgrounds include:** Accounting; Business Administration; Computer Science; Engineering; Finance; Liberal Arts; Marketing. **Benefits:** Dental Insurance; Disability Coverage; Employee Discounts; Life Insurance; Medical Insurance; Pension Plan; Profit Sharing; Tuition Assistance. **Corporate headquarters location:** Boca Raton FL. **Parent company:** Hawker Siddeley Company.

GIBRALTAR PACKAGING GROUP, INC.
2115 Rexford Road, Suite 215, Charlotte NC 28211. 704/366-2929. **Fax:** 704/366-6717. **Contact:** Human Resources. **Description:** Gilbraltar Packaging Group, Inc. designs and manufactures high-quality packaging products, serving a variety of industries including pharmaceutical, food, cosmetic, textile, toy, automotive aftermarket, specialty confectionery, and other consumer markets. The company's product line includes folding cartons, labels, tubular spiral-wound paper packaging, one-stop contract packaging and filling, flexible poly film packaging, and specialty laminated boxes. The company operates facilities in Alabama, Indiana, Nebraska, and North Carolina. The Gilbraltar Packaging Group includes Flashfold Carton (Fort Wayne, IN), GB Labels (Burlington, NC), Great Plains Packaging (Hastings, NE), Niemand Industries (Statesville, NC), and Standard Packaging (Mt. Gilead, NC). **Corporate headquarters location:** This Location. **Listed on:** NASDAQ. **Number of employees nationwide:** 950.

INGERSOLL DRESSER PUMP
PLEUGER OPERATIONS
P.O. Box 989, Statesville NC 28687. 704/872-2468. **Contact:** Ken Herrom, Director of Personnel. **Description:** Produces multistage, submersible pumps with directly coupled water-lubricated motors for municipal, industrial, and agricultural water supply; large capacity axial flow pumps for water level control systems, flood control, dewatering applications and power plants; maneuvering equipment for ships; and thruster equipment for dynamic positioning of ships. Also produces submersible motors for marine technology applications. **Common positions include:**

Accountant/Auditor; Application Engineer; Blue-Collar Worker Supervisor; Customer Service Representative; Department Manager; General Manager; Industrial Engineer; Systems Analyst. **Benefits:** Dental Insurance; Disability Coverage; Life Insurance; Medical Insurance; Pension Plan; Savings Plan; Tuition Assistance. **Corporate headquarters location:** Dallas TX. **Parent company:** Dresser Industries, Inc. **Operations at this facility include:** Manufacturing. **Listed on:** New York Stock Exchange.

KENNAMETAL INC.
P.O. Box 30700, Raleigh NC 27622-0700. 919/829-5000. **Fax:** 919/829-5148. **Contact:** Human Resources. **Description:** Manufactures, purchases, and distributes a broad range of tools, tooling systems, supplies, and services for the metalworking, mining, and highway construction industries. Kennametal specializes in developing and manufacturing metalcutting tools and wear-resistant parts using a specialized type of powder metallurgy. The company's metalcutting tools are made of cemented carbides, ceramics, cermets, and other hard materials. Kennametal manufactures a complete line of toolholders and toolholding systems by machining and fabricating steel bars and other metal alloys. The company's mining and construction cutting tools are tipped with cemented carbide and are used for underground coal mining and highway construction, repair, and maintenance. Metallurgical products consist of powders made from ore concentrates, compounds, and secondary materials. International locations include Canada, China, England, Germany, and The Netherlands. This location is part of the Metalworking Systems Division. **Corporate headquarters location:** Latrobe PA. **Listed on:** New York Stock Exchange.

LONG MANUFACTURING N.C. INC.
P.O. Box 1139, 111 Fairview Street, Tarboro NC 27886. 919/823-4151. **Fax:** 919/823-4151. **Contact:** Mike Rosenkoetter, Human Resources Director. **Description:** Develops, manufactures, and markets a broad range of farm and industrial equipment (tractors, tillers, harrows, unloading equipment, elevators, backhoes, storage bins, furnaces, and many other items), and wood-burning stoves. **Common positions include:** Administrator; Blue-Collar Worker Supervisor; Buyer; Computer Programmer; Department Manager; Draftsperson; Industrial Engineer; Manufacturer's/Wholesaler's Sales Rep.; Mechanical Engineer; Operations/Production Manager; Purchasing Agent and Manager; Quality Control Supervisor; Technical Writer/Editor. **Educational backgrounds include:** Business Administration; Computer Science; Engineering; Industrial Technology; Marketing. **Benefits:** Disability Coverage; Employee Discounts; Life Insurance; Medical Insurance; Profit Sharing. **Corporate headquarters location:** This Location. **Operations at this facility include:** Administration; Manufacturing; Research and Development; Sales; Service. **Listed on:** Privately held. **Number of employees at this location:** 326.

MURATA WIEDEMANN, INC.
10510 Twin Lakes Parkway, Charlotte NC 28269. 704/875-9280. **Contact:** Anne Steele, Director of Human Resources. **Description:** Develops, manufactures and sells computer-controlled fabrication equipment, accessories, and systems which provide flexibility and productivity for non-mass producers of parts made from flat materials (primarily sheet metal) in the world markets. Products include CNC Punch Press; Right Angle Shears; Panel Bender; Plasma Arc; and Laser Contouring Equipment. This "stand alone" equipment can be linked together in an automatic fabricating system.

RJR PACKAGING
P.O. Box 625, Winston-Salem NC 27102-0625. 910/741-6899. **Contact:** Horace A. Slate, Personnel Manager -- RJR Packaging. **Description:** A flexible packaging converter of paper, films, and foil. The parent company, RJR Nabisco, is a major tobacco and food products company. **Common positions include:** Accountant/Auditor; Adjuster; Administrative Services Manager; Biological Scientist/Biochemist; Budget Analyst; Buyer; Chemical Engineer; Chemist; Cost Estimator; Credit Manager; Customer Service Representative; Electrical/Electronics Engineer; Electrician; Financial Analyst; Food Scientist/Technologist; Human Resources Specialist; Industrial Production Manager; Manufacturer's/Wholesaler's Sales Rep.; Materials Engineer; Mechanical Engineer; Operations/Production Manager; Purchasing Agent and Manager; Science Technologist. **Educational backgrounds include:** Accounting; Art/Design; Business Administration; Engineering. **Benefits:** 401K; Daycare Assistance; Dental Insurance; Disability Coverage; Life Insurance; Medical Insurance; Pension Plan; Profit Sharing; Savings Plan; Tuition Assistance. **Corporate headquarters location:** New York NY. **Subsidiaries include:** RJ Reynolds Tobacco Company, which produces tobacco products under the brand names Winston, Salem, Camel, Doral, More, Vantage, and NOW; and RJ Reynolds International, which markets over 55 brands of tobacco products in 160 countries. Food businesses of RJR Nabisco include: Nabisco Biscuit, Life Savers, Planters, Fleischmans, Specialty Products (pet foods, sauces, cereals, and

condiments), Food Service, and Nabisco International. **Parent company:** RJR Nabisco. **Operations at this facility include:** Administration; Divisional Headquarters; Manufacturing; Research and Development; Sales. **Listed on:** New York Stock Exchange. **Number of employees at this location:** 1,050.

S-B POWER TOOL COMPANY
100 Bosch Boulevard, New Bern NC 28562-6997. 919/636-4200. **Fax:** 919/636-4323. **Contact:** Chuck Dale, Manager of Human Resources. **Description:** A manufacturer of electrical industrial power tools for woodworking and concrete applications. **Common positions include:** Accountant/Auditor; Blue-Collar Worker Supervisor; Draftsperson; Electrician; Financial Manager; General Manager; Human Resources Specialist; Industrial Engineer; Industrial Production Manager; Inspector/Tester/Grader; Machinist; Mechanical Engineer; Payroll Clerk; Precision Assembler; Secretary; Tool and Die Maker. **Educational backgrounds include:** Accounting; Engineering; Finance. **Benefits:** 401K; Dental Insurance; Disability Coverage; Employee Discounts; Life Insurance; Medical Insurance; Pension Plan; Tuition Assistance. **Special Programs:** Apprenticeships; Internships. **Corporate headquarters location:** Chicago IL. **Other U.S. locations:** Heber Springs AK; Walnut Ridge AR. **Parent company:** Bosch GmbH and Emerson Electric JV. **Operations at this facility include:** Manufacturing. **Number of employees at this location:** 350. **Number of employees nationwide:** 2,300.

SAFT AMERICA INC.
313 Crescent Street, Valdese NC 28690. 704/874-4111. **Contact:** John Hundeen, Staff Services Manager. **Description:** A manufacturer of industrial aviation batteries and numerous other storage batteries for industrial use.

SPEIZMAN INDUSTRIES INC.
508 West 5th Street, Charlotte NC 28202. 704/372-3751. **Contact:** Kay Newton, Office Manager. **Description:** Speizman Industries, Inc. is a distributor of new sock knitting machines. The company distributes technologically advanced sock knitting machines manufactured by Lonat, S.P.A. in Brescia, Italy, which is one of the world's largest manufacturers of hosiery knitting equipment. It also distributes Lonati sock and sheer hosiery knitting machines in Canada. In addition, through sales arrangements with other European textile machinery manufacturers, the company distributes other sock knitting machines, knitting machines for underwear, sweaters, collars, and trim, and other knitted fabrics and other equipment related to the manufacture of socks and sheer hosiery, principally in the United States and Canada. The company also sells dyeing and finishing equipment for the textile industry. The company sells textile machine parts and used textile equipment in the United States and a number of foreign countries. **Corporate headquarters location:** This Location. **Other locations:** Leicester, England; Montreal, Canada; Hicksville NY. **Listed on:** NASDAQ. **Number of employees at this location:** 71.

TESA TUCK, INC.
5825 Carnegie Boulevard, Charlotte NC 28209. 704/554-0707. **Contact:** Raymond L. Naseman, Vice President of Human Resources. **Description:** Engaged in the production and sale of an extensive line of masking, cellophane, electrical, cloth, and other pressure-sensitive tape products for business, industrial, and household use. Other facilities located in Carbondale, IL (industrial and retail tapes) and Sparta, MI (industrial). **Common positions include:** Accountant/Auditor; Buyer; Chemical Engineer; Chemist; Claim Representative; Computer Programmer; Credit Manager; Department Manager; Financial Analyst; Human Resources Specialist; Industrial Engineer; Manufacturer's/Wholesaler's Sales Rep.; Mechanical Engineer. **Educational backgrounds include:** Accounting; Business Administration; Chemistry; Engineering; Finance; Marketing. **Benefits:** Disability Coverage; Life Insurance; Medical Insurance. **Corporate headquarters location:** This Location. **Other U.S. locations:** Middletown NY. **Operations at this facility include:** Regional Headquarters; Research and Development.

TEXTRON, INC.
JACKSON DIVISION
3935 Westinghouse Boulevard, Charlotte NC 28273. 704/587-5987. **Contact:** Debbie Ralph, Human Resources Director. **Description:** Textron, Inc. is a diversified company with manufacturing and financial services operations. The company is one of the U.S. government's largest defense contractors. Products include helicopters, gas turbine engines, combat vehicles, air cushion landing craft, missile re-entry systems, aircraft wing structures, and aerospace materials, controls and electronics. The remainder of manufacturing primarily consists of automotive parts, outdoor products, and specialty fasteners. Financial and other services segments include Avco Financial Services, Textron Financial Corporation, Avco Insurance Services/Balboa Life and Casualty, and

83 percent-owned Paul Revere Insurance Group. **NOTE:** Ms. Ralph can be reached at 11524 Wilmont Boulevard, Charlotte, 28241.

THONET INDUSTRIES
403 Meacham Road, Statesville NC 28677. 704/878-2222. **Contact:** Carol Cockrell, Director of Human Resources. **Description:** A manufacturer of contract and institutional seating. Customers include colleges, universities, hospitals, nursing homes, offices, and public buildings.

Note: Because addresses and telephone numbers of smaller companies change rapidly, we recommend you call each company to verify the information below before inquiring about job opportunities. Mass mailings are not recommended.

Additional employers with under 250 employees:

COMMERCIAL FURNITURE AND FIXTURES

Boling Co.
S R 1938, Mount Olive NC 28365. 919/658-4947.

Davis Furniture Industries
2401 S College Dr, High Point NC 27260-8816. 910/889-2009.

Miller Desk Inc.
231 South Rd, High Point NC 27262-8152. 910/819-6500.

Miller Office Seating
4100 Cheyenne Dr, High Point NC 27263-3241. 910/861-8701.

Atlas/Soundolier Corp.
Hwy 74 Bypass E, Laurinburg NC 28352. 910/277-0239.

Broadway Salvage & Office Supply
303 E Trade St, Forest City NC 28043-3150. 704/245-6238.

Carolina Business Furniture
101 Liberty Dr, Thomasville NC 27360-4836. 910/476-6117.

Finch Fabricating & Plating
1365 Unity St, Thomasville NC 27360. 910/472-5900.

Gregson Inc.
206 E Frazier Ave, Liberty NC 27298. 910/622-2201.

Comforto
1161 Burris Blvd, Lincolnton NC 28092. 704/732-2267.

Display Fixture Co.
1501 Westinghouse Blvd, Charlotte NC 28273-6326. 704/588-0880.

Stanly Fixtures Co. Inc.
11635 Hwy 138, Norwood NC 28128. 704/474-3184.

PACKAGING PAPER AND PLASTICS FILM

Hexacomb Company
4320 Meadowridge Dr, Charlotte NC 28226-8148. 704/543-9663.

Rexham Packaging
10500 Industrial Dr, Pineville NC 28134-6522. 704/889-7262.

GASKETS, PACKING, AND SEALING DEVICES

CR Industries
55 Industrial Park Rd, Franklin NC 28734-9052. 704/524-8444.

GNC Corp.
2600 Wilco Blvd, Wilson NC 27893-9022. 919/237-6171.

GSH Corp.
310 Kingold Blvd, Snow Hill NC 28580-1306. 919/747-5947.

METAL HARDWARE

Collier-Keyworth Inc.
P.O. Box 1109, Liberty NC 27298-1109. 910/622-0120.

Endura Products Inc.
101 Little Santee Rd, Colfax NC 27235-9764. 910/668-2472.

Ilco Unican Corp.
2941 Indiana Ave, Winston-Salem NC 27105-4425. 910/725-1331.

Julius Blum Inc.
NC Highway 16, Stanley NC 28164. 704/827-1345.

Leggett & Platt Inc.
1639 Blandwood Dr, High Point NC 27260-8302. 910/889-4998.

PLUMBING FIXTURE FITTINGS AND TRIM

Thomas Co.
1024 Randolph St, Thomasville NC 27360-5727. 910/475-2131.

HEATING EQUIPMENT

Fuchs Systems Inc.
812 W Innes St, Salisbury NC 28144-4152. 704/633-2141.

Southbend
1100 Old Honeycutt Rd, Fuquay Varina NC 27526-9312. 919/552-9161.

MISC. PIPE FITTINGS AND/OR VALVES

Edward Valve Inc.
1900 S Saunders St, Raleigh NC 27603. 919/832-0525.

Kunkle Industries Inc.
1281 Old Highway 70 W, Black Mountain NC 28711-2549. 704/669-5515.

Kaiser Fluid Technologies
530 E Sugar Creek Rd, Charlotte NC 28213-6915. 704/596-3311.

Parker-Hannifin Corp.
203 Pine St, Forest City NC 28043. 704/245-3233.

Aeroquip Corp.
RR 7, Forest City NC 28043-9806. 704/286-4157.

Aeroquip Corp./Aerospace Division
Hwy 264 Alt, Middlesex NC 27557. 919/235-2121.

Parker-Hannifin Corp.
Hwy 21 N, Mooresville NC 28115. 704/664-1922.

Regtrol Inc. & Wacasco Foundry
100 Watts Rd, Spindale NC 28160. 704/286-4151.

Schrader Bellows
12415 Capital Blvd, Wake Forest NC 27587-7486. 919/556-4031.

United Brass Works Inc.
714 S Main St, Randleman NC 27317-2100. 910/498-2661.

FABRICATED PIPE AND PIPE FITTINGS

Crane Resistoflex Co.
1 Quality Way, Marion NC 28752-9410. 704/724-9524.

Whitley Products Inc.
1st & Van Raalte Sts, Franklin NC 28734. 704/369-6682.

FARM MACHINERY AND EQUIPMENT

Aeroglide Corp.
P.O. Box 29505, Raleigh NC 27626-0505. 919/851-2000.

Taylor Manufacturing
Hwy 701 S, Elizabethtown NC 28337. 910/862-2576.

CONSTRUCTION MACHINERY AND EQUIPMENT

BR Lee Industries Inc.
Hwy 16 S, Denver NC 28037. 704/483-3811.

Deere-Hitachi Construction Machinery
1000 Deere-Hitachi Rd, Kernersville NC 27284. 910/996-8100.

Grainger Industrial & Commercial Equipment
2321 Crown Centre Dr, Charlotte NC 28227-7705. 704/845-2189.

Gregory Manufacturing Co.
506 Oak Dr, Lewiston NC 27849. 919/348-2531.

CONVEYORS AND CONVEYING EQUIPMENT

FKI Material Handling Group
4601 Six Forks Rd, Raleigh NC 27609. 919/881-9312.

OVERHEAD INDUSTRIAL TRANSPORTATION EQUIPMENT

Duff-Norton Co. Inc.
Country Club Rd, Wadesboro NC 28170. 704/694-2156.

METAL CUTTING OR FORMING TOOLS

Agie USA Ltd./Elox Corp.
565 Griffith St, Davidson NC 28036. 704/892-8011.

Cleveland Twist Drill Co.
201 Yzex St, Asheboro NC 27203-3280. 910/672-3313.

DML Lineberry Inc.
151 Lineberry Rd, Wilkesboro NC 28697-8559. 910/838-3181.

Kennametal Inc.
100 Kennametal Rd, Weldon NC 27890. 919/536-2064.

Okuma Machine Tools
12200 Steele Creek Rd, Charlotte NC 28273-3736. 704/588-7000.

Wysong & Miles Co.
P.O. Box 21168, Greensboro NC 27420-1168. 910/621-3960.

MISC. INDUSTRIAL MACHINE TOOLS

LS Starrett Co.
1372 Boggs Dr, Mount Airy NC 27030-2144. 910/789-5141.

INDUSTRIAL WELDING AND SOLDERING EQUIPMENT

Thermacote Welco Co.
P.O. Box 69, Kings Mountain NC 28086-0069. 704/739-6421.

TEXTILE MACHINERY

American Barmag Corp.
1101 Westinghouse Blvd, Charlotte NC 28273-6324. 704/588-0072.

American Trutzchler Inc.
12300 Moores Chapel Rd, Charlotte NC 28214-8928. 704/399-4521.

Jenkins Metal Corp.
936 N Marietta St, Gastonia NC 28054-7301. 704/867-6394.

Leesona Corp.
2727 Tucker Street Ext, Burlington NC 27215-8859. 910/226-5511.

Lida Manufacturing
622 W 28th St, Charlotte NC 28206-2559. 704/333-7779.

Luwa Bahnson Parks Cramer
10415 Westlake Dr, Charlotte NC 28273-3740. 704/587-0105.

WOODWORKING MACHINERY

Newman Machine Co.
507 Jackson St, Greensboro NC 27403-2462. 910/273-8261.

FOOD PRODUCTS MACHINERY

APV Baker Inc.
1200 W Ash St, Goldsboro NC 27530-9739. 919/735-4570.

Fab-X/Metals Inc.
2207 N Wesleyan Blvd, Rocky Mount NC 27804-8637. 919/977-3229.

Hunter Jersey Farms
1900 N Main St, High Point NC 27262-2132. 910/883-6181.

Sealed Air Corp.
P.O. Box 98, Patterson NC 28661-0098. 704/757-4500.

SPECIAL INDUSTRIAL MACHINERY

Aeroglide Corp.
100 Aeroglide Dr, Cary NC 27511-6900. 919/851-2000.

JC Steele & Sons Inc.
710 S Mulberry St, Statesville NC 28677-5714. 704/872-3681.

Modern Machine & Metal Fabrication
920 Old Winston Rd, Kernersville NC 27284-8119. 910/993-4808.

Stork Screens America
3001 N Interstate 85 Service, Charlotte NC 28269. 704/598-7171.

PUMPS AND PUMPING EQUIPMENT

Hayward Pool Products
Hwy 161, Kings Mountain NC 28086. 704/739-9370.

Imo Industries Inc.
P.O. Box 5020, Monroe NC 28111-5020. 704/289-6511.

BALL AND ROLLER BEARINGS

American Roller Bearing Co.
307 Burke Dr, Morganton NC 28655-5334. 704/433-6641.

FANS, BLOWERS, AND AIR PURIFICATION EQUIPMENT

Farr Co.
Old Highway 70 & I-40, Conover NC 28613. 704/465-2880.

Penn Ventilator Co. Inc.
Hwy 701 Bypass, Tabor City NC 28463. 910/653-3061.

Purolator Products Inc.
207 Johnston Pky, Kenly NC
27542. 919/284-2046.

PACKAGING MACHINERY

Tipper Tie
2000 Lufkin Rd, Apex NC
27502-7068. 919/362-
8811.

INDUSTRIAL PROCESS FURNACES AND OVENS

Hankison International
170 Hankison Dr, Newport
NC 28570-9169. 919/726-
1011.

Proctor & Schwartz
2425 S Main St, Lexington
NC 27292. 704/246-5181.

POWER TRANSMISSION EQUIPMENT

Keystone Carbon Co.
100 Commerce Dr,
Cherryville NC 28021-8905.
704/435-4036.

Timken Co.
3500 Timken Pl, Randleman
NC 27317. 910/495-3700.

MISC. INDUSTRIAL MACHINERY AND EQUIPMENT

Filter Products Division
8439 Triad Dr, Greensboro
NC 27409-9018. 910/668-
4444.

High Point Sprinkler Inc.
520 Albertson Rd,
Thomasville NC 27360-
8987. 910/475-6181.

SERVICE INDUSTRY MACHINERY

AAR Power Boss Corp.
Anderson St, Aberdeen NC
28315. 910/944-2105.

Champion Industries Inc.
P.O. Box 4149, Winston-
Salem NC 27115-4149.
910/661-1556.

Pac-Fab Inc.
1620 Hawkins Ave, Sanford
NC 27330-9538. 919/774-
4151.

ENGINE PARTS

Parker-Hannifin Corp.
325 Elizabeth Brady Rd,
Hillsborough NC 27278-
9540. 919/732-9371.

INDUSTRIAL AND COMMERCIAL MACHINERY AND EQUIPMENT

Matlab Inc.
NC Highway 49 S, Asheboro
NC 27203. 910/629-4161.

Moore's Machine Co.
13120 NC Highway 902,
Bear Creek NC 27207.
910/837-5354.

NCI Inc.
401 Sweeten Creek
Industrial P, Asheville NC
28803-1729. 704/274-
4540.

Steel Heddle
1875 S Interstate 85 Service
R, Charlotte NC 28208-
2702. 704/391-8659.

Tubular Textile Machinery Corp.
P.O. Box 2097, Lexington
NC 27293-2097. 704/956-
6444.

C&S Machine Shop
4129 Hardins Farm Rd,
Sophia NC 27350-8157.
910/861-1701.

MOTORS AND GENERATORS

Buehler Products Inc.
303 Gregson Dr, Cary NC
27511-6496. 919/469-
8522.

Durham Products
3427 Industrial Dr, Durham
NC 27704. 919/471-4488.

Ohio Electric Motors Inc.
30 Paint Fork Rd,
Barnardsville NC 28709-
9711. 704/626-2901.

OMC Spruce Pine
1025 Greenwood Rd, Spruce
Pine NC 28777-3117.
704/765-4213.

MEASURING AND CONTROLLING EQUIPMENT

MTS Systems Corp.
3001 Sheldon Dr, Cary NC
27513-2007. 919/677-
0100.

Rostra Precision Control
2519 Dana Dr, Laurinburg
NC 28352-4000. 910/276-
4853.

TCOM LP
111 Kitty Hawk Ln, Elizabeth
City NC 27909-6726.
919/330-5555.

DO Creasman Electronics
1207 Smokey Park Hwy,
Candler NC 28715-9248.
704/667-2576.

OFFICE EQUIPMENT WHOLESALE

Systel Business Equipment
P.O. Box 35910, Fayetteville
NC 28303-0910. 910/483-
7114.

Young-Phillips Sales Co.
P.O. Box 25288, Winston-
Salem NC 27114-5288.
910/768-0110.

AM Multigraphics
4 Oak Branch Dr, Greensboro
NC 27407-2145. 910/299-
1051.

Eastman Kodak Company
9140 Arrow Point Blvd, Suite
100, Charlotte NC 28273-
8120. 704/523-0390.

Paul B. Williams Inc.
1048 Bragg Blvd, Fayetteville
NC 28301-4512. 910/485-
7169.

Toshiba Sales & Service
700 Forest Point Cir,
Charlotte NC 28273-5608.
704/527-8353.

COMMERCIAL EQUIPMENT WHOLESALE

Hobart Corporation
8041C Arrowridge Blvd,
Charlotte NC 28273-5604.
704/527-6381.

REFRIGERATION EQUIPMENT WHOLESALE

CC Dickson Co.
927 East Blvd, Charlotte NC
28203-5203. 704/372-
2604.

Graves Gastonia Division Pameco
809 W Airline Ave, Gastonia
NC 28052-3815. 704/866-
8726.

Pameco Corp.
337 Dalton Ave, Charlotte
NC 28206-3117. 704/377-
1567.

INDUSTRIAL MACHINERY AND EQUIPMENT WHOLESALE

Iron Peddlers
3504 N Rocky River Rd,
Monroe NC 28110-9295.
704/289-8591.

Asheville Bit & Steel Co.
Edgewood Rd, Asheville NC
28804. 704/274-3766.

EF Craven Co.
9739 Blackwell Rd SE,
Leland NC 28451-8519.
910/371-3611.

EF Craven Co.
1107 Trinity Rd, Raleigh NC
27607-4943. 919/851-
1450.

RW Moore Equipment Co.
P.O. Box 25068, Raleigh NC
27611-5068. 919/772-
2121.

Anchor Packing Co.
1295 S Park Dr, Kernersville
NC 27284. 910/996-7271.

Covington Diesel Inc.
P.O. Box 18949, Greensboro
NC 27419. 910/292-9240.

L&H Technologies
P.O. Box 7207, Charlotte NC
28241. 704/588-3670.

MacPherson Inc.
3517 W Wendover Ave,
Greensboro NC 27407-1505.
910/294-5165.

Siecor Corp.
P.O. Box 1237, Rocky Mount
NC 27802. 919/972-6000.

Western Carolina Forklift
5727 N Sharon Amity Rd #B,
Charlotte NC 28215-3984.
704/343-0077.

Dunlap Sales Inc.
8107 Arrowridge Blvd,
Charlotte NC 28273-5613.
704/529-0016.

American Schlafhorst
P.O. Box 240828, Charlotte
NC 28224-0828. 704/554-
0800.

Barco Automation Inc.
4420 Taggart Creek Rd,
Suite 101, Charlotte NC
28208-5414. 704/392-
9371.

Cattinair Corp.
8334 Arrowridge Blvd,
Charlotte NC 28273-5602.
704/523-0300.

NB Handy Co.
1005 Norwalk St,
Greensboro NC 27407-2024.
910/855-3900.

Cummins Atlantic Inc.
3700 N I-85, Charlotte NC
28206. 704/596-7690.

Dover Elevator Co.
103 J J Dr, Greensboro NC
27406-4408. 910/272-
4563.

Penhall Diamond Products
208 Quail Roost Dr, Carrboro
NC 27510-1156. 919/933-
7535.

Colder Products Co.
2002 Eastwood Rd,
Wilmington NC 28403-7218.
910/256-3098.

**Cross Sales and Engineering
Company**
8100 Arrowridge Blvd, Suite
E, Charlotte NC 28273-
5600. 704/525-7000.

Edwards and Broughton Co.
1200 Front St, Suite 113,
Raleigh NC 27609-7501.
919/833-6602.

Frischkorn Distributors
801 Weldon Rd, Roanoke
Rapid NC 27870-4713.
919/537-4169.

Parker Hannifan Corp.
125 E Meadowview Rd,
Greensboro NC 27406-4518.
910/373-1761.

Durametallic Corp.
9222 Monroe Rd, Matthews
NC 28105. 704/847-6906.

Federal Mogul Corporation
6200 Falls of Neuse Rd,
Raleigh NC 27609-3563.
919/790-2441.

Abrasives South Inc.
4018 Kynwood Dr, Trinity

NC 27370-8420. 910/861-
4776.

Leggett & Platt Inc.
1430 Sherman Ct,
Thomasville NC 27360.
910/889-2600.

National Welders Supply Co.
5315 Old Dowd Rd,
Charlotte NC 28208-5431.
704/392-7317.

National Welders Supply Co.
2526 E Market St,
Greensboro NC 27401-4816.
910/272-0900.

Howco Inc.
5001 South Blvd, Charlotte
NC 28217-2707. 704/525-
6148.

Automatic Sprinkler Corp.
622-H Guilford Jamestown
Rd, Greensboro NC 27409.
910/852-4110.

York Distributors
1305 Hodges St, Raleigh NC
27604-1431. 919/834-
5444.

**Superior Products Southern
Company**
4201 Taggart Creek Rd,
Suite 106, Charlotte NC
28208-5405. 704/399-
3394.

**SCRAP AND WASTE
MATERIALS WHOLESALE**

Texwipe Company
1210 S Park Dr, Kernersville
NC 27284-3179. 910/996-
7046.

Walker's Salvage
RR 2, Linden NC 28356-
9802. 910/893-8037.

South Carolina

COOPER INDUSTRIES INC./COOPER POWER TOOLS DIVISION
P.O. Box 1410, Lexington SC 29071. 803/359-1200. **Contact:** Jim Cloer,
Employment/ Training Manager. **Description:** The Cooper Power Tools Division of
Cooper Industries Inc. manufactures pneumatic hand tools, air motors, air feed drills,
and hoists. Overall, Cooper Industries Inc. is engaged in three primary areas of
manufacturing: tools and hardware, electrical and electronic products, and automotive
products. **Common positions include:** Accountant/Auditor; Blue-Collar Worker
Supervisor; Buyer; Commercial Artist; Computer Programmer; Customer Service
Representative; Department Manager; Draftsperson; Financial Analyst; Human
Resources Specialist; Industrial Designer; Industrial Engineer;
Manufacturer's/Wholesaler's Sales Rep.; Mechanical Engineer; Purchasing Agent and
Manager; Quality Control Supervisor; Systems Analyst. **Educational backgrounds
include:** Accounting; Business Administration; Engineering; Finance; Liberal Arts;
Marketing; Mathematics. **Benefits:** Dental Insurance; Disability Coverage; Employee
Discounts; Life Insurance; Medical Insurance; Pension Plan; Savings Plan; Tuition
Assistance. **Corporate headquarters location:** Houston TX. **Other U.S. locations:** Black
Mountain NC; Goldsboro NC. **Operations at this facility include:** Administration;
Divisional Headquarters; Manufacturing; Research and Development; Sales; Service.
Listed on: New York Stock Exchange. **Number of employees nationwide:** 45,000.

CROWN CORK & SEAL COMPANY INC.
P.O. Box 887, Cheraw SC 29520. 803/537-9794. **Contact:** Nancy Boan, Personnel Manager. **Description:** A worldwide manufacturer and distributor of a wide range of crowns, seals, and aluminum/steel cans including aerosol and beverage cans. Crown Cork & Seal also manufactures bottling equipment. **Corporate headquarters location:** Philadelphia PA. **Listed on:** New York Stock Exchange.

GREENFIELD INDUSTRIES
P.O. Box 872, Clemson SC 29633-0872. 864/654-4922. **Contact:** Personnel Department. **Description:** Produces "Chicago-Latrobe" brand and private label high-speed drills and reamers. **Corporate headquarters location:** Cleveland OH. **Parent company:** TRW is a diversified technology firm with operations in the following areas: electronics and space systems; car and truck equipment for both original equipment manufacturers and the replacement market; and a wide variety of industrial and energy components, including aircraft parts, welding systems, and electromechanical assemblies. **Listed on:** New York Stock Exchange.

HOLLINGSWORTH SACO LOWELL, INC.
P.O. Drawer 2327, Greenville SC 29602. 864/859-3211. **Fax:** 864/859-2908. **Contact:** Brent O'Shields, Human Resources Director. **Description:** Hollingsworth Saco Lowell, Inc. designs and manufactures textile machinery including parts, attachments, and accessories. The company's primary customers are textile mills. **Common positions include:** Accountant/Auditor; Adjuster; Administrative Services Manager; Advertising Clerk; Blue-Collar Worker Supervisor; Buyer; Claim Representative; Computer Programmer; Cost Estimator; Customer Service Representative; Designer; Draftsperson; Economist/Market Research Analyst; Editor; Electrical/Electronics Engineer; Electrician; Emergency Medical Technician; Environmental Engineer; Financial Analyst; General Manager; Human Resources Specialist; Industrial Engineer; Industrial Production Manager; Inspector/Tester/Grader; Machinist; Management Trainee; Manufacturer's/Wholesaler's Sales Rep.; Marketing/Advertising/PR Manager; Mechanical Engineer; Metallurgical Engineer; Millwright; Payroll Clerk; Postal Clerk/Mail Carrier; Purchasing Agent and Manager; Quality Control Supervisor; Receptionist; Sheet-Metal Worker; Systems Analyst; Technical Writer/Editor; Tool and Die Maker; Truck Driver; Typist/Word Processor; Water Transportation Specialist. **Educational backgrounds include:** Accounting; Business Administration; Computer Science; Engineering; Finance; Liberal Arts; Marketing; Mathematics; Physics. **Benefits:** Dental Insurance; Disability Coverage; Employee Discounts; Life Insurance; Medical Insurance; Pension Plan; Savings Plan; Tuition Assistance. **Corporate headquarters location:** Greenville SC. **Parent company:** Hollingsworth On Wheels. **Number of employees at this location:** 500.

SCHLUMBERGER INDUSTRIES
1310 Emerald Road, Greenwood SC 29646-8800. 864/223-1212. **Contact:** Doug Linn, Human Resources Manager. **Description:** Schlumberger Industries manufactures measurement equipment and systems for various energy applications, including petroleum meters. The parent company, Schlumberger Ltd., manufactures measurement, electronics, and testing products; and provides wellsite exploration and computer aided design. **Corporate headquarters location:** This Location. **Other U.S. locations:** West Union SC. **Parent company:** Schlumberger Ltd. (The Netherlands). **Listed on:** New York Stock Exchange.

SCOTSMAN FAIRFAX OPERATION
P.O. Box 890, Fairfax SC 29827. 803/632-2511. **Contact:** Donna Griffin, Human Resources Manager. **Description:** A manufacturer of commercial ice machines. **Common positions include:** Accountant/Auditor; Administrator; Buyer; Human Resources Specialist; Industrial Engineer; Management Trainee; Operations/Production Manager; Quality Control Supervisor. **Educational backgrounds include:** Accounting; Business Administration; Engineering. **Benefits:** Dental Insurance; Disability Coverage; Employee Discounts; Life Insurance; Medical Insurance; Pension Plan; Savings Plan; Tuition Assistance. **Corporate headquarters location:** Chicago IL. **Parent company:** Household International. **Operations at this facility include:** Manufacturing.

SONOCO PRODUCTS
North Second Street, Hartsville SC 29550. 803/383-7000. **Contact:** Grady Weaver, Employment Manager. **Description:** Sonoco Products manufactures paper and plastic cones, tubes, cores and spools; composite cans and containers; plastic bottles; plastic meter boxes and underground enclosures; specialties; partitions and pads; paperboard; aluminum and steel textile beams; machinery products; hardwood lumber; plastic grocery bags; metal, plastic, and wood reels; adhesives; fiber and plastic drums; and dual oven trays. **Other U.S. locations:** Orlando FL; Marietta GA.

STEEL HEDDLE MANUFACTURING COMPANY
P.O. Box 1867, Greenville SC 29602. 864/244-4110. **Contact:** Bill Rogers, Director of Personnel. **Description:** A manufacturer of textile machinery.

UNITED DEFENSE, L.P.
15 Windham Boulevard, Aiken SC 29801-9384. 803/649-6211. **Contact:** Robert Houston, Human Resources Manager. **Description:** United Defense, L.P. manufactures aluminum, steel, titanium, and other component parts for military ground vehicles. United Defense is the product of a partnership between the FMC Corporation and Harsco Corporation's BMY Systems Division. As one of the world's leading producers of chemicals and machinery for industry, agriculture, and government, FMC Corporation participates on a worldwide basis in selected segments of five broad markets: industrial chemicals, performance chemicals, precious metals, defense systems, and machinery and equipment. Industrial chemicals include the Alkali Chemicals Division; the Peroxygen Chemicals Division; the Phosphorus Chemicals Division; the Lithium Division; and FMC Foret, S.A. Performance chemicals includes the Agricultural Chemical Group, the Food Ingredients Division, the Pharmaceutical Division, BioProducts, and the Process Additives Division. Precious metals includes FMC Gold. Machinery and equipment includes the Energy and Transportation Equipment Group and the Food Machinery Group. FMC Corporation operates 99 manufacturing facilities and mines in 21 countries. **Corporate headquarters location:** Chicago IL.

WOVEN ELECTRONICS CORPORATION
P.O. Box 367, Greenville SC 29602. 864/233-6740. **Contact:** Bob Hunt, Director of Personnel. **Description:** Woven Electronics Corporation manufactures cable harness systems and textile narrow goods.

Note: Because addresses and telephone numbers of smaller companies change rapidly, we recommend you call each company to verify the information below before inquiring about job opportunities. Mass mailings are not recommended.

Additional employers with under 250 employees:

PACKAGING PAPER AND PLASTICS FILM

Tag & Label Corp.
2800 W Whitner St, Anderson SC 29624-1035. 864/224-2122.

METAL HARDWARE

Bommer Industries Inc.
P.O. Box 187, Landrum SC 29356-0187. 864/457-3301.

Versch Lock Manufacturing
110 Metal Park Dr, Columbia SC 29209. 803/776-7696.

PLUMBING FIXTURE FITTINGS AND TRIM

T&S Brass & Bronze Works
RR 4, Travelers Rest SC 29690. 864/834-4102.

Wolverine Brass Inc.
2951 Highway 501 E, Conway SC 29526-9514. 803/347-3121.

MISC. PIPE FITTINGS AND/OR VALVES

NIBCO Inc.
S Locust St, Denmark SC 29042. 803/793-3391.

FARM MACHINERY AND EQUIPMENT

Powell Manufacturing Co.
P.O. Box 707, Bennettsville SC 29512. 803/479-6231.

MISC. INDUSTRIAL MACHINE TOOLS

Union Butterfield Corp.
268 Beltline Rd, Gaffney SC 29341-1400. 864/489-5751.

METALWORKING MACHINERY

Huffman Corp.
1050 Huffman Way, Clover SC 29710-1400. 803/222-4561.

TEXTILE MACHINERY

Alexander Machinery Inc.
180 Neely Ferry Rd, Simpsonville SC 29680-6137. 864/963-3624.

Crosrol Inc.
P.O. Box 6488, Greenville SC 29606. 864/235-9681.

Greenville Machinery Corp.
1705 Poplar Drive, Greer SC 29651. 864/879-3011.

Morrison Textile Machinery
Highway 9, Fort Lawn SC 29714. 803/872-4401.

Sulzer Ruti Inc.
P.O. Box 5332, Spartanburg SC 29304-5332. 864/585-5255.

PAPER INDUSTRIES MACHINERY

Superior Machine Co. of SC
692 N Cashua Dr, Florence SC 29501-2006. 803/664-3001.

PRINTING MACHINERY AND EQUIPMENT

BK Industries
2812 Grandview Dr, Simpsonville SC 29680-6217. 864/963-3471.

CF Sauer Co.
P.O. Box 2346, Greenville SC 29602-2346. 864/288-3211.

SPECIAL INDUSTRIAL MACHINERY

American Foundry & Machine
1140 Memorial Park Rd, Lancaster SC 29720-2236. 803/286-4426.

BALL AND ROLLER BEARINGS

American Koyo Bearing Manufacturing
P.O. Box 967, Orangeburg SC 29116-0967. 803/536-6200.

Roller Bearing Corp. of SC
2268 S 5th St, Hartsville SC 29550-7112. 803/332-2691.

PACKAGING MACHINERY

Hartness International
1200 Garlington Rd, Greenville SC 29615-5447. 864/297-1200.

POWER TRANSMISSION EQUIPMENT

Dana Corp.
5 Technology Cir, Columbia SC 29203-9591. 803/935-0151.

MISC. INDUSTRIAL MACHINERY AND EQUIPMENT

AME Inc.
2467 Coltharp Rd, Fort Mill SC 29715-8991. 803/548-7766.

Menardi-Criswell
1 Maxwell Dr, Trenton SC 29847. 803/663-6551.

AIR-CONDITIONING, HEATING, AND REFRIGERATION EQUIPMENT

Climatic Products Inc.
1340B Old Dairy Dr, Columbia SC 29201-4838. 803/799-6599.

Palmetto Refrigerants
2521 W Palmetto St, Florence SC 29501-5925. 803/629-8536.

SERVICE INDUSTRY MACHINERY

Gen III Inc.
100 Gen III Ave, Fountain Inn SC 29644. 864/862-4742.

ENGINE PARTS

US Engine Valve Co.
7039 S Highway 11, Westminster SC 29693-3915. 864/647-2061.

INDUSTRIAL AND COMMERCIAL MACHINERY AND EQUIPMENT

Bellwright Industries Inc.
10186 Bellwright Rd, Summerville SC 29483-5403. 803/871-5030.

Bruckner Ltd. Partnership
50 International Dr, Greenville SC 29615-4832. 864/234-7111.

MOTORS AND GENERATORS

Baldor Electric Co.
2499 Deerfield Dr N, Fort Mill SC 29715-8910. 803/548-3624.

Powertec Industrial Corp.
3958 Air Way Dr, Rock Hill SC 29732-9200. 803/328-1888.

MEASURING AND CONTROLLING EQUIPMENT

ITT Conoflow
Highway 78, Saint George SC 29477. 803/563-9281.

OFFICE EQUIPMENT WHOLESALE

Lanier Worldwide
1200 Woodruff Rd Bldg C-33, Greenville SC 29607-5730. 864/297-6452.

White Business Machines
1200 Woodruff Rd #B-17,

Greenville SC 29607-5730. 864/288-1808.

INDUSTRIAL MACHINERY AND EQUIPMENT WHOLESALE

Interlake Materials Handling
P.O. Box 1734, Sumter SC 29151-1734. 803/481-3482.

Wrenn Handling Inc.
2201 Mechanic St, Charleston SC 29405-9310. 803/577-3090.

Hayssen
225 Spartangreen Blvd, Duncan SC 29334-9425. 864/439-1141.

A&P Water and Sewer Supplies
915 Oswego Hwy, Sumter SC 29153. 803/775-8341.

Associated Industrial Supply
556 Perry Ave, Greenville SC 29611-4852. 864/277-0065.

Bearing Distributors Inc.
P.O. Box 2347, Columbia SC 29202-2347. 803/799-0834.

John Crane Inc.
209 E Stone Ave, Greenville SC 29609-5654. 864/467-0068.

Bel Chemical Co.
1401 Poinsett Hwy, Greenville SC 29609-3633. 864/271-2076.

Valley Systems Inc.
148 Dahlia St, Lexington SC 29072-3622. 803/951-7444.

SCRAP AND WASTE MATERIALS WHOLESALE

Alma Alloys Recycling
413 Marietta St, Gaffney SC 29340. 864/489-1438.

For more information on career opportunities in industrial manufacturing and wholesaling:

Associations

APPLIANCE PARTS DISTRIBUTORS ASSOCIATION
228 East Baltimore Street, Detroit MI 48202. 313/875-8455. An association of wholesale parts distributors.

ASSOCIATION FOR MANUFACTURING TECHNOLOGY
7901 Westpark Drive, McLean VA 22102. 703/893-2900. A trade association.

INSTITUTE OF INDUSTRIAL ENGINEERS
25 Technology Park, Norcross GA 30092. 770/449-0460. A nonprofit organization with 27,000 members. Conducts seminars

and offers reduced rates on its books and publications.

NATIONAL ASSOCIATION OF MANUFACTURERS
1331 Pennsylvania Avenue NW, Suite 1500, Washington DC 20004. 202/637-3000. A lobbying association.

NATIONAL SCREW MACHINE PRODUCTS ASSOCIATION
6700 West Snowville Road, Brecksville OH 44141. 216/526-0300. Provides resource information.

NATIONAL TOOLING AND MACHINING ASSOCIATION
9300 Livingston Road, Fort Washington MD

20744. 301/248-1250. Reports on wages
and operating expenses. Produces monthly
newsletters. Offers legal advice.

**SOCIETY OF MANUFACTURING
ENGINEERS**
P.O. Box 930, One SME Drive, Dearborn MI
48121. 313/271-1500. Offers educational
events and educational materials on
manufacturing.

Special Programs

**BUREAU OF APPRENTICESHIP AND
TRAINING**
U.S. Department of Labor, 200 Constitution
Avenue NW, Washington, DC 20210.
202/219-6540.

MINING/GAS/PETROLEUM/ENERGY RELATED

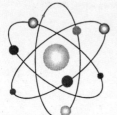

The energy industry just isn't what it used to be. In recent years, energy companies have been restructuring their operations in order to insure solid cash flows even in an era of low prices. Smaller, independent companies are now able to finance new production and land purchases with cash generated from stock sales.

Even so, jobseekers can't expect increased production to lead to much employment growth. Layoffs are expected to continue, but advanced technologies used by the energy industry continue to crop up, and jobseekers with engineering backgrounds should watch for energy-related, high-tech jobs.

In mining, earnings are much higher than average, but technological innovations, international competition, and environmental regulation will reduce employment. Best bets in the mining industry are for scientific technicians, professional specialty workers (such as geologists), and truck drivers.

North Carolina

COGENTRIX ENERGY INC.
Arrowpoint Boulevard, Charlotte NC 28273-8110. 704/525-3800. **Fax:** 704/529-5313. **Contact:** Human Resources. **Description:** Cogentrix Energy, Inc., develops, constructs, and operates non-utility electric generating facilities. The company has 10 operating facilities. **Other U.S. locations:** Singapore; Portland OR. **Listed on:** Privately held. **Number of employees nationwide:** 500.

CYPRUS FOOTE MINERAL COMPANY
348 Holiday Inn Drive, P.O. Box 686, King's Mountain NC 28086. 704/739-2501. **Fax:** 704/734-0208. **Contact:** Mr. J.E. Sanderson, Vice President of Human Resources. **Description:** Engaged in the mining, processing, and marketing of industrial raw materials. Principal products of Cyprus Foote Mineral Company include lithium and mineral products, which are used in the aluminum, ceramics, battery, pharmaceutical, and other industries. **Common positions include:** Accountant/Auditor; Blue-Collar Worker Supervisor; Budget Analyst; Buyer; Chemical Engineer; Chemist; Civil Engineer; Computer Systems Analyst; Customer Service Representative; Electrician; Financial Analyst; Human Resources Specialist; Manufacturer's/Wholesaler's Sales Rep.; Mechanical Engineer; Metallurgical Engineer; Purchasing Agent and Manager; Quality Control Supervisor. **Educational backgrounds include:** Accounting; Business Administration; Chemistry; Communications; Computer Science; Engineering; Liberal Arts. **Benefits:** 401K; Dental Insurance; Disability Coverage; Life Insurance; Medical Insurance; Pension Plan; Tuition Assistance. **Corporate headquarters location:** This Location. **Other U.S. locations:** Nationwide; New Johnsonville NV; Silver Peak NV; Duffield VA. **Parent company:** Cyprus Amax Minerals Company (Denver, CO). **Operations at this facility include:** Administration; Divisional Headquarters; Research and Development; Sales. **Listed on:** New York Stock Exchange. **Number of employees at this location:** 75. **Number of employees nationwide:** 410.

GILBARCO INC.
P.O. Box 22087, Greensboro NC 27420-2087. 910/547-5144. **Fax:** 910/292-8871. **Contact:** Dorothy Fritz, Manager, Recruiting and Placement. **Description:** A manufacturer of electronic fuel dispensing equipment and peripheral devices for the petroleum industry. **Common positions include:** Software Engineer. **Educational backgrounds include:** Engineering. **Benefits:** 401K; Dental Insurance; Disability Coverage; Employee Discounts; Life Insurance; Medical Insurance; Tuition Assistance. **Special Programs:** Internships. **Corporate headquarters location:** This Location. **Parent**

company: GEC plc. **Listed on:** Privately held. **Number of employees at this location:** 1,600.

WESTINGHOUSE ELECTRIC CORPORATION

P.O. Box 7002, Charlotte NC 28241-7002. 704/588-1220. **Contact:** Dick Baker, Manager of Human Resources. **Description:** This location of the company manufactures nuclear fuel. Overall, Westinghouse Electric Corporation is a diversified manufacturing company with interests in defense electronics, environmental services, broadcasting, mobile refrigeration units, office furniture, energy systems, and power generation. The company conducts operations through 791 locations in the U.S. and over 30 other countries. **Corporate headquarters location:** Pittsburgh PA. **Subsidiaries include:** Thermo King; The Knoll Group; Westinghouse Broadcasting. **Listed on:** New York Stock Exchange. **Number of employees nationwide:** 120,000.

Note: Because addresses and telephone numbers of smaller companies change rapidly, we recommend you call each company to verify the information below before inquiring about job opportunities. Mass mailings are not recommended.

Additional employers with under 250 employees:

OIL AND GAS FIELD MACHINERY AND EQUIPMENT

Drillers Service Inc.
1792 Highland Ave NE, Hickory NC 28601-5306. 704/322-1100.

PETROLEUM PIPELINES

Yates Construction Co.
9220 Hwy 65, Stokesdale NC 27357. 910/379-8131.

PETROLEUM AND PETROLEUM PRODUCTS WHOLESALE

Sampson-Bladen Oil Co.
P.O. Box 367, Elizabethtown NC 28337-0367. 910/862-3197.

Sampson-Bladen Oil Co.
Hwy 421 N, Clinton NC 28328. 910/592-4177.

Hydrotex Lubricants
E US 70 Hwy, Conover NC 28613. 704/459-9616.

WG Hendrix Chevron USA
5 Wendy Ct, Greensboro NC 27409-2229. 910/294-1211.

GC Quality Lubricants
1105 E Mountain St, Kernersville NC 27284-7904. 910/996-1332.

Sampson-Bladen Oil Co.
Hwy 242, Roseboro NC 28382. 910/525-4604.

South Carolina

HEWITT-ROBINS/SECO

10145 Two Notch Road, Columbia SC 29223. 803/788-1424. **Contact:** Personnel. **Description:** Manufactures rock-crushing and vibrating equipment.

INDRESCO
JEFFREY DIVISION

P.O. Box 387, Woodruff SC 29388. 864/476-7523. **Contact:** Glen Shaw, Human Resources. **Description:** Supplies underground mining equipment to a variety of customers. Indresco is an industrial company that provides products essential to infrastructure development and basic industrial production. Operations at this location include minerals and refractory products, industrial tools, and mining and construction equipment.

For more information on career opportunities in the mining, gas, petroleum and energy industries:

Associations

AMERICAN ASSOCIATION OF PETROLEUM GEOLOGISTS
P.O. Box 979, Tulsa OK 7410-0979. 918/584-2555. International headquarters for petroleum geologists.

AMERICAN GEOLOGICAL INSTITUTE
4220 King Street, Alexandria VA 22302-1507. 703/379-2480. Scholarships available. Publishes monthly *Geotimes*. Offers job listings.

AMERICAN NUCLEAR SOCIETY
555 North Kensington Avenue, La Grange Park IL 60525. 708/352-6611. Offers educational services.

AMERICAN PETROLEUM INSTITUTE
1220 L Street NW, Suite 900, Washington DC 20005. 202/682-8000. A trade association.

GEOLOGICAL SOCIETY OF AMERICA
3300 Penrose Place, P.O. Box 9140, Boulder CO 80301. 303/447-2020. Membership of over 17,000. Offers sales

items and publications. Also conducts society meetings.

SOCIETY OF EXPLORATION GEOPHYSICISTS
P.O. Box 702740, Tulsa OK 74170-2740. 918/493-3516. A membership association. Offers publications.

Directories

BROWN'S DIRECTORY OF NORTH AMERICAN AND INTERNATIONAL GAS COMPANIES
Advanstar Communications, 7500 Old Oak Boulevard, Cleveland OH 44130. 800/225-4569.

NATIONAL PETROLEUM NEWS FACT BOOK
Adams/Hunter Publishing Company, 2101 South Arlington Heights Road, Suite 150, Arlington Heights IL 60005-4142. 847/427-9512.

OIL AND GAS DIRECTORY
Geophysical Directory, Inc., P.O. Box 130508, Houston TX 77219. 713/529-8789.

Magazines

AMERICAN GAS MONTHLY
1515 Wilson Boulevard, Arlington VA 22209. 703/841-8686.

GAS INDUSTRIES
Gas Industries News, Inc., 6300 North River Road, Suite 505, Rosemont IL 60018. 312/693-3682.

NATIONAL PETROLEUM NEWS
Adams/Hunter Publishing Company, 2101 South Arlington Heights Road, Suite 150, Arlington Heights IL 60005-4142. 847/427-9512.

OIL AND GAS JOURNAL
PennWell Publishing Company, 1421 South Sheridan Road, P.O. Box 1260. Tulsa OK 74101. 918/835-3161.

PAPER AND WOOD PRODUCTS

The year 1995 was a dramatic one for the paper industry. Prices jumped higher and faster than they had at any time since World War II. According to Dean Witter, profits were up an astounding 180 percent during the year at the nation's 19 largest paper and paperboard companies.

By mid-1995, however, customers had begun to hoard paper, forcing prices back down. Luckily, even as profits soared in the early part of the year, the industry played its hand conservatively by resisting the impulse to expand capacity. Analysts expect prices to continue to stay down during 1996. That means that jobseekers shouldn't anticipate a major increase in industry hiring.

One hot trend, however, may provide opportunity. Environmental concerns should give the paper packaging segment an advantage over plastics, as companies move to become "green." The industry hopes to recycle at least half of the paper it produces by the turn of the century. Minimills, which convert cardboard into pulp, are springing up nationwide. Among the industry's recycling leaders: Weyerhaeuser and Boise Cascade.

North Carolina

ATLANTIC VENEER CORPORATION
P.O. Box 660, Beaufort NC 28516. 919/728-3169. **Contact:** Ed Nelson, Personnel Manager. **Description:** Manufactures, produces, and sells veneer, hardwood lumbers, and plywood. **Common positions include:** Accountant/Auditor; Administrator; Blue-Collar Worker Supervisor; Branch Manager; Buyer; Computer Programmer; Credit Manager; Department Manager; Financial Analyst; General Manager; Human Resources Specialist; Industrial Engineer; Industrial Production Manager; Management Trainee; Manufacturer's/Wholesaler's Sales Rep.; Operations/Production Manager; Purchasing Agent and Manager. **Educational backgrounds include:** Accounting; Business Administration; Computer Science; Engineering; Finance. **Benefits:** Disability Coverage; Life Insurance; Medical Insurance. **Special Programs:** Internships; Training Programs. **Corporate headquarters location:** This Location. **Operations at this facility include:** Administration; Manufacturing; Research and Development; Sales; Service. **Number of employees at this location:** 700.

AVERY DENNISON SOABAR
2305 Soabar Drive, Greensboro NC 27406. 910/275-9371. **Contact:** Human Resources. **Description:** Manufactures price tags for clothing.

CHAMPION INTERNATIONAL CORPORATION
P.O. Box C-10, Canton NC 28716. 704/646-2000. **Contact:** Human Resources. **Description:** This location prints and routes copy machine paper and also manufactures paperboard. Overall, Champion International Corporation is a large producer of paper, lumber, plywood, and forest products for the printing, construction, and home improvement markets. The company has the capacity to produce 6.2 million tons of paper, board, and market pulp per year. Champion International Corporation owns or controls 5.1 million acres of timberland in the United States. The company has five major business units: Printing and Writing Papers; Publication Papers; Newsprint and Kraft; Forest Products; and Marketing -- which includes nationwide newspapers, Champion Export, and Pulp Sales. Champion International Corporation also has two major foreign subsidiaries: Weldwood of Canada and Champion Papel e Celulose, Brazil. The company's paper operations include the production of business papers, coated papers, bleached paperboard, and packaging materials. **Corporate headquarters location:** Stamford CT.

CHAMPION INTERNATIONAL CORPORATION
ROANOKE RAPID MILL
P.O. Box 580, Roanoke Rapid NC 27870. 919/537-6011. **Contact:** Robert Seevers, Human Resources Manager. **Description:** This location produces kraft paper and linerboard, used to make multiwall bags and corrugated containers. This mill facility produces 507,000 tons of kraft paper and linerboard per year. Overall, Champion International Corporation is a large producer of paper, lumber, plywood, and forest products for the printing, construction, and home improvement markets. The company has the capacity to produce 6.2 million tons of paper, board, and market pulp per year. Champion International Corporation owns or controls 5.1 million acres of timberland in the United States. The company has five major business units: Printing and Writing Papers; Publication Papers; Newsprint and Kraft; Forest Products; and Marketing -- which includes nationwide newspapers, Champion Export, and Pulp Sales. Champion International Corporation also has two major foreign subsidiaries: Weldwood of Canada and Champion Papel e Celulose, Brazil. The company's paper operations include the production of business papers, coated papers, bleached paperboard, and packaging materials. **Corporate headquarters location:** Stamford CT.

ECUSTA DIVISION OF P.H. GLATFELTER
P.O. Box 200, Pisgah Forest NC 28768. 704/877-2211. **Contact:** Tom Crawford, Director of Employee Relations. **Description:** A paper plant manufacturing cigarette and Bible paper.

FEDERAL PAPER BOARD COMPANY INC.
940 North Norwood Street, P.O. Box 130, Wallace NC 28466. 910/285-4152. **Contact:** Douglas Costin, Area Manager, Land and Timber. **Description:** Office for the manufacturer of paper board and other paper-related products. Overall, the company has over 750,000 acres of forest providing material to its five sawmills and four pulp and paperboard mills. These mills provide paperboard to the company's four folding carton and printing operations, and six cup manufacturing plants.

FEDERAL PAPER BOARD COMPANY INC.
Highway 117 South, Faison NC 28341. 910/267-3751. **Contact:** Human Resources. **Description:** The wood yard for the manufacturer of paper and paper board products. Overall, the company has over 750,000 acres of forest providing material to its five sawmills and four pulp and paperboard mills. These mills provide paperboard to the company's four folding carton and printing operations, and six cup manufacturing plants.

FEDERAL PAPER BOARD COMPANY INC.
John L. Riegel Road, Riegelwood NC 28456. 910/655-2211. **Contact:** Andy Anderson, Personnel Manager. **Description:** The paper mill for the manufacturer of customized paperboard packaging products. This location produced 530,000 tons of market pulp and 310,000 tons of bleached paperboard in 1993. The mill's facilities were upgraded during 1993 and 1994. The upgrade included the rebuilding of a paperboard machine. Overall, the company produces a wide range of packaging products for pasta, coffee, laundry, and overnight envelope carriers.

FEDERAL PAPER BOARD COMPANY INC.
2221 J.R. Kennedy Drive, Wilmington NC 28405. 910/763-2921. **Contact:** Bob Hanson, Employee Relations Director. **Description:** The customized packaging facility is the largest of the company's packaging facilities. The plant, established in 1974, produces a wide range of packaging products including Muellers pasta, Folgers coffee, Purex laundry detergent, Taco Bell taco salads, and overnight carrier envelopes. The plant produces graphics by the roto gravure process and is fully equipped to perform all finishing operations on site. Overall, the company has over 750,000 acres of forest providing material to its five sawmills and four pulp and paperboard mills. These mills provide paperboard to the company's four folding carton and printing operations and six cup manufacturing plants.

FEDERAL PAPER BOARD COMPANY INC.
WOODLANDS DIVISION
P.O. Box 338, Bolton NC 28423. 910/655-5211. **Contact:** J. Marcus Lynch Jr., Employee Relations Manager. **Description:** Responsible for timberlands management and wood procurement for two pulp/paper mills and five sawmills in the Carolinas and Georgia. Overall, the company has over 750,000 acres of forest providing material to its five sawmills and four pulp and paperboard mills. These mills provide paperboard to the company's four folding carton and printing operations, and six cup manufacturing plants. **Common positions include:** Forester/Conservation Scientist. **Educational backgrounds include:** Environmental Science; Forest Management. **Benefits:** Dental

Insurance; Disability Coverage; Life Insurance; Medical Insurance; Pension Plan; Savings Plan; Stock Option; Tuition Assistance. **Corporate headquarters location:** Augusta GA. **Listed on:** New York Stock Exchange. **Number of employees nationwide:** 250.

INTERCRAFT INC.
P.O. Box 1829, Statesville NC 28687-1829. 704/873-2591. **Contact:** Kathy Pope, Human Resources Manager. **Description:** Produces miscellaneous wood products.

JEFFERSON SMURFIT CORPORATION U.S.
P.O. Box 3124, Wilson NC 27895-3124. 919/237-7121. **Contact:** Ken Wheeler, Controller. **Description:** Corrugated shipping containers represent Jefferson Smurfit's largest business segment. The container division, which operates 56 plants in the U.S., Mexico, and Puerto Rico, ranks second in U.S. production of corrugated containers and, as a part of Smurfit Group, first in the world. When it comes to recycled material usage, JSC is also an industry leader in environmental responsibility. According to the company, its average recycled content significantly exceeds both the company's nearest competitor and the industry average. In addition, JSC is the premier converter of corrugated containers made from 100 percent recycled medium and liner, both supplied by Smurfit mills. The company's strategically located plants convert more than 27 billion square feet of high-quality corrugated containers and specialty applications designed to protect, ship, store, and merchandise customers' products as economically as possible. JSC's corrugated capabilities provide an extensive variety of performance materials, as well as a wide range of graphically enhanced containers and point-of-purchase displays. Jefferson Smurfit Corporation U.S. also provides value added support to its customers through such diverse services as graphic and structural design, mechanical packaging, custom packaging, and a safe-transit certified testing center.

JORDAN LUMBER AND SUPPLY, INC.
P.O. Box 98, Mount Gilead NC 27306. 910/439-6121. **Contact:** Ronald Kincaid, Personnel Director. **Description:** A distributor of southern yellow pine lumber, wood chips, sawdust, bark, and related products. **Common positions include:** Accountant/Auditor; Blue-Collar Worker Supervisor; Department Manager; Forester/Conservation Scientist; Production Worker; Purchasing Agent and Manager; Quality Control Supervisor. **Educational backgrounds include:** High School Diploma. **Benefits:** 401K; Employee Discounts; Life Insurance; Medical Insurance; Profit Sharing; Savings Plan. **Corporate headquarters location:** This Location. **Number of employees at this location:** 150.

LEA LUMBER AND PLYWOOD
412 Hoggard Mill Road, Windsor NC 27983. 919/794-3151. **Contact:** Wanda Colfield, Director of Human Resources. **Description:** A lumber and plywood company. **Common positions include:** Accountant/Auditor; Industrial Engineer. **Educational backgrounds include:** Engineering. **Benefits:** Disability Coverage; Employee Discounts; Life Insurance; Medical Insurance; Pension Plan; Savings Plan; Tuition Assistance. **Corporate headquarters location:** High Point NC. **Operations at this facility include:** Administration; Manufacturing; Sales. **Listed on:** American Stock Exchange. **Number of employees at this location:** 265.

THOMSON CROWN WOOD PRODUCTS
P.O. Box 647, Bethel Church Road, Mocksville NC 27028. 704/634-6241. **Contact:** Dee Dee Elleman, Human Resources Manager. **Description:** Produces television cabinets for use by electronics and video manufacturers. **Common positions include:** Accountant/Auditor; Blue-Collar Worker Supervisor; Buyer; Human Resources Specialist; Industrial Engineer; Operations/Production Manager. **Educational backgrounds include:** Accounting; Engineering; Finance. **Benefits:** Dental Insurance; Disability Coverage; Life Insurance; Medical Insurance; Savings Plan; Tuition Assistance. **Parent company:** Thompson Consumer Electronics, Inc. **Operations at this facility include:** Manufacturing.

VALMET, INC.
12933 Sam Neely Road, Charlotte NC 28273. 704/588-5530. **Contact:** Ms. Daryl Price, Human Resources Manager. **Description:** Valmet, Inc. is a producer of paper and finishing systems, with production facilities located on all continents throughout the world. The company employs over 9,000 in the pulp and paper group. **Benefits:** 401K; Dental Insurance; Disability Coverage; Life Insurance; Medical Insurance; Pension Plan; Tuition Assistance. **Other U.S. locations:** Atlanta GA; Biddeford ME; Hudson Falls NY; Houston TX; Appleton WI. **Parent company:** Valmet Corporation (Helsinki, Finland). **Listed on:** Helsinki Exchange. **Number of employees nationwide:** 1,200.

WEYERHAEUSER COMPANY
Main Street Extension, P.O. Box 787, Plymouth NC 27962. 919/793-8230. **Fax:** 919/793-8098. **Contact:** Ruth Taylor, Employment Supervisor. **Description:** A pulp and paper manufacturer. **Common positions include:** Accountant/Auditor; Administrative Services Manager; Blue-Collar Worker Supervisor; Chemical Engineer; Chemist; Civil Engineer; Clerical Supervisor; Computer Programmer; Electrical/Electronics Engineer; Electrician; Financial Analyst; General Manager; Human Resources Specialist; Industrial Engineer; Licensed Practical Nurse; Management Trainee; Mechanical Engineer; Operations/Production Manager; Purchasing Agent and Manager; Quality Control Supervisor; Registered Nurse. **Educational backgrounds include:** Engineering. **Benefits:** 401K; Dental Insurance; Disability Coverage; Life Insurance; Medical Insurance; Pension Plan; Profit Sharing; Tuition Assistance. **Corporate headquarters location:** Tacoma WA. **Other U.S. locations:** Nationwide. **Operations at this facility include:** Manufacturing. **Listed on:** New York Stock Exchange. **Number of employees at this location:** 1,600.

Note: Because addresses and telephone numbers of smaller companies change rapidly, we recommend you call each company to verify the information below before inquiring about job opportunities. Mass mailings are not recommended.

Additional employers with under 250 employees:

TIMBER TRACTS

Canal Wood Corporation
318 E 5th St, Lumberton NC 28358-5586. 910/738-4423.

WOOD MILLS

Federal Wood
Armour Rd, Riegelwood NC 28456. 910/655-4106.

JW Jones Lumber Co.
1443 Northside Rd, Elizabeth City NC 27909-8531. 919/771-2497.

Louisiana-Pacific Corp.
Old Raleigh Rd, Henderson NC 27536. 919/492-4051.

Mackeys Ferry Saw Mill
SR 308, Plymouth NC 27962. 919/793-2950.

Parton Lumber Co. Inc.
Rte 2 & Hwy 64 E, Rutherfordton NC 28139-9802. 704/287-4257.

Union Camp Corp.
Hwy 186, Seaboard NC 27876. 919/589-2011.

Universal Forest Products
358 Woodmill Rd, Salisbury NC 28147-8398. 704/855-1600.

Charles D. Roberts Co.
700 W Lee St, Greensboro NC 27403-3037. 910/378-1676.

Ethan Allen Inc.
950 Riverside Dr, Asheville NC 28804. 704/252-3168.

Mannington Wood Floors
1327 Lincoln Dr, High Point NC 27260. 910/884-5600.

Oyama Woodworking
Hwy 70-A E, Conover NC 28613. 704/324-9310.

Rebel Lumber Co.
1401 Anson C R, Marshville NC 28103. 704/272-7623.

Weyerhaeuser Co.
RR 1 Box 102, Grifton NC 28530-9709. 919/746-7200.

Whiteville Plywood Inc.
630 E Main St, Whiteville NC 28472. 910/642-7114.

Zickgraf Enterprises Inc.
P.O. Box 1149, Franklin NC 28734-1149. 704/524-2131.

Certainteed Corp.
200 Certainteed Dr, Oxford NC 27565-3588. 919/693-1141.

Troy Lumber Co.
110 Leslie St #748, Troy NC 27371-2506. 910/576-6111.

MILLWORK, PLYWOOD, AND STRUCTURAL MEMBERS

Arndt & Herman Manufacturing
1708 Industrial Dr, Wilkesboro NC 28697-7345. 910/667-9075.

Carolina Hardwoods
105 Clover Dr SW, Lenoir NC 28645-8905. 704/728-8402.

Wenco of NC
5427 N Sharon Amity Rd, Charlotte NC 28215-3978. 704/535-3740.

Genwove US Ltd.
P.O. Box 310, Indian Trail NC 28079-0310. 704/821-7628.

Warvel Products
Belmont Rd, Linwood NC 27299. 704/956-2386.

Willamette Industries Inc.
306 Corinth Rd, Moncure NC 27559. 910/542-2311.

Davis Wood Products
P.O. Box 604, Hudson NC 28638-0604. 704/728-8445.

WOOD PALLETS AND SKIDS

Edwards Wood Products
1736 Old Lawyers Rd, Marshville NC 28103-7575. 704/624-5098.

WNC Pallet Co.
1414 Smokey Park Hwy, Candler NC 28715-8237. 704/667-5426.

WOOD CONTAINERS

Marvil Package Co.
1200 Castle Hayne Rd, Wilmington NC 28401-8885. 910/763-9991.

WOOD PRESERVING

Quality Forest Products
Hwy 301 S, Enfield NC 27823. 919/445-2113.

WOOD PRODUCTS

Broyhill Particleboard Co.
Miller Hill Complex, Lenoir NC 28645. 704/758-6016.

Georgia-Pacific Corp.
101 Ampac Rd, Conway NC 27820. 919/585-1323.

Weyerhaeuser Co.
Gentry Ln, Elkin NC 28621.
910/835-5100.

Blalock Manufacturing Co.
125 Sweeten Creek Rd,
Asheville NC 28803-1526.
704/274-0335.

Commercial Carving Co.
1010 Randolph St,
Thomasville NC 27360-
5727. 910/475-2301.

Cranford Woodcarving
330 19th St SE, Hickory NC
28602-4229. 704/328-
4538.

Georgia-Pacific Corp.
Highway 453, Holly Hill SC
29059. 803/496-5022.

Georgia-Pacific Corp.
1118 Russell Store Rd, Saint
Stephen SC 29479-3302.
803/567-3201.

James Gile & Co. Inc.
101 Spring St, Chester SC
29706-1559. 803/581-
5515.

PAPER MILLS

Pretty Paper Co.
900 W Academy St,
Cherryville NC 28021-3046.
704/435-4570.

Printworld Inc.
2011 N Rocky River Rd,
Monroe NC 28110-7963.
704/289-6441.

Valentine Paper
1515 W Cornwallis Dr,
Greensboro NC 27408-6334.
910/275-2922.

Carolina Paper Board
443 S Gardner Ave,
Charlotte NC 28208-3407.
704/376-7474.

Morrisette Paper Co.
5925 Summit Ave, Browns
Summit NC 27214-9704.
910/375-1515.

**PAPERBOARD CONTAINERS
AND BOXES**

Carolina Container Co.
900 Prospect St, High Point
NC 27260-8274. 910/883-
7146.

Carolina Container Co.
61 30th St NW, Hickory NC
28601. 704/328-2351.

Container Corp. of America
8080 N Point Blvd, Winston-
Salem NC 27106-3204.
910/759-7821.

Dixie Container Corp.
212 Roelee St, Trinity NC
27370. 910/434-2191.

Gaylord Container Corp.
3200 Bush St, Raleigh NC
27609-7503. 919/876-
4400.

Georgia-Pacific Corp.
200 McDowell Rd, Asheboro
NC 27203-7357. 910/629-
2151.

Highland Container Inc.
100 Ragsdale Rd,
Jamestown NC 27282-
9702. 910/887-5400.

**International Paper
Co./Container Division**
930 Meacham Rd, Statesville
NC 28677-2990. 704/872-
6541.

Jefferson Smurfit Corp.
662 Washburn Switch Rd,
Shelby NC 28150-9480.
704/482-4471.

Packaging Corp. of America
1302 N Salisbury Ave,
Salisbury NC 28144-8543.
704/633-3611.

Scotland Container Inc.
US Hwy 401 Bypass,
Laurinburg NC 28352.
910/277-0400.

St. Joe Container Co.
1201 Westinghouse Blvd,
Charlotte NC 28273-6308.
704/588-1550.

Stone Container Corp.
400 Albemarle St, Lexington
NC 27292. 704/249-9966.

Stone Container Corp.
10201 Industrial Dr, Pineville
NC 28134-6520. 704/889-
7671.

Stronghaven Inc.
760 W John St, Matthews
NC 28105-5378. 704/847-
7743.

Willamette Industries Inc.
820 Caton Rd, Lumberton
NC 28358-0458. 910/738-
6214.

Wilton Connor Packaging
3600 Westinghouse Blvd,
Charlotte NC 28273-4514.
704/588-8522.

Star Paper Tube Inc.
5620 Shattalon Dr, Winston-
Salem NC 27105-1331.
910/767-6780.

Summer Paper Tube Co.
1045 Industrial Park Dr,
Kernersville NC 27284-9481.
910/996-4165.

Colonial Carton Co. Inc.
1000 Ccc Dr, Clayton NC
27520-8015. 919/553-
4113.

Container Corp. of America
2600 E Market St,
Greensboro NC 27401-4817.
910/273-8201.

Etta Packaging Inc.
21 Burgin St, Marion NC
28752-3903. 704/652-
5511.

Universal Packaging Corp.
2801 Kenny Biggs Rd,
Lumberton NC 28358-6333.
910/738-7227.

Waldorf Corp.
400 S Center St, Taylorsville
NC 28681-3027. 704/632-
2285.

**COATED AND LAMINATED
PAPER**

Acucote Inc.
910 E Elm St, Graham NC
27253-1908. 910/578-
1800.

PAPER BAGS

Dillard Plastics Inc.
7137 Prospect Church Rd,
Thomasville NC 27360-
8839. 910/885-8131.

Sonoco Products Co.
3624 Old Mount Olive Hwy,
Mount Olive NC 28365-
8283. 919/658-6791.

**Standard Packaging &
Printing**
Hwy 73 W, Mount Gilead NC
27306. 910/439-6137.

PAPER PRODUCTS

Atlantic Envelope Co.
613 W North St Rm 1,
Raleigh NC 27603-1444.
919/832-0651.

Atlantic Envelope Co.
3434 Monroe Rd, Charlotte
NC 28205-7730. 704/334-
7661.

Carolina Pad & Paper Co.
P.O. Box 7525, Charlotte NC
28241-7525. 704/588-
3190.

**CONVERTED PAPER AND
PAPERBOARD PRODUCTS**

Atlantic Corp.
Hwy 701, Tabor City NC
28463. 910/653-3153.

Cascades Industries Inc.
805 Midway Rd, Rockingham
NC 28379-4101. 910/895-
9004.

**LUMBER AND WOOD
WHOLESALE**

McEwen Lumber Co.
P.O. Box 950, High Point NC
27261. 910/472-1900.

Chesapeake Woodyard
Foreman Mill Rd, Elizabeth
City NC. 919/335-1029.

**INDUSTRIAL PAPER AND
RELATED PRODUCTS
WHOLESALE**

Brame Specialty Co. Inc.
P.O. Box 271, Durham NC
27702. 919/683-1331.

**Southeastern Paper
Greensboro Inc.**
3500 Lake Herman Dr,
Browns Summit NC 27214-
9746. 910/375-8002.

Zellerbach A Mead Company
3600 Tarheel Dr, Raleigh NC
27609. 919/872-7210.

Old Dominion Box Co.
199 Wilshire Ave SW,
Concord NC 28025-5633.
704/782-1105.

**Packaging Services of
Carolina Inc.**
729 Palmer Rd, Rockwell NC
28138-8578. 704/279-
5650.

South Carolina

BOWATER INC.
P.O. Box 1028, Greenville SC 29602. 864/271-7733. **Contact:** Human Resources. **Description:** Bowater Inc. is a manufacturer of newsprint, coated paper, pulp, business forms, lumber, and related products. The company has integrated pulp and paper facilities in Tennessee, South Carolina, Maine, and Nova Scotia. Bowater Inc. owns 4 million acres of forestland; operates eight continuous-feed paper plants in the United States; and owns three saw mills. The company markets its computer papers and other business papers through 30 distribution centers. **Common positions include:** Accountant/Auditor; Financial Analyst; Human Resources Specialist; Marketing Specialist; Mechanical Engineer; Sales Representative. **Corporate headquarters location:** This Location. **Other U.S. locations:** Calhoun IN; Millinocket ME; Catawba SC. **Listed on:** New York Stock Exchange. **Number of employees nationwide:** 6,900.

BOWATER INC.
CAROLINA DIVISION
P.O. Box 7, Catawba SC 29704. 803/981-8000. **Contact:** Barry Baker, Human Resources. **Description:** Bowater Inc. is a manufacturer of newsprint, coated paper, pulp, business forms, lumber, and related products. The company has integrated pulp and paper facilities in Tennessee, South Carolina, Maine, and Nova Scotia. Bowater Inc. owns 4 million acres of forestland; operates eight continuous-feed paper plants in the United States; and owns three saw mills. The company markets its computer papers and other business papers through 30 distribution centers. **Common positions include:** Accountant/Auditor; Chemical Engineer; Chemist; Electrical/Electronics Engineer; Forester/Conservation Scientist; Mechanical Engineer; Registered Nurse; Software Engineer. **Educational backgrounds include:** Accounting; Business Administration; Computer Science; Engineering. **Benefits:** 401K; Disability Coverage; Life Insurance; Medical Insurance; Pension Plan; Profit Sharing; Savings Plan; Tuition Assistance. **Corporate headquarters location:** Greenville SC. **Other U.S. locations:** Calhoun IN; Millinocket ME. **Operations at this facility include:** Administration; Divisional Headquarters; Manufacturing. **Listed on:** New York Stock Exchange. **Number of employees at this location:** 1,245. **Number of employees nationwide:** 6,900.

INTERNATIONAL PAPER COMPANY
700 Kaminski Street, Georgetown SC 29440. 803/546-6111. **Contact:** Human Resources. **Description:** International Paper Company manufactures pulp and paper, packaging, and wood products as well as a range of specialty products. The company is organized into five business segments: printing papers, which includes uncoated papers, coated papers, bristles, and pulp; packaging, which includes industrial packaging, consumer packaging, and kraft and specialty papers; distribution, which includes sales of printing papers, graphic arts equipment and supplies, packaging materials, industrial supplies, and office products; specialty products, which include imaging products, specialty panels, nonwovens, chemicals, and minerals; and forest products, which includes logs and wood products. International Paper Company operates over 300 locations worldwide and controls millions of acres of timberland, making it one of the largest private landowners in the United States. **Corporate headquarters location:** Purchase NY. **Number of employees worldwide:** 72,500.

STONE CONTAINER CORPORATION
P.O. Box 100544, Florence SC 29501-0544. 803/662-0313. **Contact:** Bill Flynn, Director of Human Resources. **Description:** This location of the company makes liner board paper for cardboard boxes. Overall, Stone Container Corporation is a multinational paper and packaging company with annual sales of approximately $5 million. Its primary businesses are paperboard and paper packaging, and white paper and pulp operations. The paperboard and paper packaging segment is composed primarily of facilities which produce and sell containerboard and corrugated containers for manufacturers of consumable and durable goods and other manufacturers of corrugated containers; boxboard, folding cartons, and other products for

manufacturers of consumable goods including food, beverage, and tobacco products, and for other box manufacturers; and kraft paper and bags for supermarket chains and other retailers of consumable products, as well as for the food, agricultural, chemical, and cement industries. The white paper and pulp segment produces and sells newsprint for newspaper publishers and commercial printers; uncoated groundwood paper for producers of advertising materials, magazines, directories, and computer papers; and market pulp for manufacturers of paper products including fine papers, photographic papers, tissue, and newsprint. Other operations consist primarily of wood products operations which produce and sell lumber, plywood, and veneer for the construction and furniture industries. Including its subsidiaries and affiliates, Stone Container Corporation maintains nearly 200 manufacturing facilities and sales offices in North America, Latin America, Europe, and the Far East. **Corporate headquarters location:** Chicago IL. **Other U.S. locations:** CO; FL; MO; OH; PA; SC; TN. **Listed on:** New York Stock Exchange.

UNION CAMP CORPORATION

P.O. Box B, Eastover SC 29044. 803/353-7700. **Contact:** Kristen Krueger, Employment Manager. **Description:** A manufacturer of forest-based products. Union Camp Corporation's other fields of operation include minerals, land development, chemicals, school supplies, retail building supplies, printing machinery, packaging machinery and systems, plastic products, and cartons and containers. The company's United States facilities include pulp and paper mills, lumber mills, plywood and particleboard plants, and chemical plants. Union Camp Corporation's research and development activities are centered in Princeton, New Jersey. **Corporate headquarters location:** Wayne NJ. **Listed on:** New York Stock Exchange. **Number of employees nationwide:** 19,000.

WILLAMETTE INDUSTRIES INC.
PULP AND PAPER DIVISION

P.O. Box 678, Bennettsville SC 29512-0678. 803/479-0200. **Contact:** Donald Newton, Director of Human Resources. **Description:** This location of Willamette's Pulp and Paper Division produces copy machine paper. Willamette Industries, Inc. was founded in 1906 as the Willamette Valley Lumber Company in Dallas, Oregon. In 1967, Willamette Valley and several related firms merged to form Willamette Industries, Inc. The company is a diversified, integrated forest products company with 90 plants and mills manufacturing containerboard, bag paper, fine paper, bleached hardwood market pulp, specialty printing papers, corrugated containers, business forms, cut sheet paper, paper bags, inks, lumber, plywood, particleboard, medium density fiberboard, laminated beams, and value-added wood products. The company owns or controls 1,235,000 acres of forests. **Corporate headquarters location:** Portland OR. **Listed on:** NASDAQ. **Number of employees nationwide:** 12,500.

Note: Because addresses and telephone numbers of smaller companies change rapidly, we recommend you call each company to verify the information below before inquiring about job opportunities. Mass mailings are not recommended.

Additional employers with under 250 employees:

TIMBER TRACTS

Crescent Resources Inc.
Lancaster Rd, Great Falls SC 29055. 803/482-3221.

Federal Paperboard Land & Timber
Hwy 702, Greenwood SC 29646. 864/543-3668.

Stone Forest Products
120 Tupperway Dr, Summerville SC 29483-2520. 803/871-0892.

Westvaco Timberlands
Hwy 462, Ridgeland SC 29936. 803/726-5122.

Westvaco Timberlands
RR 4, Walterboro SC 29488-9804. 803/844-8662.

FOREST PRODUCTS AND SERVICES

Evergreen Timberlands Corp.
1511 Kendall Rd, Newberry SC 29108. 803/276-1433.

Resource Management Service
Chappells Hwy, Saluda SC 29138. 864/445-2420.

LOGGING

Coastal Lumber Co.
Highway 64 W & I-95, Walterboro SC 29488. 803/538-2866.

Collums Lumber Mill Inc.
Hwy 278 E, Allendale SC 29810. 803/584-3451.

WOOD MILLS

CM Tucker Lumber Corp.
601 N Pearl St, Pageland SC 29728. 803/672-6135.

Georgia-Pacific Corp.
Highway 278 E, Varnville SC 29944. 803/943-2523.

New South Inc.
1281 Sanders Creek Rd, Cassatt SC 29032-9289. 803/425-1810.

Standard Plywoods Inc.
Old Laurens Rd, Clinton SC 29325. 864/833-6250.

Upchurch Inc.
Highway 64 & I-95, Walterboro SC 29488. 803/538-3829.

Federal Paper Board Co.
3287 College St, Newberry
SC 29108-1637. 803/276-
4311.

Marsh Lumber Co.
6th Ave, Pamplico SC
29583. 803/493-5111.

**MILLWORK, PLYWOOD,
AND STRUCTURAL
MEMBERS**

Boozer Lumber Co. Inc.
1400 Atlas Rd, Columbia SC
29209. 803/776-1326.

Joanna Shutters
202 Pickens St, Joanna SC
29351-1430. 864/697-
6706.

Carolina Truss Systems
351 International Cir,
Summerville SC 29483-
4702. 803/875-0550.

PAPER MILLS

Carotell Paper Board Corp.
873 Alexander Rd, Taylors
SC 29687-1907. 864/244-
6221.

**PAPERBOARD CONTAINERS
AND BOXES**

Concept Packaging Group
6 Nesbitt Dr, Inman SC
29349-9425. 864/578-
0085.

Gaylord Container Corp.
100 Gordon St, Greenville
SC 29611-5024. 864/295-
1230.

Georgia-Pacific Corp.
3100 Southport Rd,
Spartanburg SC 29302-
3703. 864/573-7880.

Packaging Corp. of America
3240 Brittain Dr, Newberry
SC 29108-1510. 803/276-
3012.

Paperboard Industries Corp.
Highway 301 S, Latta SC
29565. 803/752-7121.

St. Joe Containers
Highways 221 & 385,
Laurens SC 29360.
864/682-3272.

Stone Container Corp.
128 Crews Dr, Columbia SC
29210-7202. 803/772-
5200.

Talley-Corbett Box Co.
1014 Railroad Ave,
Springfield SC 29146.
803/258-3494.

Union Camp Corp.
Highway 29 & I-85, Wellford
SC 29385. 864/439-3022.

Star Paper Tube Inc.
Alexander Dr, Taylors SC
29687. 864/244-8151.

PAPER PRODUCTS

Fiberweb North America
840 SE Main St,
Simpsonville SC 29681-
7150. 864/967-5600.

**CONVERTED PAPER AND
PAPERBOARD PRODUCTS**

Amspak
1832 N 5th St, Hartsville SC
29550-7836. 803/332-
3314.

**LUMBER AND WOOD
WHOLESALE**

**Commercial Door &
Hardware**
815 Lumber St, Myrtle Beach
SC 29577-3576. 803/448-
1711.

Horizon Forest Products Co.
240 Commerce Ct, Duncan
SC 29334-9285. 864/433-
1267.

McEwen Lumber Co.
1850 Ashley River Rd,
Charleston SC 29407-4711.
803/554-9561.

Calutie
Hwy 420, Ware Shoals SC
29692. 864/456-7984.

**For more information on career opportunities in the paper and wood products
industries:**

Associations

**AMERICAN FOREST AND PAPER
ASSOCIATION**
1111 19th Street NW, Suite 700,
Washington DC 20036. 202/463-2700. A
lobbying group that conducts informational
gatherings.

**AMERICAN FOREST AND PAPER
ASSOCIATION**
260 Madison Avenue, New York NY
10016. 212/340-0600. Headquartered in
Washington DC. A lobbying group that
conducts informational gatherings.

FOREST PRODUCTS SOCIETY
2801 Marshall Court, Madison WI 53705-
2295. 608/231-1361. An international,
nonprofit, educational association that
provides an information network for all
segments of the forest products industry.
Offers employment referral service.

NATIONAL PAPER TRADE ASSOCIATION
111 Great Neck Road, Great Neck NY
11021. 516/829-3070. Offers •
management services to wholesalers. Offers
books, seminars; and research services.

PAPERBOARD PACKAGING COUNCIL
888 17th Street NW, Suite 900,
Washington DC 20006. 202/289-4100.
Offers statistical and lobbying services.

**TECHNICAL ASSOCIATION OF THE PULP
AND PAPER INDUSTRY**
P.O. Box 105113, Atlanta GA 30348.
404/446-1400. Nonprofit. Offers
conferences and education.

Directories

**DIRECTORY OF THE FOREST PRODUCTS
INDUSTRY**
Miller Freeman Publications, Inc., 600
Harrison Street, San Francisco CA 94107.
415/905-2200.

**LOCKWOOD-POST'S DIRECTORY OF THE
PAPER AND ALLIED TRADES**
Miller Freeman Publications, Inc., 600
Harrison Street, San Francisco CA 94107.
415/905-2200.

POST'S PULP AND PAPER DIRECTORY
Miller Freeman Publications, Inc., 600
Harrison Street, San Francisco CA 94107.
415/905-2200.

Magazines

PAPERBOARD PACKAGING
Advanstar Communications, 131 West First
Street, Duluth MN 55802. 218/723-9200.

PULP AND PAPER WEEK
Miller Freeman Publications, Inc., 600
Harrison Street, San Francisco CA 94107.
415/905-2200.

WOOD TECHNOLOGIES
Miller Freeman Publications, Inc., 600
Harrison Street, San Francisco CA 94107.
415/905-2200.

PRINTING AND PUBLISHING

The big news in publishing in 1995 was the paper shortage. Paper costs account for 30 to 40 percent of the manufacturing costs of a book. Many companies compensated for the rising costs by stockpiling paper, designing books more tightly, lowering paper grades, and increasing book prices. The paper pinch also affected the magazine and newspaper industries. Newsprint prices rose more than 30 percent from early 1994 to early 1995. Magazines became noticeably shorter. One good sign for newspapers and magazines: As the economy improves, companies will increase their print advertising budgets. And, with a presidential election and a Summer Olympics on the calendar in '96, spending for advertising will increase.

Another way some publishers are balancing their books against the paper crunch is by looking to electronic media, a competitive and rapidly expanding medium. Many book publishers are offering CD-ROM versions of popular books, especially educational, reference, and children's books. Also, books-on-tape are growing in popularity. Magazines and newspapers also are joining the electronic bandwagon -- many periodicals and newspapers are now available online.

Book printing and distribution are also evolving. Traditionally, long print runs were necessary to keep costs down. But thanks to new digital presses that don't use plates, books can now be printed and distributed in small batches according to demand. Instead of printing and then distributing, publishers can now distribute and then print. Publishers will be able to use many small presses across the country, instead of one or two strategically placed large presses. The result: increased demand for computer-savvy printing professionals and dramatic cuts in shipping and warehousing.

North Carolina

AMERICAN CITY BUSINESS JOURNALS
128 South Tryon Street, Suite 2200, Charlotte NC 28202. 704/375-7404. **Contact:** Tom Wood, Human Resources Manager. **Description:** American City Business Journals publishes 27 business newspapers; a legal newspaper; the *Winston Cup Scene*, which is devoted to coverage of NASCAR motorsports racing; and also owns The Network of City Business Journals, a national advertising representation firm. American City Business Journals is one of the nation's largest publishers of local weekly business newspapers. The acquisition of the *Winston Cup Scene* at the end of 1992 marked the company's entry into sports publishing. Most of American City's business newspapers are located in the nation's top 50 markets. The company's newspapers emphasize reporting of local business news and information. Total paid circulation of the business weeklies is 313,000. Leading advertisers in the newspapers include computer and telecommunications companies, financial institutions, insurance providers, commercial real estate developers and professional organizations such as law and accounting firms. The newspapers primarily compete for readers and advertisers with the business sections of local daily newspapers. **Other U.S. locations:** Phoenix AZ; Los Angeles CA; San Francisco CA; San Jose CA; Denver CO; Washington DC; Jacksonville FL; Miami FL; Orlando FL; Tampa FL; Atlanta GA; Honolulu HI; Chicago IL; Wichita KS; Louisville KY; Baltimore MD; Detroit MI; Kansas City MO; St. Louis MO; Raleigh NC; Albany NY; Buffalo NY; New York NY; Cincinnati OH; Columbus OH; Portland OR; Houston TN; Dallas TX; San Antonio TX; Seattle WA.

BEATY'S BINDERY SERVICE
3216 Cullman Avenue, Charlotte NC 28206. 704/375-9222. **Contact:** Human Resources. **Description:** Beaty's Bindery Service is a full-service printer and binder.

BELLSOUTH ADVERTISING AND PUBLISHING CORPORATION
P.O. Box 668200, Charlotte NC 28266. 704/522-5650. **Fax:** 704/522-5506. **Recorded Jobline:** 704/522-5894. **Contact:** Eunice Smith, Manager of Employment/Recruitment. **Description:** Publishes more than 90 general Yellow Pages directories that cover North and South Carolina. These directories cover all major areas of both states, with Charlotte, NC, having the largest circulation at 750,000. **NOTE:** Experience is preferred for applicants applying to many of the job openings with BellSouth Advertising and Publishing Corporation. **Common positions include:** Advertising Sales; Marketing Specialist; Sales Associate; Sales Representative. **Educational backgrounds include:** Business Administration; College Degree; Communications; Liberal Arts; Marketing. **Benefits:** 401K; Dental Insurance; Disability Coverage; Life Insurance; Medical Insurance; Profit Sharing; Savings Plan; Tuition Assistance. **Corporate headquarters location:** Atlanta GA. **Parent company:** BellSouth Corporation. **Operations at this facility include:** Administration; Regional Headquarters; Sales; Service. **Listed on:** New York Stock Exchange.

THE CHARLOTTE OBSERVER
600 South Tryon Street, Charlotte NC 28202. 704/358-5000. **Contact:** Personnel. **Description:** A newspaper publisher. *The Charlotte Observer* is one of America's 50 largest newspapers, and was also the winner of two Pulitzers for Public Service in the 1980s. The parent company, Knight-Ridder Inc., is a newspaper publishing company which owns 28 dailies in 15 states and three non-dailies in suburban areas. Knight-Ridder also has interests in the information distribution market through Business Information Services, with subsidiaries Knight-Ridder Information, Inc., Knight-Ridder Financial, and Technimetrics. Other interests include partial ownership of the Seattle Times Company, two paper mills, a newspaper advertising sales company, and SCI Holdings. **NOTE:** *The Charlotte Observer* hires people with skills in writing, editing, business management, clerical, newspaper production, distribution, computer technology, graphics, and many other areas. **Common positions include:** Editor; Marketing Specialist; Reporter; Services Sales Representative. **Educational backgrounds include:** Business Administration; Economics; Finance; Journalism; Marketing. **Benefits:** Dental Insurance; Disability Coverage; Employee Discounts; Life Insurance; Medical Insurance; Pension Plan; Savings Plan; Tuition Assistance. **Special Programs:** Internships. **Parent company:** Knight-Ridder, Inc. (Miami, FL). **Operations at this facility include:** Administration; Sales; Service. **Listed on:** New York Stock Exchange. **Number of employees at this location:** 1,000.

R.R. DONNELLEY & SONS COMPANY
1545 St. James Church Road, Newton NC 28658. 704/464-8110. **Contact:** Dave Edgington, Human Resources. **Description:** R.R. Donnelley & Sons is a world leader in managing, reproducing, and distributing print and digital information for publishing, merchandising, and information technology customers. The company is one of the largest commercial printers in the world, producing catalogs, inserts, magazines, books, directories, computer documentation, and financial printing. R.R. Donnelley has more than 180 strategically located sales offices and production facilities. Principal services offered by the company are conventional and digital pre-press operations, computerized printing and binding, and sophisticated pool shipping and distribution services for printed products; information repackaging into multiple formats (print, magnetic, and optical media); database management, list rental, list enhancement, and direct mail production services; turnkey computer documentation services (outsourcing, translation, printing, binding, diskette replication, kitting, licensing, republishing, and fulfillment); reprographics and facilities management; creative design and communication services; and digital and conventional map creation and related services. Founded in 1864. **Corporate headquarters location:** Chicago IL. **Other U.S. locations:** Charlotte NC; Greensboro NC; Spartanburg SC. **Listed on:** New York Stock Exchange. **Number of employees worldwide:** 35,000.

R.R. DONNELLEY & SONS COMPANY
128 South Tryon Street, Suite 1720, Charlotte NC 28202-5001. 704/333-0647. **Contact:** Human Resources. **Description:** R.R. Donnelley & Sons is a world leader in managing, reproducing, and distributing print and digital information for publishing, merchandising, and information technology customers. The company is one of the largest commercial printers in the world, producing catalogs, inserts, magazines, books, directories, computer documentation, and financial printing. R.R. Donnelley has more than 180 strategically located sales offices and production facilities. Principal services offered by the company are conventional and digital pre-press operations,

computerized printing and binding, and sophisticated pool shipping and distribution services for printed products; information repackaging into multiple formats (print, magnetic, and optical media); database management, list rental, list enhancement, and direct mail production services; turnkey computer documentation services (outsourcing, translation, printing, binding, diskette replication, kitting, licensing, republishing, and fulfillment); reprographics and facilities management; creative design and communication services; and digital and conventional map creation and related services. Founded in 1864. **Corporate headquarters location:** Chicago IL. **Other U.S. locations:** Newton NC; Spartanburg SC. **Listed on:** New York Stock Exchange. **Number of employees worldwide:** 35,000.

FAYETTEVILLE PUBLISHING COMPANY
458 Whitfield Street, Fayetteville NC 28306. 910/323-4848. **Contact:** John Holmes, Personnel Director. **Description:** Publishes the *Fayetteville Observer Times*.

GENERAL MEDIA
324 West Wendover Avenue, Greensboro NC 27408. 910/275-9809. **Contact:** Human Resources. **Description:** A periodical and book publisher. **NOTE:** Please send resumes to: 277 Park Avenue, 4th Floor, New York NY 10172, attention: Iris Frank.

GRAFTECH CORPORATION
P.O. Box 30364, Charlotte NC 28230. 704/372-4286. **Contact:** Human Resources. **Description:** Graftech Corporation is a major printing company. Parent company, Cadmus Communications Corporation, is a graphic communications company offering specialized products and services in three broad areas: printing, marketing, and publishing. Cadmus is the 26th largest graphic communications company in North America. Product lines include annual reports, catalogs, direct marketing financial printing, point-of-sale marketing, promotional printing, publishing, research journals, specialty magazines, and specialty packaging. Other subsidiaries of Cadmus Communications Corporation include: American Graphics, Inc. (Atlanta, GA); Cadmus Color Center, Inc. (Richmond, VA); Cadmus Direct Marketing, Inc. (Charlotte, NC); Cadmus Interactive (Tucker, GA); Cadmus Journal Services (Linthicum, MD, Easton, MD, and Richmond, VA); Central Florida Press, L.C. (Orlando, FL); Expert Brown (Richmond, VA); Garamond, Inc. (Baltimore, MD); Marblehead Communications, Inc. (Boston, MA); Three Score, Inc. (Tucker, GA); Cadmus Charlotte W.G. (Charlotte, NC); and The William Byrd Press (Richmond, VA). **NOTE:** Please send resumes to: Cadmus Charlotte W.G., P.O. Box 31517, Charlotte NC 28231-1517. **Parent company:** Cadmus Communications Corporation.

GREENSBORO NEWS AND RECORD
P.O. Box 20848, Greensboro NC 27420. 910/373-7000. **Contact:** Linda Tatum, Human Resources Assistant. **Description:** A daily newspaper with weekday circulation of 101,000, Saturday circulation of 122,000, and Sunday circulation of 128,000.

JORDAN GRAPHICS
P.O. Box 668306, Charlotte NC 28266. 704/398-5100. **Contact:** Barry Chambers, Human Resources Director. **Description:** Produces business forms.

THE NEWS & OBSERVER
215 South McDowell Street, Raleigh NC 27601. 919/829-4500. **Contact:** Eddie Jackson, Personnel Director. **Description:** A newspaper.

PACKAGE PRODUCTS SPECIALTY
8800 South Boulevard, Charlotte NC 28273. 704/552-9211. **Contact:** Bob Floyd, Director of Human Resources. **Description:** A printing company specializing in cartons and labels.

PIEDMONT PUBLISHING COMPANY
418 North Marshall Street, Winston-Salem NC 27101. 910/727-7330. **Contact:** Randy Noftle, Director of Human Resources. **Description:** A publishing company. **Common positions include:** Accountant/Auditor; Administrative Services Manager; Administrator; Advertising Clerk; Assistant Manager; Blue-Collar Worker Supervisor; Commercial Artist; Computer Operator; Credit Clerk and Authorizer; Credit Manager; Customer Service Representative; Department Manager; Editor; Electrician; General Manager; Graphic Artist; Heating/AC/Refrigeration Technician; Human Resources Specialist; Industrial Production Manager; Instructor/Trainer; Librarian; Manufacturer's/Wholesaler's Sales Rep.; Marketing Specialist; Marketing/Advertising/PR Manager; Payroll Clerk; Photographer/Camera Operator; Photographic Process Worker; Prepress Worker; Printing Press Operator; Public Relations Specialist; Reporter; Secretary; Services Sales Representative; Technical Writer/Editor; Truck Driver;

Typist/Word Processor. **Educational backgrounds include:** Accounting; Art/Design; Business Administration; Communications; Journalism; Liberal Arts; Marketing. **Benefits:** Dental Insurance; Disability Coverage; Employee Discounts; Life Insurance; Medical Insurance; Pension Plan; Savings Plan; Tuition Assistance. **Special Programs:** Internships. **Corporate headquarters location:** Richmond VA. **Parent company:** Media General, Inc. **Operations at this facility include:** Administration; Manufacturing; Sales; Service. **Listed on:** American Stock Exchange. **Number of employees at this location:** 584.

QUALEX, INC.
3404 North Duke Street, Durham NC 27704-2130. 919/383-8535. **Contact:** Mike Kelly, Director of Human Resources. **Description:** A photofinisher. **Common positions include:** Accountant/Auditor; Attorney; Credit Clerk and Authorizer; Graphic Artist; Industrial Engineer; Market Research Analyst; Paralegal; Payroll Clerk; Purchasing Agent and Manager; Secretary. **Benefits:** Dental Insurance; Disability Coverage; Employee Discounts; Life Insurance; Medical Insurance; Pension Plan; Profit Sharing; Savings Plan; Tuition Assistance. **Corporate headquarters location:** This Location. **Parent company:** Eastman Kodak. **Number of employees at this location:** 275. **Number of employees nationwide:** 7,500.

WNC BUSINESS JOURNAL
P.O. Box 8204, Asheville NC 28814. 704/258-1322. **Fax:** 704/253-3726. **Contact:** Stephen Mason, Editor. **Description:** A monthly publication covering western North Carolina business news. WNC Business Journal also publishes *Today's Hospital Gift Shop Newsletter*, the official newsletter for all United States hospital gift shops. **Common positions include:** Accountant/Auditor; Advertising Sales; Editor; Operations/Production Manager; Reporter. **Educational backgrounds include:** Accounting; Advertising; Art/Design; Business Administration; Communications; Economics; Finance; Liberal Arts; Marketing; Sales. **Corporate headquarters location:** This Location. **Operations at this facility include:** Administration; Sales.

WALLACE COMPUTER SERVICES
P.O. Box 1577, Gastonia NC 28053. 704/864-5717. **Contact:** Scott Henley, Human Resources Manager. **Description:** A full-service commercial printer, specializing in business forms.

WASHBURN GRAPHICS, INC.
P.O. Box 31517, Charlotte NC 28231-1517. 704/372-5270. **Contact:** Ms. Chris Towson, Human Resources. **Description:** Washburn Graphics specializes in the following product lines: annual reports, promotional printing, catalogs, financial printing, and specialty packaging. Washburn Graphics has acquired the specialized equipment and production skills which enables it to offer these customers one-stop production and related services. The parent company, Cadmus Communications Corporation, is a graphic communications company offering specialized products and services in three broad areas: printing, marketing, and publishing. Cadmus is one of the largest graphic communications companies in North America. Product lines include annual reports, catalogs, direct marketing financial printing, point-of-sale marketing, promotional printing, publishing, research journals, specialty magazines, and specialty packaging. **Subsidiaries include:** American Graphics, Inc. (Atlanta GA); Cadmus Color Center, Inc. (Richmond VA); Cadmus Direct Marketing, Inc. (Charlotte NC); Cadmus Interactive (Tucker GA); Cadmus Journal Services (Linthicum MD, Easton MD, and Richmond VA); Central Florida Press, L.C. (Orlando FL); Expert Brown (Richmond VA); Garamond, Inc. (Baltimore MD); Graphtech Corporation (Charlotte NC); Marblehead Communications, Inc. (Boston MA); Three Score, Inc. (Tucker GA); Tuff Stuff Publications, Inc. (Richmond VA); and The William Byrd Press (Richmond VA). **Parent company:** Cadmus Communications Corporation (Richmond VA).

WINSTON-SALEM JOURNAL
P.O. Box 3159, Winston-Salem NC 27102. 910/727-7211. **Contact:** Randy Noftle, Director of Human Resources. **Description:** A daily newspaper. **Common positions include:** Accountant/Auditor; Customer Service Representative; Editor; Reporter; Services Sales Representative; Technical Writer/Editor. **Educational backgrounds include:** Accounting; Art/Design; Business Administration; Communications; Liberal Arts; Marketing. **Benefits:** 401K; Dental Insurance; Disability Coverage; Life Insurance; Medical Insurance; Pension Plan; Tuition Assistance. **Special Programs:** Internships. **Corporate headquarters location:** Richmond VA. **Parent company:** Media General, Inc. **Number of employees at this location:** 5,750.

Note: Because addresses and telephone numbers of smaller companies change rapidly, we recommend you call each company to verify the information below before inquiring about job opportunities. Mass mailings are not recommended.

Additional employers with under 250 employees:

NEWSPAPERS: PUBLISHING AND/OR PRINTING

Asheville Citizen Times Publishing
14 O Henry Ave, Asheville NC 28801-2604. 704/252-5611.

Daily Advance
216 S Poindexter St, Elizabeth City NC 27909-4835. 919/335-0841.

Freedom Communications
707 S Main St, Burlington NC 27215-5844. 910/227-0131.

Freedom Newspapers
2500 E Franklin Blvd, Gastonia NC 28056-9297. 704/864-3291.

Hickory Publishing Co.
1100 Park Pl, Hickory NC 28602. 704/322-4510.

High Point Enterprise
210 Church Ave, High Point NC 27262-4806. 910/888-3500.

Jacksonville Daily News
P.O. Box 196, Jacksonville NC 28541-0196. 910/353-1171.

News & Observer Publishing Co.
103 W Main St, Durham NC 27701-3638. 919/956-2423.

Rhinoceros Times
107 E Market St, Greensboro NC 27401-2805. 910/273-0885.

Times-News
1717 Four Seasons Blvd, Hendersonvlle NC 28792-2859. 704/692-0505.

Village Companies
88 McClamroch Cir, Chapel Hill NC 27514-1571. 919/968-4801.

Wilmington Star News
1003 S 17th St, Wilmington NC 28401-8023. 910/343-2000.

PERIODICALS: PUBLISHING AND/OR PRINTING

God's World Publications
85 Tunnel Rd, Asheville NC 28805-1232. 704/253-8063.

Harmon Publishing
2814 Firestone Dr, Greensboro NC 27406-4538. 910/370-0060.

Business North Carolina Magazine
506 N Gurney St, Burlington NC 27215-4820. 910/584-3899.

BOOKS: PUBLISHING AND/OR PRINTING

Business Products Division
P.O. Box 7328, High Point NC 27264-7328. 910/889-6767.

Edwards Brothers Inc.
800 Edwards Dr, Lillington NC 27546. 910/893-2717.

Colophon Publishing Services
110 Balsamwood Ct, Cary NC 27513-3456. 919/460-8874.

Oxford University Press
2001 Evans Rd, Cary NC 27513-2009. 919/677-0977.

The Real Estate Book
1210-B E Mountain St, Kernersville NC 27284. 910/996-0717.

Walsworth Publishing Co.
6101 Idlewild Rd, Suite 329, Charlotte NC 28212-0517. 704/536-6548.

COMMERCIAL PRINTING

Craftsmen Printing Co.
2700 Westinghouse Blvd, Charlotte NC 28273-6516. 704/588-2120.

Fisher-Harrison Corp.
1301 Carolina St, Greensboro NC 27401-1001. 910/378-6000.

Hickory Printing Group
2025 Brentwood St, High Point NC 27263-1805. 910/889-6767.

Hickory Printing Group
542 Main Ave SE, Hickory NC 28602. 704/322-3431.

Litho Industries Inc.
1 Litho Way, Durham NC 27703-8929. 919/596-7000.

Meredith Webb Printing Co.
334 N Main St, Burlington NC 27217. 910/228-8378.

Norling Studios Inc.
221 Swathmore Ave, High Point NC 27263-1931. 910/434-3151.

Printsouth
2605 Phoenix Dr, Greensboro NC 27406-6320. 910/292-4220.

Progress Printing Co.
22206 Torrence Chapel Rd, Davidson NC 28036-8308. 704/892-4723.

Retail Graphics Printing Co.
10911 Granite St, Charlotte NC 28273-6316. 704/588-9938.

Wesley's Business Forms
1100 Old Beltway, Rural Hall NC 27045-9537. 910/969-9101.

Finch Industries Inc.
104 Williams St, Thomasville NC 27360-3600. 910/472-4499.

Hamco Inc.
1205 Burris Rd, Newton NC 28658-1953. 704/464-6730.

Queens Group Inc.
1101 S Highway 27, Stanley NC 28164-2227. 704/263-9200.

Ringier America Inc.
8700 Red Oak Blvd, Suite J, Charlotte NC 28217-3979. 704/527-6865.

BLANK BOOKS AND BOOKBINDING

Acme Sample Books Inc.
2410 Schirra Pl, High Point NC 27263-1730. 910/883-4187.

Southeast Library Bindery
6204 Corporate Park Dr, Browns Summit NC 27214-8300. 910/375-1102.

PRINTING TRADE SERVICES

Color Response Inc.
3101 Stafford Dr, Charlotte NC 28208-3572. 704/392-1153.

WRE/Colortech
533 Banner Ave, Greensboro NC 27401-4302. 910/275-9821.

COMMERCIAL PHOTOGRAPHY

Lifetouch National School Studios
7341 W Friendly Ave, Suite H, Greensboro NC 27410-6251. 910/547-8260.

PHOTO FINISHING LABORATORIES

Amity Photo Restoration
6501 Old Pineville Rd #N, Charlotte NC 28217-4389. 704/554-1974.

Eckerd Express Photo
635 Friendly Center Rd, Greensboro NC 27408-7803. 910/632-9423.

Eckerd Express Photo
Abbey Plaza, Belmont NC 28012. 704/825-6197.

Wolf Camera & Video
328 Four Seasons Town Centre, Greensboro NC 27407. 910/299-8197.

Wolf Camera & Video
704 Pembroke Rd, Greensboro NC 27408-7610. 910/852-0358.

Wolf Camera & Video
303 E Woodlawn Rd, Charlotte NC 28217-2348. 704/523-5356.

Wolf Camera & Video
334 Cross Creek Mall, Fayetteville NC 28303-7242. 910/864-0467.

South Carolina

AIKEN STANDARD
P.O. Box 456, Aiken SC 29802. 803/648-2311. **Contact:** Judy Randall, Personnel Manager. **Description:** Publishes the *Aiken Standard*, a daily newspaper.

R.R. DONNELLEY & SONS COMPANY
300 Jones Road, Spartanburg SC 29307. 864/579-6000. **Contact:** Doug Winslow, Human Resources Manager. **Description:** This location specializes in the commercial printing of catalogs and newspaper inserts. R.R. Donnelley & Sons Company is engaged in managing, reproducing, and distributing print and digital information for publishing, merchandising, and information technology customers. The company is one of the largest commercial printers in the world, producing catalogs, inserts, magazines, books, directories, computer documentation, and financial printing. R.R. Donnelley & Sons Company has more than 180 strategically located sales offices and production facilities. Principal services offered by the company are conventional and digital pre-press operations, computerized printing and binding, and sophisticated pool shipping and distribution services for printed products; information repackaging into multiple formats (print, magnetic, and optical media); database management, list rental, list enhancement, and direct mail production services; turnkey computer documentation services (outsourcing, translation, printing, binding, diskette replication, kitting, licensing, republishing, and fulfillment); reprographics and facilities management; creative design and communication services; and digital and conventional map creation and related services. R.R. Donnelley & Sons Company was founded in 1864. **Corporate headquarters location:** Chicago IL. **Other U.S. locations:** Charlotte NC; Greensboro NC; Newton NC. **Listed on:** New York Stock Exchange. **Number of employees worldwide:** 35,000.

EVENING POST PUBLISHING COMPANY
134 Columbus Street, Charleston SC 29403. 803/577-7111. **Contact:** Paul Sharry, Human Resources Director. **Description:** An umbrella corporation for several newspaper publishing companies throughout South Carolina. The Evening Post Publishing Company owns *The Post Courier*, with a daily circulation of 115,000 and a Sunday circulation of 125,000. The Evening Post Publishing Company's business holdings also include several television stations.

GREENVILLE NEWS PIEDMONT
P.O. Box 1688, Greenville SC 29602-1688. 864/298-4100. **Contact:** Julie Sawyer, Human Resources Department Manager. **Description:** Greenville News Piedmont is a daily newspaper publisher. The company publishes *The Greenville News*, a morning paper which is printed seven days per week. *The Greenville News* has a circulation of over 100,000 on weekends and slightly less on weekdays.

THE POST & COURIER
134 Columbus Street, Charleston SC 29403-4800. 803/577-7111. **Contact:** Paul Sharry, Personnel Manager. **Description:** Publishes *The Post and Courier*, with a daily circulation of 115,000 and a Sunday circulation of 125,000.

THE STATE NEWSPAPER
P.O. Box 1333, Columbia SC 29202-9943. 803/771-6161. **Contact:** Holly Rogers, Human Resources Director. **Description:** Publishes *The State* on mornings and Sundays. Weekday circulation exceeds 145,000. The parent company, Knight-Ridder, Inc., a major newspaper publishing company, owns 28 dailies in 15 states, and three non-dailies in suburban areas. The company also produces niche publications such as Myrtle Beach's *Golf*, *CubaNews* newsletter in Miami and *Northland Outdoors* in Grand

Forks, ND. The larger papers include the *Miami Herald*, *Philadelphia Inquirer*, *Philadelphia Daily News*, *Detroit Free Press*, and *San Jose Mercury News*. Knight-Ridder also has interests in the information distribution market through Business Information Services, with subsidiaries Knight-Ridder Information, Inc., Knight-Ridder Financial, and Technimetrics. Dialog online information retrieval serves the business, scientific, technology, medical, education, and medical communities in more than 100 countries. Knight-Ridder Financial provides real-time financial news and pricing information through primary products MoneyCenter, Digital Datafeed, ProfitCenter, and TradeCenter. Knight-Ridder also has interests in cable television and other businesses. Other interests include partial ownership of the Seattle Times Company, two paper mills, a newspaper advertising sales company, and SCI Holdings. **Common positions include:** Advertising Clerk; Blue-Collar Worker Supervisor; Computer Programmer; Customer Service Representative; Editor; Manufacturer's/Wholesaler's Sales Rep.; Reporter. **Educational backgrounds include:** Communications. **Benefits:** Dental Insurance; Employee Discounts; Life Insurance; Medical Insurance; Pension Plan; Savings Plan; Tuition Assistance. **Corporate headquarters location:** This Location. **Parent company:** Knight-Ridder, Inc. (Miami, FL). **Operations at this facility include:** Administration; Manufacturing; Sales; Service. **Listed on:** New York Stock Exchange.

Note: Because addresses and telephone numbers of smaller companies change rapidly, we recommend you call each company to verify the information below before inquiring about job opportunities. Mass mailings are not recommended.

Additional employers with under 250 employees:

NEWSPAPERS: PUBLISHING AND/OR PRINTING

Beaufort Gazette
1556 Salem Rd, Beaufort SC 29902-5236. 803/524-3183.

Independent Publishing Co.
1000 Williamston Rd, Anderson SC 29621-6508. 864/224-4321.

Mid-South Management Co.
314 S Pine St, Spartanburg SC 29302-2617. 864/583-2907.

Osteen Publishing Co.
20 N Magnolia St, Sumter SC 29150-4940. 803/775-6331.

Spartanburg Herald Journal
1D Metro Dr, Spartanburg SC 29303-2754. 864/591-1606.

Sun Publishing Co. Inc.
914 Frontage Rd E, Myrtle Beach SC 29577-6700. 803/626-8555.

Thomson Newspapers
141 S Irby St, Florence SC 29501-4409. 803/669-1771.

BOOKS: PUBLISHING AND/OR PRINTING

Hart Graphics Inc.
800 SE Main St, Simpsonville SC 29681-7150. 864/967-7821.

State Printing Co. Inc.
1210 Key Rd, Columbia SC 29201-4739. 803/799-9550.

MISC. PUBLISHING

Greater Columbia Apartment Guide
3900 Bentley Dr Apt 1722, Columbia SC 29210-7989. 803/731-9588.

COMMERCIAL PRINTING

Electric City Printing Co.
730 Hampton Rd, Williamston SC 29697-9225. 864/224-6331.

Keys Printing Co.
I-385 at Roper Mountain Rd, Greenville SC 29615. 864/288-6560.

Sherwin-Williams Co.
100 N Woods Dr, Fountain Inn SC 29644-9006. 864/862-1111.

Spartanburg Herald Journal
189 W Main St, Spartanburg SC 29306-2334. 864/582-4511.

COPAC Inc.
195 Davis Chapel Rd, Spartanburg SC 29307-4300. 864/579-2554.

John H. Harland Co.
3430 Platt Springs Rd, West Columbia SC 29170-2206. 803/794-3239.

Wentworth Printing Corp.
802 Chris Dr, West Columbia SC 29169-4608. 803/796-9990.

BUSINESS FORMS

Eastern Business Forms
P.O. Box 10, Mauldin SC 29662-0010. 864/288-2451.

PRINTING TRADE SERVICES

Zenith Engraving Co.
Wilson St Ext, Chester SC 29706. 803/377-1911.

NEWS SYNDICATES

Associated Press
92 Broad St, Charleston SC 29401-2201. 803/722-1660.

For more information on career opportunities in printing and publishing:

Associations

AMERICAN BOOKSELLERS ASSOCIATION
828 South Broadway, Tarrytown NY 10591. 914/591-2665.

AMERICAN INSTITUTE OF GRAPHIC ARTS
919 3rd Avenue, 22nd Floor, New York NY 10003-3004. 212/807-1990. A 36-chapter, nationwide organization sponsoring programs and events for graphic designers and related professionals.

AMERICAN SOCIETY OF NEWSPAPER EDITORS
P.O. Box 4090, Reston VA 22090-1700.
703/648-1144.

ASSOCIATION OF GRAPHIC ARTS
330 7th Avenue, 9th Floor, New York NY
10001-5010. 212/279-2100. Offers
educational classes and seminars.

BINDING INDUSTRIES OF AMERICA
70 East Lake Street, Suite 300, Chicago IL
60601. 312/372-7606. Offers credit
collection, government affairs, and
educational services.

THE DOW JONES NEWSPAPER FUND
P.O. Box 300, Princeton NJ 08543-0300.
609/520-4000.

GRAPHIC ARTISTS GUILD
11 West 20th Street, 8th Floor, New York
NY 10011. 212/463-7730. A union for
artists.

INTERNATIONAL GRAPHIC ARTS EDUCATION ASSOCIATION
4615 Forbes Avenue, Pittsburgh PA 15213.
412/682-5170.

MAGAZINE PUBLISHERS ASSOCIATION
919 Third Avenue, 22nd Floor, New York
NY 10022. 212/752-0055. A membership
association.

NATIONAL ASSOCIATION OF PRINTERS AND LITHOGRAPHERS
780 Pallisade Avenue, Teaneck NJ 07666.
201/342-0700. Membership. Offers
consulting services and a publication.

NATIONAL NEWSPAPER ASSOCIATION
1525 Wilson Boulevard, Arlington VA
22209. 703/907-7900.

NATIONAL PRESS CLUB
529 14th St. NW, 13th Floor, Washington
DC 20045. 202/662-7500. Offers
professional seminars and career services,
conference facilities, and members-only
restaurants and a health club.

NEWSPAPER ASSOCIATION OF AMERICA
Newspaper Center, 11600 Sunrise Valley
Drive, Reston VA 22091. 703/648-1000.
The technology department publishes
marketing research.

THE NEWSPAPER GUILD
Research and Information Department,
8611 2nd Avenue, Silver Spring MD
20910. 301/585-2990. A trade union.

PRINTING INDUSTRIES OF AMERICA
100 Dangerfield Road, Alexandria VA
22314. 703/519-8100. Members are
offered publications, insurance, and political
action.

TECHNICAL ASSOCIATION OF THE GRAPHIC ARTS
68 Lomb memorial Drive, Rochester NY
14623. 716/475-7470. Conducts an
annual conference and offers newsletters.

WRITERS GUILD OF AMERICA WEST
8955 Beverly Boulevard, West Hollywood

CA 90048. 310/550-1000. A membership
association which registers scripts.

Directories

EDITOR & PUBLISHER INTERNATIONAL YEARBOOK
Editor & Publisher Company Inc., 11 West
19th Street, New York NY 10011.
212/675-4380. $100.00. Offers
newspapers to editors in both the United
States and foreign countries.

GRAPHIC ARTS BLUE BOOK
A.F. Lewis & Company, 245 Fifth Avenue,
New York NY 10016. 212/679-0770.
$80.00. Manufacturers and dealers.

JOURNALISM CAREER AND SCHOLARSHIP GUIDE
The Dow Jones Newspaper Fund, P.O. Box
300, Princeton NJ 08543-0300. 609/520-
4000.

Magazines

AIGA JOURNAL
American Institute of Graphic Arts, 164
Third Avenue, New York NY 10010.
212/752-0813. $21.50. A 56-page
quarterly magazine dealing with
contemporary issues.

EDITOR AND PUBLISHER
Editor & Publisher Company Inc., 164 Third
Avenue, New York NY 10010. 212/807-
1990.

GRAPHIC ARTS MONTHLY
249 West 49th Street, New York NY
10011. 212/463-6836.

GRAPHIS
141 Lexington Avenue, New York NY
10016. 212/532-9387. $89.00. Magazine
covers portfolios, articles, designers,
advertising, and photos.

PRINT
104 Fifth Avenue, 19th Floor New York NY
10011. 212/463-0600. Offers a graphic
design magazine. $55.00 for subscription.

PUBLISHER'S WEEKLY
249 West 17th Street, New York NY
10011. Weekly publication for book
publishers and sellers.

Special Book and Magazine Programs

THE NEW YORK UNIVERSITY SUMMER PUBLISHING PROGRAM
48 Cooper Square, Room 108, New York
NY 10003. 212/998-7219.

THE RADCLIFFE PUBLISHING COURSE
77 Brattle Street, Cambridge MA 02138.
617/495-8678.

RICE UNIVERSITY PUBLISHING PROGRAM
Office of Continuing Studies, P.O. Box
1892, Houston TX 77251-1892. 713/520-
6022.

UNIVERSITY OF DENVER PUBLISHING INSTITUTE
2075 South University Boulevard, #D-114,
Denver CO 80208. 303/871-4868.

REAL ESTATE

 *Rising interest rates in early 1995 caused housing starts to drop and sales of existing single-family homes to moderately decline. However, by mid-summer, rates began falling once more. Solid opportunities for jobseekers are available for those looking to enter the real estate field. Occupancy will go up in the office sector, as few new office properties are being built. Apartment construction, on the other hand, is on the rise. Commercial property sales will help maintain employment opportunities for real estate agents, brokers, and appraisers. The number of job openings in these occupations is expected to match the number of openings for most other careers nationwide. The majority of these openings, however, will be replacement positions, as agents return or leave the field, rather than new positions.*

Property and real estate managers will have even greater opportunities to find employment, as more openings appear for these positions than for other occupations. The people with the most qualified backgrounds for these jobs will be those with college degrees in business administration and other related studies.

North Carolina

HEITMAN PROPERTIES NORTH CAROLINA LTD.
301 North Main Street, Suite 2208, Winston-Salem NC 27111. 910/725-0294. **Contact:** Lester Burnett, Property Manager. **Description:** Operates a real estate agency.

HOWARD PERRY & WALSTON/BETTER HOMES AND GARDENS
5000 Falls of the Neuse Road, #100, Raleigh NC 27609. 919/876-8824. **Contact:** Susan Holbrook, Broker-in-Charge. **Description:** A realty agency.

LINCOLN PROPERTY COMPANY
909-1609 Brookrun Drive, Charlotte NC 28209. 704/525-8118. **Contact:** Dawn Krieg, Regional Property Manager. **Description:** A property management and development company.

WESTMINSTER HOMES
2706 North Church Street, Greensboro NC 27405. 910/375-6200. **Fax:** 910/375-6355. **Contact:** Mr. Cameron Ross, President. **Description:** A real estate and construction company. Westminster Homes specializes in single-family home development and sales in North Carolina. **Common positions include:** Accountant/Auditor; Computer Programmer; Customer Service Representative; Draftsperson; Human Resources Specialist; Manufacturer's/Wholesaler's Sales Rep.; Marketing Specialist; Operations/Production Manager; Purchasing Agent and Manager; Quality Control Supervisor. **Educational backgrounds include:** Accounting; Business Administration; Computer Science; Marketing. **Benefits:** Dental Insurance; Disability Coverage; Employee Discounts; Life Insurance; Medical Insurance; Pension Plan; Profit Sharing; Savings Plan; Stock Option; Tuition Assistance. **Special Programs:** Training Programs. **Corporate headquarters location:** This Location. **Other U.S. locations:** Cary NC. **Parent company:** Weyerhaeuser Company. **Operations at this facility include:** Administration; Sales; Service. **Listed on:** New York Stock Exchange. **Number of employees at this location:** 60. **Number of employees nationwide:** 100.

Note: Because addresses and telephone numbers of smaller companies change rapidly, we recommend you call each company to verify the information below before inquiring about job opportunities. Mass mailings are not recommended.

Additional employers with under 250 employees:

REAL ESTATE OPERATORS

CNM Associates
4020 Capital Blvd, Raleigh
NC 27604. 919/878-3955.

Gates at Quail Hollow
7040 Meeting St, Charlotte
NC 28210. 704/553-8033.

Salvation Army Booth Garden Apartments
421 N Poplar St, Charlotte
NC 28202-1727. 704/376-0763.

Timberstone Apartments
2201 Yorkhills Dr, Charlotte
NC 28217-7999. 704/523-6333.

Walden Woods Condos Association
4754 Walden Pond Dr,
Raleigh NC 27604-2707.
919/876-9391.

Windsor Harbor
3217 Shamrock Dr,
Charlotte NC 28215-3007.
704/536-6463.

Woodview Apartments
221 Hilo Dr, Charlotte NC
28206-4907. 704/596-0276.

Battleground Oaks Apartments
3803 Cotswold Ter,
Greensboro NC 27410-9355.
910/282-7368.

Brandemere Apartments Lease Office
7013 Brandemere Ln,
Winston-Salem NC 27106-2844. 910/744-0352.

Calibre Place
1820 Avent Ridge Rd,
Raleigh NC 27606-3468.
919/851-2211.

Campus Walk Apartments
455 Racine Dr, Wilmington
NC 28403-1721. 910/395-0833.

Cinnamon Ridge Apartments
835 Navaho Dr, Raleigh NC
27609-6748. 919/876-4548.

Colony Apartments
1250 Ephesus Church Rd,
Chapel Hill NC 27514-2569.
919/967-7019.

Courtyard Apartments
5312 Montague St, Charlotte
NC 28205-. 704/563-7487.

Creekwood Village Apartments
3102 Commerce Pl,
Burlington NC 27215-5157.
910/584-8498.

Cross Creek Apartments
1902 Hickory Blvd SE, Lenoir
NC 28645-6420. 704/728-0485.

Deerwood Crossing
1805 Franciscan Ter,
Winston-Salem NC 27127-7704. 910/788-2832.

East Lake Village Apartments
7428 Pebblestone Dr,
Charlotte NC 28212-0044.
704/536-7203.

Foxcroft East Apartments
4612 Simsbury Rd, Charlotte
NC 28226-5051. 704/365-1903.

Glen Alexander Apartments
420 Michelle Linnea Dr,
Charlotte NC 28262-0865.
704/547-0016.

Greenhaven Apartments
1407 Spring St, Charlotte
NC 28206-2827. 704/333-7279.

Hidden Oaks Apartments
101 Hidden Oaks Dr, Cary
NC 27513-3370. 919/481-2600.

Highland Green Apartments
4300 Furman Hall, Raleigh
NC 27612-4145. 919/783-9377.

Highlander Apartments
119 Roberts St, Red Springs
NC 28377-1513. 910/843-2389.

Homestead Lodge
I-85 & S Elm-Eugene St,
Greensboro NC 27406.
910/272-5834.

McMillan Place
8738 Fairview Rd, Charlotte
NC 28226-5100. 704/366-2471.

Misty Woods Apartments
4630 Central Ave, Charlotte
NC 28205-5802. 704/536-8571.

Murdoch Place
206 Gray Ave, Durham NC
27701-2446. 919/688-3695.

North Henderson Heights Apartments
W Andrews Av, Henderson
NC 27536. 919/492-5201.

Paces Forest
2121 Paces Forest Ct,
Raleigh NC 27612-6423.
919/783-5430.

Page Mill Apartments
100 Kempwood Dr, Cary NC
27513. 919/467-0338.

Peppertree Apartments
4311 Central Ave, Charlotte
NC 28205-5662. 704/537-5292.

Pineland Place Apartments
1007 Pineland St,
Greensboro NC 27407-2138.
910/855-1264.

Pungo Village Apartments
Pungo Village Apts, Belhaven
NC 27810. 919/943-6466.

Royal Oaks Gardens Apartments
1760 Citadel Ct, Kannapolis
NC 28083-6800. 704/933-2177.

Saint Croix Apartments
1 Saint Croix Pl, Greensboro
NC 27410-4958. 910/299-5581.

Salem Gardens Apartments
1201 Terry Rd, Winston-Salem NC 27107-1632.
910/784-5611.

Sedgefield Square Apartments
4215 Bernau Ave,
Greensboro NC 27407-4253.
910/854-0010.

Shorewood at Raintree
7907 Shorewood Dr,
Charlotte NC 28277-7814.
704/542-0011.

Simsbury Place Apartments
4428 Simsbury Rd, Charlotte
NC 28226-5047. 704/364-8762.

Summer Lake Apartments
6200 Riese Dr, Raleigh NC
27613-3037. 919/782-1393.

The Ledges
730 Anson St, Winston-Salem NC 27103-3800.
910/721-9111.

The Shire
3101A Aileen Dr, Raleigh NC
27606-3624. 919/851-6366.

Tree Top Apartments
1328 Steinbeck Dr, Raleigh
NC 27609. 919/876-1699.

Triangle Communities
3165 Hillsborough Rd,
Durham NC 27705-3002.
919/383-7491.

Tryon House Apartments
508 N Tryon St, Charlotte
NC 28202. 704/332-5009.

Village Apartments
240 Glendare Dr, Winston-Salem NC 27104-4708.
910/765-9340.

Villages of Forest Ridge Apartments
6125 Winged Elm Ct, Charlotte NC 28212-4584. 704/535-0225.

Sir Walter Apartments
400 Fayetteville Street Mall, Raleigh NC 27601-1705. 919/832-1300.

Waterford Lakes Apartments
8000 Waterford Lakes Dr, Charlotte NC 28210-7457. 704/552-5446.

Wellington Farms Apartments
4700 Twisted Oaks Rd, Charlotte NC 28212-8383. 704/532-0882.

Willow Woods Apartments
3007 Ingleside Dr Apt A, High Point NC 27265-1967. 910/869-5310.

Woodlawn House Apartments
1315 E Woodlawn Rd, Charlotte NC 28209-3058. 704/527-2822.

Woods Edge Apartments
4655 Hope Valley Rd, Durham NC 27707-5615. 919/493-8523.

Woodstream Apartments
7 Woodstream Ln, Greensboro NC 27410-6229. 910/852-8505.

Kingsborough Estates
284 Kings Pky, Raleigh NC 27610-2118. 919/231-6057.

REAL ESTATE PROPERTY LESSORS

BNE Land & Development Company
19 W Hargett St, Suite 512, Raleigh NC 27601-1350. 919/833-7289.

REAL ESTATE AGENTS AND MANAGERS

MBG Companies
6131 Falls of Neuse Rd, Suite 200, Raleigh NC 27609-3518. 919/878-8989.

University Condominium Management
8301 Univ Exec Park Dr, Suite 121, Charlotte NC 28262-3355. 704/547-8610.

Allen Tate Co.
6618 Fairview Rd, Suite 100, Charlotte NC 28210-3380. 704/365-6910.

Allen Tate Co.
Hwy 73, Davidson NC 28036. 704/896-8283.

Fonville Morisey Realty
100 Sawmill Rd, Suite 100, Raleigh NC 27615-6199. 919/847-9300.

Howard Perry & Walston
1600 E Franklin St, Chapel Hill NC 27514-2885. 919/967-9234.

Lake Jeanette Information Center
16 Canvasback Pt, Greensboro NC 27455-1327. 910/282-5253.

M I Homes Alyson Pond Sales Center
2401 Coxindale Dr, Raleigh NC 27615-3863. 919/870-9203.

Property Resources/Triad
300 N Greene St, Suite 2190, Greensboro NC 27401-2167. 910/273-2222.

Stan Byrd & Associates Inc. Realtors
10801 N Main St, Archdale NC 27263-2801. 910/861-9119.

Summit Realty Inc.
832 Shady Bluff Dr, Charlotte NC 28211-4224. 704/334-9905.

Sunchase American Ltd.
5970 Fairview Rd, Suite 710, Charlotte NC 28210-3167. 704/556-9330.

Village at Calabash
9515 Thomasboro Rd, Calabash NC 28467. 910/579-8444.

Weaver Grubar & Black
219 N Greene St, Greensboro NC 27401-2410. 910/373-8800.

Weyerhaeuser Real Estate
101 Middle St, New Bern NC 28560-2143. 919/633-6100.

Community Management Corp.
3301 Womans Club Dr, Raleigh NC 27612-4841. 919/420-0140.

One Hanover Square Associates
1 Hannover Sq, Raleigh NC 27601. 919/828-4148.

Spectrum Properties
4601 Charlotte Park Dr, Suite 120, Charlotte NC

28217-1900. 704/521-8744.

Thetford Property Management Inc.
7610 Falls of Neuse Rd, Raleigh NC 27615-3307. 919/846-8944.

Summit at Avent Ferry
1025 Avent Hl, Raleigh NC 27606-3482. 919/859-1700.

LAND SUBDIVIDERS AND DEVELOPERS

A&A Inc.
Skyline Ests, Vass NC 28394. 910/245-4442.

American Asset Corp.
5970 Fairview Rd, Charlotte NC 28210-3167. 704/554-8429.

Lingerfelt Development Corp.
2016 Cameron St Rm 222, Raleigh NC 27605-1343. 919/834-9337.

Middleton Place Clubhouse
Middleton Pl, Hendersonvlle NC 28792. 704/693-7707.

Resort Equities Inc.
402 W Trade St, Charlotte NC 28202-1627. 704/335-1925.

CEMETERY SUBDIVIDERS AND DEVELOPERS

Elmwood Cemetery
700 W 6th St, Charlotte NC 28202-1414. 704/563-2096.

Lakeview Memorial Park
3600 N O Henry Blvd, Greensboro NC 27405-2925. 910/375-4080.

Raleigh National Cemetery
501 Rock Quarry Rd, Raleigh NC 27610-3353. 919/832-0144.

Westlawn Gardens of Memory
6135 Ridgecrest Rd, Winston-Salem NC 27103-9791. 910/725-8530.

Carolina Biblical Gardens
Riverdale, Jamestown NC 27282. 910/273-0090.

Guilford Memorial Park
6000 High Point Rd, Greensboro NC 27407-7009. 910/299-5177.

Central Monument Co.
2007 English Rd, High Point NC 27262-7211. 910/884-1724.

South Carolina

BERKSHIRE PROPERTY MANAGEMENT
225 South Pleasantburg Drive, Suite I-2, Greenville SC 29607. 864/233-0025. **Contact:** Human Resources. **Description:** A property management company.

DUNES PROPERTIES OF CHARLESTON, INC.
P.O. Box 524, Isle of Palms SC 29451. 803/886-5600. **Contact:** Mary Ziegler, Personnel Department Manager. **Description:** Dunes Properties of Charleston, Inc. is a real estate management and leasing company. **Common positions include:** Accountant/Auditor; Administrator; Sales Associate. **Educational backgrounds include:** Accounting; Business Administration; Economics; Marketing. **Benefits:** Dental Insurance; Employee Discounts; Life Insurance; Medical Insurance. **Corporate headquarters location:** This Location.

INSIGNIA FINANCIAL GROUP, INC.
P.O. Box 1089, Greenville SC 29602. 864/239-1000. **Contact:** Human Resources. **Description:** Insignia Financial Group, Inc. is a real estate management and mortgage banking company. **Corporate headquarters location:** This Location. **Subsidiaries include:** IFGP Corporation; Amreal Corporation; Shelter Realty Corporation; Coventry Properties, Inc.; Dalcap Management, Inc.; First Piedmont Mortgage Company, Inc.; Insignia commercial Group, Inc.; and Insignia Management Corporation. **Number of employees nationwide:** 7,500.

RUSSELL & JEFFCOAT REALTORS INC.
10607 Two Notch Road, Elgin SC 29045. 803/699-2212. **Contact:** Mr. Collie Dyson, Broker-in-Charge. **Description:** A real estate agency.

SEA PINES ASSOCIATES, INC.
P.O. Box 7000, Hilton Head Island SC 29928. 803/785-3333. **Fax:** 803/842-1927. **Contact:** Monika Nash, Director of Human Resources. **Description:** Sea Pines Associates, Inc. is a holding company with three subsidiaries including Sea Pines Company, Inc., (also at this address) which operates all of the resort assets including three resort golf courses, a 28 court racquet club, a home and villa rental management business, retail sales outlets, food services operations and other resort recreational facilities. Sea Pines Real Estate Company, Inc. is an independent real estate brokerage firm with 11 offices serving Island residents. Sea Pines Country Club, Inc. owns and operates a full-service private country club providing golf, tennis, and clubhouse facilities for approximately 1,500 equity and associate club members. The company, through its wholly-owned subsidiary, Sea Pines/TidePointe, Inc., has a general partnership interest in TidePointe Partners. TidePointe Partners develops and constructs a continuing care retirement community with a variety of living units and amenities on Hilton Head Island, South Carolina. **Corporate headquarters location:** This Location. **Number of employees at this location:** 247.

Note: Because addresses and telephone numbers of smaller companies change rapidly, we recommend you call each company to verify the information below before inquiring about job opportunities. Mass mailings are not recommended.

Additional employers with under 250 employees:

REAL ESTATE OPERATORS

Guardian Management
37 Villa Rd, Greenville SC 29615. 864/233-5058.

J. William Pitts Apartments
150 Flora Dr, Columbia SC 29223. 803/736-2700.

Greenville Summit
201 W Washington St, Greenville SC 29601-2669. 864/242-6324.

Asbury Arms Apartments
100 Asbury Ln, West Columbia SC 29169-4829. 803/794-8052.

Cambridge Apartments
181 W Old Orangeburg Rd, Summerville SC 29483. 803/873-2158.

Crickentree
1061 Highway 17 By-Pass N, Mount Pleasant SC 29464. 803/884-4334.

Crossroads Apartments
716 Zimalcrest Dr, Columbia SC 29210-6579. 803/772-6800.

Dogwood Forest Apartments
100 Cedar St, Myrtle Beach SC 29577-5507. 803/448-6228.

Country Walk
408 Country Walk, Columbia SC 29212. 803/772-8966.

Field Village
110 Field Village Dr Apt I, Seneca SC 29678-4356. 864/885-1077.

Forest View Apartments
101 Forest View Cir, Liberty SC 29657-9156. 864/843-9755.

Foxfire Apartments
123 Meansville Rd, Union SC 29379-7752. 864/427-6301.

Foxtrot Villas
5600 Enterprise Rd, Myrtle
Beach SC 29575-6607.
803/650-3200.

Garden Manor Apartments
2400 Ashland Rd, Columbia
SC 29210-5051. 803/772-
2249.

Gateway Village Apartments
501 Boyd Ave, Simpsonville
SC 29681-2249. 864/963-
9343.

Greenbriar Apartments
1 Nancy Ln, Aiken SC
29803-5524. 803/648-
6094.

Druid Hill II
115 Beach Rd, Walterboro
SC 29488-4544. 803/538-
3522.

Highland Ridge
3549 Rutherford Rd, Taylors
SC 29687. 864/244-9141.

Hilton Head Gardens
380 Southwood Park Dr,
Hilton Head SC 29926-
2473. 803/681-2911.

Huntington Downs
1409 Roper Mountain Rd,
Greenville SC 29615-5178.
864/297-5745.

Huntington Place Apartments
517 Coachman Dr Apt A,
Sumter SC 29154-6240.
803/773-3600.

John G. Felder Apartments
104 Pearl St, St Matthews
SC 29135-9576. 803/874-
2565.

Landau Apartments
1321 S Broad St, Clinton SC
29325-9498. 864/833-
3215.

Laurens Terrace Office
P.O. Box 167, Laurens SC
29360. 864/984-2411.

Le Chateau Apartments
201 Miracle Mile Dr,
Anderson SC 29621-1398.
864/224-3033.

Meadowfield Apartments
Parsons, Summerton SC
29148. 803/485-8259.

Nance Forest Apartments
175 Nance Forest Dr,
Newberry SC 29108-1735.
803/276-0131.

Oak Ridge at Pelham
150 Oak Ridge Pl, Greenville
SC 29615. 864/297-8850.

Oakview Village Two
1900 Boling Road Ext,
Taylors SC 29687-3110.
864/268-2842.

Otranto Villas
800 Andrea Ln, Hanahan SC
29406-8631. 803/553-
7306.

**Palmetto Gardens
Apartments**
139 Oneil Ct, Columbia SC
29223-7623. 803/788-
5606.

Park Haywood Apartments
245 Congaree Rd, Greenville
SC 29607-2745. 864/297-
1122.

Parklane Apartments
8100 Bayfield Rd, Columbia
SC 29223-5658. 803/736-
2450.

Belle Ville Apartments
Hwy 56, Clinton SC 29325.
864/833-6087.

Raintree Apartments
2420 Marchbanks Ave,
Anderson SC 29621-2118.
864/224-2859.

Riverbend Apartments
100 Riverbend Dr, West
Columbia SC 29169-7449.
803/794-2948.

Riverwind Apartments
200 Heywood Ave,
Spartanburg SC 29307-
1706. 864/585-9463.

Somerset Apartments
1225 Boone Hill Rd,
Summerville SC 29483-
2444. 803/873-6555.

Springbrook Apartments
104 Springbrook Dr,
Anderson SC 29621-4102.
864/225-2892.

Springhouse Apartments
7930 Saint Ives Rd, N
Charleston SC 29406-9485.
803/572-0352.

Steeplechase Apartments
1800 Hasty Rd, Camden SC
29020-3057. 803/432-
3561.

Tanglewood Apartments
2418 Marchbanks Ave,
Anderson SC 29621-2117.
864/226-5254.

The Landings
4080 Horseshoe Rd N, Little
River SC 29566-8412.
803/248-8872.

Valley Creek Apartments
9085 Fairforest Rd,
Spartanburg SC 29301-
1100. 864/576-6830.

**Walterboro Village
Associates**
Green Pond Hwy, Walterboro
SC 29488. 803/549-2732.

Wateree Villa
970 Wateree Blvd, Camden
SC 29020-4157. 803/432-
1970.

Windsor Place
101 Bridgetown Rd, Goose
Creek SC 29445-5340.
803/553-7458.

Woodcreek Apartments
1216 E Georgia Rd,
Simpsonville SC 29681-
3960. 864/967-3516.

**Pines The Mobile Home
Community**
Highway 78, Ladson SC
29456. 803/873-6872.

**REAL ESTATE AGENTS AND
MANAGERS**

Amerolina Properties
117 N Shelby St, Blacksburg
SC 29702-1537. 864/839-
4260.

John Crosland Company
8761 Dorchester Rd,
Charleston SC 29420-7320.
803/760-3660.

Caravilla Management Corp.
6900 N Ocean Blvd, Myrtle
Beach SC 29572-3640.
803/449-4738.

**Coldwell Banker
O'Shaughnessy**
1825 Old Trolley Rd,
Summerville SC 29485-
8225. 803/871-9000.

**Coldwell Banker Tom Jenkins
Realty**
119 Amicks Ferry Rd, Chapin
SC 29036-8370. 803/345-
3700.

**Defender Resort
Management Inc.**
P.O. Box 3849, Myrtle Beach
SC 29578-3849. 803/449-
1354.

Edens & Avant Inc.
300 N Main St, Greenville SC
29601. 864/233-5011.

Fairfield Myrtle Beach
3405 S Ocean Blvd, N Myrtle
Beach SC 29582-4966.
803/449-1511.

Haig Point
10 Haig Point Ct, Hilton
Head SC 29928-3200.
803/686-2000.

**Wilson Real Estate
Development & Marketing**
1990 Augusta St, Suite 600,
Greenville SC 29605-2943.
864/232-1873.

John Crosland Company
1209 Mashie Ct, Mount
Pleasant SC 29464-8974.
803/881-1225.

Pace Homes Inc.
3294 Ashley Phosphate Rd,
Suite 1, Charleston SC
29418-8420. 803/552-
5558.

Westvaco Development
100 Hamlet Cir, Goose Creek
SC 29445-7111. 803/572-
6719.

Squires Homes Inc.
101 Lowndes Rd, Goose
Creek SC 29445-7027.
803/572-3626.

Westminster Co.
720 Gracern Rd, Suite 109,
Columbia SC 29210-7657.
803/798-6846.

Paragon Group
1 Westchase Dr, Charleston
SC 29407. 803/763-3039.

Rental Property Management
835 Lowcountry Blvd, Mount
Pleasant SC 29464-3042.
803/881-6765.

**San A Bel Towers
Maintenance Office**
1707 S Ocean Blvd, N Myrtle
Beach SC 29582-4031.
803/272-0484.

Mariner's Cove
9501 Shore Dr, Myrtle Beach
SC 29572-5133. 803/449-
3711.

Bruce Volk Real Estate
10607 Two Notch Rd, Elgin

SC 29045-8728. 803/736-
5121.

**LAND SUBDIVIDERS AND
DEVELOPERS**

Burroughs & Chapin Co.
2411 Oak St, Suite 402,
Myrtle Beach SC 29577-
3165. 803/448-5123.

Canal Forest Resources
315 Buncombe St, Edgefield
SC 29824-1069. 803/637-
5896.

Spring Island Co.
RR 6 Box 284, Ridgeland SC
29936-8928. 803/521-
1807.

For more information on career opportunities in real estate:

Associations

**INSTITUTE OF REAL ESTATE
MANAGEMENT**
430 North Michigan Avenue, P.O. Box
109025, Chicago IL 60610-9025.
312/661-1930. Dedicated to educating and
identifying real estate managers who are
committed to meeting the needs of real
estate owners and investors.

**INTERNATIONAL ASSOCIATION OF
CORPORATE REAL ESTATE EXECUTIVES**
440 Columbia Drive, Suite 100, West Palm

Beach FL 33409. 407/683-8111. An
international association of real estate
brokers.

Magazines

JOURNAL OF PROPERTY MANAGEMENT
Institute of Real Estate Management, 430
North Michigan Avenue, Chicago IL 60610.
312/661-1930.

NATIONAL REAL ESTATE INVESTOR
6151 Powers Ferry Road, Atlanta GA
30339. 404/955-2500.

RETAIL

The '90s have been turbulent times for the retail industry. During the early years of the decade, the industry struggled as the national economy remained mired in recession. Now that the recession has technically been over for several years, one would think that shoppers would be flocking back to stores. Think again.

During 1995, sales rose by only 4.5 percent, and analysts expected about the same for '96. During 1995 alone, 15,000 retailers filed for Chapter 11 bankruptcy. Many of them, according to Business Week, *were regional chains with outdated stores and merchandise.*

The problem is simple: Consumers just aren't spending like they used to, and when customers insist on cut-rate bargains, only the giants, like Wal-Mart and Target, can survive. And not even all of them are safe from the threat of red ink. Kmart, the nation's third-largest chain, is closing 70 stores; while Bradlees and Ames are both having financial problems of their own.

North Carolina

BELK STORES SERVICES INC.
2801 West Tyvola Road, Charlotte NC 28217. 704/357-1000. **Fax:** 704/357-1883. **Contact:** Tom Westall, Director of Human Resources. **Description:** Belk Stores Services provides a variety of services and administrative functions for its 280 department stores located in 14 southeastern states. **Common positions include:** Buyer; Management Trainee. **Educational backgrounds include:** Business Administration; Fashion; Home Economics; Merchandising. **Benefits:** Employee Discounts; Life Insurance; Medical Insurance; Pension Plan; Profit Sharing. **Special Programs:** Internships; Training Programs. **Corporate headquarters location:** This Location.

CAR MART
1214 South Cannon Boulevard, Kannapolis NC 28081. 704/932-3878. **Contact:** Mike Wicke, Owner. **Description:** Engaged in automotive sales and service. **Common positions include:** Automotive Mechanic/Body Repairer; Buyer; Wholesale and Retail Buyer. **Corporate headquarters location:** This Location. **Operations at this facility include:** Sales; Service. **Listed on:** Privately held. **Number of employees at this location:** 41.

CATO CORPORATION
P.O. Box 34216, Charlotte NC 28234. 704/554-8510. **Contact:** Steve Clark, Human Resources Manager. **Description:** The Cato Corporation has operated retail specialty stores for more than 44 years. The company owns over 500 stores in 22 states. The stores operate under the names "Cato," "Cato Fashions," or "Cato Plus" featuring women's popular-priced apparel for the fashion-conscious junior, misses, and large-sized customer. The company also has an off-price division (67 stores) which operates stores under the "It's Fashion!" name, featuring primarily sportswear and accessories at 20 to 80 percent off regular retail prices.

FAMILY DOLLAR STORES, INC.
10401 Old Monroe Road, P.O. Box 1017, Charlotte NC 28201-1017. 704/847-6961. **Contact:** Mr. Terry Cozort, Vice President of Human Resources. **Description:** Family Dollar Stores, Inc. owns and operates a discount store chain. In 1996, the company expected to have approximately 2,616 stores operating. The company provides low cost, basic merchandise for family and home needs. Stores are located in a contiguous 34-state area ranging as far northwest as Minnesota, northeast to New Hampshire, southeast to Florida and southwest to Texas. The stores are located in shopping centers or as freestanding buildings. **Corporate headquarters location:** This Location. **Listed on:** New York Stock Exchange. **Number of employees nationwide:** 16,500.

FOOD LION, INC.
Executive Drive, P.O. Box 1330, Salisbury NC 28145-1330. 704/633-8250. **Contact:** Andre Goodlett, Recruiting Manager. **Description:** Owns a chain of retail food stores in the southeastern United States. The company's stores sell a wide variety of groceries, produce, meats, dairy products, seafood, frozen produce, and non-food items such as tobacco, health and beauty aids, and other household and personal products.

HARRIS TEETER, INC.
P.O. Box 33129, Charlotte NC 28233. 704/845-3100. **Contact:** Mr. Jan Gillespie, Director of Personnel. **Description:** Harris Teeter, Inc. operates a regional supermarket chain with 139 stores in five southeastern states. All hiring for Harris Teeter is done at this location. The parent company, Ruddick Corporation, is a diversified holding company operating through wholly-owned subsidiaries American & Efird, Inc.; Harris Teeter, Inc.; and Ruddick Investment Company. American & Efird, located in Mount Holly, North Carolina, manufactures and distributes sewing thread for worldwide industrial and consumer markets and handles its own hiring as well. Ruddick Investment Company, a venture capital investment firm, employs less than 10 people at its Charlotte, North Carolina location. **Corporate headquarters location:** This Location. **Parent company:** Ruddick Corporation (2000 Two First Union Center, Charlotte). **Listed on:** New York Stock Exchange.

INGLES MARKETS, INC.
P.O. Box 6676, Asheville NC 28816. 704/669-2941. **Contact:** Mr. Jerry Banks, Human Resources Director. **Description:** Ingles Markets, Inc. is a supermarket chain which operates 175 supermarkets in North Carolina, South Carolina, Georgia, Tennessee, Virginia, and Alabama. The company underwent an on-going expansion, remodeling, and/or replacement program to upgrade existing supermarkets in 1995. Substantially all stores are located within a 250 mile radius of the company's warehouse and distribution center located outside of Asheville, North Carolina, which expanded in 1995 to accommodate an inventory of perishable goods and increase dry grocery storage space. Ingles Markets was among the first supermarkets in the Southeast to introduce specialty departments, including delicatessens and bakeries. In conjunction with its supermarket activities, the company owns and operates 70 neighborhood shopping centers, all but two of which contain an Ingles supermarket. The company also owns and holds for future development or sale numerous outparcels and other acreage adjacent to the shopping centers which it owns. Ingles Markets also owns and operates, as a wholly-owned subsidiary, a milk processing and packaging plant which sells approximately 53 percent of its milk and related dairy products to unaffiliated customers. The company carries not only national brands of merchandise, but also carries a wide variety of products under its own "Laura Lynn" private label. **Corporate headquarters location:** This Location. **Listed on:** NASDAQ. **Number of employees nationwide:** 9,900.

LOWE'S COMPANIES, INC.
P.O. Box 1111, North Wilkesboro NC 28656. 910/651-4000. **Fax:** 910/651-4766. **Contact:** Human Resources. **Description:** Lowe's is a discount retail distributor of consumer durables, building supplies, and home products for the do-it-yourself and home improvement markets. The company conducts operations through 311 retail stores in 20 states, mostly in south central and southeastern United States. The company's products include tools, lumber, building materials, heating, cooling and water systems, and specialty goods. **Corporate headquarters location:** This Location. **Listed on:** New York Stock Exchange.

LOWE'S FOOD STORES INC.
P.O. Box 24908, 1381 Old Mill Circle, Suite 200, Winston-Salem NC 27114-4908. 910/659-0180. **Contact:** Mike Lebo, Director of Human Resources. **Description:** A food store chain.

OFFICE DEPOT
3400-E Woodpark Boulevard, Charlotte NC 28206. 704/597-8501. **Fax:** 704/597-8501. **Contact:** Kimberly Woodall, Human Resources. **Description:** One of the nation's leading office products dealers. The company believes that since Office Depot purchases more office products from more leading manufacturers than any of its competitors, this translates into multi-billion dollar buying power, and therefore higher discounts for consumers. Both Wilson Office Products (a division of Office Depot) and Office Depot offer over 11,000 different business products, from basic supplies such as copy and printer paper to high-tech business furniture. Product categories include: furniture; desk accessories; office essentials; computer products; business machines; visual communications; safety and maintenance supplies; personalized organizers and

dated goods; writing instruments; business cases and binders; filing and storage; paper, envelopes and business forms; and labels and mailing supplies.

REVCO DISCOUNT DRUGS
2215 North Cannon Boulevard, Kannatolis NC 28083. 704/939-6000. **Contact:** Mr. Terry Summers, Director of Human Resources. **Description:** Revco Discount Drug stores offer prescription and proprietary drugs, cosmetics, toiletries, vitamins, tobacco products, sundries, and a broad line of consumer products. Most of the company's operations are centralized through its corporate headquarters in Twinsburg, Ohio. The company also has several health care products manufacturing and other unrelated subsidiaries. This location houses the regional administrative offices for the nationwide retail drugstore firm. Overall, the company operates a 1600-store, 28-state retail drugstore operation. **NOTE:** For professional positions, jobseekers may contact the Personnel Director at 1925 Enterprise Parkway, Twinsburg OH 44087. 216/425-9811. **Common positions include:** Human Resources Specialist; Management Trainee. **Benefits:** Dental Insurance; Disability Coverage; Employee Discounts; Life Insurance; Medical Insurance; Profit Sharing; Savings Plan; Tuition Assistance. **Special Programs:** Internships; Training Programs. **Corporate headquarters location:** Twinsburg OH. **Listed on:** New York Stock Exchange. **Number of employees nationwide:** 20,000.

ROSES STORES INC.
P.O. Drawer 947, Henderson NC 27536. 919/430-2600. **Contact:** Frances Burger, Recruitment Manager. **Description:** Operates a chain of retail variety stores. **Common positions include:** Management Trainee. **Special Programs:** Training Programs. **Corporate headquarters location:** This Location.

Note: Because addresses and telephone numbers of smaller companies change rapidly, we recommend you call each company to verify the information below before inquiring about job opportunities. Mass mailings are not recommended.

Additional employers with under 250 employees:

RETAIL LUMBER AND BUILDING MATERIALS

ABC Supply Co.
2900 Patterson St, Greensboro NC 27407-3337. 910/855-5030.

Carolina Builders Corp.
8800 Monroe Rd, Charlotte NC 28212. 704/535-6940.

Diamond Hill Plywood Company
601 Diamond Hill Ct, Greensboro NC 27406-4617. 910/378-1931.

Gulledge Building Supply
813 Fairview St, Kannapolis NC 28083. 704/932-6107.

Home Depot
1837 Matthews Township Pky, Matthews NC 28105-4659. 704/845-9200.

Home Depot
10210 Centrum Pky, Pineville NC 28134-8822. 704/544-2877.

Home Quarters Warehouse
3900 High Point Rd, Greensboro NC 27407-4654. 910/292-0334.

Interior Distributors
7207 Cessna Dr, Greensboro NC 27409. 910/668-3652.

LaSalle-Deitch Co.
880 Cedar Springs Rd, Salisbury NC 28147-9253. 704/636-8151.

Lowe's
US Hwy 70 W, Morehead City NC 28557. 919/247-2223.

Lowe's of Albemarle Inc.
720-6 NC 24-27 Bypass E, Albemarle NC 28001. 704/983-3111.

Lowe's of Cary
2000 Walnut St, Cary NC 27511. 919/233-7000.

Lowe's of Greenville Inc.
1055 Greenville Blvd SW, Greenville NC 27834-7021. 919/756-6560.

Lowe's of Henderson
900 S Beckford Dr, Henderson NC 27536-2974. 919/438-4411.

Lowe's of Hendersonville
109 Duncan Hill Rd, Columbus NC 28722. 704/894-3899.

Lowes of West Asheville
P.O. Box 16769, Asheville NC 28816-0769. 704/252-2300.

Lowe's of Wilson
2713 Forest Hills Rd SW, Wilson NC 27893-4432. 919/237-5211.

Morehead Builders Supply Company
2514 Bridges St, Morehead City NC 28557-3387. 919/726-6877.

Pella Window & Door Co.
415 Pinehurst Ave, Southern Pines NC 28387-7027. 910/692-3399.

Pleasants Hardware
1013 Woodward Ave, Charlotte NC 28206-2461. 704/376-3671.

Triangle Building Supply
2013 Ramsey St, Fayetteville NC 28301-4163. 910/822-2222.

Carolina Window Sales
315 US Highway 70 E, Garner NC 27529-4041. 919/779-4488.

Craftline Distribution Center
406 Tucker St, Burlington NC 27215-5962. 910/570-0010.

Malta Window Center
872 Riverside Dr, Asheville NC 28804-3222. 704/253-2646.

Robsan Fenestrations
1300 Matthews Mint Hill Rd,
Matthews NC 28105-2306.
704/845-2454.

American Overhead Door
102 West Stanly St,
Stanfield NC 28163.
704/888-8055.

Morgan Products Ltd.
647 Hargrave Rd, Lexington
NC 27292-7560. 704/956-
2000.

Passport Industries
436 W Radiance Dr,
Greensboro NC 27403-1228.
910/273-6403.

Cherokee Sanford Brick
5726 Market St, Wilmington
NC 28405. 910/452-3498.

Cherokee Sanford Group
520 Brickhaven Dr, Raleigh
NC 27606-1463. 919/828-
0541.

Clifford W. Estes Co. Inc.
2637 Old 421 Rd, Liberty
NC 27298. 910/622-2228.

Best Distributing Co.
325 N Miller Ave, Statesville
NC 28677-3731. 704/873-
4565.

**PAINT, GLASS, AND
WALLPAPER STORES**

Sherwin-Williams Co.
121 Tryon Rd, Raleigh NC
27603-3525. 919/779-
7177.

Lotus Blossom Stained Glass
3720 Battleground Ave,
Suite A, Greensboro NC
27410-2364. 910/288-
2880.

Cal-Tone Paints Inc.
305 Ashville Ave, Cary NC
27511-6667. 919/851-
4333.

**Duron Paints and
Wallcoverings**
8650 University City Blvd,
Charlotte NC 28213-3559.
704/549-4080.

Glidden Paints
511 Burkemont Ave,
Morganton NC 28655-4409.
704/438-9210.

Pritchard Paint and Glass Co.
2424 Crabtree Blvd, Raleigh
NC 27604-2233. 919/832-
4666.

Smartn' Up Wallcoverings
1809 Sardis Rd N, Charlotte
NC 28270. 704/845-1062.

Up Against The Wall
927 Lake Bay Rd, Vass NC
28394. 910/245-4712.

HARDWARE STORES

Citizens Home Center
841 Merrimon Ave, Asheville
NC 28804-2404. 704/254-
7244.

**RETAIL NURSERIES AND
GARDEN SUPPLY STORES**

Husqvarna Forest & Garden
9006 Perimeter Woods Dr,
Charlotte NC 28216-2394.
704/597-5000.

Simmons Irrigation Supply
3416 Carolina Ave, Charlotte
NC 28208-5878. 704/394-
9494.

E&E Farm Equipment Co.
Warrenton Rd, Henderson NC
27536. 919/438-4111.

**Sunshine Gardens of
Smithfield**
951 Industrial Park Dr,
Smithfield NC 27577-6019.
910/989-1177.

MOBILE HOME DEALERS

Calvary Mobile Homes
509 E New Bern Rd, Kinston
NC 28501-6739. 919/523-
4161.

Clayton Homes Sanford
3335 Hwy 87 S, Sanford NC
27330. 919/776-2110.

Clayton Mobile Home Sales
540 S Graham Hopedale Rd,
Burlington NC 27217-4322.
910/228-6213.

Freedom Homes
112 Alabama Ln, Fayetteville
NC 28306-9206. 910/424-
4600.

Freedom Homes
3404 Clarendon Blvd, New
Bern NC 28562-5220.
919/637-1773.

Freedom Homes
559 Raleigh Rd, Henderson
NC 27536-5364. 919/438-
2016.

Hometown USA
2312 New Raleigh Hwy,
Durham NC 27703-9311.
919/598-8388.

Leader Home Sales Inc.
1438 E Dixie Dr #186,
Asheboro NC 27203-8800.
910/626-7211.

Timberland Homes Inc.
Hwy 52 Bypass, Mount Airy
NC 27030. 910/789-7208.

**Wilson Mobile Home Supply
& Service**
1305 Herring Ave NE, Wilson
NC 27893-4314. 919/399-
0607.

Shoals Supply Inc.
401 Industrial Dr, Rockwell
NC 28138. 704/279-3793.

DEPARTMENT STORES

JCPenney Co. Inc.
Valley Hills Ml, Hickory NC
28602. 704/328-2661.

JCPenney Co. Inc.
Vernon Park Mall, Kinston
NC 28501. 919/527-5041.

Kmart Stores
1090 S Main St, Kernersville
NC 27284-7440. 910/993-
6919.

Wal-Mart
5511 Carolina Beach Rd,
Wilmington NC 28412-2630.
910/452-0944.

Wal-Mart
1422 E Dixie Dr, Asheboro
NC 27203-8800. 910/626-
5300.

Wal-Mart
113 Mayo St, Hillsborough
NC 27278-2573. 919/732-
9172.

Wal-Mart
2115 W Roosevelt Blvd,
Monroe NC 28110-2737.
704/289-5478.

Wal-Mart
1063 Yadkinville Rd,
Mocksville NC 27028-2077.
704/634-1266.

Wal-Mart
4540 Main St, Shallotte NC
28470-4446. 910/754-
2885.

Wal-Mart
2099 N Bridge St, Elkin NC
28621-2107. 910/526-
2636.

Wal-Mart
1227 Burkemont Ave,
Morganton NC 28655-4537.
704/433-7696.

Wal-Mart
1175 Highway 74 Byp,
Spindale NC 28160-2223.
704/287-7458.

Big Lots
2200 Westchester Dr, High
Point NC 27262-8061.
910/882-7272.

Dillard Department Store
125 Four Seasons,
Greensboro NC 27407.
910/855-5511.

Dillard Department Store
1811 S Stratford Rd,
Winston-Salem NC 27103-
5512. 910/659-1515.

Dillard Department Store
4217 Six Forks Rd, Raleigh
NC 27609-5736. 919/787-8800.

Family Dollar Store
S US 117 Hwy, Goldsboro
NC 27530. 919/734-0570.

Target Stores
1900 Matthews Township
Pky, Matthews NC 28105-4660. 704/845-0948.

Sam's Club
2811 N Park Dr, Goldsboro
NC 27534-7485. 919/778-9775.

Sam's Club
4418 W Wendover Ave,
Greensboro NC 27407-2600.
910/852-6212.

BC Moore & Sons Inc.
108 E Main St, Marshville
NC 28103-1147. 704/624-2518.

Belk
11009 Carolina Place Pky,
Pineville NC 28134-8370.
704/543-9888.

Belk
Hwy 150 & I-77, Mooresville
NC 28115. 704/664-2593.

Belk
Wesleyan Blvd & NC 43,
Rocky Mount NC 27804.
919/977-2355.

Belk
3801 Woodpark Blvd,
Charlotte NC 28206-4200.
704/598-6670.

Belk
Boone Mall, Boone NC
28607. 704/264-3886.

Belk
2766 Huffman Mill Rd,
Burlington NC 27215-9253.
910/584-9731.

Belk
600 Industrial Ave,
Greensboro NC 27406-4604.
910/378-9611.

Belk
1480 Highway 29 N,
Concord NC 28025-2933.
704/786-7111.

Belk
Lenoir Mall, Lenoir NC
28645. 704/754-2441.

Brendle's Inc.
4440 Creedmoor Rd, Raleigh
NC 27612-3866. 919/781-9710.

Hecht's
100 Cross Creek Mall,
Fayetteville NC 28303-7238.
910/864-1550.

Hecht's
700 Friendly Center Rd,
Greensboro NC 27408-7806.
910/855-7711.

Lowes of Morganton
1224 Burkemont Ave,
Morganton NC 28655-4540.
704/437-9315.

Peeble's Department Store
201 E Meadow Rd, Eden NC
27288-3415. 910/627-5241.

Stein Mart
3729 Battleground Ave,
Greensboro NC 27410-2345.
910/282-5797.

Stein Mart
4500 Falls of Neuse Rd,
Raleigh NC 27609-6274.
919/790-8060.

Super
221 The Boulevard, Eden NC
27288. 910/623-8625.

VARIETY STORES

Big Lots
656 Plaza Dr, Mooresville NC
28115-9086. 704/663-2710.

Dollar Time
11421 Granite St, Charlotte
NC 28273-6412. 704/587-0689.

Dollar Tree
North Hills Mall, Raleigh NC
27609. 919/781-8743.

Dollar Tree
Vernon Park Mall, Kinston
NC 28501. 919/527-5766.

Dollar Tree
7 S Tunnel Rd, Asheville NC
28805-2218. 704/298-6551.

Family Dollar Stores Inc.
406-B S Church St, Kenly
NC 27542. 919/284-2899.

Maxway
208 E Nash St, Wilson NC
27893. 919/237-1360.

Only One Dollar
1935 Jake Alexander Blvd
W, Salisbury NC 28147-1152. 704/636-5918.

Super 10
500 E Main St, Elizabeth City
NC 27909-4430. 919/335-0115.

Super 10
209 S Broad St, Edenton NC
27932-1931. 919/482-3771.

Super 10 Store
1329 E Main St, Albemarle
NC 28001. 704/983-1324.

Thrifty Dollar Stores Inc.
312 E Nash, Wilson NC
27893. 919/237-3120.

Variety Wholesalers Inc.
Midtown Shopping Center,
Madison NC 27025.
910/548-6607.

**MISC. GENERAL
MERCHANDISE STORES**

Dollar General
908 Washington St,
Williamston NC 27892-2652. 919/792-3282.

**GROCERY AND
CONVENIENCE STORES**

Allen's Grocery
891 W Pennsylvania Ave,
Southern Pines NC 28387-4639. 910/692-9811.

Bi-Lo Inc.
1020 Crossroads Dr,
Statesville NC 28677-8276.
704/878-6423.

Bi-Lo Inc.
2807 Hendersonville Rd,
Arden NC 28704. 704/684-5043.

Byrd's Food Stores
1232 Chapel Hill Rd,
Burlington NC 27215-7199.
910/277-1411.

Byrd's Grocery
74 Beaufort Square Shop
Center, Beaufort NC 28516-1523. 919/728-4471.

Circle K
1040 E Lexington Ave, High
Point NC 27262-2322.
910/884-4438.

Circle K Corporation
4301H Stuart Andrew Blvd,
Charlotte NC 28217-1542.
704/525-6939.

Circle K Food Store
1246 East Blvd, Charlotte
NC 28203-5777. 704/335-0040.

Citco Starmart
6908 Glenwood Ave, Raleigh
NC 27612-7140. 919/782-3548.

Community Grocerie & Grill
904 Blount St, Smithfield NC
27577-5306. 910/934-6855.

Country Corner
3320 Price Grange Rd, Eden
NC 27288-7641. 910/623-7617.

Dawson Grocery
1305 Dawson St,
Wilmington NC 28401-6027.
910/763-4135.

Edwards IGA Super Market
620 US Highway 70
Business W, Princeton NC
27569-7319. 910/936-
3021.

Family Grocery
529 S Haywood St, Raleigh
NC 27601-1929. 919/832-
3556.

Farm Fresh
Halstead Blvd, Elizabeth City
NC 27909. 919/338-0121.

**Farm Fresh Super Saving
Center**
1120 10th St, Roanoke
Rapid NC 27870. 919/537-
8083.

Fast Fare Inc.
2932 Mount Holly Huntersvil
Rd, Charlotte NC 28214-
9396. 704/392-4936.

Food Fair Stores
1415 S Hawthorne Rd,
Winston-Salem NC 27103-
4123. 910/724-9976.

Food Folks
301 N Main St, Broadway
NC 27505-9509. 919/258-
3531.

Food Folks
212 E Strawberry Blvd,
Chadbourn NC 28431-1418.
910/654-4541.

Food King
220 W Spring St, Troy NC
27371-2936. 910/572-
1917.

Food Lion
835 S Main St, Kernersville
NC 27284-3343. 910/996-
2092.

Food Lion
4151 W Vernon Ave,
Kinston NC 28501-9651.
919/523-5036.

Food Lion
Village Shopping Cntr, Hope
Mills NC 28348. 910/424-
5382.

Food Lion
358 Oak Ave, Kannapolis NC
28081-4331. 704/933-
1137.

Food Lion
2021 Lipscomb Rd E, Wilson
NC 27893-5616. 919/291-
7182.

Food Lion
3780 Battleground Ave,
Greensboro NC 27410-2344.
910/282-2206.

Food Lion
4510 Capital Blvd, Raleigh
NC 27604-4353. 919/876-
8126.

Food Lion
8700 Emerald Plantation,
Emerald Isle NC 28594.
910/354-4270.

Food Lion
1 New Clyde Hwy, Canton
NC 28716. 704/648-1550.

Food Lion
Melrose Square Shopping
Center, Shelby NC 28150.
704/487-9061.

Food Lion
Norlex Shopping Center,
Lexington NC 27292.
704/246-4637.

Food Lion
3257 Avent Ferry Rd,
Raleigh NC 27606-2720.
919/851-3584.

Food Lion
921 S Main St, Burlington
NC 27215. 910/228-0583.

Food Lion
205 E Meadow Rd, Eden NC
27288. 910/623-3294.

Food Lion
4640 W Market St,
Greensboro NC 27407-1285.
910/855-5841.

Food Lion
187 Hi House Rd, Cary NC
27511-6715. 919/467-
0256.

Food Lion
Hwy 52, Norwood NC
28128. 704/474-3118.

Food Lion
12225 Capital Blvd, Wake
Forest NC 27587-6200.
919/556-1885.

Food Lion
4709 Tuckaseegee Rd,
Charlotte NC 28208-2507.
704/399-1880.

Food Lion
463 799th W Charlotte Av,
Mount Holly NC 28120.
704/827-0588.

Food Lion
197 Timberlyn Village,
Chapel Hill NC 27514.
919/929-0458.

Food Rite Food Store Office
2321 Randleman Rd,
Greensboro NC 27406-3603.
910/373-8755.

Fresh Market
Cameron Village Shopping
Cente, Raleigh NC 27605.
919/828-7888.

Fresh Way
1406 Piney Green Rd,
Jacksonville NC 28546-
4562. 910/353-0698.

Fresh Way Food Stores
RR 8, Kinston NC 28501-
9808. 919/522-3636.

Grocery Outlet Warehouse
771 Haywood Rd, Asheville
NC 28806-3132. 704/254-
1570.

Handy Mart
Hwy 117, Faison NC 28341.
910/267-9281.

Handy Mart
Slocum Village Shp Center,
Havelock NC 28532.
919/447-1206.

Handy Pantry
9424 S Tryon St, Charlotte
NC 28273-6500. 704/588-
1689.

Handy Pantry
101 S Polk St, Pineville NC
28134-8569. 704/889-
9158.

Handy Pantry
668 W John St, Matthews
NC 28105-5351. 704/845-
1260.

Harris Supermarkets Inc.
Bell's Fork Sq, Greenville NC
27858. 919/756-2008.

Harris Teeter
7444 Creedmoor Rd, Raleigh
NC 27613-1663. 919/848-
1173.

Harris Teeter Inc.
2001 Kildaire Farm Rd, Cary
NC 27511-6613. 919/851-
1781.

Harris Teeter Inc.
7400 Creedmoor Rd, Raleigh
NC 27613-1639. 919/848-
1464.

Harris Teeter Inc.
Glenwood Village Shopping
Cent, Raleigh NC 27608.
919/787-5526.

Harris Teeter Inc.
1400 S Charles Blvd,
Greenville NC 27858-4452.
919/756-6800.

Harris Teeter Inc.
3990 NC 150 Hwy,
Mooresville NC 28115.
704/664-8881.

Harris Teeter Inc.
6325 Falls of Neuse Rd,
Raleigh NC 27615-6809.
919/872-7063.

Harris Teeter Inc.
237 W NC Highway 54,
Durham NC 27713-7512.
919/544-7715.

Harris Teeter
Abbey Plaza, Belmont NC
28012. 704/825-3727.

Harris Teeter
501 Oberlin Rd, Raleigh NC
27605-1327. 919/839-
0400.

Harris Teeter
609 College Rd, Greensboro
NC 27410-4101. 910/854-
3656.

Harris Teeter
2268 Golden Gate Dr,
Greensboro NC 27405-4302.
910/378-9971.

Harris Teeter
2800 Raeford Rd,
Fayetteville NC 28303-5465.
910/485-4139.

Harris Teeter
2485 Hope Mills Rd,
Fayetteville NC 28304-4231.
910/424-3834.

Harris Teeter
1704 Central Ave, Charlotte
NC 28205-5108. 704/375-
8491.

Harris Teeter
2950 S Church St,
Burlington NC 27215-5108.
910/584-7738.

Harris Teeter
310 N Greensboro St,
Carrboro NC 27510-1724.
919/942-8564.

Ingles Markets Inc.
214 N Main St, Boiling Spgs
NC 28017. 704/434-0096.

Ingles Markets Inc.
955 Cranberry St, Newland
NC 28657-8801. 704/733-
6086.

Ingles Markets Inc.
710 N Broad St, Brevard NC
28712-3102. 704/883-
2323.

Jan Chee Supermarket
1007 Method Rd, Raleigh NC
27606-1924. 919/834-
9888.

Circle K
4801 Central Ave, Charlotte
NC 28205-5805. 704/563-
2718.

Circle K Corp.
701 N Graham St, Charlotte
NC 28202. 704/333-6104.

Ken's Superette
1528 W May Ave, Gastonia
NC 28052. 704/865-3000.

Kroger Company
Westridge Square,
Greensboro NC 27410.
910/282-1070.

Kwik Mart
500 Raleigh Rd NW, Wilson
NC 27893. 919/291-3435.

Little Dan
525 E Main St, Lincolnton
NC 28092-3409. 704/735-
8621.

Lowe's Foods
737 W Dixie Dr, Asheboro
NC 27203-6739. 910/629-
9900.

Majik Market
3024 Central Ave, Charlotte
NC 28205-5412. 704/535-
7508.

Majik Market
3601 N Sharon Amity Rd,
Charlotte NC 28205-5931.
704/563-2433.

Minuteman Food Mart
1001 Lisbon St, Clinton NC
28328-4219. 910/592-
3556.

Pak-A-Sak Food Stores
Hwy 24, Swansboro NC
28584. 910/326-3189.

Park-N-Shop Food Centers
3512 Wilkinson Blvd,
Charlotte NC 28208-5598.
704/399-0411.

Quick Stop Food Mart
2900 Gillespie St,
Fayetteville NC 28306-3324.
910/425-4955.

Quick Stop Food Mart
504 W Saunders St, Maxton
NC 28364-1749. 910/844-
3890.

Quick Stop Food Mart
5642 Bragg Blvd, Fayetteville
NC 28303-2910. 910/868-
2927.

Quick Stop Food Mart
3002 Cumberland Rd,
Fayetteville NC 28306-2424.
910/485-1767.

Quick Stop Food Mart
1410 Fayetteville Rd,
Rockingham NC 28379-
3923. 910/895-6811.

Red Apple Market
501 W Main St,
Murfreesboro NC 27855-
1420. 919/398-5164.

Red Apple Market
102 E River St, Colerain NC
27924. 919/356-2161.

Sauratown Food Mart
4951 NC 14 Hwy, Reidsville
NC 27320. 910/623-1512.

Save-A-Center
7004 E Wt Harris Blvd,
Charlotte NC 28215-4138.
704/563-1041.

Save-A-Center
3934 Western Blvd, Raleigh
NC 27606. 919/833-9467.

Scotchman Store
6508 Yadkin Rd, Fayetteville
NC 28303-2165. 910/864-
2362.

Shop-Eze Food Stores
300 N Brown St #309,
Washington NC 27889-
5183. 919/975-2621.

T Mart Food Stores
608 Buffalo Rd, Smithfield
NC 27577-7451. 910/934-
5708.

T-Mart Food Stores
800 W Cumberland St, Dunn
NC 28334-4712. 910/892-
1025.

The Pantry
810 Hawkins Ave, Sanford
NC 27330-3312. 919/775-
7831.

The Pantry
8191 Cliffdale Rd,
Fayetteville NC 28314-5849.
910/867-1465.

The Pantry
110 W Haggard Ave, Elon
College NC 27244-9344.
910/584-2723.

The Pantry
3289 Avent Ferry Rd,
Raleigh NC 27606-2720.
919/851-4889.

**Times Turn Around Food
Store**
7915 N NC 68 Hwy,
Stokesdale NC 27357.
910/643-7036.

Wellspring Grocery
737 9th St, Durham NC
27705-4802. 919/286-
2290.

Wilson's
5309 Carolina Beach Rd,
Wilmington NC 28412-7943.
910/791-3418.

Your-Way Food Store
2436 W Florida St,
Greensboro NC 27403-3132.
910/294-6693.

Conoco
1035 Richlands Hwy,
Jacksonville NC 28540-
2914. 910/347-1767.

Dash-In Convenience Store
602 Dawson St, Wilmington
NC 28401-5712. 910/763-
6366.

Express Stop
1135 S Main St, Laurinburg
NC 28352-4740. 910/276-
2071.

**Fast Fare Convenience
Stores**
7124 Six Forks Rd, Raleigh
NC 27615. 919/847-8513.

Fast Fare Convenience Stores
8109 Falls of Neuse Rd, Raleigh NC 27615-3412. 919/847-7689.

Fast Phils
Oxford School Rd, Catawba NC 28609. 704/241-3384.

Fastop
2007 Wayne Memorial Dr, Goldsboro NC 27534-1719. 919/731-4893.

Han-Dee Hugo's
300 Northeast Blvd, Clinton NC 28328-2424. 910/592-0332.

Handy Pantry Food Stores
8016 US Hwy 29, Charlotte NC 28262. 704/548-8001.

Handy Pantry Food Stores
516 Cox Rd, Gastonia NC 28054-0627. 704/867-8717.

Handy Pantry Food Stores
5601 E Independence Blvd, Charlotte NC 28212-0509. 704/563-9029.

Handy Pantry Food Stores
4808 Bellhaven Blvd, Charlotte NC 28216-3324. 704/394-2501.

Handy Pantry Food Stores
6401 Old Statesville Rd, Charlotte NC 28269-1783. 704/597-9667.

Ice Service Food Stores
1409 Brevard Rd, Asheville NC 28806-9560. 704/665-8815.

Kountry Quik Food Mart
Hwy 24 W, Warsaw NC 28398. 910/293-3931.

Lee Mart
5338 W Market St, Greensboro NC 27409-2618. 910/316-0008.

Lewis Quick Stop
Hwy 301 S, Lumberton NC 28358. 910/738-3355.

Pete's Food Shop
104 Wilson Mills Rd, Smithfield NC 27577-3244. 910/989-7395.

Quick Stop Food Mart
3110 Sandy Ridge Rd, Colfax NC 27235. 910/993-0267.

Rebecca's Convenience Store
3209 Old Greensboro Rd, Winston-Salem NC 27101-1917. 910/722-6256.

Scotchman Store
1325 Hodges St, Raleigh NC 27604. 919/832-7751.

The Pantry
2522 Randleman Rd, Greensboro NC 27406-4312. 910/273-8197.

Wilco Food Mart
10207 US 29 Hwy, Charlotte NC 28262. 704/547-1003.

Zipmart Inc.
4330 Louisburg Rd, Raleigh NC 27604-4357. 919/872-3294.

Zipmart Inc.
3601 Sunset Ave, Rocky Mount NC 27804-3411. 919/443-4351.

Zipmart Inc.
1730 Sunset Ave, Rocky Mount NC 27804-4321. 919/442-1800.

Winn Dixie Delicatessen
265 Eastchester Dr, High Point NC 27262-7716. 910/869-6018.

Food Lion
1316 Lees Chapel Rd, Greensboro NC 27455-2602. 910/375-7482.

Food Lion
2710 N Roberts Ave, Lumberton NC 28358-2856. 910/618-0607.

Lunch Etc.
3605 Glenwood Ave, Raleigh NC 27612-4954. 919/783-7867.

MISC. FOOD STORES

John Morrell & Co.
106 Avon St, Monroe NC 28110-3014. 704/283-7080.

Colorado Prime Sales
7817 National Service Rd, Suite 5, Greensboro NC 27409-9402. 910/668-9244.

Candy Candy
400 Four Seasons Town Centre, Greensboro NC 27407. 910/547-0981.

Liberto of North Carolina
1200 Westinghouse Blvd, Charlotte NC 28273-6313. 704/588-9666.

Planter's Life Savers
8307 University Exec Park Dr, Charlotte NC 28262-3358. 704/549-9428.

Gold Medal Carolina
2119 S Elm Eugene St, Greensboro NC 27406-2826. 910/273-3346.

Flav-O-Rich
114 W Kings Hwy, Eden NC 27288. 910/623-8510.

General Nutrition Center
Randolph Mall, Asheboro NC 27203. 910/626-6440.

Herb Lizzie's Shop
149 S Main St, Kernersville NC 27284-2757. 910/996-4030.

Gloria Jean's Coffee Bean
11025 Carolina Pl Pkwy Unit A1, Pineville NC 28134-7515. 704/543-6098.

Jenny's Cupboard Inc.
101 Ward Blvd W, Wilson NC 27893-3583. 919/399-1392.

RETAIL BAKERIES

Best Foods Baking Group/Sales
2816 Trawick Rd, Suite 107, Raleigh NC 27604-3761. 919/878-1888.

Brueggers Bagel Bakery
2302 Hillsborough St, Raleigh NC 27607-7353. 919/832-6118.

Dewey's Bakery Inc.
3116 W Friendly Ave, Greensboro NC 27408-7823. 910/292-8078.

Dolly Madison
811 S Summit Ave, Charlotte NC 28208-5229. 704/342-9880.

Great American Cookie Co.
7 S Tunnel Rd, Asheville NC 28805-2218. 704/298-2849.

Merita Bakery
1397 E 5th St, Lumberton NC 28358-6031. 910/738-1000.

Merita Bread Box
4801 N Tryon St, Charlotte NC 28213-7049. 704/596-7753.

Southern Delights Bakery
1221 Memorial Dr E, Ahoskie NC 27910. 919/332-8484.

Tarheel Bagels Inc.
100 Dominion Dr, Suite 104, Morrisville NC 27560-9257. 919/469-4919.

TJ Cinnamons Bakery
2526 Hillsborough St, Suite 106, Raleigh NC 27607-7266. 919/828-9004.

Waldensian Bakeries Inc.
2579 Hendersonville Rd, Arden NC 28704-9577. 704/687-0202.

Charles Chips of Jacksonville
225 Yale Cir, Jacksonville NC 28546. 910/346-3229.

AUTO DEALERS

Leith Jaguar
400 Auto Park Blvd, Cary NC
27511-6023. 919/469-
2699.

Leith Auto Center
5601 Capital Blvd, Raleigh
NC 27604-2933. 919/876-
5432.

**Griffin Pontiac Buick GMC
Truck**
Hwy 74 W, Monroe NC
28110. 704/289-3135.

**Lowry Buick Olds Pontiac
Chevy**
1025 National Hwy,
Thomasville NC 27360-
2311. 910/472-5650.

McRae Chevrolet Buick
Hwy 27 W, Troy NC 27371.
910/572-3713.

Chris Leith Chevrolet
US 1 North, Wake Forest NC
27587. 919/832-0374.

Modern Chevrolet-Geo
800 W 4th St, Winston-
Salem NC 27101-2542.
910/722-4191.

Traders Chevrolet Co.
707 E Bessemer Ave,
Greensboro NC 27405-6906.
910/273-6971.

**Gowen Chrysler Plymouth
Jeep Eagle**
7501 South Blvd, Charlotte
NC 28273-5965. 704/554-
7420.

Hendrick-Dodge
300 MacKenan Dr, Cary NC
27511-7915. 919/319-
9225.

Capital Ford
4900 Capital Blvd, Raleigh
NC 27604-4407. 919/790-
4600.

Honda-Mazda of Asheboro
1400 E Dixie Dr, Asheboro
NC 27203. 910/629-9999.

**Anderson Nissan Lincoln
Mercury**
252 Patton Ave, Asheville
NC 28801. 704/252-1122.

Vann York Mitsubishi
416 Eastchester Dr, High
Point NC 27262-7631.
910/841-6300.

Southern States Nissan
2407 Wake Forest Rd,
Raleigh NC 27608-1709.
919/833-5733.

Liberty Pontiac GMCTruck
6111 E Independence Blvd,
Charlotte NC 28212-6838.
704/536-6000.

Flow Lexus
I-40 & Hwy 66, Kernersville
NC 27284. 910/993-0105.

Hendrick Lexus
6025 E Independence Blvd,
Charlotte NC 28212-6829.
704/568-4122.

Saturn of Chapel Hill
Chapel Hill Blvd, Chapel Hill
NC 27514. 919/929-9619.

Saturn of Winston-Salem
2575 Peters Creek Pky,
Winston-Salem NC 27127-
5657. 910/785-2222.

Car Town Inc.
2407 W Roosevelt Blvd,
Monroe NC 28110-0417.
704/283-7632.

SRS Motors
5800 High Point Rd,
Greensboro NC 27407-7005.
910/632-9900.

Club Car Inc.
3101 Petty Rd, Durham NC
27707-7105. 919/490-
0779.

CONSUMER SUPPLY STORES

**Edwards Warren Truck Tire
Center**
1036 S Interstate 85 Service
R, Charlotte NC 28208-
2312. 704/394-0138.

Itco Tire Co.
P.O. Box 641, Wilson NC
27894-0641. 919/291-
8900.

Perry Brothers Tire Service
610 Wicker St, Sanford NC
27330-4141. 919/775-
7225.

Western Auto Supply
RR 6 Box 2316, Gastonia NC
28052-9806. 704/865-
6431.

Advance Auto Parts
944 Summit Ave,
Greensboro NC 27405-7918.
910/272-9726.

Advance Auto Parts
7218 E Marshville Blvd,
Marshville NC 28103-9507.
704/624-3133.

Advance Auto Parts
314 W Boulevard St,
Williamston NC 27892.
919/792-8462.

Advance Auto Parts
1105 W Ehringhaus St,
Elizabeth City NC 27909-
6910. 919/338-6360.

Advance Auto Parts
664 S Scales St, Reidsville
NC 27320. 910/349-2926.

Advance Auto Parts
811 Tunnel Rd, Asheville NC
28805-1264. 704/298-
0995.

Advance Auto Parts
Ponderosa Shopping Cntr,
Fayetteville NC 28303.
910/864-4834.

Advance Auto Parts
2797 W 5th St, Lumberton
NC 28358-7819. 910/739-
5330.

Advance Auto Parts
2609 Castle Hayne Rd,
Wilmington NC 28401-2682.
910/763-3304.

Advance Auto Parts
1017 E Main St, Lincolnton
NC 28092-3835. 704/732-
2223.

Advantage Auto Parts
116 E Washington St, La
Grange NC 28551-1718.
919/566-4733.

Auto Supply Inc.
2910 Interstate St, Charlotte
NC 28208-3607. 704/391-
9144.

Autozone
5208 Market St, Wilmington
NC 28405-3434. 910/392-
9244.

Autozone
406 S Marine Blvd,
Jacksonville NC 28540-
3671. 910/455-7300.

Autozone
640 S Van Buren Rd, Eden
NC 27288-5365. 910/623-
3000.

Autozone
2303 E Bessemer Ave,
Greensboro NC 27405-7343.
910/275-1234.

Autozone
201 N Grace St, Rocky
Mount NC 27804-5315.
919/977-6700.

Carquest Auto Parts
1926 Spartanburg Hwy,
Hendersonvlle NC 28792-
6527. 704/693-1926.

Carquest Auto Parts
2550 Lewisville Clemmons
Rd, Clemmons NC 27012-
8711. 910/766-1636.

Carquest Auto Parts
2601 S Saunders St, Raleigh
NC 27603-2839. 919/832-
0356.

Eagle Automotive Inc.
4012 Viewmont Dr,
Greensboro NC 27406-9522.
910/299-3327.

Flowers Auto Parts Co.
75 N Main St, Granite Falls
NC 28630-1434. 704/396-
2151.

Motor Bearings & Parts Co.
509 N Mangum St, Durham
NC 27701-2413. 919/929-
5400.

Motor Bearings & Parts Co.
641 Tiffany Square Blvd,
Rocky Mount NC 27804-
1802. 919/977-1396.

Motor Bearings & Parts Co.
151 N Center St, Goldsboro
NC 27530-3620. 919/734-
4651.

NAPA Auto Parts
522 National Hwy,
Thomasville NC 27360-
3056. 910/475-9188.

NAPA Auto Parts
1303 US Highway 70 W,
Garner NC 27529-2551.
919/772-9144.

Walker Auto Stores
3738 Chapel Hill Blvd,
Durham NC 27707-6229.
919/493-1996.

Western Auto
4410 High Point Rd,
Greensboro NC 27407-4236.
910/547-8015.

Advance Auto Pdq
1205 25th Street Pl SE,
Hickory NC 28602-9658.
704/327-8272.

Exide Battery
4101 Barringer Dr #C,
Charlotte NC 28217-1509.
704/342-4800.

Tire America
2 Westgate Pky, Asheville
NC 28806. 704/251-0991.

**Firestone Tire & Service
Centers**
3737 Ramsey St,
Fayetteville NC 28311-7651.
910/822-2277.

**Merchant's Tire & Auto
Centers**
6120 Duraleigh Rd, Raleigh
NC 27612. 919/571-0071.

**Merchant's Tire & Auto
Centers**
1614 S Miami Blvd, Durham
NC 27703. 919/596-9387.

**Parrish Tire Co. Truck Tire
Center**
900 N Miami Blvd, Durham
NC 27703. 919/688-6115.

**Firestone Tire & Service
Centers**
1001 N Wesleyan Blvd,
Rocky Mount NC 27804-
1839. 919/446-4196.

**Goodyear Auto Service
Centers**
601 College Rd, Greensboro
NC 27410-4101. 910/854-
7949.

Montgomery Ward & Co.
Tarrytown Center, Rocky
Mount NC 27804. 919/443-
4111.

Parrish Tire Co. of Raleigh
8800 N Point Blvd, Winston-
Salem NC 27106-3204.
910/759-0202.

Tire Disposal
100 Pecan Ln, Clayton NC
27520-2001. 919/553-
4488.

**APPAREL AND ACCESSORY
STORES**

Casual Male Big & Tall
2397 Corporation Pky,
Burlington NC 27215-6751.
910/570-9144.

County Seat
South Square Mall, Durham
NC 27707. 919/489-0276.

Fine's Men Shop
1480-20 US Hwy 29 N,
Concord NC 28025.
704/788-7056.

J. Riggings
South Park, Charlotte NC
28211. 704/366-6020.

J. Riggings
Central Ave, Charlotte NC
28212. 704/531-1401.

Joseph A. Bank Clothiers
4217 Six Forks Rd, Raleigh
NC 27609-5736. 919/881-
9995.

**S&K Famous Brand
Menswear**
3727 Battleground Ave,
Greensboro NC 27410-2345.
910/545-1126.

S&K Menswear
1001 Airport Blvd, Morrisville
NC 27560-8935. 919/380-
7454.

Structure
Crabtree Valley Mall, Raleigh
NC 27612. 919/571-9343.

Tom James Clothiers
112 S Tryon St, Charlotte
NC 28284-0001. 704/358-
1118.

Aileen Stores Inc.
7100 S Croatan Hwy, Nags
Head NC 27959-9057.
919/441-0910.

Body Shop
3500 Oleander Dr Unit 35,
Wilmington NC 28403-0811.
910/392-0332.

Bon Worth
207 West Ave, Kannapolis
NC 28081-4334. 704/933-
5868.

Catherine's
3049 Freedom Dr, Charlotte
NC 28208-3859. 704/391-
1336.

Cato
203 US 321 Hwy Bypass,
Lincolnton NC 28092.
704/735-8403.

Closet
205 Cross Creek Mall,
Fayetteville NC 28303-7239.
910/864-2860.

Fashion Cents
4111 W Vernon Ave,
Kinston NC 28501-9672.
919/523-2444.

Fashion Cents
Brynn Marr Shp Center,
Jacksonville NC 28546.
910/353-8138.

Fiber Work Handwovens
430 Brookstown Ave,
Winston-Salem NC 27101-
5026. 910/722-7662.

Hi-Lifes
1249 Silas Creek Pky,
Winston-Salem NC 27127-
5628. 910/722-4773.

Hi-Lites
Kinston Market Pl, Kinston
NC 28501. 919/522-4772.

It's Fashion Six & Up
1307 Scotland Crossing Dr,
Laurinburg NC 28352-5414.
910/277-8617.

Lane Bryant Inc.
North Hills Mall, Raleigh NC
27609. 919/787-5122.

Lane Bryant Inc.
Crabtree Valley Mall, Raleigh
NC 27612. 919/787-9345.

Lillie Rubin-Raleigh Inc.
4325 Glenwood Ave #J246,
Raleigh NC 27612-4504.
919/787-1813.

Limited Express
Golden East Crossing Mall,
Rocky Mount NC 27804.
919/446-9103.

Liz Claiborne
1231 Plaza Dr, Burlington NC
27215-7164. 910/222-
0193.

Maurices
18 Pinecrest Plz, Southern
Pines NC 28387-4301.
910/692-7522.

Maurices Divisional Office
108 E N Fayetteville, Liberty
NC 27298. 910/622-2647.

Rainbow New York
216 Fayetteville Street Mall,
Raleigh NC 27601-1310.
919/834-8700.

Size 5-7-9 Shops
1190 Carolina Circle Mall,
Greensboro NC 27405.
910/375-1579.

Stuarts Plus
1142 Carolina Circle Mall,
Greensboro NC 27405.
910/621-5038.

Talbots
200 N Greensboro St,
Carrboro NC 27510-1833.
919/933-0242.

Talbots Specialty Shop In Park
6401 Morrison Blvd,
Charlotte NC 28211-3533.
704/364-0580.

After Thoughts
11025 Carolina Pl Pkwy Unit A4, Pineville NC 28134-7515. 704/542-3801.

Carimar Store
11025 Carolina Place Pky,
Pineville NC 28134-7515.
704/542-2826.

Claire's Boutiques
401 S Independence Blvd,
Charlotte NC 28204-2623.
704/342-5770.

Maternity Wearhouse
2402 Maple Ave, Burlington NC 27215-7116. 910/226-9814.

Victoria's Secret
Eastridge Mall, Gastonia NC
28054. 704/868-2109.

Victoria's Secret
736 Hanes Mall Blvd,
Winston-Salem NC 27103-5636. 910/760-2640.

Victoria's Secret
800 Brevard Rd, Asheville
NC 28806. 704/665-7340.

Houser Shoes
Eastridge Mall, Gastonia NC
28054. 704/867-2276.

Kid City
3441 Lackey St, Lumberton
NC 28358. 910/739-8937.

Goody's Discount Family Clothing
Jackson Plaza, Sylva NC
28779. 704/586-8867.

R&R Uniforms Inc.
333 Haywood St, Asheville
NC 28801. 704/253-2722.

Eddie Bauer Inc.
Four Seasons Town Centre,
Greensboro NC 27407.
910/292-7101.

Eddie Bauer Inc.
264 Hanes Mall Blvd,
Winston-Salem NC 27103.
910/659-9883.

Motorsport Traditions Ltd.
2835 Armentrout Dr,
Concord NC 28025-5866.
704/376-2741.

The Gap
4325 Glenwood Ave, Raleigh
NC 27612-4504. 919/571-8305.

The Gap
219 E Six Forks Rd, Raleigh
NC 27609-7725. 919/781-5204.

Personal Touch
1924 Capital Blvd, Raleigh
NC 27604-2147. 919/821-3285.

SHOE STORES

Hofheimer's Inc.
4325 Glenwood Ave, Suite
139, Raleigh NC 27612-4504. 919/787-4954.

Rack Room Shoes
8036 Providence Rd, Suite
400, Charlotte NC 28277-9701. 704/543-4622.

Rack Room Shoes
837 Highway 24 27 73 E,
Albemarle NC 28001-5359.
704/983-6158.

Roscoe-Griffin Shoes
P.O. Box 10952, Raleigh NC
27605-0952. 919/834-7978.

Foot Locker Store
Four Seasons Mall,
Greensboro NC 27407.
910/852-5320.

Lady Foot Locker
4400 Sharon Rd, Charlotte
NC 28211-3531. 704/362-3725.

Abilene Boot Company
414 E Dixie Dr, Asheboro NC
27203-6860. 910/625-8115.

Airweld Inc.
870 W Northwest Blvd,
Winston-Salem NC 27101-1214. 910/723-7303.

Burlington Shoes
1800 Skibo Rd, Suite 136,
Fayetteville NC 28303-3280.
910/864-5273.

Burlington Shoes
Berkeley Mall, Goldsboro NC
27530. 919/751-0261.

Burlington Shoes
Wilkes Mall, Wilkesboro NC
28697. 910/667-4921.

Endicott Shoes
Carolina East Mall, Greenville
NC 27834. 919/756-4103.

Foot Action USA
1058 W Club Blvd, Durham
NC 27701. 919/286-7137.

Nine West
4400 Sharon Rd, Charlotte
NC 28211-3531. 704/362-0580.

North Carolina Leather Co.
1547 English Rd, High Point
NC 27262-7231. 910/885-6827.

Pic'N Pay Shoes
842 S Van Buren Rd, Eden
NC 27288-5324. 910/627-7997.

Pic'N Pay Shoes
172 S Tunnel Rd, Asheville
NC 28805-2228. 704/298-1577.

Pic'N Pay Shoes
3124 Eastway Dr, Charlotte
NC 28205-5664. 704/536-4511.

Pic'N Pay Shoes
Cross Pointe Centre,
Fayetteville NC 28314.
910/868-4305.

Precis Shoes & Accessory Boutique
4400 Sharon Rd, Charlotte
NC 28211-3531. 704/364-2428.

Rack Room Shoes
Brassfield Shopping Center,
Greensboro NC 27410.
910/282-1250.

Rack Room Shoes
Milton Rd, Charlotte NC
28215. 704/536-3076.

Rack Room Shoes
Sutters Creek Plz, Rocky
Mount NC 27804. 919/985-4244.

Rack Room Shoes
Boulevard Plaza Shp Center,
Wilson NC 27893. 919/399-7507.

Shoe City
Cypress Bay Plz, Morehead
City NC 28557. 919/726-0550.

Shoe Show Inc.
1442 Memorial Dr E, Ahoskie
NC 27910-3926. 919/332-4034.

Shoe Show Inc.
Twin Rivers Mall, New Bern
NC 28562. 919/637-6101.

Sports World Surplus
800 Fairview Rd, Asheville
NC 28803. 704/298-6293.

The Shoe Department
110 Randolph Mall,
Asheboro NC 27203-4978.
910/629-4922.

FURNITURE STORES

Bombay Company
218 Four Season Town
Centre, Greensboro NC
27407. 910/547-9199.

Bombay Company
4325 Glenwood Ave, Suite
245, Raleigh NC 27612-
4504. 919/787-7226.

Cranford Country House
71 US Highway 321 NW,
Hickory NC 28601-5828.
704/324-1850.

Furniture Distributors
4524 South Blvd, Charlotte
NC 28209-2841. 704/523-
6332.

Heilig-Meyers Furniture Co.
1311 Town & Country Shpg
Center, Aberdeen NC 28315-
2219. 910/944-9500.

Heilig-Meyers Furniture Co.
912 Summit Ave,
Greensboro NC 27405-7918.
910/273-1180.

Heilig-Meyers Furniture Co.
1021 US Highway 17 S,
Elizabeth City NC 27909-
7628. 919/338-4111.

Heilig-Meyers Furniture Co.
1310 N Wesleyan Blvd,
Rocky Mount NC 27804-
1816. 919/972-3832.

Kimbrell's Furniture
328 Person St, Fayetteville
NC 28301-5736. 910/483-
0363.

Kimbrell's Furniture
10 Catawba St, Belmont NC
28012-3342. 704/825-
3343.

Nationwide Warehouse &
Storage Inc.
3111 Freedom Dr, Charlotte
NC 28208-3869. 704/392-
9004.

Pier 1 Imports
10501 Centrum Pky,
Pineville NC 28134-8814.
704/542-9296.

Rose Brothers Furniture
5128 Oleander Dr,
Wilmington NC 28403-7017.
910/791-1110.

Schewel Furniture Co.
220 W Kings Hwy, Eden NC
27288. 910/623-2332.

Star Furniture Co. Inc.
1920 Garland St, Durham
NC 27705. 919/286-7590.

George Thomas
Cabinetmakers
5042 Weaver Rd, Wilson NC
27893-9492. 919/291-
2282.

Builderway of Asheville
332 Haywood Rd, Asheville
NC 28806-4232. 704/252-
2493.

Cabinet Shop
929 S Chapman St,
Greensboro NC 27403-2209.
910/272-9595.

Marsh Cabinets
420F Jonestown Rd,
Winston-Salem NC 27104-
4623. 910/765-7832.

Moores Lumber and Building
Supply
Warrenton Rd, Henderson NC
27536. 919/492-2081.

MISC. HOME FURNISHINGS STORES

Dealers Supply
2640P Yonkers Rd, Raleigh
NC 27604. 919/834-7067.

Bonitz Contracting Co.
100 Southcenter Ct, Cary
NC 27511. 919/380-0084.

Heilig-Meyers Furniture Co.
4507 W Market St,
Greensboro NC 27407-1258.
910/294-0320.

Heilig-Meyers Furniture Co.
214 Ward Blvd SW, Suite 6,
Wilson NC 27893-4659.
919/291-3995.

Heilig-Meyers Furniture Co.
916 Tuckaseegee Rd,
Charlotte NC 28208-4437.
704/333-3751.

Sherwin-Williams Home
Builder
320 E Washington St,
Greensboro NC 27401-2912.
910/274-5030.

Wallpaper For Less
1650 E Franklin Blvd,
Gastonia NC 28054-4747.
704/868-4468.

Lechter's Housewares
11017 Carolina Place Pky,
Pineville NC 28134-8370.
704/541-7374.

Lechter's Inc.
100 Hanes Mall Blvd,
Winston-Salem NC 27103.
910/765-1321.

Lighting Center
1018 Asheville Hwy, Brevard
NC 28712. 704/884-7282.

Fireside & Patio Shop
3528 Wade Ave, Raleigh NC
27607. 919/828-2733.

MG Inc.
3000-36 Stoneybrook Dr,
Raleigh NC 27604. 919/878-
8073.

Linen's & Things
416 Crossroads Blvd, Cary
NC 27511-6896. 919/233-
6900.

Plej's Textile Mill Outlet
South Hills Outlet Mall,
Raleigh NC 27604. 919/876-
1330.

Pier 1 Imports
4729 South Blvd, Charlotte
NC 28217-2117. 704/523-
4846.

HOUSEHOLD APPLIANCE STORES

Ed Kelly's
6022 Duraleigh Rd, Raleigh
NC 27612-7117. 919/782-
6772.

Kelleys Home Entertainment
& Appliances
3159 Capital Blvd, Raleigh
NC 27604-3335. 919/878-
8025.

Howard Distributors
1305 Herring Ave NE, Wilson
NC 27893-4314. 919/237-
9007.

CONSUMER ELECTRONICS STORES

Honest Johnson Electronics
714 Park Ave, Greensboro
NC 27405-7810. 910/274-
9766.

Audio Encounters
540 Church St N, Concord
NC 28025-4400. 704/786-
3006.

Southern Autotronics
5409 Oak Forest Dr, Raleigh
NC 27604-4617. 919/876-
9909.

AEI Music Network Inc.
6600 Northpark Blvd,
Charlotte NC 28216-2380.
704/596-7611.

Woodworx Audio Systems
3714 Alliance Dr,
Greensboro NC 27407-2060.
910/855-5600.

COMPUTER AND SOFTWARE STORES

Avnet Computer
4421 Stuart Andrew Blvd,
Suite 60, Charlotte NC
28217-1589. 704/523-
6766.

Carolina Computer Stores
5236 E Independence Blvd,
Charlotte NC 28212-6170.
704/567-1555.

Century Data Systems
1611 E 7th St, Charlotte NC
28204-2411. 704/372-
0804.

Century Data Systems
1126 Shipyard Blvd,
Wilmington NC 28412-6496.
910/799-0851.

Compu Com Systems
700 Forest Point Cir, Suite
114, Charlotte NC 28273-
5608. 704/525-0180.

Computerland
1100 Perimeter Park Dr,
Suite 112, Morrisville NC
27560-9119. 919/460-
5260.

Data General
2709 Water Ridge Pky,
Charlotte NC 28217-4538.
704/357-0226.

Dataflow Companies Inc.
314 N Church St,
Greensboro NC 27401-3012.
910/275-3324.

**Empac Computer Systems
High Point**
10617 N Main St #J,
Archdale NC 27263-2805.
910/861-6348.

EMC
4601 Six Forks Rd, Raleigh
NC 27609-5210. 919/420-
0405.

Bottler Systems Inc.
3710 University Dr, Suite
310, Durham NC 27707-
6208. 919/490-8440.

**RECORD AND
PRERECORDED TAPE
STORES**

Blockbuster Music
Celebrations at Six Forks,
Raleigh NC 27615. 919/870-
8779.

Camelot Music
3 S Tunnel Rd, Asheville NC
28805-2221. 704/298-
5966.

CD Superstore
3707 Battleground Ave,
Greensboro NC 27410-2345.
910/282-9696.

Coconuts Music & Video
1732 Skibo Rd, Fayetteville
NC 28303-3253. 910/868-
5792.

M. Fadyen Music
136 N McPherson Church
Rd, Fayetteville NC 28303-
4455. 910/864-3600.

Record Exchange
2109 Avent Ferry Rd, Suite
144, Raleigh NC 27606-
2137. 919/831-2300.

Record Town
170 Huffman Mill Rd,
Burlington NC 27215-5113.
910/584-5933.

Starship Music & Movies
2-142 Carolina Circle Mall,
Greensboro NC 27405.
910/621-8727.

JB Video
39 W Main St, Hamlet NC
28345-3629. 910/582-
5747.

**MUSICAL INSTRUMENT
STORES**

McFadyen Music Co.
Morehead Plaza, Morehead
City NC 28557. 919/726-
1222.

DRUG STORES

Derita Drug Co.
2410 W Sugar Creek Rd,
Charlotte NC 28262-3168.
704/596-1041.

Eckerd Drugs
1002 Summit Ave,
Greensboro NC 27405-7008.
910/275-7644.

Valu-Rx Pharmacy
410 E Washington St, La
Grange NC 28551-1837.
919/566-9595.

Rite Aid Pharmacies
Byrd's Shopping Center,
Benson NC 27504. 910/894-
5764.

Rite Aid Pharmacies
3102 E Bessemer Ave,
Greensboro NC 27405-7506.
910/275-7657.

Rite Aid Pharmacies
713 W Main St, Jamestown
NC 27282-9561. 910/454-
3101.

Eckerd Drugs
3108 Weddington Rd,
Matthews NC 28105-6665.
704/841-1770.

Eckerd Drugs
6129 Plaza Road Ext,
Charlotte NC 28215-1963.
704/535-5960.

Eckerd Drugs
4716 Sharon Rd, Charlotte
NC 28210-3328. 704/553-
1078.

Eckerd Drugs
1776 Statesville Ave,
Charlotte NC 28206-3013.
704/371-3600.

Eckerd Drugs
924 NE Maynard Rd, Cary
NC 27513-4163. 919/460-
5884.

Caremark Inc.
9401-J Southern Pine Blvd,
Charlotte NC 28273.
704/523-7731.

Crown Drugs Inc.
400 Commerce Pl, Advance
NC 27006. 910/998-6800.

Kerr Drug Stores
8320 Litchford Rd, Raleigh
NC 27615-3860. 919/850-
0400.

Kerr Drug Stores
3801 Pleasant Plains Rd #H,
Matthews NC 28105-5957.
704/821-8555.

**National Prescription
Administrators**
2506 George Anderson Dr,
Hillsborough NC 27278-
8749. 919/732-2217.

Treasury Drug
Cary Town Center, Cary NC
27511. 919/467-3773.

LIQUOR STORES

Barley & Vines
300 S Sharon Amity Rd
#328, Charlotte NC 28211-
2806. 704/366-1009.

SPORTING GOODS STORES

Carolina Fitness Equipment
2411 E Millbrook Rd, Suite
101, Raleigh NC 27604-
2800. 919/876-5100.

Champ's Sports
11025 Carolina Pl Pkwy Unit
A2, Pineville NC 28134-
7515. 704/542-6983.

Champ's Sports
3500 Oleander Dr, Suite A3,
Wilmington NC 28403-0811.
910/395-1859.

Champ's Sports
1100 N Wesleyan Blvd,
Rocky Mount NC 27804-
1827. 919/446-4883.

Champ's Sports
312 Cross Creek Mall,
Fayetteville NC 28303-7242.
910/487-1495.

Dr. McSoccer
6915 Capital Blvd, Raleigh
NC 27604. 919/981-0799.

Jamestown Bicycle & Sports
118 E Main St, Jamestown
NC 27282-9531. 910/454-
5555.

Play It Again Sports
611 Tunnel Rd, Asheville NC
28805. 704/299-1221.

Sports Fantasy
Jacksonville Mall,
Jacksonville NC 28546.
910/577-4101.

Team Pride
Crabtree Valley Mall, Raleigh
NC 27612. 919/783-6839.

Thor-Lo Inc.
1072 Crossroads Dr,
Statesville NC 28677-8276.
704/873-8243.

Overton's
1331 Buck Jones Rd, Raleigh
NC 27606-3328. 919/469-
2523.

Overton's
5343 South Blvd, Charlotte
NC 28217-4117. 704/527-
8083.

BOOKSTORES

Brentano's Bookstore
Carolina Place, Pineville NC
28134. 704/541-7474.

Publishers Warehouse
401 S Independence Blvd,
Charlotte NC 28204-2623.
704/373-0070.

Diamond Comic Distributors
4901 Dwight Evans Rd,
Suite 106, Charlotte NC
28217-1441. 704/523-
1790.

STATIONERY AND OFFICE SUPPLY STORES

Hinkle's Thruway
220 S Stratford Rd, Winston-
Salem NC 27103-1818.
910/770-1598.

Forms & Supply Inc.
1314 E 5th St, Lumberton
NC 28358-6030. 910/738-
1126.

Systel Office Automation
6390 Burnt Poplar Rd #A,
Greensboro NC 27409-9716.
910/668-3443.

Harper Brothers
4921 Tallwood Dr, Raleigh
NC 27613-7001. 919/847-
0078.

Raleigh Office Supply Co.
712 Tucker St, Raleigh NC
27603-1234. 919/834-
1601.

JEWELRY STORES

Brendle's Inc.
2101 Tarboro St SW, Wilson
NC 27893-3459. 919/237-
4346.

Carlyle & Co.
11025 Carolina Pl Pkwy Unit
A2, Pineville NC 28134-
7515. 704/543-9962.

Friedman's Jewelers
1480-45 US Hwy 29 N,
Concord NC 28025.
704/784-1429.

Friedman's Jewelers
11025 Carolina Pl Pkwy Unit
C2, Pineville NC 28134-
7517. 704/542-8976.

Garibaldi and Bruns Inc.
Southpark Mall, Charlotte NC
28211. 704/366-3120.

Helzberg Diamonds
11025 Carolina Place Pky,
Pineville NC 28134-7515.
704/544-1144.

Jewel Box
Cross Creek Mall, Fayetteville
NC 28303. 910/864-0151.

Service Merchandise Co.
4501 S Tryon St, Charlotte
NC 28217-1843. 704/527-
1592.

Stereo World
2145 Lejeune Blvd,
Jacksonville NC 28546-
8251. 910/353-5500.

Whitehall Co. Jewelers
241 Cross Creek Mall,
Fayetteville NC 28303-7239.
910/487-1433.

Replacement Ltd.
1089 Knox Rd, McLeansville
NC 27301-9228. 910/697-
3000.

HOBBY, TOY, AND GAME SHOPS

Hungates Arts-Crafts & Hobbies
North Hills Mall, Raleigh NC
27609. 919/782-4436.

Janie's Craft
1602 N 4th St, Wilmington
NC 28401-2813. 910/763-
2007.

Michaels-Arts & Crafts
3721 Battleground Ave,
Greensboro NC 27410-2345.
910/282-8793.

Michaels-Arts & Crafts
8046 Providence Rd,
Charlotte NC 28277-9748.
704/543-9276.

Michaels-Arts & Crafts
7233 E Independence Blvd,
Charlotte NC 28227-9424.
704/536-0825.

Michaels-Arts & Crafts
6208 Glenwood Ave, Raleigh
NC 27612-2657. 919/781-
1184.

Old America Store
3428 Bragg Blvd, Fayetteville
NC 28303-3995. 910/487-
4481.

Ed Kelly Inc. Car Toys
1418 S Stratford Rd #200,
Winston-Salem NC 27103-
2902. 910/659-8022.

Kay-Bee Toys
Parkwood Mall, Wilson NC
27893. 919/237-3093.

Princess Street Antiques
129 Princess St, Wilmington
NC 28401-3948. 910/762-
9299.

Olde Wilmington Toy Co.
321 N Front St, Wilmington
NC 28401-3908. 910/251-
1404.

CAMERA AND PHOTOGRAPHIC SUPPLY STORES

Wolf Camera & Video
8036 Providence Rd, Suite
1100, Charlotte NC 28277-
9701. 704/541-7488.

GIFT, NOVELTY, AND SOUVENIR SHOPS

Amy's Hallmark
Biltmore Square Mall,
Asheville NC 28806.
704/665-4920.

Book Warehouse
Carolina Pottery Outlet
Center, Smithfield NC
27577. 910/934-6250.

Brame
821 Planters St, Rocky
Mount NC 27801-6021.
919/442-3154.

Cracker Barrel Old Country Store
12 Plaza Pky, Lexington NC
27292-5350. 704/242-
1212.

Cracker Barrel Old Country Store
4402 Landview Dr,
Greensboro NC 27407-2641.
910/294-0911.

Cracker Barrel Old Country Store
3375 Lackey St, Lumberton
NC 28358-9044. 910/738-
1481.

Everything's A Dollar
Carolina Circle Mall,
Greensboro NC 27405.
910/375-4589.

Kirkland's
Southpark Mall, Charlotte NC
28211. 704/364-6464.

Log Cabin
106 W Cj Thomas Rd,
Monroe NC 28110-8270.
704/282-4865.

Round & Smooth Wood Art
Hwy 64, Brasstown NC
28902. 704/837-8663.

The Nature Company
Crabtree Valley Mall, Raleigh
NC 27612. 919/783-7839.

The Nature Company
4400 Sharon Rd, Charlotte
NC 28211-3531. 704/364-
6342.

The Print Shop
North Hills Shopping Center,
Raleigh NC 27609. 919/783-
8360.

Tuesday Morning Inc.
7201 E Independence Blvd,
Charlotte NC 28227-9430.
704/535-7389.

SEWING SUPPLIES STORES

Maharam Inc.
601 S Cedar St, Suite 212,
Charlotte NC 28202-1071.
704/342-2552.

Hancock Fabrics
955 N Wesleyan Blvd #A,
Rocky Mount NC 27804-
1786. 919/985-3212.

Piece Goods Shop
5033 South Blvd, Charlotte
NC 28217-2715. 704/523-
7972.

Piece Goods Shops
406 Thompson St, Eden NC
27288-5044. 910/623-
5700.

**CATALOG AND MAIL-
ORDER HOUSES**

Ott's Discount Art Supply
714 Greenville Blvd SE,
Greenville NC 27858-5104.
919/756-9565.

Sears Roebuck and Co.
Slocum Villag Shp Center,
Havelock NC 28532.
919/223-5200.

FUEL DEALERS

Little River LP Gas
117 Ash St, Spring Hope NC
27882. 919/478-4626.

**McCracken Oil & Propane
Co.**
110 S Main St, Creedmoor
NC 27522-9701. 919/528-
9841.

**Southern States Asheville
Service**
464 Riverside Dr, Asheville
NC 28801-2532. 704/253-
9351.

Jenkins Gas and Oil Co.
P.O. Box 156, Pollocksville
NC 28573. 919/224-8911.

Amerigas
1290 N Roberts Ave,
Lumberton NC 28358-2274.
910/739-5234.

**North Carolina Propane Gas
Co.**
126 E Vance St, Zebulon NC
27597. 919/269-6930.

Synergy Gas Corporation
604 Mercury St, Raleigh NC
27603. 919/821-7255.

Thomas Gas Company
435 Church St N, Concord
NC 28025. 704/786-5899.

OPTICAL GOODS STORES

Lens Crafters
Southpark Mall, Charlotte NC
28211. 704/364-8725.

Pearle Vision Center
5330 South Blvd, Charlotte
NC 28217. 704/525-9802.

Visionworks
Cotswold Mall, Charlotte NC
28211. 704/365-6277.

Allred Optic at Statesville
Old Mocksville Rd, Statesville
NC 28677. 704/878-2854.

Western Wake Optical
200 Ashville Ave, Cary NC
27511. 919/859-5240.

MISC. RETAIL STORES

Binders Art Center
401 S Independence Blvd,
Charlotte NC 28204-2623.
704/334-4611.

Dial Page
109 W Morehead St,
Charlotte NC 28202-1826.
704/333-2337.

Page South
756 Tyvola Rd, Suite 103,
Charlotte NC 28217-3535.
704/597-0059.

Rolm A. Siemens Co.
4944 Parkway Plaza Blvd,
Charlotte NC 28217-1969.
704/357-5225.

Tekelec
3000 Aerial Center Pky,
Suite 120, Morrisville NC
27560. 919/460-5500.

**Hickory Grove True Value
Hardware & Garden**
7135 E Wt Harris Blvd,
Charlotte NC 28227-1009.
704/536-0541.

**Leslies Swimming Pool
Supplies**
4402 E Independence Blvd,
Charlotte NC 28205-7404.
704/532-5758.

Uni-Copy
7021-A Albert Pick Rd,
Greensboro NC 27409.
910/722-8061.

Frame Warehouse
3218 Silas Creek Pky,
Winston-Salem NC 27103-
3009. 910/768-7207.

Frame Warehouse
6260 Glenwood Ave, Suite
116, Raleigh NC 27612-
2612. 919/783-9354.

Lee House of Frames
1020 Central Ave, Charlotte
NC 28204. 704/333-0075.

Sungear
Central Ave, Charlotte NC
28212. 704/532-9138.

Sungear
Cross Creek Mall, Fayetteville
NC 28303. 910/487-4488.

VIDEO TAPE RENTAL

Blockbuster Video
5720 E Independence Blvd,
Charlotte NC 28212-0512.
704/536-5642.

Blockbuster Video
2237 Avent Ferry Rd,
Raleigh NC 27606-2133.
919/821-0172.

Blockbuster Video
343 S College Rd, Suite 9,
Wilmington NC 28403-1625.
910/392-9797.

Blockbuster Video
8016 Providence Rd,
Charlotte NC 28277-9748.
704/543-4073.

Blockbuster Video
3500 N Duke St, Durham NC
27704. 919/479-8466.

Blockbuster Video
1570 Four Seasons Blvd,
Hendersonvlle NC 28792-
2853. 704/697-0338.

Phar-Mor
6254 Glenwood Ave, Raleigh
NC 27612. 919/781-3361.

Phar-Mor
2105 Peters Creek Pky,
Winston-Salem NC 27127-
3712. 910/724-0689.

**Action Video Cassette
Movies Inc.**
1032 Summit Ave,
Greensboro NC 27405-7008.
910/272-9557.

Pic-A-Flick Video
3211 Eastway Dr, Charlotte
NC 28205. 704/531-7978.

Pic-A-Flick Video
3148 Freedom Dr, Charlotte
NC 28208. 704/393-0225.

South Carolina

BABY SUPERSTORE INC.
P.O. Box 100, Duncan SC 29334. 864/968-9292. **Contact:** Suzanne Thomas, Human Resources Manager. **Description:** A large format retailer of baby and young children's products. Baby Superstore Inc. was founded in 1970 and operates 46 stores in 13 states, primarily in the Southeast and Midwest. Most of the products sold by the company are directed toward newborns and children up to three years old. Baby Superstores are generally anchor tenants in strip shopping centers near major regional malls and other destination stores. Brand names offered by the company include Simmons, Graco, Bassett, Fisher-Price, Gerber, Century, Little Tikes, Kids Line, Gerry, OshKosh B'Gosh, Welsh, Red Calliope, Playskool, Brooks, Keds and Weebok. The company also markets an increasing volume of products under its own Baby Superstore brand name. The company also works with LaLeche League, Lamaze and local and national safety organizations by providing information and programs for customers at its superstores. Between 1995-1996 the company planned to open an additional 40 stores. **Common positions include:** Cashier; Management; Sales Associate; Services Sales Representative; Stock Clerk. **Corporate headquarters location:** This Location. **Other U.S. locations:** Raleigh NC; Greensboro NC; Asheville NC; Charlotte NC; North Charleston SC; Augusta SC; Columbia SC. **Listed on:** NASDAQ. **Number of employees nationwide:** 2,467.

BI-LO, INC.
P.O. Box 99, Mauldin SC 29662. 864/234-1600. **Contact:** John Gianakas, Human Resources Manager. **Description:** BI-LO, Inc. is a supermarket chain. The company has stores throughout the Southeast, including South Carolina, North Carolina, Georgia, and Tennessee. **Corporate headquarters location:** This Location.

CALE YARBOROUGH HONDA/MAZDA
2723 West Palmetto Street, Florence SC 29501. 803/669-5556. **Contact:** Robby Melton, Services Manager. **Description:** An automobile dealership that sells new and used Hondas and Mazdas as well as other vehicles. Cale Yarborough Honda/Mazda also offers automobile repair services. **Common positions include:** Automotive Mechanic/Body Repairer.

HAMRICK'S, INC.
742 Peachoid Road, Gaffney SC 29341. 864/489-6095. **Contact:** Maxine Elder, Director of Personnel. **Description:** Hamrick's, Inc. operates a chain of men's clothing stores. These stores are located in the southeastern United States at 23 different locations. **Other U.S. locations:** GA; NC; SC.

ONE PRICE CLOTHING STORES
P.O. Box 2487, Spartanburg SC 29304. 864/433-8888. **Contact:** Marsha Clifs, Director of Human Resources. **Description:** One Price Clothing Stores operates approximately 490 specialty off-price stores, featuring a wide variety of first-quality contemporary women's apparel, in season, for a uniform price of $7 per item. The company operates in 24 states. **Number of employees nationwide:** 3,273.

Note: Because addresses and telephone numbers of smaller companies change rapidly, we recommend you call each company to verify the information below before inquiring about job opportunities. Mass mailings are not recommended.

Additional employers with under 250 employees:

RETAIL LUMBER AND BUILDING MATERIALS

ABC Supply Co. Inc.
3800 Ashley Phosphate Rd, Charleston SC 29418-8503. 803/760-6811.

Ted Lansing Corporation
124 Interstate Blvd, Greenville SC 29615-5708. 864/458-7770.

Home Depot
7554 Northwoods Blvd, N Charleston SC 29406-4030. 803/569-3773.

Canal Wood Corporation
929 Church St, Georgetown SC 29440-3511. 803/527-0545.

Canco Inc.
750 W Main St, Spartanburg SC 29301. 864/583-9114.

Carolina Builders Corp.
2816 Azalea Dr, Charleston SC 29405. 803/747-7301.

Cason Builders Supply
2131 Woodruff Rd, Greenville SC 29607-5934. 864/675-9519.

Lowe's of Sumter
Hwy 378, Sumter SC 29150. 803/469-0900.

Maner Builders Supply Co.
P.O. Box 40516, N
Charleston SC 29423.
803/552-0242.

Leeds Building Products
7090 Howard St,
Spartanburg SC 29303-
1861. 864/583-3613.

**Lowe's Home Center of
Anderson**
3111 Mall Rd, Anderson SC
29625. 864/226-8587.

Morton Buildings Inc.
305 Joe S Jeffords Hwy SE,
Orangeburg SC 29115-7442.
803/533-0691.

Palmetto Brick Co.
7291 Cross County Rd, N
Charleston SC 29418-3306.
803/552-8330.

Structural Products Carolinas
30 Flatwoods Rd, Travelers
Rest SC 29690-9718.
864/855-5055.

Randolph Trucking Inc.
RR 1, Pacolet SC 29372-
9801. 864/474-2494.

Unicon Tri-County
158 Industrial Dr, Lexington
SC 29072. 803/359-5399.

Hardaway Concrete Co.
585 Calks Ferry Rd,
Lexington SC 29072-8620.
803/359-4743.

Becker Minerals
RR 3, Ridgeville SC 29472-
9803. 803/835-5868.

Glasscock Co. Inc.
P.O. Box 1384, Sumter SC
29151-1384. 803/494-
2694.

CK Supply
4311 Dorchester Rd,
Charleston SC 29405-7430.
803/747-5842.

**PAINT, GLASS, AND
WALLPAPER STORES**

Smartn' Up Wallcoverings
230 E Blackstock Rd,
Spartanburg SC 29301-
2607. 864/576-1172.

HARDWARE STORES

Tri County Ace Hardware
440 Ann St, Pickens SC
29671. 864/878-0052.

Travers Tool Co. Inc.
118 Spartangreen Blvd,
Duncan SC 29334-9424.
864/433-9000.

Ahlstrom Process Equipment
545 N Pleasantburg Dr, Suite
200, Greenville SC 29607-
2183. 864/232-0800.

**RETAIL NURSERIES AND
GARDEN SUPPLY STORES**

Lonnie's Small Engine Repair
1603 Jefferson Davis Hwy,
Camden SC 29020-3334.
803/425-5610.

Royster Southeast
Hwy 52, Kingstree SC
29556. 803/382-3661.

Northrup King Company
639 W Carolina Ave,
Hartsville SC 29550-4409.
803/332-8151.

MOBILE HOME DEALERS

Accent Mobile Homes
2359 N Pleasantburg Dr,
Greenville SC 29609-3026.
864/233-8221.

Clayton Homes
6501 Rivers Ave, N
Charleston SC 29406-4877.
803/572-2828.

Country Squire Homes
1619 E Palmetto St, Florence
SC 29506-3545. 803/667-
1494.

**Country Squire Mobile
Homes**
2446 Wilson Rd, Newberry
SC 29108-1600. 803/321-
9278.

Edisto Housing Center
1809 Augusta Hwy, West
Columbia SC 29169-5633.
803/926-9630.

Freedom Homes
2123 E Palmetto St, Florence
SC 29506-3610. 803/664-
0200.

Oakwood Homes
1006 N Anderson Rd, Rock
Hill SC 29730-2737.
803/324-2566.

Quality Housing Outlet
3060 Broad St, Sumter SC
29150-1802. 803/494-
3800.

DEPARTMENT STORES

Belk
2251 N Dave Lyle Blvd, Rock
Hill SC 29730-7939.
803/366-9471.

Kmart Stores
1457 W Hwy 123, Seneca
SC 29678. 864/882-1302.

Kmart Stores
2209 W Dekalb St, Camden
SC 29020-2070. 803/425-
0327.

Wal-Mart Discount Cities
702 Radford Blvd, Dillon SC
29536-5004. 803/841-
9800.

Wal-Mart Discount Cities
Dogwood Mall, Seneca SC
29678. 864/885-0408.

Allied Department Store
4121 W Beltline Blvd,
Columbia SC 29204-1508.
803/256-2719.

Dillard Department Stores
2121 S Beltline Blvd,
Columbia SC 29201-5111.
803/782-8910.

Dollar General Stores
10150 Dorchester Rd,
Summerville SC 29485-
8536. 803/871-2621.

Family Dollar Store
8440 Dorchester Rd,
Charleston SC 29420-7318.
803/767-9567.

Family Dollar Store
Hwy 321, Estill SC 29918.
803/625-4118.

Beacon Factory Outlet
2333 Sandifer Blvd #123,
Westminster SC 29693-
3901. 864/647-4254.

Outlet Pointe Mall
I-20 & Bush River Rd,
Columbia SC 29210.
803/798-8520.

Brendle's
3719 Clemson Blvd,
Anderson SC 29621-1316.
864/224-8855.

Belk
2060 Sam Rittenberg Blvd,
Charleston SC 29407-4696.
803/571-5420.

Belk
Rock Hill Galleria, Rock Hill
SC 29730. 803/366-9471.

Belk
Northwoods Mall, N
Charleston SC 29406.
803/797-2600.

JB White & Co.
Heritage Square, Aiken SC
29801. 803/649-1141.

VARIETY STORES

Allied Department Store
208 E Main St, Bennettsville
SC 29512-3106. 803/479-
3402.

Dollar Tree
Cross Creek Mall,
Greenwood SC 29649-1407.
864/229-0124.

Maxway
14 N Main St, Sumter SC
29150. 803/773-8166.

SH Kress & Co. 5 & 10 Store
Palmetto Plaza, Sumter SC
29150. 803/773-2367.

Super 10
118 Brooks St, Manning SC
29102. 803/435-4707.

Super 10
112 Wilkinsville Hwy,
Gaffney SC 29340-4150.
864/487-0056.

Super 10
2600 Anderson Rd,
Greenville SC 29611-6081.
864/269-2989.

**GROCERY AND
CONVENIENCE STORES**

Angler's Mini-Mart
Hwy 52-N, Moncks Corner
SC 29461. 803/761-1404.

BI-LO Inc.
212 W Columbia Ave,
Batesburg SC 29006-2123.
803/532-5943.

BI-LO Inc.
1937 Wilson Rd, Newberry
SC 29108-2201. 803/276-
1445.

BI-LO Inc.
1370 Chestnut St NE,
Orangeburg SC 29115-3451.
803/531-0670.

BI-LO Inc.
3900 Main St, Columbia SC
29203-6445. 803/252-
9967.

BI-LO Inc.
712 S Alabama Ave,
Chesnee SC 29323-1706.
864/461-3141.

BI-LO Inc.
5300 Rivers Ave, N
Charleston SC 29406-6219.
803/747-2234.

BI-LO Inc.
1621 Savannah Hwy,
Charleston SC 29407-2236.
803/556-6871.

BI-LO Inc.
8440 Dorchester Rd,
Charleston SC 29420-7318.
803/767-1328.

BI-LO Inc.
632 Highway 15-401 By-
Pass E, Bennettsville SC
29512. 803/479-6961.

BI-LO Inc.
512 Lamar Hwy, Darlington
SC 29532. 803/393-7331.

BI-LO Inc.
269 N Ron McNair Blvd,
Lake City SC 29560-2437.
803/394-5135.

BI-LO Inc.
2460 Hudson Rd, Greer SC
29650. 864/268-9811.

BI-LO Inc.
301 Brushy Creek Rd,
Taylors SC 29687-3557.
864/268-7259.

BI-LO Inc.
4435 Jefferson Davis Hwy,
Clearwater SC 29822-2000.
803/593-5142.

BI-LO Inc.
70 Pope Ave, Hilton Head SC
29928-4766. 803/842-
8691.

BI-LO Inc.
164 S Port Royal Dr, Hilton
Head SC 29928-5560.
803/681-5327.

Scotchman Store
100 E Liberty St, Marion SC
29571-4332. 803/423-
6734.

Young's Food Stores
280 S Pike Rd W, Sumter SC
29150. 803/773-4813.

Crown/Fast Fare Inc.
302 S Alabama Ave #565,
Chesnee SC 29323-1506.
864/461-8818.

Kroger Sav-On Food & Drugs
9600 N Kings Hwy, Myrtle
Beach SC 29572-4006.
803/449-9671.

Doscher's Food Store
1133 Savannah Hwy,
Charleston SC 29407-7819.
803/766-6011.

Doscher's Food Store
1750 Remount Rd, Hanahan
SC 29406-3286. 803/744-
7821.

Scotchman Stores
499 Northside Dr,
Greenwood SC 29649.
864/223-4355.

Easy Pick Up
1512 Main St, Conway SC
29526-3569. 803/248-
6551.

Easy Pick-Up
1314 4th Ave, Conway SC
29526-5029. 803/248-
4973.

Fast Fare
7624 Valley Falls Rd,
Spartanburg SC 29303-
1743. 864/578-7501.

Fast Fare
201 NE Main St, Easley SC
29640-2119. 864/859-
3764.

Fast Fare
776 College Park Rd, Ladson
SC 29456-6255. 803/797-
6105.

Markette
Highway 1, Lugoff SC
29078. 803/438-5422.

Food Lion
2250 Sunset Blvd, West
Columbia SC 29169-4750.
803/794-0413.

Food Lion
1213 Remount Rd, N
Charleston SC 29406-3433.
803/744-8890.

The Pantry
1206 Palm Blvd, Isle of
Palms SC 29451-2231.
803/886-4518.

Pantry Zone Office
1677 N Main St,
Summerville SC 29483-
7804. 803/871-6766.

Food Lion
7601 N Kings Hwy, Myrtle
Beach SC 29572-3040.
803/497-2761.

Food Lion
3890 S Kings Hwy, Myrtle
Beach SC 29577-4800.
803/238-1551.

Food Lion
2529 Broad St, Camden SC
29020-2237. 803/432-
2478.

General Food Store
316 S Main St, Bamberg SC
29003-1834. 803/245-
5829.

Good Chief
Highway 76, Mullins SC
29574. 803/464-0881.

Grocery Outlet Warehouse
1326 W Wade Hampton
Blvd, Suite E, Greer SC
29650-1156. 864/848-
9412.

Harris Teeter Inc.
2209 W Dekalb St, Camden
SC 29020-2070. 803/432-
3077.

Harris Teeter Inc.
7451 Garners Ferry Rd,
Columbia SC 29209-2602.
803/695-1588.

Harris Teeter Inc.
2660 Reidville Rd,
Spartanburg SC 29301-
3535. 864/587-1219.

Harris Teeter Inc.
2131 Old Spartanburg Rd,
Greer SC 29650-2704.
864/292-8997.

Harris Teeter Inc.
1930 W Palmetto St,
Florence SC 29501-4052.
803/678-9525.

Harris Teeter Inc.
325 Folly Rd, Charleston SC
29412-2507. 803/795-
7790.

Harris Teeter Inc.
920 Houston Nrthct Unit 14,
Mount Pleasant SC 29464-
3400. 803/881-1983.

Harris Teeter Inc.
301 Main St, Hilton Head SC
29926-1691. 803/689-
6255.

Winn-Dixie
6119l White Horse Rd,
Greenville SC 29611-3832.
864/295-2733.

Young's Food Stores
431 N Main St, Bishopville
SC 29010-1441. 803/484-
4250.

Kent's Korner
1012 Columbia Rd, Edgefield
SC 29824-9698. 803/637-
3435.

3 & 20 Food Mart
Highway 8, Easley SC
29640. 864/855-4744.

Kroger Sav-On Food & Drugs
5900 S Kings Hwy, Surfside
Beach SC 29575-4968.
803/238-1423.

Kroger Sav-On Food & Drugs
781 Main St, N Myrtle Beach
SC 29582-3029. 803/249-
9950.

**Kroger Sav-On Food and
Drugs**
817 Saint Andrews Rd,
Columbia SC 29210-5813.
803/551-1140.

Piggly Wiggly
Pinewood Rd, Sumter SC
29150. 803/773-2370.

Piggly Wiggly Carolina Co.
1005 Harbor View Rd,
Charleston SC 29412-4255.
803/762-0118.

Piggly Wiggly Carolina Co.
445 Meeting St, Charleston
SC 29403. 803/722-2766.

Piggly Wiggly Carolina Co.
119 College Park Rd, Ladson
SC 29456-3563. 803/572-
3936.

Piggly Wiggly of Camden
56 Dekalb St, Camden SC
29020. 803/432-7011.

Piggly Wiggly
1011 Broad St, Sumter SC
29150. 803/773-6011.

Piggly Wiggly Carolina Co.
8780 Rivers Ave #A, N
Charleston SC 29406-9257.
803/764-3039.

Piggly Wiggly Carolina Co.
1270 Yeamans Hall Rd,
Hanahan SC 29406-2773.
803/747-6373.

Piggly Wiggly Supermarket
Plaza at Shelter Cove, Hilton
Head SC 29928. 803/842-
4090.

Li'l Cricket Food Stores
Hwy 176, Pacolet SC
29372. 864/474-9827.

Li'l Cricket Food Stores
803 S Pinckney St, Union SC
29379-3026. 864/427-
4038.

Little General Food Store
West Front St, Iva SC
29655. 864/348-3094.

Winn Dixie
1671 Springdale Dr, Camden
SC 29020-2079. 803/432-
7091.

Pantry
5372 Sunset Blvd, Lexington
SC 29072-9260. 803/957-
2201.

Thai Market
RR 4, Sumter SC 29153-
9804. 803/469-3685.

Piez U Stores
2315 N Main St, Anderson
SC 29621-3880. 864/224-
9695.

Small's Food Center
4517 Kershaw Camden
Hwy, Heath Springs SC
29058-9127. 803/273-
2567.

Southeast Frozen Foods Co.
115 Littlejohn Rd,
Spartanburg SC 29301-
5520. 864/587-8823.

The Markette
601 S Hampton St, Kershaw
SC 29067-2002. 803/475-
4264.

Red Bank Food Center
729 S Lake Dr, Lexington SC
29072-3432. 803/359-
5226.

The Pantry
324 S Line St, Greer SC
29651. 864/879-4994.

Scotchman Stores
1598 Highway 17, Little
River SC 29566-9227.
803/249-4815.

Texaco Corner Mart
1487 Cedar Lane Rd,
Greenville SC 29611-2349.
864/246-8945.

Ridge Road Community Store
1612 Ridge Rd, Greenville
SC 29607. 864/288-0190.

Winn Dixie Deli
West Green St, Cheraw SC
29520. 803/537-3090.

The Pantry
485 Haywood Rd, Greenville
SC 29607-4304. 864/288-
8025.

Young's Food Stores
Florence Hwy, Sumter SC
29150. 803/775-8113.

Winn-Dixie
1645 Old Trolley Rd,
Summerville SC 29485-
8280. 803/875-5999.

Tuten's Bi-Rite
69 3rd St W, Estill SC
29918-9701. 803/625-
3421.

Little General Food Store
102 Westminster Hwy,
Westminster SC 29693-
1428. 864/647-2132.

RL Jordan Oil Co.
5916 Augusta Rd, Greenville
SC 29605-2748. 864/277-
8767.

General Store
409 E Carolina Av, Hampton
SC 29924. 803/943-4679.

Li'l Cricket Food Stores
310 W Butler Rd, Mauldin
SC 29662-2538. 864/297-
6753.

Food Chief
2501 Broad St, Camden SC
29020-2237. 803/432-
3531.

Circle-K Convenience Stores
1306 Redbank Rd, Goose
Creek SC 29445-4584.
803/572-4769.

EZ Shop
4137 Ladson Rd #A, Ladson
SC 29456-4993. 803/871-
0852.

Scotchman Store
1905 Maybank Hwy,
Charleston SC 29412-2110.
803/762-0869.

Circle K Stores
Hwy 17, Murrells Inlet SC
29576. 803/651-1007.

Scotchman Store
508 Johnnie Dodds Blvd,
Mount Pleasant SC 29464-
3011. 803/884-9429.

The Pantry
906 Folly Rd, Charleston SC
29412-3920. 803/762-
4838.

The Pantry
2015 State St, Cayce SC
29033-3956. 803/794-
5664.

The Pantry
620 Lake Arrowhead Rd,
Myrtle Beach SC 29572-
5513. 803/449-4014.

The Pantry
Hwy 17 Bypass, Surfside
Beach SC 29575. 803/650-
1881.

Tiger Mart
102 N Richardson St, Latta
SC 29565-1631. 803/752-
4271.

Tiger Mart
4811 Broad St, Loris SC
29569-2427. 803/756-
2626.

Scotchman Stores
3020 Highway 17, Murrells
Inlet SC 29576-7625.
803/651-1818.

The Pantry
207 Old Trolley Rd,
Summerville SC 29485-
4928. 803/875-9952.

Scotchman Stores
Hwy 544, Conway SC
29526. 803/347-4180.

Hickory Point
W C Dobbins Hwy, Laurens
SC 29360. 864/833-5832.

Hot Spot
Hwy 76, Eastover SC
29044. 803/783-2854.

Scotchman Stores
3698 Ladson Rd, Ladson SC
29456-4084. 803/873-
9452.

Food Lion
65 Sycamore Ave,
Charleston SC 29407-6705.
803/763-7289.

MISC. FOOD STORES

Southern Food Service
1200 Woodruff Rd, Suite
A1, Greenville SC 29607-
5731. 864/297-8896.

Fresh Market
300 Saint Andrews Rd,
Columbia SC 29210-4427.
803/772-4385.

General Nutrition Center
2060 Sam Rittenberg Blvd
Unit, Charleston SC 29407-
4616. 803/763-3180.

**Winter Mountain Bottled
Water**
1200 Woodruff Rd, Suite
G19, Greenville SC 29607-
5735. 864/288-7500.

RETAIL BAKERIES

Merita Bakeries
Florence Hwy, Sumter SC
29150. 803/775-0542.

**Original Great American
Chocolate Chip Cookie**
225 S Pleasantburg Dr,
Greenville SC 29607-2533.
864/235-2447.

AUTO DEALERS

Love Auto Mall
Hwy 21, Beaufort SC
29902. 803/525-4100.

**Dick Brooks Oldsmobile
Cadillac GMC Truck**
3520 Clemson Blvd,
Anderson SC 29621-1313.
864/224-2141.

Rick Hendrick Chevrolet
1500 Savannah Hwy,
Charleston SC 29407-7821.
803/571-7500.

Vic Bailey Ford
501 E Daniel Morgan Ave,
Spartanburg SC 29302-
1164. 864/233-6019.

Honda Cars of Charleston
1518 Savannah Hwy,
Charleston SC 29407-7845.
803/571-6910.

Dick Brooks Honda
745 E Wade Hampton Blvd,
Greer SC 29651-1550.
864/877-9090.

Dick Brooks Mitsubishi
3512 Clemson Blvd,
Anderson SC 29621-1313.
864/226-9090.

Ralph Hayes Toyota
3525 Clemson Blvd,
Anderson SC 29621-1312.
864/226-1571.

Saturn of North Charleston
8261 Rivers Ave, N
Charleston SC 29406-9202.
803/820-7800.

William Clarke Motors
1940 Savannah Hwy,
Charleston SC 29407-6267.
803/852-5222.

Metro Auto Sales & Finance
7716 Garners Ferry Rd,
Columbia SC 29209-3863.
803/776-7965.

Vernon Riley Truck City
1740 Jefferson Davis Hwy,
Graniteville SC 29829-9434.
803/663-4180.

CONSUMER SUPPLY STORES

Modine Piedmont Inc.
6015 Ponders Ct, Greenville
SC 29615-4601. 864/297-
8265.

Advance Auto Parts
1003 W Main St, Lexington
SC 29072-2401. 803/359-
3699.

Advance Auto Parts
204 W Columbia Ave,
Batesburg SC 29006-2123.
803/532-9001.

Advance Auto Parts
1517 Reidville Rd,
Spartanburg SC 29301-
3811. 864/574-6403.

Advance Auto Parts
403 N Duncan By-Pass,
Union SC 29379. 864/429-
8132.

Advance Auto Parts
937 Folly Rd, Charleston SC
29412. 803/795-5130.

Advance Auto Parts
5341 Dorchester Rd Unit 22,
Charleston SC 29418-5618.
803/552-1974.

Advance Auto Parts
Robertson Blvd, Walterboro
SC 29488. 803/549-7856.

Advance Auto Parts
420 Chesterfield Hwy,
Cheraw SC 29520-3053.
803/537-0927.

Advance Auto Parts
1008 N 2nd Ave, Dillon SC
29536. 803/774-3779.

Advance Auto Parts
2040 Columbia Rd NE,
Orangeburg SC 29115-2427.
803/536-3360.

Advance Auto Parts
3214 Augusta St, Greenville
SC 29605-2146. 864/277-
0007.

Advance Auto Parts
3106 N Main St, Anderson
SC 29621-2763. 864/226-
6099.

Advance Auto Parts
3033 Wade Hampton Blvd,
Taylors SC 29687-2779.
864/322-0975.

Anderson Auto Parts
540 White Horse Rd,
Greenville SC 29605-3681.
864/299-1490.

Advance Auto Parts
253 N Ron McNair Blvd,
Lake City SC 29560-2437.
803/394-3522.

ASWA Inc.
605 N Magnolia St,
Summerville SC 29483-
5170. 803/873-2230.

Western Auto
1040 Broad St, Sumter SC
29150. 803/773-4344.

Parks Auto Parts
1204 N Main St,
Summerville SC 29483-
7343. 803/875-9500.

GNB Battery Technologies
1861 Highway 20, Piedmont
SC 29673. 864/277-0682.

Carolina Tire Co.
Coastal Mall, Conway SC
29526. 803/248-5737.

Carolina Tire Co.
680 Russell St SE,
Orangeburg SC 29115-6049.
803/534-5506.

Tire Station
923 Haywood Rd, Greenville
SC 29615-3566. 864/271-
8473.

**NTW-National Tire
Warehouse**
1905 Savannah Hwy,
Charleston SC 29407-6252.
803/763-2330.

Carolina Tire Co.
6285 Rivers Ave, N
Charleston SC 29406-4928.
803/572-6691.

Carolina Tire Co.
106 Goose Creek Blvd S,
Goose Creek SC 29445-
3136. 803/764-1631.

Goodyear Carolina Tire Co.
1643 Richland Ave W, Aiken
SC 29801-3235. 803/642-
8511.

**Goodyear Auto Service
Centers**
2407 Wade Hampton Blvd,
Greenville SC 29615-1145.
864/292-0471.

**Merchant's Tire & Auto
Centers**
3419 Hwy 17 S, Murrells
Inlet SC 29576. 803/651-
4816.

Tire Station
1904 E Main St, Spartanburg
SC 29307-2305. 864/542-
8473.

Frasier Tire Service
1613 Bluff Rd, Columbia SC
29201-4913. 803/254-
5087.

**Wall Tire Maximum Auto
Care**
404 E Martintown Rd, North
Augusta SC 29841-4263.
803/278-4466.

Master Tire Co.
S Congress, Winnsboro SC
29180. 803/635-5581.

BOAT DEALERS

**Boaters World Discount
Marine Center**
1863 Sam Rittenberg Blvd,
Charleston SC 29407-4870.
803/763-8905.

E&B Discount Marine
5641 Rivers Ave, N
Charleston SC 29406-6022.
803/529-0094.

Surface Technologies Corp.
3204 Rivers Ave, Charleston
SC 29405-7739. 803/747-
6256.

**APPAREL AND ACCESSORY
STORES**

Casual Male Big & Tall
7800 Rivers Ave, Charleston
SC 29406-4057. 803/553-
1309.

Maurices Men's
2501 N Kings Hwy, Myrtle
Beach SC 29577-3054.
803/626-6772.

Tom James of Charleston
112 Pleasant Valley Dr,
Johns Island SC 29455-
5725. 803/744-4469.

Added Dimensions
Columbia Mall, Columbia SC
29223. 803/788-5312.

The Limited
10177 N Kings Hwy, Suite
G1, Myrtle Beach SC 29572-
4027. 803/272-3355.

Afterthoughts
10177 N Kings Hwy Unit 44,
Myrtle Beach SC 29572-
4028. 803/272-4475.

Carole Little
Shoppes On The Pkwy,
Hilton Head SC 29928.
803/686-4988.

Catherine's
424 Citadel Mall, Charleston
SC 29407. 803/763-0428.

Catherine's
Belvedere Shopping Center,
Anderson SC 29621.
864/226-9109.

County Seat Stores
Shelter Cove Ln #24, Hilton
Head SC 29928-3558.
803/785-9410.

Foxmoor
2060 Sam Rittenberg Blvd,
Charleston SC 29407-4616.
803/571-0654.

Hi-Lites
Festival Center, N Charleston
SC 29418. 803/552-1072.

Hi-Lites
3494 Highway 17 S, N
Myrtle Beach SC 29582-
4965. 803/272-4680.

It's Fashion
Westside Plaza, West
Columbia SC 29169.
803/796-7373.

It's Fashion
1021 S Pendleton St, Easley
SC 29642-1045. 864/850-
1110.

Jones Clothiers
781 Coachman Dr Apt A,
Sumter SC 29154-6221.
803/775-2478.

Merry Go Round
2501 N Kings Hwy, Myrtle
Beach SC 29577-3054.
803/626-3044.

The White House
128 Market St, Charleston
SC 29401-3130. 803/722-
7747.

Pontiac Factory Outlet
Hwy 1, Elgin SC 29045.
803/788-8007.

Salley Enterprises
Hwy 39, Salley SC 29137.
803/258-3426.

Westport Ltd.
Barefoot Landing, Myrtle
Beach SC 29572. 803/272-
2179.

Triangle City Factory Outlet
633 12th St, West Columbia
SC 29169-6336. 803/791-
3488.

The White House Inc.
Shelter Cove Mall, Hilton
Head SC 29928-3558.
803/785-9523.

Afterthoughts
2070 Sam Rittenberg Blvd,
Charleston SC 29407-4605.
803/763-6810.

Mitchell's Formal Wear
Northwoods Mall, N
Charleston SC 29406.
803/572-5863.

Arrow Factory Store
Outlet Park Mall III, Myrtle
Beach SC 29577. 803/236-
0826.

Goody's Family Clothing
Bay Vlg Shpng Ctr, Conway
SC 29526. 803/365-9516.

Goody's Family Clothing
7600 Greenville Hwy, Suite
15, Spartanburg SC 29301-
2500. 864/587-1506.

JCPenney Co.
1057 Broad St, Sumter SC
29150-2567. 803/778-
1871.

Merry Go Round
Jessamine Mall, Sumter SC
29150. 803/775-4941.

Structure
700 Haywood Rd Unit 1B7,
Greenville SC 29607-2781.
864/234-1444.

SHOE STORES

Rack Room Shoes
Outlet Park Mall III, Myrtle
Beach SC 29577. 803/236-
5203.

Rack Room Shoes
946 Orleans Rd, Charleston
SC 29407-4889. 803/571-
2442.

Rack Room Shoes
7800 Rivers Ave, Suite
1410, Charleston SC 29406-
4057. 803/553-0672.

Payless Shoesource
Citadel Mall, Charleston SC
29407. 803/769-0351.

Payless Shoesource
7201 Two Notch Rd #308,
Columbia SC 29223-7527.
803/699-6198.

Lady Foot Locker
2150 Northwoods Blvd, N
Charleston SC 29406-4021.
803/572-9591.

Athletic X-Press
2070 Sam Rittenberg Blvd,
Charleston SC 29407-4605.
803/766-3227.

Athletic X-Press
Cross Creek Mall,
Greenwood SC 29649-1407.
864/227-6121.

Naturalizer Shoes
Northwoods Mall, Charleston
SC 29406. 803/572-9430.

Pic'N Pay Shoes Inc.
115 E Butler Ave, Mauldin
SC 29662. 864/288-3463.

Pic'N Pay Stores Inc.
1671 Springdale Dr, Suite 1,
Camden SC 29020-2079.
803/432-2235.

Cowboy World
1412 Piedmont Hwy,
Piedmont SC 29673-9252.
864/422-9465.

Shoe Show
1872 Wilson Rd, Newberry
SC 29108. 803/276-9366.

Shoe Show
1341 N Kings Hwy, Myrtle
Beach SC 29577-3636.
803/626-5910.

FURNITURE STORES

Carolina Wicker
1450 W O Ezell Blvd, Suite
800, Spartanburg SC 29301-
1500. 864/574-8833.

**Danco Scandinavian &
Contempory Furniture**
1035 Johnnie Dodds Blvd,
Mount Pleasant SC 29464-
6154. 803/884-2256.

Farmers Furniture Co.
510 E Columbia Ave,
Leesville SC 29070-9287.
803/532-1080.

Haverty's Fine Furniture
7619 Rivers Ave, N
Charleston SC 29406-4011.
803/572-2214.

Heilig-Meyers Furniture
1750 Sam Rittenberg Blvd,
Charleston SC 29407-4938.
803/556-7533.

Heilig-Meyers Furniture
122 Shockley Ferry Road,
Anderson SC 29624.
864/225-5465.

Kimbrell Furniture Mart
127 N Main St, Fountain Inn
SC 29644-1928. 864/862-
1082.

Kimbrell Furniture Mart
1008 Meeting St, West
Columbia SC 29169-6754.
803/796-9267.

Kimbrell Furniture Mart
102 S Main St, Sumter SC
29150-5247. 803/773-
1552.

Rhodes Furniture
8570 Rivers Ave, N
Charleston SC 29406-9207.
803/572-0440.

**Columbia Supply Co.
Conway Division**
1509 3rd Ave, Conway SC
29526-5013. 803/248-
4277.

MISC. HOME FURNISHINGS STORES

Dal-Tile Corporation
2261 Technical Pky, N
Charleston SC 29406-4931.
803/824-1970.

Badcock Home Furnishings
2716 Anderson Rd,
Greenville SC 29611-5943.
864/220-5010.

Heilig-Meyers Furniture Co.
2437 Charleston Hwy,
Cayce SC 29033-1709.
803/739-0373.

Heilig-Meyers Furniture Co.
7558 Rivers Ave, Charleston
SC 29406-4661. 803/553-
6423.

Heilig-Meyers Furniture Co.
3304 Augusta St, Greenville
SC 29605-2148. 864/277-
8010.

New York Carpet World
1903 Sam Rittenberg Blvd,
Charleston SC 29407-4825.
803/571-1351.

Sherwin-Williams
533 By Pass 123, Seneca
SC 29678. 864/882-1577.

Fabric Warehouse
266 Harbison Blvd, Columbia
SC 29212-2232. 803/749-
2656.

Wallpaper for Less
3708 Liberty Hwy, Anderson
SC 29621-1309. 864/224-
1586.

Lechters
Citadel Mall, Charleston SC
29407. 803/571-6671.

Gorham Inc.
Shoppes On The Parkway,
Hilton Head SC 29928.
803/686-6637.

Ashleys Custom Vertical Blinds
654 W Main St, Spartanburg
SC 29301-2106. 864/585-
8763.

PLEJ's
2600 David H McLeod Blvd,
Florence SC 29501-4098.
803/679-0082.

PLEJ's Bath Bed & Curtains
6119 White Horse Rd,
Greenville SC 29611-3838.
864/295-6346.

PLEJ's Textile Mill Outlet
3102 N Main St, Anderson
SC 29621-2763. 864/225-
2192.

HOUSEHOLD APPLIANCE STORES

Lighthouse Electric Supply
1490 Salem Rd, Beaufort SC
29902-5258. 803/524-
8888.

Electrolux Outlet
113 1st St, Walterboro SC
29488-2807. 803/549-
5998.

Low Country Vacuum & Sew
510 College Park Rd, Ladson
SC 29456-3328. 803/824-
9444.

CONSUMER ELECTRONICS STORES

Home Cable Concepts
7268 Peppermill Pky, N
Charleston SC 29418-7403.
803/552-6531.

Videoconcepts
Citadel Mall, Charleston SC
29407. 803/571-7960.

Rex TV
3221 Mall Rd, Anderson SC
29625-1714. 864/261-
6579.

Video Concepts
7201 Two Notch Rd,
Columbia SC 29223-7527.
803/699-3326.

COMPUTER AND
SOFTWARE STORES

Babbage's Software
Haywood Mall, Greenville SC
29607-2781. 864/676-
0003.

Computer Group Inc.
1615 Wade Hampton Blvd,
Suite C, Greenville SC
29609-5049. 864/244-
6667.

Micro Media
1713 Locust Hill Rd, Greer
SC 29651-8432. 864/877-
7833.

Dove Data Products Inc.
3233 S Cashua Dr, Florence
SC 29501-6303. 803/665-
7678.

RECORD AND
PRERECORDED TAPE
STORES

Starship Records & Tapes
Aiken Mall, Aiken SC 29803.
803/648-0704.

Tape World
7201 Two Notch Rd #600,
Columbia SC 29223-7527.
803/736-8574.

Tape World
Citadel Mall, Charleston SC
29407. 803/766-2140.

Sound Shop
McAlister Square Shopping
Cent, Greenville SC 29607.
864/370-1600.

Record Town
Myrtle Square Mall, Myrtle
Beach SC 29577. 803/448-
4465.

Discjockey
Jessamine Mall, Sumter SC
29150. 803/775-3759.

MUSICAL INSTRUMENT
STORES

McFadyen Music Inc.
801 Broadway St, Myrtle
Beach SC 29577-3807.
803/448-2819.

DRUG STORES

Revco Discount Drug Center
3334 Highway 17 S, N
Myrtle Beach SC 29582-
4853. 803/272-8884.

Revco
2401 Reidville Rd,
Spartanburg SC 29301-
3655. 864/576-9268.

Miller's Liggett-Rexall Drugs
5259 Hartford Cir, N
Charleston SC 29405-4120.
803/744-6251.

Rite Aid Pharmacies
605 Main St N, New Ellenton
SC 29809-1328. 803/652-
2721.

Rite Aid Pharmacies
4124 Celanese Rd, Rock Hill
SC 29732-8100. 803/366-
5101.

**Rite Aid of SC Distribution
Center**
Hy 34 W, Ridgeway SC
29130. 803/337-8121.

Rite Aid Pharmacies
US Hwy 1 North, Batesburg
SC 29006. 803/532-2631.

Rite Aid Pharmacies
3775 Maybank Hwy, Johns
Island SC 29455-4825.
803/559-0328.

Eckerd Drugs
Westgate Village,
Spartanburg SC 29301.
864/574-0038.

Eckerd Drugs
1818 Augusta St, Greenville
SC 29605-2941. 864/233-
6689.

SPORTING GOODS STORES

Athletic Attic
Northwoods Mall, Charleston
SC 29406. 803/797-7512.

Carolina Fitness Equipment
830 Woods Crossing Rd,
Greenville SC 29607-2757.
864/234-0888.

Score Sportswear
Columbia Mall, Columbia SC
29223. 803/736-3783.

Garrett's Fishing & Marine
5365 Highway 24, Anderson
SC 29625-6051. 864/287-
9782.

Myrtlewood Golf Club
1450 48th Ave N, Myrtle
Beach SC 29577-8700.
803/449-5134.

BOOKSTORES

Books-A-Million
2465 Laurens Rd, Greenville
SC 29607-3813. 864/281-
1301.

STATIONERY AND OFFICE
SUPPLY STORES

Officemax
20 Haywood Rd, Greenville
SC 29607-3430. 864/676-
0160.

Southern Business Systems
101 Corporate Blvd, Suite
109, West Columbia SC
29169-4665. 803/791-
8340.

Forms and Supply
1133 Walter Price St, Cayce
SC 29033-3526. 803/794-
6759.

Office Depot Inc.
1812 Sam Rittenberg Blvd,
Charleston SC 29407-4868.
803/769-4576.

Vulcan Binder & Cover
1251 Shadowood Dr,
Spartanburg SC 29301-
5662. 864/576-3959.

JEWELRY STORES

Rey's Jewelers
225 S Pleasantburg Dr, Suite
D5, Greenville SC 29607-
2533. 864/370-5565.

Osterman Jewelers
700 Haywood Rd Unit 1d15,
Greenville SC 29607-2781.
864/297-1725.

Gold Gallery
700 Haywood Rd, Suite 505,
Greenville SC 29607-2748.
864/458-9752.

Golden Chain Gang
2401 Mall Dr Unit 59,
Charleston SC 29406-6511.
803/566-9685.

Golden Chain Gang
2441 Whiskey Rd, Aiken SC
29803-7606. 803/643-
0733.

Reed's Jewelers
1289 N Fraser St,
Georgetown SC 29440-
2853. 803/546-2454.

Piercing Pagoda
700 Haywood Rd Unit 2c16,
Greenville SC 29607-2781.
864/676-0288.

Cameron & Barkley Co.
2821 Azalea Dr, Charleston
SC 29405-8215. 803/745-
2820.

Friedman's Jewelers
6101 Calhoun Memorial
Hwy, Easley SC 29640-
3789. 864/859-0512.

HOBBY, TOY, AND GAME
SHOPS

Piece Goods Shop
2049 Savannah Hwy Unit 9,
Charleston SC 29407-2228.
803/763-8751.

Kay-Bee Toy Stores
Myrtle Square Mall, Myrtle
Beach SC 29577. 803/626-
3888.

Kay-Bee Toy Inc.
Northwoods Mall, N
Charleston SC 29406.
803/553-1981.

**GIFT, NOVELTY, AND
SOUVENIR SHOPS**

Carlton Cards
Haywood Mall, Greenville SC
29607-2781. 864/297-
0833.

**Cracker Barrel Old Country
Store**
126 Interstate Blvd,
Anderson SC 29621-2319.
864/225-4566.

Tuesday Morning
975 Savannah Hwy, Suite
20-06, Charleston SC
29407-7859. 803/556-
1060.

Luv
Citadel Mall, Charleston SC
29407. 803/763-7559.

Pier 1 Imports Inc. Co.
400 Congaree Rd, Greenville
SC 29607-2729. 864/676-
1080.

Potpourri Press Co. Store
2435 E North St, Suite 17,
Greenville SC 29615-1442.
864/244-6360.

Things Remembered
2501 N Kings Hwy, Myrtle
Beach SC 29577-3054.
803/626-8930.

Spencers Gifts Inc.
100 Columbiana Cir,
Columbia SC 29212-2231.
803/732-2856.

Tuesday Morning
282 Saint Andrews Rd,
Columbia SC 29210-4453.
803/772-3776.

Rainbow Bay Crafts
7400-B Rivers Av, N
Charleston SC 29406.
803/572-2262.

If It's Paper
605B N Kings Hwy, Myrtle
Beach SC 29577-3744.
803/448-6737.

SEWING SUPPLIES STORES

Fabric Warehouse
105 Verdae Blvd, Suite 520,
Greenville SC 29607-3823.
864/297-6560.

Northwest Fabrics & Crafts
1175 Woods Crossing Rd,
Suite 7, Greenville SC
29607-3552. 864/458-
8424.

Piece Goods Shop
629 Johnnie Dodds Blvd,
Mount Pleasant SC 29464-
3030. 803/881-9009.

Piece Goods Shop
125 Capital St, Greenwood
SC 29649-9105. 864/223-
9906.

96 Fabrics
910 Highway 28 By-Pass,
Anderson SC 29624.
864/226-6674.

FUEL DEALERS

Sifco Fuel
170 S Lafayette Dr, Sumter
SC 29150-5836. 803/778-
1800.

Sprott Oil Company
Main St, Summerton SC
29148. 803/485-8721.

OPTICAL GOODS STORES

Lenscrafters
Haywood Mall, Greenville SC
29607-2781. 864/234-
7200.

**Americas Best Contacts &
Eyeglasses**
5900 Rivers Ave Unit D6,
Charleston SC 29406-6082.
803/747-7700.

Opti-World
2702 N Kings Hwy, Myrtle
Beach SC 29577-3012.
803/448-5334.

Wal-Mart Vision Center
2245 Ashley Crossing Dr,
Charleston SC 29414-5704.
803/763-2204.

MISC. RETAIL STORES

Signature Signs
4211 Augusta Rd, Lexington
SC 29073-7940. 803/794-
9500.

Pet Owners Warehouse
5900 Rivers Ave Unit E2,
Charleston SC 29406-6082.
803/566-9590.

Frame Warehouse
2454 Hudson Rd, Greer SC
29650-2923. 864/322-
1218.

Visionworks
765 Haywood Rd, Suite B,
Greenville SC 29607-2772.
864/297-7990.

Charleston Ppr Co.
232 Albemarle Rd,
Charleston SC 29407-7522.
803/556-2350.

VIDEO TAPE RENTAL

Suncoast Motion Picture Co.
7201 Two Notch Rd #556,
Columbia SC 29223-7527.
803/699-1857.

Blockbuster Video
509 W Main St, Lexington
SC 29072-2501. 803/957-
0863.

Blockbuster Video
6 Hunts Bridge Rd, Greenville
SC 29611-1734. 864/294-
9041.

Blockbuster Video
5101 Ashley Phosphate Rd,
N Charleston SC 29418-
2832. 803/760-1549.

Blockbuster Video
9814 Two Notch Rd,
Columbia SC 29223-4380.
803/788-4240.

Blockbuster Video
3207 Wade Hampton Blvd,
Taylors SC 29687-2803.
864/268-3408.

Blockbuster Video
1787 N Cherry Rd, Rock Hill
SC 29732-2620. 803/329-
4548.

Blockbuster Video
399 Silver Bluff Rd, Aiken
SC 29803-6007. 803/649-
2471.

Phar-Mor
555 Haywood Rd, Greenville
SC 29607-2710. 864/297-
6491.

Phar-Mor
7800 Rivers Ave, N
Charleston SC 29406-4057.
803/764-0865.

Phar-Mor
272 Harbison Blvd, Columbia
SC 29212-2232. 803/732-
0075.

Hollywood Video
1501 Highway 17 N, Mount
Pleasant SC 29464-3342.
803/884-9425.

Hollywood Video
520 Folly Rd, Charleston SC
29412-3019. 803/795-
6301.

**Showtime Video & Music
Super**
3023 Boundary St, Beaufort
SC 29902. 803/525-4380.

**Big Jim's 24 Hour Video
Rental**
4813 Rivers Ave, N
Charleston SC 29406-6502.
803/554-7357.

For more information on career opportunities in retail:

Associations

INTERNATIONAL ASSOCIATION OF CHAIN STORES
3800 Moor Place, Alexandria VA 22305.
703/549-4525.

INTERNATIONAL COUNCIL OF SHOPPING CENTERS
665 Fifth Avenue, New York NY 10022.
212/421-8181. Offers conventions,
research, education, a variety of
publications, and awards programs.

NATIONAL AUTOMOTIVE DEALERS ASSOCIATION
8400 Westpark Drive, McLean VA 22102.
703/821-7000.

NATIONAL INDEPENDENT AUTOMOTIVE DEALERS ASSOCIATION
2521 Brown Boulevard, Suite 100,
Arlington TX 76006. 817/640-3838.

NATIONAL RETAIL FEDERATION
325 7th Street NW, Suite 1000,
Washington DC 20004. 202/783-7971.
Provides information services, industry
outlooks, and a variety of educational
opportunities and publications.

Directories

AUTOMOTIVE NEWS MARKET DATA BOOK
Automotive News, Crain Communication,
1400 Woodbridge Avenue, Detroit MI
48207-3187. 313/446-6000.

STONE, CLAY, GLASS, AND CONCRETE PRODUCTS

Growth in stone, clay, glass, concrete, and related materials is closely tied to the success of the construction industry. On the one hand, analysts believe that the fortunes of the construction industry should remain solid in the short term, despite the added pressure of an economy that has cooled from its torrid pace of growth in 1994 and early 1995. On the other hand, the longer-term forecast is for much slower growth, since infrastructure construction is dependent on declining local government budgets. In general, the stone, clay, glass, and concrete industry should see revenue growth of about 1 to 2 percent annually over the next few years.

North Carolina

APAC-CAROLINA INC.
P.O. Box 6939, Asheville NC 28816. 704/665-1180. **Contact:** Wilene Brooks, Manager of Human Resources. **Description:** APAC-Carolina Inc. is engaged in the production of asphalt. The company also offers contract asphalt paving services.

BARNHILL CONTRACTING COMPANY
P.O. Box 35376, Fayetteville NC 28303. 910/488-1319. **Contact:** Bill Surridge, Personnel Manager. **Description:** This location produces asphalt. Barnhill Contracting Company is a construction company operating in two divisions. The Building Division is engaged in non-residential building construction, such as schools and public buildings. The Paved Roads Division is involved in heavy highway construction and driveway paving. The company operates in North Carolina and parts of Virginia.

CAROLINA MIRROR COMPANY
P.O. Box 548, North Wilkesboro NC 28659-0548. 910/838-2151. **Contact:** Human Resources Department. **Description:** A manufacturer of mirrors. **Benefits:** Disability Coverage; Employee Discounts; Life Insurance; Medical Insurance; Pension Plan; Savings Plan. **Corporate headquarters location:** This Location. **Other U.S. locations:** Houston TX. **Operations at this facility include:** Administration; Divisional Headquarters; Manufacturing; Sales. **Listed on:** Privately held. **Number of employees at this location:** 575. **Number of employees nationwide:** 600.

LENOIR MIRROR COMPANY
P.O. Box 1650, Lenoir NC 28645. 704/728-3271. **Contact:** Tom Query, Human Resources Director. **Description:** A manufacturer of mirrors and other glass products.

VULCAN MATERIALS COMPANY
4401 Patterson Avenue, Winston-Salem NC 27105. 910/767-0911. **Contact:** Ed Graham, Manager of Human Resources. **Description:** Vulcan Materials Company has 21 plant locations throughout the Southeast; 14 in Georgia and seven in South Carolina. The company primarily produces crushed stone and aggregates for the highway and construction markets. **Benefits:** Dental Insurance; Disability Coverage; Life Insurance; Medical Insurance; Pension Plan; Savings Plan; Tuition Assistance. **Corporate headquarters location:** Birmingham AL. **Listed on:** New York Stock Exchange.

Note: Because addresses and telephone numbers of smaller companies change rapidly, we recommend you call each company to verify the information below before inquiring about job opportunities. Mass mailings are not recommended.

Additional employers with under 250 employees:

ASPHALT

Barnhill Contracting Co.
4425 Pleasant Valley Rd,
Raleigh NC 27612-7026.
919/787-2442.

Crowell Constructors
1100 Robeson St,
Fayetteville NC 28305-5528.
910/485-2135.

Larco Construction Co.
4130 N Glenn Ave, Winston-
Salem NC 27105-2812.
910/767-3500.

Celotex Corp.
430 Old Mount Olive Hwy,
Dudley NC 28333-5170.
919/736-7520.

**GLASS AND GLASS
PRODUCTS**

Kimble Glass Inc.
114 Wamsutta Mill Rd,
Morganton NC 28655-5551.
704/433-5000.

Owens-Brockway Glass
9698 Old US Highway 52,
Lexington NC 27292-7441.
910/764-2900.

Glassblowers
4371 Rock Hill Rd, Winston-
Salem NC 27106. 910/924-
2183.

Alumax
911 N Raleigh St,
Greensboro NC 27405-7325.
910/274-6769.

Glass Dynamics Inc.
Hwy 220 Bypass, Stoneville
NC 27048. 910/573-2393.

Interpane Glass
520 E Railroad St, Clinton
NC 28328-4304. 910/592-
7101.

Stroupe Mirror Co.
102 E Holly Hill Rd,
Thomasville NC 27360-
5818. 910/475-2181.

Glass Designs Inc.
8901 US Highway 220 Bus,
Stoneville NC 27048-8344.
910/573-3500.

CEMENT

WR Bonsal Co.
Hwy 74 E, Lilesville NC
28091. 704/848-4141.

TILE

Boren Clay Products Co.
Hwy 74 W, Monroe NC
28110. 704/283-8158.

Cherokee Sanford Group
300 Brick Plant Rd, Moncure
NC 27559. 919/774-6533.

Cunningham Brick Co.
1437 Cunningham Brick Yard
Rd, Thomasville NC 27360-
8237. 910/472-6181.

Isenhour Brick & Tile Co.
700 S Long St, East Spencer
NC 28039. 704/636-0131.

Triangle Brick Co.
6523 Apex Rd, Durham NC
27713. 919/544-1796.

**CONCRETE, GYPSUM, AND
PLASTER PRODUCTS**

NC Products Corp.
920 Withers Rd, Raleigh NC
27603-3416. 919/834-
2557.

Adams Products Co.
5701 Koppers Rd, Morrisville
NC 27560-9164. 919/467-
2218.

Dewey Brothers Inc.
705 S George St, Goldsboro
NC 27530-5717. 919/734-
3411.

**Exposaic Industries Inc. of
NC**
4101 Greensboro St,
Charlotte NC 28206-2039.
704/372-1080.

Pomona Pipe Products
4611 Dundas Dr, Greensboro
NC 27407-1613. 910/292-
8060.

Ready Mix Concrete
120 Raleigh Rd, Smithfield
NC 27577-3310. 910/934-
0385.

Ready Mixed Concrete Co.
105 E Granville St, Windsor
NC 27983-1201. 919/794-
5000.

**CUT STONE AND STONE
PRODUCTS**

North Carolina Granite Corp.
P.O. Box 151, Mount Airy
NC 27030-0151. 910/786-
5141.

EARTH AND MINERALS

KMG Minerals
P.O. Box 729, Kings
Mountain NC 28086-0729.
704/739-3616.

Unimin Corp.
Hwy 226 N, Spruce Pine NC
28777. 704/765-4283.

MINERAL PRODUCTS

Cairn Studios
200 Armitage Rd,
Mooresville NC 28115.
704/664-7128.

South Carolina

AMERICAN FLAT GLASS DISTRIBUTORS, INC. (AFGD)
148 Flint Hill Road, Fort Mills SC 29715. 803/548-3234. **Contact:** Dave Pipkin, Branch Manager. **Description:** Founded in the early 1960s, AFGD specializes in architectural insulated glass units and custom tempering. The company was originally founded as Southern Wholesale Glass, Inc. In 1983, AFG Industries, Inc. purchased Southern Wholesale Glass, Inc. and changed its name to American Flat Glass Distributors, Inc. (AFGD). Today, AFGD manufactures a complete line of insulated glass units for commercial and residential applications. Products include clear, tint, and reflective glass; wire glass; and equipment for the handling, storage, and transportation of glass. A customized order entry system allows orders to be processed upon receipt and shipped the following day. There are 19 AFGD locations throughout the United States in metropolitan areas, with the largest facilities at Marietta, GA, and Opelousas, LA. **Common positions include:** Blue-Collar Worker

Supervisor; Branch Manager; Clerical Supervisor; Customer Service Representative; Industrial Engineer; Industrial Production Manager; Management Trainee; Manufacturer's/Wholesaler's Sales Rep.; Mechanical Engineer; Metallurgical Engineer; Operations/Production Manager. **Educational backgrounds include:** Business Administration; Engineering; Finance; Marketing; Sales. **Benefits:** 401K; Disability Coverage; Life Insurance; Medical Insurance; Profit Sharing; Savings Plan; Tuition Assistance. **Corporate headquarters location:** Atlanta GA. **Subsidiaries include:** AFGD Canada. **Parent company:** AFG Industries. **Listed on:** Privately held. **Number of employees at this location:** 75. **Number of employees nationwide:** 1,000.

APAC-CAROLINA INC.
P.O. Box 521, Darlington SC 29532. 803/393-2837. **Contact:** Lou Rife, Division Controller. **Description:** APAC-Carolina Inc. is engaged in the production of asphalt. The company also offers contract asphalt paving services. **Other U.S. locations:** Nationwide.

GUARDIAN INDUSTRIES CORPORATION
LNC Railway Distribution Park, State Highway 9, Richburg SC 29729. 803/789-6100. **Contact:** Thomas Monzitta, Human Resource Manager. **Description:** This location is a float glass plant. Overall, Guardian Industries Corporation is an international manufacturer of glass, including tempered glass, reflective coatings, and insulated glass. **Common positions include:** Ceramics Engineer; Materials Engineer; Mechanical Engineer; Metallurgical Engineer. **Educational backgrounds include:** Engineering. **Benefits:** 401K; Bonus Award/Plan; Dental Insurance; Disability Coverage; Life Insurance; Medical Insurance; Pension Plan. **Corporate headquarters location:** Auburn Hills MI. **Other U.S. locations:** Nationwide. **Operations at this facility include:** Manufacturing. **Number of employees at this location:** 320. **Number of employees nationwide:** 10,000.

OWENS-CORNING FIBERGLAS CORPORATION
P.O. Box 499, Aiken SC 29801. 803/648-8351. **Contact:** Jim Jackson, Director of Personnel. **Description:** Owens-Corning Fiberglas Corporation manufactures and sells thermal and acoustical insulation products including insulation for appliances, glass fiber roofing shingles, and roof insulation and industrial asphalt. Other products of the company include windows, glass fiber textile yarns, wet process chopped strands and specialty mats, and polyester resins. **Corporate headquarters location:** Toledo OH. **Subsidiaries include:** Barbcorp, Inc.; Dansk-Svensk Glasfiber AS; Eric Co.; European Owens-Corning Fiberglas SA; IPM Inc.; Kitsons Insulations Products Ltd.; Owens-Corning AS; Owens-Corning Building Products; Owens-Corning FSC, Inc.; Owens-Corning Finance. **Listed on:** New York Stock Exchange. **Number of employees nationwide:** 17,200.

OWENS-CORNING FIBERGLAS CORPORATION
P.O. Box 1367, Anderson SC 29622. 864/296-4000. **Contact:** Jim Roser, Human Resources Manager. **Description:** Owens-Corning Fiberglas Corporation manufactures and sells thermal and acoustical insulation products including insulation for appliances, glass fiber roofing shingles, and roof insulation and industrial asphalt. Other products of the company include windows, glass fiber textile yarns, wet process chopped strands and specialty mats, and polyester resins. **Corporate headquarters location:** Toledo OH. **Subsidiaries include:** Barbcorp, Inc.; Dansk-Svensk Glasfiber AS; Eric Co.; European Owens-Corning Fiberglas SA; IPM Inc.; Kitsons Insulations Products Ltd.; Owens-Corning AS; Owens-Corning Building Products; Owens-Corning FSC, Inc.; Owens-Corning Finance. **Listed on:** New York Stock Exchange.

Note: Because addresses and telephone numbers of smaller companies change rapidly, we recommend you call each company to verify the information below before inquiring about job opportunities. Mass mailings are not recommended.

Additional employers with under 250 employees:

GLASS AND GLASS PRODUCTS

Sediver Inc.
7801 Park Pl, York SC 29745-7414. 803/684-4208.

Southeastern Fiberglass Products
Highway 78, Branchville SC 29432. 803/245-4393.

CEMENT

Blue Circle
I-26 & Highway 453, Harleyville SC 29448. 803/462-7651.

TILE

Palmetto Brick Co.
3501 Brick Yard Rd, Wallace
SC 29596-8441. 803/537-
7861.

Southern Brick Co.
624 Brickyard Rd, Ninety Six
SC 29666. 864/543-3211.

CONCRETE, GYPSUM, AND PLASTER PRODUCTS

Pre Stress Concrete Co.
2025 Cherry Hill Ln, N
Charleston SC 29405-9309.
803/577-6022.

Hardaway Concrete Co.
2001 Taylor St, Columbia SC
29204-1005. 803/254-
4350.

EARTH AND MINERALS

WR Grace & Co.
Highway 221, Enoree SC
29335. 864/969-3353.

For more information on career opportunities in stone, clay, glass, and concrete products:

Associations

THE AMERICAN CERAMIC SOCIETY
735 Ceramic Place, Westerville OH 43081.
614/890-4700. Offers a variety of
publications, meetings, information, and
educational services. Also operates Ceramic
Futures, an employment service with a
resume database.

NATIONAL GLASS ASSOCIATION
8200 Greensboro Drive, Suite 802, McLean
VA 22102. 703/442-4890.

Magazines

GLASS MAGAZINE
National Glass Association, 8200
Greensboro Drive, McLean VA 22102.
703/442-4890.

ROCK PRODUCTS
MacLean Hunter Publishing Company, 29
North Wacker Drive, Chicago IL 60606.
312/726-2805.

TRANSPORTATION

According to Labor Department estimates the number of jobs in the air transportation industry will increase faster than average. Passenger and cargo traffic should increase in response to a rise in population, incomes and business activity. Employment in other air transport activities will also increase as more aircraft are purchased for business, agriculture, and recreation. Despite this expected growth, jobseekers should expect strong competition as the number of applicants for airline jobs exceeds the number of jobs available. Not only are airline jobs highly sought after, but the industry has been going through a period of consolidation, and today more and more of the business is concentrated with a handful of the major carriers, such as American, Delta, and USAir.

In the trucking and warehousing industry, the number of jobs created is very closely related to the health of the national economy. Competition in the industry is intense, both among truckers and with the railroads. Trucking companies compete by slashing rates or offering more customized service. Motor carriers must quote rates high enough to cover costs but low enough to remain competitive. Still, job opportunities for truckers are expected to be good. In some areas, companies have had trouble recruiting well-trained drivers. Although some routes have switched to intermodal transportation and recent downturns in the economy have eased some driver shortages, turnover is relatively high. That should ensure a steady supply of jobs.

On the railroads, the use of both freight and passenger rail will climb. And according to the U.S. Commerce Department, increased trade and stronger freight rates should help the performance of U.S. flag liner companies operating in the Asian markets. Domestic use of water transportation should also increase, especially between Alaska and the lower 48 states.

North Carolina

CCAIR, INC.
dba USAIR EXPRESS
4700 Yorkmont Road, Second Floor, Charlotte NC 28208. 704/359-8990. **Contact:** Keith Noble, Supervisor of Hiring. **Description:** CCAIR, Inc. (formerly Sunbird Airlines) is an air carrier providing regularly scheduled passenger service to 25 cities in Alabama, Georgia, Kentucky, Maryland, Ohio, North Carolina, South Carolina, Virginia, and West Virginia, primarily from a hub at the Charlotte/Douglas International Airport. The company currently operates a fleet of 26 turboprop passenger aircraft with approximately 1,391 weekly departures over a route system covering approximately 230,000 miles. The company's business has involved providing service for business travelers from small- and medium-sized communities in its market area to connecting flights of major carriers, principally USAir, Inc., at the hub operations of USAir at the Charlotte/Douglas International Airport. In addition, the company operates a small number of flights to USAir's Baltimore hub and Raleigh, North Carolina. In order to market the company's services, the company has an agreement with USAir that permits the company to operate under the name "USAir Express" and to charge their joint passengers on a combined basis with USAir. **Corporate headquarters location:** This Location. **Listed on:** NASDAQ. **Number of employees nationwide:** 600.

FOUNTAIN POWERBOAT INDUSTRIES INC.
P.O. Drawer 457, Washington NC 27889. 919/975-2000. **Contact:** Carol Price, Manager of Human Resources. **Description:** Fountain Powerboat Industries Inc. designs, manufactures, and sells offshore sport boats, sport cruisers, and sport fishing boats. **Corporate headquarters location:** This Location. **Subsidiaries include:** Fountain Powerboats, Inc. **Listed on:** American Stock Exchange. **Number of employees at this location:** 280.

HATTERAS YACHTS
110 North Glenburnie Road, New Bern NC 28560. 919/633-3101. **Contact:** Linda Berry, Human Resources Manager. **Description:** Hatteras Yachts builds, sells, and repairs fiberglass yachts.

KENAN TRANSPORT COMPANY
P.O. Box 2729, Chapel Hill NC 27515-2729. 919/967-8221. **Contact:** John Krovic, Human Resources Director. **Description:** A tank truck carrier serving the petroleum, propane gas, and chemical industries in the southeastern United States. The company conducts bulk trucking operations intrastate in Virginia, North Carolina, South Carolina, Georgia, and Florida; and interstate between these five states and points throughout the continental United States. The company transports a wide variety of products including gasoline to service stations; petroleum products to wholesalers and industrial plants; propane gas to agricultural, rural, and industrial consumers and liquid and dry bulk chemicals to manufacturers. Each of the products transported requires specialized trailers. The company operates through a network of 22 terminals and a company owned fleet of 394 tractors and 567 specialized trailers. The company's terminals are located in Virginia, North Carolina, South Carolina, Georgia, and Florida near major pipeline terminals, chemical production centers, and major ports serving the Southeast. **Corporate headquarters location:** This Location. **Listed on:** NASDAQ. **Number of employees nationwide:** 740.

LANDSTAR EXPRESS AMERICA, INC.
3411 Oak Lake Boulevard, P.O. Box 19509, Charlotte NC 28219. 704/329-2626. **Toll-free phone:** 800/ 396-3278. **Contact:** Karen Gause, Director of Human Resources. **Description:** A subsidiary of one of the largest multi-modal transportation service companies in North America, Express America performs expedited and emergency air and truck freight services. Overall, the company is divided into specialized freight transportation segments. Its business is a mix of regular accounts and spot hauls, with the top 100 clients generating more than one-third of the revenue. Landstar is the only publicly traded trucking company relying on independent owner-operators rather than salaried company drivers, with the company owning just 10 percent of the trucks in its fleet. Landstar buys many trucking supplies co-op, so its drivers receive large discounts on trucks, tires, gas, and lodging, in addition to getting 75 percent of the gross revenue from a load. **Corporate headquarters location:** Shelton CT. **Other subsidiaries include:** Landstar Expedited, Inc., Landstar Gemini, Inc., Landstar Inway, Inc., Landstar ITCO, Inc., Landstar Ligion, Inc., Landstar Poole, Inc., Landstar Ranger, Inc., Landstar T.L.C., Inc., Landstar Transportation Service, Inc. **Parent company:** Landstar System, Inc.

MIDWAY AIRLINES
2400 West Terminal Boulevard, MPB #4, RDU Airport, Raleigh NC 27623. 919/840-5050. **Fax:** 919/840-5056. **Contact:** Cindy Hoard, Human Resources Manager. **Description:** An airline. **Common positions include:** Aircraft Mechanic/Engine Specialist; Flight Attendant; Ticket Agent. **Educational backgrounds include:** Business Administration. **Benefits:** Life Insurance; Medical Insurance. **Special Programs:** Internships. **Corporate headquarters location:** Chicago IL. **Operations at this facility include:** Service. **Listed on:** Privately held. **Number of employees at this location:** 500.

TRINITY INDUSTRIES, INC.
69 Bingham Road, Asheville NC 28806. 704/254-0891. **Contact:** Marvin Hyatt, Human Resources Manager. **Description:** Manufactures an assortment of railroad and construction equipment and replacement parts. Trinity also offers related services for the transportation, construction, aerospace, commercial, and industrial markets. Products include railcars, gas processing systems, petroleum transportation systems, guardrails, bridge girders and beams, airport boarding bridges, barges, tug boats, military marine vessels, and precision welding products. Trinity Industries Inc. has a fleet of 9,589 railcars and 220 barges which it leases.

Note: Because addresses and telephone numbers of smaller companies change rapidly, we recommend you call each company to verify the information below before inquiring about job opportunities. Mass mailings are not recommended.

Additional employers with under 250 employees:

LOCAL AND INTERURBAN PASSENGER TRANSIT

Fast Fayetteville Area Systems
455 Grove St, Fayetteville NC 28301-0925. 910/433-1744.

City Taxi Company
3 E Hamlet Ave, Hamlet NC 28345-2903. 910/582-9993.

Greyhound Bus Lines
5715 Westpark Dr, Suite 101, Charlotte NC 28217-3564. 704/527-9393.

Mayflower Contract Services
2434 Sunset Ave, Rocky Mount NC 27804-2531. 919/937-6387.

Piedmont Coach Lines
3427 Clinton Rd, Fayetteville NC 28301-6147. 910/323-4881.

TRUCKING

AAA Cooper Transportation
824 Purser Dr, Raleigh NC 27603-4151. 919/779-9434.

AAA Cooper Transportation
701 E Boulevard St, Williamston NC 27892. 919/792-5191.

Averitt Express
RR 6, Greenville NC 27834-9806. 919/758-1112.

Averitt Express
902 Cedar Creek Rd, Fayetteville NC 28301-6510. 910/483-6555.

Averitt Express
251 E Oakview Rd, Asheville NC 28806. 704/251-0120.

Averitt Express
3708 Westinghouse Blvd, Charlotte NC 28273-4515. 704/588-9696.

Boomerang Express Inc.
4127 Brynwood Dr, Colfax NC 27235. 910/668-0287.

Builders Transport Inc.
SR 1589, Lumberton NC 28358. 910/739-0261.

Carolina Freight Carriers Corp.
4107 Wiley Davis Rd, Greensboro NC 27407-7938. 910/299-7605.

Carolina Western Express
3845 Patterson Ave, Winston-Salem NC 27105-2657. 910/661-1720.

Carrier Haulers Inc.
1535 Salisbury Rd, Statesville NC 28677-6249. 704/871-0393.

CG Hopkins Trucking
RR 1 Box 821, Eden NC 27288-9780. 9047327177.

Chemical Leaman Tank Lines
6600 W Market St, Greensboro NC 27409-1834. 910/292-5220.

Chemical Leaman Tank Lines
120 Cowpen Landing Rd, Wilmington NC 28401-2232. 910/762-1851.

Dedicated Fleet Inc.
Jr Order Home Rd, Lexington NC 27292. 704/352-5562.

East Coast Leasing Inc.
317 Edwardia Dr, Greensboro NC 27409-2605. 910/852-4830.

Eastern Fuel Transport
P.O. Box 1386, Ahoskie NC 27910. 919/398-3121.

Epes Hauling Inc.
Groom Rd, Reidsville NC 27320. 910/349-3351.

Estes Express Lines
RR 1 Box 429, Morrisville NC 27560-9801. 919/782-7711.

Estes Express Lines Inc.
11000 Reames Rd, Charlotte NC 28269-7673. 704/597-9130.

Fredrickson Motor Express Corp.
Hwy 301 N, Wilson NC 27893. 919/291-0293.

Fredrickson Motor Express Corp.
921 E Springfield Rd, High Point NC 27263-2017. 910/434-5600.

Fredrickson Motor Express Corp.
1101 W Craighead Rd, Charlotte NC 28206-1614. 704/376-3661.

Goggin Truck Line
1155 N Roberts Ave, Lumberton NC 28358-2269. 910/739-2084.

Harold A. Puryear Trucking Co.
RR 8 Box 36B, Raleigh NC 27612-9808. 919/787-4175.

Janet & Lacy's Trucking Co.
317 Edwardia Dr, Greensboro NC 27409-2605. 910/292-0006.

KBD Services Inc.
518 Reedy Creek Rd, Cary NC 27513-4116. 919/481-4422.

Lee Williamson Trucking
P.O. Box 68, Hamlet NC 28345-0068. 910/582-2859.

Old Dominion Freight Line
5600 Wilkinson Blvd, Charlotte NC 28208-3536. 704/399-2251.

Overnite Transportation Co.
10121 Highway 70, Durham NC 27703. 919/828-0951.

PDC Trucking Company
11425 Granite St, Charlotte NC 28273-6412. 8147260982.

Pem-Kay Furniture Co.
P.O. Box 595, Conover NC 28613-0595. 704/464-2408.

Pony Express Courier Corp.
399 Northgate Park Dr, Winston-Salem NC 27105-2661. 910/744-5980.

Quality Cartage Inc.
3104 Starmount Dr, Raleigh NC 27604-3740. 919/876-5948.

Robin Hood Contnr Express Inc.
US 17 Hwy, Leland NC 28451. 910/371-6938.

Skyline Transportation
1000 Reed St, Winston-Salem NC 27107-5446. 910/785-3343.

Southeastern Freight Lines
RR 4 Box 5, Kinston NC 28501. 919/552-0593.

Southeastern Freight Lines
201 Stage Coach Trl, Greensboro NC 27409-1811. 910/852-8310.

Spartan Express
1200 Amble Dr, Charlotte NC 28206. 704/597-8060.

Spartan Express Inc.
2120 Servomation Rd,
Greensboro NC 27407-7652.
910/292-0071.

Terminal Trucking Co.
224 NC Highway 49,
Concord NC 28025.
704/786-0189.

Voyager Transportation
2665 Zion Church Rd,
Concord NC 28025-7026.
704/892-8457.

Yellow Freight System
Hwy 70 W, Raleigh NC
27612. 919/828-1005.

Swing Transport Inc.
1405 N Salisbury Ave,
Salisbury NC 28144-8544.
704/633-3567.

**Commercial Courier Express
Inc.**
P.O. Box 18527, Greensboro
NC 27419-8527. 910/665-
0893.

Byrd Motor Line Inc.
P.O. Box 828, Lexington NC
27293-0828. 704/956-
6644.

Dixie Trucking Co. Inc.
3606 N Graham St,
Charlotte NC 28206-1627.
704/335-8585.

Douglas & Sons Inc.
1025 N Chipley Ford Rd,
Statesville NC 28677-1516.
704/876-1257.

Epes Transport System
3400 Edgefield Ct,
Greensboro NC 27409-9663.
910/668-3358.

Erickson Transport Corp.
106 Cherokee Ln, Indian Trail
NC 28079-9603. 704/821-
4898.

Norton Ramsey Motor Lines
P.O. Box 487, Hickory NC
28603-0487. 704/464-
7240.

Observer Transportation Co.
1001 Pressley Rd, Charlotte
NC 28217-0910. 704/527-
2020.

Reliable Tank Line
7320 Old Mount Holly Rd,
Charlotte NC 28214-1785.
704/393-0731.

**West Brothers Transfer &
Storage**
3724 Benson Dr, Raleigh NC
27609-7321. 919/878-
8411.

Central Transport Inc.
57 Truckers Pl, Asheville NC
28805-2431. 704/298-
0443.

McLeod Trucking & Rigging
P.O. Box 26186, Charlotte
NC 28221-6186. 704/372-
3611.

AM Express Global Van Lines
1243 S Park Dr, Kernersville
NC 27284-3179. 910/996-
1391.

Burnham Service Corp.
2900 Perimeter Park Dr,
Morrisville NC 27560-9158.
919/481-9200.

Burnham Service Corp.
3211 S Miami Blvd, Durham
NC 27703-9248. 919/544-
8200.

The Shipping Department
6300 Westgate Rd, Suite D,
Raleigh NC 27613-4754.
919/782-4484.

United Van Lines Agent
1205 6th St SW, Conover
NC 28613. 704/438-1800.

COURIER SERVICES

United Parcel Service
3009 Executive Dr,
Greensboro NC 27406-5303.
910/271-0463.

**WAREHOUSING AND
STORAGE**

Colonial Storage Centers
7012 Glenwood Ave, Raleigh
NC 27612-7143. 919/782-
0191.

Storage Trust
809 Shipyard Blvd,
Wilmington NC 28412-6435.
910/799-6670.

Modern Storage Co.
Hwy 74, Marshville NC
28103. 704/624-3555.

**East Carolina Bonded
Warehouse**
312 Raleigh St, Wilmington
NC 28412-6365. 910/392-
8290.

Lake Distribution
1001-B Bond St, Charlotte
NC 28208. 704/391-9607.

Public Storage
5105 Departure Dr, Raleigh
NC 27604-1813. 919/872-
0200.

Pierce Leahy Archives
3125 Parkside Dr, Charlotte
NC 28208-3320. 704/393-
2769.

**AIR TRANSPORTATION AND
SERVICES**

Delta Air Lines Inc.
4601 Six Forks Rd, Raleigh
NC 27609-5210. 919/688-
5404.

Delta Air Lines Inc.
1901 Roxborough Rd,
Charlotte NC 28211-3482.
704/366-2546.

USAir
801 Oberlin Rd, Suite 200,
Raleigh NC 27605-1171.
919/832-8522.

Atlantic Aero Inc.
Pied Triad International Airpo,
Greensboro NC 27409.
910/668-0411.

**PASSENGER
TRANSPORTATION
ARRANGEMENT SERVICES**

AAA Travel Agency
7421 Carmel Executive Park,
Charlotte NC 28226.
704/541-7409.

American Express Travel
2810 Meridian Parkway,
Durham NC 27713-2277.
919/544-1755.

BB&T
2000 Nash St SE, Wilson NC
27893. 919/399-4181.

Da Fa Travel
4000 Wake Forest Rd, Suite
116, Raleigh NC 27609-
6859. 919/790-6898.

Sea Gate Travel
7325 W Friendly Ave, Suite
H, Greensboro NC 27410-
6211. 910/852-9119.

Wright Travel
301 S College St, Suite 265,
Charlotte NC 28202-6000.
704/338-1927.

**Solar International Shipping
Agency**
342 Shipyard Blvd,
Wilmington NC 28412-1837.
910/799-7599.

A Travel Connection Inc.
6801 Northpark Blvd,
Charlotte NC 28216-2382.
704/598-5777.

First Travelcorp
1103 N Elm St, Greensboro
NC 27401. 910/272-0111.

**Mann Travel Carlson Travel
Network**
201 S College St, Charlotte
NC 28244. 704/333-1511.

Inchcape Shipping Services
334 Shipyard Blvd, Suite 4,
Wilmington NC 28412-1837.
910/392-7700.

PACKING AND CRATING

**Chesapeake Display and
Package Co.**
540 Northridge Park Dr,
Rural Hall NC 27045-9575.
910/969-9596.

Lentz Packaging
540 Northridge Park Dr,
Rural Hall NC 27045-9575.
910/969-9920.

Transus Freight
415 Banner Ave, Greensboro

NC 27401-4301. 910/275-4822.

Shipping Connection
3104 Hillsborough St,
Raleigh NC 27607-5437.
919/821-9233.

WHOLESALE OF
TRANSPORTATION
EQUIPMENT AND SUPPLIES

Railroad Friction
P.O. Box 1349, Laurinburg
NC 28353-1349. 910/844-9700.

South Carolina

BRASWELL SERVICES GROUP INC.
60 Braswell Street, Charleston SC 29405. 803/577-4692. **Contact:** Human Resources. **Description:** Braswell Services Group Inc. runs a shipyard.

BUILDERS TRANSPORT, INC.
P.O. Box 7005, Camden SC 29020. 803/432-1400. **Contact:** John Pryor, Personnel Department Manager. **Description:** Builders Transport, Inc. is a trucking and shipping firm. The company has terminals across the country, and has a fleet of both flatbeds and vans.

EMERGENT GROUP, INC.
P.O. Box 17526, Greenville SC 29606. 864/235-8056. **Contact:** Human Resources. **Description:** A diversified holding company which operates a short-line railroad; repairs, operates, and leases railcars; offers residential mortgage and construction loans; and manufactures and markets children's clothing. **Corporate headquarters location:** This Location. **Subsidiaries include:** Carolina Investors, Inc.; Premier Financial Services, Inc.; Pickens Railroad Company; Emergent Financial Corporation; Loan Pros, Inc.; Emergent Business Capital, Inc.; and Young Generations, Inc. **Number of employees nationwide:** 250.

FARRELL LINES INC.
One Long Point Road, Mount Pleasant SC 29464. 803/881-9260. **Contact:** Human Resources. **Description:** Operates a steamship service, with extensive shipping routes to West Africa, Australia, New Zealand, Europe, the Mediterranean region, the Middle East, India, and Pakistan. **NOTE:** Please send resumes to Marge Nasco, Human Resources Manager, One Whitehall Street, New York NY 10004. **Benefits:** Dental Insurance; Disability Coverage; Life Insurance; Medical Insurance; Pension Plan; Tuition Assistance. **Corporate headquarters location:** New York NY. **Listed on:** New York Stock Exchange.

HAWTHORNE CORPORATION
P.O. Box 61000, Charleston SC 29419. 803/797-8484. **Contact:** Bill Thrift, Vice President. **Description:** Hawthorne Corporation is a holding company whose companies are engaged in a wide variety of industries including: aviation (operating airports); real estate operations (that develop land for fixed base operations; and financial services (investor services). **Corporate headquarters location:** This Location.

YELLOW FREIGHT SYSTEM
P.O. Box 4370, Lawrence SC 29501. 803/393-7434. **Contact:** Mark Sidden, Branch Manager. **Description:** Yellow Freight System is a national long-haul truckload carrier, with over 585 terminal locations in 50 states, Puerto Rico, and many Canadian provinces. The company employs 28,000 in the U.S. and Canada. **Corporate headquarters location:** Overland Park KS. **Listed on:** American Stock Exchange.

Note: Because addresses and telephone numbers of smaller companies change rapidly, we recommend you call each company to verify the information below before inquiring about job opportunities. Mass mailings are not recommended.

Additional employers with under 250 employees:

SHIP/BOAT BUILDING AND REPAIRING

Metal Trades Inc.
1905 Pittsburgh Ave,
Charleston SC 29405-9360.
803/853-8344.

Beneteau USA Inc.
Highway 76 W, Marion SC
29571. 803/423-4201.

Mason & Mason Yacht Maintenance
2103 Westrivers Rd,

Charleston SC 29412-2060.
803/767-2197.

Perception Inc.
111 Kayaker Way, Easley SC
29642-2421. 864/859-7518.

Renken Boat Manufacturing Co. Inc.
2 Farmfield Ave, Charleston SC 29407-7780. 803/795-1150.

Stingray Boat Co.
725 Railroad Ave, Hartsville SC 29550-3827. 803/383-4507.

Sunbird Boat Co.
2348 Shop Rd, Columbia SC 29201-5178. 803/799-1125.

RAILROAD EQUIPMENT

Republic Locomotive Works
131 Falls St, Greenville SC 29601-2825. 864/271-4000.

TRANSPORTATION EQUIPMENT

Holland Atlantic Hitch Co.
525 W Baruch St, Denmark SC 29042-1209. 803/793-3313.

LOCAL AND INTERURBAN PASSENGER TRANSIT

Critical Care Transports
3260 Industry Dr, N Charleston SC 29418-8478. 803/767-3369.

Ard's Lexington Cab
13 Yashica Ct, West Columbia SC 29172-2747. 803/791-5767.

TRUCKING

Atlanta Motor Lines Inc.
131 Overland Dr, West Columbia SC 29172-3910. 803/739-4672.

Averitt Express Inc.
2701 Rourk St, Charleston SC 29405-7412. 803/745-0808.

Averitt Express Inc.
2959 W Black Creek Rd, Florence SC 29501-0740. 803/661-5707.

Averitt Express Inc.
3 Shelter Dr, Greer SC 29650-4817. 864/879-0025.

Backman Trucking Co.
P.O. Box 6783, West Columbia SC 29171-6783. 803/796-3738.

Santee Carriers Division
Hwy 453, Harleyville SC 29448. 803/496-5016.

Billings Freight Systems
15 Beverly Rd, Greenville SC 29609. 864/268-7873.

Spartan Express Inc.
2650 T V Rd, Florence SC 29501-0704. 803/665-1441.

Catawba Trucking Co.
P.O. Box 111, Lancaster SC 29721-0111. 803/324-6875.

Central Division Inc.
1402 E Main St, Duncan SC 29334-9690. 864/433-0367.

Cooper Motor Lines Inc.
2841 Old Woodruff Rd, Greer SC 29651-8629. 864/879-2101.

Covenant Transport
718 Deyoung Rd, Greer SC 29651-8057. 864/877-0971.

CSI Services-Florence
4501 E Palmetto St, Florence SC 29506-4534. 803/667-7531.

Wilson Trucking Corp.
76 Bruce Rd, Greenville SC 29605-3333. 864/299-1032.

G&P Trucking Co.
1003 Lincoln Ave, Charleston SC 29405-3607. 803/554-4800.

G&P Trucking Co. Inc.
672 Bypass 72 NW, Greenwood SC 29649-1302. 864/229-5821.

Haddon House Food Products
Carolina Distribution Center, Richburg SC 29729. 803/789-3300.

MCH Transportation Co.
3240 Brittain Dr, Newberry SC 29108-1510. 803/321-1888.

Watkins Motor Lines Inc.
465 Meeting St, Charleston SC 29403-4832. 803/722-8894.

Webber Trucking
P.O. Box 660, Mc Bee SC 29101-0660. 803/335-8201.

Wilson Trucking Corp.
RR 6, Box 252, Summerville SC 29483-9806. 803/871-9528.

Spartan Express
685 Beauty Spot Rd E, Bennettsville SC 29512-3465. 803/479-7772.

Thompson Transportation
P.O. Box 12116, Florence SC 29504-0116. 803/665-9424.

Ty Pruitt Trucking
3995 Hillcrest Dr, Charleston SC 29405-7061. 803/747-6950.

Embers Express Trucking Co.
385 French Collins Rd, Conway SC 29526-8153. 803/347-3600.

Tindall Haul & Erect Corp.
P.O. Box 2648, Spartanburg SC 29304-2648. 864/576-3230.

Bankair Inc.
2406 Edmund Rd, West Columbia SC 29170-1900. 803/822-8832.

Pony Express Courier Corp.
1023 Wappoo Rd Rm A15, Charleston SC 29407-5960. 803/556-2131.

Oconee Transfer Service
Hwy 123 By-Pass, Seneca SC 29678. 864/242-3781.

American Intermodal Service Inc.
4361 Headquarters Rd, N Charleston SC 29405-7402. 803/554-8199.

Bulldog Hiway Express
P.O. Box 40247, Charleston SC 29423-0247. 803/744-1651.

Central Transport
Hwy I-85 & Pelham Rd, Greenville SC 29615. 864/288-3981.

Chemical Leaman Tank Lines
4953 Virginia Ave, Charleston SC 29405-3603. 803/747-0481.

Kenan Transport
81 Braswell St, Charleston SC 29405-9321. 803/722-5664.

Old Dominion Freight Line
323 Dreher Rd, West Columbia SC 29169-5105. 803/794-2103.

Old Dominion Freight Line
630 Leonard Rd, Duncan SC 29334-9483. 864/877-9817.

Conway Southern Express
1941 Old Dunbar Rd, West Columbia SC 29172-3918. 803/791-1975.

Nilson Van & Storage
6913 Main St, Columbia SC 29203. 803/786-1090.

Nilson Van & Storage
811 Old Augusta Rd,
Greenville SC 29605-5218.
864/277-7210.

Sellers Transfer
2800 King Street Ext,
Charleston SC 29405-8339.
803/744-5000.

Smith Dray United Van Lines
116 N Markley St, Greenville
SC 29601-2423. 864/242-
4450.

**Tru-Pak United Moving
Storage**
91 S Fairfield Rd, Greenville
SC 29605-5001. 864/299-
3367.

**WAREHOUSING AND
STORAGE**

Stockade Storage
114 N Main St, Mauldin SC
29662-2510. 864/288-
6842.

Standard Warehouse Co.
185 McQueen St, West
Columbia SC 29172-3907.
803/796-9664.

**Orangeburg Warehousing
Center**
625 Five Chop Rd,
Orangeburg SC 29115-6218.
803/534-1277.

Lanport Inc.
2045 Austin Ave, Charleston
SC 29405-9368. 803/747-
4155.

**Southeastern Wholesaling &
Distributing Inc.**
P.O. Box 3571, Spartanburg
SC 29304. 864/587-8237.

**Broad River Road Storage
Center**
3901 River Dr, Columbia SC
29201. 803/256-7505.

Morningstar Mini-Storage
Hwy 521, Sumter SC
29150. 803/469-4400.

**Smith Records Management
Service**
US Hwy 29 South & I-85,
Wellford SC 29385.
864/574-7642.

**WATER TRANSPORTATION
OF FREIGHT**

New York Line Inc.
1 Poston Rd, Suite 185,
Charleston SC 29407-3426.
803/766-3250.

Trans Freight Lines Terminal
1 Columbus St, Charleston
SC 29403. 803/722-5896.

MARINE CARGO HANDLING

Trans Continental Agencies
1 Poston Rd, Suite 183,
Charleston SC 29407-3426.
803/852-2100.

**Direct Express Courier
Service**
4025 Sunset Blvd, West
Columbia SC 29169-2439.
803/796-2760.

Rocket Express
171 Johns Rd, Greer SC
29650-4713. 864/877-
2211.

Dixie Pipeline Co.
Cola Hwy, Lexington SC
29072. 803/359-9175.

Statoravel Inc.
McAs, Beaufort SC 29902.
803/522-8673.

Travel Inc.
Columbia Metropolitan
Airport, West Columbia SC
29169. 803/822-8780.

Travel Inc.
1316 Main St #200-A,
Columbia SC 29201-3204.
803/254-0706.

Travel Inc.
60 Directors Dr, Greenville
SC 29615-3541. 864/297-
8726.

Southern Steamship Agency
635 S Fraser St, Georgetown
SC 29440-4747. 803/527-
3476.

Carlson Travel Network
200 Meeting St Unit 10,
Charleston SC 29401-3156.
803/722-4411.

Hoegh Lines Agencies
950 Houston Northcutt Blvd,
Mount Pleasant SC 29464-
3482. 803/856-1000.

Damco Maritime
4925 Lacross Rd, Suite 110,
Charleston SC 29406-6512.
803/529-4626.

PACKING AND CRATING

Intermodal
4350 Marriott Dr, Charleston
SC 29406-6519. 803/566-
8053.

3M Co./Packaging Division
1450 Perimeter Rd,
Greenville SC 29605-5467.
864/299-4208.

Scanfreight Inc.
1 Cordes St, Charleston SC
29401-2116. 803/724-
7200.

Transus Freight
2003 Cherry Hill Ln,
Charleston SC 29405-9309.
803/723-3737.

For more information on career opportunities in transportation:

Associations

**AIR TRANSPORT ASSOCIATION OF
AMERICA**
1301 Pennsylvania Avenue NW, Suite
1100, Washington DC 20004. 202/626-
4000.

AMERICAN BUREAU OF SHIPPING
2 World Trade Center, 106th Floor, New
York NY 10048. 212/839-5000.

AMERICAN MARITIME ASSOCIATION
380 Madison Avenue, 17th Floor, New
York NY 10017. 212/557-9520. A trade
association which offers collection and
bargaining services.

AMERICAN SOCIETY OF TRAVEL AGENTS
1101 King Street, Suite 200, Alexandria VA
22314. 703/739-2782. For information,
send a SASE with $.75 postage to the
attention of the Fulfillment Department.

AMERICAN TRUCKING ASSOCIATION
2200 Mill Road, Alexandria VA 22314-
4677. 703/838-1700.

ASSOCIATION OF AMERICAN RAILROADS
50 F Street NW, Washington DC 20001.
202/639-2100.

**FUTURE AVIATION PROFESSIONALS OF
AMERICA**
4959 Massachusetts Boulevard, Atlanta GA
30337. 404/997-8097. Publishes monthly
newsletter which monitors the job market
for flying jobs; a pilot employment guide,
outlining what is required to become a pilot;
and a directory of aviation employers.

**INSTITUTE OF TRANSPORTATION
ENGINEERS**
525 School Street SW, Suite 410,
Washington DC 20024-2797. 202/554-
8050. Scientific and educational

association, providing for professional development of members and others.

MARINE TECHNOLOGY SOCIETY
1828 L Street NW, Suite 906, Washington DC 20036. 202/775-5966.

NATIONAL MARINE MANUFACTURERS ASSOCIATION
401 North Michigan Avenue, Suite 1150, Chicago IL 60611. 312/836-4747. A partnership of three manufacturer groups: The National Association of Boat Manufacturers; The Association of Marine Engine Manufacturers; and The National Association of Marine Products & Services. Subscription to job listing publication is available for a fee.

NATIONAL MOTOR FREIGHT TRAFFIC ASSOCIATION
2200 Mill Road, Alexandria VA 22314-4654. 703/838-1810. Works towards the improvement and advancement of the interests and welfare of motor common carriers.

NATIONAL TANK TRUCK CARRIERS
2200 Mill Road, Alexandria VA 22314. 703/838-1700. A trade association representing and promoting the interests of the highway bulk transportation community.

Directories

MOODY'S TRANSPORTATION MANUAL
Moody's Investors Service, Inc., 99 Church Street, New York NY 10007. 212/553-0300. $12.95 per year with weekly updates.

NATIONAL TANK TRUCK CARRIER DIRECTORY
2200 Mill Road, Alexandria VA 22314. 703/838-1700.

OFFICIAL MOTOR FREIGHT GUIDE
1700 West Courtland Street, Chicago IL 60622. 312/278-2454.

Magazines

AMERICAN SHIPPER
P.O. Box 4728, Jacksonville FL 32201. 904/355-2601. Monthly.

FLEET OWNER
707 Westchester Avenue, White Plains NY 10604-3102. 914/949-8500.

HEAVY DUTY TRUCKING
Newport Communications, P.O. Box W, Newport Beach CA 92658. 714/261-1636.

ITE JOURNAL
Institute of Transportation Engineers, 525 School Street SW, Suite 410, Washington DC 20024-2797. 202/554-8050. One year subscription (12 issues): $50.

MARINE DIGEST AND TRANSPORTATION NEWS
P.O. Box 3905, Seattle WA 98124. 206/682-3607.

SHIPPING DIGEST
51 Madison Avenue, New York NY 10010. 212/689-4411.

TRAFFIC WORLD MAGAZINE
741 National Press Building, Washington DC 20045. 202/383-6140.

TRANSPORT TOPICS
2200 Mill Road, Alexandria VA 22314. 703/838-1772.

UTILITIES: ELECTRIC/GAS/WATER

With deregulation looming closer and closer, utilities are adjusting by cutting costs and providing better service. This is a good sign for the industry but a bad sign for jobseekers, as employment should remain just about flat. Job prospects in the utilities industry are probably best with large electric utilities, water supply facilities, and sanitary services right now. The most common positions with public utilities are precision production workers and operators, fabricators, and laborers.

North Carolina

CAROLINA POWER & LIGHT COMPANY
P.O. Box 1551, Raleigh NC 27602. 919/546-6475. **Contact:** Mary Anne Trollo, Corporate Recruiting Office Manager. **Description:** Carolina Power & Light Company provides electric power service to approximately one million customers. The company's service area includes portions of both North and South Carolina. Employees work at corporate headquarters, in regional and district offices, and at 16 generating plants, three of which are nuclear power plants. **Common positions include:** Accountant/Auditor; Civil Engineer; Computer Programmer; Computer Systems Analyst; Customer Service Representative; Electrical/Electronics Engineer; Electrician; Financial Analyst; Human Resources Specialist; Industrial Engineer; Management Trainee; Mechanical Engineer; Metallurgical Engineer; Systems Analyst. **Educational backgrounds include:** Computer Science; Engineering; Finance; Marketing. **Benefits:** Dental Insurance; Disability Coverage; Life Insurance; Medical Insurance; Pension Plan; Savings Plan; Tuition Assistance. **Corporate headquarters location:** This Location. **Listed on:** New York Stock Exchange. **Number of employees at this location:** 2,000. **Number of employees nationwide:** 8,000.

DUKE POWER COMPANY
422 South Church Street, Mail Code PB04J, Charlotte NC 28242-0001. 704/594-0887. **Contact:** Christopher Rolfe, Vice President of Organization Effectiveness. **Description:** Duke Power Company, founded in 1904, is one of the nation's largest investor-owned electric utilities. Duke Power and its subsidiary, Nantahala Power and Light Company, operate three nuclear generating stations, eight coal-fired stations, and 38 hydroelectric stations. The company consists of 10 business units involved in investment management, real estate development, engineering, construction, appliance sales and service, communications systems development, and water service. Except for electric service provided within Duke Power's service area, these subsidiaries are part of the Associated Enterprises Group. **Corporate headquarters location:** This Location. **Subsidiaries include:** Duke Power Electric Operation; Church Street Capital Corporation; Crescent Resources, Inc.; Duke Energy Group, Inc.; Duke Engineering & Services, Inc.; Duke/Flour Daniel; Duke Merchandising; DukeNet Communications, Inc.; Duke Water Operations; Nantahala Power and Light Company. **Listed on:** New York Stock Exchange. **Number of employees nationwide:** 17,000.

PIEDMONT NATURAL GAS
P.O. Box 33068, Charlotte NC 28233. 704/364-3120. **Contact:** Virginia Parker, Director of Personnel. **Description:** Piedmont Natural Gas is engaged in the distribution of natural gas in the Piedmont region of North Carolina and South Carolina, and in the Nashville, Tennessee area. The company is also engaged in oil and gas exploration. **Number of employees nationwide:** 1,916.

PUBLIC SERVICE COMPANY OF NORTH CAROLINA, INC.
400 Cox Road, P.O. Box 1398, Gastonia NC 28053-1398. 704/864-6731. **Contact:** Human Resources. **Description:** Delivers natural gas products and services to residential, commercial, industrial, transportation, electric power generation customers, and other local distribution companies. Public Service Company of North Carolina's products and services include natural gas distribution, interstate and

intrastate pipeline services, supply and capacity brokering, natural gas vehicle fueling, and natural gas appliance sales, installation, and service. The company serves natural gas customers in 89 cities and communities in a 10,000 square mile area with a population of over 2.3 million people. **Corporate headquarters location:** This Location. **Listed on:** NASDAQ.

Note: Because addresses and telephone numbers of smaller companies change rapidly, we recommend you call each company to verify the information below before inquiring about job opportunities. Mass mailings are not recommended.

Additional employers with under 250 employees:

ELECTRIC SERVICES

Blue Ridge Electric Membership Corp.
1216 Blowing Rock Blvd, Lenoir NC 28645-3649. 704/758-2383.

Carolina Power and Light Co.
228 S Madison Blvd, Roxboro NC 27573-5428. 910/599-2196.

Carolina Power and Light Co.
300 S Center St, Goldsboro NC 27530-4807. 919/735-0121.

Cliffside Station
US Hwy 221A, Mooresboro NC 28114. 704/657-6314.

Davidson Electric Membership Corp.
15 W Salisbury St, Denton NC 27239-6925. 704/869-3700.

Duke Power Company
P.O. Box 1011, Durham NC 27702-1011. 919/687-3000.

Duke Power Company
1163 Highway 74 Byp, Suite G, Spindale NC 28160-2200. 704/287-7301.

Jones Onslow Electric Membership
520 Hwy 210, Sneads Ferry NC 28460. 910/327-2770.

Lumbee River Electric Membership Corp.
605 E 4th Ave, Red Springs NC 28377-1668. 910/843-4131.

Nantahala Power & Light Co.
17 W Main St, Franklin NC 28734-3005. 704/524-2121.

North Carolina Power
201 West Blvd, Williamston NC 27892-2143. 919/809-4100.

Piedmont Electric Membership Corp. NC
Hwy 86, Hillsborough NC 27278. 919/732-2123.

Rutherford Electric Membership Corp.
202 Hudlow Rd, Forest City NC 28043-2537. 704/245-1621.

Southport Municipal Electric Department
201 E Moore St, Southport NC 28461-3900. 910/457-6911.

Buck Generating Station
P.O. Box 2629, Salisbury NC 28145-2629. 704/642-3300.

Cliffside Generating Station
P.O. Box 306, Cliffside NC 28024-0306. 704/657-6314.

Riverbend Steam Station
175 Steam Plant Rd, Mount Holly NC 28120-9740. 704/827-4931.

GAS UTILITY SERVICES

Amerigas
219 E Wilmington St, Maxton NC 28364-1841. 910/844-5423.

Guilford Gas Service
1904 S Main St, High Point NC 27260-4465. 910/869-4454.

Public Service Co. NC
P.O. Box 2008, Durham NC 27702-2008. 919/682-5661.

Public Service Co. NC
322 E Front St, Statesville NC 28677-5907. 704/872-7404.

Public Service Co. NC
130 S Main St, Hendersonvlle NC 28792-5082. 704/692-0511.

Suburban Propane
1333 Berryhill Rd, Charlotte NC 28208-4009. 704/375-1721.

COMBINATION UTILITY SERVICES

French Board Electric Membership Corp.
P.O. Box 9, Marshall NC 28753. 704/649-2051.

South Carolina

SCANA CORPORATION
1426 Main Street, Columbia SC 29201. 803/748-3000. **Recorded Jobline:** 803/748-3001. **Contact:** Human Resources. **Description:** An energy-based holding company with 12 direct wholly-owned subsidiaries engaged in electric and natural gas utility operations and other energy-related businesses. South Carolina Electric & Gas company, SCANA's principal subsidiary, is a regulated public utility engaged in the generation, transmission, distribution, and sale of electricity and the purchase and sale of natural gas in South Carolina. South Carolina Electric & Gas provides electric service to approximately 482,000 customers, and natural gas to approximately 238,000 customers. SCANA's nonregulated operations include oil and natural gas exploration and production; natural gas marketing and propane storage; the purchase, delivery, and sale of propane; fiber-optic-based telecommunications and personal communications services; and power plant management and support services. **NOTE:** SCANA Corporation does not accept unsolicited resumes. Please apply only for

positions advertised on the company's jobline. **Corporate headquarters location:** This Location. **Listed on:** New York Stock Exchange.

SOUTH CAROLINA ELECTRIC AND GAS COMPANY
Mail Code: 092, Columbia SC 29218. 803/799-9000. **Recorded Jobline:** 803/748-3001. **Contact:** Human Resources Department. **Description:** A public service organization which produces and distributes electricity and natural gas. **Common positions include:** Accountant/Auditor; Administrative Worker/Clerk; Customer Service Representative; Electrical/Electronics Engineer; Mechanical Engineer. **Educational backgrounds include:** Accounting; Engineering. **Benefits:** Dental Insurance; Disability Coverage; Life Insurance; Medical Insurance; Pension Plan; Profit Sharing; Savings Plan; Tuition Assistance. **Special Programs:** Internships; Training Programs. **Corporate headquarters location:** This Location. **Operations at this facility include:** Administration. **Listed on:** New York Stock Exchange. **Number of employees nationwide:** 4,000.

SOUTH CAROLINA ELECTRIC AND GAS COMPANY
1115 East Main Street, Lake City SC 29560. 803/394-8043. **Contact:** Human Resources Department. **Description:** A public service organization which produces and distributes electricity and natural gas. **NOTE:** Please send resumes care of the Human Resources Department, South Carolina Electric & Gas, Mail Code: 092, Columbia 29218. 803/799-9000. **Corporate headquarters location:** Columbia SC. **Listed on:** New York Stock Exchange. **Number of employees nationwide:** 4,000.

WESTINGHOUSE SAVANNAH RIVER COMPANY
THE DEPARTMENT OF ENERGY
616 Road One, Aiken SC 29802. 803/725-6211. **Contact:** George Harley, Director of Human Resources. **Description:** The Westinghouse Savannah River Company serves as part of the Department of Energy's nuclear power facility.

Note: Because addresses and telephone numbers of smaller companies change rapidly, we recommend you call each company to verify the information below before inquiring about job opportunities. Mass mailings are not recommended.

Additional employers with under 250 employees:

ELECTRIC SERVICES

Aiken Electric Cooperative
P.O. Box 417, Aiken SC 29802-0417. 803/649-6245.

Berkeley Electric Cooperative Inc.
P.O. Box 1234, Moncks Corner SC 29461-1234. 803/761-8200.

Blue Ridge Electric Cooperative
W Main St, Box 277, Pickens SC 29671-2222. 864/878-6326.

Board of Public Works
210 E Frederick St, Gaffney SC 29340. 864/488-8800.

Carolina Power & Light Co.
P.O. Box 100519, Florence SC 29501. 803/661-4120.

Carolina Power & Light Co.
2220 W Old Camden Rd, Hartsville SC 29550-8304. 803/332-2633.

Ware Shoals Power & Water
135 S Greenwood Avenue Ext, Ware Shoals SC 29692. 864/456-3492.

Duke Power Company
1629 Bypass NE, Greenwood SC 29649. 864/459-9291.

Duke Power Company
18 Piedmont Hwy, Piedmont SC 29673-1036. 864/242-3261.

Duke Power Company
111 Covenant St, Lancaster SC 29720-6122. 803/283-4171.

Edisto Electric Cooperative
Marlboro Av, Barnwell SC 29812. 803/259-3717.

Fairfield Electric Cooperative Inc.
Highway 321 N, Winnsboro SC 29180. 803/425-1059.

Hollidays Bridge Station
1000 Holiday Dam Rd, Honea Path SC 29654-9204. 864/338-7514.

Santee Electric Co-op
1201 Main St, Suite 1710, Columbia SC 29201-3261. 803/771-8939.

Santee Electric Co-op
Hwy 260, Manning SC 29102. 803/473-4036.

Santee Electric Co-op
P.O. Box 548, Kingstree SC 29556-0548. 803/354-6187.

Seneca Light & Water Department
P.O. Box 4773, Seneca SC 29679-4773. 864/885-2715.

South Carolina Electric & Gas
4481 Leeds Pl W, N Charleston SC 29405-8402. 803/554-7234.

South Carolina Electric & Gas
3495 Ashley Phosphate Rd, Charleston SC 29418-8410. 803/745-6065.

South Carolina Public Service Authority
553 Cross Station Rd, Pineville SC 29468. 803/351-4545.

Walnut Grove Generating Station
1395 Blackstock Rd, Pauline SC 29374. 864/582-2944.

Westinghouse Electric Corp.
25 Woods Lake Rd, Suite 314, Greenville SC 29607-2723. 864/232-5696.

**Charleston Resource
Recovery Facility**
1801 Shipyard Creek Rd,
Charleston SC 29405-8396.
803/566-9322.

Winyah Generating Station
3097 Pennyroyal Road,
Georgetown SC 29440.
803/546-4171.

GAS UTILITY SERVICES

South Carolina Pipelines
P.O. Box 6317, Columbia SC
29260. 803/788-3220.

Carotane Propane Gas
1331 Dutch Fork Rd, Irmo
SC 29063-8788. 803/749-
1296.

Ferrellgas
Hwy 170, Ridgeland SC
29936. 803/726-4124.

Suburban Propane Gas
818 N Main St, Bishopville
SC 29010-1846. 803/484-
5411.

**GAS AND/OR WATER
SUPPLY**

Kiawah Island Utility Inc.
31 Sora Rail Rd, Johns Island
SC 29455. 803/768-0641.

Spartanburg Water System
200 N Commerce St,
Spartanburg SC 29306-
5159. 864/583-7361.

Spartanburg Water System
8515 Highway 9, Inman SC
29349. 864/592-2240.

For more information on career opportunities in the utilities industry:

Associations

AMERICAN PUBLIC GAS ASSOCIATION
Lee Highway, Suite 102, Fairfax VA
22030. 703/352-3890. Publishes a weekly
newsletter.

**AMERICAN PUBLIC POWER ASSOCIATION
(APPA)**
2301 M Street NW, Washington DC
20037. 202/467-2970. Represents
publicly-owned utilities. Provides many
services including: government relations,
educational programs, and industry-related
information publications.

AMERICAN WATER WORKS ASSOCIATION
6666 West Quincy Drive, Denver CO
80235. 303/794-7711.

**NATIONAL RURAL ELECTRIC
COOPERATIVE ASSOCIATION**
1800 Massachusetts Avenue NW,
Washington DC 20036. 202/857-9500.

Directories

MOODY'S PUBLIC UTILITY MANUAL
Moody's Investors Service, Inc., 99 Church
Street, New York NY 10007. 212/553-
0300. Annually available at libraries.

Magazines

PUBLIC POWER
2301 M Street NW, Washington DC
20037. 202/467-2900.

NOTE: *While every effort is made to keep the addresses and phone numbers of these companies up-to-date, employment services often move or change hands and are therefore more difficult to track. Please notify the publisher if you find any discrepancies.*

TEMPORARY EMPLOYMENT AGENCIES OF NORTH CAROLINA

DP PROS INC.
P.O. Box 2229, Burlington NC 27216. 910/222-8030. **Contact:** Babs Thomasson, Manager of Sales Administration. Temporary Agency. **Specializes in the areas of:** MIS/EDP. **Positions commonly filled include:** Computer Programmer; Systems Analyst. Company pays fee. **Number of placements per year:** 1 - 49.

DEBBIE'S STAFFING
4431 North Cherry, Suite 50, Winston-Salem NC 27105. 910/759-9999. **Fax:** 910/759-9255. **Contact:** Debbie Lambie, President. Temporary Agency.

FORBES TEMPORARY STAFFING
6401 Carmel Road, Suite 107, Charlotte NC 28226. 704/542-0312. **Contact:** Frieda Smith, President. Temporary Agency. **Specializes in the areas of:** Apparel; Computer Hardware/Software; Food Industry; Health/Medical; Hotel/Restaurant; Office Support; Technical and Scientific; Textiles.

INTERIM PERSONNEL, INC.
6404 Falls of the Neuse Road, Suite 110, Raleigh NC 27615. 919/872-3800. **Contact:** Mr. Chris Gardner, Client Service Manager. Temporary Agency. **Specializes in the areas of:** Banking; Clerical. **Positions commonly filled include:** Administrative Worker/Clerk; Construction Trade Worker; Data Entry Clerk; Draftsperson; Driver; Factory Worker; Legal Secretary; Light Industrial Worker; Marketing Specialist; Medical Secretary; Nurse; Purchasing Agent and Manager; Quality Control Supervisor; Receptionist; Secretary; Statistician; Stenographer; Technical Writer/Editor; Technician; Typist/Word Processor; Underwriter/Assistant Underwriter. **Number of placements per year:** 200 - 499.

MEBANE TEMPORARY SERVICES
P.O. Box 248, Mebane NC 27302. 919/563-1115. **Contact:** Nancy H. Berry, Partner. Temporary Agency. **Specializes in the areas of:** Clerical; Construction; Food Industry; Manufacturing; Sales and Marketing; Secretarial; Technical and Scientific. **Positions commonly filled include:** Administrative Assistant; Bookkeeper; Claim Representative; Clerk; Computer Programmer; Construction Trade Worker; Credit Manager; Customer Service Representative; Data Entry Clerk; Draftsperson; Driver; EDP Specialist; Factory Worker; Hotel Manager/Assistant Manager; Legal Secretary; Light Industrial Worker; Marketing Specialist; Medical Secretary; Public Relations Specialist; Purchasing Agent and Manager; Receptionist; Sales Representative; Secretary; Typist/Word Processor.

OLSTEN STAFFING
2301 West Meadowview Road, The Henderson Building, Suite 100, Greensboro NC 27407. 910/852-0500. **Contact:** Meridith Loy, Customer Service Representative. Temporary Agency. **Specializes in the areas of:** Clerical; Manufacturing. **Positions commonly filled include:** Accountant/Auditor; Administrative Assistant; Bank Officer/Manager; Bookkeeper; Clerk; Computer Operator; Computer Programmer; Construction Trade Worker; Customer Service Representative; Data Entry Clerk; Draftsperson; Driver; EDP Specialist; Factory Worker; General Manager; Human Resources Specialist; Legal Secretary; Light Industrial Worker; Medical Secretary; MIS Specialist; Operations/Production Manager; Public Relations Specialist; Purchasing Agent and Manager; Quality Control Supervisor; Receptionist; Sales Representative; Secretary; Stenographer; Systems Analyst; Technician; Typist/Word Processor. **Number of placements per year:** 1000 +.

OLSTEN TEMPORARY SERVICES OF WILMINGTON
513 Market Street, Wilmington NC 28401. 910/343-8763. **Contact:** Fran Young, Owner. Temporary Agency. **Specializes in the areas of:** Non-Specialized. **Positions commonly filled include:** Administrative Worker/Clerk; Bookkeeper; Clerk; Computer Operator; Construction Trade Worker; Customer Service Representative; Data Entry

Clerk; Draftsperson; Driver; Factory Worker; Financial Analyst; Legal Secretary; Light Industrial Worker; Medical Secretary; Receptionist; Secretary; Stenographer; Technical Writer/Editor; Technician; Typist/Word Processor. Company pays fee. **Number of placements per year:** 1000+.

PERSONNEL SERVICES UNLIMITED, INC.
824 South Dekalb Street, Shelby NC 28150. 704/484-0344. **Contact:** Tim Blackwell, Vice President. Temporary Agency. **Specializes in the areas of:** Clerical; Insurance; Legal; Manufacturing. **Positions commonly filled include:** Administrative Assistant; Bookkeeper; Clerk; Computer Operator; Customer Service Representative; Data Entry Clerk; Factory Worker; Legal Secretary; Light Industrial Worker; Receptionist; Secretary; Typist/Word Processor.

QUALITY PLUS TEMPORARIES, INC.
5200 Park Road, Suite 131, Charlotte NC 28209. 704/522-7587. **Contact:** Marjorie M. Rich, Owner. Temporary Agency. **Specializes in the areas of:** Health/Medical. **Positions commonly filled include:** Health Services Worker; Nurse. **Number of placements per year:** 1000+.

TEMPORARY STAFFING SYSTEMS
P.O. Box 672, Lincolnton NC 28092. 704/732-1116. **Contact:** Shonta Ramsey, Service Coordinator. Temporary Agency. **Specializes in the areas of:** Non-Specialized. **Positions commonly filled include:** Administrative Assistant; Clerk; Engineer; Factory Worker; General Manager; Industrial Designer; Light Industrial Worker; Secretary.

TEMPORARY STAFFING SYSTEMS
P.O. Box 87, Gastonia NC 28053-0087. 704/861-1516. **Contact:** David Cline, President. Temporary Agency. **Specializes in the areas of:** Non-Specialized. **Positions commonly filled include:** Administrative Assistant; Clerk; Engineer; Factory Worker; General Manager; Industrial Designer; Light Industrial Worker; Secretary.

TEMPORARY EMPLOYMENT AGENCIES OF SOUTH CAROLINA

ACCEL TEMPORARY SERVICES
P.O. Box 10422, Greenville SC 29603. 864/232-9921. **Contact:** Theresa Pelligrino, President/Owner. Temporary Agency. **Specializes in the areas of:** Computer Hardware/Software; Engineering; Manufacturing; Personnel/Labor Relations; Technical and Scientific. **Positions commonly filled include:** Aerospace Engineer; Biological Scientist/Biochemist; Biomedical Engineer; Ceramics Engineer; Chemical Engineer; Chemist; Civil Engineer; Draftsperson; Electrical/Electronics Engineer; Human Resources Specialist; Industrial Designer; Industrial Engineer; Mechanical Engineer; Metallurgical Engineer; Quality Control Supervisor; Statistician; Technician. Company pays fee. **Number of placements per year:** 50 - 99.

ADVANTAGE STAFFING
P.O. Box 2952, Spartanburg SC 29304. 864/585-6562. **Contact:** Kathy Chandler, President. Temporary Agency. **Specializes in the areas of:** Clerical; Manufacturing; Secretarial. **Positions commonly filled include:** Accountant/Auditor; Administrative Assistant; Bookkeeper; Clerk; Computer Programmer; Construction Trade Worker; Data Entry Clerk; Draftsperson; Factory Worker; Legal Secretary; Light Industrial Worker; Purchasing Agent and Manager; Receptionist; Secretary; Stenographer; Typist/Word Processor. Company pays fee. **Number of placements per year:** 1000+.

ROPER SERVICES
220 Executive Center Drive, Columbia SC 29210. 803/798-8500. **Contact:** Sharon Geiger. Temporary Agency. **Specializes in the areas of:** Clerical; Construction; Manufacturing; Sales and Marketing; Secretarial. **Positions commonly filled include:** Bookkeeper; Ceramics Engineer; Civil Engineer; Clerk; Construction Trade Worker; Data Entry Clerk; Draftsperson; Electrical/Electronics Engineer; Factory Worker; Human Resources Specialist; Industrial Designer; Industrial Engineer; Legal Secretary; Light Industrial Worker; Mechanical Engineer; Medical Secretary; Receptionist; Secretary; Stenographer; Telemarketer; Typist/Word Processor. Company pays fee. **Number of placements per year:** 1000+.

TALENT TREE
25 Woods Lake Road, Suite 222, Greenville SC 29607. 864/233-4301. **Contact:** Jennifer Waltz, Operations Manager. Temporary Agency. **Specializes in the areas of:** Non-Specialized. **Positions commonly filled include:** Administrative Worker/Clerk; Clerk; Computer Operator; Construction Trade Worker; Data Entry Clerk; Driver; Factory Worker; Light Industrial Worker; Receptionist; Typist/Word Processor. **Number of placements per year:** 1000+.

PERMANENT EMPLOYMENT AGENCIES OF NORTH CAROLINA

A FIRST RESOURCE PERSONNEL SERVICE
KLS ENTERPRISES, INC.
8025 North Point Boulevard, Winston-Salem NC 27106. 910/784-5898. **Contact:** Karen L. Siburt, President. Employment Agency. **Specializes in the areas of:** Accounting/Auditing; Administration/MIS/EDP; Finance; Food Industry; General Management; Industrial; Manufacturing; Sales and Marketing; Secretarial. **Positions commonly filled include:** Accountant/Auditor; Advertising Clerk; Branch Manager; Buyer; Chemist; Civil Engineer; Claim Representative; Clerical Supervisor; Computer Programmer; Computer Systems Analyst; Construction Contractor and Manager; Counselor; Credit Manager; Customer Service Representative; Draftsperson; Economist/Market Research Analyst; Electrical/Electronics Engineer; Food Scientist/Technologist; General Manager; Hotel Manager/Assistant Manager; Human Service Worker; Industrial Engineer; Industrial Production Manager; Management Trainee; Manufacturer's/Wholesaler's Sales Rep.; Mechanical Engineer; Medical Records Technician; Paralegal; Public Relations Specialist; Purchasing Agent and Manager; Restaurant/Food Service Manager; Services Sales Representative; Social Worker; Software Engineer; Transportation/Traffic Specialist. Company pays fee. **Number of placements per year:** 50 - 99.

A-1 STAFFING AND PERSONNEL
25 Heritage Plaza, Asheville NC 28806. 704/252-0708. **Fax:** 704/253-7973. **Contact:** Janice Hurd, Manager. Employment Agency. **Specializes in the areas of:** Accounting/Auditing; Advertising; Architecture/Construction/Real Estate; Banking; Finance; Food Industry; General Management; Legal; Manufacturing; Personnel/Labor Relations; Printing/Publishing; Retail; Sales and Marketing; Secretarial. **Positions commonly filled include:** Accountant/Auditor; Adjuster; Administrative Services Manager; Advertising Clerk; Automotive Mechanic/Body Repairer; Bank Officer/Manager; Blue-Collar Worker Supervisor; Branch Manager; Broadcast Technician; Buyer; Chemical Engineer; Clerical Supervisor; Clinical Lab Technician; Collector; Computer Programmer; Counselor; Credit Manager; Customer Service Representative; Editor; Electrical/Electronics Engineer; Electrician; Food Scientist/Technologist; General Manager; Hotel Manager/Assistant Manager; Human Resources Specialist; Human Service Worker; Industrial Engineer; Industrial Production Manager; Investigator; Landscape Architect; Management Analyst/Consultant; Management Trainee; Manufacturer's/Wholesaler's Sales Rep.; Mechanical Engineer; Operations/Production Manager; Paralegal; Property and Real Estate Manager; Public Relations Specialist; Purchasing Agent and Manager; Quality Control Supervisor; Restaurant/Food Service Manager; Securities Sales Rep.; Services Sales Representative; Technical Writer/Editor; Travel Agent; Wholesale and Retail Buyer. **Number of placements per year:** 200 - 499.

ACTION PERSONNEL SERVICES
P.O. Box 241536, Charlotte NC 28224. 704/527-9710. **Fax:** 704/527-9714. **Contact:** Richard T. Langdon, CPC. Employment Agency. **Specializes in the areas of:** Engineering; Insurance; Manufacturing.

ALPHA OMEGA PERSONNEL SERVICES
P.O. Box 24013-171, Winston-Salem NC 27114. 910/659-9001. **Fax:** 910/659-9206. **Contact:** CPC. Employment Agency. **Specializes in the areas of:** Accounting/Auditing; Engineering; Finance; Manufacturing.

AYERS & ASSOCIATES
P.O. Box 16065, Greensboro NC 27416. 910/378-1761. **Fax:** 910/275-8232. **Contact:** Dick Ayers, Owner. Employment Agency. **Specializes in the areas of:** Apparel; Manufacturing; Textiles. **Positions commonly filled include:** Buyer; Chemist;

Industrial Engineer; Mechanical Engineer; Operations/Production Manager; Quality Control Supervisor; Textile Manager; Transportation/Traffic Specialist. Company pays fee. **Number of placements per year:** 100 - 199.

CAREER STAFFING

800 Clanton Road, Suite W, Charlotte NC 28217. 704/525-8400. **Fax:** 704/525-8682. **Contact:** Jim Chambers, President. Employment Agency. **Specializes in the areas of:** Banking; Clerical; Computer Hardware/Software; Secretarial. **Positions commonly filled include:** Administrative Assistant; Bank Officer/Manager; Bookkeeper; Clerk; Computer Programmer; Construction Trade Worker; Credit Manager; Data Entry Clerk; Draftsperson; Driver; EDP Specialist; Factory Worker; Financial Analyst; Legal Secretary; Light Industrial Worker; Medical Secretary; Receptionist; Secretary; Stenographer; Systems Analyst; Typist/Word Processor. Company pays fee. **Number of placements per year:** 200 - 499.

CAREERS UNLIMITED INC.

1911 Hillandale Road, Suite 1210, Durham NC 27705. 919/383-7431. **Fax:** 919/383-5706. **Contact:** Phyllis Carswell, CPC. Employment Agency. **Specializes in the areas of:** Accounting/Auditing; Computer Science/Software; Finance; Office Support; Sales and Marketing; Temporary Assignments.

CORPORATE STAFFING CONSULTANTS, INC.

P.O. Box 221739, Charlotte NC 28222. 704/366-1800. **Fax:** 704/366-0070. **Contact:** Alan W. Madsen, CPC. Employment Agency. **Specializes in the areas of:** Computer Science/Software; Engineering; Environmental; Temporary Assignments.

DATA MASTERS

P.O. Box 14548, Greensboro NC 27415-4548. 910/373-1461. **Fax:** 910/373-1501. **Contact:** Paula White, Manager. Employment Agency. **Specializes in the areas of:** Computer Science/Software. **Positions commonly filled include:** Computer Programmer; Computer Systems Analyst; Science Technologist. Company pays fee. **Number of placements per year:** 50 - 99.

DURHAM JOB SERVICE OFFICE

1105 South Briggs Avenue, Durham NC 27703. 919/560-6880. **Contact:** Manager. Employment Agency. **Specializes in the areas of:** Non-Specialized. **Positions commonly filled include:** Accountant/Auditor; Actuary; Administrative Assistant; Advertising Clerk; Aerospace Engineer; Agricultural Engineer; Architect; Attorney; Bank Officer/Manager; Biological Scientist/Biochemist; Biomedical Engineer; Bookkeeper; Buyer; Ceramics Engineer; Chemical Engineer; Chemist; Civil Engineer; Claim Representative; Clerk; Commercial Artist; Computer Operator; Computer Programmer; Construction Trade Worker; Credit Manager; Customer Service Representative; Data Entry Clerk; Dietician/Nutritionist; Draftsperson; Driver; Economist/Market Research Analyst; EDP Specialist; Electrical/Electronics Engineer; Factory Worker; Financial Analyst; Food Scientist/Technologist; General Manager; Hotel Manager/Assistant Manager; Human Resources Specialist; Industrial Designer; Industrial Engineer; Insurance Agent/Broker; Legal Secretary; Light Industrial Worker; Marketing Specialist; Mechanical Engineer; Medical Secretary; Metallurgical Engineer; Mining Engineer; MIS Specialist; Nurse; Operations/Production Manager; Petroleum Engineer; Physicist/Astronomer; Public Relations Specialist; Purchasing Agent and Manager; Quality Control Supervisor; Receptionist; Reporter; Sales Representative; Secretary; Statistician; Stenographer; Systems Analyst; Technical Writer/Editor; Technician; Typist/Word Processor; Underwriter/Assistant Underwriter. **Number of placements per year:** 1000 +.

ELITE PERSONNEL AND JOB FORCE

P.O. Box 52029, Durham NC 27717-2029. 919/493-1449. **Contact:** Ms. Lise Gussow, President. Employment Agency. **Specializes in the areas of:** Office Support; Temporary Assignments.

ELLIS ASSOCIATES

P.O. Box 98925, Raleigh NC 27624. 919/676-1061. **Contact:** Mr. Lee Douglas, Vice President. Employment Agency. **Specializes in the areas of:** Biotechnology; Pharmaceutical.

F-O-R-T-U-N-E PERSONNEL CONSULTANTS OF RALEIGH, INC.

P.O. Box 98388, Raleigh NC 27624-8388. 919/848-9929. **Fax:** 919/848-9666. **Contact:** Rick Deckelbaum, Vice President. Employment Agency. **Specializes in the areas of:** Accounting/Auditing; Banking; Computer Science/Software; Engineering; Finance; Food Industry; Manufacturing; Personnel/Labor Relations. **Positions commonly filled include:** Accountant/Auditor; Aerospace Engineer; Biomedical Engineer; Ceramics

Engineer; Chemical Engineer; Chemist; Civil Engineer; Computer Programmer; Computer Systems Analyst; Electrical/Electronics Engineer; Financial Analyst; General Manager; Human Resources Specialist; Industrial Engineer; Materials Engineer; Mechanical Engineer; Metallurgical Engineer; Petroleum Engineer; Software Engineer; Statistician. Company pays fee. **Number of placements per year:** 200 - 499.

FRIDAY STAFFING
1944 Hendersonville Road, Asheville NC 28803. 704/684-1788. **Contact:** Kathy Jarvis. Employment Agency. **Specializes in the areas of:** Non-Specialized. **Positions commonly filled include:** Accountant/Auditor; Administrative Assistant; Bookkeeper; Customer Service Representative; Data Entry Clerk; Draftsperson; Factory Worker; Light Industrial Worker; Medical Secretary; Receptionist; Secretary; Typist/Word Processor.

FRIDAY STAFFING
227 Duncan Hill Road, Hendersonville NC 28792. 704/697-1507. **Contact:** Ruth Langston. Employment Agency. **Specializes in the areas of:** Non-Specialized. **Positions commonly filled include:** Accountant/Auditor; Administrative Assistant; Bookkeeper; Customer Service Representative; Data Entry Clerk; Draftsperson; Factory Worker; Light Industrial Worker; Medical Secretary; Receptionist; Secretary; Typist/Word Processor.

GRAHAM & ASSOCIATES
2100-J West Cornwallis Drive, Greensboro NC 27408. 910/288-9330. **Contact:** Gary Graham, CPC, President. Employment Agency. **Specializes in the areas of:** Accounting/Auditing; Banking; Clerical; Computer Hardware/Software; Engineering; Legal; Manufacturing; MIS/EDP; Personnel/Labor Relations; Technical and Scientific. **Positions commonly filled include:** Accountant/Auditor; Administrative Assistant; Aerospace Engineer; Agricultural Engineer; Attorney; Bank Officer/Manager; Bookkeeper; Buyer; Ceramics Engineer; Chemical Engineer; Chemist; Civil Engineer; Clerk; Computer Operator; Computer Programmer; Credit Manager; Customer Service Representative; Data Entry Clerk; Draftsperson; Economist/Market Research Analyst; EDP Specialist; Electrical/Electronics Engineer; Factory Worker; Financial Analyst; General Manager; Human Resources Specialist; Industrial Designer; Industrial Engineer; Legal Secretary; Light Industrial Worker; Marketing Specialist; Mechanical Engineer; Medical Secretary; Metallurgical Engineer; Mining Engineer; Operations/Production Manager; Petroleum Engineer; Physicist/Astronomer; Purchasing Agent and Manager; Quality Control Supervisor; Receptionist; Secretary; Stenographer; Systems Analyst; Technical Writer/Editor; Technician; Typist/Word Processor. Company pays fee. **Number of placements per year:** 200 - 499.

GRANITE PERSONNEL SERVICE
4 Park Avenue, Granite Falls NC 28630. 704/396-2369. **Contact:** James Terrell, President. Employment Agency. **Specializes in the areas of:** Administration/MIS/EDP; Clerical; Sales and Marketing; Technical and Scientific. **Number of placements per year:** 50 - 99.

GREER PERSONNEL
5500 McNeely Drive, Suite 102, Raleigh NC 27612. 919/571-0051. **Fax:** 919/571-7450. **Contact:** Deborah G. Greer, CPC. Employment Agency. **Specializes in the areas of:** Accounting/Auditing; Bookkeeping; Clerical; Engineering; Finance; Legal; Office Support.

ROBERT HALF INTERNATIONAL
300 North Greene Street, Suite 275, Greensboro NC 27401. 910/274-4253. **Fax:** 910/273-2882. **Contact:** Patricia Murray, Placement Manager. Employment Agency. **Specializes in the areas of:** Accounting/Auditing; Administration/MIS/EDP; Computer Hardware/Software; Finance. **Positions commonly filled include:** Accountant/Auditor; Bookkeeper; Clerk; Computer Operator; Computer Programmer; CPA; Credit Manager; Data Entry Clerk; Software Engineer; Systems Analyst. Company pays fee.

KELLY SERVICES
620 Green Valley Road, Suite 206, Greensboro NC 27408. 910/292-4371. **Fax:** 910/852-6822. **Contact:** Delane Hooper, Office Manager. Employment Agency. **Specializes in the areas of:** Accounting/Auditing; Administration/MIS/EDP; Advertising; Banking; Computer Science/Software; Engineering; Finance; General Management; Industrial; Insurance; Legal; Manufacturing; Personnel/Labor Relations; Printing/Publishing; Sales and Marketing; Secretarial; Technical and Scientific. **Positions commonly filled include:** Accountant/Auditor; Administrative Assistant; Bookkeeper; Clerk; Computer Operator; Computer Programmer; Customer Service Representative; Data Entry Clerk; Designer; Human Resources Specialist; Insurance Agent/Broker;

Legal Secretary; Light Industrial Worker; Marketing Specialist; MIS Specialist; Purchasing Agent and Manager; Receptionist; Records Manager; Secretary; Technical Writer/Editor; Typist/Word Processor. **Number of placements per year:** 1000+.

KELLY SERVICES
2701 Coltsgate Road, Suite 102, Charlotte NC 28211. 704/364-4790. **Fax:** 704/364-6616. **Contact:** Jenny Mehaffey, Office Manager. Employment Agency. **Specializes in the areas of:** Accounting/Auditing; Administration/MIS/EDP; Advertising; Banking; Computer Science/Software; Engineering; Finance; General Management; Industrial; Insurance; Legal; Manufacturing; Personnel/Labor Relations; Printing/Publishing; Sales and Marketing; Secretarial; Technical and Scientific. **Positions commonly filled include:** Accountant/Auditor; Administrative Assistant; Bookkeeper; Clerk; Computer Operator; Computer Programmer; Customer Service Representative; Data Entry Clerk; Designer; Human Resources Specialist; Insurance Agent/Broker; Legal Secretary; Light Industrial Worker; Marketing Specialist; MIS Specialist; Purchasing Agent and Manager; Receptionist; Records Manager; Secretary; Technical Writer/Editor; Typist/Word Processor. **Number of placements per year:** 1000+.

MANAGEMENT RECRUITERS OF CONCORD/KANNAPOLIS
305 South Main Street, Kannapolis NC 28081. 704/938-6144. **Fax:** 704/938-3480. **Contact:** Tom Whitley, President. Employment Agency. **Specializes in the areas of:** Computer Science/Software. **Positions commonly filled include:** Computer Programmer; Computer Systems Analyst. Company pays fee. **Number of placements per year:** 50 - 99.

MEDICAL PROFESSIONALS
P.O. Box 837, Wrightsville Beach NC 28480. 910/256-8115. **Fax:** 910/256-6961. **Contact:** Donna Paap, President. Employment Agency. **Specializes in the areas of:** Health/Medical. **Positions commonly filled include:** Physician. **Number of placements per year:** 1 - 49.

MERRICK & MOORE
P.O. Box 8816, Asheville NC 28804. 704/258-1831. **Contact:** M.B. Parker, President. Employment Agency. **Specializes in the areas of:** Banking; Engineering; Health/Medical; Manufacturing; Technical and Scientific. **Positions commonly filled include:** Accountant/Auditor; Aerospace Engineer; Attorney; Bank Officer/Manager; Biological Scientist/Biochemist; Chemist; EDP Specialist; Electrical/Electronics Engineer; Financial Analyst; Health Services Worker; Industrial Engineer; Mechanical Engineer; Systems Analyst. Company pays fee. **Number of placements per year:** 1 - 49.

MYERS & ASSOCIATES
13420 Reese Boulevard West, Huntersville NC 28078. 704/875-8300. **Fax:** 704/875-8891. **Contact:** Joseph N. Myers, Sr., President. Employment Agency. **Specializes in the areas of:** Administration/MIS/EDP; Engineering; Health/Medical; Industrial; Manufacturing. **Positions commonly filled include:** Accountant/Auditor; Buyer; Chemical Engineer; Computer Programmer; Computer Systems Analyst; Electrical/Electronics Engineer; Industrial Engineer; Mechanical Engineer; Metallurgical Engineer; Occupational Therapist; Physical Therapist; Respiratory Therapist; Software Engineer. Company pays fee. **Number of placements per year:** 1 - 49.

NATIONAL CAREER CENTERS
P.O. Box 447, Fayetteville NC 28302. 910/483-0413. **Fax:** 910/487-0298. **Contact:** James Robert Smith, President. Employment Agency. **Specializes in the areas of:** Computer Science/Software; Engineering; Sales and Marketing.

PERSONNEL PLACEMENT INC.
2426 Reynolda Road, Weston NC 27106. **Contact:** Irene Littleton, Senior Recruiter. Employment Agency. **Specializes in the areas of:** Computer Science/Software; Finance; Manufacturing. **Positions commonly filled include:** Computer Programmer; Computer Systems Analyst. **Number of placements per year:** 50 - 99.

PERSONNEL SERVICES OF EASTERN NORTH CAROLINA
105 Oakmont Drive, Suite A, Greenville NC 27858. 919/756-5820. **Fax:** 919/756-0697. **Contact:** Lori D. Nease, CPC, President. Employment Agency. **Specializes in the areas of:** Non-Specialized.

REP & ASSOCIATES
P.O. Box 55, Washington NC 27889. 919/946-6643. **Contact:** Richard Phelan, Recruiter. Employment Agency. **Specializes in the areas of:** Computer Science/Software.

SNELLING PERSONNEL
P.O. Box 1800, Lexington NC 29071. 803/359-7644. **Contact:** Ms. Jina Robbins-McCuen, Owner. Employment Agency. **Specializes in the areas of:** Accounting/Auditing; Banking; Clerical; Manufacturing; Technical and Scientific. **Positions commonly filled include:** Accountant/Auditor; Administrative Assistant; Advertising Clerk; Architect; Bank Officer/Manager; Biological Scientist/Biochemist; Bookkeeper; Buyer; Chemical Engineer; Chemist; Civil Engineer; Claim Representative; Clerk; Commercial Artist; Computer Operator; Computer Programmer; Credit Manager; Customer Service Representative; Data Entry Clerk; Dietician/Nutritionist; Draftsperson; Driver; EDP Specialist; Electrical/Electronics Engineer; Factory Worker; Financial Analyst; Human Resources Specialist; Industrial Engineer; Insurance Agent/Broker; Legal Secretary; Light Industrial Worker; Marketing Specialist; Mechanical Engineer; Medical Secretary; Metallurgical Engineer; Nurse; Public Relations Specialist; Purchasing Agent and Manager; Quality Control Supervisor; Receptionist; Reporter; Sales Representative; Secretary; Statistician; Stenographer; Systems Analyst; Technician; Typist/Word Processor. Company pays fee. **Number of placements per year:** 200 - 499.

WADDY R. THOMSON ASSOCIATES
233 South Sharon Amity Road, Charlotte NC 28211. 704/366-1956. **Contact:** Waddy Thomson, Principal. Employment Agency. **Specializes in the areas of:** Industrial; Manufacturing. **Positions commonly filled include:** Environmental Engineer; Environmental Scientist; Safety Engineer; Safety Specialist. Company pays fee. **Number of placements per year:** 1 - 49.

THE UNDERWOOD GROUP/ACCREDITED PERSONNEL
2840 Plaza Place, Suite 211, Raleigh NC 27612. 919/782-3024. **Contact:** Mark Underwood, Owner/President. Employment Agency. **Specializes in the areas of:** Data Processing; Engineering. **Positions commonly filled include:** Computer Programmer; Electrical/Electronics Engineer; Mechanical Engineer; MIS Specialist; Software Engineer; Systems Analyst.

WOODS-HOYLE, INC.
P.O. Box 9902, Greensboro NC 27429. 910/273-4557. **Contact:** Anne Marie Woods, President. Employment Agency. **Specializes in the areas of:** Computer Science/Software; Data Processing.

PERMANENT EMPLOYMENT AGENCIES OF SOUTH CAROLINA

DUNHILL OF GREENVILLE
96 Villa Road, Greenville SC 29615. 864/271-7180. **Contact:** Duke Haynie, President. Employment Agency. **Specializes in the areas of:** Data Processing; Engineering. **Positions commonly filled include:** Computer Programmer; Industrial Engineer; Manufacturing Engineer; Systems Analyst.

DUNHILL PERSONNEL OF SAINT ANDREWS
Interstate Center, 16 Berry Hill Road, Suite 120, Columbia SC 29210. 803/772-6751. **Fax:** 803/798-0874. **Contact:** Kristyne Hamilton, Account Executive. Employment Agency. **Specializes in the areas of:** Engineering; Industrial; Manufacturing; Sales and Marketing; Textiles. **Positions commonly filled include:** Accountant/Auditor; Aerospace Engineer; Computer Programmer; Computer Systems Analyst; Electrical/Electronics Engineer; Human Resources Specialist; Industrial Engineer; Industrial Production Manager; Manufacturer's/Wholesaler's Sales Rep.; Materials Engineer; Mechanical Engineer; Meteorologist; Operations/Production Manager; Quality Control Supervisor; Software Engineer. Company pays fee. **Number of placements per year:** 50 - 99.

THE HAMPTON GROUP
27 Gamecock Avenue, Suite 200, Charleston SC 29407. 803/763-0532. **Contact:** Nyle Martin, Owner. Employment Agency. **Specializes in the areas of:** Engineering; Technical and Scientific. **Positions commonly filled include:** Industrial Engineer; Legal Secretary; Mechanical Engineer; Operations/Production Manager; Secretary.

HARVEY PERSONNEL, INC.
P.O. Box 1931, Spartanburg SC 29304. 864/582-5616. **Fax:** 864/582-3588. **Contact:** Howard L. Harvey, CPC, President. Employment Agency. **Specializes in the

areas of: Accounting/Auditing; Administration/MIS/EDP; Computer Hardware/ Software; Engineering; General Management; Industrial; Manufacturing; Personnel/ Labor Relations; Technical and Scientific. **Positions commonly filled include:** Accountant/Auditor; Biological Scientist/Biochemist; Biomedical Engineer; Buyer; Ceramics Engineer; Chemical Engineer; Chemist; Civil Engineer; EDP Specialist; Electrical/Electronics Engineer; Industrial Engineer; Manufacturing Engineer; Manufacturing Supervisor; Mechanical Engineer; Metallurgical Engineer; MIS Specialist; Operations/Production Manager; Plastics Engineer; Purchasing Agent and Manager; Quality Control Supervisor; Software Engineer; Systems Analyst. Company pays fee. **Number of placements per year:** 1 - 49.

PRL & ASSOCIATES, INC.
P.O. Box 340, Lexington SC 29071. 803/957-3222. **Contact:** Perrin R. Love, President. Employment Agency. **Specializes in the areas of:** Accounting/Auditing; Banking; Engineering; Finance; General Management; Manufacturing; Personnel/Labor Relations; Technical and Scientific. **Positions commonly filled include:** Accountant/Auditor; Bank Officer/Manager; Biomedical Engineer; Branch Manager; Buyer; Chemical Engineer; Civil Engineer; Electrical/Electronics Engineer; Financial Analyst; General Manager; Human Resources Specialist; Industrial Engineer; Mechanical Engineer; Metallurgical Engineer; Operations/Production Manager; Quality Control Supervisor; Structural Engineer; Transportation/Traffic Specialist. Company pays fee. **Number of placements per year:** 1 - 49.

PHELPS PERSONNEL
P.O. Box 4177, Greenville SC 29608. 864/232-8139. **Fax:** 864/271-1426. **Contact:** Ronald A. Phelps, CPC. Employment Agency. **Specializes in the areas of:** Engineering.

SEARCH AND RECRUIT INTERNATIONAL
2501 Northforest Drive, North Charleston SC 29420. 803/572-4040. **Fax:** 803/572-4045. **Contact:** Les Callahan, Southeast Regional Manager. Employment Agency. **Specializes in the areas of:** Accounting/Auditing; Administration/MIS/EDP; Computer Science/Software; Engineering; Finance; Food Industry; Health/Medical; Industrial; Manufacturing; Nuclear Power; Technical and Scientific. **Positions commonly filled include:** Accountant/Auditor; Biological Scientist/Biochemist; Biomedical Engineer; Ceramics Engineer; Chemical Engineer; Civil Engineer; Computer Programmer; Computer Systems Analyst; Electrical/Electronics Engineer; Electrician; Financial Analyst; Geologist/Geophysicist; Industrial Engineer; Industrial Production Manager; Materials Engineer; Mechanical Engineer; Medical Records Technician; Metallurgical Engineer; Nuclear Engineer; Nuclear Medicine Technologist; Occupational Therapist; Operations/Production Manager; Pharmacist; Physical Therapist; Physician; Quality Control Supervisor; Respiratory Therapist; Software Engineer; Speech-Language Pathologist; Stationary Engineer; Structural Engineer. Company pays fee. **Number of placements per year:** 100 - 199.

STAFFING RESOURCES
1755 St. Julian Place, Columbia SC 29204. 803/765-0820. **Contact:** Frank Staley, Owner. Employment Agency. **Specializes in the areas of:** Banking; Computer Hardware/Software; Health/Medical; Insurance; Manufacturing; Office Support; Temporary Assignments. **Positions commonly filled include:** Accountant/Auditor; Administrative Assistant; Computer Operator; Computer Programmer; Controller; CPA; Financial Manager; Receptionist; Secretary; Systems Analyst; Typist/Word Processor.

SYSTEMS CAREERS
P.O. Box 969, Columbia SC 29202. 803/771-6454. **Fax:** 803/765-1431. **Contact:** Stephanie Parkinson, Personnel Consultant. Employment Agency. **Specializes in the areas of:** Computer Science/Software; Data Processing.

EXECUTIVE SEARCH FIRMS OF
NORTH CAROLINA

BENNETT ALLEN & ASSOCIATES
7422 Carmel Executive Park Drive, Charlotte NC 28226. **Contact:** Ben Liebstein, President. Executive Search Firm. **Specializes in the areas of:** Engineering. **Positions commonly filled include:** Aerospace Engineer; Agricultural Engineer; Electrical/Electronics Engineer; Mechanical Engineer; Mining Engineer; Structural Engineer. Company pays fee.

ANDREWS & ASSOCIATES
6100 Fairview Road, Suite 1420, Charlotte NC 28210. 704/556-0088. **Contact:** Dwight L. Andrews, Principal. Executive Search Firm. **Specializes in the areas of:** Accounting/Auditing; Administration/MIS/EDP; Finance; Health/Medical. **Positions commonly filled include:** Accountant/Auditor; Bookkeeper; Computer Programmer; EDP Specialist; MIS Specialist. Company pays fee. **Number of placements per year:** 1 - 49.

ATCHISON & ASSOCIATES, INC.
612 Pasteur Drive, Suite 106, Greensboro NC 27403. 910/855-5943. **Contact:** Bill Atchison. Executive Search Firm. **Specializes in the areas of:** Accounting/Auditing; Engineering; Industrial; Manufacturing; Personnel/Labor Relations; Technical and Scientific. **Positions commonly filled include:** Accountant/Auditor; Chemical Engineer; Chemist; Civil Engineer; Computer Programmer; Electrical/Electronics Engineer; Industrial Engineer; Manufacturing Engineer; Mechanical Engineer; Metallurgical Engineer; Quality Control Supervisor; Software Engineer. Company pays fee. **Number of placements per year:** 1 - 49.

BANK SEARCH
P.O. Box 491, Ayden NC 28513. 919/355-8282. **Contact:** David Melvin, Owner. Executive Search Firm. **Specializes in the areas of:** Banking. **Positions commonly filled include:** Bank Officer/Manager. Company pays fee. **Number of placements per year:** 1 - 49.

BULLINGTON ASSOCIATES
3700 National Drive, #214, Raleigh NC 27612. 919/781-1350. **Fax:** 919/781-5947. **Contact:** Hal Keyser, Manager. Executive Search Firm. **Specializes in the areas of:** Sales and Marketing. Company pays fee. **Number of placements per year:** 1 - 49.

S.L. COLLINS ASSOCIATES
P.O. Box 472181, Charlotte NC 28247-2181. 704/365-9889. **Fax:** 704/365-9890. **Contact:** Steve Collins, President/Owner. Executive Search Firm. **Specializes in the areas of:** Biology; Engineering; Manufacturing; Pharmaceutical; Technical and Scientific. **Positions commonly filled include:** Agricultural Scientist; Biological Scientist/Biochemist; Biomedical Engineer; Ceramics Engineer; Chemical Engineer; Chemist; Clinical Lab Technician; Electrical/Electronics Engineer; Industrial Engineer; Industrial Production Manager; Materials Engineer; Mechanical Engineer; Medical Records Technician; Metallurgical Engineer; Operations/Production Manager; Quality Control Supervisor; Science Technologist; Technical Writer/Editor. Company pays fee. **Number of placements per year:** 50 - 99.

EASTERN SEARCH GROUP
P.O. Box 4655, Wilmington NC 28406. 910/799-7700. **Fax:** 910/392-6266. **Contact:** Fred Wells, President. Executive Search Firm. **Specializes in the areas of:** Apparel; Computer Science/Software; Engineering; Industrial; Manufacturing; Textiles. **Positions commonly filled include:** Accountant/Auditor; Chemical Engineer; Computer Programmer; Computer Systems Analyst; Electrical/Electronics Engineer; Industrial Engineer; Industrial Production Manager; Mechanical Engineer; Quality Control Supervisor. Company pays fee. **Number of placements per year:** 50 - 99.

EXECUTIVE RECRUITMENT SPECIALISTS, INC.
6407 Idlewild Road, Suite 210-10, Charlotte NC 28212. 704/536-8830. **Fax:** 704/536-8893. **Contact:** Eric Sklut, President. Executive Search Firm. **Specializes in the areas of:** Computer Science/Software; Engineering; Finance; General Management; Government; Health/Medical; Manufacturing. **Positions commonly filled include:** Accountant/Auditor; Biomedical Engineer; Electrical/Electronics Engineer; General Manager; Health Services Manager; Licensed Practical Nurse; Mechanical Engineer; Medical Records Technician; Nuclear Medicine Technologist; Occupational Therapist; Physical Therapist; Quality Control Supervisor; Radiologic Technologist; Recreational Therapist; Registered Nurse; Respiratory Therapist; Software Engineer; Speech-Language Pathologist. Company pays fee. **Number of placements per year:** 50 - 99.

INFORMATION SYSTEMS PROFESSIONALS, INC.
5904 Castlebrook Drive, Raleigh NC 27604. 919/954-9100. **Fax:** 919/954-1947. **Contact:** Brad Moses, President. Executive Search Firm. **Specializes in the areas of:** Administration/MIS/EDP; Computer Science/Software. **Positions commonly filled include:** Computer Programmer; Computer Systems Analyst; Management Analyst/Consultant; Software Engineer; Technical Writer/Editor. **Number of placements per year:** 1 - 49.

INSURANCE PROFESSIONAL SEARCH
6869 Fairview Road, Suite 200, Charlotte NC 28210. 704/362-5638. **Contact:** Susan Belton, Owner. Executive Search Firm. **Specializes in the areas of:** Insurance. **Positions commonly filled include:** Accountant/Auditor; Actuary; Adjuster; Claim Representative; Collector; Insurance Agent/Broker; Investigator; Underwriter/Assistant Underwriter. Company pays fee. **Number of placements per year:** 1 - 49.

R.E. LOWE ASSOCIATES, INC.
7621 Little Avenue, Suite 216, Charlotte NC 28226. 704/543-1111. **Fax:** 704/543-0945. **Contact:** R. Patrick Perkins, President. Executive Search Firm. **Specializes in the areas of:** Accounting/Auditing; Administration/MIS/EDP; Engineering; Finance; Industrial; Manufacturing; Personnel/Labor Relations; Secretarial. **Positions commonly filled include:** Accountant/Auditor; Credit Manager; Customer Service Representative; EDP Specialist; Electrical/Electronics Engineer; Industrial Engineer; Legal Secretary; Manufacturing Engineer; MIS Specialist; Secretary. Company pays fee. **Number of placements per year:** 100 - 199.

MRI/SALES CONSULTANTS
107 Edinburgh South, Suite 210, Cary NC 27511. 919/460-9595. **Contact:** Donna Durkin, Administrative Assistant. Executive Search Firm. **Specializes in the areas of:** Accounting/Auditing; Administration/MIS/EDP; Advertising; Architecture/ Construction/ Real Estate; Banking; Communications; Computer Hardware/Software; Design; Electrical; Engineering; Food Industry; General Management; Health/Medical; Insurance; Legal; Manufacturing; Operations Management; Personnel/Labor Relations; Printing/Publishing; Procurement; Retail; Sales and Marketing; Technical and Scientific; Textiles; Transportation.

MANAGEMENT RECRUITERS
22 South Pack Square, Suite 302, Asheville NC 28801. 704/258-9646. **Fax:** 704/252-0866. **Contact:** Paul Rumson, President. Executive Search Firm. **Specializes in the areas of:** Administration/MIS/EDP; Computer Science/Software; Engineering; General Management; Industrial; Manufacturing; Personnel/Labor Relations; Technical and Scientific. **Positions commonly filled include:** Aerospace Engineer; Chemical Engineer; Chemist; Computer Programmer; Computer Systems Analyst; Designer; Draftsperson; Electrical/Electronics Engineer; Human Resources Specialist; Industrial Engineer; Industrial Production Manager; Materials Engineer; Mechanical Engineer; Mining Engineer; Purchasing Agent and Manager; Quality Control Supervisor; Software Engineer; Structural Engineer. Company pays fee. **Number of placements per year:** 1 - 49.

MANAGEMENT RECRUITERS
5509 Creedmoor Road, Suite 206, Raleigh NC 27612-2812. 919/781-0400. **Contact:** Phillip Stanley, Manager. Executive Search Firm. **Specializes in the areas of:** Accounting/Auditing; Administration/MIS/EDP; Advertising; Architecture/ Construction/ Real Estate; Banking; Communications; Computer Hardware/Software; Design; Electrical; Engineering; Food Industry; General Management; Health/Medical; Insurance; Legal; Manufacturing; Operations Management; Personnel/Labor Relations; Printing/Publishing; Procurement; Retail; Sales and Marketing; Technical and Scientific; Textiles; Transportation.

MANAGEMENT RECRUITERS
P.O. Box 6077, Hickory NC 28603. 704/495-8233. **Contact:** Byron King, Manager. Executive Search Firm. **Specializes in the areas of:** Accounting/Auditing; Administration/MIS/EDP; Advertising; Architecture/Construction/Real Estate; Banking; Communications; Computer Hardware/Software; Design; Electrical; Engineering; Food Industry; General Management; Health/Medical; Insurance; Legal; Manufacturing; Operations Management; Personnel/Labor Relations; Printing/Publishing; Procurement; Retail; Sales and Marketing; Technical and Scientific; Textiles; Transportation.

MANAGEMENT RECRUITERS
P.O. Box 399, Cedar Mountain NC 28718. 704/884-4118. **Contact:** Frank Schoff, President. Executive Search Firm. **Specializes in the areas of:** Accounting/Auditing; Administration/MIS/EDP; Advertising; Architecture/Construction/Real Estate; Banking; Communications; Computer Hardware/Software; Design; Electrical; Engineering; Food Industry; General Management; Health/Medical; Insurance; Legal; Manufacturing; Operations Management; Personnel/Labor Relations; Printing/Publishing; Procurement; Retail; Sales and Marketing; Technical and Scientific; Textiles; Transportation.

MANAGEMENT RECRUITERS
835 Highland Avenue SE, Hickory NC 28602. 704/324-2020. **Contact:** Scott Volz, Manager. Executive Search Firm. **Specializes in the areas of:** Accounting/Auditing;

Administration/MIS/EDP; Advertising; Architecture/Construction/Real Estate; Banking; Communications; Computer Hardware/Software; Design; Electrical; Engineering; Food Industry; General Management; Health/Medical; Insurance; Legal; Manufacturing; Operations Management; Personnel/Labor Relations; Printing/Publishing; Procurement; Technical and Scientific; Textiles; Transportation.

MANAGEMENT RECRUITERS
P.O. Box 1186, Rocky Mount NC 27802-1186. 919/442-8000. **Contact:** Bob Manning, Manager. Executive Search Firm. **Specializes in the areas of:** Accounting/Auditing; Administration/MIS/EDP; Advertising; Architecture/ Construction/ Real Estate; Banking; Communications; Computer Hardware/Software; Design; Electrical; Engineering; Food Industry; General Management; Health/Medical; Insurance; Legal; Manufacturing; Operations Management; Personnel/Labor Relations; Printing/Publishing; Procurement; Retail; Sales and Marketing; Technical and Scientific; Textiles; Transportation.

MANAGEMENT RECRUITERS INTERNATIONAL
5701 Westpark Drive, Suite 110, Charlotte NC 28217. 704/525-9270. **Fax:** 704/527-0070. **Contact:** Ev Fuller, General Manager. Executive Search Firm. **Specializes in the areas of:** Art/Design; Computer Science/Software; Engineering; Finance; Food Industry; General Management; Health/Medical; Industrial; Insurance; Manufacturing; Personnel/Labor Relations; Printing/Publishing; Sales and Marketing; Technical and Scientific; Transportation. **Positions commonly filled include:** Administrative Services Manager; Bank Officer/Manager; Biomedical Engineer; Branch Manager; Buyer; Chemical Engineer; Chiropractor; Computer Programmer; Computer Systems Analyst; Construction Contractor and Manager; Customer Service Representative; Dentist; Designer; EEG Technologist; EKG Technician; Financial Analyst; General Manager; Health Services Manager; Industrial Engineer; Industrial Production Manager; Management Analyst/Consultant; Manufacturer's/Wholesaler's Sales Rep.; Occupational Therapist; Operations/Production Manager; Pharmacist; Physical Therapist; Physician; Purchasing Agent and Manager; Quality Control Supervisor; Recreational Therapist; Registered Nurse; Respiratory Therapist; Securities Sales Rep.; Software Engineer; Surveyor; Transportation/Traffic Specialist; Underwriter/Assistant Underwriter; Veterinarian. Company pays fee. **Number of placements per year:** 200 - 499.

MANAGEMENT RECRUITERS OF DURHAM
5102 Chapel Hill Durham Boulevard, Durham NC 27707. 919/489-6521. **Contact:** Ann Phillips, Manager. Executive Search Firm. **Specializes in the areas of:** Accounting/Auditing; Administration/MIS/EDP; Advertising; Architecture/ Construction/ Real Estate; Banking; Communications; Computer Hardware/Software; Design; Electrical; Engineering; Food Industry; General Management; Health/Medical; Insurance; Legal; Manufacturing; Operations Management; Personnel/Labor Relations; Printing/Publishing; Procurement; Retail; Sales and Marketing; Technical and Scientific; Textiles; Transportation.

MANAGEMENT RECRUITERS OF FAYETTEVILLE
951 South McPherson Church Road, Suite 105, Fayetteville NC 28303. 910/483-2555. **Fax:** 910/483-6524. **Contact:** John Semmes, Manager. Executive Search Firm. **Specializes in the areas of:** Accounting/Auditing; Administration/MIS/EDP; Advertising; Architecture/Construction/Real Estate; Banking; Communications; Computer Hardware/Software; Design; Electrical; Engineering; Food Industry; General Management; Health/Medical; Insurance; Legal; Manufacturing; Operations Management; Personnel/Labor Relations; Printing/Publishing; Procurement; Retail; Sales and Marketing; Technical and Scientific; Textiles; Transportation.

MANAGEMENT RECRUITERS OF GREENSBORO
324 West Wendover Avenue, Suite 230, Greensboro NC 27408. 910/378-1818. **Fax:** 910/378-0129. **Contact:** Mitch Oakley, Manager. Executive Search Firm. **Specializes in the areas of:** Accounting/Auditing; Administration/MIS/EDP; Advertising; Architecture/Construction/Real Estate; Banking; Communications; Computer Hardware/Software; Design; Electrical; Engineering; Food Industry; General Management; Health/Medical; Insurance; Legal; Manufacturing; Operations Management; Personnel/Labor Relations; Printing/Publishing; Procurement; Retail; Sales and Marketing; Technical and Scientific; Textiles; Transportation.

MANAGEMENT RECRUITERS OF KINSTON
P.O. Box 219, Kinston NC 28502. 919/527-9191. **Fax:** 919/527-3625. **Contact:** William Thomas, President/Owner. Executive Search Firm. **Specializes in the areas of:** Engineering; Food Industry; Health/Medical; Industrial; Manufacturing; Paper. **Positions commonly filled include:** Electrical/Electronics Engineer; Industrial Engineer; Mechanical

Engineer; Nuclear Medicine Technologist; Occupational Therapist; Physician; Quality Control Supervisor; Radiologic Technologist. Company pays fee. **Number of placements per year:** 50 - 99.

MANAGEMENT RECRUITERS OF LOUISBURG
P.O. Box 8, Louisburg NC 27549. 919/496-2153. **Fax:** 919/496-1417. **Contact:** Darrell Perry, Manager. Executive Search Firm. **Specializes in the areas of:** Accounting/Auditing; Administration/MIS/EDP; Advertising; Architecture/ Construction/ Real Estate; Banking; Communications; Computer Hardware/Software; Design; Electrical; Engineering; Food Industry; General Management; Health/Medical; Insurance; Legal; Manufacturing; Operations Management; Personnel/Labor Relations; Printing/Publishing; Procurement; Retail; Sales and Marketing; Technical and Scientific; Textiles; Transportation.

MANAGEMENT RECRUITERS OF WINSTON-SALEM
P.O. Box 17054, Winston-Salem NC 27116-7054. 910/723-0484. **Contact:** Mike Jones, Manager. Executive Search Firm. **Specializes in the areas of:** Accounting/Auditing; Administration/MIS/EDP; Advertising; Architecture/ Construction/ Real Estate; Banking; Communications; Computer Hardware/Software; Design; Electrical; Engineering; Food Industry; General Management; Health/Medical; Insurance; Legal; Manufacturing; Operations Management; Personnel/Labor Relations; Printing/Publishing; Procurement; Retail; Sales and Marketing; Technical and Scientific; Textiles; Transportation.

MARK III PERSONNEL INC.
Suite 604, 4801 East Independence Boulevard, Charlotte NC 28212. 704/535-5883. **Contact:** Mr. Lindsay Allen, President. Executive Search Firm. **Specializes in the areas of:** Banking; Engineering; Environmental. **Positions commonly filled include:** Bank Officer/Manager; Chemical Engineer; Mechanical Engineer. Company pays fee. **Number of placements per year:** 1 - 49.

MOFFITT INTERNATIONAL, INC.
1316A Patton Avenue, Park Terrace Center, Asheville NC 28806. 704/251-4550. **Fax:** 704/251-4555. **Contact:** Tim Moffitt, President. Executive Search Firm. **Specializes in the areas of:** Architecture/Construction/Real Estate; Biology; Engineering; Food Industry; General Management; Health/Medical; Legal; Manufacturing; Pharmaceutical; Sales and Marketing; Technical and Scientific; Transportation. **Positions commonly filled include:** Attorney; Biological Scientist/Biochemist; Biomedical Engineer; Chemical Engineer; Chemist; Civil Engineer; Clinical Lab Technician; Construction and Building Inspector; Construction Contractor and Manager; Cost Estimator; Dental Lab Technician; Dietician/Nutritionist; EEG Technologist; EKG Technician; Electrical/Electronics Engineer; Emergency Medical Technician; Food Scientist/Technologist; Geologist/Geophysicist; Health Services Manager; Industrial Engineer; Industrial Production Manager; Landscape Architect; Licensed Practical Nurse; Manufacturer's/Wholesaler's Sales Rep.; Mechanical Engineer; Medical Records Technician; Nuclear Medicine Technologist; Occupational Therapist; Operations/Production Manager; Paralegal; Petroleum Engineer; Pharmacist; Physical Therapist; Physician; Purchasing Agent and Manager; Quality Control Supervisor; Radiologic Technologist; Recreational Therapist; Registered Nurse; Respiratory Therapist; Restaurant/Food Service Manager; Software Engineer; Speech-Language Pathologist; Structural Engineer; Surgical Technician; Technical Writer/Editor; Transportation/Traffic Specialist; Urban/Regional Planner; Water Transportation Specialist. Company pays fee. **Number of placements per year:** 200 - 499.

NATIONAL SERVICES, INC.
P.O. Box 6505, Raleigh NC 27628-6505. 919/787-8000. **Contact:** Bill Poole, President. Executive Search Firm. **Specializes in the areas of:** Accounting/Auditing; Computer Hardware/Software; Engineering; General Management; Manufacturing; Personnel/Labor Relations; Technical and Scientific. **Number of placements per year:** 1 - 49.

ROMAC & ASSOCIATES
2000 West 1st Street, Suite 616, Winston-Salem NC 27104. 910/725-1933. **Fax:** 910/725-1994. **Contact:** Michael J. Lavallee, Managing Partner. Executive Search Firm. **Positions commonly filled include:** Computer Programmer; Computer Systems Analyst. Company pays fee. **Number of placements per year:** 1 - 49.

SAIN-WADE CORPORATION
400 West Market Street, Suite 208, Greensboro NC 27401. 910/274-3336. **Contact:** Mary Sain-Wade, President. Executive Search Firm. **Specializes in the areas of:**

Accounting/Auditing; Administration/MIS/EDP; Health/Medical; Industrial; Manufacturing; Technical and Scientific. **Positions commonly filled include:** Accountant/Auditor; Chemical Engineer; Designer; Industrial Engineer; Manufacturing Engineer; MIS Specialist; Secretary; Systems Analyst. Company pays fee. **Number of placements per year:** 1 - 49.

SALES CONSULTANTS OF CONCORD, INC.
254 Church Street NE, Concord NC 28025. 704/786-0700. **Fax:** 704/782-1356. **Contact:** Anna Lee Pearson, President. Executive Search Firm. **Specializes in the areas of:** Computer Science/Software; General Management; Health/Medical; Sales and Marketing; Technical and Scientific; Telecommunications. **Positions commonly filled include:** Branch Manager; Customer Service Representative; Economist/Market Research Analyst; Electrical/Electronics Engineer; General Manager; Health Services Manager; Management Analyst/Consultant; Manufacturer's/Wholesaler's Sales Rep.; Marketing/Advertising/PR Manager; Physical Therapist; Physician; Product Manager; Psychologist; Sales Manager; Services Sales Representative; Software Engineer. Company pays fee. **Number of placements per year:** 1 - 49.

SALES CONSULTANTS OF HIGH POINT
2411 Penny Road, Suite 101, High Point NC 27265. 910/883-4433. **Contact:** Tom Bunton, Pervis Greene, Co-Managers. Executive Search Firm. **Specializes in the areas of:** Accounting/Auditing; Administration/MIS/EDP; Advertising; Architecture/Construction/Real Estate; Banking; Communications; Computer Hardware/Software; Design; Electrical; Engineering; Food Industry; General Management; Health/Medical; Insurance; Legal; Manufacturing; Operations Management; Personnel/Labor Relations; Printing/Publishing; Procurement; Retail; Sales and Marketing; Technical and Scientific; Textiles; Transportation.

JOHN R. WILLIAMS & ASSOCIATES
2102 North Elm Street, Suite H, Greensboro NC 27408. 910/279-8800. **Contact:** John R. Williams, President and Owner. Executive Search Firm. **Specializes in the areas of:** Accounting/Auditing; Banking; Engineering; General Management; Industrial; Manufacturing; Personnel/Labor Relations. **Positions commonly filled include:** Attorney; Bank Officer/Manager; Chemical Engineer; Civil Engineer; Electrical/Electronics Engineer; General Manager; Human Resources Specialist; Industrial Engineer; Industrial Production Manager; Mechanical Engineer; Quality Control Supervisor. Company pays fee. **Number of placements per year:** 1 - 49.

EXECUTIVE SEARCH FIRMS OF SOUTH CAROLINA

BOCK & ASSOCIATES
2375 East Main Street, Suite A105, Spartanburg SC 29307. 864/579-7396. **Contact:** Kevin Bock, Owner/Manager. Executive Search Firm. **Specializes in the areas of:** Engineering; Industrial; Manufacturing; Personnel/Labor Relations; Technical and Scientific. **Positions commonly filled include:** Chemical Engineer; Chemist; Human Resources Specialist; Industrial Engineer; Mechanical Engineer. Company pays fee. **Number of placements per year:** 1 - 49.

DUNHILL PROFESSIONAL SEARCH
Six Village Square, 231 Hampton Street, Greenwood SC 29646. 864/229-5251. **Contact:** Hal Freese, President. Executive Search Firm. **Specializes in the areas of:** Accounting/Auditing; Computer Hardware/Software; Engineering; Manufacturing.

FIRST CHOICE STAFFING
1624 Ebenezer Road, Rock Hill SC 29732. 803/324-2424. **Contact:** Bill Gregory, President. Executive Search Firm. **Specializes in the areas of:** Textiles.

HEALTH CARE SEARCH ASSOCIATES
P.O. Box 17334, Greenville SC 29606-8334. 864/242-1999. **Fax:** 864/271-1426. **Contact:** David Gahan, Owner/Manager. Executive Search Firm. **Specializes in the areas of:** Health/Medical. **Positions commonly filled include:** Medical Records Technician; Nuclear Medicine Technologist; Radiologic Technologist; Registered Nurse; Speech-Language Pathologist. Company pays fee. **Number of placements per year:** 1 - 49.

MANAGEMENT RECRUITERS OF AIKEN
P.O. Box 730, Aiken SC 29802-0730. 803/648-1361. **Contact:** Michael Hardwick, Manager. Executive Search Firm. **Specializes in the areas of:** Apparel; Computer Hardware/Software; Electronics; Health/Medical; Medical Software; Metals; Plastics; Textiles. Company pays fee. **Number of placements per year:** 500 - 999.

MANAGEMENT RECRUITERS OF ANDERSON
P.O. Box 2874, Anderson SC 29622. 864/225-1258. **Fax:** 864/225-2332. **Contact:** Rod Pagan, Owner. Executive Search Firm. **Specializes in the areas of:** Automotive; Computer Science/Software; Data Processing; Health/Medical; Pharmaceutical. **Positions commonly filled include:** Accountant/Auditor; Biological Scientist/Biochemist; Biomedical Engineer; Buyer; Chemical Engineer; Chemist; Computer Programmer; Computer Systems Analyst; Electrical/Electronics Engineer; General Manager; Human Resources Specialist; Industrial Engineer; Mechanical Engineer; Purchasing Agent and Manager. Company pays fee. **Number of placements per year:** 50 - 99.

MANAGEMENT RECRUITERS OF COLUMBIA
1201 Hampton Street, Suite 2B, Columbia SC 29201. 803/254-1334. **Fax:** 803/254-1527. **Contact:** Bob Keen, Manager. Executive Search Firm. **Specializes in the areas of:** Accounting/Auditing; Administration/MIS/EDP; Advertising; Architecture/Construction/Real Estate; Banking; Communications; Computer Hardware/Software; Design; Electrical; Engineering; Food Industry; General Management; Health/Medical; Insurance; Legal; Manufacturing; Operations Management; Personnel/Labor Relations; Printing/Publishing; Procurement; Retail; Sales and Marketing; Technical and Scientific; Textiles; Transportation.

MANAGEMENT RECRUITERS OF GREENVILLE
330 Pelham Road, Suite 109B, Greenville SC 29615. 864/370-1341. **Contact:** Office Manager. Executive Search Firm. **Specializes in the areas of:** Accounting/Auditing; Administration/MIS/EDP; Advertising; Architecture/Construction/Real Estate; Banking; Communications; Computer Hardware/Software; Design; Electrical; Engineering; Food Industry; General Management; Health/Medical; Insurance; Legal; Manufacturing; Operations Management; Personnel/Labor Relations; Printing/Publishing; Procurement; Retail; Sales and Marketing; Technical and Scientific; Textiles; Transportation.

MANAGEMENT RECRUITERS OF ORANGEBURG
2037 Saint Matthews Road, Orangeburg SC 29118. 803/531-4101. **Fax:** 803/536-3714. **Contact:** Dick Crawford/Ed Chewning, Co-Managers. Executive Search Firm. **Specializes in the areas of:** Accounting/Auditing; Administration/MIS/EDP; Advertising; Architecture/Construction/Real Estate; Banking; Communications; Computer Hardware/Software; Design; Electrical; Engineering; Food Industry; General Management; Health/Medical; Insurance; Legal; Manufacturing; Operations Management; Personnel/Labor Relations; Printing/Publishing; Procurement; Retail; Sales and Marketing; Technical and Scientific; Textiles; Transportation.

MANAGEMENT RECRUITERS OF ROCK HILL
1925 Ebenezer Road, Rock Hill SC 29730. 803/324-5181. **Fax:** 803/324-3431. **Contact:** Herman Smith, Manager. Executive Search Firm. **Specializes in the areas of:** Accounting/Auditing; Administration/MIS/EDP; Advertising; Architecture/Construction/Real Estate; Banking; Communications; Computer Hardware/Software; Design; Electrical; Engineering; Food Industry; General Management; Health/Medical; Insurance; Legal; Manufacturing; Operations Management; Personnel/Labor Relations; Printing/Publishing; Procurement; Retail; Sales and Marketing; Technical and Scientific; Textiles; Transportation.

PENN HILL ASSOCIATES
P.O. Box 1367, Pawley's Island SC 29585. 803/237-8988. **Fax:** 803/237-9220. **Contact:** Conrad L. Kohler, CPC. Executive Search Firm. **Specializes in the areas of:** Consumer Finance.

PHILLIPS RESOURCE GROUP
P.O. Box 5664, Greenville SC 29606. 864/271-6350. **Fax:** 864/271-8499. **Contact:** Mr. A.M. Hicks, President. Executive Search Firm. **Specializes in the areas of:** Administration/MIS/EDP; Engineering; Manufacturing; Personnel/Labor Relations; Sales and Marketing; Technical and Scientific. **Positions commonly filled include:** Accountant/Auditor; Chemical Engineer; Chemist; Computer Programmer; EDP Specialist; Electrical/Electronics Engineer; Industrial Engineer; Manufacturing Engineer; Marketing Specialist; Mechanical Engineer; Metallurgical Engineer; MIS Specialist. Company pays fee. **Number of placements per year:** 100 - 199.

JOHN SHELL ASSOCIATES, INC.
P.O. Box 23291, Columbia SC 29224. 803/788-6619. **Fax:** 803/788-1758. **Contact:** John C. Shell III, CPA, President. Executive Search Firm. **Specializes in the areas of:** Accounting/Auditing; Finance. **Positions commonly filled include:** Accountant/Auditor; Bookkeeper.

SOUTHERN RECRUITERS
P.O. Box 2745, Aiken SC 29802. 803/648-7834. **Contact:** Ray Fehrenbach, President. Executive Search Firm. **Specializes in the areas of:** Computer Hardware/Software; Engineering; Manufacturing; MIS/EDP; Technical and Scientific. **Positions commonly filled include:** Accountant/Auditor; Aerospace Engineer; Attorney; Bank Officer/Manager; Biomedical Engineer; Ceramics Engineer; Civil Engineer; Computer Programmer; EDP Specialist; Electrical/Electronics Engineer; Financial Analyst; Human Resources Specialist; Mechanical Engineer; Metallurgical Engineer; Petroleum Engineer; Purchasing Agent and Manager; Systems Analyst. Company pays fee. **Number of placements per year:** 50 - 99.

RESUME/CAREER COUNSELING SERVICES OF NORTH CAROLINA

KING CAREER CONSULTING
2915 Providence Road, Suite 300, Charlotte NC 28211. 704/366-1685. **Fax:** 704/364-9678. **Contact:** Jerry King, President. Career/Outplacement Counseling. **Specializes in the areas of:** Executives; General Management. **Number of placements per year:** 50 - 99.

INDEX OF PRIMARY EMPLOYERS

NOTE: *Below is an alphabetical index of primary employer listings included in this book. Those employers in each industry that fall under the headings "Additional employers" are not indexed here.*

Your Job Hunt
Your Feedback

Comments, questions, or suggestions? We want to hear from you. Please complete this questionnaire and mail it to:

The JobBank Staff
Adams Media Corporation
260 Center Street
Holbrook, MA 02343

Did this book provide helpful advice and valuable information which you used in your job search? Was the information easy to access?

Recommendations for improvements. How could we improve this book to help in your job search? No suggestion is too small or too large.

Would you recommend this book to a friend beginning a job hunt?

Name: _____

Occupation: _____

Which JobBank did you use? _____

Address: _____

Daytime phone: _____

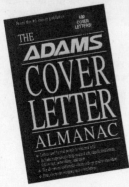